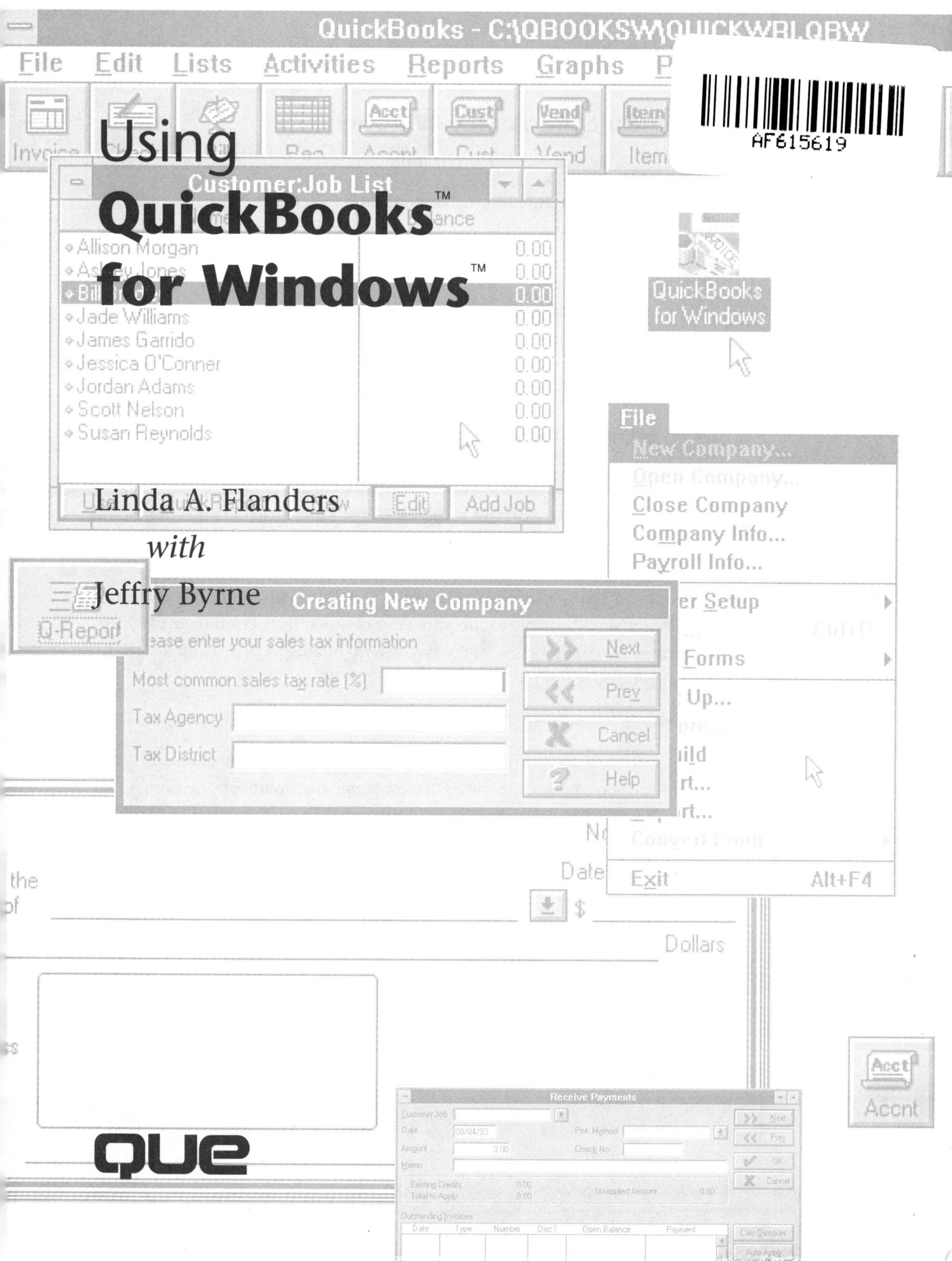

Using QuickBooks™ for Windows™

Linda A. Flanders

with

Jeffry Byrne

QUE

Using QuickBooks for Windows™

Library of Congress Catalog No.: 93-86248

ISBN: 1-56529-283-9

95 94 93 5 4 3 2 1

Interpretation of the printing code: the rightmost double-digit number is the year of the book's printing; the rightmost single-digit number, the number of the book's printing. For example, a printing code of 93-1 shows that the first printing of the book occurred in 1993.

Screen reproductions in this book were created using Collage Plus from Inner Media, Inc., Hollis, NH.

Publisher: David P. Ewing

Director of Publishing: Michael Miller

Managing Editor: Corinne Walls

Marketing Manager: Ray Robinson

Dedication

To my three wonderful daughters, who make everything feel special.

Linda Flanders

Credits

Publishing Managers
Don Roche, Jr.
Shelley O'Hara

Acquisitions Editor
Nancy Stevenson

Product Directors
Joyce J. Nielsen
Kathie-Jo Arnoff

Development Editor
Janice A. Snyder

Production Editor
Joy M. Preacher

Editors
William A. Barton
Elsa Bell
Lori Cates
Thomas F. Hayes
Patrick Kanouse
Heather Kaufman
Lori A. Lyons
Virginia Noble
Pamela Wampler

Technical Editor
Susan Twer

Book Designer
Amy Peppler-Adams

Cover Designer
Jay Corpus

Editorial Assistant
Jill Stanley

Production Team
Jeff Baker
Angela Bannan
Claudia Bell
Charlotte Clapp
Karen Dodson
Brook Farling
Caroline Roop
Amy L. Steed
Tina Trettin
Donna Winter

Indexer
Michael Hughes
Johnna VanHoose

Composed in *1StoneSerif* and *MCPdigital*
by Que Corporation.

About the Authors

Linda A. Flanders is a Certified Public Accountant and holds a B.S. degree in accounting from Indiana University. She has worked in public accounting for Arthur Andersen & Co., and private accounting for Mayflower Group, Inc., where she specialized in taxation. She currently operates a small individual tax practice. She is the author of *Using Turbo Tax: 1992 Edition, CheckFree Quick Reference, Quicken 5 Quick Reference, 10 Minute Guide to Quicken 5,* and *Using Microsoft Money.*

Jeffry Byrne lives in Portland, Oregon, with his wife, Marisa, and three dogs and two cats. He is also the author of *Paradox 4 QuickStart.* In addition to writing for Prentice Hall Computer Publishing, he has written books and user manuals for accounting, spreadsheet, database, and point-of-sale programs.

Acknowledgments

Thanks to Susan Twer for her thoroughness and technical expertise.

Thanks to Jeff Byrne for pinch-hitting for me.

And, as always, thanks to the people at Que, who do an excellent job and make mine that much easier.

Linda Flanders

Thank you to my wife, Marisa, for her help in this project, and to Linda Flanders, my co-author, who provided the backbone for this book. For all her help and encouragement, thanks to Nancy Stevenson, and thanks to the rest of the Prentice Hall Computer Publishing staff who went to great efforts to complete this book.

Jeff Byrne

Trademarks

Contents at a Glance

Introduction 1

Getting Started **13**

1 Preparing To Use QuickBooks for Windows 15

2 Learning Your Way Around QuickBooks for Windows 29

3 Setting Up Your Company in QuickBooks for Windows 63

4 Working with Accounts 83

5 Using QuickBooks for Windows Lists 111

Getting Started

Tracking Customers **167**

6 Creating Invoices 169

7 Tracking Sales Tax 205

8 Printing Invoices, Statements, and Other Forms 223

9 Receiving and Depositing Customer Payments 247

10 Using the Accounts Receivable Register 275

Tracking Customers

Paying Bills **291**

11 Entering and Paying Bills 293

12 Using the Accounts Payable Register 307

13 Writing and Printing Checks 325

14 Entering Transactions in the Check Register 353

Paying Bills

Maximizing QuickBooks **377**

15 Speeding Up Your Work in QuickBooks for Windows 379

16 Reconciling Your Bank Account 409

17 Using Other Accounts To Perform Tasks 423

Maximizing QuickBooks

Analyzing Business Data **465**

18 Preparing Budgets 467

19 Creating and Printing Reports 477

20 Creating Graphs 513

Analyzing Business Data

Managing QuickBooks **531**

21 Managing QuickBooks for Windows Files 533

22 Customizing QuickBooks for Windows 549

Managing QuickBooks

Appendixes 567

A Installing QuickBooks for Windows 569

B Using QuickPay with QuickBooks for Windows 575

C QuickBooks versus Quicken: Which Is Best for You? 583

D QuickBooks for Canadian Users 589

Index 595

Appendixes

Contents

Introduction 1

Overview of QuickBooks for Windows ... 3
Who Should Read This Book? ... 6
What Is in This Book? ... 7
- Part I—Getting Started ... 7
- Part II—Tracking Customers ... 8
- Part III—Paying Bills ... 9
- Part IV—Maximizing QuickBooks ... 9
- Part V—Analyzing Business Data ... 10
- Part VI—Managing QuickBooks ... 10
- Part VII—Appendixes ... 11

Conventions ... 11

I Getting Started 13

1 Preparing To Use QuickBooks for Windows 15

Converting Your Manual System to QuickBooks for Windows ... 15
Ordering Checks, Invoices, and Supplies ... 16
Gathering Information ... 19
Starting QuickBooks for Windows for the First Time ... 22
Registering Your Program ... 24
Setting Up Your Printer ... 26
Summary ... 27

2 Learning Your Way Around QuickBooks for Windows 29

Starting the Program ... 29
Working with the Mouse and Keyboard ... 30
- Using the Mouse ... 30
- Using the Keyboard ... 31
- Using Quick Keys ... 32

Understanding the Windows Environment ... 33
- Examining the Title Bar ... 34
- Activating a Window ... 34
- Manipulating Windows ... 35
- Scrolling through Windows ... 40
- Working with Dialog Boxes ... 41

Using QuickBooks for Windows Menus ... 45
- Accessing Menus from the Menu Bar ... 46
- Choosing Menu Commands and Options ... 47
- Removing Menus from the Screen ... 47

Using the Iconbar To Choose Menu Commands and Options ... 47
Changing the Iconbar Display ... 49
Eliminating the Iconbar ... 49
Switching between Windows ... 50
Arranging the Desktop ... 50
Arranging Windows and Icons ... 50
Saving the Desktop When Exiting ... 51
Getting Help ... 52
Using Qcards ... 53
Using QuickBooks' On-Line Help System ... 54
Using the QuickBooks Tutorial ... 57
Using Sample Company Data To Learn QuickBooks ... 59
Exiting the Program ... 60
Summary ... 61

3 Setting Up Your Company in QuickBooks for Windows 63

Creating a New Company File ... 63
Converting Your QuickBooks for DOS System to QuickBooks for Windows ... 69
Setting Up Your Company from Quicken Data ... 73
Examining Changes to Quicken Accounts ... 76
Examining Changes in Accounts Receivable ... 78
Examining Changes in Accounts Payable ... 79
Editing Company Information ... 79
Summary ... 81

4 Working with Accounts 83

Understanding the Chart of Accounts ... 83
Reviewing Balance Sheet Accounts ... 86
Reviewing Income and Expense Accounts ... 87
Accessing the Chart of Accounts ... 88
Adding Accounts ... 89
Adding a Balance Sheet Account ... 90
Adding Income and Expense Accounts ... 93
Creating Subaccounts ... 95
Working with Numeric Accounts ... 97
Modifying the Chart of Accounts ... 99
Editing Accounts and Subaccounts ... 99
Deleting Accounts and Subaccounts ... 100
Moving Accounts ... 102
Combining Accounts ... 104
Changing the Color of an Account ... 105
Printing the Chart of Accounts ... 107
Summary ... 109

5 Using QuickBooks for Windows Lists 111

Working with QuickBooks for Windows Lists ... 111
Exploring QuickBooks for Windows Lists ... 112
Entering List Items in Fields ... 114
Accessing QuickBooks for Windows Lists ... 114

Designing the Customer:Job List 115
- Adding a Customer 116
- Editing Customer Information 118
- Creating Customer Notes 119
- Deleting a Customer 121
- Tracking Jobs 122

Designing the Vendor List 125
- Adding a Vendor 126
- Editing Vendor Information 128
- Creating Vendor Notes 128
- Deleting a Vendor 129

Designing the Employee List 130
- Adding an Employee 131
- Editing Employee Information 132
- Creating Employee Notes 132
- Deleting an Employee 133

Designing the Other Names List 133
- Adding an Other Name 134
- Editing an Other Name 135
- Deleting an Other Name 136

Designing the Invoice Items List 136
- Adding an Item 138
- Editing an Invoice Item 140
- Deleting an Invoice Item 141

Designing the Class List 142
- Turning On Class Tracking 142
- Adding a Class 143
- Adding a Subclass 144
- Moving Classes 144
- Editing a Class 145
- Deleting a Class 145

Designing the Customer Type List 146
- Adding a Customer Type 147
- Editing a Customer Type 147
- Deleting a Customer Type 148

Designing the Vendor Type List 148
- Adding a Vendor Type 149
- Editing a Vendor Type 150
- Deleting a Vendor Type 150

Designing the Payment Method List 151
- Adding a Payment Method 151
- Editing a Payment Method 152
- Deleting a Payment Method 152

Designing the Terms List 152
- Adding a Payment Term 154
- Editing a Payment Term 154
- Deleting a Payment Term 155

Designing the Ship Via List 155
- Adding a Shipping Method 156
- Editing a Shipping Method 156
- Deleting a Shipping Method 157

Designing the Customer Message List 157
Adding a Customer Message 158
Editing a Customer Message 159
Deleting a Customer Message 159
Adding to Lists on the Fly 160
Reorganizing QuickBooks for Windows Lists 161
Using the Mouse To Reorganize Lists 161
Re-sorting Lists Alphabetically 162
Printing QuickBooks for Windows Lists 162
Summary 165

II Tracking Customers 167

6 Creating Invoices 169

Accessing the Create Invoices Window 169
Selecting the Invoice Format To Use 170
Reviewing the Create Invoices Window 172
The Customer:Job Field 173
The Class Field 173
The Account Field 173
The Invoice 173
Command Buttons 174
Memo and Balance Due Fields 175
Moving Around in the Create Invoices Window 175
Writing an Invoice 175
Completing Customer:Job, Class, and Account Information 177
Completing the Invoice Header 178
Completing the Line-Item Area 180
Understanding Line Items 183
Inserting Line Items 188
Deleting Line Items 188
Adding Reimbursable Expenses to Invoices 189
Completing the Invoice 193
Editing an Invoice 195
Deleting an Invoice 196
Voiding an Invoice 198
Changing the Invoice Title 198
Entering Historical Invoices 199
Entering Unpaid Invoices 199
Entering Paid Invoices 202
Preparing Job Estimates 203
Summary 204

7 Tracking Sales Tax 205

Setting Up QuickBooks To Track Sales Tax 205
Setting Up Tax Rates for Auto Tax 206
Setting Up Sales Tax Line Items 209

Applying Sales Tax to Invoices 211
Using Auto Tax To Calculate Sales Tax 211
Entering Sales Tax Line Items on Invoices 212
Reviewing Sales Taxes Owed 214
Viewing the Sales Tax Payable Register 216
Paying Sales Tax 219
Summary 222

8 Printing Invoices, Statements, and Other Forms 223

Ordering Invoices and Other Supplies 223
Setting Up Your Printer 224
Previewing Invoices 228
Positioning Invoices in Your Printer 229
Printing Invoices 233
Selecting Invoices to be Printed 234
Reprinting Invoices 235
Printing Statements 237
Printing Mailing Labels 241
Printing Rotary Index Cards 245
Summary 246

9 Receiving and Depositing Customer Payments 247

Entering a Customer Payment 248
Applying Payments to Invoices 248
Applying Early Payment Discounts 254
Handling Overpayments, Down Payments, and Prepayments 256
Editing Applied Payments 258
Entering Cash Sales 259
Making Deposits 262
Editing Deposited Payments 266
Recording Returns 267
Issuing a Credit Memo 267
Voiding an Invoice 270
Tracking American Express Charges 270
Using American Express and Cash Sales 271
Handling the American Express Deposit 272
Summary 273

10 Using the Accounts Receivable Register 275

Displaying the Accounts Receivable Register 275
Reviewing the Accounts Receivable Register 276
Moving around the Register 280
Editing Accounts Receivable Transactions 281
Deleting Accounts Receivable Transactions 282
Viewing a Transaction History 284
Using QuickReport To View Customer Records 286
Adding Customer or Job Notes 287
Printing the Accounts Receivable Register 288
Summary 290

III Paying Bills 291

11 Entering and Paying Bills 293

Entering Bills 293
Changing the Calculated Pay Date 299
Paying Bills 300
Entering Credits from Vendors 302
Using Reminders To Pay Bills 303
Summary 305

12 Using the Accounts Payable Register 307

Displaying the Accounts Payable Register 307
  Reviewing the Accounts Payable Register 309
  Moving Around in the Register 311
Entering Bills into the Accounts Payable Register 313
Editing Bills in the Accounts Payable Register 315
Viewing a Transaction History 317
Entering Accounts Payable Historical Transactions 319
  Entering Outstanding Bills 319
  Entering Bills Paid This Year 320
Using QuickReport To View Vendor Records 320
Adding Vendor Notes 321
Printing the Accounts Payable Register 322
Summary 323

13 Writing and Printing Checks 325

Viewing the Write Checks Window 326
  Reviewing the Write Checks Window 326
  Moving Around the Write Checks Window 329
Writing a Check 329
  Writing Checks from One Checking Account 329
  Filling Out the Check 330
  Filling In Detail Lines 332
Editing a Check 337
Voiding a Check 338
Deleting a Check 339
Printing Checks 340
  Ordering Checks 341
  Positioning Checks in Your Printer 342
  Printing Checks 346
  Reprinting Checks 349
  Printing a Logo on Checks 349
Summary 351

14 Entering Transactions in the Check Register 353

Displaying the Check Register 353
  Reviewing the Check Register 354
  Moving Around the Check Register 356

Entering Transactions 358
Editing Transactions 363
Splitting Transactions 364
  Editing a Split Transaction 367
  Deleting a Split Transaction Line 367
Deleting Transactions 368
Voiding Transactions 369
Entering a Transfer Transaction 370
  Finding Transfer Transactions 370
  Editing and Deleting a Transfer Transaction 370
Entering Historical Transactions 371
Entering a Summary Transaction 372
Printing the Check Register 374
Summary 376

IV Maximizing QuickBooks 377

15 Speeding Up Your Work in QuickBooks for Windows 379

Using the Windows Calculator 379
Finding Transactions 383
Using Memorized Transactions 387
  Memorizing a Transaction 387
  Recalling a Memorized Transaction 389
  Editing a Memorized Transaction 390
  Deleting a Memorized Transaction 391
Using Memorized Invoices 392
  Memorizing an Invoice 392
  Recalling a Memorized Invoice 394
  Editing and Deleting Memorized Invoices 394
Using Transaction Groups 395
  Creating a Transaction Group 396
  Using a Transaction Group 400
  Editing and Deleting Transactions in a Group 401
  Editing a Transaction Group 403
  Deleting a Transaction Group 403
Copying and Pasting Transactions 404
Working with the Windows Clipboard 405
Using Reminders 406
Summary 408

16 Reconciling Your Bank Account 409

Starting To Reconcile Your Account 410
  Adjusting Opening Balance Differences 413
  Marking Cleared Transactions 414
  Entering Missing Transactions 415
  Leaving the Reconciliation 416

Completing the Reconciliation When Your Account Balances ... 416
Completing the Reconciliation When Your Account Doesn't Balance ... 417
Resolving Reconciliation Differences ... 417
Letting QuickBooks Reconcile the Differences ... 418
Printing a Reconciliation Report ... 420
Summary ... 421

17 Using Other Accounts To Perform Tasks 423

Understanding Balance Sheet Accounts ... 424
Updating Account Values ... 425
Working with Credit Card Accounts ... 428
Adding a Credit Card Account ... 428
Entering Credit Card Transactions ... 429
Editing, Deleting, or Voiding a Credit Card Transaction ... 431
Reconciling Your Credit Card Account ... 432
Making Credit Card Payments ... 435
Working with Current Asset Accounts ... 437
Working with Fixed Asset Accounts ... 439
Adding a Fixed Asset Account ... 439
Adding an Accumulated Depreciation Account ... 440
Entering Depreciable Assets ... 442
Entering Depreciable Transactions ... 443
Selling Depreciable Assets ... 445
Working with Payroll Accounts ... 447
Adding Payroll Tax Accounts ... 448
Assigning Payroll Liability Accounts to Transactions ... 449
Paying Payroll Taxes ... 452
Working with Liability Accounts ... 454
Adding a Liability Account ... 454
Tracking Loans ... 455
Working with Equity Accounts ... 457
Adding an Equity Account ... 458
Making Transfers from the Opening Balance Equity Account ... 459
Recording Draws ... 460
Sole Proprietorships ... 460
Partnerships ... 460
Corporations ... 460
Recording Draws ... 460
Recording Capital Investments ... 461
Completing the Year-End Transactions ... 462
Closing Your Books...Or Not ... 462
Making Adjusting Entries ... 463
Freezing Last Year's Transactions ... 464
Summary ... 464

V Analyzing Business Data 465

18 Preparing Budgets 467

Creating the Budget ... 467
- Filling Varied Budget Amounts ... 469
- Filling in Constant Budget Amounts ... 472
- Budgeting by Customer, Job, or Class ... 473

Changing the Budget ... 474
Viewing a Budget Report ... 475
Summary ... 476

19 Creating and Printing Reports 477

Using QuickReports To View Transactions ... 478
Using QuickBooks' Preset Reports ... 480
- Profit and Loss Reports ... 481
- Balance Sheet Reports ... 484
- Accounts Receivable Reports ... 485
- Sales Reports ... 487
- Accounts Payable Reports ... 488
- Budget Reports ... 489
- Transaction Reports ... 491
- Other Reports ... 492

Customizing a Report with the Report Window ... 494
- Using the Report Button Bar ... 494
- Viewing the Entire Report On-Screen ... 505
- Recalling a Memorized Report ... 506
- Editing and Deleting Memorized Reports ... 507

Printing Reports ... 508
Summary ... 511

20 Creating Graphs 513

Overview of QuickBooks for Windows Graphs ... 513
- Bar Graphs ... 514
- Pie Charts ... 514
- Other Graphs ... 515

Creating Graphs ... 516
- Income and Expense Graphs ... 516
- Sales Graphs ... 518
- Accounts Receivable Graphs ... 519
- Accounts Payable Graphs ... 519
- Net Worth Graph ... 521
- Budget vs. Actual Graphs ... 521

Using the Button Bar To Customize Graphs ... 523
Examining Graph Detail by Using QuickZoom ... 526
Printing Graphs ... 529
Summary ... 530

VI Managing QuickBooks 531

21 Managing QuickBooks for Windows Files 533

Adding Company Files ... 534
Opening a Company File ... 537
Closing a Company File ... 538
Backing Up and Restoring Company Files ... 538
    Backing Up a File ... 539
    Restoring a File ... 540
Using the Utilities ... 542
    Rebuilding a Company File ... 542
    Verifying a Company File ... 542
Importing Data to QuickBooks ... 543
Exporting QuickBooks Data ... 544
Using Passwords ... 545
    Assigning Passwords ... 545
    Changing a Password ... 547
    Eliminating Password Protection ... 548
Summary ... 548

22 Customizing QuickBooks for Windows 549

Customizing Your Company File ... 549
    Setting Transaction Preferences ... 550
    Setting Invoice Preferences ... 552
    Setting Check Preferences ... 554
    Setting Reporting Preferences ... 555
    Setting Sales Tax Preferences ... 557
    Setting Password Preferences ... 559
Customizing the QuickBooks Program ... 559
    Setting View Preferences ... 559
    Setting Data Entry Preferences ... 561
    Setting Reminder Preferences ... 563
    Setting Graph Preferences ... 565
Summary ... 565

VII Appendixes 567

A Installing QuickBooks for Windows 569

Reviewing the Program Requirements ... 569
    Hardware Requirements ... 569
    Software Requirements ... 570
Performing the Installation ... 570
    Using Express Installation ... 570
    Customizing Installation ... 572

B Using QuickPay with QuickBooks for Windows 575

What QuickPay Does ... 575
What You Need To Run QuickPay with QuickBooks ... 577
How To Run QuickPay ... 577

C QuickBooks versus Quicken: Which Is Best for You? 583

Using Quicken for Home Finances ... 583
Using QuickBooks for Small Businesses ... 584

D QuickBooks for Canadian Users 589

Ordering Cheques, Invoices, and Other Supplies ... 589
Adapting the Chart of Accounts ... 589
Tracking Goods and Services Taxes (GST) ... 590
- Adding Liability Accounts for GST ... 590
- Using Specialized Accounts in Quebec ... 590
- Using Auto Tax ... 591
- Adding a GST Invoice Item ... 591
- Entering GST on Invoices ... 591
- Entering Bills with GST ... 592
- Paying GST ... 592

Index 595

Introduction

Whether you own or work in a small business, you know how much time the bookkeeping aspect of your business takes—hours and hours. You also know how frustrated you can become working with accounting software packages that require you to have a high level of accounting knowledge before you even get started. As a business owner, you would rather spend your time managing your business, which you know the most about. As a bookkeeper in a small business, you don't want to be bogged down with the tedium of double-entry accounting when you can achieve the same results with a powerful and accurate bookkeeping system that doesn't force you to deal with debits and credits, posting to journals, making closing entries, and so on.

The bookkeeping task of a small business, however, should not be underemphasized. Without an effective system for recording transactions, you have no way of knowing the operating results of the business. Because all small businesses exist to make money, it is extremely important that these results be determined and assessed at regular intervals so that you, as owner, can make the necessary changes in your business to improve results.

QuickBooks for Windows is your solution. Whether your current bookkeeping system is manual or computerized using Quicken or some other double-entry accounting software, the switch to QuickBooks for Windows is well worth the financial investment.

If you're using Quicken for Windows, switching to QuickBooks for Windows couldn't be easier. QuickBooks for Windows uses the same types of menu commands and windows (checks and reports, for example) that you are accustomed to seeing in Quicken. Many of the tasks that you perform in Quicken are done the same way in QuickBooks for Windows. You write checks, for example, in the Write Checks window in QuickBooks for Windows just as you do in Quicken for Windows. (QuickBooks for Windows checks, however, look more like business checks, including a voucher area.)

You create QuickBooks for Windows reports in the same way that you create reports in Quicken, from a Reports menu that lists all the available reports. You also can customize reports the same way that you do in Quicken. You even reconcile your checking account the same way in QuickBooks for Windows as you do in Quicken. These few examples should give you an idea of how QuickBooks for Windows and Quicken operate in similar ways. You can see that a Quicken user has a minimal learning period with QuickBooks for Windows. You can be up and running in no time!

If you currently use a manual bookkeeping system, you're probably anxious to make the switch to a computerized system so that you can spend less time writing customer invoices, entering invoices in the Accounts Receivable ledger, tracking Accounts Receivable balances, writing checks, entering transactions in your Check register, subtracting transactions from your account balance, and putting together financial reports (such as profit and loss statements and balance sheets). With QuickBooks for Windows, you enter transaction information once, and QuickBooks records the information in the appropriate register. When you write a check, for example, QuickBooks for Windows records the transaction in the Check register and subtracts the check amount from your checking account balance. Additionally, the transaction is assigned to an expense account so that you know exactly how monies are being spent.

Likewise, QuickBooks records invoices in the Accounts Receivable register, and adjusts the receivables balance by customer and in total accordingly. Payments from customers need only be entered once to credit the customer's account and to update Accounts Receivable simultaneously. As you can see, whereas a manual bookkeeping system requires several steps to do one task, QuickBooks for Windows most often requires just one step.

In this age of high technology, almost anything you do at a desk can be accomplished with a computer. Bookkeeping for your small business is no exception. With well-designed software, you can write checks and invoices, record transactions, set up a budget, reconcile your checking account, and create the reports and graphs you need to monitor the operating results of your business. You can accomplish these tasks in a fraction of the time that you are now spending with your manual system or your double-entry accounting package. For the majority of small businesses, QuickBooks for Windows offers a solution to the hours spent with a pencil or the hours of frustration when working with a complex accounting system.

With QuickBooks for Windows, you never need to know a debit from a credit, or any other accounting jargon for that matter. QuickBooks for Windows speaks to you in plain English and displays invoices and Check registers in a manner that's most familiar to you.

Overview of QuickBooks for Windows

QuickBooks for Windows, published by Intuit, is a computerized bookkeeping system for small businesses developed for use with Microsoft Windows. Intuit designed QuickBooks for Windows to work with its Windows product so that the user can learn and use QuickBooks for Windows in an easier and friendlier environment. Windows is an environment surrounding DOS, the disk operating system. With Windows, you can accomplish the same tasks that you can with DOS, but through the use of a graphical user interface, which provides visual choices and options for performing tasks. With Windows programs, all your choices are visible, which provides you with easier access to program features. When working in a Windows program, you can load other programs and quickly switch from one to another.

QuickBooks for Windows is suitable for any small business, cash or accrual; however, it is probably not the right program for a small business that has extensive inventories and needs a precise inventory tracking system.

Intuit is also the publisher of Quicken (DOS and Windows versions), the best-selling financial management program for home use. Quicken was designed for personal use, but also can be used in a small business (although not without some deficiencies). With Quicken, you can write and print checks, reconcile your checking account, keep track of your assets and liabilities, print reports, display graphs, track your investments, and create budgets.

Although you can use Quicken in a small business, it has some shortcomings for this type of use. With Quicken, a small business cannot write invoices, create customer statements, or adequately track accounts receivable and accounts payable. Also, Quicken's terminology is not always appropriate for small business use. Instead of *categories* to assign transactions related to one kind of income or expense, for example, QuickBooks for Windows actually uses the terms *Income* and *Expense accounts* to track transactions related to income or expenses of the business. QuickBooks for Windows is Intuit's answer to the growing small-business market's need for a simple, powerful, and effective bookkeeping system that doesn't require any accounting knowledge.

The following are some of the many capabilities available to you through QuickBooks for Windows:

- *Write and print invoices.* The process of invoicing and sending statements to your customers is a breeze with QuickBooks for Windows on-screen invoices, which are easy to fill out and print. QuickBooks for Windows provides three invoice formats from which to choose. End-of-month (or any other specified period) statements are automatically created by QuickBooks for Windows and are ready to print whenever you need them.

- *Track and bill for reimbursable expenses.* You can easily track expenses that will be reimbursed by your customers or clients. Then when it's time for billing, QuickBooks for Windows automatically enters these expenses on the invoices.

- *Record customer payments.* Payments received from your customers can be credited to their accounts to keep an up-to-date record of your accounts receivable. You also can handle overpayments or discounts with QuickBooks for Windows.

- *Prepare deposits.* After receiving payments, you can record deposits to your checking account (or other bank account) and print a deposit summary that you can include with your bank deposit slip.

- *Write and print checks.* You can fill in the information for a check in a window that looks just like the check you will be printing for your business.

- *Keep company lists.* You can keep an up-to-date list of your customers, jobs, vendors, employees, payment and shipping methods, customer and vendor types, payment terms, invoice items, and even the customer messages that you print on invoices. These lists not only give you the information you need, but make writing invoices and checks fast and easy.

- *Reconcile your checking account.* You can enter your bank statement information and reconcile your checking account in just minutes.

- *Enter bills from vendors.* To keep track of your Accounts Payable, you can enter bills from your vendors. To avoid late payment penalties or to take advantage of early payment discounts, you can have QuickBooks for Windows alert you when it's time to pay bills.

- *Pay bills.* QuickBooks for Windows can prepare checks to pay the bills that you have entered in the Accounts Payable register, which you can limit to bills with a due date through a specified date, selected bills, or partial payment of a bill.
- *Create cash flow forecasts.* Using QuickBooks for Windows to create cash flow forecasts helps you predict your business' cash flow needs.
- *Track fixed assets.* You can set up asset accounts for each or all of your fixed assets and enter depreciation and improvements to keep the basis of your fixed assets up-to-date.
- *Track your total equity.* You can set up asset and liability accounts, other than the accounts that are predefined by QuickBooks for Windows, to record all your assets and liabilities. Then you can create a balance sheet that lists your assets, liabilities, and the total equity in your small business.
- *Create and print reports.* At any given time, you can create and print reports to give yourself an accurate assessment of the operations of your business. You can customize reports to include as little or as much information as necessary.
- *Print reports to disk.* You can print any QuickBooks for Windows report to disk so that you can use the report in a spreadsheet such as Lotus 1-2-3 or in a word processor such as WordPerfect.
- *Create graphs.* You can create on-screen graphs to compare your income with expenses, net sales by month, accounts receivable by aging interval, accounts payable by aging period, net worth by month, and actual amounts with budget amounts.
- *Set up a budget.* You can set up budget amounts for the income and expense accounts you use in QuickBooks for Windows. QuickBooks for Windows compares budgeted amounts with actual amounts and creates a report that shows differences.
- *Transfer company data from Quicken or QuickBooks DOS.* If you have been using Quicken for your small business or QuickBooks for DOS, you easily can transfer your company data to QuickBooks for Windows. Your Quicken data and your QuickBooks DOS data remain intact.

- *Generate a 1099 report.* You can generate a report that lists the vendors to whom you paid more than $600 each year. You then can use this report to prepare Form 1099 at the end of the year.
- *Create new company files.* QuickBooks for Windows enables you to set up as many company files as you need so that you can keep the books for more than one company.
- *Receive reminder messages.* QuickBooks for Windows reminds you when you have checks to print, bills to pay, or overdue invoices from customers.
- *Generate sales-tax payable reports.* You can create sales-tax payable reports that summarize how much sales tax was billed for any given period.
- *Produce aging reports.* To find out how much your customers owe and for how long, you can produce an Accounts Receivable aging report with just a few keystrokes.
- *Get instant help.* With QCards, you get on-screen help when you display most forms.
- *Tour QuickBooks for Windows.* To get an overview of the program, how it works, and what it can do for you, QuickBooks for Windows provides a Quick Tour tutorial that you can view when you first start QuickBooks or any time down the road when you want to learn more.

Who Should Read This Book?

If you want to buy a bookkeeping system for your small business but cannot decide which program best meets your needs, you should read *Using QuickBooks for Windows* to get a feel for what the program offers. This Introduction identifies the general features included in QuickBooks for Windows. Reading the rest of the book will show you how easy QuickBooks for Windows is to use and will help you determine whether it is the right program for your particular business situation.

If you have just purchased QuickBooks for Windows, good for you! You already have recognized what a powerful tool QuickBooks for Windows is and are anticipating many hours saved by managing the finances of your small business with QuickBooks for Windows. Read *Using QuickBooks for Windows* to learn how to use the program and all its vast capabilities. In this book, you not only learn how to use QuickBooks for Windows efficiently and effectively, but also how to work with examples that can help you with some of the tasks that you most often encounter in your business.

If you are a first-time computer user, *Using QuickBooks for Windows* is written for you, too. This book helps you feel at ease in front of the computer and takes you step by step through the installation and use of QuickBooks for Windows.

Are you an accomplished computer user who is fairly proficient with financial and business programs? You also can benefit from reading *Using QuickBooks for Windows* because it contains numerous financial tips that are the result of CPA experience and practice.

If you're already using Quicken in your small business, this book will teach you the differences between the two programs and show you how to transfer your Quicken data to QuickBooks for Windows.

What Is in This Book?

Using QuickBooks for Windows takes a tutorial approach to familiarize you with the material. This book contains everything you need to know—from installing the program to creating and printing reports to show the results of your work. Of utmost value are the CPA Tips you find throughout this book. These tips contain advice and information to help you better manage your business finances. *Using QuickBooks for Windows* is divided into 7 parts, consisting of 22 chapters and 4 appendixes.

Part I—Getting Started

Part I shows you how to start QuickBooks for Windows and set up your company in the program. You also learn how to set up and modify accounts to meet the needs of your business situation and how to work with company lists (customer, vendor, employee, and so on).

Chapter 1, "Preparing To Use QuickBooks for Windows," gives you the information you need to start QuickBooks for Windows. This chapter shows you what information you should gather before sitting down with QuickBooks for Windows, how to decide when to start automating your system, how to start QuickBooks, and how to register your program with Intuit.

Chapter 2, "Learning Your Way Around QuickBooks for Windows," teaches you how to work with windows, move around in the program, use QuickBooks menus, get help when you need it, and exit the program when you are finished.

Chapter 3, "Setting Up Your Company in QuickBooks for Windows," describes how to create your company file and how to convert your QuickBooks DOS system or Quicken data to QuickBooks for Windows. Because you cannot do anything in QuickBooks for Windows until you set up your company file, this chapter is a must.

Chapter 4, "Working with Accounts," shows you how to set up the accounts with which you will be working.

Chapter 5, "Using QuickBooks for Windows Lists," explains the lists that QuickBooks for Windows uses to make filling out invoices and checks quick and easy. You also learn how to add your own items to a list and how to edit items in a list as well as delete those items that you don't need.

Part II—Tracking Customers

Part II describes how to create invoices and manage your Accounts Receivable. You learn how to track sales tax charged to your customers, how to print invoices and statements that you can send to customers, and how to enter customer payments in the Accounts Receivable register.

Chapter 6, "Creating Invoices," describes how to fill out an invoice to send to your customers. You also learn some shortcuts for making invoicing fast and easy.

Chapter 7, "Tracking Sales Tax," explains how to set up tax rates and taxing agencies in QuickBooks for Windows so that you can keep track of the sales tax that you collect from customers.

Chapter 8, "Printing Invoices, Statements, and Other Forms," teaches you how to print QuickBooks for Windows invoices, how to create and print customer statements, and how to print mailing labels and rotary index cards.

Chapter 9, "Receiving and Depositing Customer Payments," shows you how to enter the payments that you receive from your customers. You learn how to credit payments to a customer's account, how to handle overpayments and returns, and how to apply discounts. This chapter also explains how to enter cash sales and how to record deposits and print deposit summaries that you can include with your bank deposit slip.

Chapter 10, "Using the Accounts Receivable Register," shows you how to edit transactions in the Accounts Receivable register, view customer records using the QuickReport feature, and create a Transaction History Report.

Part III—Paying Bills

Part III teaches you how to enter and pay bills in the Accounts Payable register. You also learn how to write and print checks, and how to enter transactions in the Check register.

Chapter 11, "Entering and Paying Bills," teaches you how to enter bills that you owe your vendors and then shows you how to pay bills, how to add credits from vendors, and how to use the Reminders List to notify you when a bill is due for payment.

Chapter 12, "Using the Accounts Payable Register," shows you how to enter and edit bills in the Accounts Payable register, how to view a transaction history, and how to use the QuickReport feature to display vendor records.

Chapter 13, "Writing and Printing Checks," describes how to fill out the on-screen check window. You also learn how to assign check amounts to accounts so that you know exactly what you're paying for and how to print checks.

Chapter 14, "Entering Transactions in the Check Register," teaches you how to enter checks in the Check register if you are not using QuickBooks for Windows to write and print checks and how to enter other types of transactions that affect your checking account, such as deposits and bank charges. You also learn how to split a transaction so that you can assign more than one account, customer, or job (or all) to a check amount. This chapter describes how to edit, delete, and void transactions and how to enter a transfer transaction (a transaction assigned to another balance sheet account).

Part IV—Maximizing QuickBooks

Part IV shows you how to speed up your work in QuickBooks for Windows. Part IV teaches you how to reconcile your bank account and how to use other accounts, such as Credit Card, Current Asset, Fixed Asset, Payroll, Liability, and Equity accounts to complete your financial picture.

Chapter 15, "Speeding Up Your Work in QuickBooks for Windows," shows you how to enter transactions quickly and easily by using memorized transactions and transaction groups, as well as how to find transactions in the Check register (or any other QuickBooks for Windows register).

Chapter 16, "Reconciling Your Bank Account," explains how to reconcile your bank account quickly and easily, and how to search for and correct errors when you reconcile your accounts.

Chapter 17, "Using Other Accounts To Perform Tasks," shows you how to make your financial picture more complete by creating Balance Sheet accounts so that you can enter other types of transactions, such as depreciation of fixed assets or prepaid expenses. You learn how to enter transactions into these accounts and how to update account values.

Part V—Analyzing Business Data

Part V explains how to use QuickBooks for Windows beyond the basics to help you analyze your finances through budgeting, reports, and graphing financial results.

Chapter 18, "Preparing Budgets," explains how to set up a monthly budget and create a Budget report.

Chapter 19, "Creating and Printing Reports," discusses the different types of reports you can create with QuickBooks for Windows and tells how to generate and print those reports. You also learn how to customize reports to fit your business's reporting needs, how to memorize and recall reports, and how to examine report detail with the QuickZoom feature.

Chapter 20, "Creating Graphs," describes the new QuickBooks graph feature. If you want to see comparisons between income and expenses, net sales by month, actual versus budget amounts, and so on, read this chapter to learn about the various graphs that you can create on-screen and print.

Part VI—Managing QuickBooks

Part VI shows you how to manage your QuickBooks company files and customize the program to better fit the needs of your business.

Chapter 21, "Managing QuickBooks for Windows Files," teaches you how to create new company files and switch between company files so that you can enter more than one company's data in QuickBooks for Windows. You also learn how to back up and restore files, import and export data, and assign passwords to QuickBooks for Windows files and activities to prevent unauthorized use.

Chapter 22, "Customizing QuickBooks for Windows," explains how to customize your company file or the QuickBooks for Windows program to better suit your needs. You learn how to customize your company file by changing the invoice type, the method for receiving payments, the way classes are tracked, and so on, and how to customize the program so it works the way you want. This chapter also shows you how to use Reminders to remind you of checks to print, bills that are due, or overdue invoices.

Part VII—Appendixes

Appendix A, "Installing QuickBooks for Windows," lists the system requirements for running QuickBooks for Windows and explains how to install the program on your computer.

Appendix B, "Using QuickPay with QuickBooks for Windows," describes how to use Intuit's QuickPay program for preparing payroll along with your QuickBooks for Windows program.

Appendix C, "QuickBooks versus Quicken: Which Is Best for You?," gives an overview of QuickBooks for Windows as it relates to Quicken and explains how to transfer Quicken data to the QuickBooks for Windows program.

Appendix D, "QuickBooks for Canadian Users," explains how users should modify their QuickBooks for Windows system to accommodate Canadian needs, such as the use of the European date format and tracking of Goods and Services Taxes.

Conventions

The conventions used in this book have been established to help you learn to use QuickBooks for Windows quickly and easily.

- Information you are to type (usually found in examples with numbered steps) is indicated by boldface type (for example, "Type **c:\qbooksw** in the Directory text box to indicate the directory where you want to install the QuickBooks for Windows program") or is indented and set on a line by itself.

- Names of menus are shown with the initial letter capitalized.

- Options are shown with headline-style capital letters to help them stand out to the reader, although QuickBooks uses sentence-style capitals. For example, QuickBooks' Show icons only option appears as Show Icons Only in this book.

- The *mnemonic* key, which is the key that you can press to quickly choose a command or option, appears in boldface type (for example,

"From the **F**ile menu, choose **O**pen"). Mnemonic letters are underlined in QuickBooks.

- Messages and prompts that appear on-screen appear in a `monospace font`.
- Words or phrases defined for the first time appear in *italics*.
- Key combinations called *quick keys* are used to quickly choose menu commands or options. Quick keys are shown as Ctrl+A, for example, to indicate that you press the Ctrl key simultaneously with the A key.

This book also contains CPA Tips, which appear as sidebars with headings, that contain advice and information to help you better manage your business finances.

Part I

Getting Started

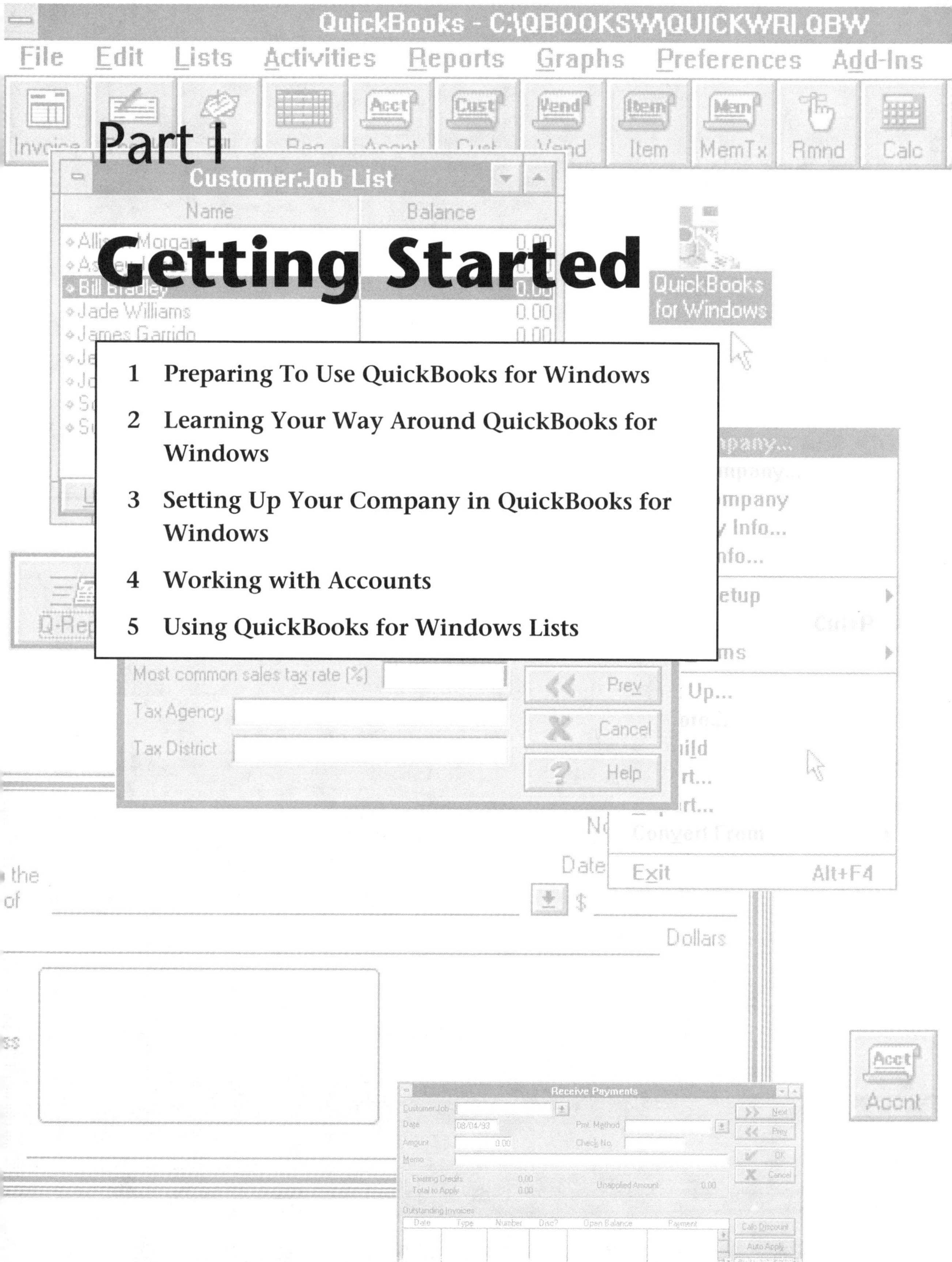

1 Preparing To Use QuickBooks for Windows

2 Learning Your Way Around QuickBooks for Windows

3 Setting Up Your Company in QuickBooks for Windows

4 Working with Accounts

5 Using QuickBooks for Windows Lists

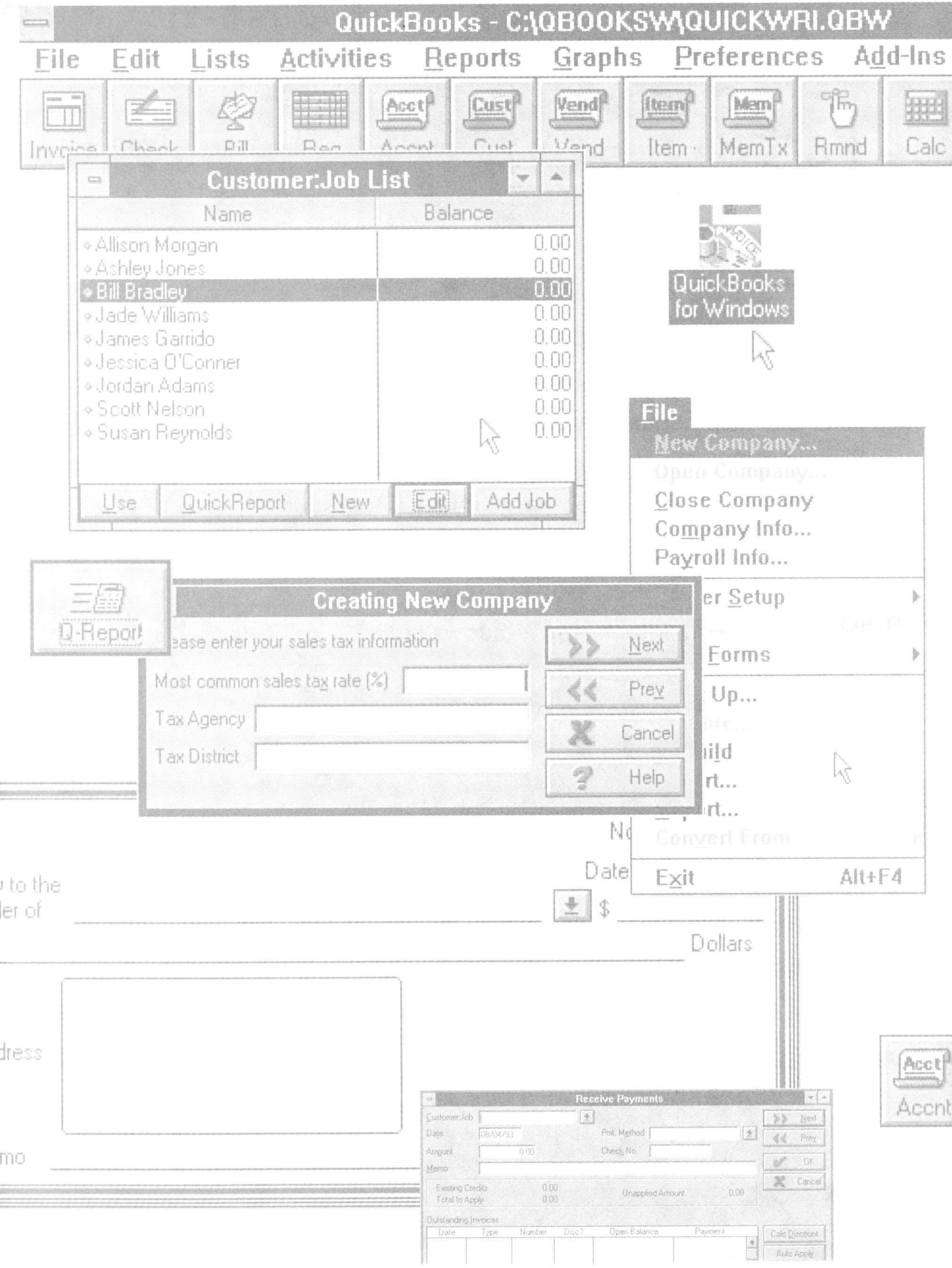

QuickBooks - C:\QBOOKSW\QUICKWRI.QBW
File Edit Lists Activities Reports Graphs Preferences Add-Ins
Vend Item MemTx Rmnd Calc
Customer:Job List
Name Balance
Allison Morgan 0.00
Ashley Jones 0.00
Bill Bradley 0.00
Jade Williams 0.00
James Garrido 0.00
Jessica O'Conner 0.00
Jordan Adams 0.00
Scott Nelson 0.00
Susan Reynolds 0.00
Use QuickReport New Edit Add Job
QuickBooks for Windows
File
New Company...
Open Company...
Close Company
Company Info...
Payroll Info...
Exit Alt+F4
Q-Report
Creating New Company
Please enter your sales tax information
Most common sales tax rate (%)
Tax Agency
Tax District
Next
Prev
Cancel
Help
Date
$
Dollars
Receive Payments
Accnt

Chapter 1

Preparing To Use QuickBooks for Windows

In this chapter, you learn how to do the following:

- Choose the best time to convert your manual bookkeeping system to QuickBooks for Windows
- Order checks, invoices, and supplies
- Gather information so you know which items and documentation you need before working with QuickBooks
- Start QuickBooks for Windows for the first time
- Register your QuickBooks program
- Set up your printer to print from Windows

QuickBooks for Windows makes bookkeeping tasks for your small business easy and quick. The introduction aquainted you with many of QuickBooks' capabilities, including writing and printing invoices, recording customer payments, keeping company lists, tracking Accounts Payable, and creating financial reports and graphs. Now you can begin setting up your QuickBooks system.

Converting Your Manual System to QuickBooks for Windows

Although you may have just purchased QuickBooks for Windows and are ready to get started, you should give due consideration to when you should stop using your manual system (hand-writing checks and entries into journals or registers) and automate your bookkeeping system with QuickBooks.

The ideal time to start using QuickBooks is January 1, or the first day of your fiscal year. Starting QuickBooks on January 1 allows you to enter a full year of transactions and makes reporting easier. If January 1 has come and gone, you still can start using QuickBooks; however, you may want to go back and enter all your transactions from the beginning of the year so that you can use QuickBooks to provide complete year-to-date reports. This task is time-consuming if you must enter eight to ten months of transactions. If that's the case, you might want to wait until January 1 of the next year to start using QuickBooks.

If you're unable to start using QuickBooks on January 1, and you don't want to go back and enter transpired data, start using QuickBooks at the beginning of a month. Then, at the end of the year, you can add the completed full months from your manual transactions to the totals in your QuickBooks system.

Suppose that you start using QuickBooks on August 1. You record your transactions in QuickBooks from August 1 to December 31. Then, when you compile year-end reports—such as profit and loss statements—just add the seven full months (January through July) of transactions from your manual bookkeeping system to the totals from QuickBooks to arrive at year-end totals.

CPA TIP: Using Data from Both Systems for Income Tax Purposes

If you are using data from both your manual system and your QuickBooks system for income tax purposes, make sure that you provide adequate worksheets or documentation for the income and expenses of your business. In this case, you must show that amounts reported on income tax forms and schedules are derived from two sources: your manual system and your QuickBooks system.

If you want your QuickBooks records to be complete and include all transactions from the beginning of your fiscal year, you can enter all historical transactions or just one summary transaction that includes year-to-date amounts for each account. To learn more about entering historical transactions, see Chapter 6, "Creating Invoices," Chapter 11, "Entering and Paying Bills," and Chapter 14, "Entering Transactions in the Check Register."

Ordering Checks, Invoices, and Supplies

You can use QuickBooks for Windows simply as an electronic bookkeeping system to record the transactions of your business, calculate the ending balance in your checking account, track Accounts Receivable and Accounts Payable, reconcile your checking account, and produce reports and graphs. But the power of QuickBooks lies in its invoice- and check-printing capabilities, its biggest time-saving feature. Printing checks with QuickBooks is faster and easier than hand-writing checks. You will need a pen only to sign the checks to make them valid.

Printing checks with QuickBooks not only saves time, but also saves on clerical errors. And printing invoices with QuickBooks for Windows is faster and easier than typing or using a word processor to prepare invoices.

Preprinted checks, invoices, and statements are available from Intuit. (If you prefer not to use preprinted invoices or statements, you can use plain paper or your company letterhead.) Envelopes and mailing labels are also available. Your QuickBooks package contains a supply catalog and order form that you can use to place an order with Intuit, or you can print an order form by using your QuickBooks program. Ordering invoices and other supplies is discussed in Chapter 8, "Printing Invoices, Statements, and Other Forms." Ordering checks is discussed in more detail in Chapter 13, "Writing and Printing Checks."

If your printer uses continuous-feed paper, you can choose from three types of invoices:

- Multipart product invoices
- Multipart service invoices
- Multipart professional invoices

Nine types of checks are available for use with continuous-feed printers:

- Classic standard nonvoucher, one part only
- Classic standard nonvoucher, multiple parts (provides a carbonless copy of each check)
- Classic voucher, one part only
- Classic voucher, multiple parts (provides a carbonless copy of each check)
- Prestige voucher, one part only
- Prestige voucher, two parts (provides a carbonless copy of each check)
- Prestige standard nonvoucher, one part only
- Prestige standard nonvoucher, two parts (provides a carbonless copy of each check)
- Antique standard nonvoucher, one part only

If you have a laser or inkjet printer, you can choose from three types of invoices:

- Product invoices: one part, triplicate, or quadruplicate (last part is a packing slip)
- Service invoices: one part or triplicate
- Professional invoices: one part or triplicate

Seven types of checks are available for laser or inkjet printers:

- Classic laser voucher, one part only
- Classic laser voucher, duplicate parts
- Classic laser standard nonvoucher, one part only
- Prestige laser voucher, one part only
- Prestige laser voucher, duplicate parts
- Prestige laser standard nonvoucher, one part only
- Antique laser standard nonvoucher, one part only

Note

Voucher checks include a bottom stub for payroll or Accounts Payable information. Standard logos can be printed (free of charge) on checks or invoices. If your small business has a customized logo that you want to use, enclose black-and-white, camera-ready artwork with your order. You will be charged a one-time fee for customized logos.

You can also order the following items from Intuit to make your bookkeeping tasks fast and easy:

- Multipart customer statements
- Forms leader for continuous-feed or inkjet printers
- Preprinted deposit slips
- Mailing labels

- Double-window check envelopes (envelopes with a window for the addressee and a window for the return address)
- Endorsement and return address stamps

Intuit guarantees that your order will be printed as submitted and error-free, that your checks and invoices will work in your printer, and that the checks you order will be accepted by your bank.

To place an order, look through the *Intuit Checks and Invoices Catalog* that came packaged with your QuickBooks software and fill out the order form included in the package. You can print additional order forms from the QuickBooks program. See Chapter 8, "Printing Invoices, Statements, and Other Forms," and Chapter 13, "Writing and Printing Checks," to learn how to print order forms.

Gathering Information

With QuickBooks for Windows, you can start writing invoices and checks with as little or as much information as you want to enter. To begin using QuickBooks, you *must* enter your company name (so that QuickBooks can create a company file to store your data) and set up the account that you will be using to write checks (your business checking account). If you want to get the most out of your QuickBooks system, however, you will want to gather more information before using QuickBooks. The following is a list of items you might want to gather before starting your system:

- *Company information.* Although you can set up your company file in QuickBooks just by entering the name of your business, you will want to enter more information if you plan to show company information on customer invoices. Additional company information you can add includes the address, employer identification number, shipping location, and the usual shipping method. Chapter 3, "Setting Up Your Company in QuickBooks for Windows," shows you how to enter this information.
- *List of accounts.* When you set up your company, QuickBooks asks which preset income, expense, and balance sheet accounts you want to use. Accounts are preset based on the type of business. You can modify (add to, delete, or edit) these accounts to fit your particular business

needs. The best summary of the types of accounts that your business uses is from your profit and loss statement and the balance sheet. The profit and loss statement lists Income and Expense accounts, and the balance sheet lists Asset and Liability accounts. Have your latest statements ready so that you can customize the account list to fit your business. See Chapter 4, "Working with Accounts," to learn how to set up accounts in your company file.

- *Checking account information.* You must set up an account to record your financial activities. Most likely, this account will be your business checking account, where cash inflows are deposited and cash outflows are withdrawn. Checking account information should include your bank account name and account number. You learn how to set up a checking account in Chapter 4, "Working with Accounts."

- *Bank statement.* When adding your checking account in QuickBooks, you must enter the account balance (opening balance) as of a specific date. Several options are available for entering the account balance, and they are discussed later in this chapter. If you choose to enter your ending bank statement balance as the opening balance in your checking account in QuickBooks, however, you should have your latest bank statement handy. Chapter 4, "Working with Accounts," shows you how to enter bank statement information for your checking account.

- *Customer List.* QuickBooks makes entry fast and easy by storing lists of your customers so that you don't have to enter the same information each time you enter an invoice or receive a payment. QuickBooks adds the customer to the Customer List each time you enter new customer information. You may want to enter your Customer List up front, however, to save time after you begin using QuickBooks. Chapter 5, "Using QuickBooks for Windows Lists," shows you how to add to the Customer List.

- *Vendor List.* QuickBooks automatically adds a new vendor to the Vendor List as you enter the vendor information in the Accounts Payable register. If you want a complete Vendor List before you begin using QuickBooks to track payables, enter each vendor from your Vendor List up front. Chapter 5, "Using QuickBooks for Windows Lists," shows you how to add to the Vendor List.

- *Employee List.* If your small business has several employees, you may want to go ahead and add them to the QuickBooks Employee List. Chapter 5, "Using QuickBooks for Windows Lists," shows you how to add to the Employee List.

- *List of invoice items.* Invoice items are listed as line item detail on customer invoices. These items describe what product or services you are billing your customer for. Have a complete list of your products and services handy so that you can complete this list. Chapter 5, "Using QuickBooks for Windows Lists," shows you how to add these items.

- *Check register.* If you want to enter transactions before the date you are starting your QuickBooks system, you will need your check register. (See Chapter 14, "Entering Transactions in the Check Register.")

- *Accounts Receivable transactions.* If you want QuickBooks to show correct balances for Accounts Receivable, you must enter outstanding invoices. (See Chapter 6, "Creating Invoices.")

- *Accounts Payable transactions.* If you want QuickBooks to show correct balances for Accounts Payable, you must enter any outstanding bills. (See Chapter 11, "Entering and Paying Bills.")

- *Schedule of assets.* If you set up an asset account for each business asset, you need documentation that establishes the value of those assets. You might not have one document that lists all of your assets. You can use original purchase documentation for fixed assets, however, or your latest brokerage statement for investment assets. Fixed assets should be recorded at their original cost, with a separate account for depreciation. Chapter 17, "Using Other Accounts To Perform Tasks," teaches you more about asset accounts.

- *Schedule of loans.* If you set up liability accounts for each outstanding business loan, you need loan schedules or amortization schedules so that you can enter the outstanding loan balances. QuickBooks for Windows does not perform amortization calculations, so you must obtain these schedules from your bank or creditor, or set up your own amortization schedule by using a spreadsheet program such as Lotus 1-2-3. Chapter 17, "Using Other Accounts To Perform Tasks," teaches you how to set up a liability account.

Quicken includes a loan amortization feature that you can use to determine outstanding loan balances. If you're switching from Quicken to QuickBooks, you might want to keep your Quicken system intact (don't delete your Quicken program files) so that you can use this feature.

Other items you might want to gather before using QuickBooks are a list of your payment terms, shipping methods, and payment methods.

You can begin using QuickBooks without entering some of the preceding information. If you want your QuickBooks system to serve as your complete financial software system, however, you eventually will need to enter the majority of the suggested information. By entering all your financial and business information, you can use QuickBooks to generate invoices, statements, checks, financial reports, graphs, and budgets. You will not need to supplement your QuickBooks system with any other system to effectively and efficiently manage your business finances.

Starting QuickBooks for Windows for the First Time

After you have properly installed QuickBooks, as explained in Appendix A, "Installing QuickBooks for Windows," you are ready to start the program and begin setting up your system. To start QuickBooks, follow these steps:

1. At the DOS prompt, type **win** and press Enter.
2. From the Windows opening screen, move the mouse pointer to the QuickBooks for Windows icon in the QuickBooks window, as shown in figure 1.1. When you ran the QuickBooks for Windows install program, the QuickBooks program was installed in the QuickBooks group window (unless you chose to install the program in a different program group). Notice that the group windows in your Windows opening screen might not look like the ones in figure 1.1, which are displayed in cascade format.
3. Double-click (press the left mouse button twice in quick succession) the QuickBooks for Windows icon to start the program. (Chapter 2, "Learning Your Way Around QuickBooks for Windows," explains mouse operations in greater detail.)

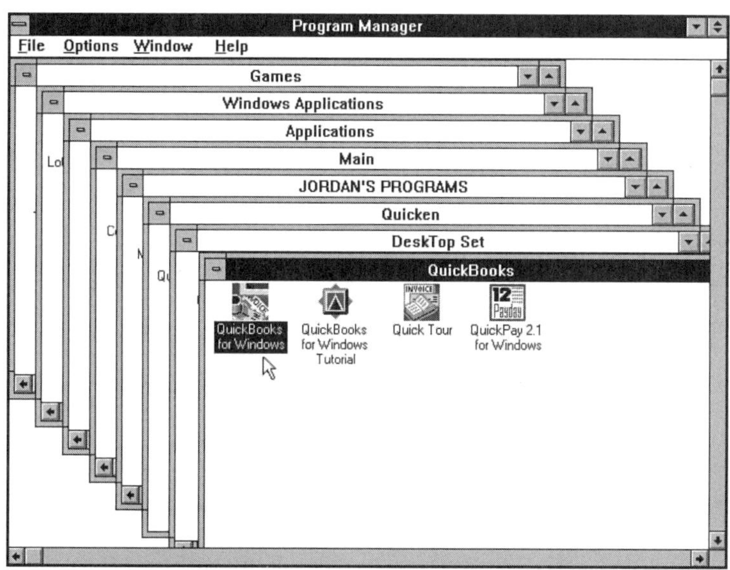

Fig. 1.1
Click the QuickBooks for Windows icon in the QuickBooks program group to start QuickBooks.

The first time you start QuickBooks, the Welcome to QuickBooks screen appears (see fig. 1.2). You have two options: start the program or start the QuickBooks tutorial. To start the program itself, point to the **S**tart QuickBooks button and click. To start the tutorial, point to the **Q**uick Tour button and click. The tutorial consists of eight lessons from which you can choose to get an on-screen overview of how QuickBooks works. You will learn some of the more specific activities performed in the program, like creating a company file, adding to lists, writing invoices and checks, entering bills, preparing reports and graphs, and so on. In Chapter 2, "Learning Your Way Around QuickBooks for Windows," you'll learn how to use the tutorial. For now, click the **S**tart QuickBooks button.

When you start QuickBooks, the QuickBooks for Windows application window displays, as shown in figure 1.3.

The QuickBooks for Windows application window is essentially blank, except for the title bar and menu bar that appear at the top of the screen. Chapter 2, "Learning Your Way Around QuickBooks for Windows," goes into greater detail about the QuickBooks for Windows application window.

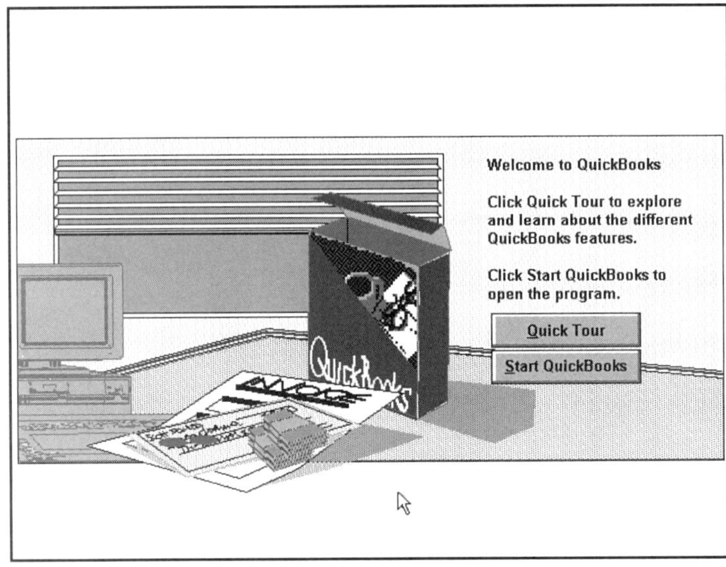

Fig. 1.2
The Welcome to QuickBooks window is displayed the first time you start the program.

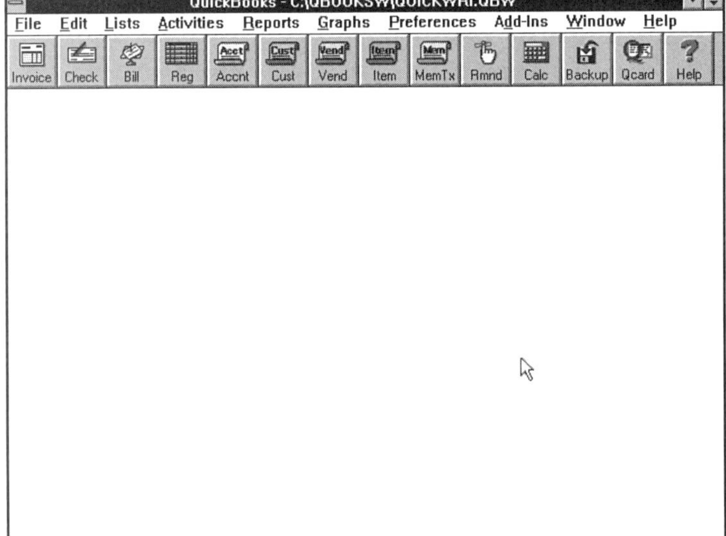

Fig. 1.3
The QuickBooks for Windows application window displays when you start QuickBooks.

Registering Your Program

To take advantage of technical support from Intuit, to receive notification of upgrades, and to learn about subsequent special offerings to QuickBooks customers, you must register your QuickBooks software. The second time that you start QuickBooks, the Product Registration dialog box shown in figure 1.4 displays.

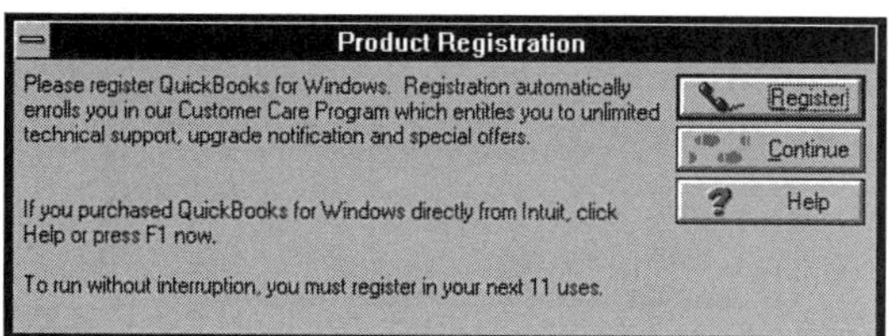

Fig. 1.4
The Product Registration dialog box displays each time you start QuickBooks until you register your software.

Caution

You will only be able to use QuickBooks for Windows 25 times without registering your software with Intuit. If you have not registered your software and start QuickBooks for the 26th time, you will see only the Product Registration dialog box, and you will not be able to use the program! It is *vitally* important that you register your QuickBooks software *now!*

If you purchased your QuickBooks software directly from Intuit, make sure that you have your eight-digit Customer Number before you register your software. Your Customer Number is located in the upper-left corner of the packing slip you received with your QuickBooks software. If you did not buy QuickBooks from Intuit, follow the instructions in the Note after step 3 in the following list.

To register your QuickBooks software, follow these steps:

1. From the Product Registration dialog box shown in figure 1.4, choose **R**egister.

   If the Product Registration dialog box is not displayed, from the **A**ctivities menu, choose the Register **Q**uickBooks option. To choose this option, choose **A**ctivities on the menu bar at the top of the QuickBooks for Windows screen. QuickBooks displays the Activities menu. Then choose Register **Q**uickBooks (the last option on the Activities menu).

   Chapter 2, "Learning Your Way Around QuickBooks for Windows," provides additional information on selecting program options and using the mouse and keyboard.

2. QuickBooks displays the Register QuickBooks for Windows dialog box shown in figure 1.5.

3. If you purchased your QuickBooks program directly from Intuit, type your Customer Number in the Customer Number text box.

Fig. 1.5
Enter your eight-digit customer number in the Register QuickBooks for Windows dialog box.

> **Note**
>
> If you *did not* purchase your QuickBooks software directly from Intuit, call the toll-free telephone number shown in the Register QuickBooks for Windows dialog box. (Representatives from the United States or Canada are available 24 hours a day, seven days a week.) Give the QuickBooks representative the QuickBooks for Windows serial number displayed in your Register QuickBooks for Windows dialog box. After you give the representative your name, address, daytime telephone number, and preferred floppy disk size, you will receive your eight-digit Customer Number.

4. Choose OK or press Enter. QuickBooks displays a dialog box that thanks you for registering the program.

5. Choose OK or press Enter.

After you have registered your QuickBooks software, the Register **Q**uickBooks option is no longer available from the **A**ctivities menu.

QuickBooks stores your Customer Number; you can retrieve it quickly by choosing the **A**bout QuickBooks option from the Help menu. QuickBooks displays your Customer Number in the lower-right corner of the QuickBooks information window. You must have your Customer Number handy if you need to call Intuit for technical support.

Setting Up Your Printer

If you've been printing reports or documents using other Windows applications, your printer is already set up to print invoices, statements, checks, reports, lists, graphs, labels, and rotary index cards with QuickBooks. If you have not printed from a Windows application, you must set up Windows to use your printer or printers before you can print from QuickBooks.

To set up Windows to use your printer(s), follow these steps:

1. Type **win** at the `C:\` prompt, and press Enter to start the Windows program.

2. Make sure that the Program Manager window is active. If it is not, double-click the Program Manager icon or press Ctrl+Esc to display the Windows Task List. From the Windows Task List, click Program Manager, or use the arrow keys to highlight Program Manager, and press Enter.

3. From the Program Manager, locate the Control Panel icon (usually in the Main Group). Double-click the Control Panel icon to display the Control Panel window.

4. From the Control Panel window, double-click the Printers icon to display the Printers dialog box.

5. Examine the printers shown in the Default Printer box to see whether the correct default printer and printer port (such as LPT1) appears. If not, select a printer from the Installed **P**rinters list box and choose S**e**t As Default Printer.

6. If you want to install other printers to use with QuickBooks, choose **A**dd and select a printer name from the list. Then choose **I**nstall and follow the on-screen instructions.

To learn how to customize printer settings to use other printers, to print logos, or to choose a different paper size and orientation, see Chapter 8, "Printing Invoices, Statements, and Other Forms," Chapter 13, "Writing and Printing Checks," Chapter 19, "Creating and Printing Reports," and Chapter 20, "Creating Graphs."

Summary

In this chapter, you learned about converting your manual system to QuickBooks for Windows. You also learned what information you need to gather before starting your first QuickBooks session; how to order checks, invoices, and other supplies; how to register your QuickBooks program; and how to make sure that you're ready to print from QuickBooks.

You're now ready to get into the program. The next chapter teaches you the basics of QuickBooks. You learn how to work with windows (activate, move, resize, and so on), dialog boxes, and menus. You also learn how to use the Iconbar to choose menu commands and options, how to get on-line help when you need it, and how to exit the program when your work is finished.

Chapter 2

Learning Your Way Around QuickBooks for Windows

In this chapter, you learn how to do the following:

- Start the program
- Use the mouse and keyboard
- Become familiar with Windows basics
- Use the Iconbar to choose menu commands and options
- Use Qcards for step-by-step help
- Exit from the program when your work is finished

Now that you have registered your QuickBooks for Windows system, you're ready to learn the basics of the QuickBooks program. Notice that you cannot begin using QuickBooks until you have set up your company file. You learn how to set up a company file in Chapter 3, "Setting Up Your Company in QuickBooks for Windows." This chapter is confined to QuickBooks for Windows basics. The steps in the later sections of this chapter require that you have a company file set up so that you can open windows, choose commands, and so on. If you want to follow along with those steps, go to Chapter 3 first and set up your company. Then return to this chapter so that you can follow the steps that teach you the QuickBooks basics.

Starting the Program

In Chapter 1, "Preparing To Use QuickBooks for Windows," you learned how to start QuickBooks for the first time. You start your second session almost the same way; however, you don't have to bother with program registration this time.

To start QuickBooks, follow these steps:

1. At the DOS prompt, type **win** and press Enter.
2. From the Windows opening screen, move the mouse pointer to the QuickBooks for Windows icon in the QuickBooks window, and

double-click it to start the program. (Mouse operations are explained in more detail later in this chapter.) You can also start QuickBooks by highlighting the QuickBooks for Windows icon in the QuickBooks window and pressing Enter.

3. QuickBooks starts and opens the last company file that you used.

Working with the Mouse and Keyboard

QuickBooks, as with most Windows programs, works equally well with a mouse or the keyboard to move around the screen or select menus and commands. You'll probably find that using the mouse makes it easier to learn and search through the program menus. Sometimes, however, using a combination of the mouse and keyboard is the most efficient way to work within QuickBooks.

Using the Mouse

A mouse lets you open menus, select commands, and perform other operations. You probably noticed that the mouse pointer on-screen is in the shape of an arrow. Actually, the shape of the mouse pointer can change depending on the operation you are performing.

The following table lists the basic mouse shapes that you will see on-screen and their functions:

Mouse Shape On-Screen	Function
Arrow pointer	Selects or chooses menus, commands, or options
I-beam	Moves the cursor or selects text to be edited
Hourglass	Waits while the program works
Right arrow or Left arrow	Moves the window to a different place on-screen

To move the mouse pointer around the screen, move the mouse on your desk or mouse pad in the same direction that you want the mouse pointer to move. When you have moved the mouse pointer where you want it, you can follow any of these procedures:

- *Click.* Press the left mouse button once.
- *Double-click.* Press the left mouse button twice in quick succession.
- *Drag.* Hold down the left button while moving the mouse on your desk or mouse pad.

Throughout this book, the preceding terms are used to explain how to select menus, commands, and options with a mouse.

Using the Keyboard

You enter text and numbers into QuickBooks fields by using the keys on the keyboard. You can also use the keyboard to choose menus, commands, and options. To choose a menu and select a command from the menu bar (explained later in this chapter), follow these steps:

1. Press the Alt key together with the underlined letter in the name of the menu item. This underlined letter is called a *mnemonic*; in this book, mnemonics are shown in boldface type. For example, to choose the **F**ile menu, press Alt plus the F key to pull down the menu shown in figure 2.1. Throughout this book, instructions for using the Alt key and letter combination (known as *quick keys*) appear as Alt+*letter* (Alt+F in this example). The letter key you press can be upper- or lowercase.

Fig. 2.1
The File pull-down menu is accessed by pressing Alt+F.

2. When the pull-down menu appears, follow either one of these procedures:

   Use the up- and down-arrow keys to move the highlight bar to the command or option that you want to select, and press Enter.

or

Press the mnemonic in the command or option name that you want to select.

Using Quick Keys

Quick keys can save you steps in selecting menus, commands, or options when using the keyboard. Quick keys usually combine the Ctrl or Alt keys with a letter key or a function key but also may be a single key such as the Tab, Enter, Del, Esc, or arrow keys or a single function key. Quick keys are listed to the right of the command or option name in the menu, as shown in figure 2.2.

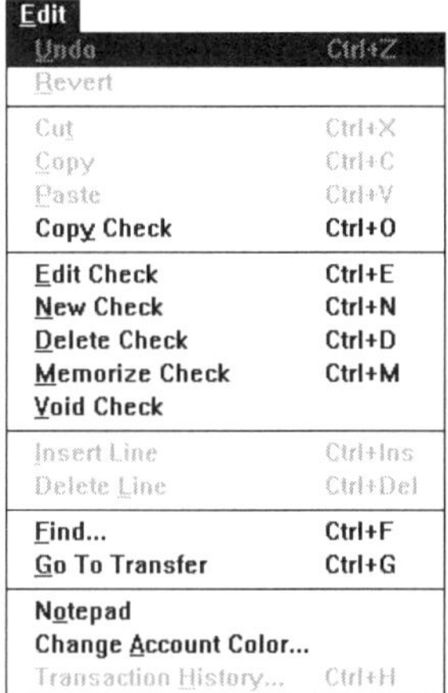

Fig. 2.2 Quick keys are listed to the right of the menu command or option.

Table 2.1 lists the quick keys used in QuickBooks to access menus, select commands and options, and move more quickly within the program.

Table 2.1. Quick Keys

Quick key	Function
Ctrl+A	Access the Chart of Accounts List
Ctrl+C	Copy to Windows Clipboard
Ctrl+D	Delete an invoice or a transaction
Ctrl+E	Edit a transaction
Ctrl+F	Display the Find window to search for an invoice or transaction
Ctrl+G	Go to transfer transaction

Quick key	Function
Ctrl+H	Display a transaction history
Ctrl+I	Display the Create Invoices window
Ctrl+J	Access the Customer:Job List
Ctrl+M	Memorize an invoice or transaction
Ctrl+N	Create a new invoice or write a new check
Ctrl+O	Copy a transaction to the Windows Clipboard
Ctrl+P	Print
Ctrl+R	Use a register
Ctrl+T	Access the Memorized Transactions List
Ctrl+V	Paste from the Windows Clipboard
Ctrl+W	Display the Write Checks window
Ctrl+X	Cut (remove) and place in the Windows Clipboard
Ctrl+Z	Undo the last edit
Ctrl+Ins	Insert a line
Ctrl+Del	Delete a line
Alt+F4	Exit QuickBooks
F1	Get help on current window or menu
F2	Access the QuickBooks tutorial

Understanding the Windows Environment

QuickBooks works with the Microsoft Windows operating system, version 3.1. To learn how to use QuickBooks, you should first be familiar with the Windows environment and how to navigate through the windows displayed on-screen. If you are a proficient Windows user, skip this section of the chapter.

Programs that run in the Windows environment display your work in rectangular windows that allow you to work with more than one application at the same time. For example, in Windows you can work with a word processing program, a spreadsheet program, and a database program at the same time, and copy and move information between programs.

Although you can work with more than one window or application, only one at a time can be active. For example, when you switch from one window to another, the window you move to becomes the active window. The window you leave remains open, but not active.

QuickBooks is set up to work from within the Windows environment and uses several different windows: Create Invoices, Write Checks, Enter Bills, Check Register, Accounts Receivable Register, Accounts Payable Register, and so on. You can also work with these windows simultaneously.

All windows in Windows applications such as QuickBooks have the same characteristics. The following section explains these common elements. Some of the operations performed with the Windows commands that you learn about next can be performed in QuickBooks through the menu bar displayed at the top of the QuickBooks for Windows screen. Commands and options from the QuickBooks menu bar are explained later in this chapter.

Examining the Title Bar

The title bar is located at the top of a window and displays a name to help you identify the contents of the window and the current file name. In figure 2.3, you see the name QuickBooks-`C:\QBOOKSB\SAMPLE.QBW-[Write Checks-Checking]` in the title bar at the top of the window that indicates the name of the program (QuickBooks), the file name (C:\QBOOKSB\SAMPLE.QBW) and the contents of the window (Write Checks-Checking).

Activating a Window

Before you can work in a window, the window must be active. As stated earlier, you can work with more than one window at a time but only one window can be active at a time. When a window is active, the title bar of that window is highlighted. To activate a window, follow these steps:

1. Place the mouse pointer on the title bar of the window that you want to activate.

2. Click the title bar. QuickBooks moves the window to the foreground of the screen and highlights the title bar to show that the window is active and that you can begin working in it.

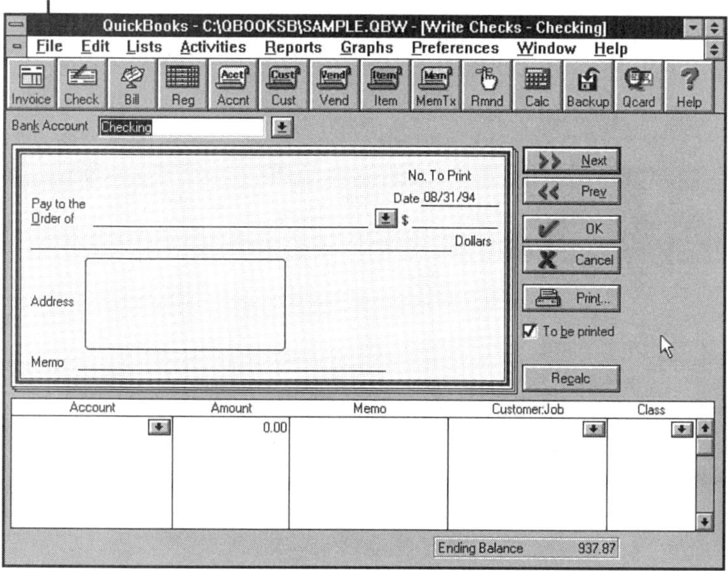

Fig. 2.3 The title bar for the Write Checks window in the SAMPLE.QBW file.

Manipulating Windows

The Control menu box is a small box in the left corner of the title bar. When you click this box or press Alt+space bar, the Control menu shown in figure 2.4 appears. The Control menu contains options for manipulating and switching among windows.

Fig. 2.4 The Control menu box and the Control menu are used to manipulate windows.

You can also resize windows by using the Minimize, Maximize, and Restore buttons in the right corner of the title bar, as shown in figure 2.5.

Restoring Windows. The first item in the Control menu is the Restore command. You can use it to enlarge windows or reduce windows to an icon at the bottom of the screen. *Icons* are small pictures that represent QuickBooks windows, as shown in figure 2.6. When you choose Restore, QuickBooks returns the window to the size it was before it was enlarged or reduced.

If, for example, you enlarge an icon to a window, and then you choose the Restore command from the Control menu for that window, the window is restored to an icon.

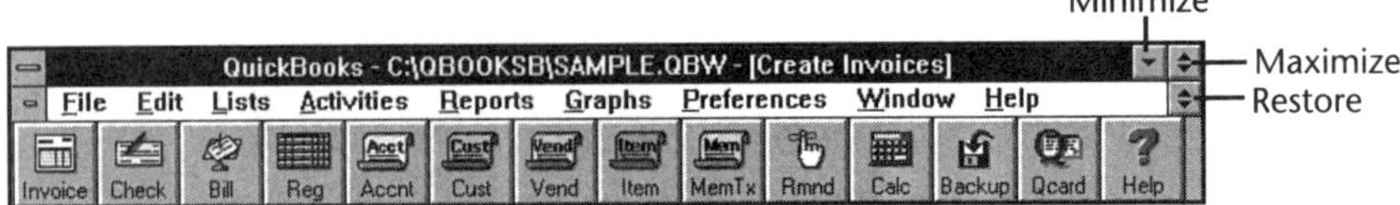

Fig. 2.5 The Minimize, Maximize, and Restore buttons are used to change the size of a window.

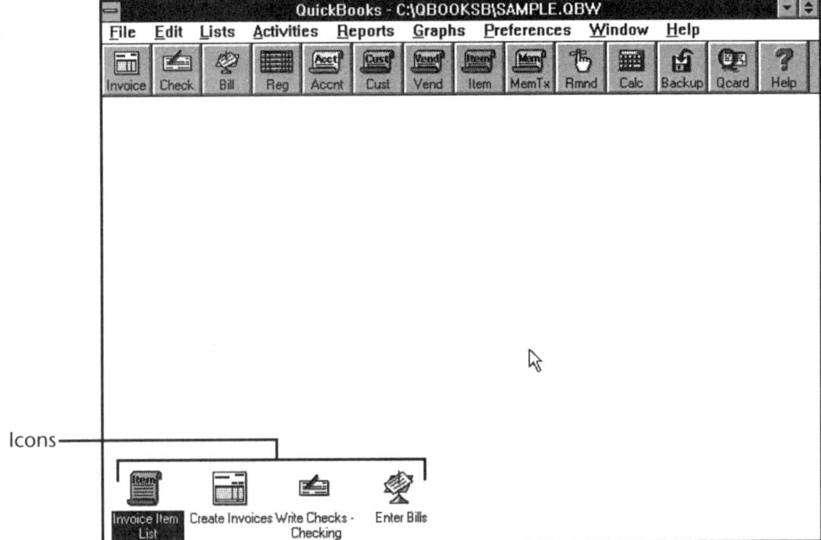

Fig. 2.6 Icons representing QuickBooks windows.

To restore a window by using the Restore command, follow these steps:

1. Place the mouse pointer on the window that you want to restore.
2. Click the Control menu box to open the Control menu.
3. Choose the **R**estore command by clicking it or pressing R. QuickBooks restores the window to its original size.

If you are using a mouse, you can restore a reduced window by completing these steps:

1. Place the mouse pointer on the icon that you want to restore.
2. Double-click the left mouse button.

To restore an enlarged window to the size it was previously when using a mouse, follow these steps:

1. Place the mouse pointer on the Restore button on the title bar (refer to fig. 2.5).

2. Click the Restore button to restore the window to its original size.

Moving Windows. You can move windows to help organize the information on-screen. You may want to move the window in which you are working, for example, so that you can see the information in another window while you are working. The Move command from the Control menu can be used in combination with a mouse to move windows.

To move windows by using the Move command from the Control menu, follow these steps:

1. Place the mouse pointer on the title bar of the window that you want to move, and click to either activate the window or move it to the foreground of the screen.

2. Click the Control menu box to open the Control menu.

3. From the Control menu, choose the **M**ove command by clicking it or by pressing M.

4. Use the arrow keys to move the pointer to the position on-screen where you want to place the window.

5. Press Enter. QuickBooks positions the window in its new location.

You can also move windows with the mouse alone by following these steps:

1. Place the mouse pointer on the title bar of the window that you want to move.

2. Press and hold the left mouse button.

3. Drag the mouse pointer (which changes shape, as explained in the earlier section "Using the Mouse") to the position on-screen where you want to place the window. When you move the mouse, the outline of the window follows the mouse pointer.

4. Release the mouse button. The window is moved to its new location. Figures 2.7 and 2.8 show the Write Checks window moved from the upper-left part of the screen to the lower-right part of the screen.

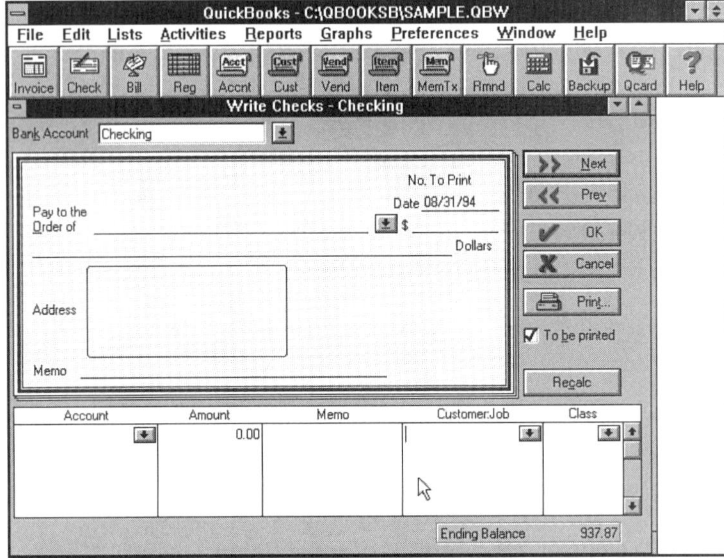

Fig 2.7
The Write Checks window positioned in the upper-left part of the screen.

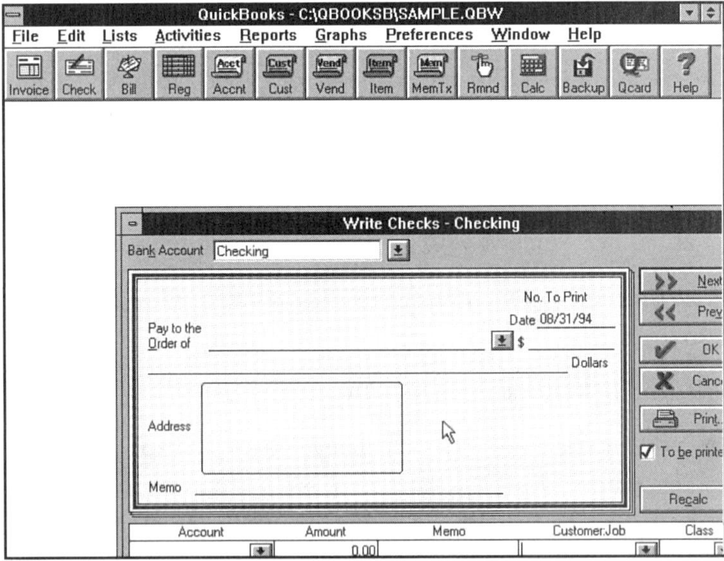

Fig 2.8
The Write Checks window moved to the lower-right part of the screen.

Resizing Windows. You can change the size of a window by enlarging the window to fill the screen, shrinking the window to an icon, or changing the height or width of a window. When you shrink or reduce the size of a window, the window is inactive but still open for you to use later. You can enlarge or shrink windows by using the Size, Minimize, and Maximize commands from the Control menu. Or you can use the Minimize and Maximize buttons in the right corner of the title bar (refer to fig. 2.5).

Changing Window Height and Width. To change the height or width of a window by using the Size command from the Control menu, follow these steps:

1. Place the mouse pointer on the title bar of the window that you want to resize, and click to activate the window or move it to the foreground of the screen.
2. Click the Control menu box to open the Control menu.
3. From the Control menu, choose **S**ize.
4. Use the arrow keys to move the pointer to the border or corner that you want to move.
5. When the pointer is properly positioned, use the arrow keys to resize the window.
6. Press Enter. The window changes size.

To change the height or width of a window by using a mouse, follow these steps:

1. Place the mouse pointer on the corner of the window that you want to resize. The pointer shape changes to a double arrow.
2. Press and hold the left mouse button.
3. Drag the mouse pointer to move the corner of the window to the size that you want. An outline of the window borders follows the pointer as you move it.
4. Release the mouse button. The window changes size.

Maximizing Windows. To enlarge a window to fill the screen by using the Maximize command from the Control menu, follow these steps:

1. Place the mouse pointer on the title bar of the window that you want to enlarge, and click to activate the window or move it to the foreground of the screen.

2. Click the Control menu box to open the Control menu.

3. From the Control menu, choose the Ma**x**imize command. QuickBooks enlarges the window to fill the screen.

To maximize a window by using the Maximize button on the title bar, follow these steps:

1. Place the mouse pointer on the title bar of the window that you want to enlarge. If this window is not active, click the title bar to activate the window or move it to the foreground of the screen.

2. Place the mouse pointer on the Maximize button (refer to fig. 2.5) and click. QuickBooks enlarges the window to fill the screen.

Minimizing Windows. To shrink a window to an icon by using the Minimize command from the Control menu, follow these steps:

1. Place the mouse pointer on the title bar of the window that you want to shrink, and click to activate the window or move it to the foreground of the screen.

2. Open the Control menu, and choose the Mi**n**imize command. The window is minimized to an icon.

To minimize a window by using the Minimize button on the title bar, follow these steps:

1. Place the mouse pointer on the title bar of the window that you want to shrink. If this window is not active, click the title bar to activate the window or move it to the foreground of the screen.

2. Place the mouse pointer on the Minimize button (refer to fig. 2.5) and click. The window becomes an icon, or small picture, at the bottom of the screen.

Scrolling through Windows

If you want to display different parts of the window on-screen, you can scroll through the contents of a window by using the scroll bar on the right side of the window. The scroll bar, as shown in figure 2.9, moves the contents of the window up or down. Scroll bars also can appear at the bottom of the window in some cases. Scroll bars at the bottom of the window allow you to move the contents of the window right or left. The scroll box, shown in figure 2.9, indicates your relative position within the contents of a window. For example, if the scroll box is positioned in the middle of the scroll bar, then you know that you are in the middle of the contents in the window.

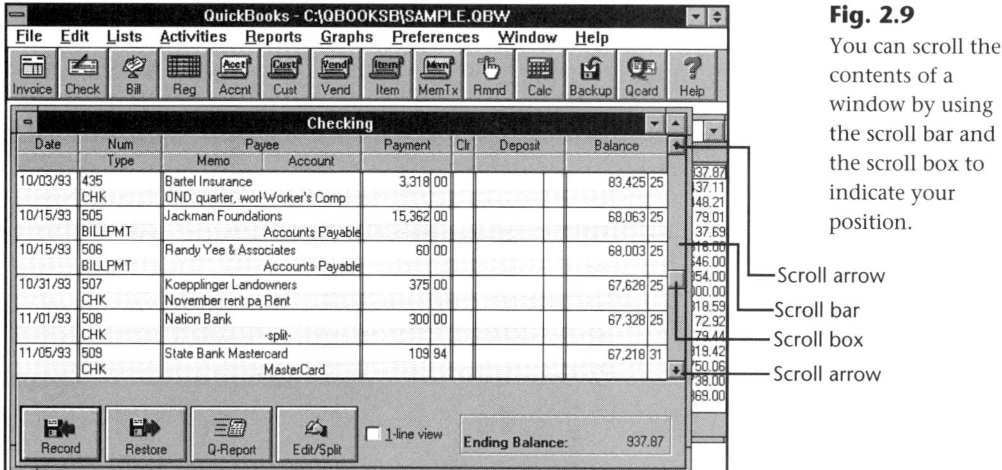

Fig. 2.9
You can scroll the contents of a window by using the scroll bar and the scroll box to indicate your position.

To scroll the contents of a window, you can also use the arrow keys or the PgUp and PgDn keys if you are using the keyboard. To scroll the contents of a screen by using the scroll bars, follow either of these procedures:

- Click the arrows at either end of the scroll bar to move the contents of the window up or down a short distance.

  or

- Place the mouse pointer anywhere in the scroll bar to represent the part of the window that you want to display, and click. For example, if you want to quickly move to the middle of the contents of a window, place the mouse pointer in the middle of the scroll bar and click.

Working with Dialog Boxes

A *dialog box* is a box displayed within a window after you select a command or option or begin a particular procedure. Three types of boxes are found within dialog boxes that you will see in QuickBooks: text boxes, list boxes, and drop-down lists. A *text box* asks you to type information, such as a customer name, employee name, and so on. A *list box* asks you to make a selection from a list of options, such as choosing an account from the Chart of

Accounts List. A *drop-down list* also asks you to make a selection from a list; however, the list is not displayed until you instruct QuickBooks to display the list. QuickBooks uses drop-down lists to display lists of items to select such as customers, vendors, and employees.

Entering Information in Text Boxes. To enter information in a text box, as shown in figure 2.10, follow these steps:

1. Place the cursor in the text box by positioning the mouse pointer on the text box and clicking.

2. Type the text, and then press Tab.

Fig. 2.10 You use a text box to enter information.

If you need to edit the information in a text box, place the cursor within the text and press Backspace to delete characters to the left, or press Delete to remove characters to the right. Then type the new text. If you want to delete the entire text, place the cursor at the beginning of the text and press Delete, or place the cursor at the end of the text and press Backspace.

Choosing Options in Dialog Boxes. Some dialog boxes display options as a list within which you move up or down to select, and other dialog boxes display options with radio buttons and check boxes.

To select an option from a list in a dialog box, as shown in figure 2.11, follow these steps:

1. Move down the list by using the mouse, or use the up and down arrows to highlight the item that you want to select.

2. Click the mouse button or press Enter.

To open a drop-down list, as shown in figure 2.12, follow these steps:

1. Point to the boxed arrow to the right of the list box and click, or press Alt+down arrow.

2. Click the arrows in the scroll bar to move up and down the list or use the up and down arrows.
3. Highlight the item that you want to select from the list, and click or press Enter.

Press Esc if you don't want to make a selection from the drop-down list.

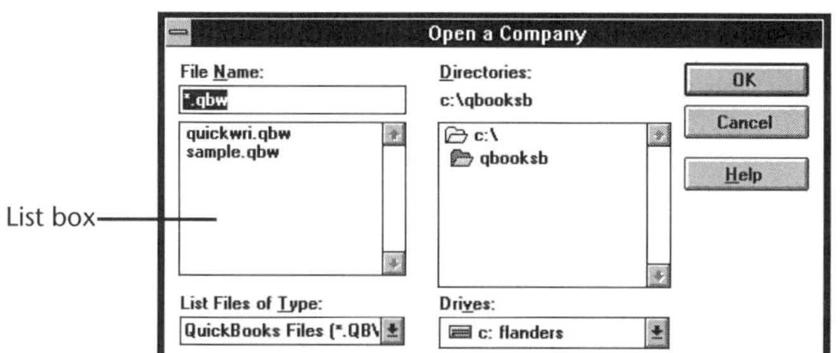

Fig. 2.11
You can select an item from a list in a dialog box.

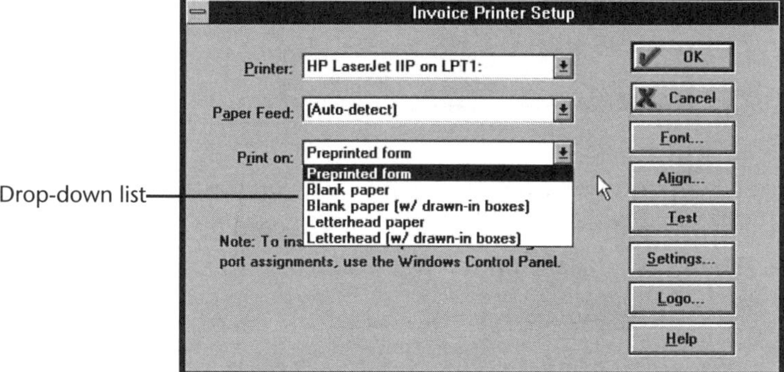

Fig. 2.12
You can open a drop-down list to select an item from the list.

Use the mouse or the keyboard to select an option by using an option button, as shown in figure 2.13.

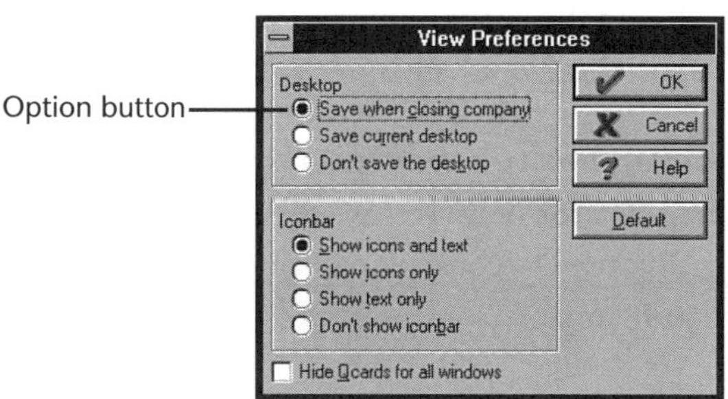

Fig. 2.13
You can choose an option in a dialog box by selecting an option button.

To select an option button by using the mouse, place the mouse pointer on the button next to the option that you want to select, and click. QuickBooks blackens the button for the option that you select. Click the option button again if you decide that you don't want to select the option.

To select an option button option by using the keyboard, follow these steps:

1. Press Tab to enclose the option buttons within the dialog box with dotted lines.

2. Use the arrow keys to highlight the option that you want to select.

3. Press Enter. The option button turns black.

Use the mouse or the keyboard to select a check box option, as shown in figure 2.14.

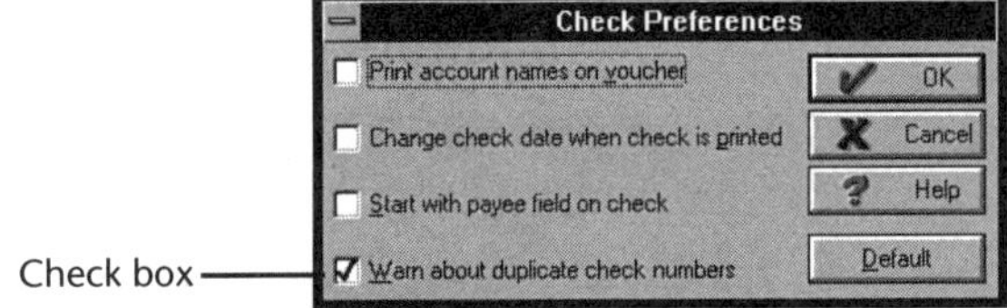

Fig. 2.14
You can select a check box option in a dialog box.

To select a check box option using the mouse, place the mouse pointer on the check box that you want to select, and click. QuickBooks places a check mark or an X in the box next to the option that you select. Click the option a second time to deselect the option.

To select a check box option using the keyboard, follow these steps:

1. Press Tab to enclose the option that you want to select from within the dialog box with dotted lines.

2. Press the space bar to select the option. QuickBooks places a check mark or an X in the box next to the option that you select. Press the space bar again to remove the check mark or X from the check box.

Activating Options in Dialog Boxes. After you have made the selections in a dialog box, they must be activated or saved into the program. Dialog box options are activated by using the OK command button on the right side of the dialog box, as shown in figure 2.15.

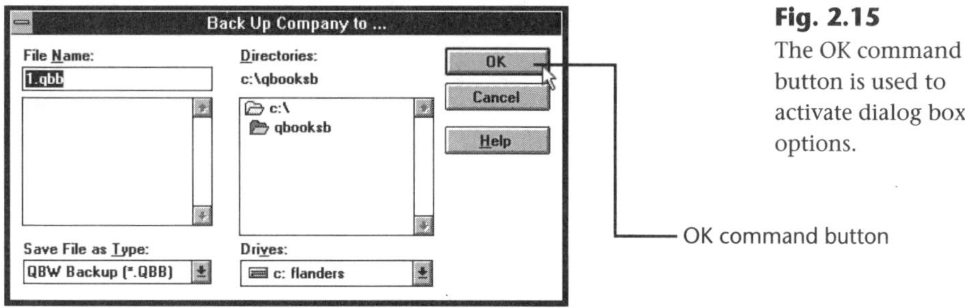

Fig. 2.15
The OK command button is used to activate dialog box options.

To choose the OK command from a dialog box, perform one of the following procedures:

- Place the mouse pointer on the OK command button and click.

  or

- Press Tab until the OK command is enclosed by dotted lines, and then press Enter or the space bar.

Closing Dialog Boxes. Several ways are available to close a dialog box without activating options. To close a dialog box, perform any one of these procedures:

- Choose the Cancel command.
- Press Esc.
- Double-click the Control menu box.
- Press Alt+F4.

Using QuickBooks for Windows Menus

QuickBooks operates through commands and options. You access QuickBooks commands from separate menus contained in the menu bar at the top of the QuickBooks application window. QuickBooks commands are used to initiate an operation or procedure within the program, to display another menu of commands, or to display dialog boxes to select options. Options define how certain QuickBooks operations and procedures are performed and allow you to make selections.

Figure 2.16 shows the QuickBooks menu bar, which contains nine different menus: **F**ile, **E**dit, **L**ists, **A**ctivities, **R**eports, **G**raphs, **P**references, **W**indow, and **H**elp. These menus contain various QuickBooks commands. When you choose a menu from the menu bar, the menu is pulled down and displayed below the menu bar.

Fig. 2.16
The QuickBooks menu bar contains nine menus.

Accessing Menus from the Menu Bar

To access menus from the QuickBooks menu bar, follow one of these procedures:

- Place the mouse pointer on the menu name in the menu bar that you want to select and click.
- Press Alt or F10 to display the highlight bar in the menu bar, and then use the right and left arrows to move the highlight bar to the menu name in the menu bar that you want to select, and press Enter.
- Press the Alt key in combination with the mnemonic key in the menu name within the menu bar. For example, press Alt+F to access the **F**ile menu.

When you access a menu from the menu bar, QuickBooks displays the pull-down menu, as shown in figure 2.17.

Fig. 2.17
A pull-down menu displayed by accessing a menu from the menu bar.

A quick way to view all the QuickBooks menus or lists of commands is to use the right- and left-arrow keys to move the highlight bar from one menu name to another when a pull-down menu is displayed.

Choosing Menu Commands and Options

You can choose commands from a menu by using the mouse or the keyboard. To choose commands from a menu by using the mouse, place the mouse pointer on the command that you want to choose, and click.

To choose commands by using the keyboard, use one of the following procedures:

- Use the up and down arrows to highlight the command you want to select, and press Enter.

  or

- Press the mnemonic key within the command name. For example, to select the **D**elete command from the **A**ctivities menu, press D.

You can select some commands by using quick keys. A list of quick keys appeared earlier in this chapter in table 2.1. A Quick key is listed to the right of the command in the menu.

Choosing a command from a pull-down menu that is followed by three dots (ellipses) causes QuickBooks to display another window or dialog box. For example, when you choose the **V**iew... command from the **P**references menu, QuickBooks displays the View Preferences dialog box (shown later in fig. 2.18).

Removing Menus from the Screen

If you don't want to select a command from a menu displayed on-screen, follow one of these procedures:

- Click the menu name in the menu bar.

  or

- Press Esc to remove the menu. **Note:** the highlight bar remains in the Menu bar until you press Esc again.

Using the Iconbar To Choose Menu Commands and Options

QuickBooks displays an Iconbar beneath the menu bar at the top of the screen. The Iconbar contains 14 icons (or pictures) along with text (or labels) so that you can quickly select a QuickBooks window, list, or feature.

Table 2.2 lists the icons contained on the Iconbar.

Table 2.2. Icons on the Iconbar

Icon	Function
Invoice	Displays the Create Invoices window
Check	Displays the Write Checks window
Bill	Displays the Enter Bills window
Reg	Displays the register for the current account
Accnt	Displays the Chart of Accounts List
Cust	Displays the Customer:Job List
Vend	Displays the Vendor List
Item	Displays the Invoice Items List
MemTx	Displays the Memorized Transaction List
Rmnd	Displays the Reminders List
Calc	Displays the QuickBooks calculator
Backup	Displays the Backup Company to dialog box
Qcard	Hides/shows the Qcard for the current window or dialog box
Help	Accesses the QuickBooks Help system

To choose a function from the Iconbar, point to the icon with the mouse pointer, and click.

Changing the Iconbar Display

If you want to continue to display the Iconbar but want to change its size so that more of the application window is visible, you can choose to show icons only or text only.

To change the Iconbar display, follow these steps:

1. Choose **P**references on the menu bar. The Preferences menu appears.

2. From the Preferences menu, choose **V**iew. The View Preferences dialog box appears, as shown in figure 2.18.

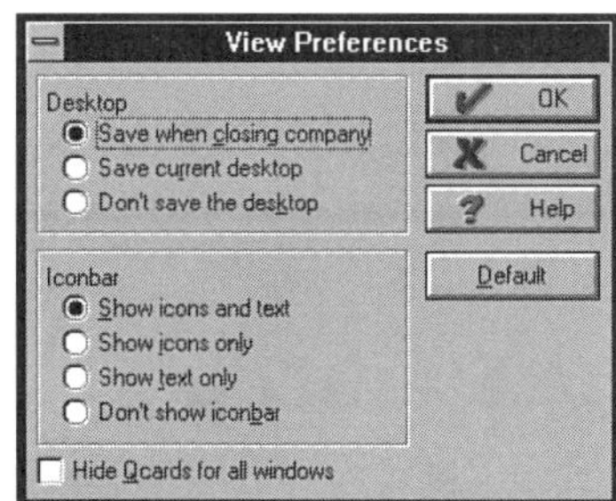

Fig. 2.18
The View Preferences dialog box.

3. Click the Show Icons Only option button if you want icons only displayed in the Iconbar. Click the Show Text Only option button if you want text only displayed in the Iconbar. QuickBooks blackens the selected option button.

4. Click OK. QuickBooks displays the Iconbar as you selected in step 3.

Eliminating the Iconbar

If you want to see more of your application window and don't want to use the Iconbar, you can eliminate it from the screen.

To eliminate the Iconbar from the screen display, follow these steps:

1. Choose **P**references on the menu bar. The Preferences menu appears.

2. From the Preferences menu, choose **V**iew. The View Preferences dialog box appears.

3. Click the Don't Show Iconbar option button. QuickBooks blackens the selected option button.

4. Click OK. QuickBooks displays the Iconbar as you selected in step 3.

Switching between Windows

If you are currently working with one QuickBooks window and want to switch to another QuickBooks window, the program saves your work in the current window. To switch to another window, follow these steps:

1. Choose **W**indow on the menu bar to display the Window menu.
2. Click the window that you want to switch to or press the mnemonic key in the name of the window that you want to switch to.

You can also switch between windows by clicking on the title bar of the window you want to switch to.

A third option for switching between windows is to use the Nex**t** command from the Control menu by pressing the mnemonic key or pressing Ctrl+F6.

Arranging the Desktop

The *Desktop* refers to the way your screen is currently arranged with respect to open windows and their position within the screen. Open windows can be arranged in a *cascading* (overlapping) format or can be *tiled* (side-by-side) on-screen. If you have windows that have been reduced to icons, you can also arrange the icons within the QuickBooks screen. You can also clear your screen by closing all windows. Options from the **W**indow menu are used to arrange your desktop.

Once you have the desktop the way you want it, with certain windows open and in the positions you want, you can save the desktop so that each time you open your company file, windows and their positions are exactly the same as during the previous work session.

Arranging Windows and Icons

You can arrange windows in a cascade or tile windows both vertically and horizontally. You may want to arrange windows so that you can see more than one window at a time. For example, if you're working in the Create Invoices window, you can open the Accounts Receivable register and have it displayed behind (cascade) or next to (tile) the Create Invoices window. When you cascade windows, the window that appears on top is the active window. When you tile windows, the window with the highlighted title bar is the active window.

You can also arrange icons (windows that you have reduced to small pictures). When you arrange icons, QuickBooks places all icons horizontally at the bottom of the screen.

To cascade windows, from the **W**indow menu choose **C**ascade. Figure 2.19 shows how QuickBooks windows appear when they are cascaded. Notice that the Write Checks window is the active window because it appears on top.

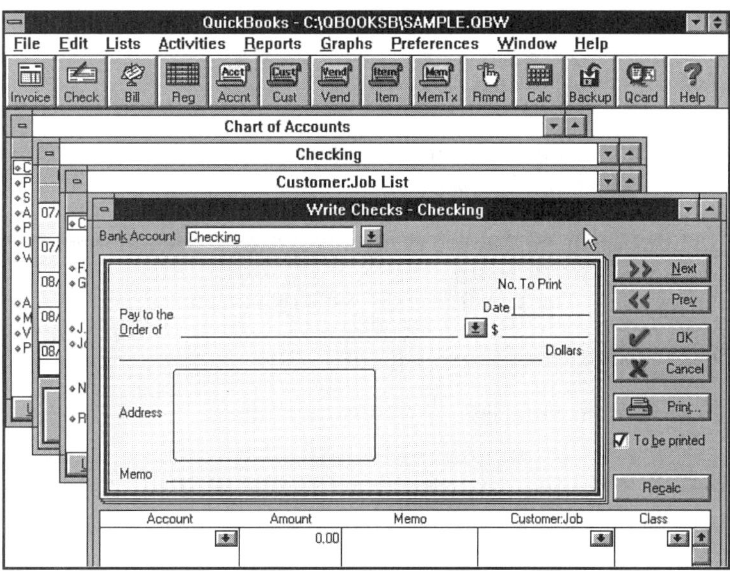

Fig. 2.19 Cascading QuickBooks windows. The active window appears on top.

To tile windows, from the **W**indow menu choose Tile **V**ertically or Tile **H**orizontally.

To arrange icons horizontally at the bottom of the screen, from the **W**indow menu, choose Arrange **I**cons.

If you want to clear your screen, you can close all open windows by choosing Close **A**ll from the **W**indow menu.

Saving the Desktop When Exiting

As you are working in QuickBooks for Windows, you may prefer to have the same windows open each time you start the program. You can instruct QuickBooks to remember the open windows and their positions from when you last closed the file or to keep the same windows open each time that you return to the file. You can also instruct QuickBooks to close all open windows when you return to the company file.

To save the current desktop and display the current windows each time your company file is opened, follow these steps:

1. From the menu bar, choose **P**references. The Preferences menu appears.
2. Choose **V**iew. The View Preferences dialog box appears.
3. Click the Save Cu**r**rent Desktop option button if you want the windows that are currently open to automatically be opened each time you open your company file. This option does not affect other company files.
4. Click OK to save the desktop setting.

To save the open windows and their positions from when you last closed your company file, follow these steps:

1. From the menu bar, choose **P**references. The Preferences menu appears.
2. Choose **V**iew. The View Preferences dialog box appears.
3. Click the Save When **C**losing option button.
4. Click OK to save the desktop setting.

If you want all windows closed when you exit your company file or exit QuickBooks, follow these steps:

1. From the menu bar, choose **P**references. The Preferences menu appears.
2. Choose **V**iew. The View Preferences dialog box appears.
3. Click the Don't Save the Des**k**top option button.
4. Click OK to save the desktop setting.

Getting Help

QuickBooks provides a significant amount of on-screen help for users. Almost anytime you get stuck, you can turn to QuickBooks for help. On-screen information provides step-by-step help with menu options so that you can learn the exact procedure for performing an activity. You can access the QuickBooks Help system at any time from almost any screen.

For beginning users, QuickBooks provides Qcards that serve as on-screen "cues" to help with each field in a window or dialog box. The QCard is displayed within a window or beside a dialog box and explains each part of the window or dialog box.

Using Qcards

QuickBooks provides help and tips on various fields in a window or dialog box in rectangular boxes called *Qcards*. Qcards are on-screen cues to help you fill out each field in a window or dialog box. As you move from field to field, QuickBooks displays the appropriate Qcard for the current field. Each Qcard presents help for the current field and, when applicable, shows the page number to turn to in the QuickBooks for Windows *User's Guide* for more information. Figure 2.20 shows the Qcard for the Customer:Job field in the Create Invoices window.

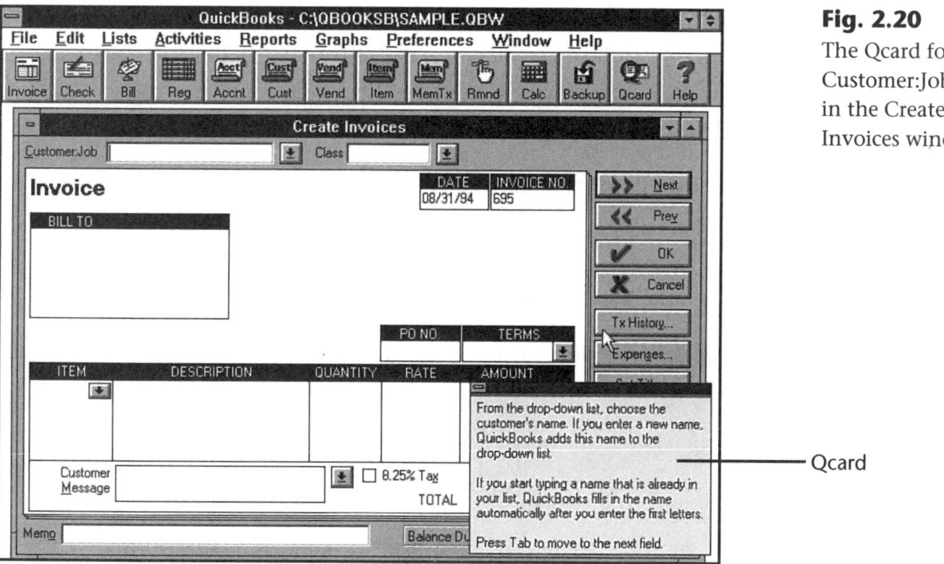

Fig. 2.20
The Qcard for the Customer:Job field in the Create Invoices window.

The display of Qcards on-screen does not interfere with entering information or data in windows or dialog boxes. Qcards are always displayed within the current window or beside the current dialog box and do not prevent you from seeing the current field.

After you become comfortable with QuickBooks, you may want to turn off the Qcard for the current window or turn off the Qcard feature completely. The next two sections show you how.

Turning Off Qcards in the Current Window. You can turn off or remove Qcards from the current window without turning off Qcards for other windows or dialog boxes by using a variety of methods.

To turn off Qcards in the current window, use any of these methods:

- Click the Qcard button on the Iconbar.
- Click the Close button (refer to fig. 2.20) in the upper-left corner of the Qcard.
- Click the Control menu button in the upper-left corner of the window, and then click the Show Qcards for this window option.
- Choose the Show Qcards for Active Window option from the **H**elp menu.

Turning Off Qcards throughout the Program. If you're feeling comfortable with QuickBooks and don't need the added help from the Qcards for any window or dialog box, you can turn off the Qcards feature completely (disable it) so that Qcards no longer appear.

To turn off Qcards throughout the program, follow these steps:

1. From the menu bar, choose **P**references. The Preferences menu appears.
2. Choose **V**iew. The View Preferences dialog box appears.
3. Click the Hide **Q**cards for All Windows check box. QuickBooks places a check mark in the box.
4. Click OK.

If you need to turn the Qcards back on, click the check box in the View Preferences dialog box again to clear the check mark from the Hide Qcards for All Windows check box.

Using QuickBooks' On-Line Help System

QuickBooks' on-line Help system assists with menu commands and options, provides definitions of QuickBooks terms, explains QuickBooks procedures (such as reconciling a bank account or making deposits), and gives tips for using the program.

To get help information from the Help system, follow these steps:

1. From the menu bar, choose **H**elp. The Help menu appears.

2. Choose **H**elp.

You can also access the Help system by pressing F1.

All Help screens in the QuickBooks Help system are set up like the screen you see in figure 2.21. Notice that the Help system has its own menu bar at the top of the screen and six command buttons below the menu bar.

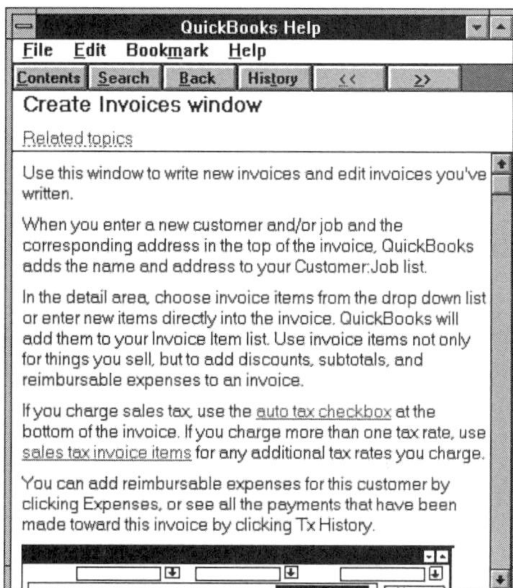

Fig. 2.21
The QuickBooks Help screen has its own menu and command buttons.

The following table lists the menus on the Help menu bar, with their commands and functions:

Menu	Command	Function
File		
	Open	Opens a new Help file
	Print topic	Prints the topic currently displayed in the help screen
	P**r**int Setup	Sets printer options
	E**x**it	Exits from the help system and saves any annotations or bookmarks

(continues)

(continued)

Menu	Command	Function
Edit		
	Copy	Copies the text of the help screen in the Windows Clipboard
	Annotate	Adds your own notes or comments on the current help topic
Book**m**ark		
	Define	Lets you place bookmarks at help topics
Help		
	Using **H**elp	Accesses the Index to Using Help
	About Help	Displays copyright information

Not all command buttons are active at any given time; active command buttons are highlighted. Below is a list of the command buttons and their functions:

Command Button	Function
Contents	Displays the Help topics
Search	Displays a dialog box used to define the Help topic for which you are looking
Back	Returns to last Help topic displayed
His**t**ory	Lists the Help topics that you have viewed in the order they were selected
<<	Displays the preceding Help window
>>	Displays the next Help window

To select a command button, place the mouse pointer on the button and click or press the Alt key together with the mnemonic letter in the command button name. For example, to select the **B**ack command button, press Alt+B.

To select a topic from within a Help screen, place the mouse pointer on any of the underlined topics, and click. The mouse pointer changes to the shape of a pointed finger when you point to a topic.

Using the QuickBooks Tutorial

When you started QuickBooks the first time (refer to Chapter 1, "Preparing To Use QuickBooks for Windows"), you may have selected the **Q**uickTour option from the Welcome to QuickBooks window. If so, you saw the Tour QuickBooks screen (see fig. 2.22), which is used to select lessons from the QuickBooks tutorial.

Fig. 2.22
Select the lesson you want to view from the Tour QuickBooks screen.

The Tour QuickBooks screen contains eight lessons from which you can choose to learn more about the program. The following lessons are included in the tutorial:

- *QuickBooks* ***O****verview.* Gives you a general overview of the program and what it can do for you.
- ***S****tarting QuickBooks.* Explains how to create a QuickBooks company file, how to change the Chart of Accounts, and how to determine the opening balance for accounts.
- *Working with* ***L****ists.* Describes QuickBooks' company lists and how to add, edit, or delete list items.
- ***A****ccounts Receivable.* Explains how to create invoices, enter customer payments, deposit payments, and record cash sales.

- *Checking.* Teaches you about bank accounts and how to write checks, make deposits, use the check register, and reconcile your bank account.
- *Accounts Payable.* Explains how to enter bills, pay bills, and use the Accounts Payable register.
- *Reports & Graphs.* Describes the various QuickBooks reports and graphs and explains how to prepare and customize reports and graphs.
- *Quick Tips.* Shows you the numerous time-saving tips; adding accounts on-the-fly, QuickReports, displaying a transaction history, using memorized transactions, using Quicken data in QuickBooks, saving the desktop, using QuickFill and AutoRecall to enter data, using QuickZoom to examine report and graph detail, and using the cash or accrual method in reports.

Selecting a Lesson. To select a lesson from the Tour QuickBooks screen, follow these steps:

1. Click a lesson button from the Tour QuickBooks screen (refer to fig. 2.22). QuickBooks displays the Topic Menu for the topics covered in the lesson. Figure 2.23 shows the Topic Menus that display when you select the Checking lesson.

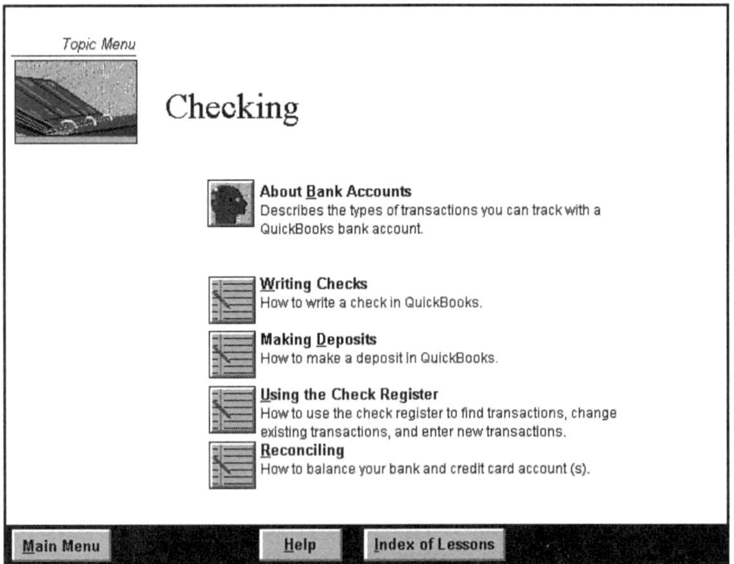

Fig. 2.23
QuickBooks displays a Topic Menu for each lesson.

Note

You can quickly go to the tutorial for the area in which you're working by pressing F2. For example, if you're working in the Create Invoices window and press F2, QuickBooks displays the Topic Menu for Accounts Receivable.

2. Click the button for the topic that you want to see. QuickBooks begins the tutorial for the topic that you select. To continue to the next tutorial screen, click the Next button or press Enter. To go back to the previous screen, click the Back button.

If you need help using the tutorial, click the **H**elp button at the bottom of the Learn QuickBooks screen.

Viewing Topics in the Tutorial. To see an index of all lessons in the tutorial, click the **I**ndex of Lessons button at the bottom of the Tour QuickBooks screen, the Topic Menu, or the tutorial screen. QuickBooks displays the list of topics covered in the tutorial. To select a topic, point to the topic and double-click.

Exiting the Tutorial. You can exit the tutorial at any time and return to your work in QuickBooks.

To exit the tutorial, follow these steps:

1. Return to the Tour QuickBooks screen by clicking the **M**ain Menu button at the bottom of the screen.

2. At the Tour QuickBooks screen, click the E**x**it button. QuickBooks returns to the window in which you were working before you viewed the tutorial.

Using Sample Company Data To Learn QuickBooks

QuickBooks includes sample data from a fictitious six-person construction company called Macadamia Construction. The company's fiscal year runs from September to August, and the sample company includes two years worth of data. Macadamia Construction invoices its customers for labor hours and resale products. The company makes full use of QuickBooks by using Accounts Payable to track bills, job tracking, payroll, and reimbursable expenses. You may want to view the sample data before you start using QuickBooks in your small business so that you can see just how the program works, without making mistakes with your own company's books.

To view the sample data, follow these steps:

1. From the menu bar, choose **F**ile. The File menu appears.

2. Choose **O**pen Company. If the Open Company option is not available (is dimmed), choose **C**lose Company to close the current company file; then choose **O**pen Company.

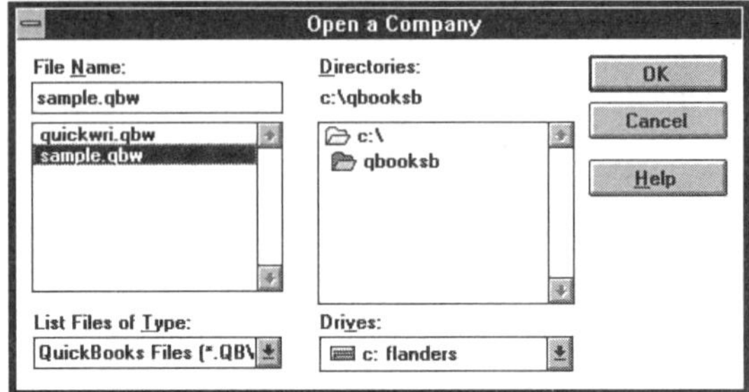

Fig. 2.24 Select the sample.qbw file from the Open a Company dialog box to view the sample company data.

3. QuickBooks displays the Open a Company dialog box shown in figure 2.24. Select the file `sample.qbw` from the File **N**ame box.

4. Click OK. QuickBooks opens the sample company file, and you're ready to experiment with the program by entering data, creating reports or graphs, changing items in lists, displaying windows, and so on.

To remove the sample data and to access your own company file, from the **F**ile menu choose **C**lose Company.

Exiting the Program

When you're finished working in QuickBooks, you'll need to exit so that you don't risk losing or damaging any of your company data. When you exit QuickBooks for Windows via the E**x**it command from the **F**ile menu, your QuickBooks company file automatically is saved.

To exit QuickBooks for Windows and to save your company file, follow these steps:

1. From the menu bar, choose **F**ile. The File menu appears.

2. From the File menu, click E**x**it or press X.

You can also exit QuickBooks for Windows by pressing Alt+F4.

Caution

Do not exit QuickBooks for Windows by turning off your computer. If you turn off your computer, data from your current work session will not be saved!

CPA TIP: Backing Up Your Files before Exiting

No matter what level of computer experience you have, it's **always** advisable to keep backup copies of your company files. You can back up your QuickBooks company files each time you exit the program by selecting the Back Up command from the File menu. See Chapter 21, "Managing QuickBooks for Windows Files," for more information on backing up your files before exiting QuickBooks.

Summary

In this chapter, you got a general view of Windows programs and learned how to get around in QuickBooks for Windows. You also learned how to use QuickBooks menus, select menu commands and options, use the Iconbar, get on-line help when you need it, and exit the program when your work is done.

The next chapter teaches you how to set up your company file in QuickBooks and how to add information to your company file. If you use QuickBooks for DOS or Quicken, you learn how to convert your data to QuickBooks. You also learn how to set up QuickBooks to work with your printer so that you can use the program to print invoices, checks, reports, or graphs.

Chapter 3

Setting Up Your Company in QuickBooks for Windows

In the first two chapters, you learned what you need to start using QuickBooks for Windows: starting the program, selecting menu commands and options, working with windows, obtaining Help, exiting QuickBooks, and so on.

Now you are ready to create your company file. If you are new to QuickBooks, you must first create a company file and then enter into the file information about your company, customers, vendors, employees, and so on. If you already use QuickBooks for DOS, you needn't duplicate earlier efforts. You can quickly convert your QuickBooks DOS system to QuickBooks for Windows without losing any data. If you use Quicken (DOS versions 5 or 6 or Windows versions 1 or 2), you can use your Quicken data to create your company file in QuickBooks for Windows. Data created in QuickInvoice or In-House Accountant also can be converted to QuickBooks.

In this chapter, you learn how to do the following:

- Create a new company file in which to store your company's financial data
- Convert your QuickBooks DOS system to QuickBooks for Windows (if applicable)
- Set up your QuickBooks company by using data from your Quicken system (if applicable)
- Edit your company information

Creating a New Company File

Before you can use QuickBooks for your small-business bookkeeping tasks, you must set up your company or business entity. Whether your business entity is organized as a corporation, a partnership, a sole proprietorship, a nonprofit organization, or even a division, you must set up a QuickBooks "company" so that QuickBooks can create a company file in which to store your data. Setting up your company takes just a few steps. Most steps are performed by QuickBooks after you enter a name and choose preset Balance Sheet, Income, and Expense accounts (the *Chart of Accounts*).

Note

If your company information changes or if you make a mistake in entering information as you set up your company file, you can edit this information later. See the section "Editing Company Information" later in this chapter.

To set up your company in QuickBooks, follow these steps:

1. From the File menu, choose New Company. QuickBooks displays the Creating New Company dialog box, as shown in figure 3.1.

Fig. 3.1 Enter information about your company in the Creating New Company dialog box.

2. In the Name text box, type your company name or the name you want to use in QuickBooks, and then press Tab. Company names can be up to 29 characters long and can include numbers, letters, and other characters in any combination. You also can include spaces in your company name.

3. In the Address text box, type your company address. (The address can be up to five lines long.) If you use plain-paper invoices, the address you enter here appears on those invoices. Type your company's telephone number as the last line of this address if you want the number also to appear on your plain-paper invoices.

4. Move the insertion point to the First Month in Your Fiscal Year drop-down list box. Type the beginning month in this box, or click the arrow next to the list box (or press Ctrl+L) to open the drop-down list, and select a month from the list.

5. Choose Next or press Enter to open the Creating New Company dialog box for selecting invoices, as shown in figure 3.2.

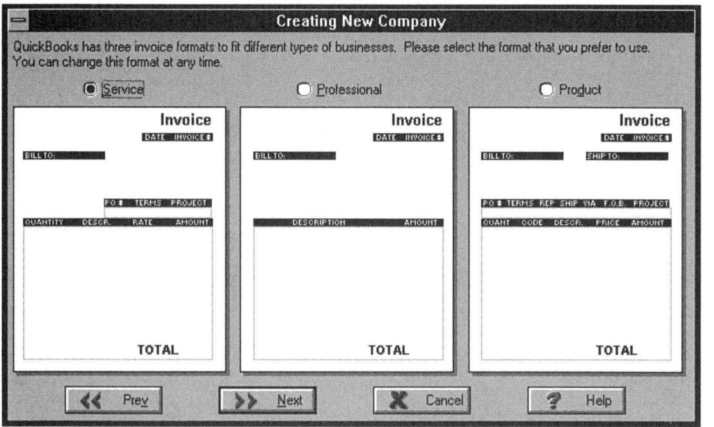

Fig. 3.2
The second Creating New Company dialog box enables you to select the invoice format you want to use.

6. Choose the option button for the invoice format you want. QuickBooks uses the following three invoice formats:

   - *Service*. For service-oriented businesses that do not sell products, such as interior design, house painting, and gardening businesses.

   - *Professional*. For businesses that provide professional services such asaccounting, legal, and medical services.

   - *Product*. For businesses that sell products such as auto parts, computers, and books. (If your business sells both products and services, use this type of invoice.)

7. Choose Next or press Enter. QuickBooks asks whether you charge sales tax to your customers. Choose Yes if you charge sales tax. If you do not charge sales tax, choose No and skip to step 9.

   If you charge sales tax (and answered Yes in step 7), QuickBooks displays the Creating New Company dialog box for entering sales tax information (see fig. 3.3).

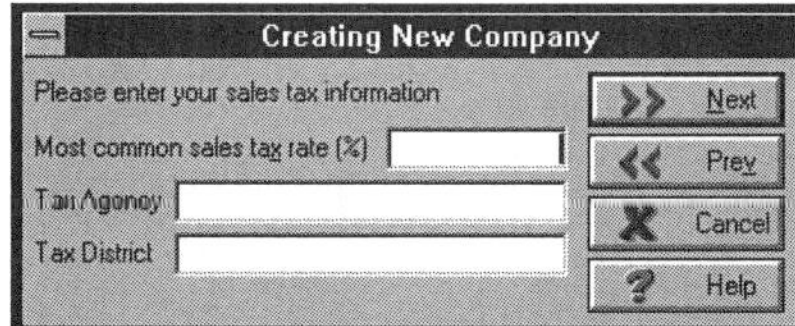

Fig. 3.3
If you charge sales tax to your customers, enter sales tax information in the Creating New Company dialog box.

8. In the first text box, type the most common sales tax rate that you charge to customers, and press Tab. In the Tax Agency text box, type the name of the tax agency for which you most commonly collect sales tax. Press Tab again. Type the name of the tax district for which you most commonly collect sales tax in the Tax District text box. After this sales tax information is complete, choose **N**ext or press Enter.

> **Note**
>
> The sales tax rate you enter in the Most Common Sales **T**ax Rate (%) text box is the rate used by QuickBooks to calculate sales tax on invoices automatically. Chapter 7, "Tracking Sales Tax," explains automatic sales tax calculations.

> **Note**
>
> If you collect sales tax for more than one tax agency, enter in the Most Common Sales **T**ax Rate (%) text box the sales tax rate of the district for which you most often collect the tax. You can enter other sales tax rates as you set up Sales Tax invoice items. You learn how to set up Sales Tax invoice items in Chapter 5, "Using QuickBooks for Windows Lists."

QuickBooks now displays the Creating New Company dialog box that lists company types (see fig. 3.4).

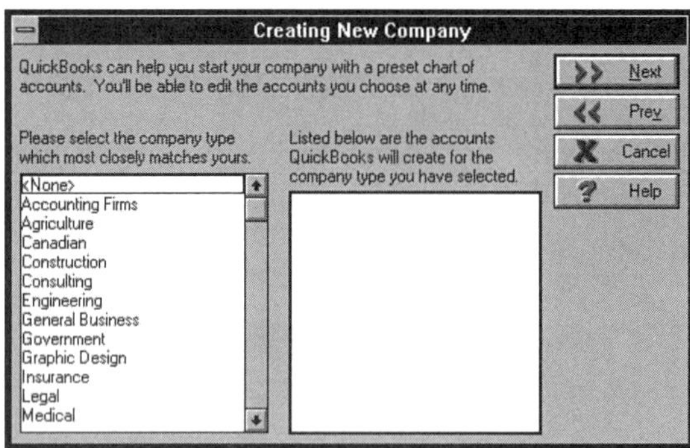

Fig. 3.4
The Creating New Company dialog box for selecting your company type.

9. Select the type of company you are creating from the list box in the lower-left area of the window. (If your type of company does not appear in the list box, scroll down the list until you find the type you want.)

Choose the exact company type (if listed) or the company type that most closely describes your business.

After you select a company type, QuickBooks automatically adds a preset list of Income, Expense, and Balance Sheet (asset and liability) accounts to your company file. As you highlight a company type in the list box, its preset Chart of Accounts appears in the box to the right of the list.

If you do not want QuickBooks to add a preset Chart of Accounts to your company file, select the first entry in the company type list: `<None>`. If you select `<None>`, QuickBooks creates your company file without any accounts. You therefore must create each account you want to use in your company file. In Chapter 4, "Working with Accounts," you learn how to add accounts to the Chart of Accounts.

Note

After QuickBooks adds preset accounts to your company file, you can add accounts to the list, edit accounts, or delete accounts. Chapter 4, "Working with Accounts," describes how to edit accounts.

10. After you select a company type, choose Next or press Enter.

Caution

This is your only opportunity to select a preset list of accounts to use for your company. After setting up a company file, you cannot go back and choose a different group of preset accounts. You can, however, access this account list at any time and add, edit, or delete accounts from the list. Chapter 4, "Working with Accounts," tells you how to change accounts.

QuickBooks displays the New Company Summary dialog box, containing all the information you entered for your company (see fig. 3.5).

11. Review the information in the New Company Summary dialog box to make sure that it is accurate. Revise any information you need to change.

12. Choose OK or press Enter to accept the new company information.

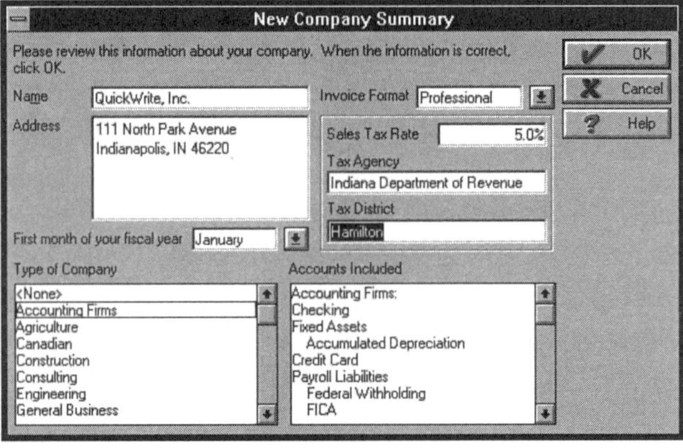

Fig. 3.5
The New Company Summary dialog box contains all the information about your company as entered in the Creating New Company dialog boxes.

The Filename for New Company dialog box appears (see fig. 3.6). You now must tell QuickBooks where to store your new company file. QuickBooks proposes a file name for your company file as well as a directory in which to store the file.

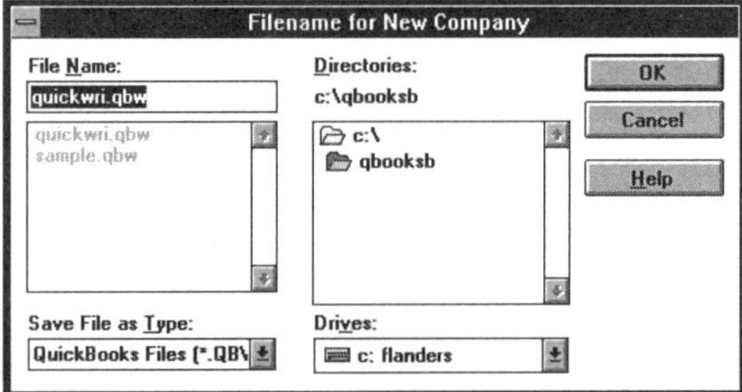

Fig. 3.6
In the Filename for New Company dialog box, QuickBooks proposes a file name, a directory, and a drive for your new company file.

13. To change the suggested name of your new company file, type a new name in the File Name text box (or choose one from the File Name list box). To change directories, choose a new directory from the Directories list box. To accept the file name and directory suggested by QuickBooks, go to step 14.

14. Choose OK or press Enter to create your company file.

QuickBooks creates the company files, sets up Income and Expense accounts for your type of business, creates Balance Sheet accounts, and sets up appropriate lists (payment terms, invoice memos, and so on).

Note

QuickBooks changes the company name you typed in the Creating New Company window to a valid, eight-character DOS file name for purposes of naming the data file. If the company name you typed includes spaces, QuickBooks replaces the spaces with underline characters. If you change the company file name, make sure that you follow the rules for a DOS file name. You may want to change the DOS file name if you are setting up separate divisions within the same company. If you set up companies with the same prefix name and a different division name—Hyatt-Computers and Hyatt-Printers, for example—QuickBooks names the first data file HYATTCOM and the second data file HYATTPRI. You may want to change these data file names so that they are identified as HYATT1 and HYATT2.

Converting Your QuickBooks for DOS System to QuickBooks for Windows

If you already use QuickBooks for DOS, you can easily convert your company file to QuickBooks. Before you convert your DOS file to Windows, however, take some time to become familiar with the following new features in QuickBooks:

- QuickBooks uses drop-down lists to enable you to select items instead of the diamond lists used in QuickBooks for DOS.

- QuickBooks supplies on-screen forms for you to use in entering almost every transaction. These forms resemble actual paper forms, such as credit card slips and deposit form slips. In QuickBooks for DOS, many transactions are entered directly into registers.

- The term *classes* is used in QuickBooks, in place of *projects* in QuickBooks for DOS, to track income and expenses by project. However, you use classes the same way you use projects in QuickBooks for DOS.

- QuickBooks includes a new job tracking feature. Jobs are entered in the Customer:Job list so that each job is associated with a customer. (In QuickBooks for DOS, you use projects to track jobs.)

- The Automatic Sales Tax calculation feature is new in QuickBooks. If you choose the Automatic Sales Tax option, QuickBooks adds up the sales tax for invoice items marked as taxable.

- You can now track and bill your clients or customers for reimbursable expenses. Just assign a job or a customer to the reimbursement expense when you enter the expense. Then, as you create an invoice for a customer, a list of reimbursable expenses appears so that you can add the appropriate expense to the invoice.
- With QuickBooks, you can enter cash sales on the Enter Cash Sales form and print a sales receipt for customers who pay with cash. (QuickBooks for DOS does not have a specific entry for cash sales.)
- QuickBooks includes a new command to credit or refund customers for returns.
- The new QuickReport feature displays a predefined report from any company list. The QuickReport shows you all open invoices, for example, after you select the QuickReport button from the Customer list.
- QuickBooks includes several new reports that enable you to compare data from different periods. You can create a Trial Balance report or a General Ledger report, for example, in QuickBooks.
- The new QuickZoom feature enables you to examine the detail behind entries in reports.
- Graphing is a new capability in QuickBooks. Preset graphs include Profit and Loss, Sales, Accounts Receivable, Accounts Payable, New Worth, and Budget Variance graphs.
- You get *Reminders* in QuickBooks, which appear after you start QuickBooks. Reminder messages alert you to print checks or invoices that are due, to deposit customer payments, and so on.
- In QuickBooks, you can group invoice items so that the items or services you sell are not shown in detail on invoices.
- As in all Windows programs, QuickBooks includes the Copy and Paste features that enable you to copy data from QuickBooks to another Windows program.
- QuickBooks includes a window for general journal entries.
- QuickBooks incorporates some payroll changes: The single FICA liability accounts and MCARE accounts in QuickBooks for DOS, for example,

are split into two liability accounts for each FICA and MCARE account—one for company contributions and one for employee contributions.

Although several differences do exist between QuickBooks for Windows and QuickBooks DOS, most of your DOS data converts easily to QuickBooks for Windows. Before converting from the DOS to the Windows version, however, be aware that a few program features change in the conversion or cannot be converted at all. These features or items are listed in the following table.

QuickBooks DOS	QuickBooks for Windows
Projects	Changes to Classes
Memorized reports	Not converted (because of the difference in reports)
Memorized transactions	Not converted
Transaction groups	Not converted
Company files stored	Automatically combines four DOS files into one file

Note

If you have set up more than one company in QuickBooks for DOS and you want to convert all company files to QuickBooks for Windows, you must convert each company file separately.

To convert a company file in QuickBooks for DOS to QuickBooks for Windows, follow these steps:

1. Close the current company file by opening the File menu and then choosing Close Company.

2. From the File menu, choose Convert From. The menu that appears lists the programs from which you can convert data to QuickBooks for Windows.

3. Choose QuickBooks. QuickBooks for Windows displays the Convert a DOS QuickBooks File dialog box, as shown in figure 3.7.

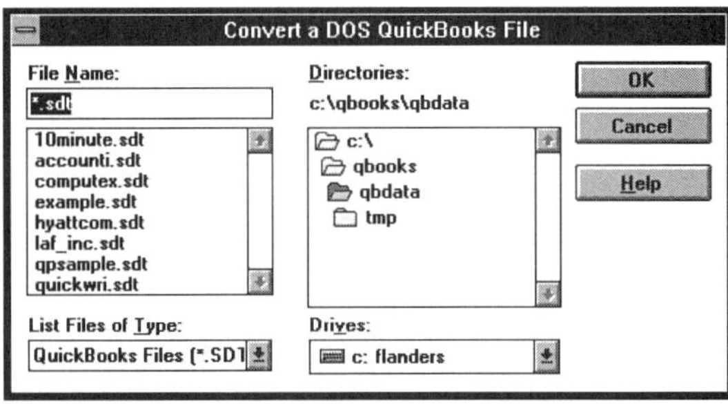

Fig. 3.7
Select the QuickBooks for DOS file you want to convert from the Convert a DOS QuickBooks File dialog box.

4. In the File Name list box, select the QuickBooks DOS file you want to convert. If necessary, change the directory in the Directories list box to the directory in which your QuickBooks DOS files are stored.

5. Choose OK, or press Enter. QuickBooks for Windows displays the Create a New QuickBooks for Windows File dialog box, as shown in figure 3.8.

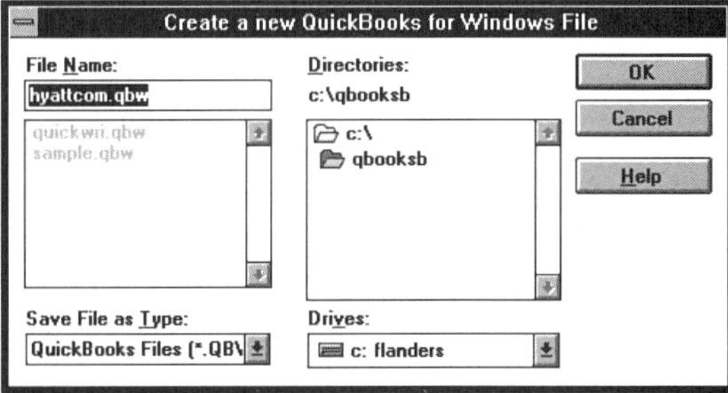

Fig. 3.8
QuickBooks enters in the Create a New QuickBooks for Windows File dialog box the name of the DOS file you want to convert.

6. In the File Name text box, type a file name for your new QuickBooks file.

   QuickBooks for Windows stores the converted company file in the C:\QBOOKSW directory. If necessary, change the directory in which QuickBooks for Windows stores the converted file by selecting a new directory from the Directories list box.

Caution

As you enter a file name for the converted file name, make sure that you do not enter a QuickBooks company file name that already exists. If you do use an existing file name, the existing QuickBooks file is overwritten with the converted file data.

7. Choose OK or press Enter to convert your QuickBooks DOS file to QuickBooks for Windows. A message appears on-screen to tell you that the conversion is complete.

Caution

QuickBooks for Windows is unable to convert QuickBooks for DOS files created before version 1.9 of that program. Make sure that you update your QuickBooks DOS program by using the 1.9 upgrade disks sent to all registered users of QuickBooks 1.0. Version 1.9 upgrade disks were sent to registered QuickBooks users to correct some of the bugs in the original version of the program. If you did not receive version 1.9, contact Intuit for a copy of this upgrade *before* you convert your DOS data to QuickBooks for Windows.

Setting Up Your Company from Quicken Data

If you use Quicken for DOS version 5 or 6 or Quicken for Windows version 1 or 2 in your small business, you can easily convert your Quicken data to QuickBooks for Windows in just minutes. QuickBooks copies your Quicken accounts and data to your company file.

Note

If you use an earlier version of Quicken for DOS (version 1, 2, 3, or 4), you must update your Quicken program to version 5 or 6 before you can convert your data to QuickBooks for Windows. Intuit provides free upgrades for registered users of Quicken. Contact Intuit at 1-800-624-8742. If you use QuickPay, you must have version 2.1 or later to convert your QuickPay data to QuickBooks for Windows.

Before you use your Quicken data in QuickBooks for Windows, you need to be aware of a few differences in the terminology used by the two programs. The following table lists these differences.

Quicken Term	QuickBooks for Windows Term
File	Company
Accounts	Balance Sheet account
Category	Income or Expense account
Blanks	Fields
Category and Transfer List and Account List	Chart of Accounts

For a discussion of the differences in features used by Quicken and QuickBooks, see Appendix C, "QuickBooks versus Quicken: Which Is Best for You?"

To set up your company from Quicken data, follow these steps:

1. Close the current company file by opening the **File** menu and choosing Close Company.
2. From the **File** menu, choose Con**v**ert From. The Convert From menu appears, listing the programs from which you can convert data to QuickBooks.
3. Choose **Q**uicken from this menu. QuickBooks displays the Convert a Quicken File dialog box, as shown in figure 3.9.

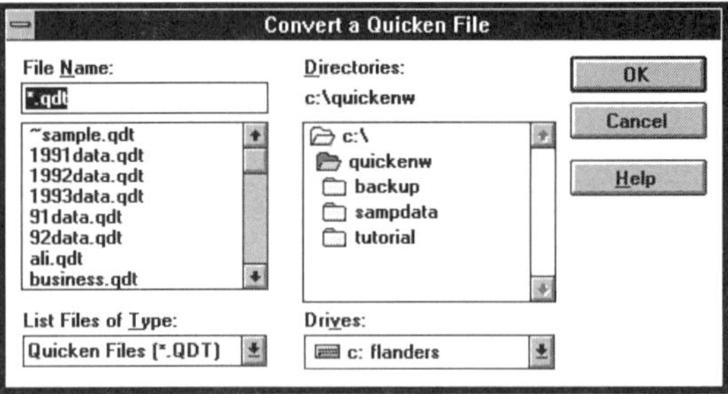

Fig. 3.9
From the Convert a Quicken File dialog box, choose the Quicken file you want to convert to QuickBooks.

4. In the File **N**ame list box, select the Quicken file containing the data you want to use in QuickBooks. If necessary, change the directory in the **D**irectories list box to the directory in which your Quicken files are stored.

5. Choose OK or press Enter. QuickBooks displays the Create a New QuickBooks for Windows File dialog box (refer to fig. 3.8).

6. In the File **N**ame text box, type a file name for your new QuickBooks file.

   QuickBooks stores the converted Quicken file in the C:\QBOOKSW directory. If necessary, change the directory in which QuickBooks stores the converted file by choosing a new directory from the **D**irectories list box.

Caution

When you enter a file name for the converted file name, make sure that you do not enter a QuickBooks company file name that already exists. If you do enter an existing name, the existing QuickBooks file is overwritten with the converted file data.

7. Choose OK or press Enter to convert your Quicken file to QuickBooks. A message appears telling you that QuickBooks is converting your Quicken data.

8. During conversion, QuickBooks asks whether you use Quicken to track Accounts Receivable. Choose **Y**es if you track Accounts Receivable in your Quicken file; choose **N**o if you don't track Accounts Receivable in Quicken.

   If you answered No in step 8, QuickBooks continues the conversion and displays a message on-screen to tell you that the conversion is complete.

   If you answered Yes in step 8, QuickBooks displays the Quicken Convert dialog box, as shown in figure 3.10.

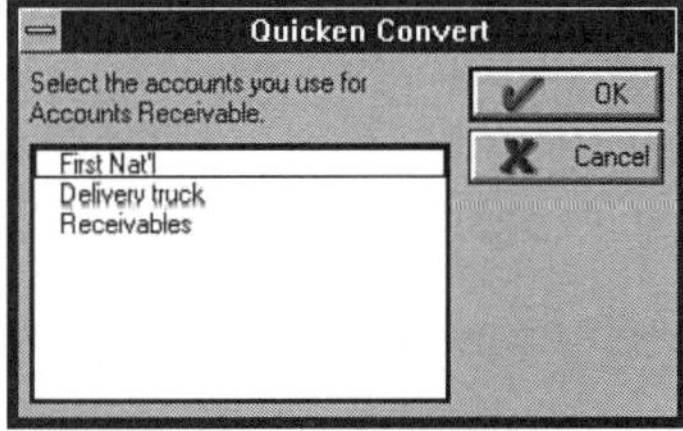

Fig. 3.10
Use the Quicken Convert dialog box to convert accounts used to track Accounts Receivable.

9. In the account list of the Quicken Convert dialog box, choose the account or accounts that you use in Quicken to track Accounts Receivable.

> **Note**
>
> If you use QuickInvoice, follow steps 1 through 9 in this section to convert your Accounts Receivable accounts to QuickBooks accounts. QuickBooks automatically converts all the QuickInvoice data that has been posted in Quicken. QuickBooks does not convert any invoices that are not yet posted.

10. Choose OK or press Enter after you select the account or accounts that you use in Quicken to track Accounts Receivable. QuickBooks continues the conversion of your Quicken data and displays a message telling you that the conversion is complete.

> **Note**
>
> When you convert your Quicken data to QuickBooks, the data in your Quicken files remains intact and unchanged. QuickBooks creates a new set of data files for you to use with QuickBooks. You can continue to use your Quicken data files. Quicken and QuickBooks are not connected, so changes you make to your Quicken data do not affect your company file data in QuickBooks.

You can continue to use your Quicken file for your personal finances. If you use Quicken to track investments, you need to continue using Quicken for that purpose, because QuickBooks does not have an investment feature.

Examining Changes to Quicken Accounts

For each Quicken account you convert, QuickBooks creates a Balance Sheet account of the type closest to the Quicken account type. The following table lists the equivalent Quicken and QuickBooks account types.

Quicken Account Type	QuickBooks for Windows Account Type
Bank	Bank
Credit Card	Credit Card
Cash	Bank
Other Asset	Other Current Asset
Other Liability	Other Current Liability
Investment	Other Current Asset

QuickBooks automatically creates an Accounts Receivable account, an Accounts Payable account, a Sales-tax Payable account, and an Undeposited Funds account in your company file, whether or not these accounts were present in the original Quicken file. If your Quicken data does include these accounts, QuickBooks changes the names to Quicken A/R, Quicken A/P, Qsales Tax A/P, and Qundeposited Fund, respectively, so that you can recognize your Quicken data in the QuickBooks Chart of Accounts.

In Quicken, Income and Expense accounts are set up as categories and subcategories. If you use Quicken 5 or Quicken, QuickBooks creates from your converted Quicken files a list of Income and Expense accounts in the same outline structure as those categories and subcategories used in Quicken.

If you have a category in Quicken named Computer Repairs, for example, QuickBooks creates an Expense account by the same name. If any unused categories or subcategories are in your Quicken file, QuickBooks omits them in your company file. For each transaction copied from Quicken, QuickBooks changes the category and subcategory to the corresponding QuickBooks Income or Expense account and subaccount.

QuickBooks creates an Open Bal Equity account, which is the account QuickBooks uses to keep your balance sheet in balance as you set up your accounts (assets minus liabilities equals owner's equity). For more information on the Open Bal Equity account, see Chapter 17, "Using Other Accounts To Perform Tasks."

In Quicken 6 and 7, all categories, subcategories, and transfer accounts (Balance Sheet accounts) are listed in the Category and Transfer List. Categories and subcategories are listed first in the Category and Transfer List, followed by transfer accounts. QuickBooks replaces the Category and Transfer List with the Chart of Accounts and rearranges accounts by listing the Balance Sheet accounts first, followed by Income accounts and then Expense accounts.

After your Quicken data is in QuickBooks for Windows format, you are ready to begin using QuickBooks. If you had a checking account set up in your Quicken file, you need not set one up in QuickBooks. The checking account was added when you set up your company from your Quicken data. Review your QuickBooks Chart of Accounts, however, to make sure that it includes all the accounts you need to perform your bookkeeping tasks. Chapter 4, "Working with Accounts," teaches you how to edit accounts, add accounts, or delete accounts from the QuickBooks Chart of Accounts.

Note

If you convert your Quicken data to QuickBooks, you cannot select one of the preset Chart of Accounts lists from the Creating New Company window. Your Chart of Accounts is determined by the Quicken categories and subcategories you use.

Examining Changes in Accounts Receivable

If you use Quicken to track Accounts Receivable, you need to be aware of how QuickBooks treats converted Accounts Receivable data. QuickBooks converts the Accounts Receivable transactions entered in your converted Quicken file as described in the following table.

Quicken Accounts Receivable	Converted to
A transaction that increases Accounts Receivable balance	An invoice
A transaction that decreases Accounts Receivable balance and has only one split line	A payment*
A transaction that decreases Accounts Receivable balance and has more than one split line	A credit memo

Quicken Accounts Receivable	Converted to
Each payee	A customer
Each category	An invoice item and an Income account

**Each payment that QuickBooks converts from your Quicken data is assigned to the oldest invoice first.*

To make sure that your Accounts Receivable data is how you want it, you may need to make some changes to the converted data. You can change account names or invoice items. Chapter 4, "Working with Accounts," describes how to make changes to the Chart of Accounts, and Chapter 5, "Using QuickBooks for Windows Lists," describes how to edit invoice items.

Examining Changes in Accounts Payable

If you used Quicken to track Accounts Payable, you either used a Quicken Bank account and entered outstanding bills as postdated checks (a cash-basis system) or you used an Other Liability account to enter outstanding bills (an accrual-basis system). Notice that after you convert your Quicken data, regardless of the method you use in Quicken, QuickBooks automatically sets up a new account named Accounts Payable in your Chart of Accounts.

If your converted Quicken data contains postdated checks for outstanding bills, treat checks already entered as you usually do. For all future bills, however, enter each bill in the new QuickBooks Accounts Payable account by using the Enter Bills window. Chapter 11, "Entering and Paying Bills," explains how to enter bills in Accounts Payable.

If your converted Quicken data contains outstanding bills entered in the Other Liability account, QuickBooks converts the accounts to a Current Liability account. Continue to use this account for bills that have already been entered. For all future bills, however, enter each bill in the new QuickBooks Accounts Payable account by using the Enter Bills window. Chapter 11, "Entering and Paying Bills," explains how to enter bills in Accounts Payable.

Editing Company Information

If you need to change your company name, address, or fiscal year start month, or if you want to add your company's Employer ID number, you can edit your company information to do so at any time.

CPA TIP: Applying for Your Employer ID Number

Apply for your Employer ID number before you open your doors for business. You may be surprised at how often you need this number; an Employer ID number is required on payroll returns, W-2s, 1099s, and federal and state tax returns, among other forms. You must complete an SS4 form to obtain this number. If you feel uncomfortable completing an IRS form on your own, ask your accountant for help.

To edit company information, follow these steps:

1. From the File menu, choose Company Info. QuickBooks displays the Company Info dialog box, as shown in figure 3.11.

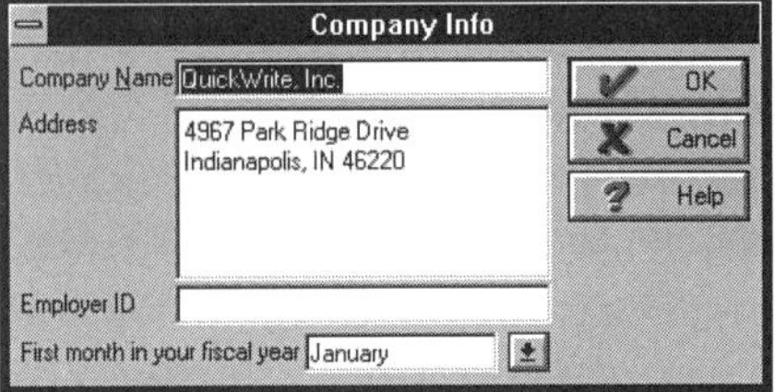

Fig. 3.11
The Company Info dialog box, in which you can change the company information you entered earlier or add an Employer ID number.

2. Place the insertion point in the field you want to change, and replace the existing information with the new information. If you change your company name, for example, move to the Company Name text box, and type the new name.

   You also can add your Employer ID number to its text box in this window.

   To change the fiscal year start date, type a new month in the list box, or click the arrow next to the First Month in Your Fiscal Year drop-down list box (or press Ctrl+L), and then select a different month from the drop-down list.

3. After you make all the changes you want to your company information, choose OK or press Enter to return to the window in which you were working.

Summary

In this chapter, you learned how to set up a new company file in which to store your data and how to convert QuickBooks for DOS and Quicken data to QuickBooks for Windows. You also learned how to edit company information in your company file.

In the next chapter, you learn about the Chart of Accounts and how to add, edit, delete, or rearrange your QuickBooks accounts so that they better fit the needs of your small business.

Chapter 4

Working with Accounts

Now that you know how to set up your QuickBooks for Windows system and how to move through the program's menu system, you can start working with the preset Chart of Accounts that the program set up after you selected a company type. If you did not select a company type for your company file, you must now set up your accounts before you can begin to enter daily transactions.

As you set up your company in QuickBooks for Windows, as described in Chapter 3, "Setting Up Your Company in QuickBooks for Windows," you entered the name of your company or small business along with other company information. You also selected a company type that best describes your type of business. Based on this information, QuickBooks created your company file, using a valid, eight-digit DOS file name, and set up a preliminary Chart of Accounts (the accounts you use in your business). You can add to or change the Chart of Accounts to better meet the needs of your small business.

In this chapter, you learn how to do the following:

- Develop an understanding of the QuickBooks for Windows Chart of Accounts
- Access the Chart of Accounts
- Add Balance Sheet, Income, and Expense accounts to the Chart of Accounts
- Modify the Chart of Accounts
- Print the Chart of Accounts

Understanding the Chart of Accounts

After you set up your company and company type, QuickBooks for Windows creates a Chart of Accounts in your company file. QuickBooks determines what accounts to include in your Chart of Accounts, based on your type of business. Those unfamiliar with accounting often misunderstand the Chart of Accounts. *Chart of Accounts* is an accounting term that refers to the list of accounts you use to classify your day-to-day transactions. Whether you are recording your rent payment or the interest you earned on your bank account balance, you must classify or assign these transactions to an account.

You can, for example, assign your office rent payment to an Expense account named Rent Expense. By assigning transactions to accounts, you know exactly the types of expenses your business is incurring and from where you are generating business income.

CPA TIP: Different Charts of Accounts for Different Businesses

The number of accounts and account names in the Chart of Accounts varies among businesses or companies. A catering business, for example, has accounts significantly different from those of a printing business.

The Chart of Accounts includes Balance Sheet, Income, and Expense accounts. Accounts affecting your company's net worth are called *Balance Sheet accounts*, which include accounts such as assets, liabilities, and owner's equity. The three types of Balance Sheet accounts are explained as follows:

- *Assets* are cash or noncash resources, such as accounts receivable, office equipment, land, or patents.
- *Liabilities* are creditor's claims against your business's assets, such as accounts payable, credit card balances, working capital loans, and real estate loans.
- *Owner's equity* represents the owner's interest in the business's assets. Owner's equity can be a confusing concept. Just remember that owner's equity is the money or value of assets that the owner puts into the business. Future earnings of the business increase owner's equity; future losses of the business decrease owner's equity.

CPA TIP: What Is Owner's Equity?

You may understand the concept of owner's equity better if you look at it this way: If your business is discontinued, owner's equity is what is left after all assets are sold and all liabilities are paid.

Your Chart of Accounts can be as simple or as complex as you want, depending on the amount of detail you want QuickBooks to provide. You can classify all your income into one Income account or separate income into several different Income accounts. If your catering business, for example, offers services for private parties, wedding receptions, business seminars, and other events, you can set up an Income account for each type of service. At the end of your fiscal year, you can easily assess how well your business is doing in regard to each type of service.

Table 4.1 lists the accounts and account types in QuickBooks for Windows.

Table 4.1. QuickBooks for Windows Accounts

Account	Account Type
Bank	Asset
Accounts Receivable	Asset
Other Current Asset	Asset
Fixed Asset	Asset
Other Asset	Asset
Accounts Payable	Liability
Credit Card	Liability
Other Current Liability	Liability
Long-Term Liability	Liability
Capital/Equity	Liability
Income	Income
Cost of Goods Sold	Expense
Expense	Expense
Other Income	Income
Other Expense	Expense

If you add an account to the QuickBooks for Windows Chart of Accounts, you must choose for this new account one of the account types listed in table 4.1. You add an office supplies purchases account, for example, as an Expense account. Similarly, you add an investment income account as an Income account. You learn how to add an account and choose an account type in the later section "Adding Accounts."

If you choose a company type at the time you set up your company, you have a head start in establishing your Chart of Accounts. QuickBooks sets up a preliminary Chart of Accounts for your company type that serves as a starting point for organizing your small-business accounts. Because each small business is unique, you probably need to add, edit, delete, rearrange, or combine some accounts in the Chart of Accounts supplied by QuickBooks. You learn how to view the Chart of Accounts in the later section "Accessing the Chart of Accounts."

If you chose `<None>` from the QuickBooks list of company types when you set up your company, you must now enter all your accounts. QuickBooks does not create a Chart of Accounts for you. If you access the Chart of Accounts, which you learn how to do later in this chapter, no accounts appear. In this chapter, you also learn how to add accounts so that you can start writing invoices and checks and recording other business transactions with QuickBooks.

If you chose a company type when you set up your company, however, QuickBooks sets up the basic Balance Sheet accounts for you—although you probably need to add to or modify these accounts to meet your company's particular needs. In this chapter, you learn not only how to add accounts but also how to edit, delete, rearrange, and combine accounts in the Chart of Accounts. (For more information, refer to the later section "Modifying the Chart of Accounts.")

Reviewing Balance Sheet Accounts

QuickBooks provides nine Balance Sheet account types that you can add to your Chart of Accounts to track various items, as described in table 4.2.

Table 4.2. QuickBooks Balance Sheet Account Types

Account Type	Tracks
Bank	Checking, savings, and money market accounts.
Accounts Receivable (A/R)	Transactions between you and your customers: invoices, payments, deposits, refunds, credit memos, and statements.
Other Current Asset	Any assets you need to convert to cash or use in one year or less: petty cash, prepaid expenses, security deposits, and advances or notes receivable due in 12 months or less.

Account Type	Tracks
Fixed Assets	Capital equipment that your business owns: equipment, furniture, or real estate. Certificates of Deposit and long-term notes. Any other assets that you don't convert to cash or use during regular operations.
Accounts Payable	Outstanding bills.
Credit Card	Credit card transactions and lines of credit.
Other Current Liability	Liabilities scheduled to be paid within one year: accrued sales tax, accrued payroll tax, accrued salaries, short-term notes, and the current portion of long-term liabilities.
Long-Term Liability	Liabilities scheduled to be paid over periods longer than one year: long-term loans and mortgages.
Capital/Equity	Owner's equity, retained earnings, capital stock, capital investments, draws, partners' salaries.

CPA TIP: Which Balance Sheet Accounts to Add

If you are just starting your small business, talk to your accountant to determine which Balance Sheet accounts to add. If you need to track an item that is not listed, have your accountant decide which account type to use for this item, based on the available QuickBooks account types.

Reviewing Income and Expense Accounts

Income and Expense accounts are used to track your revenues (income) and your expenses. Most daily transactions affect either an Income account or an Expense account. If you sell a product to a customer, for example, you enter the amount of the sale as income. The sale also affects a Balance Sheet account: either cash or Accounts Receivable (if the customer purchased the product on credit). After you pay a vendor, the transaction is entered to an Expense account, such as supplies expense, maintenance expense, or utilities expense.

Income and Expense account balances accumulate over one year—your fiscal year. The net income of your business is determined by subtracting total expenses from total income. The balances in Income and Expense accounts do not carry over to the next fiscal year. Income and Expense account balances are closed out at the end of the year. The net Income and Expense account balances are transferred to the owner's equity account at the end of the year, thereby increasing the owner's equity in profitable years or decreasing the equity in loss years. At the beginning of your fiscal year, therefore, account balances for Income and Expense accounts are zero. You learn more about account balances at year end in Chapter 17, "Using Other Accounts To Perform Tasks."

Accessing the Chart of Accounts

Before you make additions or changes to QuickBooks' preliminary Chart of Accounts, make sure that you have your business's recent financial reports (income statement and balance sheet) handy so that you can determine the accounts your business currently uses. You then access the QuickBooks for Windows Chart of Accounts and compare its listed accounts with your business's current accounts to decide which accounts you need to add or change.

You can access the QuickBooks Chart of Accounts by performing any of the following actions:

- Choose the Accnt (Account) button from the Iconbar.
- From the **L**ists menu, choose Chart of **A**ccounts.
- Press Ctrl+A.

QuickBooks displays the Chart of Accounts window, as shown in figure 4.1.

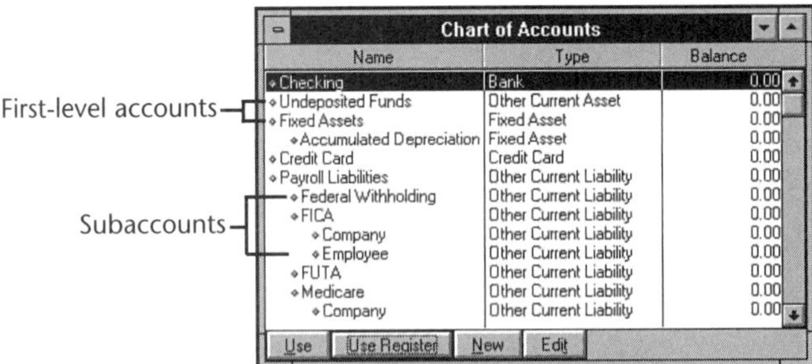

Fig. 4.1
The Chart of Accounts window lists all the accounts for the current company file.

QuickBooks first lists in the Chart of Accounts the Balance Sheet accounts and then lists the Income accounts followed by the Expense accounts. You can scroll through the Chart of Accounts by using the up- or down-arrow keys, the PgUp or PgDn keys, or the vertical scroll bar. As you scroll through the Chart of Accounts, QuickBooks highlights the selected account. You can perform various actions on a selected Balance Sheet account: You can use (**U**se), view (U**s**e Register), set up (**N**ew), or change (Edi**t**) the account. The following actions can be performed on a selected Income or Expense account: You can use (**U**se) the account, display a list of transactions for the account (**Q**uickReport), set up (**N**ew) an account, or change (Edi**t**) an account. You also can delete accounts from the Chart of Accounts, move accounts within the Chart of Accounts, or combine two accounts.

Note

You can prevent unauthorized users from changing your accounts by assigning a password to the delete, add, edit, and move account activities. Chapter 21, "Managing QuickBooks for Windows Files," teaches you how to assign a password to these activities.

Adding Accounts

After reviewing your small business's current accounts, you may decide to add some accounts to the QuickBooks for Windows Chart of Accounts. You can add accounts from the Chart of Accounts window even if no existing accounts appear in this window (which is the case if you chose `<None>` from the QuickBooks company types list when you set up your company).

If you add a Balance Sheet account to the Chart of Accounts, you must enter the opening balance for the account as you are entering other information for the account. The opening balance refers to the amount in the account as of your QuickBooks start date. You learn about entering the opening balance for a balance sheet account in the next section.

You can add an account as a *first-level account* or as a *subaccount*. A first-level account does not serve as a subaccount to another account; therefore, all accounts that are not subaccounts are first-level accounts. The section "Creating Subaccounts" later in this chapter teaches you how to add subaccounts to your Chart of Accounts.

Adding a Balance Sheet Account

If you determine that you need other Balance Sheet accounts to accurately reflect the activity of your business, you can add a Balance Sheet account at any time.

To add a Balance Sheet account, follow these steps:

1. From the **L**ists menu, choose Chart of **A**ccounts; from the Iconbar, choose the Accnt button; or press Ctrl+A. The Chart of Accounts displays (refer to fig. 4.1).

2. In the Chart of Accounts window, choose **N**ew. QuickBooks displays the New Account window, as shown in figure 4.2.

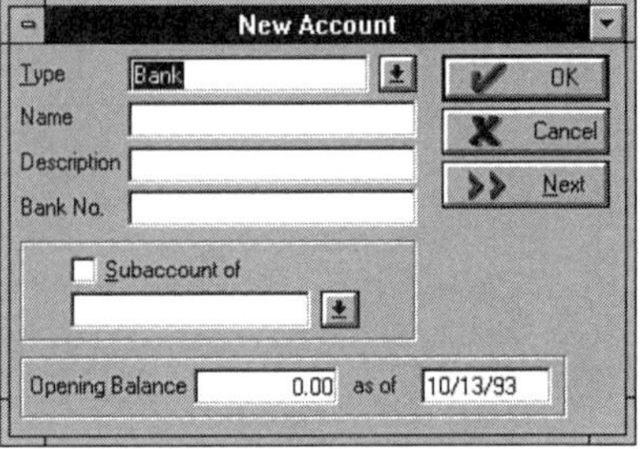

Fig. 4.2
The New Account window, used for adding a new account to the Chart of Accounts.

3. Click the down arrow to the right of the **T**ype text box to display the drop-down list of account types, and select from the list the type of Balance Sheet account you want to add (Bank, Accounts Receivable, Other Current Asset, and so on).

4. In the Name text box, type the name of the new account. Account names can contain up to 15 characters, including numbers, letters, and spaces.

5. In the Description text box, type an optional description of the account to provide more detail about the account's contents. For a Fixed Asset account, for example, you may enter a description of the type of fixed asset to which the account pertains, such as Real Estate, Computer Equip, or a CD.

   The next text box available depends on the type of account you are adding. If you add a Bank account, for example, a Bank No. text box appears so that you can enter the account number for the Bank account you are setting up (refer to fig. 4.2). If you add a Credit Card account, you enter your credit card number in the Card No. text box that appears. For other types of accounts, such as Accounts Receivable and Accounts Payable, the Note text box appears so that you can enter additional information about the account.

6. Type the necessary information in the text box that appears.

Note

The next area in this window relates to subaccounts. This section only explains how to set up a Balance Sheet account. The section "Creating Subaccounts," later in this chapter, describes how to set up a Balance Sheet subaccount.

7. In the Opening Balance text box at the bottom of the window, enter the opening balance for the account you are adding. See the next section "Entering the Opening Balance for a Balance Sheet Account" for more information.

8. Type in the As Of text box the date that relates to the opening balance that you entered in step 7. If you enter the account balance for a Bank account of $5,000, for example, type the date on which the account balance was $5,000.

9. Choose OK or press Enter to add the Balance Sheet account to the QuickBooks for Windows Chart of Accounts.

QuickBooks updates the Chart of Accounts to include the account you just added. The program arranges Balance Sheet accounts by account type and then alphabetically by account name within the account type.

Entering the Opening Balance for a Balance Sheet Account. If you add Balance Sheet accounts, you also must enter the correct opening balance for each account you add. You enter the account's opening balance in the Opening Balance text box in the New Account window (refer to fig. 4.2). After you add a new Balance Sheet account with an opening balance, QuickBooks automatically enters an Opening Balance transaction in the register for the account.

The guidelines offered in table 4.3 can help you determine the opening balance for various accounts.

Table 4.3. Guidelines for Determining Opening Balance

Account	Opening Balance
Checking and savings (Bank)	Dollar amount in the bank on the date you start QuickBooks or add the account.
Other Current Asset	Value of the asset on your QuickBooks start date.
Fixed Asset	Net book value of the asset (cost less accumulated depreciation) on your QuickBooks start date.
Other Current Liability	Loan balance on your QuickBooks start date.
Long-Term Liability	Loan balance on your QuickBooks start date.
Credit Card	Dollar amount owed to the credit card company on your QuickBooks start date.
Owner's Equity	Amount invested in the business as of your QuickBooks start date.
Prior Earnings	Any profits reinvested or not taken out of your business as of your QuickBooks start date or any losses incurred as of your QuickBooks start date.
Accounts Receivable	Enter **0** as the opening balance and then enter actual invoices that were unpaid as of your QuickBooks start date to determine the opening balance. Or Enter **0** as the opening balance and then enter each customer's balance as of your QuickBooks start date to determine the opening balance.*
Accounts Payable	Enter **0** as the opening balance and then enter actual outstanding bills as of your QuickBooks start date to determine the opening balance. Or Enter **0** as the opening balance and then enter the amount owed to each vendor as of your QuickBooks start date to determine the opening balance.**
Multiple: Fixed Asset Current Asset Current Liability Long-Term Liability	Enter **0** (and then enter individual transactions in the account register, using the net book value (original cost less accumulated depreciation) of the asset or net value of the liability on your QuickBooks start date).

**Chapter 6, "Creating Invoices," describes how to enter invoices and customer balances.*

***Chapter 12, "Using the Accounts Payable Register," describes how to enter outstanding bills and vendor balances.*

For accounts that you add to your Chart of Accounts when you set up your QuickBooks system, use the same start dates for all accounts as of your start date. For accounts that you add at a later date, enter the opening balance as of the date that you enter the account in the Chart of Accounts.

If you don't know the opening balance for an account when you add it, enter **0** as the opening balance and later edit this amount from the account's register. Enter an opening balance of **0** for all accounts in which you want to track multiple assets or liabilities individually. You may, for example, want to track each piece of equipment in a Fixed Asset account or each individual loan in a Long-Term Liability account. Tracking multiple assets or liabilities is explained in Chapter 17, "Using Other Accounts To Perform Tasks."

You can correct an account's opening balance at any time by changing the Opening Balance transaction amount in the account's register. Working with account registers is covered in later chapters of *Using QuickBooks for Windows*.

Entering Opening Balance Transactions. You can enter an opening balance of **0** for an account and then add opening balance transactions in the account register for the value of assets or liabilities as of your QuickBooks start date. You may find this feature particularly useful for tracking multiple assets or liabilities within one account. If you add a Fixed Asset account for your computer equipment, for example, enter **0** for the account balance as of the date you add the account. Then access the Computer Equipment account register, and enter a transaction for each existing piece of equipment. Make sure that you date each transaction with the starting date chosen for your QuickBooks system. For Asset or Liability accounts, enter the opening balance transaction in the Increase field in the account's register. Working with multiple asset accounts is described in more detail in Chapter 17, "Using Other Accounts To Perform Tasks."

Make sure that you assign the Open Bal Equity account to any opening balance transaction that you enter. The Open Bal Equity account also is discussed in Chapter 17.

Adding Income and Expense Accounts

Income and Expense accounts are used to track revenues and the expenses of your business. QuickBooks automatically adds some Income and Expense accounts to your Chart of Accounts based on the company type you selected when you created your company file. You may, however, need to set up additional Income and Expense accounts for your particular business situation.

To add Income and Expense accounts to the QuickBooks for Windows Chart of Accounts, follow these steps:

1. From the **L**ists menu, choose Chart of **A**ccounts; from the Iconbar, choose the Accnt button; or press Ctrl+A. The Chart of Accounts Displays (refer to fig. 4.1).

2. In the Chart of Accounts window, choose **N**ew. QuickBooks displays the New Account window (refer to fig. 4.2).

3. Click the down arrow to the right of the **T**ype text box to display the drop-down list of account types. Select from the account type list Income, Cost of Goods Sold, Expense, Other Income, or Other Expense.

4. In the Name text box, type the name of the new account. Account names can contain up to 15 characters, including numbers, letters, and spaces.

5. In the Description text box, type an optional description of the account to provide more detail about the account's contents. For a Supplies account, for example, you may want to enter a description of the types of supplies involved, such as office, computer, or janitorial.

6. Type additional information about the account in the Note text box in the New Account window. The Note text box appears (instead of the Bank No. text box that you see in figure 4.2) when adding an Income or Expense account type.

Note

The Subaccount Of check box and the following drop-down list box in the New Account window relate to subaccounts only. This section explains only how to set up Income and Expense accounts. The section "Creating Subaccounts," later in this chapter, teaches you how to set up a Balance Sheet subaccount.

7. Choose OK or press Enter to add the account to the Chart of Accounts.

After you add an account, QuickBooks updates the Chart of Accounts to include the new account. The program organizes accounts alphabetically within the appropriate section (Balance Sheet or Income/Expense) of the Chart of Accounts window. Bank accounts are always listed first in the Chart of Accounts, followed by all other types of Balance Sheet accounts, listed alphabetically. The Income/Expense accounts are listed after the Balance Sheet accounts, also in alphabetical order.

Note

If you add an Expense account that relates to reimbursable expenses, you must set one of the Invoice preferences (track Reimbursed Expenses as Income) so that the New Account window includes a check box to indicate that the expense is a reimbursable expense. When this preference is set, QuickBooks also adds an account drop-down list box to designate the account in which reimbursements should be assigned. If this preference is not set, a check box does not appear in the window. See Chapter 6, "Creating Invoices," to learn how to set up Expense accounts as reimbursable accounts.

Note

If you choose an Income or Expense account from the Chart of Accounts, the **U**se Register button at the bottom of the Chart of Accounts window changes to the **Q**uickReport button. After you choose the **Q**uickReport button, QuickBooks displays an on-screen report that shows year-to-date transactions for the Income or Expense account you select. See Chapter 19, "Creating and Printing Reports," to learn more about QuickReports.

Creating Subaccounts

You learned in the preceding section how to add accounts to the Chart of Accounts. Unless you specify an account as a *subaccount*, the account stands alone; it is not a subaccount of any other account in the Chart of Accounts. If the Investment Inc. account, for example, stands alone in the Chart of Accounts, and you assign transactions relating to investment income to this account only, then Investment Inc. is not a subaccount, but rather a *first-level account*.

Subaccounts further divide an account into second-, third-, fourth-, or fifth-level accounts. Most QuickBooks for Windows users do not divide accounts into more than three subaccounts. If you want to divide the Repairs Expense account, for example, so that you can track expenses for repairing your building, office equipment, and computer equipment separately, you can set up three second-level Expense subaccounts called Bldg, Equip, and Cmptr.

QuickBooks first lists the Repairs Expense account, followed by these three subaccounts. Notice that the program indents subaccounts to show their relationship to an account in the Chart of Accounts window (refer to fig. 4.1).

To create a subaccount, follow these steps:

1. From the **L**ists menu, choose Chart of **A**ccounts; from the Iconbar, choose the Accnt button; or press Ctrl+A. The Chart of Accounts displays.

2. In the Chart of Accounts window, choose **N**ew. QuickBooks displays the New Account window (refer to fig. 4.2).

3. Click the down arrow to the right of the **T**ype text box to display the drop-down list of account types. Select from the list the type of account that you want to add as a subaccount.

4. In the Name text box, type the name of the new subaccount. Subaccount names can contain up to 15 characters, including numbers, letters, and spaces.

5. (Optional) Type a description and notes about the subaccount in those text boxes.

6. Select the Subaccount Of check box.

7. Click the arrow next to the Subaccount Of text box to display the drop-down list of accounts. Select from the list the *parent*, or higher-level, account for this subaccount.

8. Choose OK or press Enter to add the subaccount to the Chart of Accounts.

QuickBooks organizes subaccounts alphabetically under their higher-level accounts.

You create subaccounts of subaccounts the same way you create subaccounts for accounts. Follow steps 1 through 6 in the preceding steps. Then choose the higher-level subaccount from the Subaccount Of drop-down list.

You may need to convert an account to a subaccount of another account or change a subaccount to a first-level account. You can *move* a first-level account so that it becomes a subaccount or move a subaccount to a first-level account. See the section "Moving Accounts," later in this chapter, for more information.

Working with Numeric Accounts

If you prefer to number rather than name your accounts, you can use account numbers in QuickBooks.

If you use a numeric Chart of Accounts, QuickBooks sorts accounts first by type (Bank, Accounts Receivable, Other Current Asset, Fixed Asset, Other Asset, Accounts Payable, Credit Card, Other Current Liability, Long-Term Liability, Capital/Equity, Income, Cost of Goods Sold, Expense, Other Income, and Other Expense) and then numerically (ascending order) within each type. Your numeric Chart of Accounts must be based on account "names" containing a consistent number of digits and must follow a numbering system similar to that of the partial list of accounts shown in the following table.

First-Level Account	Subaccount	Account Type	Description
1000		Bank	Checking account
1200		Accounts Receivable	A/R account
1300		Current Asset	Petty cash
1500		Fixed Asset	Office equipment
2000		Accounts Payable	A/P account
2100		Accounts Payable	Sales tax payable
2200		Credit Card	American Express
2300		Current Liability	Bank loan
2400		Long-Term Liability	Real estate loan
2900		Equity	Owner's equity
	2999	Equity	Opening balance equity
3000		Income	Revenue
	3020	Income	Sales income
4500		Expense	Selling expense
	4520	Expense	Advertising expense

In the preceding Chart of Accounts, notice that the account types are ordered by type (Bank, Accounts Receivable, Current Asset, and so on) and then ordered alphabetically within type ("A/P account" comes before "Sales tax payable").

Because account names can be up to 15 characters long, QuickBooks can accommodate almost any numbering system, even if you have hundreds of accounts.

CPA TIP: Numbering Your Accounts

Because your account numbers also can include hyphens, you may want to include two- or three-digit prefixes to designate departments within the account numbers. One department, for example, may have the prefix 10 so that accounts relating to this department have account numbers such as 10-1000, 10-1200, and 10-2000. Another department may have a different prefix, such as 20, with account numbers such as 20-1000, 20-1200, and 20-2000.

With the program's customized reporting capabilities, you can easily generate reports for each department by filtering transactions to include only those with certain account names or numbers.

To set up QuickBooks to use a numeric Chart of Accounts, follow these steps:

1. From the **P**references menu, choose **T**ransactions. QuickBooks displays the Transaction Preferences dialog box, as shown in figure 4.3.

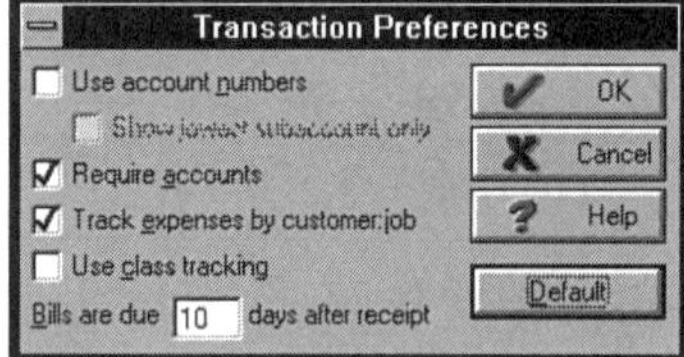

Fig. 4.3
The Transaction Preferences dialog box includes preferences you can set that enable you to track information as transactions are entered.

2. Select the Use Account **N**umbers check box.
3. Choose OK, or press Enter.

QuickBooks displays the Chart of Accounts with numbers to the left of each account name. If you add a new account, QuickBooks also displays a Number text box in the New Account window (see fig. 4.4).

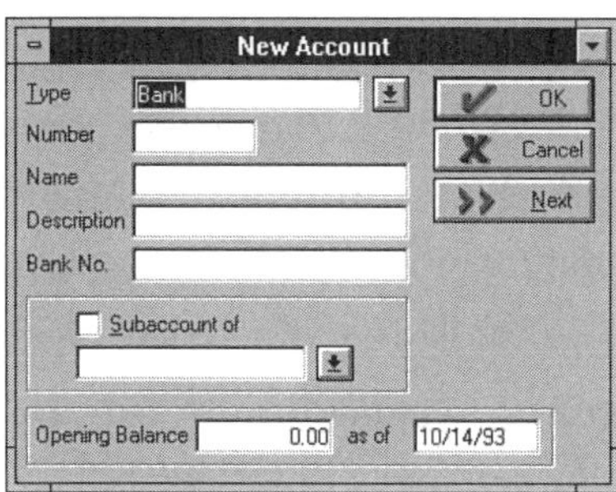

Fig. 4.4
The New Account window, with the Number text box added for entering a numeric account.

Modifying the Chart of Accounts

You can change the name of an account or subaccount or any information relating to an account in the Chart of Accounts. After you change an account, QuickBooks automatically makes changes to the account in any existing transactions assigned to the account.

You also can delete accounts and subaccounts that you no longer need. You cannot, however, delete accounts that contain transactions, accounts that were entered in the Payroll Information window, or accounts to which invoice items are assigned.

Accounts and subaccounts can be moved to new positions in the Chart of Accounts. Although QuickBooks arranges accounts alphabetically (and numerically, if using a numeric system), you can move the accounts to positions that best fit your needs.

If two of your accounts are very similar or track similar items, you may want to combine the accounts so that your balance sheet or profit and loss statement is clearer and more condensed. For example, if you have a Fixed Asset account called Furniture and another called Fixtures, you may want to combine the two accounts and call the new account Furn & Fixtures.

Editing Accounts and Subaccounts

You can edit any existing accounts or subaccounts in the Chart of Accounts. After you rename or change an account or subaccount assigned to previous transactions, QuickBooks for Windows changes the account information in all existing transactions and invoices. You may, for example, want to change an Income account name from "Inv Inc" (for investment income) to "Dividends" so that the type of investment income is more accurately described.

To rename or change information for an Income or Expense account or subaccount, follow these steps:

1. From the **L**ists menu, choose Chart of **A**ccounts; from the Iconbar, choose the Accnt button; or press Ctrl+A. The Chart of Accounts appears.

2. At the Chart of Accounts window, choose Edi**t**. QuickBooks displays the Edit Account window, as shown in figure 4.5. This Edit Account window displays the same information that was entered when the account was set up by QuickBooks or when you added the account.

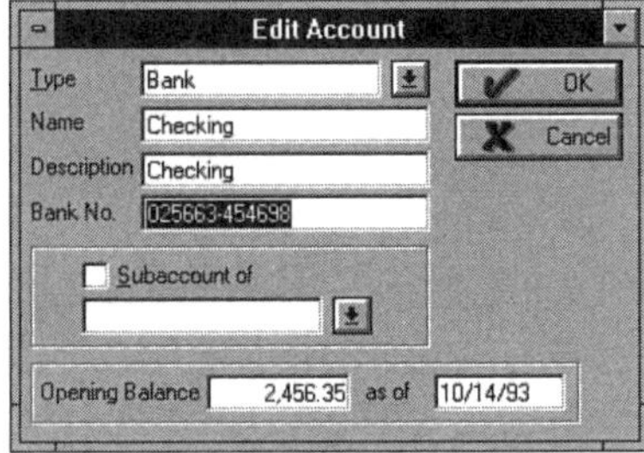

Fig. 4.5
You can change account information using the Edit Account window.

3. Go to the text box you want to change. Replace the existing information with the new information.

4. Choose OK or press Enter to save the changes to the account.

Note

If you rename an account or subaccount, QuickBooks for Windows changes the account name in all previous transactions assigned to that account. If you don't want the account name changed on previous transactions, create a new account and begin assigning transactions to this new account name.

Deleting Accounts and Subaccounts

You may need to delete an account or subaccount you no longer use. You cannot, however, delete the following accounts:

- Accounts assigned to transactions.
- Accounts entered in the Payroll Information window.
- Accounts assigned to invoice items.

QuickBooks will not allow the deletion of these accounts because they are crucial to your past financial data. For example, if an account assigned to previous transactions is deleted, those transactions will no longer be assigned to an account. Transactions that are not assigned to an account cannot be included in financial statements and reports. Therefore, your financial data is incomplete.

If you delete a subaccount assigned to previous transactions, QuickBooks automatically assigns the higher-level account to those transactions.

To delete an account or subaccount, follow these steps:

1. From the **L**ists menu, choose Chart of **A**ccounts; from the Iconbar, choose the Accnt button; or press Ctrl+A. The Chart of Accounts appears.
2. Choose from the Chart the account or subaccount you want to delete.
3. From the **E**dit menu, choose **D**elete Account (or press Ctrl+D). QuickBooks displays a confirmation message asking if you're sure that you want to delete the account.
4. To delete the account, choose OK or press Enter. Choose Cancel or press Esc to keep the account in your Chart of Accounts.

Warning

If you attempt to delete an account that includes subaccounts, QuickBooks displays a message that you must first delete all subaccounts.

CPA TIP: Retain Accounts Used in Prior Periods

If you plan to create reports that use comparison data, be careful not to delete accounts you used in prior periods. Your reports need to show consistent accounts from year to year. If you are not using the account this year, wait until the end of the next year to delete the account.

Moving Accounts

You can change a first-level account to a subaccount or change a subaccount to a first-level account or to a higher-level account. This process is called *moving* accounts. You also can move a subaccount so that it is under a different account.

To illustrate how subaccounts move within accounts and subaccounts, assume that your Chart of Accounts has a first-level account for telephone expenses, with three subaccounts as follows:

Telephone

    Local
    Long Distance
    Yellow Pages Ad

You can change a subaccount to a first-level account so that it is no longer subordinate to an account. In this example, you can change the Yellow Pages Ad subaccount to a first-level account, or you can move the Yellow Pages Ad subaccount to another first-level account, such as Advertising. You also can move—or *demote*—the first-level account, Telephone, to make it a subaccount. If you demote an account that has subaccounts, such as the one in the example, its subaccounts move along with the account. If you demote the Telephone account to a subaccount under another account, such as Communications, for example, all three subaccounts move with the Telephone account (as subaccounts of Telephone, which is now a subaccount of Communications).

Caution

You cannot move an account under a different account type. You cannot make an Income account a subaccount of an Expense account, for example, or move an Income account to the Expense account section of the Chart of Accounts. All accounts within the same account type must be positioned together.

To move accounts in the Chart of Accounts, follow these steps:

1. From the **L**ists menu, choose Chart of **A**ccounts; from the Iconbar, choose the Accnt button; or press Ctrl+A. The Chart of Accounts appears.

2. Move the mouse pointer to the small diamond to the left of the name of the account you want to move. As you point to the diamond, the mouse pointer changes its appearance and becomes a four-pointed arrow. The four-pointed arrow indicates that the account can be moved up, down, left, or right within the Chart of Accounts.

   If you move a subaccount to the left, the subaccount becomes a higher-level account. If you move accounts or subaccounts to the right, they become subaccounts of the higher-level account immediately above them in the Chart of Accounts. Accounts moved up or down are repositioned within the Chart of Accounts.

> **Note**
>
> If an account is already a first-level account (its name is positioned all the way to the left on the Chart of Accounts), the mouse pointer does not display a left arrow; you cannot move that account any farther to the left.

3. Drag (move) the account to the desired location. If you move an account that has subaccounts, its subaccounts move with it.

Figure 4.6 shows the Chart of Accounts before the Billing Adjustments account and the Accounting Services' subaccounts are moved.

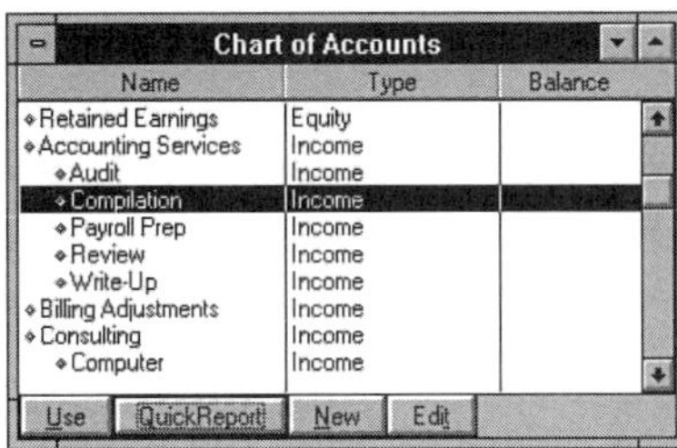

Fig. 4.6
The Chart of Accounts window before subaccounts under Accounting Services are moved.

Figure 4.7 shows the Chart of Accounts after the Billing Adjustments account is changed to a subaccount of the Accounting Services account and after the subaccounts of the Accounting Services account are rearranged.

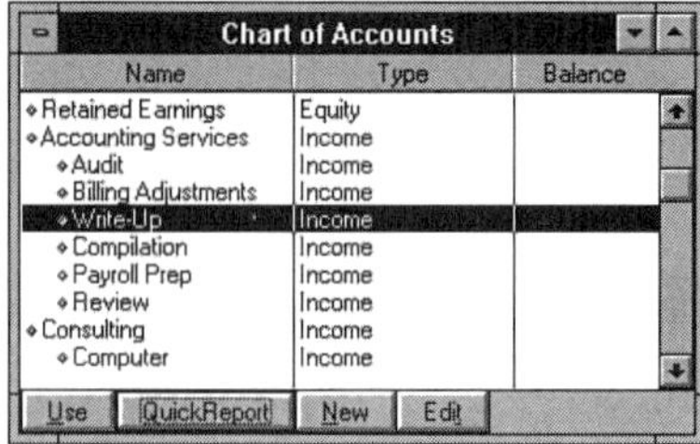

Fig. 4.7 The Chart of Accounts after accounts are moved.

Combining Accounts

You can combine or merge two accounts in one company file's Chart of Accounts. You can merge two accounts if, for example, you want to combine two companies, change a Balance Sheet account's type, or eliminate Balance Sheet accounts you no longer need. You can combine two Income accounts, two Expense accounts, or two Balance Sheet accounts. Be aware, however, of the restrictions described in the following table.

This Account Type	Combines Only with This Account Type
Income	Income
Expense	Expense
Accounts Receivable	Accounts Receivable
Accounts Payable	Accounts Payable
All other types	Any type except Income, Expense, Accounts Receivable, or Accounts Payable

If you combine two accounts (A and B), QuickBooks deletes Account A, and only Account B remains. The program also reassigns all Account A transactions to Account B.

If you combine an asset account with a liability account, QuickBooks automatically changes the sign (positive or negative) for transactions to produce the appropriate effect on your balance.

Caution

If you combine a Bank account with another account, make sure that you first print any checks you still need to print. You can print checks from a Bank account only.

To combine two accounts within the same company file, follow these steps:

1. From the **L**ists menu, choose Chart of **A**ccounts; from the Iconbar, choose the Accnt button; or press Ctrl+A. The Chart of Accounts appears.
2. Select from the Chart of Accounts the account you want to merge into another account.

   If the account you want to merge is not of the same level as the account with which you want to merge it, you must first move the account to make it the same level as that of the other account. Refer to the earlier section "Moving Accounts" for information on how to move the account to the appropriate level.
3. Choose the Edi**t** button. QuickBooks displays the Edit Account window (refer to fig. 4.5).
4. In the Name text box, type the *exact* name of the account into which you want to merge the selected account.
5. Choose OK or press Enter.
6. QuickBooks displays a message that the name you have entered is already being used and asks whether you would like to merge the two accounts. Choose **Y**es to merge the two accounts.

Caution

Before combining accounts, make a backup of your company file. After you combine two accounts, you cannot separate them. Chapter 21, "Managing QuickBooks for Windows Files," describes how to back up your company file.

Changing the Color of an Account

The *color* of an account refers to the appearance of the account's register and any data entry forms, such as invoices for Accounts Receivable accounts or checks for Bank accounts. If the color of one of your Bank accounts is green, for example, the Bank account register is green, and the check form in the Write Checks window also is green.

The color of any account with a register (Balance Sheet accounts) can be changed. Changing the color of an account is helpful if you have more than one account of the same account type. If you have more than one Credit Card account, for example, you may want to choose a different color for each one so that you don't mistakenly enter credit card transactions in the wrong account.

To change the color of an account, follow these steps:

1. Display the register for the account of which you want to change the color. You can display the register by choosing the account from the Chart of Accounts and choosing **U**se Register.

2. From the **E**dit menu, choose Change **A**ccount Color. QuickBooks displays the Change Account Color dialog box, as shown in figure 4.8.

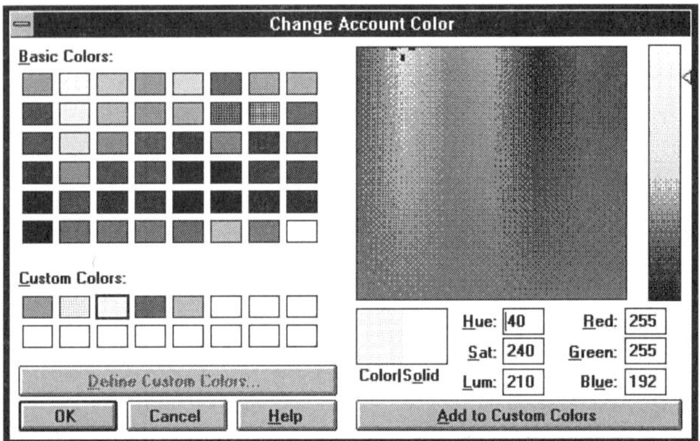

Fig. 4.8 The Change Account Color dialog box is used to change the color of a Balance Sheet account.

You can choose a new color for your account from the **B**asic Colors palette in this dialog box. You also can customize a color by choosing the **D**efine Custom Colors button and then creating your color from the color schemes displayed on the right side of the Change Account Color dialog box. After you create a new color, you choose the **A**dd to Custom Colors button, and the newly created color appears in the **C**ustom Colors palette.

3. Choose a new color for your account from either the **B**asic Colors palette or the **C**ustom Colors palette (after you create a custom color) by clicking the appropriate color box. You can also choose a color by pressing Alt+B (for basic colors) or Alt+C (for custom colors) and using the right- and left-arrow keys to highlight the appropriate color box.

4. Choose OK or press Enter to change the color of the account.

Printing the Chart of Accounts

After you customize the QuickBooks Chart of Accounts by adding, editing, moving, or deleting accounts, you should print and review a copy of your revised Chart of Accounts in its entirety.

Before you print your Chart of Accounts, you must make sure that QuickBooks is set up to print lists. QuickBooks includes separate options to set up the program to print invoices, statements, checks, and labels. The Report/List Printer option is used to set up QuickBooks to print reports, graphs, lists, registers, deposit summaries, and any other forms that don't have a separate setup option.

To set up QuickBooks to print lists, follow these steps:

1. From the **F**ile menu, choose Printer **S**etup.
2. From the Printer **S**etup menu, choose **R**eport/List Printer. The Report Printer Setup dialog box appears, as shown in figure 4.9.

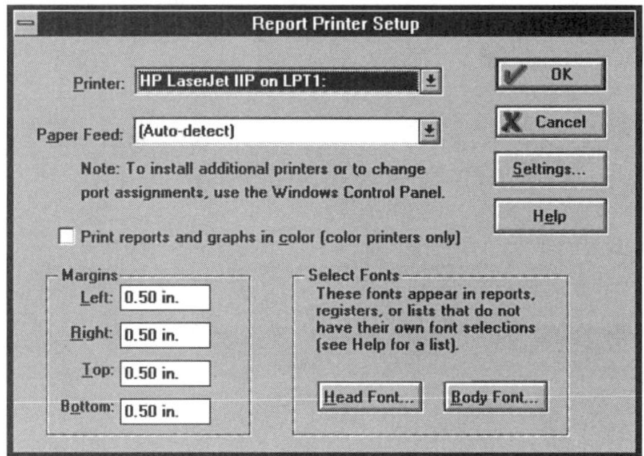

Fig. 4.9
Set up QuickBooks to print lists to your printer using the Report Printer Setup dialog box.

3. Select your installed printer from the **P**rinter drop-down list.
4. If the paper feed shown in the P**a**per Feed drop-down list box is not correct for your installed printer, select the appropriate paper feed from the P**a**per Feed drop-down list. (QuickBooks uses the Auto-detect option, shown as the default setting in the P**a**per Feed text box, to determine whether your printer is continuous-feed or page-oriented.)

5. If you use a color printer and want to print the Chart of Accounts in color, select the Print Reports and Graphs in **C**olor check box. (You must have a color printer installed to use this option.)

6. Check the **L**eft, **R**ight, **T**op, and **B**ottom margins. If necessary, enter larger or smaller values than the preset values QuickBooks uses as its defaults.

7. To change the type font for the heading or body of the Chart of Accounts list, choose the **H**ead Font or **B**ody Font button. QuickBooks displays the Report Default Headline Font dialog box or the Report Default Font dialog box.

   In these dialog boxes, you can change the font type, font style, font size, printing effects (strikeout or underline), and print color. After the head and/or body fonts are as you want them, choose OK or press Enter to return to the Report Printer Setup dialog box.

8. Choose the **S**ettings command button to change other print settings, such as the paper tray, paper size, orientation, and number of copies. QuickBooks displays the Other Settings dialog box for your installed printer.

   Make any necessary changes in this dialog box, and choose OK or press Enter to return to the Report Printer Setup dialog box.

9. Choose OK or press Enter to save the printer settings.

After QuickBooks is set up to print lists, follow these steps to print your Chart of Accounts:

1. Access the Chart of Accounts.

2. From the **F**ile menu, choose **P**rint List (or press Ctrl+P). QuickBooks displays the Print Report dialog box, as shown in figure 4.10.

3. To print to your printer, choose the P**r**inter option button. You also can save your Chart of Accounts to an ASCII Disk File, a tab-delimited disk file, or a 123[.PRN] Disk File or Screen to preview the Chart of Accounts list on-screen by choosing the option buttons for those options.

4. Choose the Print in Color check box to print the Chart of Accounts in color. (You must have a color printer installed to print the list in color.) Choose the Print in Draft Mode check box if you want to print a draft copy of the Chart of Accounts only.

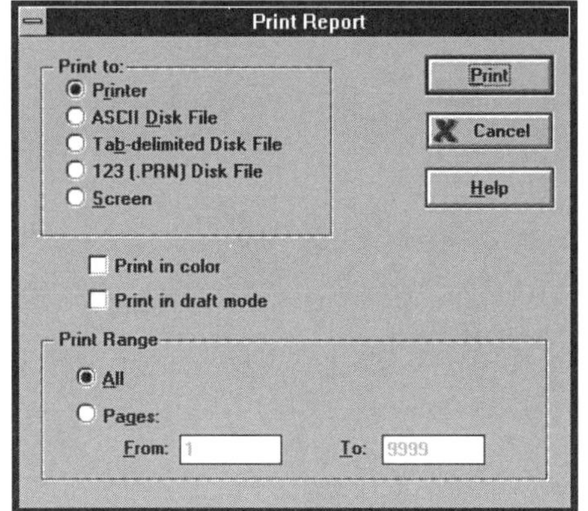

Fig. 4.10
QuickBooks displays the Print Report dialog box when you press Ctrl+P from the Chart of Accounts window.

5. Choose the Print Range. Choose **A**ll to print all pages of the Chart of Accounts list. Otherwise, choose Pa**g**es and specify in the **F**rom and **T**o text boxes which pages you want to print.

6. Choose **P**rint or press Enter to begin printing the Chart of Accounts.

CPA TIP: Printing Your Chart of Accounts

If you are setting up your business and just beginning to use QuickBooks, print a copy of your Chart of Accounts for your accountant or financial advisor to review. He or she may suggest additional accounts you may need to record your business transactions.

Summary

In this chapter, you gained a better understanding of the QuickBooks Chart of Accounts and learned how to add, delete, edit, move, and combine accounts.

In the next chapter, you learn how to customize and edit QuickBooks lists so that they contain information specific to your small business.

Chapter 5

Using QuickBooks for Windows Lists

QuickBooks for Windows provides several lists that can save you time entering transactions and ensure that information is consistent in every transaction. QuickBooks for Windows lists store information about your customers, jobs, vendors, employees, and standard items on invoices. You also can record customer and vendor types, payment terms, shipping and payment methods, and even customer messages that you include on invoices in QuickBooks for Windows lists. QuickBooks lists, therefore, serve as valuable tools, not only saving you time but also providing you with a database of vital information for your small business.

You also learn about all QuickBooks lists and how to use them in your QuickBooks work sessions.

In this chapter, you learn how to do the following:

- Add to QuickBooks for Windows lists
- Edit items in a list
- Delete items from a list
- Reorganize QuickBooks for Windows lists
- Print QuickBooks for Windows lists

Note

In this chapter, you learn how to customize QuickBooks lists so that the items in each list are specific to your small business. Some lists include predefined items based on your business type. You can, however, edit or delete items from these predefined lists to fit your needs.

Working with QuickBooks for Windows Lists

Although QuickBooks for Windows features several helpful lists, you need not use all the lists the program provides; use only those lists that help you track information important to you and your business. Neither must you add customized items to any of the program's predefined lists before you can perform standard QuickBooks tasks, such as writing invoices and checks or entering transactions into an account register.

You can add an item to a QuickBooks list at the same time you enter a transaction. If you enter an invoice for a new customer not already part of the Customer:Job List, for example, QuickBooks displays the Customer Not Found dialog box. You can add only the name of the customer (a Quick Add), or you can enter new information for the customer (a Set Up). Adding list items as you enter transactions—or adding to lists *on the fly*—is explained in the section "Adding to Lists on the Fly" later in this chapter.

You can, therefore, add information to QuickBooks lists in either of two ways: You can access a QuickBooks list directly and enter all the information at that time, or you can add information to a list after being prompted by QuickBooks during a transaction.

CPA TIP: Adding to Lists before You Begin

If you have numerous customers, vendors, employees, or invoice items, the most efficient way to add information to the appropriate QuickBooks for Windows lists is to do so before you begin entering transactions. Have all the information right in front of you, access the list, and then begin entering customers, vendors, employees, invoice items, and so on. After you complete your QuickBooks lists, you can then enter transactions quickly and easily, because most required information about your customers, vendors, employees, and invoice items is instantly available from your QuickBooks lists. You simply choose an item from a list to complete a field on an invoice, check, register, and so on.

Exploring QuickBooks for Windows Lists

QuickBooks provides the following lists, in which you can store business information and then use this data to complete invoice, check, or register fields:

- *Customer:Job List.* Lists customers' names and outstanding balances. Select an item from the Customer List to enter a customer's name in the Bill To field on an invoice. Jobs are associated with a particular customer, so customers and jobs are listed together. Adding jobs to your Customer:Job list enables you to keep track of income and expenses for the various jobs you perform for any one customer.

- *Vendor List.* Lists your vendors' names and the current balance you owe to each vendor. Select Vendor List items to enter transactions in the Accounts Payable register or the Credit Card register.
- *Employee List.* An alphabetized list of employee names and initials. Use Employee List items to complete the Rep field on product invoices or the Sales Representative in the Customer List.
- *Other Names List.* Includes names you want to store other than those of customers, vendors, or employees. If you enter a new name in the Write Checks window or the Enter Credit Card Charges window, you can add the name to the Other Names List so that QuickBooks stores the name for the next time you need to use it.
- *Invoice Items List.* Includes information about the items you sell or the services you provide. Use the Invoice Items List to complete invoices quickly and to perform calculations on invoices based on prices in this list.
- *Class List.* Helps you track income and expenses by project, property, location, department, or any grouping specific to your small business. Select an item from the Class List to complete the Class field on invoices.
- *Customer Types List.* Lists the types of customers with whom you do business, such as retailers, wholesalers, and so on. Select a Customer Types List item to add a customer to the Customer List.
- *Vendor Types List.* Keeps track of the types of vendors from whom you purchase goods or services. Select a Vendor Types List entry if you add a vendor to the Vendor List.
- *Payment Methods List.* Includes all methods of payment you accept. This list enables QuickBooks to sort payments by payment method as you prepare deposits.
- *Terms List.* Includes the various payment terms you offer to your customers. Use the Terms List if adding a customer to the Customer List. As you write an invoice, QuickBooks automatically fills in that customer's payment terms. QuickBooks also applies the appropriate discount at the time you receive a payment.
- *Ship Via List.* Includes all shipping methods your business uses. QuickBooks uses this information to complete the Via field on an invoice.

- *Customer Message List.* Includes memos you can print at the bottom of a customer invoice, such as "Thank you for your prompt payment" or "Invoice is past due—please remit."

Entering List Items in Fields

Using QuickBooks for Windows makes data entry in forms and registers quick and easy. You can enter list items quickly by using any of the following methods:

- *QuickFill.* After you type a few characters in a field in which list items are used, such as the Customer:Job field in an invoice, QuickBooks searches the Customer:Job List to find a matching list item. If QuickBooks for Windows finds a match, the QuickFill feature fills in the rest of the Customer:Job name. You learn more about QuickFill in Chapter 6, "Creating Invoices," Chapter 13, "Writing and Printing Checks," and Chapter 14, "Entering Transactions in the Check Register."

- *Drop-Down Lists.* Drop-down list fields display a down arrow at the end of the field. After you click the arrow, QuickBooks displays the appropriate list, from which you can select an item. QuickBooks enters the item you select in the field.

- *Ctrl+L.* You can press Ctrl+L at any field that can be filled by a list item. QuickBooks displays the appropriate list for you to use in selecting an item for the field. QuickBooks then enters the item you select in the field.

Accessing QuickBooks for Windows Lists

To access any QuickBooks for Windows list, choose the desired list from the **L**ists menu. The selected list is displayed. To access the Vendor List, for example, open the **L**ists menu and then choose **V**endors.

After you access a QuickBooks list, you can add, edit, or delete items in the list. In this chapter, you learn how to perform these actions as you learn about the individual QuickBooks lists.

Tip
Some QuickBooks lists, such as the Customer List, Vendor List, and Invoice Item List, can be accessed from the Iconbar.

Note

You can prevent unauthorized persons from deleting, adding, or editing items in the Customer, Vendor, and Employee Lists by using passwords. Assigning passwords to these activities is explained in Chapter 21, "Managing QuickBooks for Windows Files."

Designing the Customer:Job List

Because your customers are so important to your business, your Customer:Job List is equally important among your QuickBooks lists. The Customer:Job List contains the following vital information about your customers: name, mailing address, shipping address, customer type, contact person, alternative contact person, telephone number, alternative telephone number, fax number, credit limit, resale number, payment terms granted to a customer, whether the customer is taxable at your automatic sales tax rate, and the customer's opening account balance. You select items from the Customer:Job List to complete the invoice's Customer:Job field quickly.

After you select a name from the Customer:Job List to complete an invoice's Customer:Job field, QuickBooks automatically adds the customer's address and other required information to the invoice.

To access the Customer List, click the Cust (Customer) button on the Iconbar; or from the **L**ists menu, choose **C**ustomer:Job.

QuickBooks displays the Customer:Job List, as shown in figure 5.1. Notice that only the customer name, name of the job, and customer balance appear in the Customer:Job List. QuickBooks stores all other customer information, such as address and customer type, and displays this data only if you choose to edit information about an existing customer.

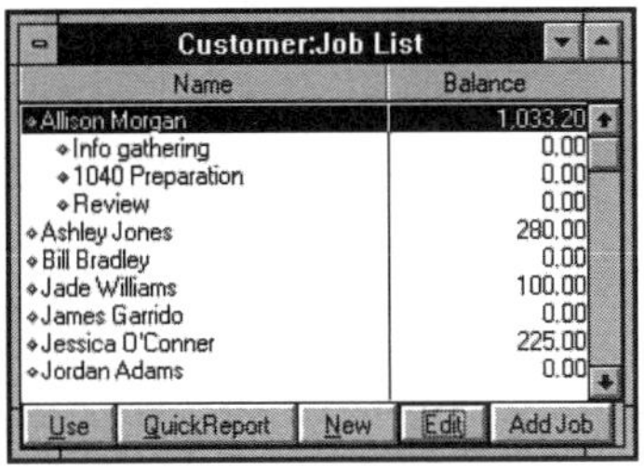

Customer:Job List

Name	Balance
◆Allison Morgan	1,033.20
◆Info gathering	0.00
◆1040 Preparation	0.00
◆Review	0.00
◆Ashley Jones	280.00
◆Bill Bradley	0.00
◆Jade Williams	100.00
◆James Garrido	0.00
◆Jessica O'Conner	225.00
◆Jordan Adams	0.00

Use QuickReport New Edit Add Job

Fig. 5.1
The Customer:Job List provides a list of your customers, jobs, and customer account balances.

In the Customer:Job List, you can add, edit, and delete customers and/or jobs from the list. You also can view a QuickReport that lists all unpaid invoices and unapplied payments or credits for a selected customer or job. You can print the Customer List from the File menu. For more information on printing the Customer:Job List, see the section "Printing QuickBooks for Windows Lists," later in this chapter.

Adding a Customer

You can add a customer to the Customer List at any time—for example, when you first start your QuickBooks for Windows system or when you sell your product or service to a new customer. If you add a customer to the list, you can include as much information as you want, including the customer's name, address, shipping address (if different), customer type, contact person's name and telephone number, and so on.

To add a customer to the Customer:Job List, follow these steps:

1. In the Customer:Job List, choose the **N**ew button (refer to fig. 5.1). QuickBooks displays the New Customer window, as shown in figure 5.2.

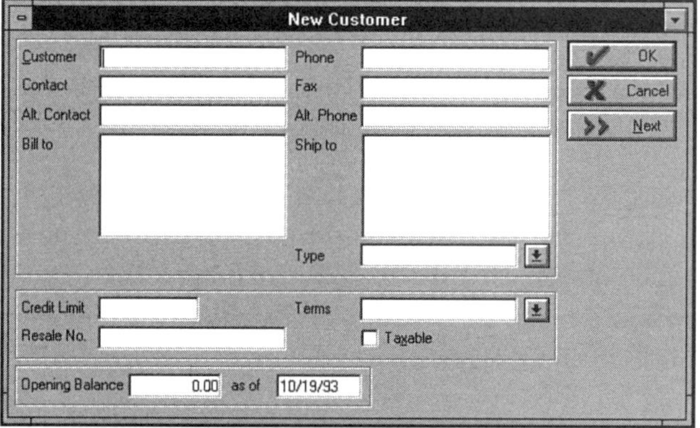

Fig. 5.2
Enter information about a customer in the New Customer window.

2. In the **C**ustomer text box, type the customer's name, using up to 24 characters.

   You cannot enter a customer name that already appears in the Customer:Job List. If you add a customer who has the same name as an existing customer, you must include a phrase that distinguishes the new customer from the existing one.

   To enable you to sort your customers alphabetically by last name, enter the last name first.

3. Type the contact person's name in the next text box.

4. If the customer has a second contact person, enter this name in the Alt. Contact text box.

5. Type the customer's billing address beginning on the second line in the Bill To text box. (QuickBooks automatically enters the customer's name in the first line when you move to the Bill To text box.) You can include up to four 24-character lines in the billing address. To sort customers by ZIP code, make sure that you enter the ZIP code as the last information on the line. The Postal Service requires that no information follow the line containing the ZIP code. To send invoices to the attention of a specific person, type that person's name directly below the customer name. After you finish the last line in the address, press Tab to move to the next text box.

6. In the Phone text box, type the customer's telephone number.

7. If the customer has a fax number, type the number in the Fax text box.

8. If the customer has a second telephone number, type that number in the Alt. Phone text box.

9. In the Ship To text box, type the customer's shipping address if it is different from the mailing address. You can enter up to four 24-character lines in the shipping address. If both addresses are the same, press the " (Shift+apostrophe) key to copy the address from the Bill To text box.

10. Click the drop-down list arrow to the right of the Type text box (or press Ctrl+L) to display the Customer Type List. Select the customer type from the list. Notice that, if you have not yet added customer types to the Customer Type List, this list is empty. Designing the Customer Type List is explained later in this chapter.

11. If a credit limit applies to this customer, type this amount in the Credit Limit text box. QuickBooks tracks each customer's credit balance and warns you if a customer exceeds the specified credit limit.

12. If the customer purchases items for resale, enter the customer's resale number in the Resale No. text box. Usually, sales tax is not charged to customers who buy items for resale.

13. Click the drop-down list arrow to the right of the Terms text box (or press Ctrl+L) to display the Payment Terms List, and then select from this list the payment terms granted to this customer. Notice that, if you have not yet added payment terms to the Terms List, this list is empty. The Terms List is explained in the section "Designing the Terms List," later in this chapter.

14. Select the Taxable check box if you normally charge sales tax to this customer. If this check box is selected, QuickBooks uses the automatic sales tax rate to charge sales tax when you write an invoice for this customer. If you don't select the Taxable check box, you can still charge sales tax to the customer by selecting the Tax check box when writing an invoice in the Create Invoices window.

15. If you did not enter outstanding invoices for customers at the time you started your QuickBooks for Windows system, type the customer's balance as of the current date in the Opening Balance field. Then enter the date that relates to the outstanding balance in the As Of text box. Do not enter an opening balance if you enter actual invoices for customers with outstanding balances.

16. Click OK or press Enter to add the customer to the Customer:Job List.

Editing Customer Information

If customer information changes—a customer moves, for example, or you change the customer's credit limit—you must edit the customer information in the Customer:Job List. You also may need to rename a customer in the list if a customer's name changes—if a female customer marries, for example, and changes her last name. From time to time, you also may need to view information on a customer from the list.

To edit or view customer information or to rename a customer, follow these steps:

1. Access the Customer:Job List by accessing the **L**ists menu and choosing **C**ustomers:Jobs, clicking the Cust button from the Iconbar, or pressing Ctrl+J.

2. Scroll through the Customer:Job List to select the customer whose information you want to edit.

3. Choose the Edi**t** button. QuickBooks displays the Edit Customer window, which contains the same information entered when you added the customer to the Customer:Job List (see fig. 5.3).

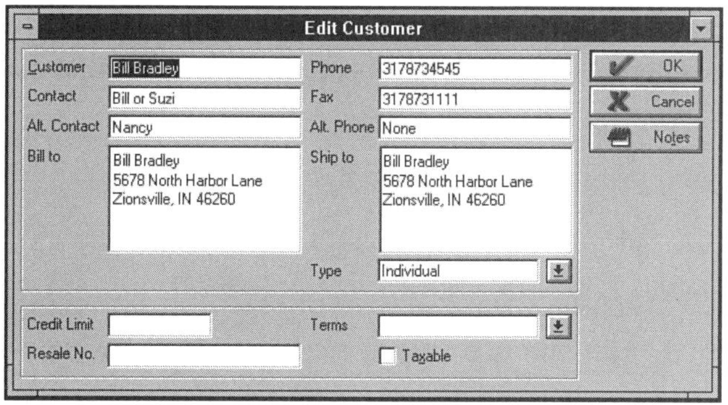

Fig. 5.3
You change customer information in the Edit Customer window.

4. To rename a customer, type the new name to replace the existing name. Notice that, if you change the customer name in the Customer text box, you also must change the name in the Bill To and the Ship To text boxes. To edit other customer information, move to the fields you want to change and type the new information to replace the existing information.

5. After you make the appropriate changes, click OK or press Enter.

After you change the customer name or any other information on the first line in the Bill To text box, QuickBooks changes the information on existing invoices. Changes you make to other fields in the Edit Customer window are not reflected on existing invoices but are used on future invoices.

Tip
To change the customer's name on future invoices only, add a new customer with this new name to the Customer:Job List, and then use this new customer listing for all future invoices.

CPA TIP: Spotting Problem Accounts

As you review the A/R Aging Summary report, look at customer accounts that show an abnormal increase in size and peculiarities in the pattern of payments. Such changes can indicate problem accounts. You also can use the A/R Aging Summary report to determine the overall effectiveness of your credit policy. You may find that your policies are too lenient in regard to some customers and need to be modified. Chapter 19, "Creating and Printing Reports," explains how to create the A/R Aging Summary report.

Creating Customer Notes

You can create notes about a customer by using the QuickBooks for Windows Notepad, available from the Edit Customer window. The Notepad can store up to 10 windows of text for each customer. You also can print notes from the Notepad. Use the Notepad to write reminders for any of the following: your telephone conversations with a customer, special requests from a customer, or payment agreements between you and a customer. Using the QuickBooks Notepad eliminates loose paper or sticky notes that easily get lost.

To create a customer note, follow these steps:

1. From the Customer:Job List, select the customer for whom you want to write a note.

2. Choose the Edi**t** button to display the Edit Customer window.

3. Choose the No**t**es button to display the Notepad.

4. Type the text of your note in the Notepad (see fig. 5.4).

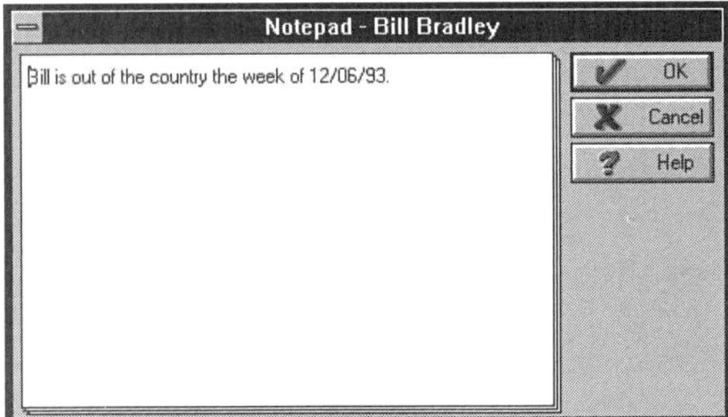

Fig. 5.4
Create a customer note in the QuickBooks Notepad.

You can use the following keys to help you create a note:

Keys	**Function**
Enter	Starts a new line of text.
Ins	Inserts text in existing note.
Ins again	Deactivates Insert mode.
Ctrl+I	Moves to first Tab point.
Ctrl+Del	Deletes the current line.
Del	Deletes characters to the right of the cursor.
Backspace	Deletes characters to the left of the cursor.

5. After your note is complete, click OK or press Enter to record it in the Notepad. Click Cancel or press Esc to discard the note.

You also can create notes from a transaction in the Create Invoices windows or in the Accounts Receivable register. To create a note from these windows, highlight any transaction for the customer for whom you want to create a note, open the **E**dit menu, and choose N**o**tepad to access the Notepad. Then follow the preceding steps for creating a note.

Deleting a Customer

You can always delete a customer from the Customer:Job List, as long you have no existing invoices for that customer. To ensure that your Accounts Receivable records are accurately reflected, QuickBooks does not allow you to delete an existing customer if you have written invoices for that customer.

To delete a customer from the Customer:Job List, follow these steps:

1. Access the Customer:Job List by opening the **L**ists menu and choosing **C**ustomers:Jobs, clicking the Cust button from the Iconbar, or pressing Ctrl+J.
2. Scroll through the Customer:Job List to select the customer you want to delete.
3. From the **E**dit menu, choose **D**elete Customer; or press Ctrl+D. QuickBooks displays a confirmation message asking whether you are sure that you really want to delete the customer.
4. To delete the customer, click OK or press Enter. Click Cancel or press Esc to keep the customer on your list.

Note

If invoices exist for a customer, QuickBooks displays a message informing you that you cannot delete the customer from the Customer:Job List.

CPA TIP: Deleting Customers

Never delete a customer with whom you still do business or have done business in the current year. Keep this important information in your QuickBooks for Windows system so that your Accounts Receivable and aging schedules for the customer are reflected accurately. If you discontinue business with a customer, you can delete the customer from your Customer:Job List the following year.

Tracking Jobs

Jobs in the Customer:Job List are used to track jobs, projects, or services for a particular customer. Each job, therefore, must be related to a specific customer within the list. If, for example, your accounting business provides tax preparation, auditing, and write-up services to a customer, you can set up these services as jobs for that particular customer. If you never perform more than one job, project, or service for customers, you may not want to enter jobs in the Customer:Job List. If you don't want to track jobs, you can simply turn off the job-tracking feature in QuickBooks.

Adding a Job. Tracking jobs helps you track the various services you perform for each of your customers or clients. Although assigning jobs to customers is not required, job tracking is very useful in determining how profitable each job is. You can identify expenses by job, write invoices by job, invoice customers for reimbursable expenses by job, and create reports by job.

To add a job to the Customer:Job List, follow these steps:

1. In the Customer:Job List, select the customer for whom you want to add a job.

2. Choose the Add Job button. QuickBooks displays the New Job window, as shown in figure 5.5.

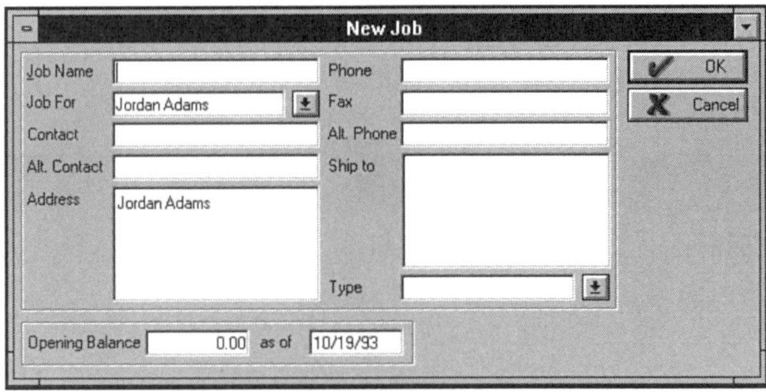

Fig. 5.5
Enter the information about a job, project, or service in the New Job window.

3. In the **J**ob Name text box, type a descriptive job name.

   The customer's name selected in step 1 appears in the Job For field. To change the customer, click the drop-down arrow to display the list of customers from the Customer:Job List. Then select a different customer name from this list.

4. Click OK or press Enter to add the job to the Customer:Job List.

   QuickBooks adds jobs alphabetically under the customer to which they apply. Job names are indented to distinguish them from customer names in the Customer:Job List.

Editing Job Information. You can change the job name for a job in the Customer:Job List, or you can even change the customer to whom the job relates.

To edit job information, follow these steps:

1. In the Customer:Job List, select the job you want to change.

2. Choose the Edi**t** button. QuickBooks displays the Edit Job window (which is similar to the New Job window except for the Opening Balance and As Of fields).

3. To change the job name, type over the existing name in the Job Name text box.

   The customer's name to whom the job relates appears in the Job For text box. To change the customer to whom the job relates, click the drop-down arrow to display the list of customers from the Customer:Job List. Then select a different customer name from this list.

4. Click OK or press Enter to change the job information.

Creating Job Notes. You create notes about jobs the same way you create customer notes. To add additional information about the jobs you perform or provide for customers, use the Notepad to write notes or reminders to yourself.

To create a job note, follow these steps:

1. In the Customer:Job List, select the job for which you want to write a note.

2. Choose the Edi**t** button to display the Edit Job window.

3. Choose the No**t**es button to display the Notepad (similar to the one shown in fig. 5.4).

4. Type the text of your note in the Notepad, using the same keys as listed in the table in the section "Creating Customer Notes," earlier in this chapter.

5. Click OK or press Enter to save the note in the Notepad.

Deleting a Job. You can delete jobs from the Customer:Job List just as you can delete customer names. You cannot, however, delete jobs that have been used in transactions.

To delete a job, follow these steps:

1. Access the Customer:Job List by opening the **L**ists menu and choosing **C**ustomers:Jobs, clicking the Cust button from the Iconbar, or pressing Ctrl+J.

2. Scroll through the Customer:Job List to select the job you want to delete.

3. From the **E**dit menu, choose **D**elete Customer; or press Ctrl+D.

4. QuickBooks displays a confirmation message. To delete the job, click OK or press Enter. Click Cancel or press Esc to keep the job in your list.

Moving Jobs. You can move a job in the Customer:Job List to a different customer's name. If your landscaping business sets up a mulching job for John Smith, for example, but you no longer provide this service to John Smith, you can move the job to another customer in the Customer:Job List—such as Scott Jones.

You also can move jobs so that they become sub-jobs of another, *higher-level job*. In the Customer:Job List, jobs are listed alphabetically and indented under the customer's name to whom they relate. Sub-jobs also are listed alphabetically and indented under the higher-level job to which they relate. An accounting firm, for example, may break down the job 1040 Preparation into several smaller jobs (or sub-jobs) such as information gathering, data entry, printing, and review. In the Customer:Job List, the sub-jobs for information gathering, data entry, and so on are listed under the job 1040 Preparation. The process of moving jobs within the Customer:Job List is similar to that of moving accounts within the Chart of Accounts, as described in Chapter 4, "Working with Accounts."

To move a job, follow these steps:

1. Access the Customer:Job List by opening the **L**ists menu and choosing **C**ustomers:Jobs, clicking the Cust button on the Iconbar, or pressing Ctrl+J.

2. Move the mouse pointer to the small diamond located to the left of the job name you want to move. As you point to the diamond, the mouse pointer changes its appearance to a four-pointed arrow. The four-pointed arrow indicates that the job can be moved up, down, left or right within the Customer:Job List.

   If you move a job to the left, you make the job a higher-level job. If you move jobs to the right, they become sub-jobs. Jobs moved up or down are repositioned within the Customer:Job List.

3. Drag the job to its new location in the list. If you move a job that has sub-jobs, its sub-jobs move with it.

Turning Off Job Tracking. If you don't want to track jobs by customer, you can turn off the QuickBooks job tracking feature. After you install QuickBooks for Windows, job tracking is automatically turned on.

To turn off job tracking, follow these steps:

1. From the **P**references menu, choose **T**ransactions. QuickBooks displays the Transactions Preferences dialog box.

2. Select the Track **E**xpenses by Customer:Job check box to remove the check mark and turn off job tracking.

3. Click OK or press Enter. Job tracking is now off.

Designing the Vendor List

The Vendor List includes the name, contact person, address, a first and second telephone number, fax number, vendor type, the name you want printed on checks to the vendor, your credit limit with the vendor, taxpayer ID number, and opening balance and date. The Vendor List makes it easy to complete fields in the Enter Bills window and the Accounts Payable and Credit Card registers when you enter or pay bills. The Vendor List also provides the information you need to file an IRS 1099 report for vendors to whom you pay more than $600 per year.

To access the Vendor List, click the Vend (Vendor) button on the Iconbar, or from the **L**ists menu, choose **V**endors.

QuickBooks displays only the vendor name and balance in the Vendor List window, as shown in figure 5.6. The program stores all other information about a vendor—such as address and vendor type—and displays this information only if you choose to edit the vendor information.

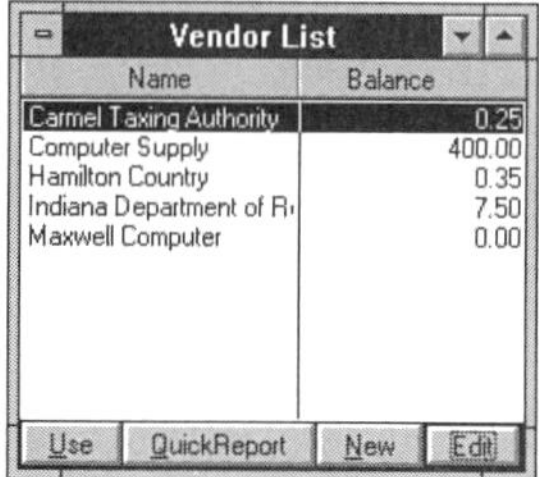

Fig. 5.6
The Vendor List displays a list of your vendors and your account balance with each one.

From the Vendor List, you can add, edit, and delete vendors from the list. You also can print the Vendor List. For more information on printing a vendor list, see the section "Printing QuickBooks for Windows Lists," later in this chapter.

Adding a Vendor

You can add a vendor to the Vendor List at any time. You enter the vendor's name, address, vendor type, and so on when you add a vendor to the Vendor List.

To add a vendor to the Vendor List, follow these steps:

1. In the Vendor List, select the **N**ew button. QuickBooks displays the New Vendor window, as shown in figure 5.7.

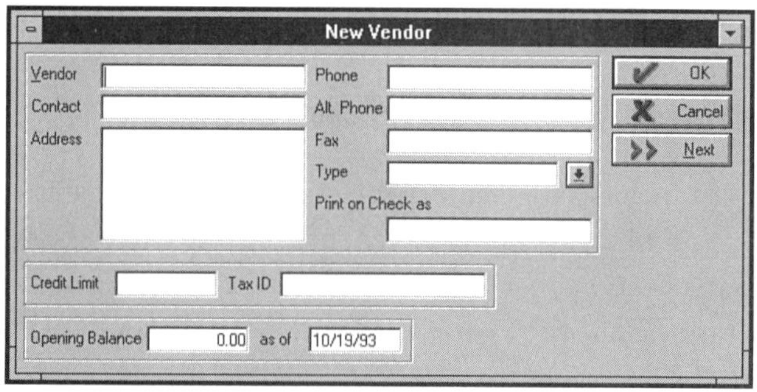

Fig. 5.7
Enter information in the New Vendor window about a vendor you want to add to your Vendor List.

2. In the **V**endor text box, type the vendor's name, using up to 24 characters.

You cannot enter a vendor name that already appears in the Vendor List. If you add a vendor who has the same name as an existing vendor, you must include a phrase that distinguishes the new vendor from the existing one.

To list your vendors alphabetically by last name, enter the last name first.

3. In the Contact text box, type the name of the contact person for this vendor.
4. Beginning on the second line of the Address text box, type the vendor's address, using up to four lines for the address. (QuickBooks automatically enters the name of the vendor on the first line.)
5. In the Phone text box, type the vendor's telephone number.
6. If this vendor has more than one telephone number, type the other number in the Alt. Phone text box.
7. Type the vendor's fax number in the Fax text box.
8. Select the vendor type by clicking the arrow next to the Type text box or by pressing Ctrl+L. QuickBooks displays a drop-down list of vendors from the Vendor Type List. The Vendor Type List is explained later in this chapter.
9. If you want a different vendor name printed on checks, type the name in the Print on Check As text box exactly as you want it to appear on the checks. If a vendor is named "A & L Arts" in your Vendor List, for example, you can print the vendor's legal name, "A & L Arts Supply Company, Inc.," on checks.
10. In the Credit Limit text box, type the amount of credit that the vendor has granted you.
11. If you expect to file a 1099 for this vendor, enter the vendor's taxpayer ID number next in the Tax ID text box.
12. If you didn't enter any outstanding bills from vendors at the time you started your QuickBooks for Windows system, type the outstanding balance owed to this vendor as of the current date in the Opening Balance text box. Then enter the date that relates to the outstanding balance in the As Of text box. Do not enter an opening balance if you enter actual bills from vendors with outstanding balances.
13. Click OK or press Enter to add the vendor to the Vendor List.

Editing Vendor Information

To edit or view vendor information or to rename a vendor, follow these steps:

1. From the **L**ists menu, choose **V**endors, or click the Vend (Vendor) button from the Iconbar to display the Vendor List.
2. Scroll through the Vendor List to select the vendor you want to edit.
3. Choose the Edi**t** button to display the Edit Vendor window, as shown in figure 5.8.

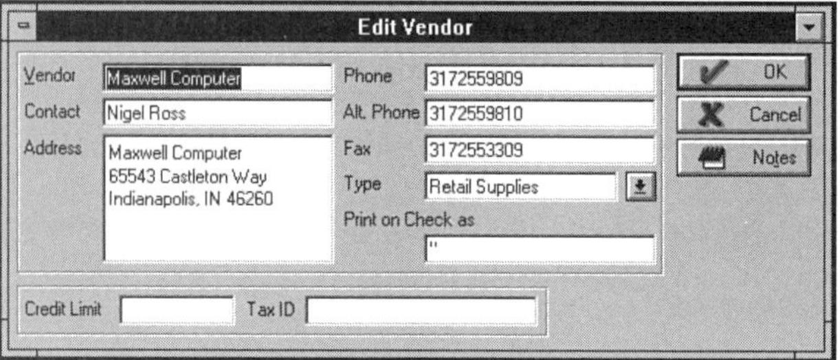

Fig 5.8
You can change information about a vendor in the Edit Vendor window.

4. To rename the vendor, type the new vendor name to replace the existing vendor name. If you change the vendor name, you must also change the name in the Address text box. To edit other vendor information, move to the text box you want to edit, and type over the existing information.
5. After making the appropriate changes, click OK or press Enter.

CPA TIP: Changing the Vendor Name

If you change the vendor name, QuickBooks changes the information in existing transactions. To change the vendor's name in future transactions only (leaving the former vendor name in existing transactions), add a new vendor with this new name to the Vendor List, and then use this new vendor on all future transactions. Do not rename the vendor unless you want all existing transactions updated.

Creating Vendor Notes

You can create notes about a vendor by using the QuickBooks Notepad, which also is available from the Edit Vendor window. The Notepad can store up to 10 windows of text for each vendor. You also can print notes from the Notepad. Use the Notepad to write reminders for any of the following: your telephone conversations with a vendor, special requests you make to a vendor, or payment agreements between you and a vendor. Using the Notepad eliminates loose paper or sticky notes that easily get lost.

To create a vendor note, follow these steps:

1. From the Vendor List, select the name of the vendor for whom you want to write a note.

2. Choose the Edi**t** button to display the Edit Vendor window.

3. Select the No**t**es button to display the Notepad (similar to the one shown in figure 5.5 for a customer note).

4. Type the text of your note in the Notepad, using the keys listed in the earlier section "Creating Customer Notes" to create the note.

5. After your note is complete, click OK or press Enter to record it in the Notepad. Click Cancel or press Esc to discard the note.

You also can create notes from a transaction in the Enter Bills window or in the Accounts Payable register. To create a note from these windows, highlight any transaction containing the vendor for whom you want to create a note, and from the **E**dit menu, select N**o**tepad to access the Notepad. Then follow the preceding steps for creating a note.

Deleting a Vendor

You can always delete a vendor from the Vendor List, provided that you have no existing transactions for that vendor. (You cannot delete a vendor for whom you have entered bills. This ensures that your accounts payable records are accurately reflected.)

To delete a vendor from the Vendor List, follow these steps:

1. To access the Vendor List from the **L**ists menu, choose **V**endors; or click the Vend button on the Iconbar.

2. Scroll through the Vendor List and select the name of the vendor you want to delete.

3. From the **E**dit menu, choose **D**elete Vendor; or press Ctrl+D. QuickBooks displays a confirmation message asking whether you are sure you want to delete the vendor.

4. To delete the vendor, click OK or press Enter. Click Cancel or press Esc to keep the vendor in your list.

Note

If you have existing transactions for a vendor, QuickBooks does not allow you to delete that vendor. If you try to delete a vendor for whom transactions exist, QuickBooks displays a message indicating that the current vendor cannot be deleted. QuickBooks needs this vendor information to generate Accounts Payable reports.

Designing the Employee List

The Employee List is used to store information about your employees. QuickBooks sorts the Employee List alphabetically by the name that you enter first. If you add employees to the list by entering their first names first, for example, QuickBooks sorts the Employee List alphabetically by employees' first names. When you write an invoice, QuickBooks enters employees' initials in the Rep field of the invoice so that you can track sales by employee. If you pay employees on a commission basis, this feature is particularly useful.

To access the Employee List, open the **L**ists menu and choose **E**mployees. QuickBooks displays the Employee List (see fig. 5.9).

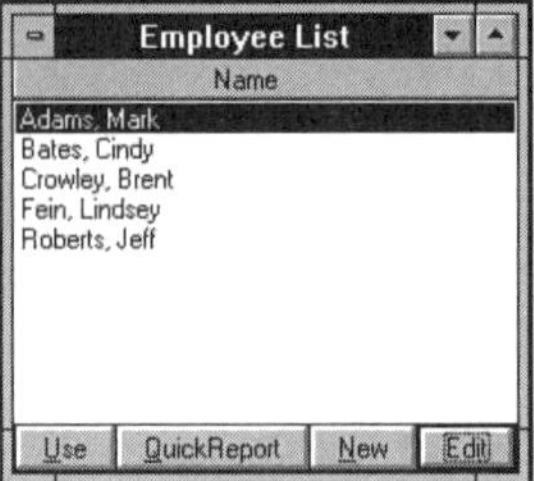

Fig. 5.9
Employee names are listed alphabetically in the Employee List.

From the Employee List, you can add, edit, and delete employees. You also can print the Employee List. See the later section "Printing QuickBooks for Windows Lists" for more information on printing an Employee List.

Adding an Employee

If you add an employee to the Employee List, you enter the employee's name, initials, social security number, up to two telephone numbers, and address. The employee's initials are used to identify the employee as the sales representative on a customer invoice.

To add an employee to the Employee List, follow these steps:

1. From the Employee List, select the **N**ew button to display the New Employee window, as shown in figure 5.10.

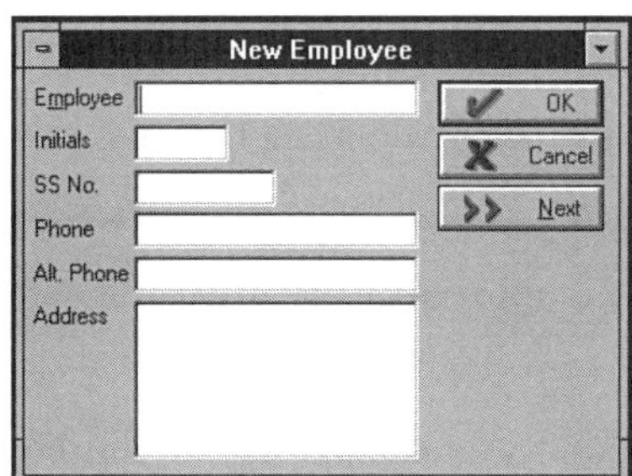

Fig. 5.10
Enter information about an employee in the New Employee window.

2. In the E**m**ployee text box, type the employee's name, using up to 24 characters.

   You cannot enter an employee name that already appears in the Employee List. If you add an employee who has the same name as an existing employee, you must include a phrase that distinguishes the new employee from the existing one.

   If you want to list your employees alphabetically by last name, enter the last name first.

3. To assign different initials to the employee, type the modified initials in the Initials field. Otherwise, QuickBooks automatically enters the employee's initials based on the name that you entered in the Employee text box. Initials are used in the Rep field of an invoice or a cash sale receipt to identify the employee who sold items to a customer.

4. In the SS No. text box, type the employee's social security number.

5. In the next two text boxes, type the employee's telephone number and, if applicable, a second telephone number for the employee.

6. Beginning on the second line of the Address box, type the employee's address, using up to four lines. (QuickBooks automatically enters the employee's name in the first line of the Address box.)

7. Click OK or press Enter to add the employee to the Employee List.

Editing Employee Information

If employee information changes, you must edit the Employee List to reflect the changes. You also may need to view employee information at some point, perhaps to get an employee's address.

To edit or view employee information, follow these steps:

1. Access the Employee List by opening the **L**ists menu and choosing **E**mployees.

2. Scroll through the Employee List to select the name of the employee you want to edit.

3. Choose the Edi**t** button to display the Edit Employee window (which is similar to the New Employee window shown in figure 5.10).

4. To change the employee name, type the new employee name to replace the existing name. If you change the employee name in the Employee text box, you also must change the name in the Address box. To edit other employee information, press Tab to move to the text box you want to edit, and type the new information to replace the existing information.

5. After making the appropriate changes, click OK or press Enter.

Creating Employee Notes

You can add notes that relate to employees in your Employee List by using the Notepad. The Notepad can store such additional information about employees as their hire date, their spouse's name, children's' names, and so on.

To create an employee note, follow these steps:

1. From the Employee List, select the employee for whom you want to write a note.

2. Choose the Edi**t** button to display the Edit Employee window.

3. Choose the No**t**es button to display the Notepad (similar to the one shown in figure 5.5 for a customer note).
4. Type the text of your note in the Notepad, using the keys listed in the section "Creating Customer Notes" earlier in this chapter to create a note.
5. After your note is complete, click OK or press Enter to record it in the Notepad. Click Cancel or press Esc to discard the note.

Deleting an Employee

You can always delete an employee from the Employee List by following these steps:

1. From the **L**ists menu, choose **E**mployees to access the Employee List.
2. Scroll through the Employee List to select the employee whose name you want to delete.
3. From the **E**dit menu, choose **D**elete Employee; or press Ctrl+D. QuickBooks displays a confirmation message asking whether you really want to delete the employee.
4. To delete the employee name, click OK or press Enter. Click Cancel or press Esc to keep the employee in your list.

Designing the Other Names List

The Other Names List is a "catchall" list for names of anyone with whom you deal other than customers, vendors, or employees. QuickBooks requires that names entered in the Write Checks window or the Enter Credit Card Charges window be part of a list. If you write a check to a person who is not listed in the Vendor List, you must add that person's name to a list. If you do not want the name included in your Vendor List, you can choose to add it to the Other Names List. If you make a one-time contribution to the Boys Scouts of America, for example, you can add this name to the Other Names List.

Adding names to the Other Names List helps speed up data entry in QuickBooks by enabling you to quickly fill in list fields by using QuickFill or the drop-down lists. (QuickFill is explained in more detail in Chapter 13, "Writing and Printing Checks.")

Adding an Other Name

If you enter a new name in the Payee text box in the Write Checks window or in the Purchased From text box in the Enter Credit Card Charges window, QuickBooks asks whether you want to add the name to the Other Names List. You can add the name only (Quick Add) or add the name and other information (Set Up). You can also add a name to the Other Names List by accessing the list itself and entering the name and any other pertinent information.

To add a name to the Other Name List, follow these steps:

1. From the **L**ists menu, choose Other **N**ames. QuickBooks displays the Other Names List, as shown in figure 5.11.

Fig. 5.11 The Other Names List includes names of anyone with whom you deal other than customers, vendors, or employees.

2. Choose the **N**ew button. QuickBooks displays the New Name window, as shown in figure 5.12.

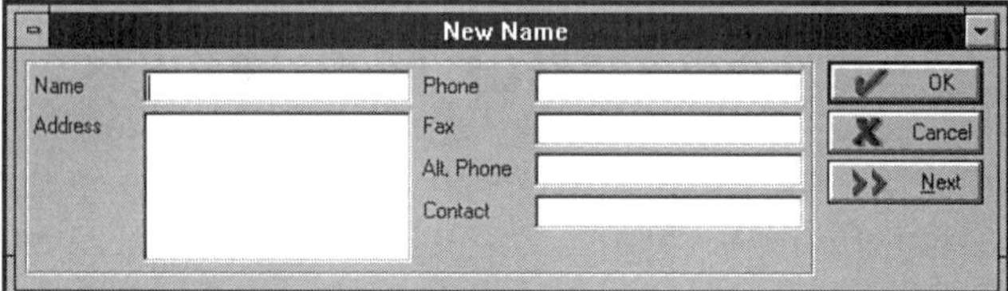

Fig. 5.12 Add a name to the Other Name List by entering information in the New Name window.

3. Type the name, address, telephone number, fax number, alternative telephone number, and contact person in their respective text boxes. (You can enter as little or as much information for the name as you want.)

4. Click OK or press Enter to add the name to the Other Names List.

Alternatively, you can simply enter a new name in the Payee text box of the Write Checks window or in the Purchased From text box of the Enter Credit Card Charges window. If the name does not already appear in the Customer, Vendor, or Employee List, QuickBooks asks whether you want to add the other name by using Quick Add or Set Up. Choose **S**et Up to display the Select Name Type dialog box (see fig. 5.13). Then choose the **O**ther option button, and click OK or press Enter to display the New Name window.

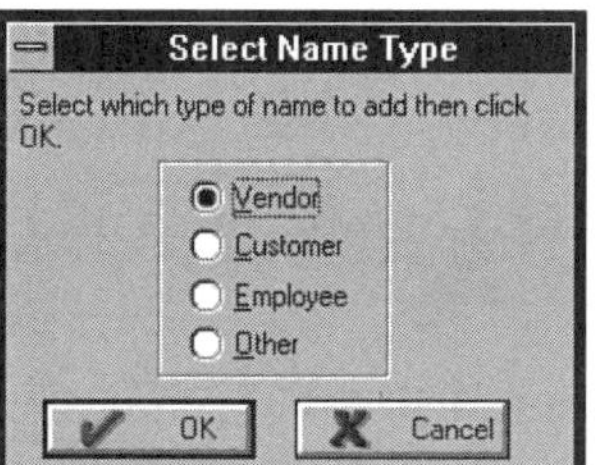

Fig. 5.13
Specify in the Select Name Type dialog box to which list you want to add the new name.

Editing an Other Name

If you add a name to the Other Names List and then decide that you want the name included in, for example, your Vendor List, you can change the name's type. You also can change any of the other information for a name that appears in the Other Names List.

To change the name's type, or to change any other information about the name, follow these steps:

1. From the **L**ists menu, choose **O**ther Names to access the Other Names List.
2. Scroll through the list of names, and select the name you want to change.
3. Choose the Edi**t** button to display the Edit Name window (which is similar to the New Name window shown in figure 5.12, except for the Notes and **C**hange Type buttons).
4. To change the name type, choose the **C**hange Type button. QuickBooks displays the Select Name Type dialog box.
5. In the Select Name Type dialog box, choose the option button for the name type to which you want to change the name, and click OK or press Enter. QuickBooks returns to the Edit Name window.
6. To change other information in the Edit Name window, press Tab to move to the text box that you want to change, and type the new information to replace the existing information.

Tip
You also can create notes for a name in the Other Names List. To create a note, follow the steps for creating Customer, Vendor, or Employee notes, as explained in those sections earlier in this chapter.

7. Click OK or press Enter after you finish changing the information for the selected name in the Other Names List.

Deleting an Other Name

If you no longer use a name in the Other Names List, you can delete the name by following these steps:

1. Access the Other Names List by opening the **L**ists menu and choosing **O**ther Names.
2. Scroll through the list to select the name you want to delete.
3. From the **E**dit menu, choose **D**elete Name; or press Ctrl+D. QuickBooks displays a confirmation message asking whether you really want to delete the name.
4. To delete the name, click OK or press Enter. Click Cancel or press Esc to keep the name in the Other Names List.

Designing the Invoice Items List

The Invoice Items List contains extremely useful information about the products you sell or the services you provide to your customers. You design the Invoice Items List to include the line items you frequently enter on customer invoices. If you are an interior designer, for example, you probably bill your customers or clients for the following: consulting fees, design fees, furnishings, fabrics, labor, and installation. You can set up a line item for each type of item or service you provide along with its price. To write a customer invoice, you simply choose an item from the Invoice Item List, and QuickBooks completes the lines on the invoices and calculates the total price per line item. You also use the Item List to enter another sales tax rate (other than your normal sales tax rate), discounts, a subtotal, refunds, and payments.

QuickBooks includes eight invoice item types you can add to the Invoice Item List. Three of these invoice types (Service, Part, and Other Charge) relate to the goods or services your business offers. The other five invoice item types (Subtotal, Discount, Payment, Group, and Sales Tax) deal with invoice calculations. The following table explains the functions of these invoice item types.

Item Type	Function
Part	Inventory or tangible items; Quantity, Price Each, and Amount fields on invoices are positive for Part item types.
Service	Services provided to customers; quantity usually is in terms of hours.
Other Charges	Identifies miscellaneous charges to customers, such as markups or freight; the Balance Forward item (preset by QuickBooks for Windows) is an Other Charge.
Subtotal	Shows a subtotal on an invoice; subtotals all previous lines following the preceding subtotal.
Discount	Discounts line items; has a negative dollar or percentage value in the Price Each field.
Payment	Payments received the same time you issue an invoice; QuickBooks automatically makes payment items negative so that they are subtracted from the customer's invoice.
Group	Hides details on an invoice by grouping more than one invoice item.
Sales Tax	Used if you collect sales tax from more than one tax district. Calculates the appropriate sales tax by multiplying the tax rate by the amount in the immediately preceding line.

You also must define an invoice item code for every invoice item you add to the Invoice Item List. Item codes enable QuickBooks to link Income, Expense, and Balance Sheet accounts to your invoice items. Item codes also help you recognize your invoice items and distinguish individual invoice items within the Invoice Item List. You should assign an item code to each inventory item or service you provide to your customers.

Note

Unless you assign more than 100 item codes, you can use words or phrases to define an item code. If you do assign more than 100 item codes, you probably should use numbers. Notice that you also can include special characters, such as a hyphen (-), in an item code. QuickBooks organizes the Invoice Item List by item type and then alphabetically (or in ascending numeric order) by item code. Because item codes can contain up to 13 characters, you can easily assign numeric item codes to thousands of items of each item type.

You also assign Income, Expense, or Balance Sheet accounts to invoice items so that QuickBooks automatically assigns the invoice items to the appropriate accounts when you enter items on an invoice.

To access the Invoice Item List, click the Item button from the Iconbar, or from the **L**ists menu, choose **I**nvoice Items. QuickBooks displays the Invoice Item List, as shown in figure 5.14.

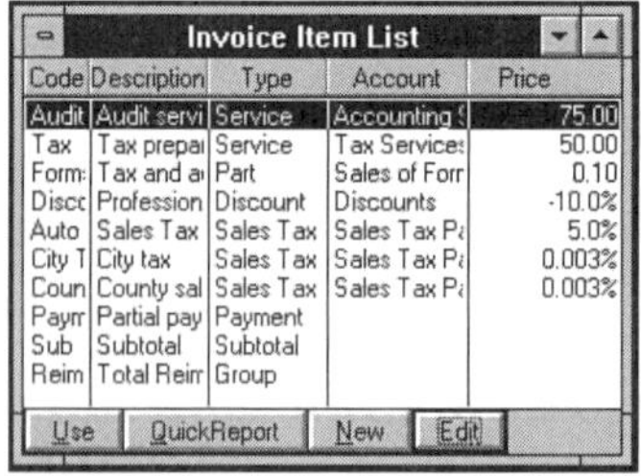

Code	Description	Type	Account	Price
Audit	Audit servi	Service	Accounting S	75.00
Tax	Tax prepar	Service	Tax Services	50.00
Form:	Tax and a	Part	Sales of Forr	0.10
Discc	Profession	Discount	Discounts	-10.0%
Auto	Sales Tax	Sales Tax	Sales Tax Pa	5.0%
City T	City tax	Sales Tax	Sales Tax Pa	0.003%
Coun	County sal	Sales Tax	Sales Tax Pa	0.003%
Paym	Partial pay	Payment		
Sub	Subtotal	Subtotal		
Reim	Total Reim	Group		

Fig. 5.14
The Invoice Item List includes the line items you use to write invoices.

As you first access the Invoice Item List, you see only the one item that QuickBooks added at the time you set up your company (if, that is, you charge sales tax to your customers): the Auto Sales Tax item. This item appears as *Auto* in the Code column of the list window. The Auto Sales Tax item is used by QuickBooks to calculate sales tax, based on your most common sales-tax rate.

Adding an Item

You need to add items specific to your small business to the Invoice Item List. Subsequently, you may need to edit or delete an invoice item. You can easily accomplish these tasks from the Invoice Item List window.

To add an item to the Invoice Item List, follow these steps:

1. From the **L**ists menu, choose **I**nvoice Items to access the Invoice Item List.
2. Choose the **N**ew button. QuickBooks displays the New Item window, as shown in figure 5.15.
3. Click the arrow next to the **T**ype text box to display the drop-down list of invoice item types. Select an invoice item type from the list.

Note

The text boxes in the New Item window change depending on the type of invoice item you select to add.

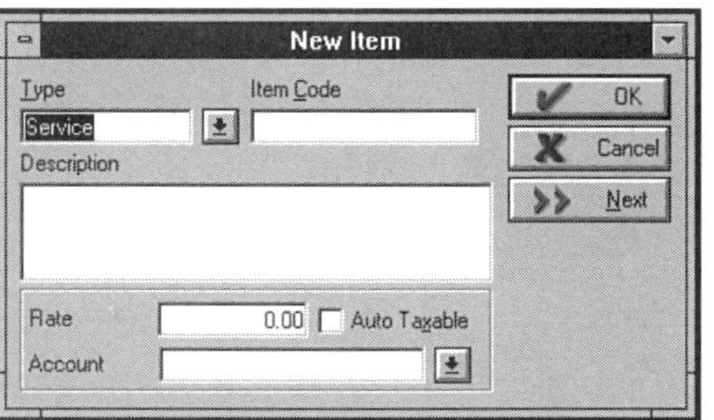

Fig. 5.15
Enter information about a new invoice item in the New Item window.

4. In the Item Code field, type a unique identifying code for the invoice item, using up to 13 characters.

5. Type in the Description text box a one- to three-line description of the invoice item; the description's first line appears on invoices.

   The next several fields vary depending on the invoice item type you are adding.

6. Follow the appropriate step for the invoice item type you are adding.

   - For Service, Part, or Other Charge invoice item types, enter the Rate (hourly rate for services) or Unit Price (price per item) in the next field.

     Select the Auto Taxable check box if you want QuickBooks to automatically calculate sales tax on the item, using your most common sales tax rate.

     In the Account text box, assign an Income, Expense, or Balance Sheet account to the invoice item you are adding. Click the drop-down arrow to display the list of accounts and select an account from the list.

   - For the Discount item type, enter the discount amount or percentage rate in the Amount of % text box.

Select the Auto Taxable check box if you want QuickBooks to automatically calculate sales tax on the discount item, using your most common sales tax rate.

In the Account text box, assign an Income, Expense, or Balance Sheet account to the discount invoice item you are adding. Click the drop-down arrow to display the list of accounts, and select an account from the list.

- For the Sales Tax invoice item type, enter the sales tax rate in the Rate text box.

  Select the agency for which you collect sales tax in the Tax Agency drop-down list, and then type the name of the Tax District in that text box.

- For the Payment invoice item type, click the drop-down arrow next to the Payment Method text box to select a payment method from the drop-down list. After you assign a payment method to a Payment invoice item, QuickBooks enables you to group the money received by payment method. This feature is useful if you create deposit slips.

- For the Group invoice item type, select the Print Items in Group check box if you want invoice items detailed on invoices. (If you leave the check box blank, QuickBooks enters only the group item description on invoices.)

  Then select items from your Invoice Items List that you want included in the group. Click the arrow next to the Item field, and select the Item Code from the drop-down list. The appropriate description is entered in the Description column.

  Entering group invoice items is explained in Chapter 6, "Creating Invoices."

7. After the New Item window is complete, click OK or press Enter to add the invoice item to the list.

Editing an Invoice Item

If your invoice items change at any time—for example, you change the price of an item—you can edit the invoice item from the Invoice Item List.

To edit an invoice item from the Invoice Item List, follow these steps:

1. Access the Invoice Item List by opening the **L**ists menu and choosing **I**nvoice Items.

2. Scroll through the Invoice Item List to select the invoice item you want to edit.

3. Choose the Edi**t** button. QuickBooks displays the Edit Item window (which is similar to the New Item window, shown in fig. 5.15).

4. Move to the field you want to change, and type the new information to replace the existing information or make a different selection from the drop-down list.

5. Click OK or press Enter to change the invoice item.

QuickBooks updates all existing invoices to reflect the changes you make to an invoice item. To change the invoice item type for an invoice item (from Part to Other Charges, for example), rename the invoice item so that existing invoices continue to have the same item code. (If you delete line items, QuickBooks removes the item code from existing invoices.) You then add a new invoice item, using the old invoice item name, but selecting the new item type.

Deleting an Invoice Item

If you no longer need certain invoice items—for example, if you discontinue selling an item or providing a particular service—you can delete the invoice item from the Invoice Item List. You cannot, however, delete an invoice item that has been assigned to existing invoices.

To delete an invoice item from the Invoice Item List, follow these steps:

1. From the **L**ists menu, choose **I**nvoice Items to access the Invoice Item List.

2. Scroll through the Invoice Item List to select the invoice item you want to delete.

3. From the **E**dit menu, choose **D**elete Item; or press Ctrl+D. QuickBooks displays a confirmation message asking if you are sure that you want to delete the item.

4. To delete the invoice item, click OK or press Enter. Click Cancel or press Esc to keep the invoice item in your list.

Designing the Class List

If you use Quicken's classes to track income and expenses by project or class, you will find that the QuickBooks for Windows Class List enables you to handle these numerous levels of information more efficiently. You can set up as many as five levels of information in a QuickBooks Class List—a *first-level class* (parent class) and four lower-level classes, called *subclasses*. Subclasses are similar to subaccounts, because they further divide the detail of a class. (See Chapter 4, "Working with Accounts," for more information on subaccounts.)

QuickBooks' new job-tracking feature tracks income and expenses by customer. Classes, however, classify your income and expenses by department, business office, or location; separate properties you own; or distinguish any other breakdown specific to your business.

To track, for example, income and expenses that relate to each unit of real estate you own, you set up a class for each unit. A retail store, on the other hand, may add a class for each department so that the owner can compare sales by department.

Notice that using classes in your QuickBooks system is completely optional. Unless you turn on the Use Class Tracking option, QuickBooks does not display the Class text box in the windows in which you enter invoices, checks, bills, credit card charges, and other transactions.

Turning On Class Tracking

Before you begin to design your Class List, you need to turn on the Class Tracking option so that the Create Invoices window, Write Checks window, Enter Bills window, and so on, display the Class text box. If you do not turn on Class Tracking, you cannot assign classes to transactions.

To turn on class tracking in QuickBooks, follow these steps:

1. From the **P**references menu, choose **T**ransactions. QuickBooks displays the Transaction Preferences dialog box.

2. Select the Use **C**lass Tracking check box.

3. Click OK or press Enter.

Adding a Class

After you turn on the class tracking feature in QuickBooks, you can begin adding items to the Class List. QuickBooks does not include any predefined classes in the Class List, because classes vary from business to business. You must add any classes you want to use in your QuickBooks system to the Class List.

To add a first-level class, follow these steps:

1. From the **L**ists menu, choose C**l**asses. QuickBooks displays the Class List window, as shown in figure 5.16.

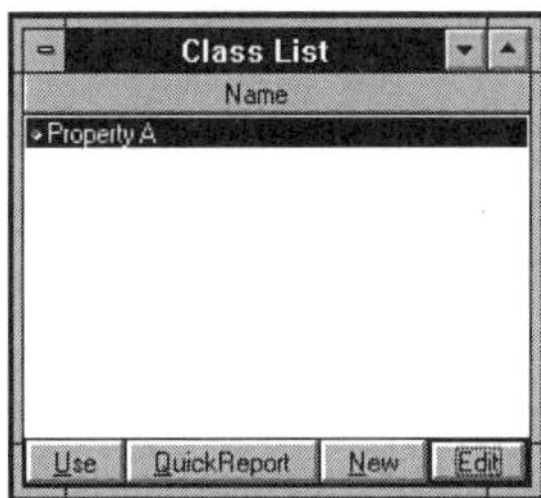

Fig. 5.16
The Class List window includes an alphabetical list of all classes you set up to track income and expenses.

2. Choose the **N**ew button to display the New Class window, as shown in figure 5.17.

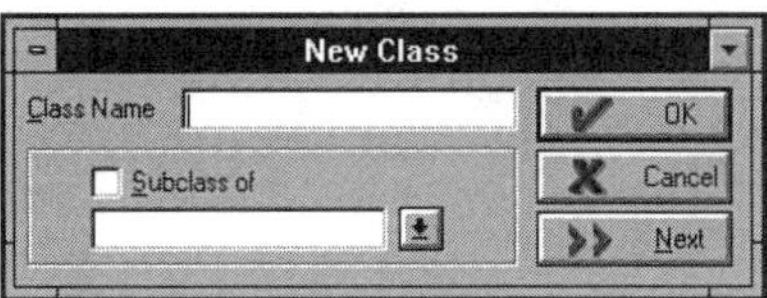

Fig. 5.17
You set up a class in the New Class window.

3. In the **C**lass Name field, type the class's name, such as a client's name, property address, office location, or department. You can enter up to 15 characters in this field, including letters, numbers, and special characters, such as %, @, #, &, and so on.

4. Click OK or press Enter to add the class to the Class List.

Note

You learn how to assign classes to transactions in Chapter 11, "Entering and Paying Bills," Chapter 13, "Writing and Printing Checks," and Chapter 14, "Entering Transactions in the Check Register."

Adding a Subclass

A *subclass* further divides the classifications you have established. Use subclasses if you want a more detailed breakdown of income and expenses by project, department, property, and so on. You may, for example, establish a class for each apartment building that you own and specify subclasses for each apartment unit within each building.

To add a subclass to the Class List, follow these steps:

1. From the **L**ists menu, choose C**l**asses. QuickBooks displays the Class List window.
2. Choose the **N**ew button to display the New Class window.
3. In the **C**lass Name text box, type the subclass's name.
4. Select the **S**ubclass Of check box.
5. Click the drop-down arrow next to the following text box to display the drop-down list of classes. Select the parent class of the subclass you entered in the Class Name text box.
6. Click OK or press Enter to add the subclass to the Class List. The subclass is indented under the parent class in the Class List.

Note

You learn how to assign subclasses to transactions in Chapter 11, "Entering and Paying Bills," Chapter 13, "Writing and Printing Checks," and Chapter 14, "Entering Transactions in the Check Register."

Moving Classes

Like accounts and subaccounts in the Chart of Accounts or customers and jobs in the Customer:Job List, you can change the relationship of classes and subclasses by moving them in the Class List. You can demote a class to a subclass or promote a subclass to a class. To change or move a subclass to a higher-level class, follow these steps:

1. From the **L**ists menu, choose C**l**asses to access the Class List.
2. Scroll through the Class List to select the subclass you want to move to a higher level.
3. Move the mouse pointer to the small diamond located to the left of the

subclass name you want to move within the Class List. After you point to the diamond, the mouse pointer changes to a four-pointed arrow. The four-pointed arrow indicates that the subclass can be moved up, down, left, or right within the Class List.

If you move a subclass to the left, you make the class a higher-level subclass or change the subclass to a class. If classes are moved to the right, they become subclasses. Subclasses moved up or down are repositioned within the Class List and become subclasses of a different class.

4. Drag (move) the subclass to its new location within the Class List. If you move a class that has subclasses or a subclass with subclasses, its subclasses also move with it.

Editing a Class

To edit or rename a class in the Class List, follow these steps:

1. From the **L**ists menu, choose C**l**asses to access the Class List.

2. Scroll through the Class List to select the class or subclass you want to edit or rename.

3. Choose the Edi**t** button to display the Edit Class window, which is similar to the New Class window shown in figure 5.17.

4. Type the new name of the class or subclass to replace the existing name in the Class Name field.

5. Click OK or press Enter.

Deleting a Class

You can always delete a class or subclass from the Class List. If you delete a class assigned to existing transactions, QuickBooks removes the class name and assigns a blank to those transactions. You can go back and reassign a class to those transactions from which the class name is deleted. QuickBooks does not permit you to delete a class or subclass that has subclasses. You must first delete the subclasses for the class or subclass you want to delete.

To delete a class or subclass from the Class List, follow these steps:

1. From the **L**ists menu, choose C**l**asses to access the Class List.

2. Scroll through the Class List to select the class or subclass you want to delete.

3. From the **E**dit menu, choose **D**elete Class; or press Ctrl+D. QuickBooks displays a confirmation message asking whether you really want to delete the class.

4. To delete the class or subclass, click OK or press Enter. Click Cancel or press Esc to keep the class or subclass in your list.

Designing the Customer Type List

You can use the Customer Type List to track the types of customers with whom you do business. You then can create reports that show your customers grouped by type. If you are in the landscaping business, for example, you can set up the following customer types: residential, commercial, and municipal. You can periodically review your Customer Type reports to determine the customer type for which you provide the most services.

Based on the business type you select when you set up your company, QuickBooks adds some customer types to the Customer Type List for you. You then can add, edit, or delete items to customize the Customer Type List for your small business. Using the Customer Type List, however, is completely optional.

You need the Customer Type List, in fact, to complete only the Customer Type text box in the New Customer window. You do not, however, need to enter information in the Customer Type text box. You can simply skip this field when adding a new customer.

You also can further divide customer types into subtypes. You can add customer types to define your customers as residential or commercial, for example, and then add subtypes for their geographic locations. You could, therefore, track all residential customers by city, county, or state and all commercial customers also by city, county, or state.

To access the Customer Type List, open the **L**ists menu, and choose C**u**stomer Types. QuickBooks displays the Customer Type List, as shown in figure 5.18.

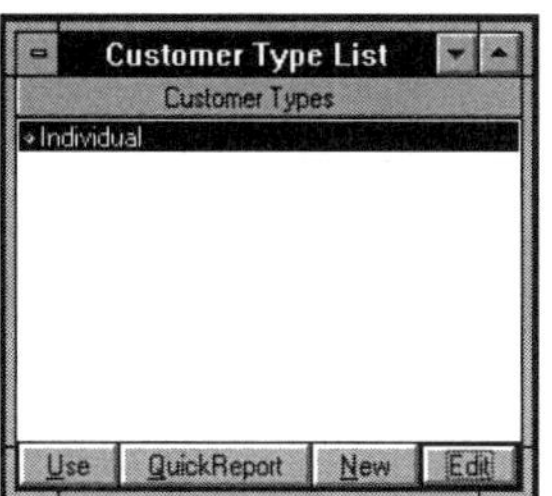

Fig. 5.18
The Customer Type List is an alphabetical list of the types of customers with whom you do business.

Adding a Customer Type

Customer types classify your customers into specific categories. You can add new customer types at any time.

To add a customer type or subtype to the Customer Type List, follow these steps:

1. From the **L**ists menu, choose C**u**stomer Types to access the Customer Type List.

2. Choose the **N**ew button to display the New Customer Type window.

3. Type a descriptive name in the Customer **T**ype field.

4. If adding a subtype, select the **S**ubtype Of check box, and then click the drop-down arrow to display the drop-down list of customer types, from which you can select the parent customer type.

5. Click OK or press Enter to add the customer type or subtype to the Customer Type List.

Editing a Customer Type

To edit a customer type or subtype, follow these steps:

1. From the **L**ists menu, choose C**u**stomer Types to access the Customer Type List.

2. Choose the Edi**t** button to display the Edit Customer Type window, which is similar in appearance to the New Customer Type window.

3. Change the name of the customer type by typing the new type to replace the existing type in the Customer Type text box. Change a subtype to a parent customer type by deselecting the **S**ubclass Of check box. Change the parent customer type of a subclass by selecting a new customer type from the drop-down list.

4. Click OK or press Enter.

Deleting a Customer Type

If you no longer have customers of a certain type or subtype, you can delete that customer type or subtype from the Customer Type List. You cannot, however, delete a customer type or subtype that relates to customers to whom you have written previous invoices.

To delete a customer type or subtype, follow these steps:

1. From the **L**ists menu, choose C**u**stomer Types to access the Customer Type List.
2. Scroll through the Customer Type List to select the customer type or subtype you want to delete.
3. From the **E**dit menu, choose **D**elete Customer Type; or press Ctrl+D. QuickBooks displays a confirmation message asking whether you are sure you want to delete the type.
4. To delete the customer type or subtype, click OK or press Enter. Click Cancel or press Esc to keep the customer type or subtype in your list.

Designing the Vendor Type List

The Vendor Type List contains a listing of every type of vendor from whom you purchase goods and services. You may find this list helpful for determining the vendors from whom you purchase certain materials or supplies or those vendors on whom you are relying too heavily. You are most likely to classify vendors by the type of supplies, materials, or services you purchase, such as computers, consultations, and office supplies.

CPA TIP: Purchasing from More than One Vendor

Unless you receive a substantial volume discount from a certain vendor from whom you purchase a particular material or supply, you probably should diversify your purchases so that you do not rely too heavily on one vendor. If relations should become strained between you and that vendor, or if the vendor changes his payment terms, you may need to purchase the supplies necessary to run your business from another vendor. Having another vendor relationship also gives you additional leverage if you need to negotiate new payment terms with an existing vendor.

You can add, edit, or delete types to customize the Vendor Type List for your small business. You also can add vendor subtypes to further divide the vendor types in your Vendor Type List. Using the Vendor Type List, however, is completely optional.

You use the Vendor Type List, in fact, to complete only the Type field in the New Vendor window. You can, however, simply skip this field when you add a new vendor to the Vendor List.

To access the Vendor Type List, open the **L**ists menu, and choose Ven**d**or Types. QuickBooks displays the Vendor Type List. (The Vendor Type List is similar to the other lists shown in this chapter: the Employee List, shown in fig. 5.9; the Other Names List, shown in fig. 5.11; and the Class List, shown in fig. 5.16).

Adding a Vendor Type

You set up vendor types to classify the vendors with whom you do business. If you begin purchasing from a vendor who doesn't fall into one of the vendor types from your Vendor List, you can add a new vendor type to the list. You also can add vendor subtypes to further break down the vendor types into smaller groups. You may have vendor types for plumbing subcontractors, for example, and then set up a subtype for each geographic region in which these subcontractors are located.

To add a vendor type or subtype to the Vendor Type List, follow these steps:

1. From the **L**ists menu, choose Ven**d**or Types to access the Vendor Type List.
2. Choose the **N**ew button to display the New Vendor Type window.
3. Type a descriptive name in the Vendor **T**ype field.
4. If adding a subtype, select the **S**ubtype Of check box, and then click the drop-down arrow to open the drop-down list from which you select the parent vendor type.
5. Click OK or press Enter to add the vendor type or subtype to the Vendor Type List.

Editing a Vendor Type

You can change vendor types in your Vendor Type List at any time.

To edit a vendor type, follow these steps:

1. From the **L**ists menu, choose Ven**d**or Types to access the Vendor Type List.
2. Scroll through the Vendor Type List to select the vendor type you want to edit.
3. Choose the Edi**t** button to display the Edit Vendor Type window.
4. Change the name of the vendor type by typing a new type to replace the existing type in the Vendor Type text box. Change a subtype to a parent vendor type by deselecting the **S**ubclass Of check box. Change the parent vendor type of a subclass by selecting a new vendor type from the drop-down list.
5. Click OK or press Enter.

Deleting a Vendor Type

If you find that you no longer conduct business with vendors of a certain vendor type or subtype included in the Vendor Type List, you can delete that vendor type or subtype. You cannot, however, delete a vendor type or subtype for a vendor for whom you have entered bills in the Enter Bills window.

To delete a vendor type or subtype, follow these steps:

1. From the **L**ists menu, choose Ven**d**or Types to access the Vendor Type List.
2. Scroll through the Vendor Type List to select the vendor type or subtype you want to delete.
3. From the **E**dit menu, choose **D**elete Vendor Type; or press Ctrl+D. QuickBooks displays a confirmation message asking whether you are sure you want to delete the vendor type.
4. To delete the vendor type or subtype, click OK or press Enter. Click Cancel or press Esc to keep the vendor type or subtype in your list.

Designing the Payment Method List

The Payment Method List includes all common methods of payment that you accept from your customers, such as cash, check, American Express, VISA, and MasterCard. After you receive a payment, select an item from the Payment Method List to complete the Pmt Method field on the invoice. QuickBooks then displays the Pmt Method field in the Make Deposit window so that you can identify payments and print deposit slips sorted by payment method.

You can, however, add, edit, or delete items from the Payment Method List so that it contains only those methods of payment that your small business accepts.

To access the Payment Method List, open the **L**ists menu, and choose Pa**y**ment Methods. QuickBooks displays the Payment Method List, as shown in figure 5.19.

Fig. 5.19
The Payment Method List is an alphabetical listing of all the payment methods you accept from your customers.

Adding a Payment Method

A payment method that is used by a customer but does not appear on the Payment Method List can easily be added.

To add a payment method to the Payment Method List, follow these steps:

1. From the **L**ists menu, choose Pa**y**ment Methods to access the Payment Method List.
2. Choose the **N**ew button to display the New Payment Method window.
3. Type a descriptive name in the Payment **M**ethod text box, using up to 24 characters.
4. Click OK or press Enter to add the payment method to the Payment Method List.

Editing a Payment Method

If you need to change a payment method, you can edit the Payment Method List at any time.

To edit a payment method, follow these steps:

1. From the **L**ists menu, choose Pa**y**ment Methods to access the Payment Method List.
2. Select from the list the payment method you want to edit, and then choose the Edi**t** button. QuickBooks displays the Edit Payment Method window.
3. Change the payment method by type a new payment method to replace the existing payment method.
4. Click OK or press Enter to save your changes to the Payment Method List.

Deleting a Payment Method

You can delete from the Payment Method List any payment methods your customers no longer use. You cannot, however, delete a payment method you have already entered in the Receive Payments window for payments from customers.

To delete a payment method, follow these steps:

1. From the **L**ists menu, choose Pa**y**ment Methods to access the Payment Method List.
2. Select from the list the payment method you want to delete.
3. From the **E**dit menu, choose **D**elete Payment Method; or press Ctrl+D. QuickBooks displays a confirmation message asking whether you are sure you want to delete the payment method.
4. To delete the payment method, click OK or press Enter. Click Cancel or press Esc to keep the payment method in your list.

Designing the Terms List

You can include every payment term you grant your customers in the Terms List. Payment terms indicate when payment is expected (usually the number of days) and what discount, if any, can be taken if payment is made within the expected payment term. A payment term of *2% 10 Net 30*, for example, means that if the customer pays the invoice amount within 10 days of the invoice date, the customer may take a 2% discount; otherwise, the full amount is due 10 to 30 days after the invoice date. Payment terms of *Net 30* mean that the net amount of the invoice is due within 30 days of the invoice date, with no discount allowed.

CPA TIP: Formulating Credit Policies

The payment terms you offer your customers or clients are up to your discretion; you should, however, formulate credit policies that are in line with other businesses of the same nature. If you own a catering business, for example, and other established caterers offer a 1% discount for payments made within 10 days of the invoice date, you probably need to offer the same payment terms to your customers to stay competitive.

Whatever the payment terms you decide to offer your customers, remember that you can be selective as to whom you extend favorable payment terms. Carefully evaluate each customer's credit history before offering payment terms with discounts or long payment periods.

After you add a new customer, you can complete the Terms text box by selecting an item from the Terms List. As you write an invoice for a customer, QuickBooks automatically adds the correct payment terms for that customer. After you receive payments, QuickBooks checks the date and applies any discount if the payment terms are met.

You can customize the Terms List for your small business by adding, editing, or deleting terms.

CPA TIP: Selecting Shorter Payment Periods

The time period in which you allow a customer to pay the net invoice is specific to your credit policies; most businesses, however, allow a 30- to 90-day period. If you allow a customer to pay an invoice within 30 or more days, you are providing credit to the customer and delaying the flow of cash into your business. If you are just starting out, cash inflows are extremely important to enable you to meet your monthly obligations. Consider allowing shorter net due periods (10 days or 15 days) to speed up the flow of cash into your business. As your business matures, you can always loosen your payment terms to allow longer net-due periods.

To access the Payment Terms List, follow these steps:

1. From the **L**ists menu, choose Invoice **O**ptions. QuickBooks displays the Invoice Options menu.

2. Choose **T**erms. QuickBooks displays the Terms List.

Adding a Payment Term

To add a payment term to the Terms List, follow these steps:

1. Access the Terms List, as described in the preceding steps.

2. Choose the **N**ew button to display the New Terms window, as shown in figure 5.20.

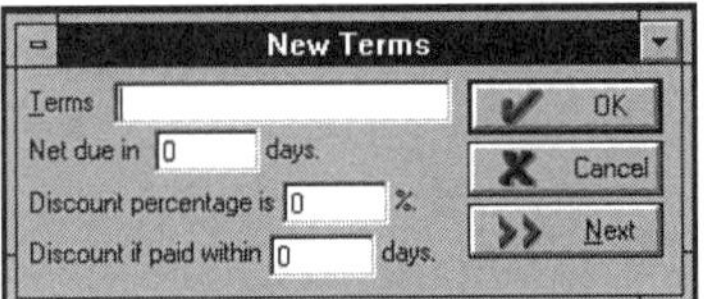

Fig. 5.20
Add information about a new payment term in the New Terms window.

3. In the **T**erms text box, type a descriptive name for the new payment terms. These terms then appear on customer invoices. Commonly, payment terms are shown with the discount percentage first, followed by the number of days the customer has to qualify for the discount and the number of days when the net invoice amount is due (2% 10 Net 30).

4. Enter the number of days in which the net amount of the invoice is due.

5. Type the discount percentage in the next text box. This is the discount allowed to a customer if payment is made within a specified period.

6. In the last field, type the number of days for which an early payment discount can be taken.

7. Click OK or press Enter to add the new payment term to the Terms List.

Tip
For Due on Receipt or Prepaid payment terms, enter zeros in all text boxes in the New Terms window.

Editing a Payment Term

If you need to change your payment terms, you can edit the Terms List at any time.

To edit a payment term, follow these steps:

1. From the **L**ists menu, choose Invoice **O**ptions, and then choose **T**erms to access the Terms List.

2. Scroll through the Terms List to select the payment term you want to edit.

3. Choose the Edi**t** button to display the Edit Terms window, which is similar to the New Terms window shown in figure 5.20.

4. Move to the text box you want to change and type the new information to replace the existing information.

5. Click OK or press Enter to save your changes to a payment term.

Deleting a Payment Term

If you no longer extend a payment term included in your Terms List, you can delete that payment term from the list. You cannot, however, delete a payment term you have entered on an existing invoice.

To delete a payment term, follow these steps:

1. From the **L**ists menu, choose Invoice **O**ptions, and then choose **T**erms to access the Terms List.

2. Scroll through the Terms List to select the payment term you want to delete.

3. From the **E**dit menu, choose **D**elete Terms; or press Ctrl+D. QuickBooks displays a confirmation message asking whether you are sure you want to delete the term.

4. To delete the payment term, click OK or press Enter. Click Cancel or press Esc to keep the payment term in your list.

QuickBooks does not change existing invoices to reflect payment terms you change.

Designing the Ship Via List

The Ship Via List contains the methods you frequently use to ship your products to your customers. You can add, edit, or delete items in the Ship Via List so that it contains only the methods you use in your small business. You select items from the Ship Via List to complete the Ship Via field as you write product invoices.

To access the Ship Via List, follow these steps:

1. From the **L**ists menu, choose Invoice **O**ptions. QuickBooks displays the Invoice **O**ptions menu.

2. Choose **S**hip Via. QuickBooks displays the Ship Via List. (The Ship Via List is similar in appearance to other lists shown in this chapter: the Employee List, shown in fig. 5.9; the Other Names List, shown in fig. 5.11; and the Class List, shown in fig. 5.16).

Adding a Shipping Method

If your small business begins using a new shipping method, you can add that method to the Ship Via List.

To add a shipping method to the Ship Via List, follow these steps:

1. Access the Ship Via List, as described in the preceding steps.

2. Choose the **N**ew button to display the New Shipping Method window.

3. In the Shipping Method text box, type a descriptive name for the new shipping method, using up to 15 characters. This name appears in the Ship Via field on product invoices.

4. Click OK or press Enter to add the new shipping method to the Ship Via List.

Editing a Shipping Method

If a shipping method changes, just edit that method in the Ship via List.

To edit a shipping method, follow these steps:

1. Access the Ship Via List, as described earlier in this section.

2. Scroll through the Ship Via List to select the shipping method you want to edit.

3. Choose the Edi**t** button to display the Edit Shipping Method window.

4. Type a new shipping method name to replace the existing name in the Shipping Method text box.

5. Click OK or press Enter to save your change to the Ship Via List.

Deleting a Shipping Method

Shipping methods you no longer use can be deleted from the Ship via List at any time. You cannot, however, delete a shipping method you have entered on an existing invoice.

To delete a shipping method, follow these steps:

1. Access the Ship Via List, as described earlier in this section.
2. Scroll through the Ship Via List to select the shipping method you want to delete.
3. From the **E**dit menu, choose **D**elete Shipping Method; or press Ctrl+D. QuickBooks displays a confirmation message asking whether you are sure you want to delete the shipping method.
4. To delete the shipping method, click OK or press Enter. Click Cancel or press Esc to keep the shipping method in your list.

QuickBooks does not change existing invoices to reflect shipping methods that you change.

Designing the Customer Message List

Use the Customer Message List to store memos that you repeatedly print at the bottom of customer invoices, such as `Please remit`, `Past due!`, or `Thank you for your continued business`. If you have a unique memo for a particular customer, you can type this memo on that invoice only. Your Customer Message List should contain only those memos you use repeatedly.

To access the Customer Message List, follow these steps:

1. From the **L**ists menu, choose Invoice **O**ptions. QuickBooks displays the Invoice **O**ptions menu.
2. Choose Customer **M**essages. QuickBooks displays the Customer Message List, as shown in figure 5.21.

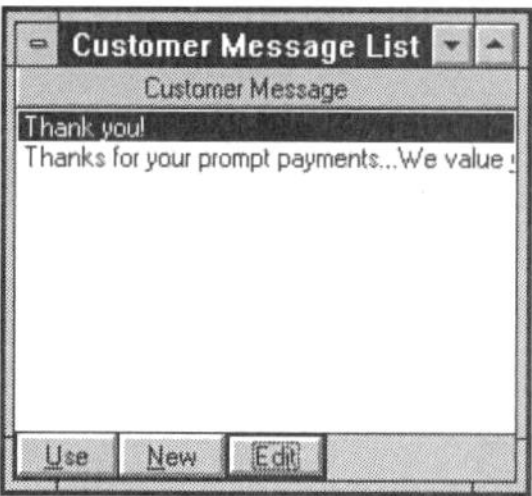

Fig. 5.21
QuickBooks stores in the Customer Message List the messages that print on invoices.

Adding a Customer Message

If you decide to include a customer message on your invoices that is not listed in the Customer Message List, just add it to the list.

To add a message to the Customer Message List, follow these steps:

1. Access the Customer Message List, as described in the preceding steps.

2. Choose the **N**ew button to display the New Customer Message window, as shown in figure 5.22.

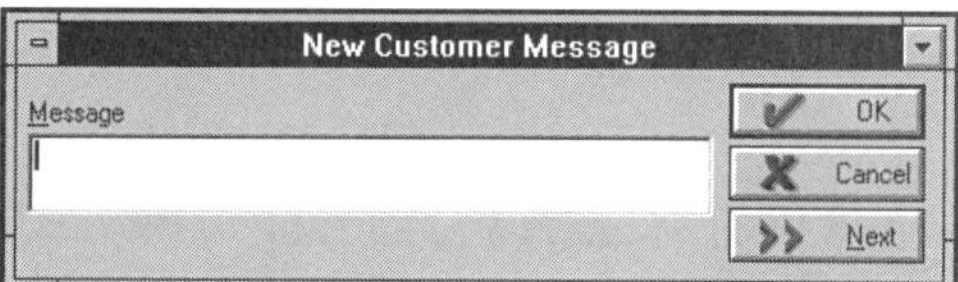

Fig. 5.22
Type the text of your message in the New Customer Message window.

3. In the Message text box, type the text of your customer message. Press Enter at the end of a line to move to the next line. QuickBooks prints the text on invoices exactly as it appears in the New Customer Message window, so be careful not to make typing errors. To correct a typing error, press the Backspace key to delete a character before the cursor or the Del key to delete a character after the cursor.

4. After your customer message is correct and complete, click OK or press Enter to add the message to the Customer Message List.

Editing a Customer Message

Messages in the Customer Message List can be changed if you decide you want to reword the message.

To edit a customer message, follow these steps:

1. Access the Customer Message List, as described earlier in this section.
2. Scroll through the Customer Message List to select the message you want to edit.
3. Choose the Edi**t** button to display the Edit Customer Message window, (which looks similar to the New Customer Message window, as shown in figure 5.22).
4. Make any necessary changes to the message.
5. Click OK or press Enter to save the changes.

If you change a customer message, QuickBooks does not change the message on existing invoices.

Deleting a Customer Message

You can delete customer messages you no longer use from the Customer Message List. You cannot, however, delete a customer message you have entered on existing invoices.

To delete a customer message, follow these steps:

1. Access the Customer Message List, as described earlier in this section.
2. Scroll through the Customer Message List to select the message you want to delete.
3. From the **E**dit menu, choose **D**elete Customer Message; or press Ctrl+D. QuickBooks displays a confirmation message asking whether you are sure you want to delete the message.
4. To delete the customer message, click OK or press Enter. Click Cancel or press Esc to keep the customer message in your list.

Adding to Lists on the Fly

In preceding sections, you learned how to add to QuickBooks lists by first accessing the list and adding all the information for an item. This method is most efficient if you are just starting your QuickBooks for Windows system and are just beginning to write invoices, write checks, and enter other transactions. Your lists, therefore, are complete as you start to use QuickBooks in your business.

You can, however, also add an item to any list at the same time you enter a transaction. Suppose, for example, that you just performed services for a new customer and now want to create an invoice. You do not need to first access the Customer:Job List to add the new customer to the list. You can simply type the new customer's name in the Customer:Job field of the invoice, and add the customer as you write the invoice. This method is called adding to a list *on the fly*. If you add an item to a list on the fly, you can add all the information relating to the item by using the Quick Add option or add only the name to the list by using the Set Up option.

To add to lists on the fly, follow these steps:

1. Type the new list item in a field in any of QuickBooks forms or registers. (You learn how to access forms and registers and enter transactions in QuickBooks in Parts II and III of this book.)

2. If QuickBooks looks through the appropriate list and does not find the name, a message appears on-screen (similar to the one shown in figure 5.23) telling you that the item is not found.

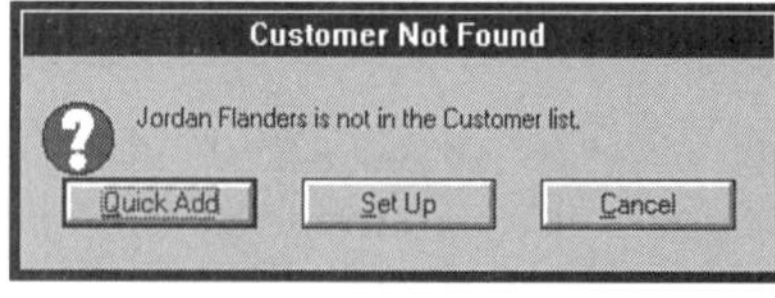

Fig. 5.23
The message displayed if QuickBooks for Windows does not find an item in a list.

3. To add to the appropriate list all the information for the item, choose Set Up. QuickBooks for Windows displays the appropriate window to enable you to add information for the item. If you enter a new customer in the Customer:Job text box in an invoice, for example, and then choose Set Up, QuickBooks displays the New Customer window.

To just add the name to the list, choose Quick Add. QuickBooks adds the name to the appropriate list and enables you to continue entering data in the current form or register.

Reorganizing QuickBooks for Windows Lists

QuickBooks sorts lists alphabetically; you can, however, reorganize the following lists any way you want:

- Chart of Accounts (Refer to Chapter 4, "Working with Accounts," to learn about the Chart of Accounts list.)
- Customer:Job List
- Class List
- Customer Type List
- Vendor Type List
- Memorized Transaction List (See Chapter 15, "Speeding Up Your Work in QuickBooks for Windows," to learn how to use the Memorized Transaction List.)

You can reorganize lists by using the mouse to drag list items to other locations within the list. If you decide later that you want the list back in alphabetical order, you can access the **L**ists menu and choose the Re-**s**ort List command to return the list to its original, alphabetical order. Notice that the Re-**s**ort List command is not available unless one of the list windows is open.

Using the Mouse To Reorganize Lists

You can reorganize lists simply by dragging a list item to the location within the list that you prefer. You can move parent items and subitems. You also can make a parent item a subitem and make a subitem a parent item. You can even move items farther to the right to create up to five levels of subitems.

To reorganize lists, follow these steps:

1. Access the list you want to reorganize.

2. Move the mouse pointer to the small diamond to the left of the item you want to move. As you point to the diamond, the mouse pointer changes to a four-pointed arrow. The four-pointed arrow indicates that the item can be moved up, down, left, or right within the list.

   If you move an item to the left, you make the item a higher-level item. If you move items to the right, they become subitems. Items moved up or down are repositioned within the list.

3. Drag (move) the item to the desired position within the list. If you move a parent item that has subitems, its subitems also move with it.

Re-sorting Lists Alphabetically

If you reorganize one of the lists described at the beginning of this section and later decide you want to re-sort your list alphabetically, you can put the list back in alphabetical order by opening the **L**ists menu and choosing the Re-**s**ort List command. Re-sorting lists returns any subitems to their original parent item.

To re-sort lists alphabetically, follow these steps:

1. Access the list you want to re-sort.
2. From the **L**ists menu, choose Re-**s**ort List.
3. Click OK or press Enter to re-sort the list alphabetically. Click Cancel or press Esc to keep the list in its current order.

Printing QuickBooks for Windows Lists

QuickBooks enables you to print lists either to your printer or to a disk. You can use the printed lists as references, and you can use the disk file in your word processing program.

Before you print a QuickBooks list, you must make sure that QuickBooks is set up to print lists. The program includes separate options to set up the program to print invoices, statements, checks, and labels. The **F**ile menu's **R**eport/List Printer option is used to set up QuickBooks to print reports, graphs, lists, registers, deposit summaries, and any other forms that do not have a separate setup option.

To set up QuickBooks to print lists, follow these steps:

1. From the **F**ile menu, choose Printer **S**etup. QuickBooks displays the Printer **S**etup menu.

2. Choose **R**eport/List Printer to display the Report Printer Setup dialog box, as shown in figure 5.24.

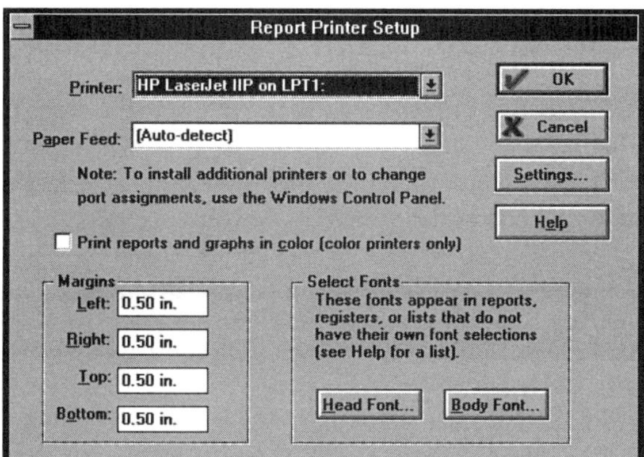

Fig. 5.24
Use the Report Printer Setup dialog box to set up QuickBooks to print lists.

3. Select your installed printer from the P**r**inter drop-down list.

4. If the paper feed is not correct, open the P**a**per Feed drop-down list to select the appropriate paper feed for your installed printer. (QuickBooks uses the Auto-detect option to determine whether your printer is continuous-feed or page-oriented.)

5. If you use a color printer and want to print the QuickBooks company list in color, select the Print Reports and Graphs in **C**olor check box. You must have an installed color printer to use this option.

6. Check the **L**eft, **R**ight, **T**op, and **B**ottom margins. If you want a larger or smaller margin than the preset values that QuickBooks uses, change the value in the appropriate field.

7. If you want to change the type font for the heading or body of the list, choose the **H**ead Font or **B**ody Font button in the Select Fonts area. QuickBooks displays the Report Default Headline Font dialog box or the Report Default Font dialog box. From here, you can change the font type, font style, font size, printing effects (strikeout or underline), and print color. After the Head and/or Body fonts are how you want them, click OK or press Enter to return to the Report Printer Setup dialog box.

You also can change other print settings, such as the paper tray, paper size, orientation, and number of copies.

8. To change other print settings, choose the **S**ettings button. QuickBooks displays the Other Settings dialog box for your installed printer. Make the necessary changes in this dialog box, and click OK or press Enter to return to the Report Printer Setup dialog box.

9. Click OK or press Enter to save the printer settings.

Now that QuickBooks is set up to print lists, follow these steps to print any list:

1. Access the QuickBooks list you want to print.

2. From the **F**ile menu, choose **P**rint List; or press Ctrl+P.

   QuickBooks displays the Print Report dialog box, as shown in figure 5.25.

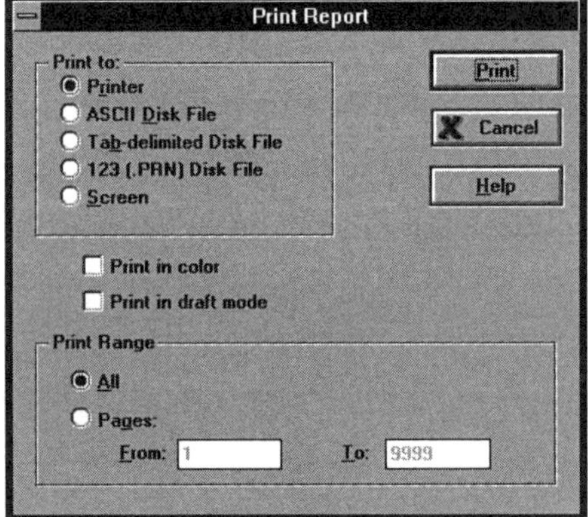

Fig. 5.25 The Print Report dialog box appears after you press Ctrl+P from any list window.

3. To print to your printer, choose the P**r**inter option button. You also can save your list to an ASCII disk file, a tab-delimited disk file, or a 123[.PRN] disk file, or preview the list on-screen, by choosing the button for one of those options.

4. Select the Print in Color check box to print the list in color. You must have a color printer installed to print the list in color. Select the Print in Draft Mode check box if you want to print a draft only.

5. Choose the Print Range; choose the **A**ll option button to print all pages of the list. To print only certain pages of the list, choose the Pa**g**es option button and specify the pages you want to print in the **F**rom and **T**o fields.

6. Choose the **P**rint button or press Enter to print the list.

Summary

This chapter showed you how to access QuickBooks for Windows lists and how to design lists to include items specific to your small business. You also learned how to add customer, job, vendor, and employee notes and how to re-sort lists. Finally, you learned how to print QuickBooks lists.

In the next chapter, you learn how to create invoices in QuickBooks. You discover just how easy creating an invoice and having QuickBooks do all your accounting work can be.

Part II

Tracking Customers

6 Creating Invoices

7 Tracking Sales Tax

8 Printing Invoices, Statements, and Other Forms

9 Receiving and Depositing Customer Payments

10 Using the Accounts Receivable Register

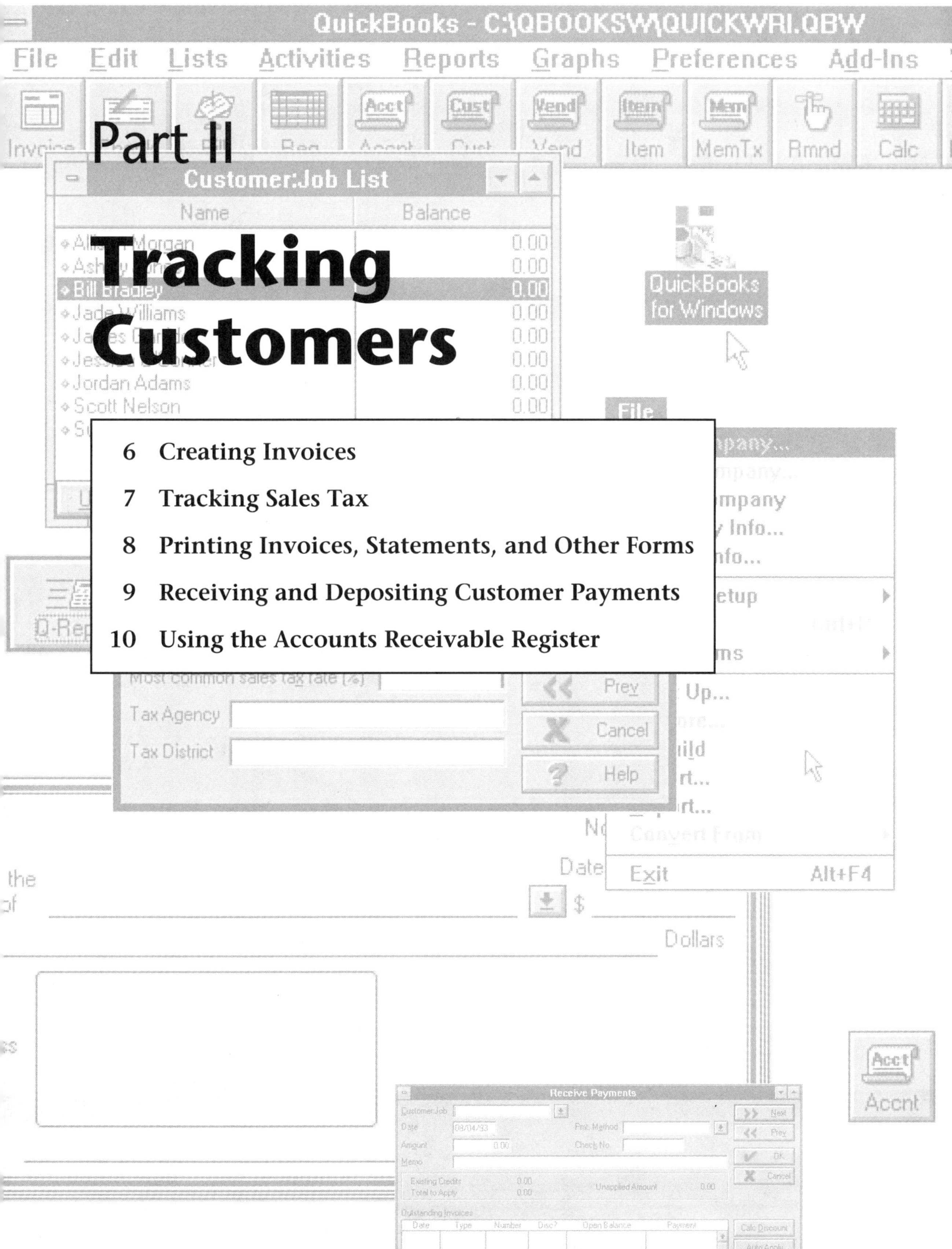

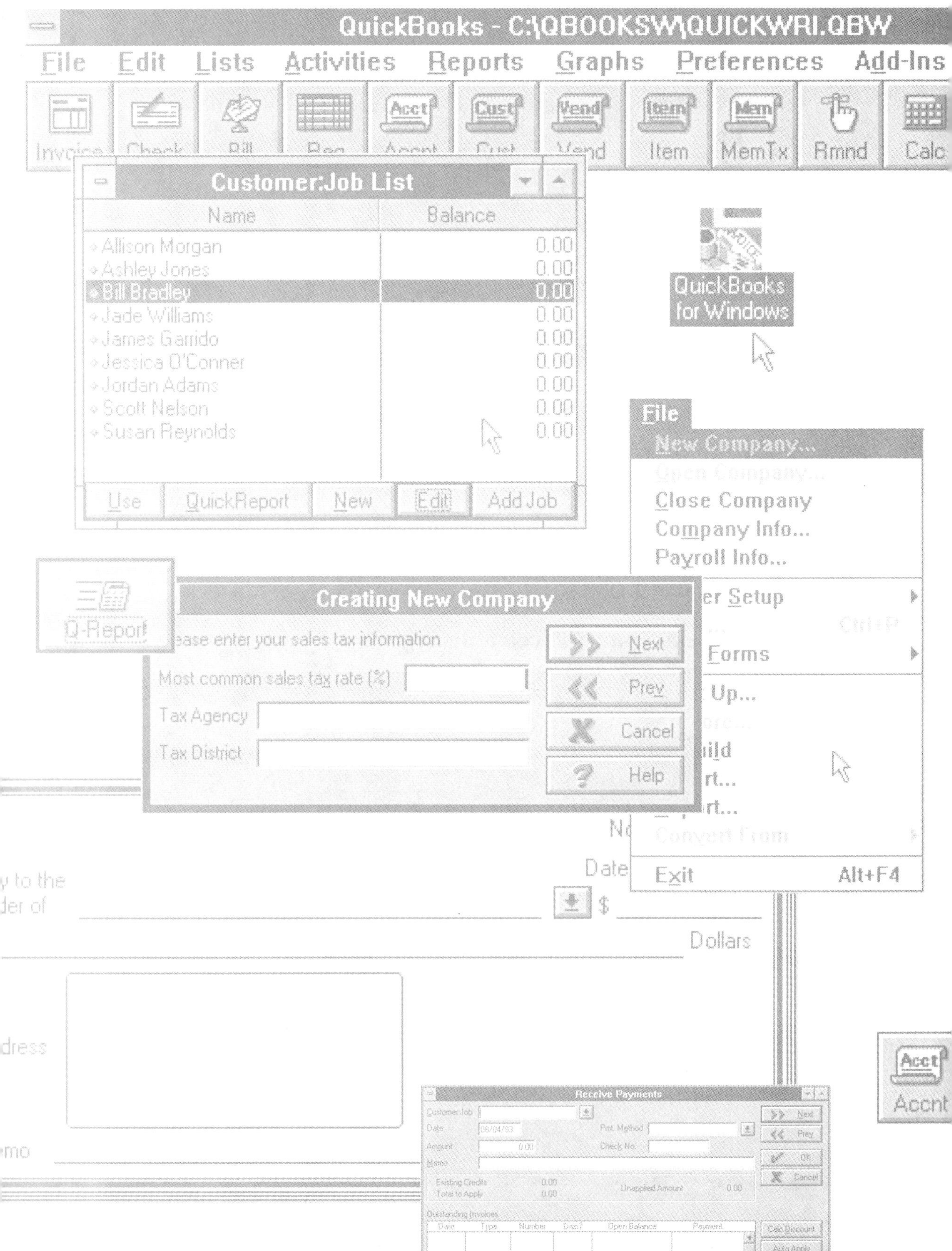

QuickBooks - C:\QBOOKSW\QUICKWRI.QBW
File Edit Lists Activities Reports Graphs Preferences Add-Ins
Item MemTx Rmnd Calc
Customer:Job List
Name Balance
Allison Morgan 0.00
Ashley Jones 0.00
Bill Bradley 0.00
Jade Williams 0.00
James Garrido 0.00
Jessica O'Conner 0.00
Jordan Adams 0.00
Scott Nelson 0.00
Susan Reynolds 0.00
Use QuickReport New Edit Add Job
QuickBooks for Windows
File
New Company...
Close Company
Company Info...
Payroll Info...
Exit Alt+F4
Q-Report
Creating New Company
Most common sales tax rate (%)
Tax Agency
Tax District
Next
Prev
Cancel
Help
Date
Dollars
Acct
Accnt
Receive Payments

Chapter 6

Creating Invoices

You probably have been typing your customer invoices manually, or maybe even writing them one by one. With QuickBooks for Windows, you can write an invoice, print it, and mail it to your customer. Your invoices look more professional and consistent when you use QuickBooks for Windows. Better yet, you don't have to calculate sales tax, discounts, subtotals, or totals; QuickBooks makes all invoice calculations for you. Best of all, QuickBooks for Windows automatically updates your Accounts Receivable register each time you write an invoice. The Accounts Receivable register is an asset account that keeps track of money owed to you. QuickBooks for Windows also helps you track reimbursable expenses and enter those as line items on invoices.

If you're worried that QuickBooks invoices are not appropriate for your business, don't be. QuickBooks provides three different formats for invoices: service, professional, and product. If your business sells services, such as catering, window cleaning, or interior design, you should use the service invoice. Use the professional invoice if your business sells professional services such as accounting, legal, or medical services. If your business sells products, such as toys, medical supplies, or playground equipment, use the product invoice.

In this chapter, you learn how to do the following:

- Select the invoice format for your business
- Move around the Create Invoices window
- Complete an invoice
- Enter and delete line items
- Group line items
- Add reimbursable expenses to invoices
- Edit, delete, and void an invoice
- Enter historical invoices
- Prepare job estimates

Accessing the Create Invoices Window

When you're ready to write or review a customer invoice, you first access the Create Invoices window. Printed invoices remain in the Create Invoices window so that you can display and review them. QuickBooks for Windows sorts invoices in chronological order and always places a blank invoice at the end of the list.

To access the Create Invoices window, use one of the following methods:

- Choose the Invoice button on the Iconbar.
- Choose Create **I**nvoices from the **A**ctivities menu.
- Press Ctrl+I.

QuickBooks displays the invoice type you selected when you set up your company. In Chapter 3, "Setting Up Your Company in QuickBooks for Windows," you learned how to select an invoice format. Figure 6.1 shows the service invoice displayed on-screen.

Selecting the Invoice Format To Use

When you set up your company in QuickBooks, you selected an invoice format. The following invoice formats are available in QuickBooks for Windows:

- *Service invoice.* Used for service-oriented businesses that do not sell products, such as interior design, house painting, and gardening businesses. A service invoice is shown in figure 6.1.

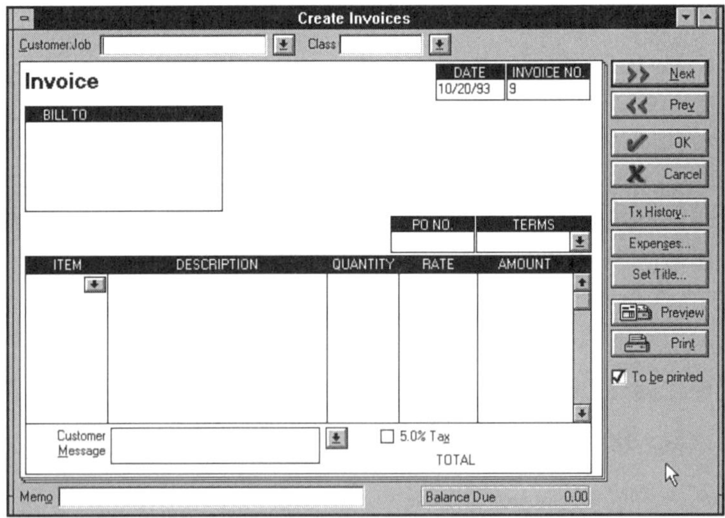

Fig. 6.1
Use the service invoice to bill your customers for services that you provide.

- *Professional invoice.* Used for businesses that provide professional services such as accounting, legal, and medical services. Figure 6.2 shows an example of a professional invoice.

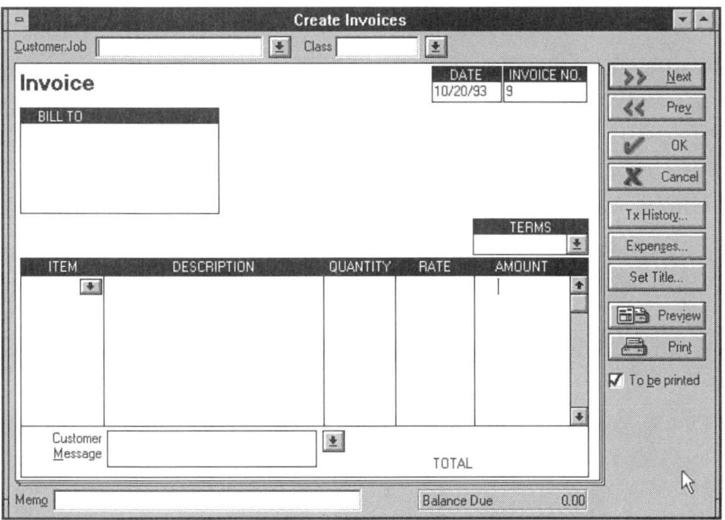

Fig. 6.2
Use the professional invoice to bill your customers for professional services that you provide, such as legal, accounting, or consulting services.

- *Product invoice.* Used for businesses that sell products, such as auto parts, computers, and books. If your business sells both products and services, use this type of invoice. Figure 6.3 shows a product invoice.

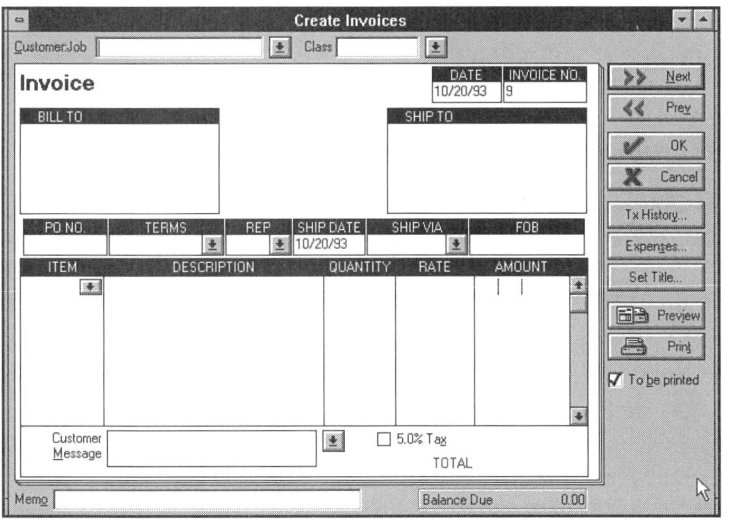

Fig. 6.3
Use the product invoice to bill your customers for just products, or both products and services.

Each invoice format is different to enable you to enter the appropriate information. The product invoice, for example, includes fields for shipping information, such as the shipping address, PO number, ship date, method of shipment, and how freight charges are handled.

You're not stuck with the same invoice format that you chose when you set up your company. You can change the invoice format at any time. You may change your invoice type to write only one invoice, and then change back to your first invoice type selection.

To change the invoice format, follow these steps:

1. From the **P**references menu, choose **I**nvoices. QuickBooks for Windows displays the Invoice Preferences dialog box, shown in figure 6.4.

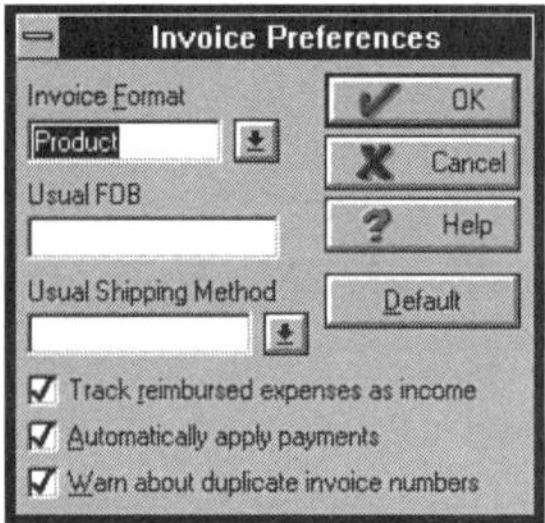

Fig. 6.4 The Invoice Preferences dialog box.

2. Click the drop-down arrow in the Invoice Format field, or press Ctrl+L. Then select the invoice format: service, product, or professional.

3. Choose OK or press Enter.

Reviewing the Create Invoices Window

When you access the Create Invoices window, QuickBooks displays the invoice in the detail view, which shows more information than appears on the customer's printed invoice. While you are writing an invoice, you can choose the Pre**v**iew button to see how the invoice will look when printed—exactly the invoice your customers will see.

Regardless of the invoice format that you use, the Create Invoices window includes these common elements: the Customer:Job field, the Class field (if you choose to track transactions by class), the Account field (only available if you have more than one Accounts Receivable account set up in QuickBooks for Windows), the actual invoice, the command buttons to the right of the invoice, and the Memo and Balance Due fields. The following sections describe each element of the Create Invoices window.

The Customer:Job Field

You use the Customer:Job field to identify the customer to whom you are selling goods and services. If you track jobs by customer, enter the job that relates to the invoice. Fill in the Customer:Job field using the drop-down list box to display the Customer:Job List, and then select a customer and/or job from the list. The Customer:Job List is explained in Chapter 5, "Using QuickBooks for Windows Lists."

The Class Field

The Class field is used to classify the invoice with others of its type. QuickBooks for Windows does not display the Class field unless you turn on the Class tracking feature. Refer to Chapter 5, "Using QuickBooks for Windows Lists," to learn how to turn on Class tracking. Fill in the Class field using the drop-down list box to display the Class List, and then select a class from the list.

The Account Field

If you have more than one Accounts Receivable account set up in your Chart of Accounts, QuickBooks displays an Account field at the top of the Create Invoices window. If you have only one Accounts Receivable account, this field is not displayed. Fill in the Account field using the drop-down list box to display the Chart of Accounts, and then select the Accounts Receivable account to which you want the current invoice recorded.

The Invoice

QuickBooks displays the actual invoice in the middle of the Create Invoices window. For service and professional invoice formats, QuickBooks displays more fields than are displayed on the printed invoice. The product invoice that you see on-screen is exactly as it appears in print. The fields that QuickBooks includes in an invoice are dependent on the invoice format.

The top or header of the invoice includes the following fields: Date, Invoice Number, Bill To, Ship To (on product invoice only), PO Num (on service and product invoices only), Terms, and on product invoices only, the Rep, Ship Date, Ship Via, and FOB fields. The bottom part of the invoice—the line item area—includes fields for the Item code, Description, Quantity, Rate, and Amount.

You can use the QuickBooks for Windows lists that you learned about in Chapter 5, "Using QuickBooks for Windows Lists," to complete several fields in the Create Invoices window. At any field followed by a drop-down arrow, you just click the arrow or press Ctrl+L to display a list from which you can choose an item to complete the field. If you have not entered items into QuickBooks lists before you begin writing invoices, you can enter items as you go.

The invoice also includes a field in which to enter a customer message that will appear on printed invoices. Use the Customer Message field to show payment instructions (`Please return one copy with your payment`), payment reminders (`Your balance is past due. Please remit`), seasonal greetings (`HAPPY HOLIDAYS`), your Taxpayer Identification Number, or just to tell your customer `Thank You`.

Finally, the % Tax check box at the bottom of the invoice tells QuickBooks to calculate sales tax on the line items marked as taxable using the Auto Tax feature.

Command Buttons

The command buttons on the right side of the Create Invoices window provide the commands you use to write invoices (refer to fig. 6.3). The following command buttons are available from the Create Invoices window:

- *Next.* Moves to the next invoice.
- *Prev.* Moves to the previous recorded invoice.
- *OK.* Records the current invoice.
- *Cancel.* Cancels the current invoice information and removes the Create Invoices window from the screen.
- *Tx History.* Displays a transaction history for the customer in the current invoice.
- *Expenses.* Displays the list of reimbursable expenses from which you can select to enter on an invoice.
- *Set Title.* Displays a dialog box to change the title of the current invoice only.
- *Preview.* Displays the preview of the current invoice as will appear when printed.
- *Print.* Prints the current invoice.

The To Be Printed check box follows the command buttons. This check box is used to mark an invoice to be printed.

Memo and Balance Due Fields

The Memo field, at the bottom of the Create Invoices window, is used to enter a memo that will appear on customer statements (not printed invoices). If you don't send statements, you can use this field to make notes or reminders to yourself about a particular invoice.

The Balance Due field shows the balance due from the customer for this invoice. The Balance Due field is automatically calculated by QuickBooks for Windows based on the information you entered in the line item area of the invoice.

Moving Around in the Create Invoices Window

The keys in the following table enable you to move around in the Create Invoices window quickly and easily.

Key	Function
Tab	Moves forward one field or to the next line within a field
Shift+Tab	Moves backward one field or to the preceding line within a field
Home	Moves to beginning of the current field
End	Moves to end of the current field
Ctrl+right arrow	Moves forward one word within a field
Ctrl+left arrow	Moves backward one word within a field

Writing an Invoice

QuickBooks displays an on-screen invoice that makes writing an invoice as easy as filling in the blanks. In addition, by using QuickBooks for Windows lists, you don't need to type much information. You just select an item from a list, and QuickBooks enters your selection into the field.

To use QuickBooks most efficiently, you should enter your customers, employees, invoice items, and so on in the appropriate list before you begin writing invoices. (Refer to Chapter 5, "Using QuickBooks for Windows Lists," to learn how to enter items in lists.) Using lists makes writing invoices quick and easy because you complete the fields by selecting rather than typing items. Using lists also provides for consistency in your invoices; you will not send an invoice to John A. Smith one time and to J.A. Smith another time.

If you have not entered items in lists, you still can start writing invoices. QuickBooks enables you to add items to lists "on the fly," or as you write invoices. When you type a customer's name that QuickBooks doesn't find in the Customer:Job List, the program prompts you to add that name to your Customer:Job List through Quick Add or Set Up. Adding to lists "on the fly" is explained in Chapter 5, "Using QuickBooks for Windows Lists." You do not have to add customers with which you do business on a one-time basis to the Customer:Job List. You can add them to the Other Names List.

When you write a QuickBooks invoice, you must fill in the Customer:Job field. The Class field, however, is optional. If you have more than one Accounts Receivable account set up in QuickBooks, an Account field appears; you must select the Accounts Receivable account in which to record the current invoice. You then complete the actual invoice, which consists of two parts: the header and the line-item area. In the header, you enter the date, invoice number, payment terms, and so on. You enter the items for which you are billing your customer in the line-item area.

To speed up data entry in invoices, QuickBooks uses the QuickFill feature. When you type a few characters in a field where list items are used, such as the Customer:Job field in an invoice, QuickBooks searches the Customer:Job List to find a matching list item. When QuickBooks finds a match, the QuickFill feature fills in the rest of the Customer:Job name. If the Customer:Job name is not the one that you want, just type the next letter of the customer name, and QuickBooks fills in the next name on the Customer:Job List that matches the letters that you have typed. For example, if you type the first letter **A** in the Customer:Job field, QuickBooks enters the first name in the Customer:Job List that begins with *A*, like Amanda Jones. If Amanda Jones is not the name that you want entered in the Customer:Job field, just type the second letter of the customer's name—N, for example; QuickBooks enters the next name on the Customer:Job List, Anne Fein.

Completing Customer:Job, Class, and Account Information

To speed up the process of writing invoices, the first information you enter is the customer and/or job for the invoice. If you've entered your customers and jobs in the Customer:Job List, QuickBooks automatically enters all related information for the customer and job (if applicable) that you enter in the Customer:Job field.

To complete the Customer:Job field, follow these steps:

1. Click the arrow in the Customer:Job field to display the Customer: Job List.
2. Scroll through the list to find the customer to whom the invoice relates. Click the customer's name. QuickBooks enters the customer's name in the Customer:Job field.
3. If you are tracking jobs for this customer, scroll through the customer's jobs to find that job for which the invoice relates. Click the job.

   QuickBooks for Windows enters the customer and job name (if applicable) in the Customer:Job field. If you entered other information for the customer in the Customer:Job List, QuickBooks enters the same information in the appropriate fields in the invoice.

> **Note**
>
> If you don't want to track jobs by customer, you can turn off the job tracking feature. Refer to Chapter 5, "Using QuickBooks for Windows Lists," to learn how to turn off job tracking.

If you use classes to classify invoices by department, property, and so on, you can assign a class to each invoice. To complete the Class field, click the arrow to display the Class List, and then select a class from the list.

If you have more than one Accounts Receivable account in your Chart of Accounts, QuickBooks displays an Account field next to the Class field. To complete the Accounts field, click the arrow to display the Chart of Accounts, and then select an Accounts Receivable account from the list.

Tip
You can enter a new customer's name in the Customer:Job field by typing the customer's name. You can then add the customer to the Customer:Job List by using Quick Add or Set Up.

Completing the Invoice Header

Some of the information in the invoice header is automatically completed by QuickBooks for Windows when you enter a customer in the Customer:Job field. This information is only entered, however, if you enter a customer that is listed in the Customer:Job List and you have also entered other information for the customer: address, shipping address, and terms.

To complete the invoice header, follow these steps:

1. Access the Create Invoices window. QuickBooks displays the invoice format you selected when you set up your company or the invoice format that you changed to in the Invoice Preferences dialog box (refer to fig. 6.4).

2. QuickBooks automatically enters today's date in the Date field. If you want the invoice to show a different date, press Tab or Shift+Tab to move to the Date field, and then enter a new date. To quickly change the date, press the + (plus) key to increase the date by one day or press the – (minus) key to decrease the date by one day. You enter dates in the format MM/DD/YY. Notice that you do not have to type the slashes (/). After you type the date, press Tab to move to the Invoice No. field.

3. QuickBooks also automatically enters the next invoice number in the Invoice No field. You can edit this number, however, by typing a new number. To quickly change the invoice number, press the + (plus) key to increase the invoice number by one or press the – (minus) key to decrease the invoice number by one.

> **Note**
>
> You enter invoices that you write manually in the Create Invoices window just as you would enter any other invoice. Because you will not print this invoice, type the number you assigned the manual invoice in the Invoice No field.

4. In the Bill To field, QuickBooks enters the customer's name and address, provided you typed an address when you added the customer to the Customer:Job List. If necessary, type the customer's address in the Bill To field. If you need to change the customer name or address, press Tab to move to the appropriate line, and type over the existing information.

5. When you enter a customer in a product invoice, QuickBooks automatically completes the Ship To field, provided you entered this information when you added the customer to the Customer:Job List. If the Ship To field isn't completed, press Tab to move to the field, and type the customer's shipping address.

6. In the Po No field, enter the customer's purchase order number (if applicable), and press Tab. Notice that QuickBooks does not include the Po No field on a professional invoice.

7. In the next field, click the drop-down arrow or press Ctrl+L to select the payment terms that you are providing this customer from the Terms List.

8. The product invoice's header includes fields for the sales rep (Rep), shipping date (Ship Date), shipping method (Ship Via), and shipping site (FOB). For each field followed by a drop-down list arrow, click the arrow or press Ctrl+L to select an item from a list. Complete the following fields:

   - In the Rep field, click the drop-down arrow or press Ctrl+L to select the initials of the employee who sold the product or service to the customer you are invoicing.

   - In the Ship Date field, enter the date that the product was shipped to the customer.

   - In the Ship Via field, enter the shipping method used to ship products to your customer.

   - In the FOB field, enter the site from which you ship merchandise or products, using up to 13 characters.

QuickBooks for Windows may have completed the Ship Via and/or the FOB field for you if you entered your usual shipping method and ship site as invoice preferences. Refer to Chapter 22, "Customizing QuickBooks for Windows," to learn how to set these preferences.

CPA TIP: Accounting for Each Invoice

Although QuickBooks for Windows numbers invoices for you, you should make sure that invoice numbers are in sequence for accountability. If you engage an accounting firm to audit your books, you most certainly will be asked to account for any missing invoice numbers.

Completing the Line-Item Area

You enter the items for which you are billing your customer in the line-item area in the lower portion of the invoice. A line item includes a full line of information, including the invoice item, description, quantity, price, and the total amount for the item. In the line-item area of an invoice, you include the quantity of items, whether these items are products or hours of service. Enter each item for which you are billing your customer on a separate line. You also enter discounts, refunds, markups, sales tax, and subtotals on separate lines in the invoice's line-item area. If you incur expenses that are to be reimbursed by customers, you can include those expenses in the line-item area of the invoice.

In Chapter 5, "Using QuickBooks for Windows Lists," you learned about the Invoice Items List and the eight line-item types. The following three line-item types are used to identify the goods or services that your business sells:

- *Part.* Defines the products or merchandise that you sell.
- *Service.* Defines the services that you provide.
- *Other Charges.* Defines miscellaneous items such as markups or freight charges.

The remaining five line-item types are used to calculate invoices:

- *Subtotal.* Calculates the total of all line items above this line.
- *Discount.* Defines point-of-sale discounts to be applied to customer invoices.
- *Payment.* Allows a payment line on the invoice so that you can enter partial payments at the time of purchase. (Notice that full payments are entered as cash sales; see Chapter 9, "Receiving and Depositing Customer Payments," to learn how to enter a cash sale.)
- *Group.* Hides details on an invoice by grouping more than one invoice item.
- *Sales Tax.* Defines the sales tax rates (other than the most common sales tax rate calculated by Auto Tax) to be applied to customer charges.

You can complete the invoice's line-item area most efficiently by selecting line items from the Invoice Item Lists. By using Invoice Item Lists, you not only speed up the invoice entry process, but you ensure that all your invoices contain consistent information. To access the Invoice Item List, click the drop-down arrow in the Item field in the invoice's line-item area, or press Ctrl+L. From this list, you choose a line item for QuickBooks to enter in the invoice. If a line item requires a calculation, QuickBooks makes the calculation for you. You never have to calculate, for example, the sales tax on an invoice.

When you select the sales tax line item from the Item List, QuickBooks multiplies the sales tax rate by the number in the line that immediately precedes the Sales Tax field in the Amount field of the invoice. The program then displays the result of the sales tax calculation in the Amount field of the sales tax line. In the next section of this chapter, you learn more about how line items work and how to use them on an invoice.

It is important that each line item that you enter has an item code. You may remember from Chapter 5, "Using QuickBooks for Windows Lists," that QuickBooks uses item codes to distinguish line items from one another, but more important, item codes link income and expense accounts to your line items. If you do not assign an item code to a line item, you also do not assign an income or expense account to the line item. When you enter a line item without an item code, QuickBooks cannot properly classify the invoice transaction and lumps the amount into the Income-Other account on reports.

To complete an invoice's line-item area, follow these steps:

1. Press Tab to move to the first line in the line-item area of the invoice. You can add up to 30 line items on the invoice.

2. In the Item field, click the drop-down arrow or press Ctrl+L to display the Invoice Item List shown in figure 6.5.

3. Select the invoice item you want. QuickBooks completes the Description and Rate fields automatically when you select a line item from the Invoice Item List. You also can type a new description or a new rate in the appropriate fields.

4. In the Quantity field, type the quantity of parts, merchandise, or hours for which you are billing your customer. If you are billing your customer or client for legal services, for example, enter the number of hours in the Quantity field. If your business sells computer supplies, enter the number of a specific product you sold to your customer. Press Tab.

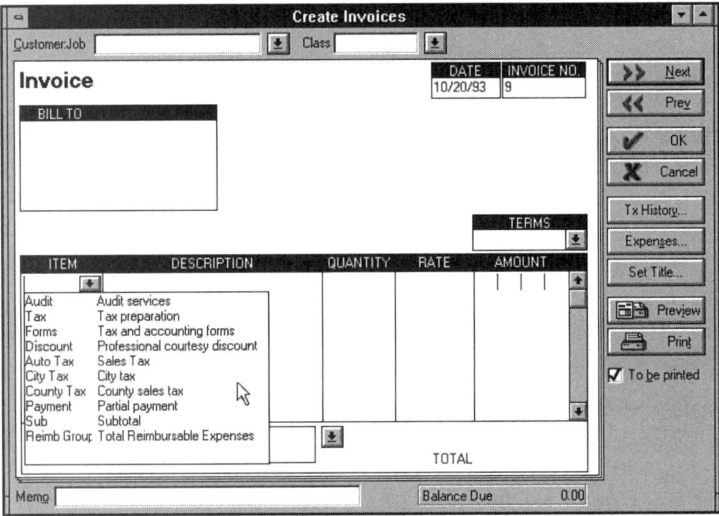

Fig. 6.5
The Invoice Item List displays from the Item field in an invoice.

5. QuickBooks multiplies the quantity by the Rate as soon as you provide this information, and enters the result in the Amount field. The program updates the Total and Balance fields each time a new line item appears in the Amount field.

   After you enter a line item, you can change the information in any of its fields: the number in the Quantity field, text in the Description field, or the number in the Rate field.

Repeat steps 1 through 5 as often as necessary to continue entering line items into the invoice's line item area.

> **Note**
>
> QuickBooks enters a T after invoice items that are taxable. You designate invoice items as taxable when you add an item to the Invoice Items List. Refer to Chapter 5, "Using QuickBooks for Windows Lists," to learn how to designate an invoice item as taxable.

You complete the invoice when you finish the line item area. You also can enter an invoice memo if you want. See the section "Completing the Invoice" later in this chapter for more information.

Understanding Line Items

Although line items describe the product, merchandise, or service that you sell to your customer, you also use line items to identify discounts, markups, sales tax, payments, and subtotals. When you add an item to the Invoice Item List, you assign an item code (refer to Chapter 5). Item codes distinguish one line item from another, but they also link line items to income, expense, or balance sheet accounts. When you enter a line item on an invoice, QuickBooks automatically assigns the amount to the appropriate income, expense, or balance sheet account. The account, however, never appears on the invoice.

After you have set up the invoice line items that you use in your business (see Chapter 5 to learn how to set up invoice line items), you easily can complete the invoice's line item area by selecting from the Invoice Item List. QuickBooks enters the selected line item information and performs calculations to determine the amount of each invoice line item, the sales tax (if applicable), and the total amount of the invoice.

Entering Part, Service, or Other Charges Line Items. For part, service, or other charges line items, QuickBooks enters the description and Rate and then calculates the amount for each line item. If, for example, you enter 100 in the Quantity field and then select a service line item with a rate per hour of $15, QuickBooks multiplies 100 x 15 and enters 1,500 in the Amount field. Figure 6.6 shows how a service line item appears on an invoice.

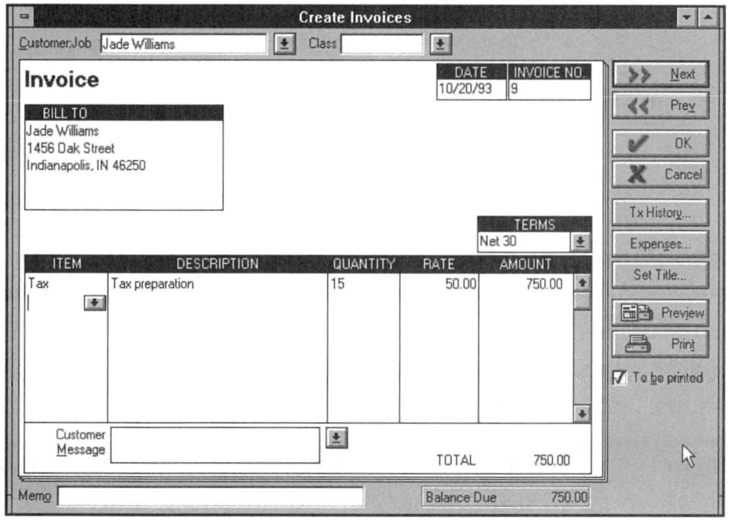

Fig. 6.6
Entering a service line item on an invoice.

Entering Discount Line Items. When you add a discount item type to the Invoice Item List, you can express the discount either in dollars or as a percentage. When you enter a discount line item, QuickBooks enters a dollar amount as a negative amount in the Amount field. For percentage discount line items, QuickBooks multiplies the number in the immediately preceding line item's Amount field by the discount percentage and enters the result in the discount line item's Amount field. You can offer a customer separate discounts on different items by entering two different discount line items on the invoice. If you did not enter discount line items on the invoice, you can apply a discount when you receive payment from the customer by using the Receive Payment window (see Chapter 9, "Receiving and Depositing Customer Payments"). Notice, however, that you can apply only one discount per invoice by using the Receive Payment window. Figure 6.7 shows how a discount line item appears on an invoice.

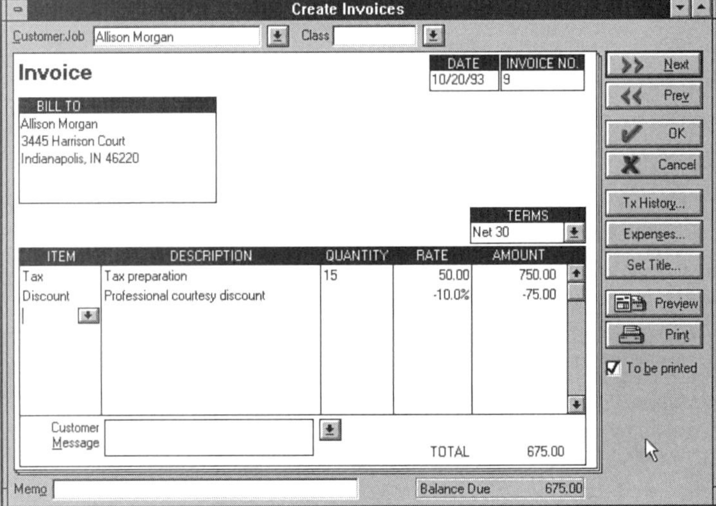

Fig. 6.7 Entering a discount line item on an invoice.

Entering Subtotal Line Items. When you select the subtotal line item, QuickBooks adds the amounts of all preceding line items that follow the preceding subtotal line item. If the invoice does not contain other subtotal lines, QuickBooks adds the amounts of all preceding line items, including the invoice's first line item, when you select a subtotal line item.

To compute the total amount of the invoice, select another subtotal line item immediately after you select one subtotal line item. You will need to break an invoice into subtotals if you are billing your customer for items that are taxable and items that are not taxable. See the next section "Entering Sales Tax Line Items" to see how subtotal line items work with sales tax line items. You also may want a subtotal line to show the customer the total amount billed for services and the total billed for products. The invoice shown in figure 6.8 contains subtotal line items.

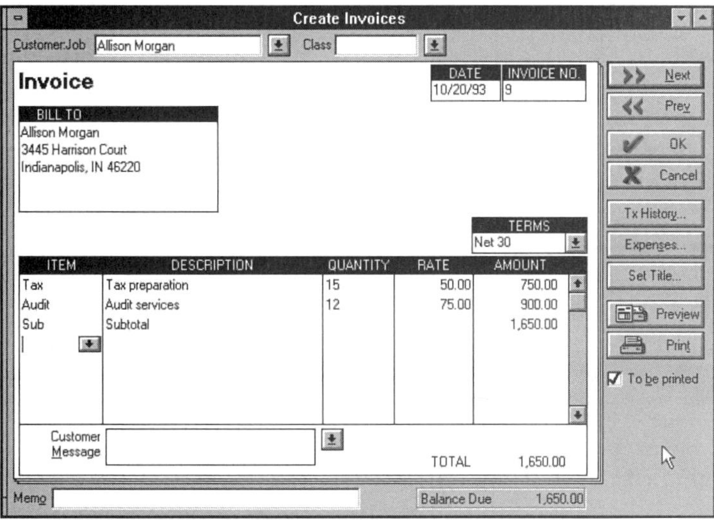

Fig. 6.8
When you enter a subtotal line item on an invoice, QuickBooks adds all lines immediately preceding the subtotal line.

Entering Sales Tax Line Items. If you collect sales tax for more than one tax agency, you can enter a sales tax line item in the line item area of an invoice. If you collect sales tax for just one tax agency, QuickBooks calculates sales tax automatically using the Auto Tax feature and the most common sales tax rate that you entered when you set up your company. You do not have to enter a sales tax line item on invoices if you pay tax to only one tax agency.

For sales tax line items entered in the line item area of an invoice, QuickBooks multiplies the sales tax rate (defined when you added the sales tax line item to the Invoice Item List) by the number in the immediately preceding line item's Amount field. QuickBooks ignores the immediately preceding line item if it uses a percentage to calculate the amount in the Amount field (discount line items, or other sales tax line items, for example). If you have more than one taxable line item, you first select a subtotal line item and then select the sales tax line item. QuickBooks then multiplies the number in the subtotal line item's Amount field by the sales tax rate.

If you have both taxable and nontaxable line items, group together the taxable line items, subtotal them, and then select the sales tax line item. Figure 6.9 shows an invoice with taxable and nontaxable line items.

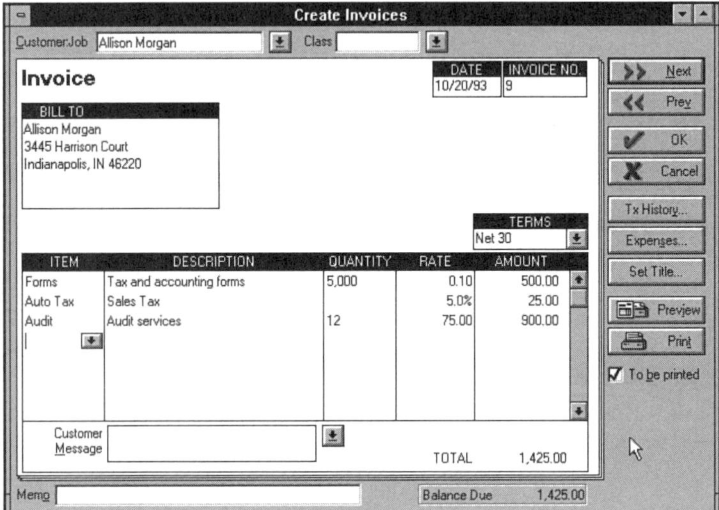

Fig. 6.9
Entering taxable and nontaxable line items on an invoice.

As mentioned earlier, if you collect sales tax for more than one sales tax jurisdiction—for example, state and county—you set up additional sales tax line items in the Invoice Item List. You can enter more than one sales tax line item on an invoice. Again, QuickBooks ignores a line item that immediately precedes the sales tax line when this line item uses a percentage to calculate the amount in the Amount field. Two sales tax line items are shown on the invoice in figure 6.10.

QuickBooks adds a sales tax payable account to your Chart of Accounts if you indicate that you collect sales tax when you set up your company. QuickBooks assigns the amounts calculated by sales tax line items to the sales tax payable account. If you collect sales tax for more than one jurisdiction, don't add other sales tax accounts. QuickBooks tracks each tax jurisdiction as a separate vendor in the sales tax payable account; therefore, it is not necessary to have more than one sales tax payable account. When it's time to submit the sales tax that you have collected for each tax jurisdiction, you easily will be able to determine which taxes go where by generating a Sales Tax Report. See Chapter 7, "Tracking Sales Tax," to learn more about setting up QuickBooks for Windows to track sales tax, applying sales tax to invoices, and paying sales tax.

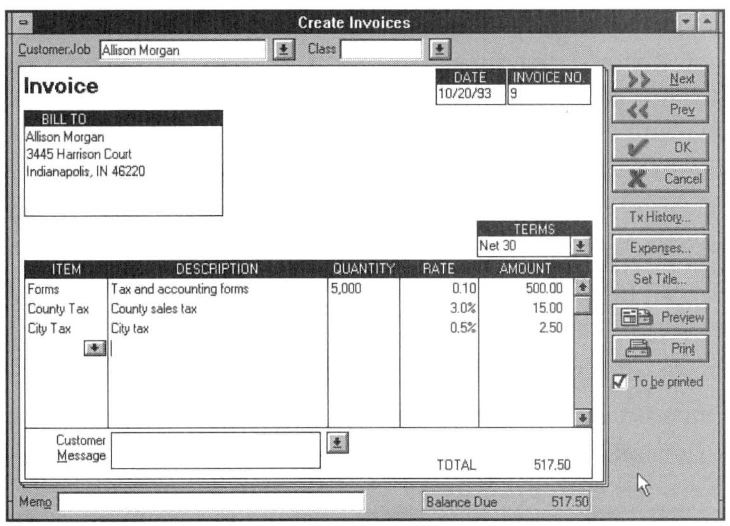

Fig. 6.10
Entering two sales tax line items on an invoice.

Entering Payment Line Items. Use the payment line item to enter partial payments that you receive from a customer at the time you issue the invoice. QuickBooks enters a negative amount in the Amount field when you enter a payment line item. If you receive total payment for an invoice, enter the sale as a cash sale. See Chapter 9, "Receiving and Depositing Customer Payments," to learn how to enter cash sales. Figure 6.11 shows an invoice with a payment line item.

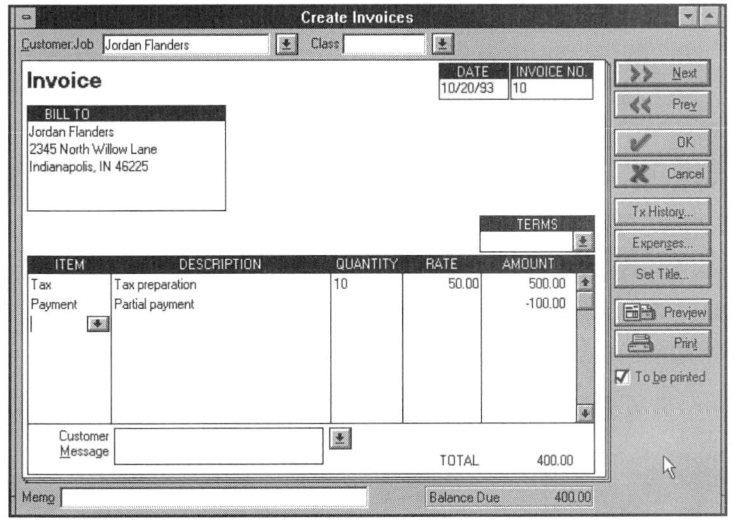

Fig. 6.11
Entering a partial payment on an invoice.

Grouping Line Items. QuickBooks allows you to group line items so that you can just show a single item on the customer's invoice without the detail. Grouping line items allows you to detail jobs and projects for sales report purposes without disclosing the same details to your customers on invoices. For example, if you break out a job into several categories, such as materials, labor, markup, and so on, you can group these line items so they appear as just one item on the invoice. Grouping line items prevents your customer from seeing some of the detail that may be relevant only to you. Refer to Chapter 5, "Using QuickBooks for Windows Lists," to learn how to group line items.

To see more examples of invoice line items, load QuickBooks for Windows' sample company data and access the Create Invoices window to review the sample invoices. Refer to Chapter 2, "Learning Your Way Around QuickBooks for Windows," to learn how to load the sample company.

Inserting Line Items

Provided you have not exceeded QuickBooks for Windows' 30 line-item limit, you can insert another line item within the line item area. If you have entered 6 line items, for example, and decide that you need to enter a line item in the third line (instead of the seventh), you can insert a blank line between the second and third line items and enter a new line item between the two existing lines.

To insert a line item, follow these steps:

1. Highlight the line item directly after the position in which you want to insert a line. To insert a line item between the second and third lines, for example, highlight the third line.

2. From the **E**dit menu, choose **I**nsert Line, or press Ctrl+Ins. QuickBooks inserts a blank line just above the line you highlighted in step 1.

Deleting Line Items

Tip
If you want to space the line items on the printed invoice, insert a blank line between each line item.

If you mistakenly add a line item to an invoice, you easily can delete the line from the invoice's line item area.

To delete a line item, follow these steps:

1. Highlight the line item you want to delete.

2. From the **E**dit menu choose Delete **L**ine, or press Ctrl+Del. QuickBooks deletes the line item and recalculates the invoice.

CPA TIP: Returned Items

If a customer returns an item, you should issue a credit memo invoice instead of deleting the line item. A credit memo cancels all or part of the original invoice and shows the customer that you received the returned item. You learn how to issue a credit memo in Chapter 9, "Receiving and Depositing Customer Payments."

Adding Reimbursable Expenses to Invoices

If you incur expenses that are attributable to jobs that you perform on behalf of your clients or customers, you can easily track these expenses as reimbursable expenses and include them on customer invoices. Before you can add a reimbursable expense to an invoice, however, you must first do the following:

1. Turn on the job tracking feature in QuickBooks. If job tracking is not turned on, the Customer:Job field does not appear when you record expenses. Refer to Chapter 5, "Using QuickBooks for Windows Lists," to learn how to turn on job tracking.

2. If you want to track reimbursable expenses as they are incurred in one account (an expense account) and the customers' reimbursements in another account (an income account), you must first select the Track Reimbursable Expense Accounts preference. You learn how to select this preference later in this section.

3. Set up the expense as reimbursable when you enter the expense in QuickBooks. You learn how to set up expenses as reimbursable later in this section.

All reimbursable expenses are included in the Choose Reimbursable Expenses dialog box. As you are writing an invoice, you can display this window as described later in this section and select Reimbursable Expenses from the list of expenses. You can mark up reimbursable expenses and either show the markup on the invoice or hide the markup.

Selecting the Track Reimbursable Expense Account Preference. When you record a reimbursable expense, the transaction is assigned to an expense account (or an asset account if you are purchasing a capital asset for the customer). The expense, therefore, shows up in your profit and loss statement as an expense. When the customer reimburses you for the expense, the reimbursement is recorded as a negative expense. For example, if you pay travel expenses of $500 on behalf of a client or customer, the $500 increases your travel expense account. When you bill your client or customer for the travel expenses and receive reimbursement, the $500 received is recorded as a negative expense. Therefore, the amount in your travel expense account decreases by $500.

You can track reimbursed expenses in Income accounts by selecting the Track Reimbursable Expense Accounts preference. When you select this preference, QuickBooks puts an additional check box and Account drop-down list box in the New Account window for the Expense account. You can then specify that an Expense account is a reimbursable expense and specify the Income account to which reimbursements should be assigned.

To select the Track Reimbursable Expense Accounts preference, follow these steps:

1. From the **P**references menu, choose **I**nvoices to display the Invoice Preferences dialog box.
2. Choose the Track **R**eimbursed Expenses as Income check box.
3. Choose OK or press Enter.

After you select the Track **R**eimbursed Expenses as Income preference, make sure that you enter the income account that you want QuickBooks to assign to reimbursed expenses. Enter the income account in the New Account window when setting up a new account or the Edit Account window for an account that is already in your Chart of Accounts. Refer to Chapter 4, "Working with Accounts," to learn how to set up new accounts or edit existing accounts.

Setting Up Expenses as Reimbursable. Each time that you enter a transaction for a reimbursable expense in QuickBooks, you must assign the client and job so that the expense is added to the Choose Reimbursable Expenses dialog box. Only those expenses included in the Choose Reimbursable Expenses dialog box can be added as a line item on an invoice. Reimbursable expenses are entered in the Enter Bills window when you receive a bill for a reimbursable expense or the Write Checks window when you write a check for a reimbursable expense. See Chapter 11, "Entering and Paying Bills," to learn how to enter expenses in the Enter Bills window. See Chapter 13, "Writing and Printing Checks," to learn how to write a check for an expense.

Entering a Reimbursable Expense to an Invoice. Reimbursable expenses are entered on an invoice in the line item area. To enter a reimbursable expense to an invoice, follow these steps:

1. In the Create Invoices window, display the invoice for which you want to enter a reimbursable expense. Make sure that you have at least filled in the Customer:Job field before you proceed to step 2.

2. Choose the Expen**s**es button on the right side of the Create Invoice window. QuickBooks displays the Choose Reimbursable Expenses dialog box shown in figure 6.12. This window includes all reimbursable expenses for this customer.

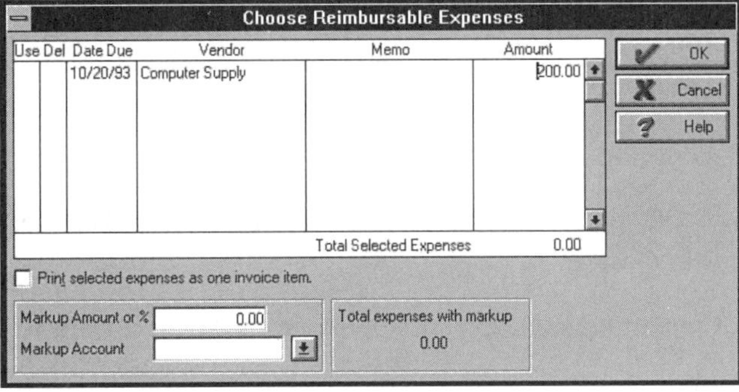

Fig. 6.12
The Choose Reimbursable Expenses dialog box lists all expenses paid on behalf of the customer you are invoicing.

3. Scroll through the list of reimbursable expenses for this customer. Select the expense or expenses that you want to enter on the invoice by clicking the Use column. If you will never invoice this customer for an expense that appears in the Choose Reimbursable Expenses dialog box, click the Del (Delete) column for that expense. Just leave the expense blank if you might include it on a future invoice but do not want to include it on the current invoice.

4. If you have more than one reimbursable expense and want to show only one line item on the invoice, choose the Prin**t** Selected Expenses as One Invoice Item check box. QuickBooks totals all reimbursable expenses selected, plus any markup, and enters the amount as one line item on the invoice with the description `Total reimbursable expenses.`

Note

Each reimbursable expense appears on the on-screen invoice. If you chose the Print Selected Expenses as One Invoice Item check box, reimbursable expenses are grouped together on the printed invoice. To see how the printed invoice appears, choose the Preview button.

5. Choose OK or press Enter to enter the reimbursable expenses to the invoice.

Marking Up a Reimbursable Expense. If you mark up items that you purchase for your customers or clients, you can have QuickBooks calculate the markup, add it to the reimbursable expense on the invoice, and assign a markup account so that you can track markup income. You can mark up one, several, or all reimbursable expenses for each customer.

To mark up a reimbursable expense, follow these steps:

1. Access the Choose Reimbursable Expenses dialog box (refer to fig. 6.12) as explained earlier.
2. Select the reimbursable expense or expenses that you want to mark up.
3. In the Markup Amount or % field, type a markup dollar amount or a markup percentage. For percentages, type the percent sign after the percentage rate—for example, 5%.
4. Click the arrow at the Markup Account drop-down list, or press Ctrl+L, and select an income account to track your markup income.
5. If you do not want the markup amount shown on the invoice, select the Print Selected Expenses as One Invoice Item check box. QuickBooks adds the markup to the reimbursable expense and enters only the total on the invoice with the description `Total reimbursable expenses`.

Note

Each reimbursable expense appears on the on-screen invoice. If you selected the Print Selected Expenses as One Invoice Item check box so that the markup does not show separately, the markup and expenses are grouped together on the printed invoice. To see how the printed invoice appears, choose the Preview button.

6. Choose OK or press Enter.

To mark up some—but not all—of the reimbursable expenses, follow these steps:

1. Access the Choose Reimbursable Expenses dialog box as explained earlier.
2. Select the reimbursable expenses that you want to mark up.
3. In the Markup Amount or % field, type a markup dollar amount or a markup percentage. For percentages, type the percent sign after the percentage rate—for example, 5%.
4. Click the arrow at the Markup Account drop-down list, or press Ctrl+L, and select an income account to track your markup income.
5. Choose OK or press Enter. QuickBooks enters the reimbursable expense and the markup on the invoice.
6. Choose the Expenses button again to access the Choose Reimbursable Expenses dialog box.
7. Select the reimbursable expenses that you do not want to mark up.
8. Choose OK or press Enter to enter these reimbursable expenses on the invoice.

Completing the Invoice

After you've entered the items for which you're invoicing your customer and the calculation items (subtotals, discounts, and so on), you're ready to complete the rest of the invoice and record the invoice so that QuickBooks enters the invoice transaction in the Accounts Receivable register.

To complete the invoice and record the invoice transaction in the Accounts Receivable register, follow these steps:

1. Move to the Customer Message field. If you entered customer messages in the Customer Message List (see Chapter 5, "Using QuickBooks for Windows Lists"), click the drop-down arrow or press Ctrl+L to select a message from the list.

   To enter a message that is not in the Customer Message List, just type the new message in the Customer Message field and press Tab.

QuickBooks tells you that the message was not found in the Customer Message List and allows you to add the entire message to the Customer Message List using Quick Add or add just what you typed using Set Up.

Remember that the customer message prints exactly as it appears on-screen, so be careful not to make typing errors or misspell words. As mentioned earlier, you can use customer messages to show the following: payment instructions (`Please return one copy with your payment`), payment reminders (`Your balance is past due. Please remit`), seasonal greetings (`HAPPY HOLIDAYS`), your Taxpayer Identification Number, or just to tell your customer `Thank You`.

2. If you have turned on the automatic sales tax feature and you want QuickBooks to automatically calculate sales tax on the invoice items that are marked as taxable in the line item area, select the % Ta**x** check box. The percentage that QuickBooks enters to the right of this check box is the tax rate that you entered as the most common sales tax rate when you set up your company or turned on the automatic sales tax feature. See Chapter 7, "Tracking Sales Tax," to learn how to turn on the automatic sales tax feature and enter your sales tax rate.

   If the customer for this invoice was designated as taxable in the Customer:Job List, QuickBooks automatically selects the check box. If no sales tax should be calculated to this particular invoice, however, just click the check box to deselect it.

   When you select to have QuickBooks automatically calculate sales tax, the program calculates the sales tax amount and enters it to the right of the % Ta**x** check box.

   Note

   The automatic sales tax calculation is not applicable for professional invoices; therefore, the % Ta**x** check box does not appear.

3. In the Mem**o** field, type a memo or reminder for this invoice. If you send statements to your customer, the memo that you enter in the Memo field also appears on the statement as a reference to this invoice. Memos do appear in the Accounts Receivable register but do not appear on printed invoices.

4. If you want to include this invoice in a list of invoices to print later, select the To **B**e Printed check box. See Chapter 8, "Printing Invoices, Statements, and Other Forms," to learn how to print invoices.

5. Review all invoice information and choose **N**ext to record the invoice and enter the invoice transaction in the Accounts Receivable register. QuickBooks displays the next blank invoice.

If the customer for whom you are recording an invoice has exceeded his or her credit limit, QuickBooks displays a warning message, telling you the amount by which the customer's credit limit is exceeded and the customer's current balance. To record the invoice, regardless of the customer's credit status, choose Record or press Enter. If you don't want to record the invoice, choose Cancel or press Esc. QuickBooks returns to the invoice so that you can change or delete it.

CPA TIP: Increasing a Customer's Credit Limit

If you're writing an invoice, you already may have extended credit beyond the customer's credit limit by shipping goods or providing services in advance of payment. To decide whether to increase the customer's credit limit, first scrutinize the customer's transaction history or aging status schedule. If the customer has a good payment history, you may decide to increase the credit limit, keep the credit limit the same and add an invoice memo, or call to advise the customer that he has exceeded his credit limit and is not eligible for future credit sales.

Editing an Invoice

Before you print invoices that you have written and recorded, you should review them to ensure the following: the customer information is correct, the invoice shows the proper payment terms, the line items are accurate and complete, and the customer message is appropriate. QuickBooks organizes invoices in chronological order and always displays a blank invoice when you access the Create Invoices window. Because the Create Invoices window displays only one invoice at a time, you must use the **N**ext button to move to the next invoice in numerical sequence, or the Pre**v** button to move to the previous invoice in numerical sequence.

If the invoice that you want to edit is several invoices from the current invoice, you can access the invoice more quickly from the Accounts Receivable register. Access the Accounts Receivable register, and then scroll through the register to find the invoice or use the Find command, if necessary, to find the invoice that you want to edit. See Chapter 10, "Using the Accounts Receivable Register," to learn how to access and move around in the Accounts Receivable register.

You can restrict unauthorized access to the invoice-editing activity in QuickBooks by assigning passwords. Any person trying to edit an invoice then must enter the appropriate password; otherwise, QuickBooks denies access to this feature. To learn how to assign passwords to particular QuickBooks activities, see Chapter 21, "Managing QuickBooks for Windows Files."

To edit an invoice, follow these steps:

1. In the Create Invoice window, display the invoice you want to edit by using the Pre**v** and the **N**ext buttons. If you've located the invoice transaction in the Accounts Receivable register, double-click the transaction, from the **E**dit menu choose **E**dit Invoice, or press Ctrl+E to display the invoice that you want to edit.

2. Use the keys listed in this chapter in the earlier section "Moving Around in the Create Invoices Window" to move to the field that you want to change.

3. Make the necessary changes to the field.

4. When you finish editing the invoice, choose the **N**ext button to record it. To cancel the changes you made to an invoice, choose Cancel or press Esc before you record the invoice.

Deleting an Invoice

You can delete an invoice that you wrote inadvertently or as a practice invoice. Although QuickBooks enables you to delete a recorded invoice, you should not delete the following invoices:

- *An invoice with an error.* Instead, edit the invoice and correct the error. If you already have mailed the invoice to the customer, send a corrected invoice and either change the title of the invoice to Corrected Invoice (must be printed on blank paper only) or enter a customer message that explains the correction. See the section "Changing the Invoice Title" later in this chapter to learn how to change the invoice's title.

- *An invoice to which you already have applied a payment.* QuickBooks does not allow you to delete an invoice to which you have applied a payment.

- *An invoice for a product that the customer subsequently cancels or returns.* You should issue a credit memo to give the customer credit or a refund. See Chapter 9, "Receiving and Depositing Customer Payments," to learn about credit memos.

- *An invoice that the customer paid with a check which is subsequently returned for insufficient funds.* Instead of deleting this invoice, write another invoice or a debit memo. A debit memo is simply a new invoice that you write, charging a customer again for the same item or service. Add a message to the invoice telling the customer why they are being billed again, such as `Your check was returned for non-sufficient funds. Please remit immediately.`

When you delete an invoice, QuickBooks permanently deletes all information for the invoice from the Accounts Receivable register.

Notice that you can delete written and recorded invoices either from the Create Invoices window or from the Accounts Receivable register. You learn how to use the Accounts Receivable register in Chapter 10, "Using the Accounts Receivable Register."

To delete an invoice from the Create Invoices window, follow these steps:

1. In the Create Invoices window, display the invoice that you want to delete by using the Pre**v** and **N**ext buttons.

2. From the **E**dit menu choose **D**elete Invoice, or press Ctrl+D. QuickBooks displays the Delete Transaction dialog box.

3. Choose OK or press Enter to delete the invoice. Choose Cancel or press Esc if you don't want to delete the invoice.

When you delete an invoice, QuickBooks removes the invoice from the Create Invoices window and the invoice transaction from the Accounts Receivable register.

Voiding an Invoice

Voiding an invoice keeps the invoice detail in QuickBooks for Windows but doesn't add the total of the voided invoice to Accounts Receivable. When you void an invoice, the invoice remains; however, QuickBooks changes the invoice amount to zero and enters the word VOID in the Memo field. If you originally entered an invoice memo, QuickBooks inserts VOID before it. Voiding invoices provides a better "audit trail" because you can still account for every invoice.

To void an invoice, follow these steps:

1. In the Create Invoices window, display the invoice that you want to void by using the Pre**v** and **N**ext buttons.
2. From the **E**dit menu, choose **V**oid Invoice. QuickBooks voids the invoice and enters VOID in the Memo field.

To unvoid an invoice, follow these steps:

1. In the Create Invoices window, display the invoice that you want to unvoid by using the Pre**v** and **N**ext buttons.
2. From the **E**dit menu, choose **R**evert. QuickBooks unvoids the invoices by entering the invoice total to the invoice and in the Accounts Receivable register. VOID is removed from the Memo field.

Changing the Invoice Title

Unless you change the title of an invoice, the printed version of the invoice is titled "Invoice." You may, for example, want to change the title to "Duplicate Invoice," for an invoice that may have been lost in the mail, or "Amended Invoice," for an invoice with a correction.

Notice, however, that QuickBooks will not print a different title on preprinted invoice forms or letterhead. To print an invoice with a different title, you must print the invoice on plain paper.

To change the invoice title, follow these steps:

1. In the Create Invoices window, display the invoice for which you want to change the title.

2. Choose the Set Title button to display the Invoice Title dialog box shown in figure 6.13.

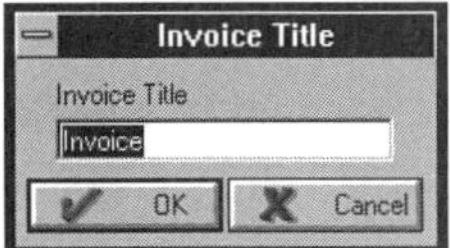

Fig. 6.13
Use the Invoice Title dialog box to change the title of an invoice.

3. Type a word or phrase as the new invoice title, using up to 19 characters.

4. Choose OK or press Enter to change the invoice title.

Note

When you change the invoice title, the title is changed on the current invoice only. The next or previous invoice titles are not changed.

Entering Historical Invoices

Even if you start using QuickBooks at the beginning of your fiscal year, you most likely will have some outstanding invoices (written invoices for which you have not received payment). The total of your outstanding invoices makes up your Accounts Receivable balance at any given time.

In QuickBooks, you don't enter an opening balance for the Accounts Receivable account. The program determines the opening Accounts Receivable balance based on the invoices you enter. You must, therefore, enter all outstanding invoices (as of the beginning of your fiscal year) so that your Accounts Receivable account's beginning balance is accurate. If you begin your QuickBooks for Windows system at any time other than the beginning of your fiscal year, you must enter outstanding invoices that you wrote during the current and prior years. Regardless of when you wrote these outstanding invoices, you should enter them in your QuickBooks for Windows system.

Entering Unpaid Invoices

Any invoices that are outstanding, or unpaid, when you start your QuickBooks system should be entered so that your Accounts Receivable balance is accurate as of your starting date and so that you can effectively track customer balances with QuickBooks. You can enter unpaid invoices in two ways: by individual invoice or by customer. You can enter each individual invoice for which you have an unpaid balance, or you can enter the outstanding balance for each customer in the New Customer window as of the date you start QuickBooks.

To enter individual invoices for customers in the Customer:Job List, follow these steps:

1. Choose the Invoice button from the Iconbar to display a blank invoice.
2. For each invoice, enter the invoice number and the original date of the invoice.
3. Complete the remaining invoice fields as you usually would.
4. Choose **N**ext to record the invoice and display the next blank invoice.

QuickBooks enters the invoice information in the Accounts Receivable register.

To enter each customer's outstanding balance, follow these steps:

1. Choose the Cust (Customer) button from the Iconbar to access the Customer:Job List.
2. Choose the **N**ew button to display the New Customer window. Fill in the New Customer window with your customer information. Refer to Chapter 5, "Using QuickBooks for Windows Lists," to learn how to complete the New Customer window.
3. In the Opening Balance field, type the outstanding balance for this customer.
4. In the As Of field, type the date of the outstanding balance in step 3. This should be your QuickBooks start date.
5. Choose OK or press Enter.

QuickBooks for Windows records each customer's opening balance as a separate invoice and records the invoice transaction in the Accounts Receivable register.

If you've already added your customers in the Customer:Job List, follow these steps to enter an opening balance:

1. Choose the Invoice button from the Iconbar to display a blank invoice.
2. Enter the customer in the Customer:Job field.
3. In the Date field, type your QuickBooks start date.
4. In the line item area of the invoice, type **Bal Fwd** in the Item field.
5. If Bal Fwd is not found in the Invoice Item List, choose the Set Up option to add this item in the New Item window.
6. Choose Other Charge in the Type field of the New Item window.
7. Type a description, such as **Opening Balance Invoice**, in the Description field.
8. Select the account in which you want all customer opening balances to be recorded, such as **Uncategorized Sales** or any other income account that you want to use.
9. Choose OK in the New Item window to add the Bal Fwd item to the Invoice Item List.

   QuickBooks returns to the invoice and enters the new Bal Fwd item in the Item field along with the description.
10. Type the customer's opening balance in the Amount field.
11. Choose **N**ext to record the opening balance invoice.

To edit a customer's opening balance, follow these steps:

1. Choose the Accnt (Account) button from the Iconbar to access the Chart of Accounts window.
2. From the Chart of Accounts window, highlight the Accounts Receivable account and choose the U**s**e Register button.
3. QuickBooks displays the Accounts Receivable register. (The Accounts Receivable register is explained in detail in Chapter 10, "Using the Accounts Receivable Register.")
4. Scroll through the register to find the opening balance transaction for the customer whose balance you want to edit.
5. Choose the Edit/Split button at the bottom of the register to display the opening balance invoice that QuickBooks created.

6. Type over the invoice amount in the Amount field.

7. Choose OK or press Enter to change the opening balance.

Entering Paid Invoices

If you want complete customer aging reports, current sales reports, and balance sheets that reflect the actual Accounts Receivable balance as of January 1 (or the first day of your fiscal year), you must enter all invoices that were paid during the current year.

Notice that you should enter your historical, or year-to-date, Accounts Receivable transactions before you enter your year-to-date checking transactions. QuickBooks automatically enters transactions that relate to customers in the check register as you enter these transactions into Accounts Receivable. If you receive payment from a customer, for example, and record the payment and deposit in Accounts Receivable, QuickBooks enters the deposit transaction into the check register.

During the current year, you probably have received payment for invoices that you wrote in the preceding year. Suppose that you received a payment on January 12, 1994, for an invoice that you wrote on December 15, 1993. Because the invoice is outstanding on January 1, 1994, you must enter it so that QuickBooks adds the outstanding amount to your Accounts Receivable balance. During the current year, you also probably have written other invoices for which you have received payment in the current year.

To enter paid invoices, you need to enter all invoices written in the prior and current years for which you received payment this year.

Invoices Written in the Prior Year. To enter invoices written in the prior year, enter a summary line item for each customer with an outstanding balance as of the beginning of your fiscal year. To enter a summary invoice for each customer, follow the same steps for entering a summary invoice for unpaid invoices as outlined in the preceding section. Be sure to date the invoices in the year they were written and use the Bal Fwd line item so that QuickBooks updates Accounts Receivable as of January 1, or the first day of your fiscal year.

Invoices Written in the Current Year. You should enter invoices written between the beginning of the year and the date you started your QuickBooks system so that QuickBooks for Windows' sales reports accurately reflect your current year sales. If you want the program to produce complete sales reports and customer transaction histories, you must enter each individual invoice you wrote during the period between the beginning of your fiscal year and the date you started using QuickBooks. By entering individual invoices, you can supply line-item detail so that QuickBooks can assign line items to the proper income, expense, or balance sheet accounts.

To enter individual invoices, follow these steps:

1. Choose the Invoice button from the Iconbar to display a blank invoice.
2. Enter the invoice number and the original date of the invoice.
3. Enter the remaining invoice information as usual, selecting line items from the Invoice Item List.
4. Enter individual payments on invoices as payment line items.
5. Choose OK or press Enter to record the invoice.

Preparing Job Estimates

You can use invoices to prepare job estimates for current or potential customers or clients. On the invoice, you can enter a line item for each part or service that you will provide and print the invoice to show your customer or client. Then, if the customer accepts the job as proposed, you already have the invoice entered.

To prepare a job estimate, follow these steps:

1. Choose the Invoice button from the Iconbar to display a blank invoice.
2. In the Customer:Job field, enter the customer for which you are estimating the job.
3. Complete the invoice header as you usually would.
4. In the line item area of the invoice, enter the quantity and the line item for each part or service required to perform the job.
5. Choose the Set Title button and change the title of the invoice to "Job Estimate" or whatever phrase you use for job estimates and proposals.
6. Choose OK or press Enter to record the job estimate invoice.

7. Print the invoice on plain paper so that the new title is printed with today's date and give it to your customer or client. (See Chapter 8, "Printing Invoices, Statements, and Other Forms," for instructions on printing invoices.)

8. After you print the job estimate, replace the invoice date with a future date so that QuickBooks does not include this invoice transaction in statements that you soon may send to the customer.

9. If the customer or client accepts the job estimate, delete the words `Job Estimate`, or whatever you entered as a description, change the invoice date to the date on which you want to send the invoice for parts sold or services rendered, and change the title back to `Invoice`. You can make adjustments to line items, but be careful not to change line items on which you and your customer already have agreed. Delete the job estimate invoice if your customer or client does not accept your proposal.

CPA TIP: Dating Job Estimates

It's important to date job estimates or proposals with the current date, or at least the date through which you're willing to provide parts or services at the estimated costs. A job estimate or proposal with a future date obligates you to provide those parts or services at stated costs on the proposal until that date. Because your costs of doing business increase rapidly, you don't want to obligate yourself to doing a job for less than is profitable.

Summary

In this chapter, you learned about the Create Invoices window, the three different invoice types (service, professional, and product) and, most importantly, how to write an invoice by using QuickBooks for Windows. You learned how to group invoice items and how to bill your customers for reimbursable expenses. You also learned how to edit, delete, and void invoices.

In the next chapter, you learn how to track the sales tax that you collect, how to pay sales tax due, and how to view the sales tax payable register.

Chapter 7

Tracking Sales Tax

Many of you in the business of selling goods also must help support your state, county, or city by collecting and paying a sales tax. If you are required to collect a sales tax, you must track its collection. For many businesses, keeping track of how much sales tax is owed to the local tax authority is a major headache. QuickBooks for Windows alleviates many problems for you by automatically charging sales taxes on an invoice and keeping the amount due in a separate account. QuickBooks can then remind you that sales taxes are due. You will need to add a memorized transaction for QuickBooks to remind you of this. Memorized Transactions are covered in Chapter 15, "Speeding Up Your Work in QuickBooks for Windows." The Sales Tax Liability Report will show you how much is owed for the period. If you are required to track more than one type of sales tax and/or tax district, QuickBooks can easily handle this requirement as well. In some localities, you may be required to collect multiple taxes. For example, you may be required to collect a state sales tax of 5 percent, and a local, city, or county sales tax of 1.5 percent.

In this chapter, you learn how to do the following tasks:

- Use Auto Tax for your primary sales tax
- Create additional sales taxes as line items
- Apply sales tax to an invoice
- Use QuickBooks' Sales Tax Liability Report to help you pay sales tax
- View the Sales Tax Payable Register

Setting Up QuickBooks To Track Sales Tax

You can easily set up QuickBooks to track more than one type of sales tax at a time. If you must answer to a primary tax authority, set up the program to use the Auto Tax feature for this tax authority. Auto Tax automatically calculates the taxable amount due and then adds it to every invoice necessary. At times, however, you may sell items to another reseller and thus not need to charge sales tax. With only a few keystrokes or a single mouse click, you can instruct QuickBooks not to add the sales tax to this invoice.

You may have more than one sales tax rate to track and apply to invoices. Use Auto Tax for your primary tax. You will use this tax rate most often in your business, or collect the most money for this tax (for example, your state sales tax). Secondary sales taxes, such as those levied by a city, county, or other taxing districts, are entered on an invoice as a sales tax line item. In this section you learn how to create a sales tax line item, and in the next section you learn how to use it in an invoice.

Tip
Collection of sales taxes is required by certain states, and municipalities. You must keep careful track of all amounts owed. Whenever possible, automating the collection function helps reduce the potential for human error.

Before you can use its sales tax functions, however, you must first tell QuickBooks for which tax agencies you must collect a sales tax as well as the rates you must collect. As described in Chapter 5, "Using QuickBooks for Windows Lists," you must check the Auto Taxable box in the New Item dialog box whenever you add a new invoice item. If you do not, Auto Tax does not consider this item taxable.

Note

Keeping your sales and sales-tax accounts separate helps you make better business decisions. If you keep only a single account, combining your sales and sales tax receipts, you are using overstated information to make these decisions. By using separate QuickBooks accounts, however, you can base your business decisions on actual sales, not on the inflated figure of your sales plus the sales tax collected.

Setting Up Tax Rates for Auto Tax

You must turn on the Auto Tax feature before QuickBooks uses it in invoice calculations. If you do not enable Auto Tax when you install QuickBooks and set up your company, you can do so at any time afterward. You also can change the tax rate, the tax agency, or the tax district to which you pay the sales tax.

To set up tax rates for Auto Tax, follow these steps:

1. From the **P**references menu, choose **S**ales Tax. QuickBooks displays the Sales Tax Preferences dialog box, as shown in figure 7.1.

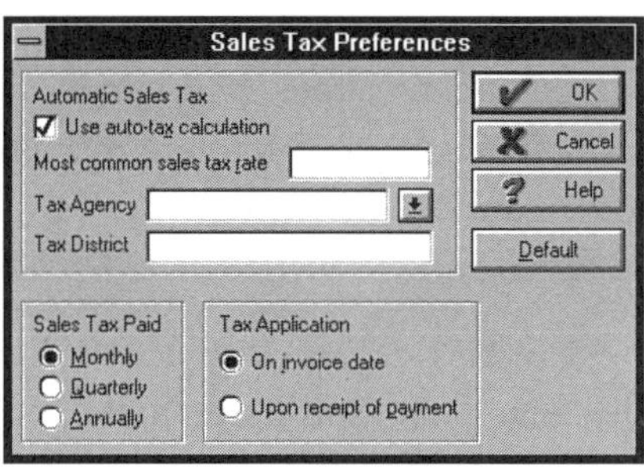

Fig. 7.1
From the Sales Tax Preferences dialog box, you can turn Auto Tax on or off and make other adjustments to your sales-tax collection methods.

2. Turn on the Auto Tax feature by selecting the Use auto-ta**x** calculation check box, if it is not already selected (checked). If you do not plan to use Auto Tax, make sure that this check box is deselected.

3. Enter the tax rate in the Most common sales tax **r**ate text box. If you must collect sales tax for more than one tax agency, use the rate for the agency you pay most often, whether this rate is for the state, county, or city tax agency.

   Enter a tax rate of 6.5%, for example, as **6.5**, not .065. You do not need to add the percent sign; QuickBooks does this for you.

4. In the Tax Agency drop-down list box, enter the name of the tax agency to which you pay this sales tax. QuickBooks uses a feature called *QuickFill* as you begin to type in the text box. As you type a letter, QuickBooks fills in the text box with the first closest matching item, in this case *vendor*. If the first selection that QuickBooks enters is not the correct choice, type the next letter. Continue typing until the correct vendor is displayed. If you cannot make a match, you also can select the agency from the Tax Agency drop-down list by clicking the arrow next to the list box (or pressing Ctrl+L) to display the list.

   If your Tax Agency does not appear in the drop-down list, simply type the name in the list box. After you press Tab to move to the next field, QuickBooks displays a dialog box containing the warning `Vendor Not Found`. You then can choose the **Q**uick Add or **S**et Up button to add the tax agency to the QuickBooks Vendor List or choose the **C**ancel button to cancel this vendor, and return to the Sales Tax Preferences dialog box. You must either choose an existing vendor from the drop-down list box, or enter a different name for your new tax agency/vendor. A tax agency is considered by QuickBooks to be a vendor because you write checks to them, and so must be included in the Vendor List.

5. Enter in the Tax District text box the name of the specific tax district in which you collect sales tax. (This is optional and is necessary only if you pay another sales tax to the same tax agency in a separate tax district.)

   The Tax District is an optional item. In some circumstances, you may collect taxes for more than one tax district that you pay to a single tax agency. The tax agency then redirects the taxes back to the districts. For example, you may collect a 2 percent tax for the city in which you are located, and 1 percent for the local transit authority. You are required to remit the taxes collected to a single tax agency. You would enter the city as the tax district because they have the higher of the tax rates.

6. Select the appropriate option button for Sales Tax Paid: **M**onthly, **Q**uarterly, or **A**nnually. If you pay sales tax to the agency listed in step 4 every month, for example, select the **M**onthly radio button.

   QuickBooks uses this information as the basis for its Sales Tax Liability Report. If **M**onthly is selected, the report is based on information from the previous month.

7. Select in the Tax Application area the radio button that corresponds to your sales tax liability as determined by your tax agency.

   This selection determines when your sales tax liability is accrued. The correct selection depends on your specific situation.

   Select the On **I**nvoice Date option if you become liable for the sales tax on the same date that you charge your customer—usually the invoice date. QuickBooks handles your sales tax liability on an accrual basis, even if you select the cash accounting basis.

Choose the Upon Receipt of **P**ayment option if you are not liable for a sales tax until the date you actually receive payment from your customer. QuickBooks handles your tax liability on a cash basis, even if you use an accrual accounting basis.

8. Choose OK or press Enter to save your changes and addition to the Sales Tax Preferences dialog box. Figure 7.2 shows how a completed dialog box may appear.

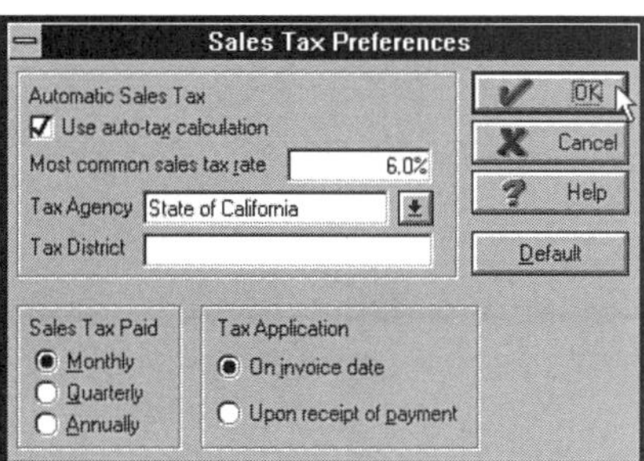

Fig. 7.2
A completed Sales Tax Preferences dialog box contains all the necessary sales tax information for your most commonly used sales tax rate.

Choose the Cancel button to leave the Sales Tax Preferences dialog box without saving any of your changes.

Choosing the Help button accesses on-screen help for the Sales Tax Preferences dialog box.

Choosing the **D**efault button deletes all the selections you have made, leaving the dialog box on-screen with its field blank or at the default settings, similar to its appearance in figure 7.1.

Setting Up Sales Tax Line Items

If a secondary sales tax must be applied to your transactions, you can set up this additional tax as a *sales tax line item*. You also can use this option if you occasionally apply an alternative tax rate to an invoice. Additional sales tax rates must be added to the Invoice Items List.

To add a sales tax line item, follow these steps:

1. From the **L**ists menu, choose **I**nvoice Items. The Invoice Item List appears, as shown in figure 7.3.

Fig. 7.3
The Invoice Item List contains all QuickBooks line items that can be used on an invoice. The list has columns for the item code, a description, item type, account assigned, and the retail price.

Invoice Item List

Code	Description	Type	Account	Price
T-DGWD-P	Tree - Dog Wood - Pink	Part	Sales	15.00
T-WPCHRY-F	Weeping Cherry - Flowering Pink	Part	Sales	125.00
Discount	Discount on Invoice	Discount	Cash Discounts	0.00
Auto Tax	Sales Tax	Sales Tax	Sales Tax Payable	6.0%

Use | QuickReport | New | Edit

2. Choose the **N**ew button. The New Item dialog box appears, as shown in figure 7.4.

3. Open the Type drop-down list, and select from the list the Sales Tax new item type.

4. Enter a descriptive code for this sales tax line item in the Item Code text box.

5. Enter up to a three-line description for this sales tax in the Description box. (Remember that only the first line of this description appears on an invoice.)

6. Enter the tax percentage in the Rate text box. Remember to enter the percentage as 1.5 for .015.

7. Open the Tax Agency drop-down list and select from the list the tax agency for which you collect the sales tax. If the agency does not appear as a vendor in the Vendor List, QuickBooks enables you to add it to that list now.

8. Enter the name of the tax district for which the tax is collected in the Tax District text box, if applicable. You now have a sales tax item that looks similar to the one shown in figure 7.4.

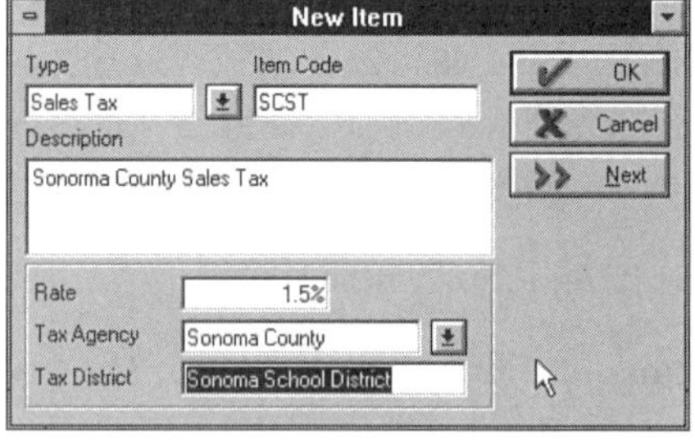

Fig. 7.4
You use the New Item dialog box for creating new inventory and sales line items. An item does not have to be an actual piece of inventory to be included here. You also can include services, discounts, or subtotals.

9. Choose OK or press Enter to enter this new item as a sales tax line item into the Invoice Item List.

Applying Sales Tax to Invoices

After you set up your sales tax rates (and enter the tax agencies as vendors if you have not already done so), you can apply a sales tax to an invoice. Using QuickBooks to track the sales taxes you collect—and then pay—can save you time and money, by preventing costly errors that may result in assessed penalties or late fees.

Using Auto Tax To Calculate Sales Tax

By using Auto Tax when creating an invoice, you take all the guesswork from your calculations. By entering a check mark in the Auto Ta**x**able box when you create or edit an invoice line item, you are telling QuickBooks that this item is a taxable item. In most cases, actual items that you purchase such as cars, lamps, paper, and so on, are subject to the sales tax. Items such as food, medicine, and services are not. Depending on your specific situation, you may not be required to charge sales tax to some customers. If you sell to both retail and wholesale customers, you may be required to collect the sales tax from your retail customers and not wholesale, or customers who will resell the item. By checking the Ta**x**able box in the New or Edit Customer dialog box, you can designate a customer as one from whom you will collect a sales tax, and one from whom you will not.

To use Auto Tax on an invoice, follow these steps:

1. Open the Create Invoices window by clicking the Invoice button on the Iconbar, by opening the **A**ctivities menu and choosing Create **I**nvoices, or by pressing Ctrl+I.

2. Enter the required data for an invoice, as described in Chapter 6, "Creating Invoices." Figure 7.5 shows a completed invoice.

   Each time you enter into an invoice an item marked as taxable, QuickBooks indicates this by placing a small, capital letter "T" to the right of the subtotal in the Amount column. You can see this "T" in figure 7.5. If you do not see this taxable designator on a line item in an invoice, QuickBooks does not calculate the Auto Tax by using this item. Figure 7.5 shows two taxable line items, and so QuickBooks has automatically calculated the sales tax on both items.

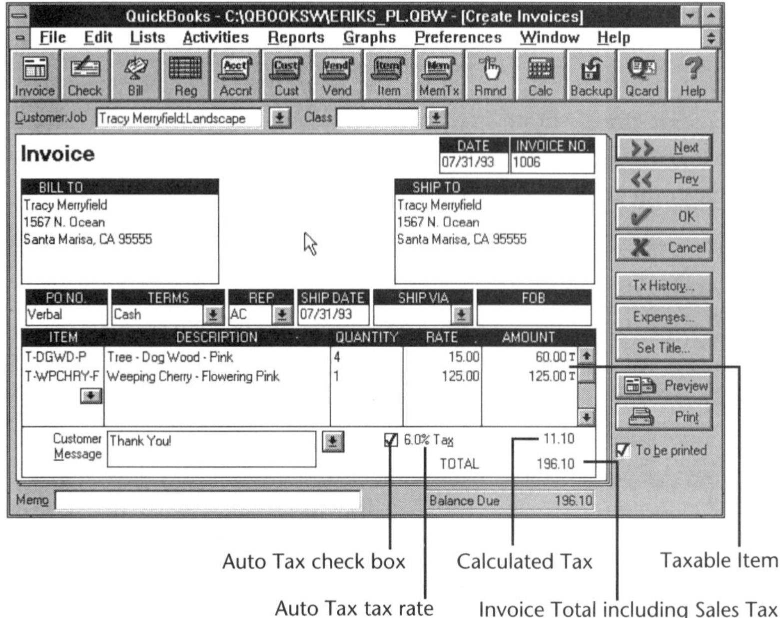

Fig. 7.5
Shown is the completed invoice. Because both line items are taxable, QuickBooks has used Auto Tax to enter the tax rate and add the calculated tax to the invoice. You can turn Auto Tax off by unchecking the Auto Tax check box.

As you can see, Auto Tax can greatly simplify calculating the sales tax that a customer must pay.

Entering Sales Tax Line Items on Invoices

Adding a second sales tax to an invoice requires only a little more effort than using Auto Tax. If a second sales tax is used, however, you must take some care as to how you arrange the line items on the invoice.

To enter a sales tax line item to an invoice, follow these steps:

1. Enter all the information required for an invoice, except for the line items.

2. Add to the invoice all nontaxable line items, if any. Nontaxable items may include medications, food items, or some services.

3. After all the nontaxable items are entered, add a subtotal line item to the invoice. Your invoice should look similar to the one shown in figure 7.6.

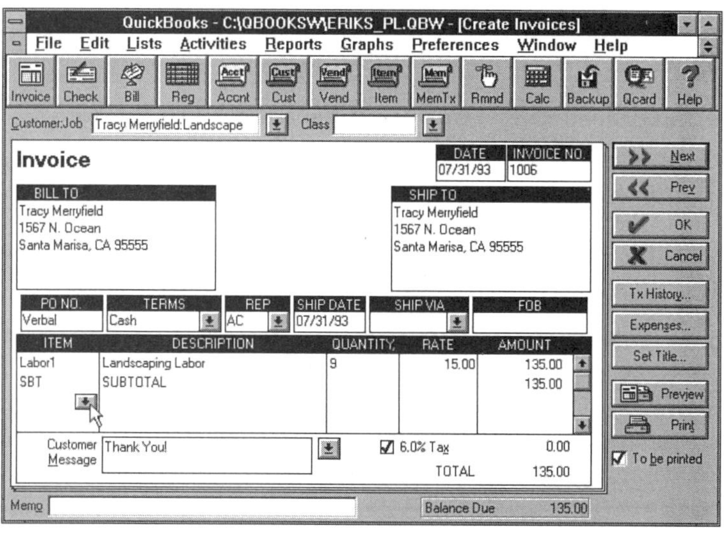

Fig. 7.6
An invoice listing a nontaxable line item and a subtotal line item.

Notice that the Auto Tax feature has not included this nontaxable line item as part of its automatically calculated tax.

4. Add all taxable items to the invoice. The invoice should now look similar to that shown in figure 7.7.

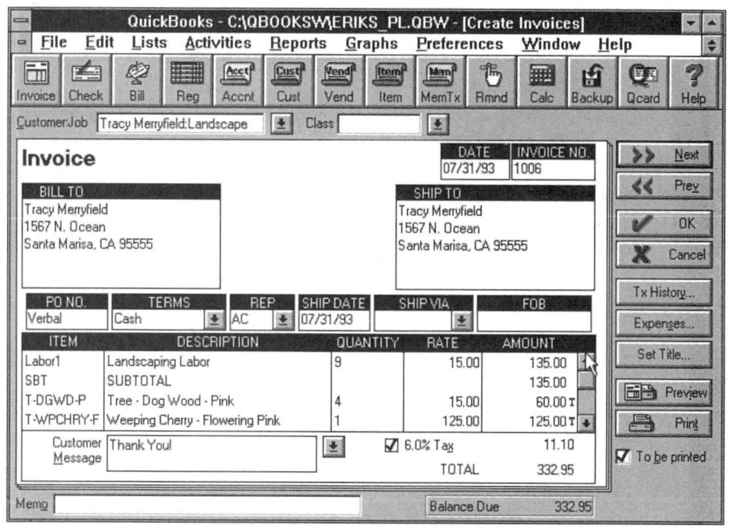

Fig. 7.7
The same invoice, now listing both nontaxable and taxable line items.

Notice that the Auto Tax has now calculated the total tax due on the taxable items: $11.10.

5. Add to the end of the list of line items a subtotal line item for the taxable items.

   A subtotal line item only subtotals those items below the previous subtotal line item. In this example, you have a single nontaxable item and its subtotal, followed by two taxable items and their subtotal.

6. Enter the secondary tax rate line item after the last subtotal line item.

   As shown in figure 7.8, the completed invoice lists two taxable items, a subtotal item, and finally a secondary tax item. Notice that the Auto Tax has not included the amount of the secondary sales tax in its calculation of sales tax due.

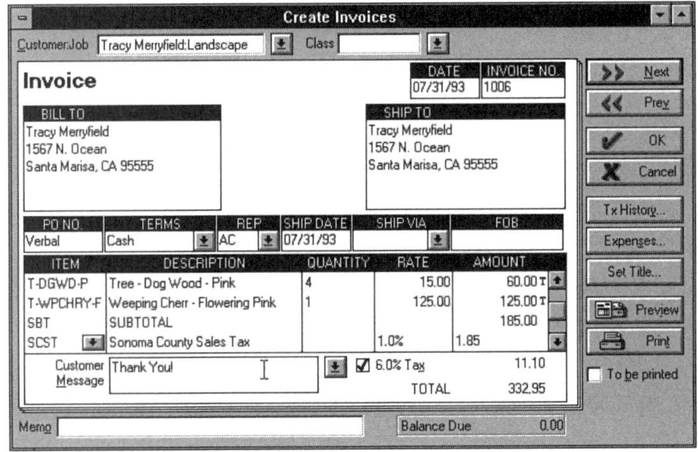

Fig. 7.8
The completed invoice, listing a secondary sales tax line item along with the nontaxable and taxable line items and their subtotals.

7. Choose OK to record the invoice.

Reviewing Sales Taxes Owed

Now that you know how to collect sales taxes from your customer, you must at some time gather that tax information for the tax agency. If you previously used a manual system, you may have saved each month's sales receipts and then laboriously reviewed each one to extract the amount of the sales taxes paid. You then recorded each total and added together the entire month's tax receipts for a grand total. (And how often did you need to run out three or four ten-foot lengths of adding machine tape trying to arrive at the same total twice?) QuickBooks now does all this work for you. With a few simple keystrokes, you can create and print a copy of your *Sales Tax Liability Report*, which lists the amount of sales tax you owe.

The QuickBooks Sales Tax Liability Report shows or prints a report detailing your current sales tax liability. The report lists each of the agencies to which you pay a sales tax. The next column shows the total taxable sales during the period selected for each agency. The final column displays the total tax that is currently owed to the agency for the selected period. You can then use this report to help fill out the required tax forms. This report can be created at any time, allowing you to estimate your cash requirements for payment of this tax.

To create and print the Sales Tax Liability Report, follow these steps:

1. From the **R**eports menu, choose **A**/P Reports. The **A**/P Reports menu opens.

2. Choose the **S**ales Tax Liability Report option from this menu.

   QuickBooks creates the Sales Tax Liability Report, as shown in figure 7.9.

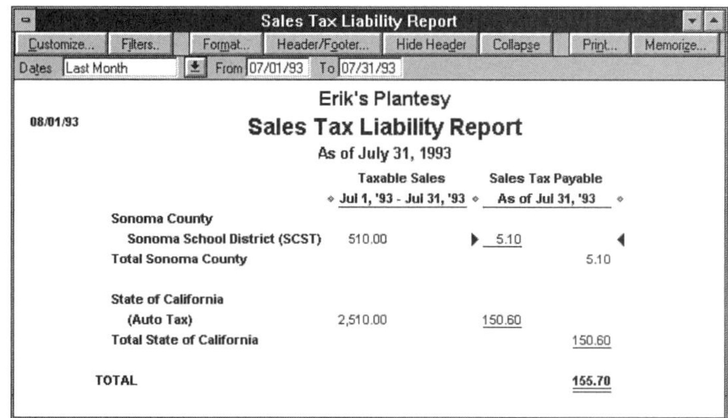

Fig. 7.9
The Sales Tax Liability Report for the previous month, showing sales tax collected for the Sonoma County School District and the state of California.

   In this report you can clearly see to whom you owe a sales tax payment, the amount of that payment, and the taxable sales for the period covered by this report.

3. Print the Sales Tax Liability Report by choosing one of the following print options:

- Click the Pri**n**t button with the mouse.
- Press Alt+P to choose the Pri**n**t button.
- From the **F**ile menu, choose **P**rint Report.
- Press Ctrl+P.

Regardless of which option you choose, the Print Report dialog box appears. In the Print Report dialog box, you can choose where to print the report, how the report is to be printed, and how much of the report to print. (Refer to Chapter 4, "Working with Accounts," for information on the Print Report dialog box and its options.)

4. Choose the Pri**n**t button in the dialog box to print the report.

You now know how much sales tax you must pay to each of the tax agencies to which you are liable. In Chapter 13, "Writing and Printing Checks," you learn how to use QuickBooks to create checks so that you can pay the tax you owe.

Viewing the Sales Tax Payable Register

As you create an invoice listing any sales tax collected, QuickBooks adds this amount to the register of your Sales Tax Payable account. The Sales Tax Payable account is one that QuickBooks may have automatically added to your Chart of Accounts when you installed the program, if you had answered Yes to the question: `Do you charge your customers sales tax?` Most businesses have only a single Sales Tax Payable account. QuickBooks can track in this single account all the sales taxes you must collect and the different tax agencies for which you collect sales taxes.

Each account listed in the Chart of Accounts is backed by a *register*. As the Chart of Accounts contains a list of each account that QuickBooks maintains for your business, the register contains a detailed listing of each transaction for that account. Figure 7.10 shows an example of a Sales Tax Payable register. Remember, you can display any of the account registers by opening the Chart of Accounts window, selecting the account from the list, and clicking the U**s**e Register button.

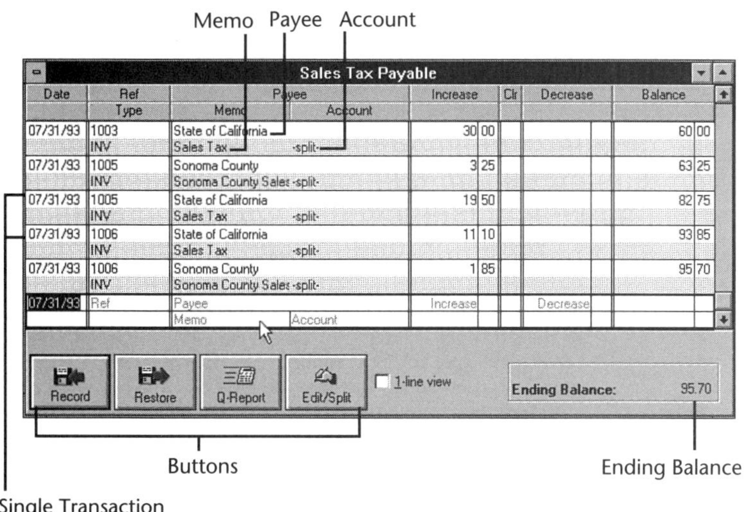

Fig. 7.10
The Sales Tax Payable register lists each transaction that added or subtracted from it. When you collect a sales tax on an invoice, the sales tax part of the transaction appears in this register.

The various QuickBook account registers are similar in their function and construction. Registers include two basic areas: transactions and functions. Following are two tables that describe the transaction area and the register functions/displays area, respectively.

Transaction Area

Item	Description
Date	The date each transaction was completed.
Ref	The reference number of the transaction. In the Sales Tax Payable register, this number refers to the invoice on which the sales tax was collected or the check number that paid the taxes due.
Type	The type of transaction. In the Sales Tax Payable register, you see INV, for invoice, or CHK, for check.
Payee	The agency to which the tax is owed.
Memo	Any note you entered. In the Sales Tax Payable register, this is the description you entered when you added the sales tax line item.
Account	The name of the account to which the transaction has been assigned. In the Sales Tax Payable register, the transaction often is split between more than one account, because the original transaction—the invoice—is split between the Sales account and the Sales Tax Payable account.

(continues)

Transaction Area Continued

Item	Description
Increase	This column includes all transaction amounts that increase the account balance. In the Sales Tax Payable register, the Increase column includes all amounts collected as sales taxes from customer Invoices and Sales Receipts. The name of this column may vary, depending on the register in which you are working; a Checking account uses Deposit; a Credit Card account uses Charge.
Decrease	This column includes all transaction amounts that decrease the account balance. In the Sales Tax Payable register, the Decrease column includes amounts that have been remitted to the taxing agency, and amounts that are credited back to a customer on a Credit Memo. The name of this column also will vary, depending on the register; a Checking account uses Payment; a Credit Card account uses Payment.
Clr	Used to clear the transaction from the register. After you pay a transaction and have reconciled the payment with your bank statement, placing an X in this column clears the transaction.

Register Functions and Displays

Item	Description
Balance	A running total of all transactions listed in the register.
Record button	Records any changes you make to the selected transaction.
Restore button	Enables you to clear any changes you have made. Use this button to restore the transaction to its original state.
Q-Report button	Displays a QuickReport listing all transactions related to the payee.
Edit/Split button	Displays the selected transaction in its original form. This enables you to edit a transaction, to split the transaction amount among different accounts, or to classify the transaction as a reimbursable expense. After editing the transaction, choose OK to return to the register.
1-Line View	Selecting this check box changes the register display to display only a single line for each transaction, as shown in figure 7.11. Deselect the check box to restore the register to its normal two-line mode.
Ending Balance	The final balance for the register.

Sales Tax Payable

Date	Ref	Payee	Account	Increase	Clr	Decrease	Balance
07/31/93	1002	State of California	-split-	30 00			30 00
07/31/93	1003	State of California	-split-	30 00			60 00
07/31/93	1005	Sonoma County	-split-	3 25			63 25
07/31/93	1005	State of California	-split-	19 50			82 75
07/31/93	1006	State of California	-split-	11 10			93 85
07/31/93	1006	Sonoma County	-split-	1 85			95 70
07/31/93	Ref	Payee	Account	Increase		Decrease	

Record Restore Q-Report Edit/Split 1-line view Ending Balance: 95.70

Fig. 7.11
The Sales Tax Payable register with its entries displayed in single lines after the **1**-Line View check box is selected.

Paying Sales Tax

Earlier sections in this chapter describe how to use the Auto Tax feature of QuickBooks, how to create a sales tax line item, how to add sales tax to an invoice, how to create the Sales Tax Liability Report, and how to use the Sales Tax Payable register. At some point, however, the tax agency for which you collect sales taxes is going to want to be paid. Fortunately, QuickBooks easily separates your sales taxes payments from the payments for your everyday business bills.

To use QuickBooks to pay a sales tax, follow these steps:

1. From the **A**ctivities menu, choose Pay Sales **T**ax. The Pay Sales Tax dialog box appears, as shown in figure 7.12.

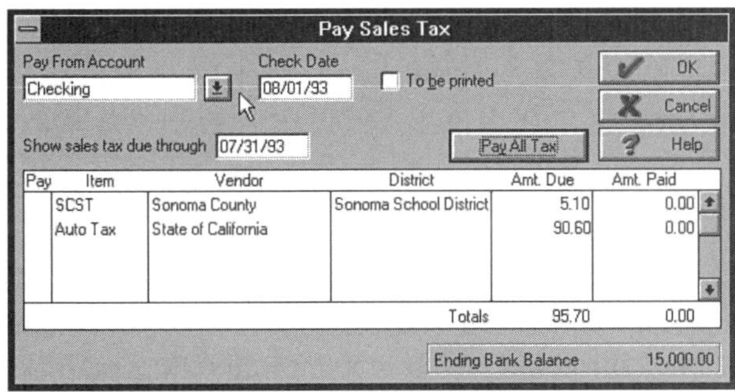

Fig. 7.12
Use the Pay Sales Tax dialog box to select the account from which to pay the taxes due, the date to show on your check, and the date used to calculate the sales tax owed.

2. Open the Pay From Account drop-down list. If you pay sales taxes from another checking account, select it from the drop-down list (or by pressing Ctrl+L).

3. Enter a date in the Check Date text box if you are recording a handwritten check. If you plan to have QuickBooks print your check for you, you will be able to enter the date that appears on your check at that time.

4. Select the To **b**e printed check box to add this check to the Select Checks to Print list, if you want to have QuickBooks print your check in the next check run.

   If you write this check by hand, be sure that this box is not checked. QuickBooks then automatically assigns the next available check number to the transaction and records it in the appropriate registers.

5. Verify that the Show Sales Tax Due Through text box is correct. Adjust the date in this text box, if necessary.

6. If you want to pay all of the taxes owed to each agency, choose the Pa**y** All Tax button. A check mark appears in the Pay column beside each of the agencies listed. Notice that the button label changes to Clear Pa**y**ments. This button toggles between these choices.

   If you do not want to pay all the tax agencies listed at this time take one of the following actions:

   - Position the mouse pointer in the Pay column for the agency to be paid, and click. This places a check mark in the Pay column for that agency only. If you change your mind and decide not to pay this agency now, clicking again removes the check mark from the Pay column, and changes the Amt.Paid to 0.00.

   - Choose the Pa**y** All Tax button. Then press the Tab key until the Amt. Paid column for the agency not to be paid is highlighted. Change the amount in this column to **0.00**, and press Tab again. The check mark is removed from the Pay column of that agency.

7. To change the amount to be paid to a specific agency, press Tab until the amount to be changed in the Amt. Paid column is highlighted. Then edit this amount to reflect the amount to actually be paid. Figure 7.13 shows the completed Pay Sales Tax dialog box.

   You also can use the mouse, by placing the mouse pointer on the figure to be changed in the Amt. Paid column and clicking once. Edit this figure to the required amount.

8. Press the OK button to save this transaction.

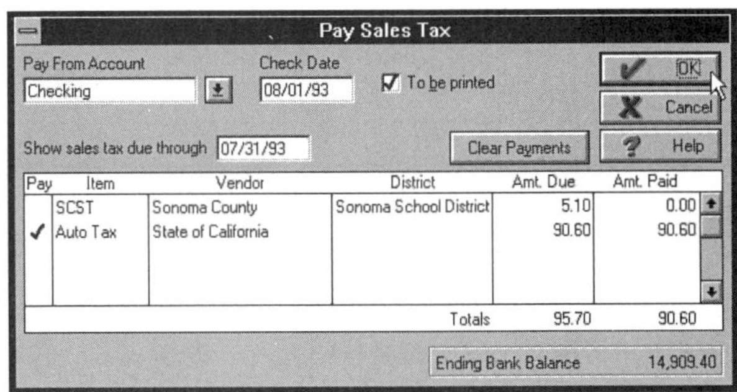

Fig. 7.13
The completed Pay Sales Tax dialog box, showing how much sales tax is due and which agency is being paid.

After you complete the Pay Sales Tax dialog box, open the Sales Tax Payable register. That register now reflects the payment made in the Pay Sales Tax dialog box, as shown in figure 7.14.

Sales Tax Payable

Date	Ref / Type	Payee / Memo	Account	Increase	Clr	Decrease	Balance
07/31/93	1005	Sonoma County		3 25			63 25
	INV	Sonoma County Sales	-split-				
07/31/93	1005	State of California		19 50			82 75
	INV	Sales Tax	-split-				
07/31/93	1006	State of California		11 10			93 85
	INV	Sales Tax	-split-				
07/31/93	1006	Sonoma County		1 85			95 70
	INV	Sonoma County Sales	-split-				
08/01/93		State of California				90 60	5 10
	SLSTAXPMT		Checking				
07/31/93							

Record | Restore | Q-Report | Edit/Split | 1-line view | Ending Balance: 5.10

Fig. 7.14
The Sales Tax Payable register, listing the sales tax payment just made.

II Tracking Customers

Summary

In this chapter, you learned how to use QuickBooks to track the sales taxes you collect and owe. You learned how to set up the Auto Tax feature, how to create a sales-tax line item, and how to apply these sales taxes to an invoice. You also learned how to display and print the Sales Tax Liability Report. Finally, you learned how to access and view the Sales Tax Payable register and to pay sales taxes due by using the Pay Sales Tax dialog box.

In the next chapter, you learn how to print invoices, statements, and other QuickBooks forms.

Chapter 8

Printing Invoices, Statements, and Other Forms

In this chapter, you learn how to do the following:

- Order invoices and other supplies from Intuit
- Print invoices
- Create statements for your customers
- Print mailing labels
- Print rotary index cards from your vendor and customer lists

One problem in any business is the amount of paper generated in a single day. By using QuickBooks for Windows, you can reduce some of this paperwork by reducing the number of incorrect invoices or statements sent out. But even if it doesn't reduce the quantity of your paperwork, QuickBooks can improve its quality.

Your regular customers know you mainly by the goods or services you provide them. But what about customers with whom you do business only infrequently? These customers remember you only when they receive your invoice or statement in the mail. QuickBooks helps ensure that they remember your invoice or statement as a thoroughly professionally prepared document.

Ordering Invoices and Other Supplies

You can use QuickBooks simply as an electronic bookkeeping system to record the transactions of your business, calculate the ending balance in your checking account, track Accounts Receivable and Accounts Payable, reconcile your checking account, and produce reports. The power of QuickBooks, however, lies in its check- and invoice-writing capabilities—its most important time-saving features.

You can use your QuickBooks system to print a check or a customer invoice for each transaction you enter in QuickBooks. Printing invoices in QuickBooks is faster and easier than using a typewriter or even a word processor to prepare invoices. Preprinted checks and invoices are available from Intuit. Your QuickBooks package contains a supply catalog and an order form you can use to make orders from Intuit; you can even print such an order form by using QuickBooks itself.

Using QuickBooks to order supplies from Intuit is easy. As a standard supplies order form is included among QuickBooks' preset forms, you can never misplace your order forms.

To print the Intuit supplies order form, follow these steps:

1. From the **A**ctivities menu, choose Supplies **O**rder Form. The Supplies Order Form dialog box appears, as shown in figure 8.1.

Fig 8.1
The Intuit Supplies Order Form dialog box. Use this dialog box to print a copy of the Supplies Order Form.

2. Choose the Prin**t** button to print the supplies order form. The form is three pages in length.

If your printer is not yet set up (see the following section) or you decide not to print the order form at this time, choose the **D**one or Cancel button to return to the desktop.

When you have finished printing the Supplies Order Form, take a few moments with the catalog that arrived with your QuickBooks package and decide on the forms or checks that you want to order. Fill out the order form and send or fax it off. Be sure to include all required information, including a copy of a voided check if you are having checks printed.

Setting Up Your Printer

You must tell QuickBooks what printer you intend to use for each type of print function. You can use one printer for printing checks and another for printing reports and invoices. If you have a single printer, you tell QuickBooks about that printer for each print function. (Before you can choose a printer in QuickBooks, however, you must use the Windows Control Panel to correctly install the printer. See your Windows documentation for information on installing printers through the Control Panel.)

From this Invoice Printer Setup dialog box, you can set several options for the printer you intend to use for invoice printing. Each Printer Setup dialog box is very similar in its available options. The differences in each dialog box are described later in this book when the specific item to be printed is discussed. The following options are available in the Invoice Printer Setup dialog box, similar settings are used in the other Printer Setup dialog boxes:

- *Printer.* To access a list of printers, click the down arrow button next to the **P**rinter drop-down list box, or press Alt+down arrow. All printers you set up in the Windows Control Panel appear in the list. Select the printer you want to use for the function you are setting up—in this case, printing invoices. Remember that a laser printer cannot print continuous-feed invoice forms. If you use this form type, plan on using a nonlaser printer for your invoices.

- *Paper Feed.* This option gives you three choices for type of paper feed:

  (Auto-detect). This is the default option. QuickBooks automatically detects the type of form you use based on your printer and its settings. Use this setting unless you are having problems with your printer.

  Continuous. Use this option if QuickBooks cannot detect that you are using continuous feed forms in your printer.

  Page-oriented. Use this option if QuickBooks cannot detect that you are using single-sheet forms or paper in your printer.

- *Print On.* This option enables you to choose the type of form on which you intend to print your invoices, as shown in figure 8.2.

  From the Print on drop-down list box, you can choose among the following five options:

  Preprinted form. Select this option if you print your invoice on a preprinted invoice form. These forms can be ordered from Intuit, and can be ordered with your logo, company name, and address preprinted on

Tip
If QuickBooks has problems detecting your use of single sheet-forms or letterhead in your dot-matrix printer, make sure that you changed your printer's selector lever from tractor to single-sheet feed.

the form. Blocks for all invoice fields will be printed on this type of form. These forms can be page-feed or continuous-feed.

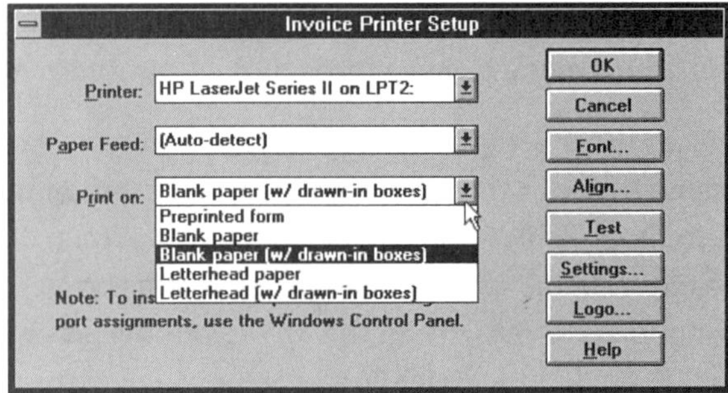

Fig. 8.2
The Invoice Printer Setup dialog box displaying the various paper options available for printing invoices.

Blank paper. Choose this option if you need only a simple invoice or receipt. When selected, this option prints your company's name and address on the invoice in the upper-left corner. By selecting this option, QuickBooks prints the different headings (such as Ship To or Description) for the different invoice fields, but does not draw boxes around these headings.

Blank paper (with drawn-in boxes). This option is similar to that for blank paper, except that QuickBooks prints the field titles and draws boxes around titles and between invoice line-item columns. This option is a good one if your company has not yet decided to invest in preprinted forms, but does need to provide the customer with an invoice. You can use this option while you are waiting for your preprinted forms to arrive.

Letterhead paper. This option prints an invoice exactly as does the blank paper option, except the company name and address are not included. You must use letterhead that is 8 1/2 by 11 inches. Your company name and address must also be printed only within the upper 1.9 inches of the paper, or QuickBooks may print part of the invoice on top of your masthead.

Letterhead (with drawn-in boxes). This option prints as does the Blank paper with drawn-in boxes, except without printing your company name and address. The letterhead restrictions of the previous choice apply. This option is a good one if you need a professional-appearing invoice to send to a client but do not use preprinted invoice forms.

- ***F**ont button.* This button displays the Invoice Printing Font dialog box, enabling you to select fonts for the invoice. The options available vary depending on your printer, any font cartridges installed, and any soft-fonts you may have installed (such as TrueType fonts).
- *Al**i**gn button.* Displays the Printer Alignment dialog box. This option is discussed in the later section "Printing Invoices."
- ***T**est button.* Enables you to test print an invoice. Make sure that the correct printer is selected and the correct invoice's forms are loaded before you use this option.
- ***S**ettings button.* This option enables you to adjust your printer settings. The dialog box this button accesses is similar in function to the settings window in the Windows Control Panel. The title bar of this dialog box lists the name of the printer that you have selected.
- ***L**ogo button.* This option displays the Invoice Artwork dialog box, which enables you to select a logo to print on your invoices. This artwork can be either a Windows bitmap file (*.BMP) or a piece of artwork cut from another application and placed in the Windows Clipboard. After you select the logo artwork, it is displayed in the Selected Artwork area.
- ***H**elp button.* Accesses the on-line Help screen for this dialog box.

To set up your printer, follow these steps:

1. From the **F**ile menu, choose Printer **S**etup.
2. From the Printer **S**etup menu, choose **I**nvoice Printer for this example. The Invoice Printer Setup dialog box appears, as shown in figure 8.3. Setting up a Statement, Check, Report, or Label printer follows this same process.

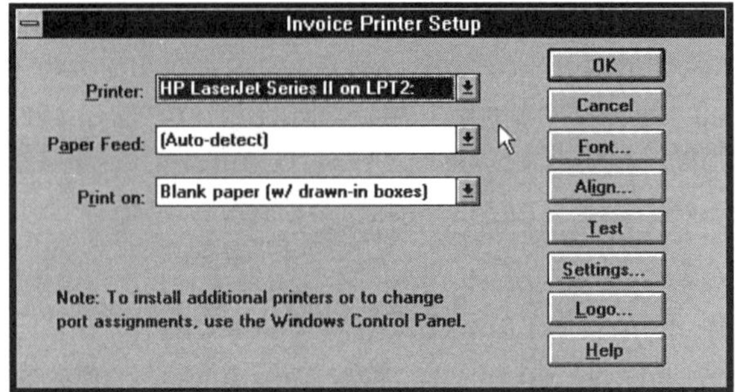

Fig. 8.3
The Invoice Printer Setup dialog box. Use this dialog box to set up or change the printer used for invoices. Other options available by selecting the button are described later.

Note

Use the Invoice Printer Setup dialog box for printing invoices, credit memos, and cash sales receipts, regardless of whether you use preprinted forms, blank paper, or letterhead.

3. After you make the selections you require for invoice printing, click the OK button or press Enter to save your settings.

Previewing Invoices

At times you may want to view an invoice before you print it. The service and professional invoice formats print differently than they appear in the Create Invoice window. Several of the different fields contain information needed by QuickBooks, but do not print on the invoice. QuickBooks enables you to preview an invoice before you print it.

To preview an invoice, follow these steps:

1. Click the Invoice button on the Iconbar; or from the **A**ctivities menu, choose Create **I**nvoices. This action opens the Create Invoice window.

2. Choose an invoice to preview by choosing the **N**ext or Pre**v** buttons.

3. After the invoice you want to preview appears on-screen, choose the Prev**i**ew button. The Print Preview window appears, as shown in figure 8.4.

   As is evident in figure 8.4, the entire invoice cannot be viewed at one time. You can use the mouse to move up, down, left, or right in the Print Preview window to view the entire invoice by clicking the arrows on the scroll bars or by dragging a scroll box in the direction you want to move. There are no keyboard equivalents, you must have a mouse.

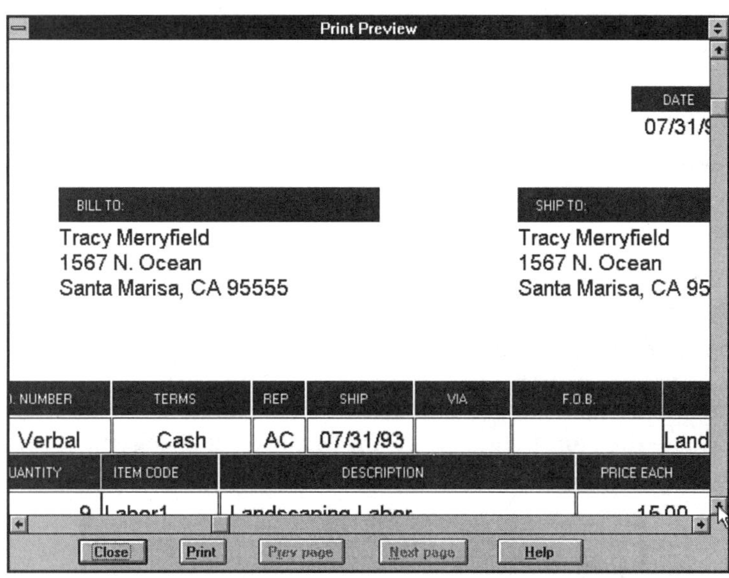

Fig. 8.4
The Print Preview window. You must use the scroll bars to view other areas of the invoice.

The Print Preview window contains the following command buttons, located at the bottom of the screen:

- *Close*. Closes the Print Preview window and returns you to the document window.
- ***P**rint*. Opens the Print Invoice (or other document) dialog box.
- *P**r**ev page*. Displays the previous page of the document. Because this invoice is a single-page document, this and the following button are dimmed. If you preview a multiple page invoice these buttons would be available.
- ***N**ext page*. Displays the next page of the document.
- ***H**elp*. Displays the on-line Help screen for this window.

Positioning Invoices in Your Printer

Among the most difficult print jobs on a computer is printing such pre-printed forms as checks and invoices. QuickBooks, however, makes this job much easier. QuickBooks provides two ways to align text to fit your forms.

If you use blank paper invoices or letterhead, you probably need make no printing alignment adjustments at all.

Earlier versions of QuickBooks—and Quicken—offered several different methods of aligning forms, depending on your printer type—laser, using single-page (or *page-oriented*) forms, or dot-matrix, using continuous feed (or *tractor*) forms. QuickBooks for Windows, and now Quicken 2 for Windows, however, simplifies this job by using the same methods for all printers and form types.

To adjust the alignment of forms in your printer, follow these steps:

1. Display the invoice to be printed in the Create Invoices window by opening the Create Invoice window and selecting an invoice by pressing the Pre**v** button until it appears in the window.

2. Choose the Prin**t** button. The Print One Invoice dialog box appears, as shown in figure 8.5.

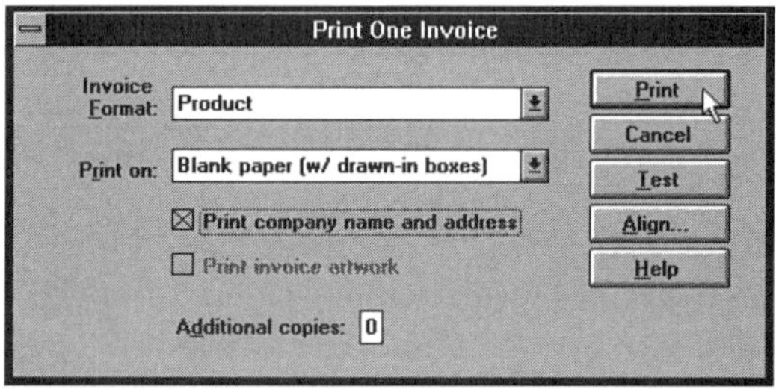

Fig. 8.5
The Print One Invoice dialog box describing an invoice to be printed in the product invoice format on blank paper with drawn-in boxes; the company name and address also are included.

In this dialog box, you can adjust some of the settings you already made for the invoice printer. Steps 3 through 7, which adjust these settings, however, are optional. If the settings you made when you set up your printer still are valid and do not need adjustment, skip to step 8.

3. (Optional) Change the format listed in the Invoice **F**ormat drop-down list box if you require a different format for this specific invoice. Steps 8 through 12 show you how to print and align a test invoice, and are optional if you do not need to check the alignment of your printing.

4. (Optional) Use the P**r**int On drop-down list to change the default form selection. (Remember that this option was chosen when you first set up your invoice printer.)

5. (Optional) Select the Print Company Name and Address check box if you want your company's name and address printed on your invoice. (This option is not available if you selected either of the Letterhead options in step 4.)

6. (Optional) Select the Print Invoice Artwork check box to print your company logo on your invoice. (This option is available only if you selected the logo option when you set up your invoice printer.)

7. (Optional) Enter in the A**d**ditional Copies text box the number of extra copies of this invoice you want to print. (This option is not available if you selected Preprinted Forms in step 3 or if that is your default selection.)

   The Print One Invoice dialog box is complete. You can now print your invoice, or you can print a test invoice. The test invoice is a dummy invoice that you can print to check your printer's alignment with paper or forms, without the risk of adding to your sales or receivables an incorrectly printed invoice. Information on the dummy test invoice is never added to your QuickBooks accounts. If you are testing the alignment of your printer and paper, it is highly recommended that you use the test invoice.

   To print the test invoice, and to check the alignment of your printing, continue with steps 8 through 12. If you are sure of your printer's alignment, skip to step 13.

8. (Optional) Choose the **T**est button. You print the test invoice to Jane Doe.

   After the test invoice is printed, the Is the Alignment OK? dialog box appears, as shown in figure 8.6.

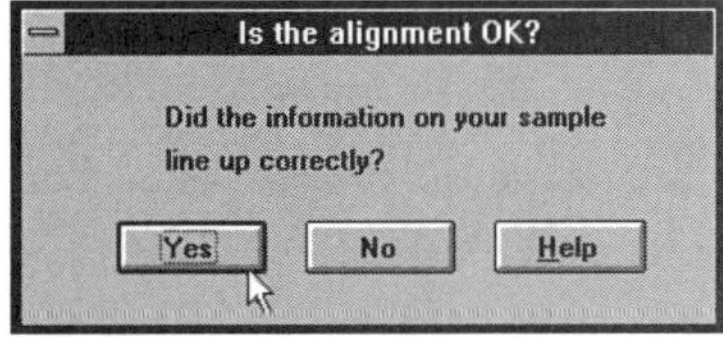

Fig. 8.6
The Is the Alignment OK? dialog box asks if the just-printed test invoice is aligned correctly.

9. (Optional) Check your printed test invoice before you choose one of the buttons in this dialog box. Check the alignment on the test printing to see whether the text is aligned within the boxes on the preprinted

invoice form or, if you use letterhead or blank paper, that the invoice is correctly centered on the page.

10. (Optional) If the test invoice is printed correctly, click the Yes button or press Enter.

If the test invoice is misaligned, click the No button. The Printer Alignment dialog box appears, as shown in figure 8.7. Notice that the shape of the mouse pointer has changed in this dialog box.

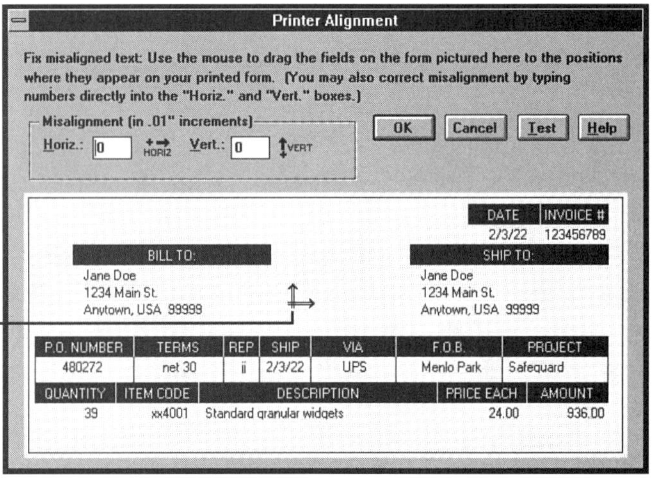

Fig. 8.7
The Printer Alignment dialog box, used to adjust where an invoice prints on the page. Notice the new shape of the mouse pointer.

Mouse pointer

11. Drag the text by clicking and holding the left mouse button, and move the text until your screen looks like your printed test invoice.

You now have a picture on-screen of the top half of the printed invoice, with all of the text misaligned just as your printed copy is. Basically, what you have done is to create a picture of your invoice so that QuickBooks knows how your printer holds paper, and how it prints. QuickBooks uses this picture to calculate the adjustments needed for your printer. These adjustments are saved when you choose OK. You will not need to adjust your printer again for an invoice, unless you change the type of invoice or printer you use.

You also can use the keyboard to make these adjustments by entering numbers into the **H**oriz text box or the **V**ert text box. The increments in these boxes are in .01 inches; this means that if you need to adjust the printing by a quarter inch, enter **25** (25 one-hundredth inches).

Alignment Problem	Make this Adjustment
Text prints too far to the right	Increase the number in the **H**oriz text box.
Text prints too far to the left	Decrease the number in the **H**oriz text box. (You can use negative numbers.)
Text prints too high	Increase the number in the **V**ert text box.
Text prints too low	Decrease the number in the **V**ert text box. (You can use negative numbers.)

Note

If the horizontal alignment (left or right) is off by more than a quarter-inch and you use a tractor feed printer, try adjusting the tractor paper clamps. Check your printer manual for details. Print another test invoice and fine-tune your adjustments with the Printer Alignment dialog box, if necessary.

12. You can check the changes you make in the Printer Alignment dialog box by choosing the **T**est button in this dialog box.

    You return to the Printer Alignment dialog box after the test invoice is printed. You can make any further adjustments that may be needed. After the alignment is correct, choose OK to save the adjustments. QuickBooks returns to the Print One Invoice dialog box.

13. Choose the **P**rint button to print this invoice.

Printing Invoices

In the preceding section, you learn how to print a single invoice. More often, however, you enter several invoices in the Create Invoices windows at one time and then print them as a batch. This saves you the time and effort involved in changing the paper in your printer for every single invoice you print.

With QuickBooks, you can print a single invoice, two or more selected invoices of a group, or all the invoices that are ready to print. As you create an invoice you can print it immediately, if you so choose, or print it at a later date. If you do not want to print invoices at this time, you tell QuickBooks that this invoice is to be printed later by selecting the To **b**e printed check box at the bottom right of the Create Invoices window, as shown in figure 8.8.

Fig. 8.8
A completed invoice shown in the Create Invoices window, with the To **b**e printed check box selected for later printing.

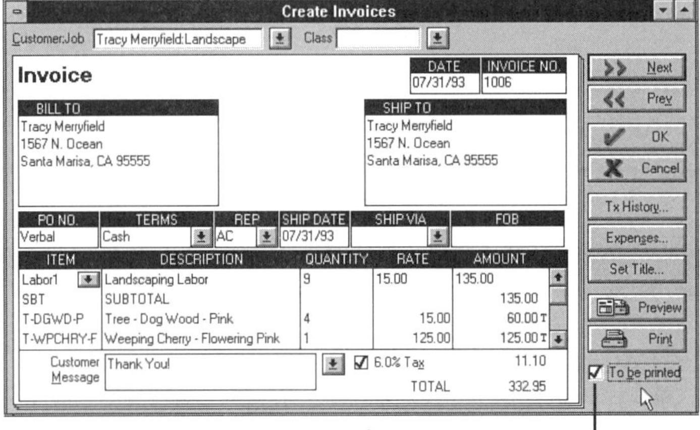

The To Be Printed check box

Selecting Invoices to be Printed

When you are ready to print the invoices that you have already created, you must decide whether to print all invoices that are ready to be printed or to select only certain invoices for printing. QuickBooks makes either option quick and easy.

To select certain invoices for printing, follow these steps:

1. From the **F**ile menu, choose Print **F**orms. The Print **F**orms menu lists a variety of forms you can print.

2. Choose Print **I**nvoices/Credit Memos. The Select Invoices/Credit Memos to Print dialog box appears, as shown in figure 8.9.

3. Select the specific A/R (Accounts Receivable) account in the A/**R** Account text box, to which the selected invoices will be added after they are printed. Type the account name, or choose from the drop-down list.

   All the invoices are selected for printing when you first open this dialog box, as indicated by the check marks in the first column.

4. Choose the Select **N**one button to deselect all the invoices, removing all the check marks from the first column. (Choose the Select **A**ll button if you change your mind and want to reselect all invoices for printing.)

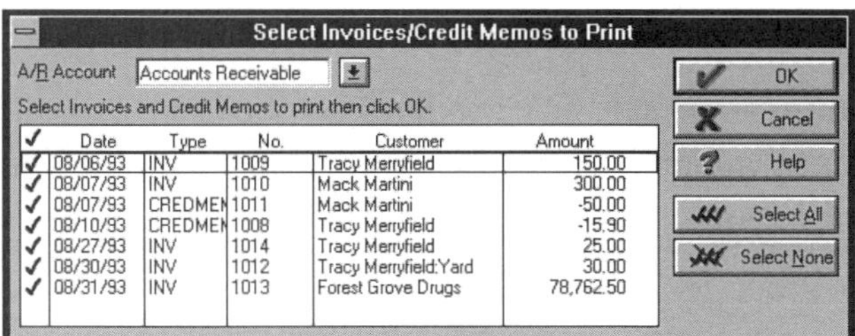

Fig. 8.9
The Select Invoices/Credit Memos to Print dialog box, listing all the invoices you can print.

5. Select the invoices to be printed from the list of invoices displayed in the dialog box by using either the keyboard or the mouse.

   Notice in figure 8.9 that the first invoice, number 1009, has a block around the entire line. Use the up- or down-arrow keys to move the selection block to another invoice. Press the spacebar to select (or deselect) the invoice marked by the selection block, placing a check mark at the beginning of the line.

   You also can select or deselect an invoice by positioning the mouse anywhere on the line for that invoice and clicking. This action both selects or deselects the invoice and moves the selection block around this invoice line.

6. After you finish making your selections, choose OK or press Enter.

7. Use the Print Invoices/Credit Memos dialog box just as you used the Print One Invoice dialog box, as described in the preceding section in this chapter. All the options and your choices are the same. Choose the **P**rint button to print the selected invoices.

Reprinting Invoices

QuickBooks provides several ways to reprint an invoice. If the invoice did not print correctly (the paper jammed in the printer, etc.), QuickBooks enables you to reprint the invoice immediately. Figure 8.10 shows the Did Invoice(s) print OK? dialog box that appears immediately after printing either invoices or credit memos.

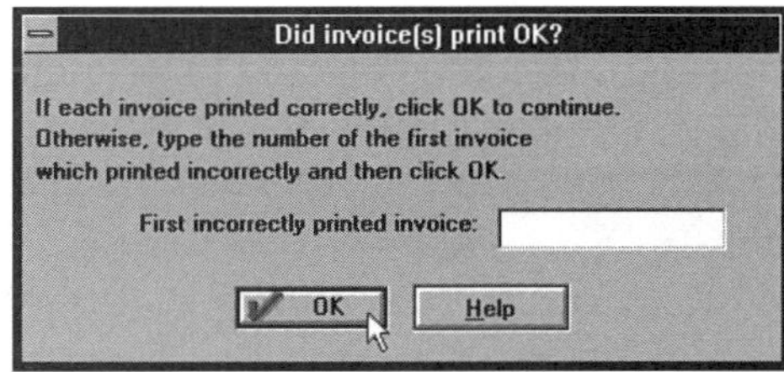

Fig. 8.10
The Did Invoice(s) Print OK? dialog box, used to reprint either invoices or credit memos.

To reprint an invoice from this dialog box, follow these steps:

1. Enter into the First incorrectly printed invoice text box the invoice/credit memo number that appears for that invoice in the Number column of the invoice list of the Select Invoices/Credit Memos to Print dialog box.

2. Click the OK button or press Enter. The invoice is added back to the list of memos to print in the Select Invoices/Credit Memos to Print dialog box.

3. Reprint the Invoice or Credit Memo by following the steps in the preceding section. Essentially, it is as if you had never printed it in the first place.

If you choose OK in step 1 instead of entering a number in the text box, QuickBooks assumes that all the invoices printed are correct and removes these invoices from the print list in the Select Invoices/Credit Memos to Print dialog box. To add an invoice back to the print list, you must display the specific invoice in the Create Invoice window, and recheck the To **B**e Printed check box. QuickBooks deselects this option when an invoice is printed. An invoice does not appear in the Select Invoices/Credit Memos to Print dialog box list if the To **B**e Printed check box is not checked.

To add an invoice back to the print list in the Select Invoices/Credit Memos to Print dialog box, follow these steps:

1. Click the Invoice button on the Iconbar; or from the **A**ctivities menu, choose Create **I**nvoices; or press Ctrl+I. The Create Invoices window appears.

2. Choose the **N**ext or Pre**v** buttons until the invoice you want to reprint appears on-screen.

3. Select the To **B**e Printed check box.

4. Choose OK. This invoice is added back to the print list in the Select Invoices/Credit Memos to Print.

   As noted in the section "Selecting Invoices to be Printed," all invoices and credit memos are automatically selected or checked for printing.

After the invoice is added back to the print list, use the steps described in the section "Selecting Invoices to be Printed," earlier in this chapter, to reprint the invoice.

Tip
Use the Edit menu's Find command to quickly jump to the invoice you want reprinted. Searching screen by screen for an invoice many numbers away from the one currently onscreen may take a while. (The Find command is described in Chapter 15, "Speeding Up Your Work in QuickBooks for Windows.")

Printing Statements

QuickBooks can print statements as well as invoices. *Statements* show a customer's account activity for a selected period of time—usually a month. QuickBooks can create a statement that displays all activity for a customer, or you can choose a statement for each job for a customer. QuickBooks creates and prints statements based on information in the Accounts Receivable register, and your selections in the Select Statements to Print dialog box. Each statement includes the following elements:

Table 8.1. Elements of a Statement

Field	Description
Statement Headings	
Date	Date the statement is created.
To	Customer's name and address.
Amount Due	Total amount owed.
Amount Enc	Space for customer to fill out when sending their payment.
Statement Body	
Date	Ending date of previous period, invoice date, payment date, or date of other activity.
Transaction	Description of the transaction. May include an invoice number, job title, payments, and credits.
Amount	Amount due or paid on each transaction.
Balance	Running total of all transactions listed.

(continues)

Table 8.1. Continued

Field	Description
Statement Footer	
Current	Portion of balance that is not past the terms granted to the customer.
1-30 Days Past Due	Amount of total due that is 1-30 days past terms.
31-60 Days Past Due	Amount of total due that is 31-60 days past terms.
61-90 Days Past Due	Amount of total due that is 61-90 days past terms.
Over 90 Days Past Due	Amount of total more than 90 days past terms.
Amount Due	Total owed by customer.

Statements can be used to remind a customer of payments due or past due. The statements can be helpful for use as an account summary, and in identifying disputed transactions. You may quickly find that some of your previously notorious slow-pay customers begin to pay their bills on time. Some companies find paying their bills by statement to be much easier because all of the transactions are listed. These companies don't have to spend the time gathering all their invoices and deciding which ones are due.

To print statements, follow these steps:

1. Choose **F**ile, Print **F**orms, Print **S**tatements. QuickBooks displays the Select Statements to Print dialog box, as shown in figure 8.11.

   The Select Statements to Print dialog box is used to choose the statements to be printed. QuickBooks creates statements based on the selections that you make, and then extracts the necessary information from the Accounts Receivable register.

2. Enter the beginning and ending dates for statements in the **D**ated Between text boxes.

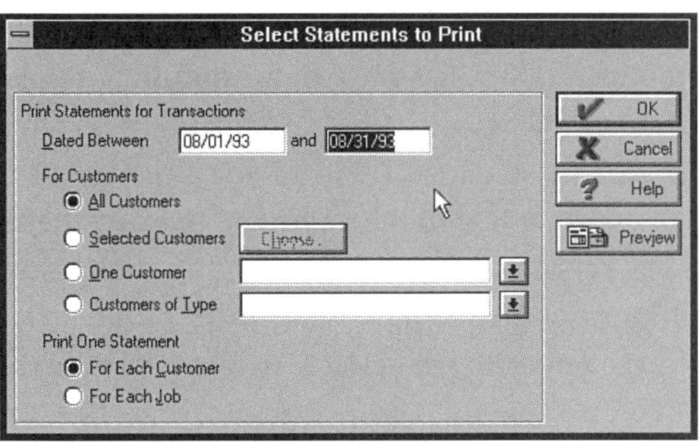

Fig. 8.11
The Select Statements to Print dialog box is used to select when and for whom to print statements.

For example, to include all transactions in the last half of July 1993, type the dates **07/15/93** and **07/31/93** in the text boxes. All outstanding invoices prior to the beginning date appear as a single Balance Forward amount. Invoices dated after the end date do not appear on the statement at all.

CPA TIP: Accounts Receivable and Your Cash Flow

Accounts Receivable, invoices on which you have extended terms or trade credit, often are a small business's largest current asset. As a small-business owner, you need to balance the total dollar amount of receivables that you carry at any one time. Monitor the terms and the aging of the receivables report. If a customer begins to carry larger receivables balances or to extend the date that payment is remitted to you, you probably need to reconsider the terms you are granting. Contact the customer; that customer may simply be having a temporary cash-flow problem or business may have suddenly increased. While we can all understand the issue of a customer with a cash-flow problem, a sudden increase in business is another matter. Just because your customer's business has increased by 25 percent and he is now buying considerably more from you, does not mean that his own cash inflows have also increased by 25 percent. He may have increased his X by granting extend terms or by lowering his prices. If his own cash inflow is slower because of either of these items, his payments to you may also suffer. You need to discover the reasons behind any unusual shift in your receivables, however, before you experience a cash-flow problem of your own.

3. Click the applicable radio button in the For Customers section. Your choices are as follows:

   - *All Customers*. This selection prints statements for all customers with outstanding invoices within the selected date range.

- *Selected Customers.* Selecting this button activates the C**h**oose button next to it. Click the C**h**oose button to display the Print Statements dialog box. Use the scrolling list box to select customers or jobs for statements. By clicking a customer's name or moving the selector box to the name and pressing the spacebar, you will see a check mark entered beside the name. This customer or job is now selected to have a statement printed. Press the OK button to return to the Select Statements to Print dialog box.

- *One Customer.* This option prints a statement for a single customer. Type the customer's name in the text box, or select the name from the drop-down list that appears when you click the down arrow next to the text box.

- *Customers of Type.* This option enables you to print statements by a selected customer type. Type the name of the customer type in the text box, or select the customer type from the drop-down list that appears after you click the down-arrow button next to the text box.

4. Select the type of statement you want to print: a single statement for each customer or a single statement for each job. Choose either of the following:

   *For Each **Customer**.* Select this option to consolidate all invoices and jobs for a customer into a single statement.

   *For each **Job**.* Prints a single statement for each job.

5. Choose the Pre**v**iew button to view the statement on-screen prior to printing. If you do not need to preview the statement, go to step 6.

6. Choose OK to begin printing your statements. The Print Statements dialog box appears, as shown in figure 8.12.

   Use the options in the Print Statements dialog box if you need to make any last-minute changes before you actually print your statements. You can change the following:

   - Select the type of paper on which the statements will be printed. By selecting the P**r**int On option, you can choose to print your statements on preprinted forms, blank paper, or letterhead.

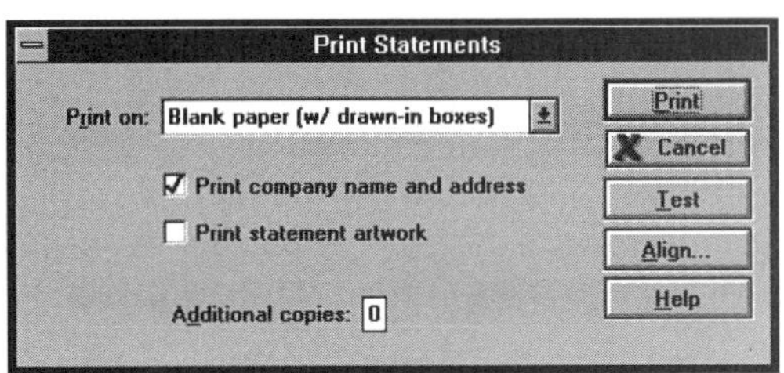

Fig. 8.12
Use the Print Statements dialog box to choose the statement form type to print on and other options.

- Choose Print Company Name and Address by placing a check mark in the box beside the option if you want to print your company's name and address on your statements. This option is available only if you have selected the Blank Paper option above.
- Check the Print Statement Artwork check box if you want QuickBooks to print your selected artwork on your statements. This option is available only if you selected a piece of artwork when you set up your statement printer, as you learned in the earlier section "Setting Up Your Printer."
- Enter a number in the A**d**ditional Copies box. QuickBooks prints the indicated number of extra copies of each statement.

7. Choose the **P**rint button or press Enter to print the statements.

Printing Mailing Labels

At various times of the year, you may want to send your customers or vendors a mailing, perhaps just to remind them you are still in business or to advertise a new service or product you now offer. QuickBooks enables you to easily print mailing labels for such times from your customer or vendor database. QuickBooks uses a standard label that comes on sheets or continuous forms. The labels are four inches by one inch, and come two labels side by side, also known as *2 up* labels.

QuickBooks also can print a set of rotary index cards for you. Although you may already have your own set of rotary index cards on your desk, how many of these cards have names and phone numbers crossed out and rewritten? By using QuickBooks, you can keep your rotary index up-to-date. If the information on a card changes, simply print out a new one.

To print mailing labels for your customers or vendors, follow these steps:

1. Choose **F**ile, Print **F**orms, Print **M**ailing Labels. The Print Mailing Labels dialog box appears, as shown in figure 8.13.

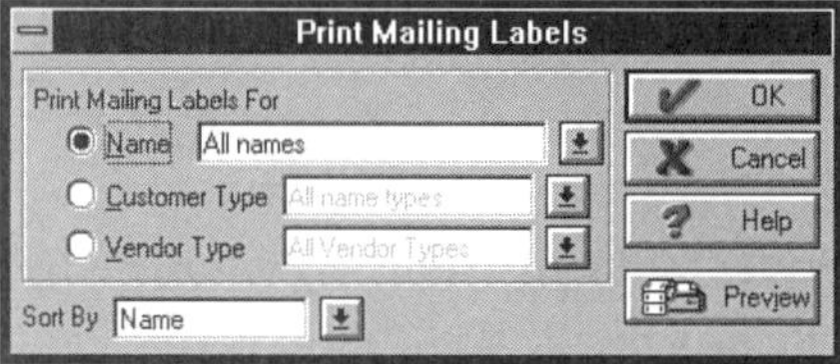

Fig. 8.13 The Print Mailing Labels dialog box, used to select individual mailing labels to print.

2. Choose one of the three radio buttons in the Print Mailing Labels For area of the dialog box to determine for whom you print the mailing labels.

   Choose the **N**ame radio button to print mailing labels by name. The default value in the text box is All Names. If you do not want to print mailing labels for all your customers or vendors, click the down-arrow button next to the text box, or press Ctrl+L, to display the Name drop-down list, as shown in figure 8.14.

Fig. 8.14 The Name drop-down list of the Print Mailing Labels dialog box.

   From this list, you can choose a specific person for whom to print a label, or you can select all customers, all vendors, all employees, or all names in the Other Names List.

   Choose the **C**ustomer Type radio button to print mailing labels for selected customers by type. Type the customer type in the text box, or click the arrow next to the text box (or press Ctrl+L) to select a customer type from the drop-down list. This option can be effective for a targeted advertising campaign.

Choose the **V**endor Type radio button to print labels for selected vendors by type. Type the vendor type into the text box, or click the arrow next to the text box (or press Ctrl+L) to select a vendor type from the drop-down list.

3. Select a sort option for your labels by clicking the arrow next to the Sort By text box (or pressing Ctrl+L) and then selecting an option from the drop-down list or by typing in the text box how you want your labels sorted.

   If you plan to use U.S. Postal Service bulk mail rates, for example, select the Postal Code Sort By option. QuickBooks then prints all your labels in ZIP/postal code order. Using this option saves you both time and money when using bulk mail rates.

   If you are not using a bulk mail postal rate, QuickBooks prints the mailing label list faster if you choose the Name option, because with this option, your database does not need to be sorted first.

4. Choose the Pre**v**iew button to view your labels on-screen before printing them. The primary reason to preview labels is to be sure that you have selected the right group if you have restricted your label selection in step 2. If necessary, reselect your group.

5. Choose the OK button to display the Print Labels dialog box, as shown in figure 8.15.

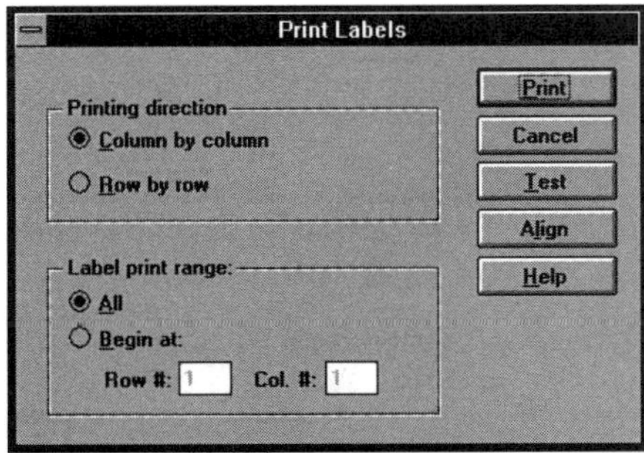

Fig. 8.15
The Print Labels dialog box, used to tell QuickBooks how to print your labels.

6. Choose one of the two radio buttons in the Printing Direction area to choose a printing direction for your labels.

Choose **C**olumn by Column to print a single wide label for each name in your selected mailing list. Each name follows the next. Labels are printed from the left column down the page and then the right column down the page.

Choose **R**ow by Row to print two names side by side across the page. Use label sheets that are two labels wide, commonly called 2 up labels.

7. Choose one of the two radio buttons in the Label Print Range area of the dialog box to determine how many labels to print.

- Choose **A**ll to print all your labels. This is the usual choice if you use a dot-matrix printer and continuous feed labels.
- Choose **B**egin At to print a range of labels that begins or ends on a partial page. This option is most commonly used if you print labels on a laser or page printer. If you use this type of label and you used a partial sheet in your last mailing label job, save it. You can use this partial page as the first page in your current mailing label print job.

  If you choose **B**egin At, enter the row number of the first label remaining on the page, starting from the top of the sheet, in the Row # text box. Enter the column number of the first label, starting from the left, in the Col # text box.

8. Choose the **P**rint button to print your mailing labels.

Print a single test label by pressing the **T**est button on the Print Labels dialog box.

QuickBooks prints a single label. Check the name and address to be sure that it is aligned correctly on your label. If it is, press the Yes button in the Is the Alignment OK? dialog box, and you will return to the Print Labels dialog box; go on to step 9. If the alignment is not OK, select the No button. The Printer Alignment dialog box is displayed. Align your label as described in the earlier section "Positioning Invoices in Your Printer." The procedure is the same for aligning labels. You can also access the Printer Alignment dialog box by selecting the A**l**ign button in the Print Labels dialog box.

Printing Rotary Index Cards

To set up your printer to print rotary index cards, follow these steps:

1. Choose **F**ile, Printer **S**etup, **L**abel Printer. The Label Printer Setup dialog box appears, as shown in figure 8.16.

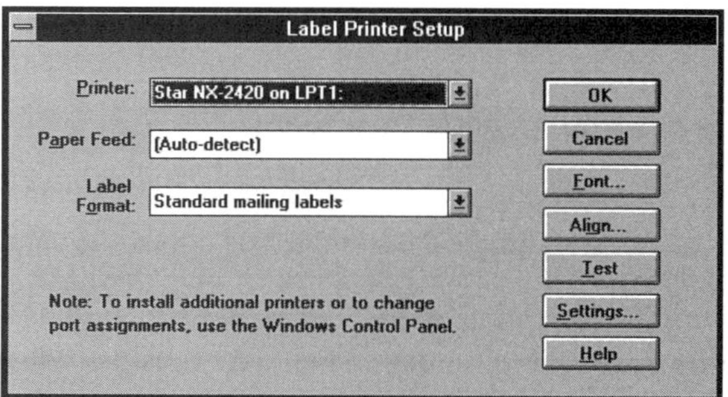

Fig. 8.16
The Label Printer Setup dialog box. From this dialog box you can set up your printer for mailing labels or rotary index cards.

2. Select from the **P**rinter drop-down list the printer you intend to use for printing rotary index cards. (Access the list by clicking the down arrow next to the Printer text box.) You also can type the name of the printer in the text box, if you know its designation, or press Alt+down arrow.

   You should not have to change the selection QuickBooks has made in the P**a**per Feed option. You should not have to adjust this unless you have an unusual printer that QuickBooks or Windows does not fully support.

3. Select the format you want from the Label F**o**rmat drop-down list. Click the down-arrow button or press Alt+down arrow to display the drop-down list, as shown in figure 8.17. This list contains the following three format options:

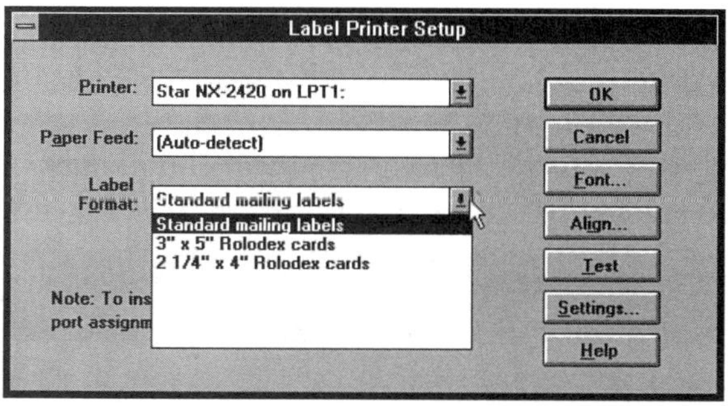

Fig. 8.17
The Label Printer Setup dialog box, with the Label Format drop-down list displayed.

II

Tracking Customers

Standard mailing labels (15/16 x 3 1/2 inches).

3" x 5" rotary index cards.

2 1/4" x 4" rotary index cards.

Select the rotary index card option that fits the size of your rotary index card holder.

4. Choose OK to save these settings.

To print rotary index cards, follow these steps:

1. To print your rotary index cards, choose **F**ile, Print **F**orms, Print **M**ailing Labels. The Print Mailing Labels dialog box appears (refer to fig. 8.13).
2. In the Print Mailing Labels dialog box, select which rotary index cards to print by using the techniques described in the preceding section on printing labels.
3. Choose the Pre**v**iew button to view your rotary index cards on-screen before printing them.
4. Choose the OK button to display the Print Labels dialog box (refer to fig. 8.15).
5. Use this dialog box to select the Printing Direction and Label Print Range options for your rotary index cards as described for labels in the preceding section.
6. Choose the **P**rint button to print your rotary index cards.
7. (Optional) If you find that your rotary index cards are not aligned correctly, you can use the A**l**ign button to access and use the Printer Alignment dialog box to adjust the alignment of your cards, as described earlier in this chapter.

Summary

In this chapter, you learned how to order supplies from Intuit. You also learned to select and print invoices and statements for your customers. Finally, you learned to create mailing labels and rotary index cards.

In the next chapter, you learn to receive customer payments and apply the payment to their accounts and to make deposits to your income accounts. You also learn to deal with customer returns and issue credit memos.

Chapter 9

Receiving and Depositing Customer Payments

In the preceding chapters, you learned to invoice your customers for services rendered and products sold. You also learned how to keep track of and collect sales taxes and how to print invoices, statements, labels, and rotary index cards.

In this chapter, you learn how to receive payments from your customers and then to create the deposit slip for your bank. By using QuickBooks for Windows, you can easily apply payments to a customer's account, apply an early payment discount, handle overpayments, and update your Accounts Receivable.

In this chapter, you learn how to do the following:

- Apply payments and early payment discounts to specific invoices
- Edit payments applied to invoices
- Create a cash sale
- Handle a customer return and issue credit memos
- Track American Express charges

CPA TIP: Why You Need an A/R Collections Policy

Accounts Receivable are considered a current asset of your business, because they are assumed to be highly liquid and to be converted to cash within one year. As a small business owner, however, your Accounts Receivable can represent a strain on your cash resources. If your business sells products, you still must pay your vendors for products you sell on credit. Even if your customers pay on time, you still must tie up your cash. As a result, meeting your own financial obligations may prove difficult. Make sure, therefore, that you maintain an effective collection policy so that your Accounts Receivable do not become a burden to your business.

Entering a Customer Payment

After you receive payments from your customers for the invoices you sent them by using QuickBooks, you can see even more clearly the value of QuickBooks to you and your business. With only a few keystrokes, you can record a payment to a customer's account, view the customer's current account balance, and obtain a list of outstanding invoices. QuickBooks enables you to handle not only a payment on an outstanding invoice, but also a down payment for future work or products.

Payments received from customers and applied to their accounts are held by QuickBooks in a special account called *Undeposited Funds*. All receipts are held in this account until deposited into your checking account.

Applying Payments to Invoices

As payment is received from customers, whether in the form of cash, checks, or credit cards, you must apply these payments to your customers' accounts. If a customer has outstanding invoices, you can choose either to pay specific invoices or to apply the payment to the oldest transactions.

Most businesses pay and receive payments for specific invoices. This system is known as *payment per invoice*. As a payment is received, it is applied directly to a specific invoice. This method is preferred because invoices that are disputed or paid short—or even overpaid—are noticed immediately and can be dealt with.

The other alternative is to receive payment for invoices in a *balance forward* system. Balance forward applies payments to the oldest invoice first, continuing to apply a payment until the entire payment has been applied. If an invoice remains partially paid, its balance will be the first one paid when the next payment is received. Balance forward is a very simple system, but it has a greater potential for inaccuracies. By automatically applying a customer's payment to the oldest invoice, you will usually never show an invoice that is past terms. What you do not show is that your customer has disputed, or paid short an invoice because of some dissatisfaction, and has not paid the invoice. For example, the following transactions are recorded in your Accounts Receivable register for a customer. The customer's Accounts Payable (the money they owe you) is also shown.

Your Accounts Receivable register shows the following:

Date	Transaction	Amount	Balance
7/1/93	INV 1000 for 10,000 Widgets	$10,000	$10,000
7/15/93	INV 1250 for 5,000	$ 5,000	$ 5,000
8/1/93	Payment received & applied to INV 1000	($ 8,000)	$ 7,000
8/15/93	Payment received & applied as:	($ 5,000)	$ 2,000
	$2,000 to INV 1000—now shows paid-in-full		
	$3,000 to INV 1250—now shows balance due of $2,000		

Your customer's Accounts Payable register shows the following transactions and notes:

Date	Transaction	Amount	Balance
7/2/93	INV 1000 for 10,000 Widgets	$10,000	$10,000
	Received only 8,000 widgets.		
	Placed missing portion in dispute.		
	Do not pay until resolved.	($ 2,000)	$ 8,000
	Vendor notified 7/3/93.		
7/15/93	INV 1250 for 5,000	$ 5,000	$ 5,000
8/1/93	Payment made on undisputed portion of INV 1000	($ 8,000)	$ 5,000
8/15/93	Payment made on INV 1250	($ 5,000)	$ 0,000
	$8,000 to INV 1000—undisputed portion		
	$2,000 to INV 1000—disputed, will not be paid until resolved		
	$5,000 to INV 1250—paid-in-full		

According to your system, your customer still owes $2,000 on invoice 1250. Your customer, on the other hand, believes that invoice 1250 is paid-in-full, and invoice 1000 is partially disputed. The balance forward system that you are using does not flag this problem, and unless your sales staff is communicating with your bookkeeper, the accounting staff may not even know about the problem the customer claims to have with the nonreceipt of some of the merchandise. Although the per invoice system may not alleviate a lack of communication, it will flag a possible problem much sooner than balance forward. Problems such as this example shows can conceivably remain hidden for months, at which time it can be very difficult and time-consuming to trace what had happened.

To apply payments to a customer's outstanding invoices, follow these steps:

1. From the **A**ctivities menu, choose Receive Pa**y**ments. The Receive Payments window appears, as shown in figure 9.1.

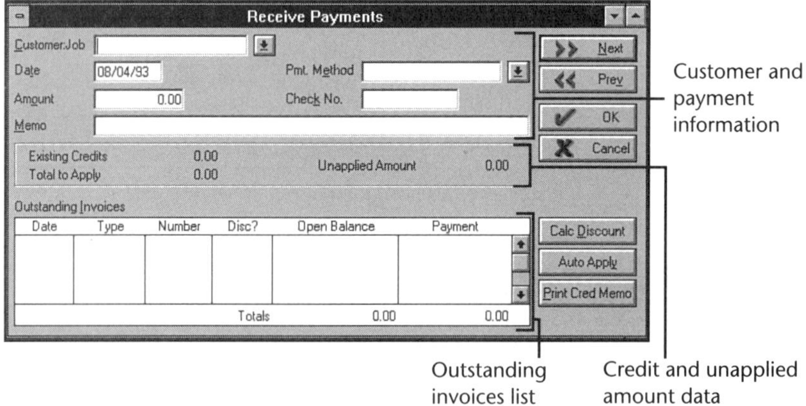

Fig. 9.1
The Receive Payments window, used to apply payments to a customer's account.

The credit and unapplied area in the Receive Payments window displays the following information:

- *Existing Credits.* Whether the customer has any existing credits due from an overpayment, return of merchandise, or a prepayment for work to be completed.
- *Total to Apply.* The amount of the payment received, plus any existing credits.
- *Unapplied Amount.* Initially, an amount identical to that given for Total to Apply. As you apply payments to invoices, however, the Unapplied Amount decreases. If a balance remains as an

unapplied amount after all outstanding invoices are paid, the balance remaining is kept by QuickBooks as a credit in the customer's account. The next time you open the Receive Payments window, this same amount appears as an existing credit.

2. Enter the customer's name in the **C**ustomer:Job text box. You also can select the Customer:job by clicking the down-arrow button next to the text box, or pressing Alt+down-arrow to display the Customer:Job drop-down list. You also can press Ctrl+L to show the Customer:Job window, and choose the Customer:job there. Press the **U**se button to select a Customer:job.

Caution

Make sure that you select the correct customer:job account. QuickBooks does not apply payments from one customer:job to a different job for the same customer. Suppose, for example, that you receive a $687.15 payment from your customer Tracy Merryfield, which pays her account in full. You have set up two job accounts for her: Yard Service and Landscaping. She owes $15 on the Yard Service job and $672.15 on the Landscaping job. If you merely choose the customer Tracy Merryfield from the drop-down list, however, the Outstanding Invoice section of the Receive Payments window remains blank. You must make sure that you break the payment up manually across the several job accounts. You will show the receipt of check number 1000 for $672.15 and apply it to Tracy Merryfield:Landscape. You will then receive check number 1000 for $15.00 again, and apply it to Tracy Merryfield:Yard Service.

3. Enter in the Date text box the date on which you received the payment. QuickBooks uses this date when calculating whether the customer is due a discount off the invoice total.

4. Enter in the Amount text box the amount of the payment received. If the amount received is larger than the total amount due, you need to determine whether the customer has other outstanding invoices in another job account.

   QuickBooks automatically applies the payment in the balance forward method, as soon as the cursor leaves the Amount text box. You will see the Auto Apply button changes labels to read Clear Pa**y**ments. The Unapplied Amount field is reduced to 0.00 if the account total has more than the check amount, or shows the remaining unapplied amount that will be carried as a credit.

5. Enter in the Pmt. Method text box the form in which the payment is received. You also can select the payment method from the drop-down list, accessed by clicking the down-arrow button next to the text box, or pressing Alt+down arrow. If the payment is not listed here, you can add it to the Payment Method List by typing the payment name in the text box. QuickBooks then displays the Payment Method Not Found dialog box. Select one of the following options:

   - *Quick Add.* This option (which is the quick method) adds the new payment method to the Payment Method List. No other information is added to the list when this option is used. If the item requires other information, you need to go to the list and add the other required information. In the case of the Payment Method, no other information is required.

   - *Set Up.* This button opens the Set Up dialog box, and you can enter all the necessary information for this particular item. In the case of a Payment Method, no other information is needed.

   - *Cancel.* This option returns to the previous text box. Use this option if you decide to select an existing option and not add a new item.

   You also can press Ctrl+L to display the Payment Method List window. Choose the payment method for this transaction, and then press the Use button to return to the Receive Payments window.

6. (Optional) Enter the check or other reference number in the Check No. text box. If you receive payment in the form of cash, you do not need to enter a reference number.

7. (Optional) Add a notation related to this payment in the Memo text box. This memo appears in your Accounts Receivable and on reports.

   QuickBooks uses the balance forward system by default and automatically applies a payment to the oldest invoice first. After the payment has been completely applied, any credits due the customer are applied to any remaining invoices. If this is the system that you are using, go to step 10 and record this transaction. If you want to apply payments using the per invoice system, continue with step 8.

8. Press the Clear Payments button to delete the automatically applied balance forward payments. QuickBooks again displays the check amount in the Unapplied Amount field.

9. Move the cursor to the Outstanding Invoices area. QuickBooks allows you to make entries only in the Payment column. To manually apply the payment to selected invoices, or partial payments to more than one invoice, enter the invoice payment amount in the same row that lists the invoice.

   Figure 9.2 shows how a $400 payment has been partially applied to an invoice. Notice that the Unapplied Amount shows $200 yet to be disbursed in the account. The memo notes that the customer wants to divide her payment between two invoices. The remaining $200 is to be applied to the next invoice. This leaves an outstanding balance on both invoices.

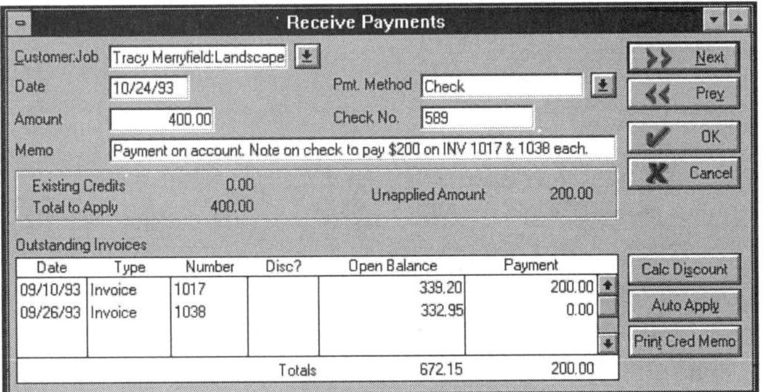

Fig. 9.2
The Receive Payments window, showing a payment that partially pays two outstanding invoices.

   If you decide to apply the previous payment in a balance forward method, you can clear the payments applied by pressing the Clear Payments button and then pressing the Auto Apply button. QuickBooks then applies $339.20 to Invoice 1017. This invoice is now paid in full. The remaining balance of $60.80 is then applied to Invoice 1038, leaving an outstanding balance to be carried forward.

10. Choose the **N**ext button to record this transaction and enter a payment in another account. Choose Pre**v** to move to a prior transaction to which you need to make adjustments. Choose OK after you finish entering all payments.

Applying Early Payment Discounts

You may want to give discounts to your customers to encourage prompt payments. Discounts for early payments are different from discounts given on an invoice. The latter discount is already accounted for in your sales figures, while the former is not. Common payment terms are as follows:

2% 10 Net 30	This means that if the invoice is paid in full within 10 days of the invoice date, the customer can deduct 2% from the total. Otherwise, the full amount is due 30 days from the invoice date.

> **Note**
>
> Use early payment cash discounts only if required in your competitive situation. If other businesses of the same type and size as yours offer a discount for early payment, you also may want to offer the same discount. If you need to speed up your own cash-flow, offering a discount for prompt payment also may help that situation. You may find, however, that discontinuing such a discount at a future date is difficult after it has been offered to a customer.

To apply a discount for early payment of an invoice, follow these steps:

1. Open the Receive Payments window, and select the customer or Customer:job in the **C**ustomer:Job text box to which the payment is to be applied.

   If you granted this customer terms that include a discount for early payment, the word `Avail` appears in the Disc? column in the Outstanding **I**nvoices block. Figure 9.3 shows a customer account with two invoices that are eligible for an early payment discount.

2. Choose the Calc **D**iscount button. The Calculate Discount dialog box appears, as shown in figure 9.4.

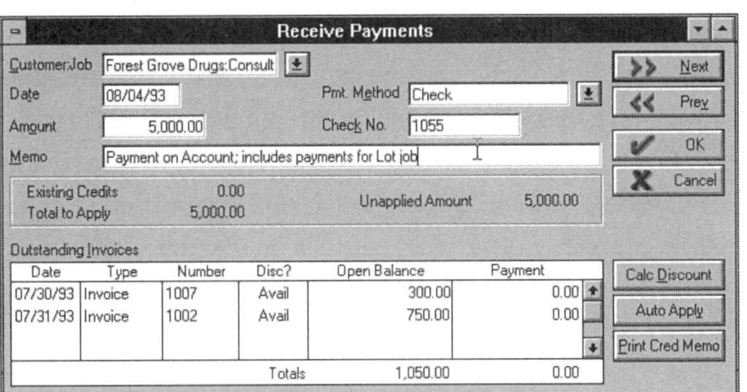

Fig. 9.3
The Receive Payments window, showing a customer who has an early payment discount available to his account.

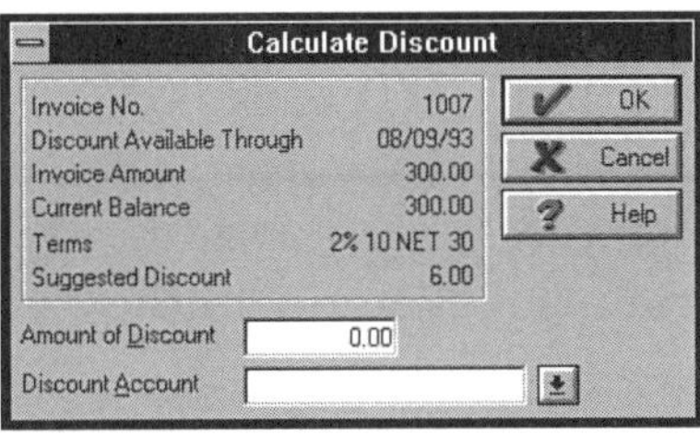

Fig. 9.4
The Calculate Discount dialog box, used to calculate and apply an early payment cash discount.

This dialog box displays information about the selected invoice or about the first invoice for which a discount is noted as being available. The information shown in the dialog box includes: the invoice number, the date through which the discount is available, the total invoice amount, the current balance of the invoice, the terms extended, and a suggested (calculated) discount that is due by these terms.

You can choose to give the customer the discount calculated by QuickBooks, to enter another amount in the Amount of **D**iscount text box, or not to grant any discount at all.

3. Enter in the Amount of **D**iscount text box the discount of `6.00` suggested by QuickBooks.

   You also can enter a greater or lesser discount by simply entering that amount into the Amount of **D**iscount text box. If you decide not to apply any discount, select the Cancel button. You will return to the Receive Payments window.

4. Enter in the Discount **A**ccount text box the account name to which to credit the discount, which you can select by typing or choosing from the account list. If you extend cash discount terms to customers,

QuickBooks sets up an account called Cash Discounts. If you prefer to use a different expense account, you can instead enter the name of that account into the text box. You also can click the down arrow next to the text box (or press Alt+down arrow or Ctrl+L) to display a drop-down list of all your QuickBooks Expense accounts and then select one from the list. You must choose an expense account for any discount that you apply. A discount is considered by QuickBooks to be an expense against your sales account.

5. Click the OK button to apply the discount. QuickBooks returns you to the Receive Payment window and applies the discount to the invoice, and the Open Balance amount of the invoice is reduced by the amount of the discount.

6. Apply the customer's payments as appropriate. After the early payment discount has been applied, you can apply the payment made by the customer to the remaining balance. Click the OK button to save the transaction.

Note

You also can use the Calculate Discount dialog box to record a bad debt. Open the Receive Payments window, select the customer or customer:job in the **C**ustomer:Job text box. Choose the invoice in the Outstanding Invoices list that is to be written off as a bad debt, and press the Calc Di**s**count button.

Enter the amount of the bad debt in the Amount of **D**iscount text box, and select the account that you use to record bad debts—for example, Bad Debt Expense—in the Discount **A**ccount text box, and then press the OK button. QuickBooks returns to the Receive Payments window. Record the bad debt by pressing the OK button.

Handling Overpayments, Down Payments, and Prepayments

If you receive a payment from a customer for more than the amount due, QuickBooks shows this overpayment as a credit balance in the customer's account. QuickBooks handles a down payment or prepayment the same way. Generally, a down payment is a partial payment in advance of work to be performed or goods to be delivered. A prepayment is usually full payment in advance of services or goods.

Overpayments generally arise in one of two ways: The customer double pays an invoice, or he does not take the early payment discount granted by the terms of the invoice. QuickBooks automatically carries an overpayment as a credit due in the customer's account. The next time you open the Receive Payments window for this customer, the credit amount appears in the Existing Credits field.

Tip

Whenever performing work for a customer before receiving payment—or special ordering for that particular customer material that cannot easily be resold to another—make sure that you always negotiate a certain percentage of the price to be paid in advance.

Note

If a customer pays an invoice early but does not take the early payment discount, you can take either of two actions: You can apply the discount, print up a credit memo, and notify the customer that he has an outstanding credit, or you can simply apply the payment in whole and not apply any discount. As a business owner, you must decide whether to notify a customer of any discount owed them. Both actions have their pros and cons.

The first choice, informing the customer of the discount, has the big plus that your customer may prefer to do even more business with you. On the negative side, you must create and mail a credit memo, and then track it within your receivables system, which will involve additional expenses to you: the cost of the credit memo, mailing fees, and additional accounting time to track the credit. These expenses are above the expense that you incurred with the early payment discount.

The second choice, not applying a discount, involves the potential negative of making customers dissatisfied with you because you did not inform them of the discount. You can, of course, tell the customers at that point that you would give them the discounts that are due, and also remind them that your invoice does indicate in the terms that the discount is available. One advantage of not informing the customers is that you will not incur the additional expenses involved with the first choice.

To record down payments and prepayments, follow these steps:

1. Open the Receive Payments window, and select the customer or customer:job account to which the monies received are to be applied, as described in the section "Applying Payments to Invoices" earlier in this chapter.

   If the payment received is a down payment for a specific job, make sure that you enter the payment into this account. Then you can easily apply the down payment to all invoices billed to this job.

2. Enter the amount of the payment, date received, the payment method, and the check number, if any, into the appropriate text boxes of the Receive Payments window.

3. (Optional) Add to the **M**emo text box a note regarding the reason for the down payment or prepayment. Although this step is optional, it is highly recommended.

4. Record the payment in the customer's account by clicking the OK button or by choosing the **N**ext or Pre**v** buttons. To print a receipt for the customer, see the section "Issuing a Credit Memo" later in this chapter.

Editing Applied Payments

If a payment has been misapplied to the wrong invoice or to the wrong customer account, QuickBooks enables you to edit the application of the payment so that you can correct the error.

Caution

QuickBooks does not allow a payment that has been deposited to be edited, unless you first reverse the deposit transaction, as discussed in the section "Editing Deposited Payments" later in this chapter. Once this is done, you can reapply a payment transaction.

To edit the application of a payment, follow these steps:

1. Open the Receive Payments window by selecting **A**ctivities, Receive Pa**y**ments from the menu.

2. Choose the Pre**v** button—and continue to choose it—until the payment transaction you need to correct appears in the window.

3. Make any adjustments necessary to correct the transaction.

   If you originally selected the wrong customer or customer:job, select the correct customer or customer:job from the drop-down list of the **C**ustomer:Job text box.

   To change the application of the payment received to different invoices, or to split the payment differently between invoices, click the Clear Pa**y**ments button. This deletes all previous applications of the payment. Now enter the payment as if this was the first time. See the section "Applying Payments to Invoices" earlier in this chapter for further details. Remember, the Clear Pa**y**ments and Auto Appl**y** buttons are toggles; when you use them, their functions change.

Adjust any other errors you may have made, such as entering the incorrect amount received, check number, date, and so on, by editing the information in the appropriate text box.

4. Click the OK button to save your changes.

Payments also can be connected directly in the Accounts Receivable register, as discussed in Chapter 10, "Using the Accounts Receivable Register," in the section "Editing Accounts Receivable Transactions."

Entering Cash Sales

You also can use QuickBooks to handle your cash sales. QuickBooks considers any sale for which you are immediately paid to be a cash sale. You can use these cash sales to summarize your daily sales. This can be especially useful if your business processes only a few sales transactions a day.

Note

Cash sales include all point-of-sale payments—checks, credit cards, or cash. Point-of-sale transactions include any sale for which you receive full payment at the time of the sale. Cash sales do not include any transaction for which you create an invoice, such as sales "on-account or terms," or sales that involve third-party finance companies. If you create a sale that involves an Accounts Receivable transaction, it is not a cash sale. If you create an invoice and an accounts receivable, you must use the Receive Payments window to record the payment received from the customer.

To create a cash sale, follow these steps:

1. From the **A**ctivities menu, choose Enter Cash **S**ales. The Enter Cash Sales window appears, as shown in figure 9.5.

   The Enter Cash Sales window is very similar in appearance to the Create Invoices window. The only differences are the title of the receipt (`Sales Receipt` instead of `Invoice`); a Sale No. field in place of the one for an invoice number; and the Check No. field replacing the PO number field.

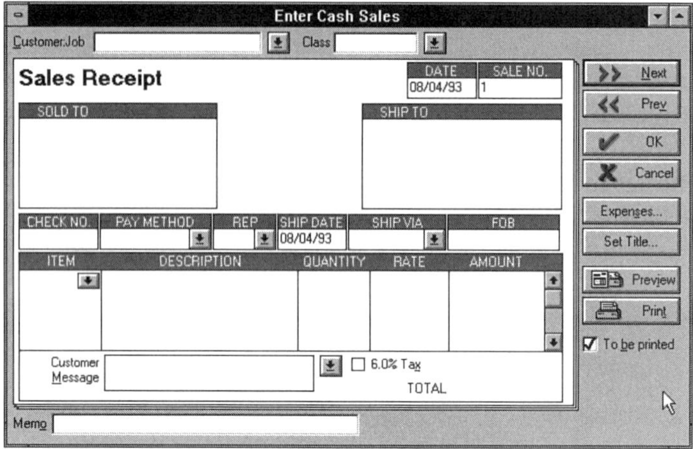

Fig. 9.5 The Enter Cash Sales window, used to create a receipt for a point-of-sale payment.

2. Enter the customer or customer:job account into the **C**ustomer:Job text box.

> **Note**
>
> The use of the Customer:Job text box is optional. Use this text box only if the sale is to a regular customer or if you want to add this customer to the database.

> **Note**
>
> If you are required to collect a sales tax on some of your line items, you may want to set up a dummy customer account for use with cash sales. You can use such a cash sale customer even if you do not have to collect a sales tax. You can add such a dummy customer account from the Enter Cash Sales window at step 2, or open the Customer:Job List by pressing Ctrl+J and using the **N**ew button to add the account. For a simple cash sale, enter the **C**ustomer text box with "Cash," the Bill to text box with "Cash Sale," and check the Ta**x**able box, if necessary. Save the new customer by choosing OK. Now when you use the Enter Cash Sales window, enter "Cash" into the **C**ustomer:Job text box. QuickBooks then fills in the Sold To text box with "Cash Sale" and checks the Ta**x** box for you.

3. (Optional) Enter in the Class text box the class of the sale. Classes can be used to further categorize your information. For example, you may have two stores. You could use class "A" for one, and class "B" for the

other. You may want to classify your customers by the advertisement that brought them to your store.

4. Enter the customer's name in the Sold To box. If you do not need the customer's name on the receipt, you can use something as simple as "Cash Sale" as a descriptive line.
5. Enter the check number in the Check No. field, if applicable.
6. Select the appropriate payment method in the Pay Method field.
7. Enter the required information in the Rep, Ship Date, Ship Via, and FOB fields, if applicable. (Remember that these fields appear only on the product type of invoice/sales receipt.)
8. Enter the line items sold, and add any discounts given, into the Item, Description, Quantity, and Rate fields. Use the same procedures that you learned in Chapter 6, "Creating Invoices."
9. Add to the Customer **M**essage text box any messages you want to appear on the sales receipt.
10. Select the Ta**x** box to apply the Auto Tax rate, if applicable.

Caution

If you must collect a sales tax, but you have not selected a customer:job account, QuickBooks does not automatically apply your primary sales tax. You must remember to check the Auto Tax check box.

11. Choose the Print button to print the Sales Receipt. The Print One Sales Receipt dialog box appears.
12. Make the appropriate selections in the Print One Sales Receipt dialog box, and then choose **P**rint. Refer to Chapter 8, "Printing Invoices, Statements, and Other Forms," for information on the options available in a Print dialog box. You are then returned to the Enter Cash Sale where you complete the print procedures.
13. Save the receipt and the sale by clicking OK or by choosing the **N**ext button to go to the next sales receipt or the Pre**v** button to select a previous transaction (if you need to make a correction).

Making Deposits

When you are ready to deposit your receipts at the bank, you must tell QuickBooks to take all—or selected—monies from the Undeposited Funds account and to add these funds to the account to which you are making your deposit.

You can deposit receipts only into a Bank type account. You may have several Bank type accounts in your Chart of Accounts, and you can deposit funds into any of them—a checking account, for example, or a money market or savings account.

To make a deposit, follow these steps:

1. From the **A**ctivities menu, choose Make **D**eposits. The Payments to Deposit dialog box appears, as shown in figure 9.6.

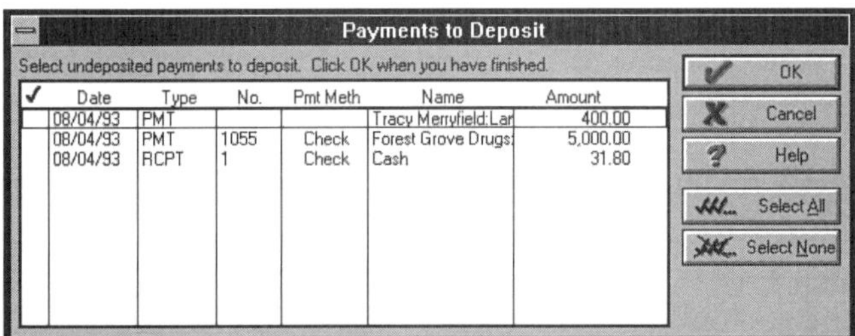

Fig. 9.6
The Payments to Deposit dialog box. This dialog box lists all payments that have been received and currently held by the Undeposited Funds account.

   The Payments to Deposit dialog box lists all payments that you have received, either through the Receive Payments window, or from the Enter Cash Sales window. As you receive money, QuickBooks automatically enters it into an account called Undeposited Funds. As you deposit money to your checking or other account, you transfer it from the Undeposited Funds account to the account to which you are making the deposit. The Payments to Deposit dialog box shows you the date on which you received each payment, type of payment, reference number, payment method, from whom you received the money, and the amount that you received.

2. Select in this dialog box the payments you want to deposit.

   Payments are selected by using the up- and down-arrow keys to move the selection box to different payments in the list and then pressing the spacebar to place a check mark in the far-left column. The payment is selected for deposit after it is checked. You also can use the mouse to select a payment by clicking once on that payment in the list.

You can select all the payments listed in the dialog box by choosing the Select **A**ll button.

Notice that all payments in this dialog originate from an invoice or from a cash sale. Monies received from other sources such as refund of deposits, tax refunds, or interest or dividends from business investments, do not appear here.

CPA TIP: Deposits and Bank Reconciliation

To make your bank reconciliation as easy as possible, group your deposits in the same categories that your bank uses. Your bank, for example, may separate deposits by checks, cash, MasterCard, and VISA. Instead of selecting everything listed in the Payments to Deposit dialog box, choose all the checks, or all the VISA deposits. Group your selections as your bank groups your deposits on your bank statement. When you go through the reconciliation process, your deposits should match the deposits that your bank lists. This method of creating your deposit can save you much time later. If you deposit all of your receipts, cash, credit cards, and checks as one lump sum, you will then have to try and match this one large amount to possibly four or more smaller deposits that your bank has categorized as your single deposit.

3. Click the OK button after you are satisfied with your selections. The Make Deposits window appears, as shown in figure 9.7. QuickBooks transfers the items that you have selected in the Payments to Deposit dialog box to the Make Deposits window.

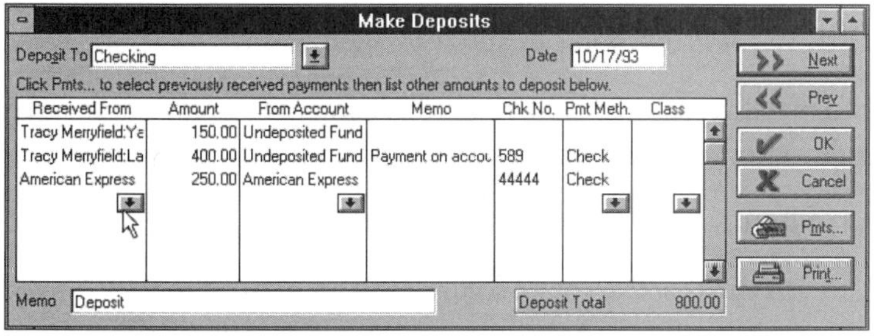

Fig. 9.7
You use the Make Deposits window to record your deposit into the accounts that are to receive the money. QuickBooks also prints a deposit slip for you.

The Make Deposits window is used to select the account to which the deposited funds will be transferred. Remember, you have selected payments from the Undeposited Funds account and will now transfer this money to a bank account. From the Make Deposits window you also can add other funds that you want to deposit to the bank account. You may receive money from an investment, or refunds from vendors and other sources, that you can now deposit. You will add these additional transactions into the detail area of the Make Deposits window. When you open the Make Deposits window, the four down arrow buttons are not displayed until you actually enter the cursor into the detail area, by either clicking the mouse anywhere in this area, or by pressing the Tab key until the first deposit transaction is selected.

4. Select from the Deposit To drop-down list the account to which you want to deposit the payment. (Remember that this must be a Bank type of account; you cannot deposit monies to an Accounts Receivable account or back to the Undeposited Funds account.)

5. Enter in the Date text box the date of the deposit. QuickBooks enters "today's" date automatically here. You can change the date if necessary. If you are actually making this deposit in QuickBooks on Saturday, but won't take it to the bank until Monday, enter Monday's date.

6. Add other deposits in the detailed area in the middle of the Make Deposits window by moving the cursor to the Received From column, positioning it below the last deposit recorded, and typing in this column the name of the payment you are depositing (or the name of the person from whom the payment was received). You also can click the down arrow button displayed, or press Alt+down arrow to display a drop-down list and select from whom this item was received. If the name is not listed, you can add it by typing it in now.

   You may list here deposits you are making of interest income, refunds from vendors, or transfers from one of your other bank accounts.

7. Enter in the Amount column the amount of the deposit.

8. Select in the From Account column the account from which the deposit is coming. This should be either another Income account, such as Interest Income, or another Balance Sheet account if you are transferring money. Type the account name, or press the down arrow button (or Alt+down arrow) to display a drop-down list that you can choose from.

9. Enter a note in the Memo field if you need it to remind you later what this specific transaction is for. Any memo that you entered for this transaction in the Receive Payment window is displayed in this field.

10. Enter the check number in the Chk No. column.

11. Enter in the Pmt Meth. column the payment method, or select from the drop-down list.

12. Select the Class type if you use classes. You can choose from the drop-down list.

13. Type a note regarding this entire deposit in the Memo text box at the bottom of the window.

    The completed Make Deposits window now appears very similar to that shown in figure 9.8.

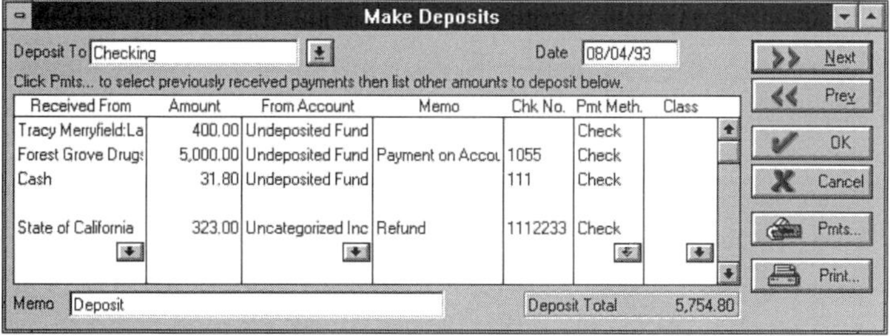

Fig. 9.8
The completed Make Deposits window.

14. Choose the Pmts button to select additional payments from the Payments to Deposit window. The Payments to Deposit dialog box is redisplayed, allowing you to choose additional payments to be included in this deposit. Repeat steps 2 and 3 in the preceding section.

    This option is especially helpful if you take your deposit to the bank every few days. You can add new receipts to the deposit slip each day until you actually go to the bank. This saves you from having to rush to get a deposit ready for the bank late in the day. When you are ready to print your deposit summary, go to step 15.

15. Select the Prin**t** button in the Make Deposit window to access the Print Report dialog box. Now select the **P**rint button in the Print Report dialog box to print your deposit summary.

You learn about the other options in the Print Report dialog box in Chapter 19, "Creating and Printing Reports."

16. Click the OK button to save the deposit transaction.

Editing Deposited Payments

Because QuickBooks does not enable you to edit a payment after it is deposited directly, you must first reverse the deposit, and then edit the payment transaction.

To edit a deposited payment, follow these steps:

1. From the **L**ists menu, choose Chart of **A**ccts (or press Ctrl+A) or click the Accounts button in the Iconbar to open the Chart of Accounts. Select from the Chart of Accounts the account to which the payment was deposited.

2. Click the **U**se Register button located at the bottom of the Chart of Accounts.

3. Select the deposit that contains the payment you want to edit, and then double-click the Account field or click the Edit/Split button. The Make Deposit window appears, listing all the transactions that make up the deposit. You also can press the Tab key until the Edit/Split button is selected and then press Enter.

4. Select the transaction in the detail area you want to edit, and then delete it from the Make Deposits window by pressing Ctrl+D or choosing **E**dit, Delete **L**ine (from the menus). The transaction is now undeposited.

   Press the OK button in the Make Deposits window. You return to the account register and the deposit transaction.

5. Edit or delete the transaction in the Receive Payments window as described in the section "Editing Applied Payments," earlier in this chapter. After the payment transaction is corrected, you can redeposit the payment in the Make Deposits window, as described in the preceding section.

Note

After you deposit a payment, you cannot change how it was applied to invoices without first reversing the deposit transaction. Once you undeposit the payment, you can reapply it as necessary and then deposit it again.

Recording Returns

Every business must deal with customer returns and canceled orders. Even if you own a service business with no inventory, a customer can cancel an order for your business's service. If you already recorded an invoice and payment—or a cash sale—for an order that is canceled or returned, you can create a credit memo or refund to reverse the transaction.

Note

When creating your customer returns policy, you must be careful to balance both customer service and your own business needs. Know your vendors' return policies before you create your own policy. After all, you do not want to take back merchandise because a customer didn't quite like the color and has used the item, and you can't return it to the manufacturer or distributor. You can go out of business very quickly by being too lenient.

Issuing a Credit Memo

As a business owner, you must keep your customers satisfied. You also must decide whether to exchange a defective product, refund the customer's money, or issue the customer a store credit. Knowing your vendor's return policies can help you make your own decisions about how to handle returns.

For any product you purchase from a vendor, for example, you need to know how long you have to return a product to the vendor, whether you must have all the packaging for the product, whether the vendor charges a restock fee, what to do about returning a defective product, and whether you need a Return Merchandise Authorization (RMA) number from the vendor before you can return an item. Remember that, for a product-oriented business, part of the cost of doing business is the cost of returns, including any costs for handling, paperwork, and time; shipping and packaging charges; and any possible restock fees. Although you must be fair to your customers, you can't let yourself be taken advantage of. If you have a fair return policy, then stick to it. Returned merchandise that you can neither return to the vendor nor resell is your money down the drain.

To record a customer return, follow these steps:

1. From the **A**ctivities menu, choose Create Credit Memos/Re**f**unds. The Create Credit Memos/Refunds window appears, as shown in figure 9.9.

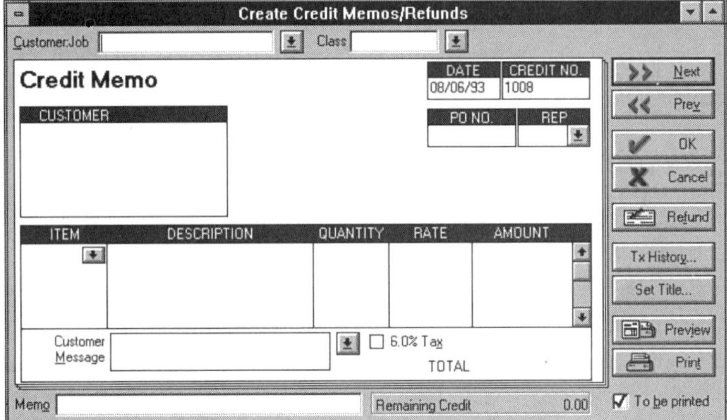

Fig. 9.9 The Create Credit Memos/Refunds window, used to record a return from a customer for a paid invoice or a cash sale.

2. Enter in the **C**ustomer:Job text box—or select from the drop-down list—the account to which this credit memo or refund is to be applied. (Optional if a refund is from a cash sale.)

3. (Optional) Enter in the Class text box—or select from the drop-down list—the class of the account, if you use classes.

   QuickBooks automatically enters today's date and the Credit No. You can change these, if required, by selecting and typing the new information.

4. Enter in the Customer area of the credit memo the customer's name and address or any other information, as necessary. If you select a customer:job account in step 2, the information in this area is filled in by QuickBooks.

5. (Optional) Enter in the Po No. and Rep fields a purchase order number, if applicable, and the initials of the sales representative, if you track sales by salesperson, respectively. These two fields are displayed only if you use the Product Invoice type.

6. Enter the line items returned. Use the same steps you learned to enter invoice line items in Chapter 6, "Creating Invoices."

Caution

If the customer returning the item does not have a receipt, make sure that you check the original invoice for the sale. You do not want to credit or refund a sale at full price if you gave the customer a discount on the original sale, nor do you want to give credit or cash back if someone did not purchase the item from you.

7. (Optional) Enter in the Customer **M**essage text box a note about the credit or return if you plan to print a credit memo for the customer. You may want to print a message telling the customer that a refund will be mailed, a `We're sorry` message, or some other type of message.
8. (Optional) Enter in the Mem**o** text box a note about the credit or return. This note does not print on the credit memo but appears in your Accounts Receivable register. This note could refer to the original invoice number, or some private note about the transaction that you do not want printed on the credit memo.
9. Choose the Prev**i**ew button to view the credit memo before printing it.
10. Choose the Prin**t** button to access the Print One Credit Memo dialog box, and then print the Credit Memo, as described in Chapter 8, "Printing Invoices, Statements, and Other Forms." The procedure is the same.
11. Save the transaction by clicking the OK button or by choosing the **N**ext or Pre**v** buttons, if you are creating another credit memo or editing a previous one.

If you plan to write a refund check for this credit/return, you can do so easily. By choosing the Ref**u**nd button in the Create Credit Memos/Refunds window, QuickBooks displays the Write Checks window. You see a completely filled out check displayed on-screen. In Chapter 13, "Writing and Printing Checks," you learn all about using the Write Checks window. For now, simply record this check by choosing the OK button in the Write Checks window. You then return to the Create Credit Memos/Refunds window.

Voiding an Invoice

If you have not yet received a payment on an invoice, you may want to consider voiding the invoice. If you void an invoice, QuickBooks retains the transaction but makes a notation that it has been voided in the Mem**o** text box and changes the amount to $0.00.

To void an invoice, follow these steps:

1. Open the Create Invoices window, and then choose the Pre**v** button to display the invoice to be voided.

2. From the **E**dit menu, choose **V**oid Invoice.

   Your invoice now displays zeros in the amount column for all line items, and QuickBooks enters the note `VOID` into the Mem**o** field. If you already entered a note in the Memo field, QuickBooks places the void notation in front of your note.

   If you find that you voided the wrong invoice, access the **E**dit menu and choose **R**evert. The transaction reverts to how it was before you voided it.

   Caution

   The **R**evert option works only if you notice your mistake before saving the transaction again. After you click the OK, **N**ext, or Pre**v** buttons, you cannot unvoid the transaction.

3. Click the OK button or choose the **N**ext or Pre**v** button to save the voided transaction.

Tracking American Express Charges

American Express, unlike VISA and MasterCard, maintains its own payment and service bureau. You cannot simply deposit your American Express charge slips with your bank; you must send them to American Express for payment. The company then sends you a check for the amount of charge slips that you have sent, less its fees.

To track American Express charges, you first must create an account in the Chart of Accounts to record American Express transactions. To create this account, follow these steps:

1. Open the Chart of Accounts, and select the **N**ew account button.
2. Enter in the **T**ype text box (or select from the drop-down list) **Other Current Asset** as the account type.
3. Enter in the Name text box (or select from the drop-down list) **American Express** as the name of the account.
4. Enter in the Description text box **Due from American Express** as the description.
5. (Optional) Enter in the Bank No. text box your merchant number.
6. Enter in the Opening Balance text box the amount that American Express currently owes you.
7. Enter the date in the next text box.
8. Press the OK button. You return to the Chart of Accounts window. Your new account also is highlighted.

Using American Express and Cash Sales

If a customer uses an American Express card to pay for purchases, you do not receive the cash immediately as you do if payment is made by VISA or MasterCard.

To record an American Express payment of a cash sale, follow these steps:

1. Add a cash sale as described in the section "Entering Cash Sales," earlier in this chapter, by using the Enter Cash Sales window.
2. Enter **American Express** as the payment method for the sale, in the Pay Method field.
3. Complete the cash sale, enter the necessary line items, and save the transaction.

In a sale that is invoiced, you needn't be concerned about the form of the payment because there is no payment option in the Create Invoice window. Merely record the transaction as usual. When you receive the customer's payment, simply select American Express as the payment method.

> **Note**
>
> If you know that a customer uses an American Express card (or another credit card) to pay invoices, consider whether you want to extend payment terms that offer an early payment discount. If you give the customer a 2% discount for early payment and then you are charged by the bank—or by American Express—another 1% to 3% credit-card fee, you are in effect giving a much greater discount than you may have anticipated.

Handling the American Express Deposit

When you are ready to send your charge slips to American Express, put together your normal American Express invoice and charge slip bundle, and send it off.

To deposit the charge slips in QuickBooks, follow these steps:

1. From the **A**ctivities menu, choose Make **D**eposits to open the Payments to Deposit dialog box (refer to fig. 9.6).
2. In the Payments to Deposit dialog box, select all payments that are noted in the Pmt Meth. column as American Express, and then choose OK to open the Make Deposits window (refer to fig. 9.7).
3. Select from the Deposit To drop-down list the American Express account as the account to which payment is deposited.
4. Enter in the Date text box the date on which you mail the deposit.
5. Choose OK to save the transaction.

After you receive your payment from American Express for the charge slips you sent, you deposit the payment to your bank account. Because you do not actually receive the full amount recorded in your American Express account, follow these steps:

1. Open the Make Deposits window, as described in steps 1 and 2 of the preceding steps.
2. Select from the Deposit To drop-down list the account in which you are depositing the check received from American Express. (This is most likely your checking account; it is *not* your American Express account.)
3. Enter **American Express** in the Received From column or select from the drop-down list. If you have not yet entered American Express as a vendor, do so now.

4. Enter the total amount due from American Express; this amount is *not* the amount of the check received.

5. Enter **American Express** in the From Account column.

6. Enter a memo in the Memo field, if needed for your records.

7. Enter the check number, payment method, and class in the appropriate columns.

8. Start a new line to record the credit card fee taken by American Express by entering **American Express** again in the Received From column.

9. Enter in the Amount column the amount of the credit card fee. Make sure that you enter this as a negative number.

10. Enter **Credit Card Fee** in the From Account column. You are not required to fill in the remaining fields in this portion of the transaction.

11. The Deposit Total field should now equal the check you received. Figure 9.10 shows how the Make Deposits now appears.

12. Choose OK to save the transaction.

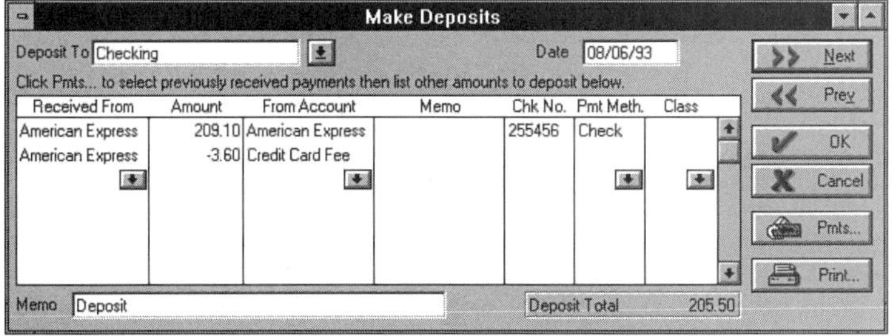

Fig. 9.10
The Make Deposits window, showing a payment received from American Express.

Summary

In this chapter, you learned how to apply customer payments and discounts to invoices and how to handle overpayments and down payments. You also learned how to enter cash sales and make deposits. You then learned how to record customer returns, issue credit memos, and track American Express payments.

In the next chapter, you learn how to use the Accounts Receivable register and how to edit, delete, or void Accounts Receivable transactions. You also learn how to view an Accounts Receivable Transaction History, use QuickReport to view a customer's records, add customer notes, and print the Accounts Receivable register.

Chapter 10

Using the Accounts Receivable Register

In earlier chapters of Part II, "Tracking Customers," you worked with QuickBooks transactions that affect your Accounts Receivable account. For many small businesses, Accounts Receivable may be one of the largest current assets on the Balance Sheet. Accounts Receivable are the monies owed to you by customers to whom you have sold goods or services. QuickBooks keeps track of that money by entering a transaction in the Accounts Receivable register each time you write an invoice, create a credit memo, apply a discount to an invoice, or deposit a payment from a customer.

In this chapter, you learn how to do the following:

- Display and move around the Accounts Receivable register screen
- Edit and delete transactions from the Accounts Receivable register
- View a transaction history
- Create a report about a customer with QuickReport
- Add customer or job notes
- Print the Accounts Receivable register

Displaying the Accounts Receivable Register

The Accounts Receivable register is a listing of all the transactions that have occurred when you have invoiced a customer for goods or services. Cash sales don't go through the Accounts Receivable account; they go directly to the Income Account "Sales," and the money received goes to the Undeposited Funds Account. Each time you create an invoice, receive payment on an invoice, or apply a discount to an invoice, you create a new transaction entry in the Accounts Receivable register. The Accounts Receivable register is similar to the Sales Tax Payable register, which you learned about in Chapter 7, "Tracking Sales Tax."

To open the Accounts Receivable register, follow these steps:

1. Open the Chart of Accounts by choosing the Accnt button from the Iconbar; choosing Lists, Chart of Accounts; or pressing Ctrl+A.

2. Choose the Accounts Receivable account from the list, and select the Use Register button. You now see the Accounts Receivable register on-screen, as shown in figure 10.1.

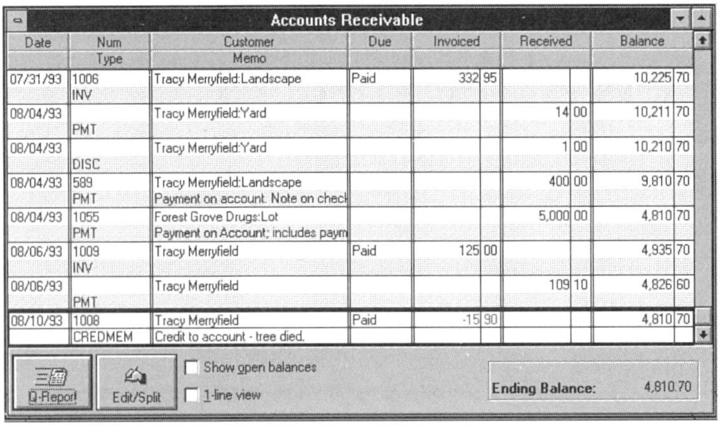

Fig. 10.1
The Accounts Receivable register displayed in the standard two-line view.

Accounts Receivable

Date	Num / Type	Customer / Memo	Due	Invoiced	Received	Balance
07/31/93	1006 INV	Tracy Merryfield:Landscape	Paid	332 95		10,225 70
08/04/93	PMT	Tracy Merryfield:Yard			14 00	10,211 70
08/04/93	DISC	Tracy Merryfield:Yard			1 00	10,210 70
08/04/93	589 PMT	Tracy Merryfield:Landscape / Payment on account. Note on check			400 00	9,810 70
08/04/93	1055 PMT	Forest Grove Drugs:Lot / Payment on Account; includes paym			5,000 00	4,810 70
08/06/93	1009 INV	Tracy Merryfield	Paid	125 00		4,935 70
08/06/93	PMT	Tracy Merryfield			109 10	4,826 60
08/10/93	1008 CREDMEM	Tracy Merryfield / Credit to account - tree died.	Paid	-15 90		4,810 70

Q-Report | Edit/Split | Show open balances | 1-line view | Ending Balance: 4,810.70

Reviewing the Accounts Receivable Register

The Accounts Receivable register (often simply called A/R) is where all invoiced sales are recorded. The Accounts Receivable register includes a transaction line for each invoice, payment, credit memo, and deposit transaction. The Accounts Receivable register is a listing of the various transactions; you can't enter or edit a transaction from the register. QuickBooks does, however, allow you to access the window from which a transaction originated, so that you can edit or delete a transaction.

The Accounts Receivable register is made up of several parts. Table 10.1 lists these parts and their contents:

Table 10.1. The Accounts Receivable Register

Field	Contains
Date	The date the transaction was entered into QuickBooks.
Num	The reference number of the transaction. This field may be blank. If you do not enter a reference of some type in the check number field in the Receive Payments window, the payment displays a blank field in the Accounts Receivable register. The Receive Payments window was discussed in Chapter 9, "Receiving and Depositing Customer Payments."

Field	Contains
Type	The type of transaction. Some of the codes in the Accounts Receivable register are as follows:
	INV refers to an invoice.
	PMT refers to a payment.
	CREDMEM refers to a credit memo.
	DISC refers to an early payment discount applied to an invoice.
	CHK refers to a check being paid, usually a refund check in the case of the Accounts Receivable register.
Customer	The customer name and/or job listing.
Memo	A message that you enter into the memo field of an invoice, credit memo, or Receive Payments window if you entered one.
Due	The date that an invoice is due. When the invoice is paid, the field displays the word `Paid`, instead of the date.
Invoiced	The amount that was invoiced or credited to an account.
Received	The amount that was paid.
Balance	A running total of all transactions. This balance figure shows the running total, as of the transaction on that line.
Ending Balance	The current balance as of the latest transaction.

The Accounts Receivable register also includes two buttons and two check boxes, as follows:

Button	Function
Q-Report	Displays a report listing all transactions for a selected customer.
Edit/Split	Allows you to edit a selected transaction. The transaction appears in the window from which it was created.

Check boxes	Function
Show **O**pen Balances	Select this box to display only open balances remaining on all transactions in the register.
1-Line View	Select this box to display the Accounts Receivable register in a 1-line per transaction view. This is handy when you want to view many transactions quickly.

You learn more about Q-Report and Edit/Split later in this chapter.

QuickBooks normally displays the register in a two-line format—with the first line in white, and the second line in a color—and shows all invoiced and received amounts, as shown in figure 10.1. Selecting the Show **O**pen Balances check box displays a register like the one shown in figure 10.2, and selecting the **1**-Line View check box displays a register like the one shown in figure 10.3.

Accounts Receivable

Date	Num / Type	Customer / Memo	Due	Invoiced	Received	Balance
07/30/93	1007 INV	Forest Grove Drugs:Consult	08/29/93	300 00		300 00
07/31/93	1000 INV	Tracy Merryfield:Yard / Opening balance	Paid			315 00
07/31/93	1001 INV	Tracy Merryfield:Landscape / VOID: Opening balance	Paid			315 00
07/31/93	1002 INV	Forest Grove Drugs:Consult	08/30/93	750 00		1,065 00
07/31/93	1003 INV	Forest Grove Drugs:Lot	Paid			1,595 00
07/31/93	1004 INV	Forest Grove Drugs:Lot	07/31/93	3,480 00		9,545 00
07/31/93	1005 INV	Forest Grove Drugs	07/31/93	347 75		9,892 75
07/31/93	1006 INV	Tracy Merryfield:Landscape	Paid			10,225 70

Q-Report | Edit/Split | ☑ Show open balances | ☐ 1-line view | Ending Balance: 4,810.70

Fig. 10.2
The Accounts Receivable register with the Show **O**pen Balances checked.

Accounts Receivable

Date	Num	Customer	Due	Invoiced	Received	Balance
07/30/93	1007	Forest Grove Drugs:Consult	08/29/93	300 00		300 00
07/31/93	1000	Tracy Merryfield:Yard	Paid	15 00		315 00
07/31/93	1001	Tracy Merryfield:Landscape	Paid	0 00		315 00
07/31/93	1002	Forest Grove Drugs:Consult	08/30/93	750 00		1,065 00
07/31/93	1003	Forest Grove Drugs:Lot	Paid	530 00		1,595 00
07/31/93	1004	Forest Grove Drugs:Lot	07/31/93	7,950 00		9,545 00
07/31/93	1005	Forest Grove Drugs	07/31/93	347 75		9,892 75
07/31/93	1006	Tracy Merryfield:Landscape	Paid	332 95		10,225 70
08/04/93		Tracy Merryfield:Yard			1 00	10,224 70
08/04/93	Cash	Tracy Merryfield:Yard			14 00	10,210 70
08/04/93	589	Tracy Merryfield:Landscape			400 00	9,810 70
08/04/93	1055	Forest Grove Drugs:Lot			5,000 00	4,810 70
08/06/93	1009	Tracy Merryfield	Paid	125 00		4,935 70
08/06/93		Tracy Merryfield			109 10	4,826 60
08/10/93	1008	Tracy Merryfield	Paid	-15 90		4,810 70

Q-Report | Edit/Split | ☐ Show open balances | ☑ 1-line view | Ending Balance: 4,810.70

Fig. 10.3
The Accounts Receivable register with the **1**-line view box checked.

Notice that all amounts, except outstanding balances, have been hidden. This view is especially useful to quickly scan the register, looking for open balances that are large amounts. This can be faster than creating a report. An open balance refers to an amount that is still owed, whether this be an invoice or a credit memo. When Show Open Balances is selected, QuickBooks suppresses the display of any amount in either the Invoiced or Received columns that nets to a zero amount, or reduces an amount to the net value. For example, you have some transactions like the ones in the following table listed in your Accounts Receivable register, and displayed in an abbreviated form without Show Open Balances checked:

Type	Customer	Invoiced	Received	Balance
INV 100	Company A	100.00		100.00
INV 101	Company B	200.00		300.00
PMT	Company A		100.00	200.00
INV 102	Company A	150.00		350.00
PMT	Company B		100.00	250.00

Once Show Open Balances is selected, QuickBooks displays the register as shown in the following table:

Type	Customer	Invoiced	Received	Balance
INV 100	Company A			100.00
INV 101	Company B	100.00		300.00
PMT	Company A			200.00
INV 102	Company A	150.00		350.00
PMT	Company B			250.00

Now, you quickly can see the balances that are still outstanding without having to create a report or try to visually match invoices to payments on-screen.

By hiding the type and memo fields, this view becomes useful by not showing as much detail. You can then display a greater number of transactions.

You also can combine both of these options, displaying a single line for all transactions, and displaying only the open balances by selecting both options.

Moving around the Register

QuickBooks makes it easy to move around in the Accounts Receivable register. The selected transaction is surrounded by a black-lined box, and the colored line becomes white.

You can use several methods of moving the selection box to another transaction. If you can see the transaction on-screen, simply place the mouse pointer on the transaction and click. The selector box jumps to the selected transaction. You can also use the up- or down-arrow keys to move the selector box. If you have a large distance to move, such as several months of transactions, use the vertical scroll bar on the right side of the window. Click and drag the scroll box on the scroll bar up or down the scroll bar. Up moves the selector box to past transactions, and down moves to current transactions. As you drag the scroll box, you will notice the pop-up date box that appears as shown in figure 10.4. As you quickly scroll through the transactions, the date changes in the box. This helps to give you an idea of where you are in the register. Once you release the mouse from the scroll box, the register shifts to display the portion of the register that you have selected.

Fig. 10.4
Scrolling through the Accounts Receivable register and the pop-up date box.

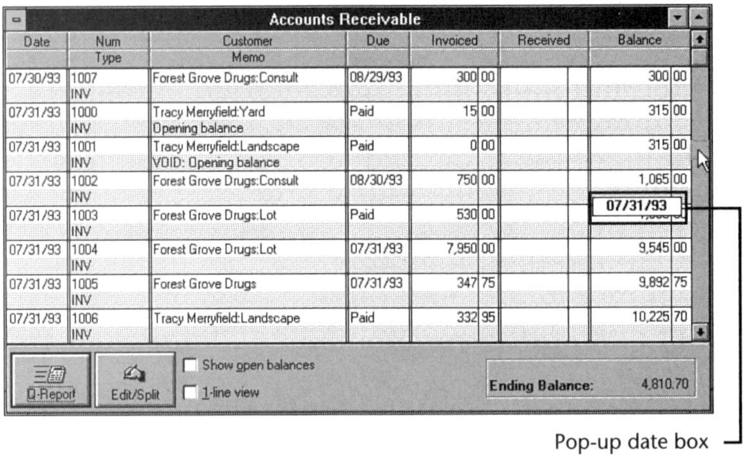

You can also use the keyboard to move through the register. Table 10.2 lists the keyboard strokes and tells how you can use them to move about in the register.

Table 10.2. Keyboard Movement Keys

Press These Keys	To Move
Up arrow	Up one transaction
Down arrow	Down one transaction
PgUp (Page Up)	Up one screen of transactions
PgDn (Page Dn)	Down one screen of transactions
Ctrl+PgUp	To the beginning of the previous month of transactions
Ctrl+PgDn	To the beginning of the next month of transactions
Ctrl+Home, or Home+ Home+Home+Home	To the beginning of the register
Home+Home+Home	To the beginning of screen
Ctrl+End, or End+ End+End+End	To the end of the register
End+End+End	To the end of the screen

Editing Accounts Receivable Transactions

The Accounts Receivable register is a listing of all the transactions that you have created. You cannot edit an Accounts Receivable transaction directly in the Accounts Receivable register. QuickBooks allows you to edit a transaction from the window in which it was created.

To edit an Accounts Receivable transaction, follow these steps:

1. Open the Accounts Receivable register by selecting it in the Chart of Accounts and either double-clicking it or pressing the Use Register button.

2. Select the transaction to be edited. Move the selection box—with the mouse or keyboard—until the transaction you want to edit is selected.

3. Edit the selected transaction by doing one of the following:

   - Double-click the transaction with the mouse.
   - Select the Edit/Split button.
   - From the Edit menu, choose Edit (transaction type). The name of this specific option varies depending on the transaction that you have selected: Edit Payment, Edit Invoice, or Edit Credit Memo.
   - Press Ctrl+E.

   Depending on the transaction you are editing, QuickBooks opens the window where the selected transaction originated. Selecting an invoice transaction opens the Create Invoice window, and a payment transaction opens the Receive Payments window.

4. Make the necessary changes, and choose OK. Another window asks you to confirm that you do want to make the changes. Choose Yes to record the changes.

Deleting Accounts Receivable Transactions

You cannot delete a transaction directly from the Accounts Receivable register. You can, however, use the Accounts Receivable register to access the window from which you originally created the transaction. You can delete the transactions from there.

A credit memo or invoice can be deleted, but a payment transaction can be deleted only if it has not yet been deposited. Once a payment transaction is deposited, you must first reverse the deposit from the bank account, and then remove the payment transaction from the deposit. You can then delete the payment transaction. You learned to edit and delete both payments and deposits in Chapter 9, "Receiving and Depositing Customer Payments."

To delete an invoice or credit memo, follow these steps:

1. Select the transaction to be deleted in the Accounts Receivable window.
2. From the Edit menu, choose Delete Invoice, Delete Credit Memo, or Delete Payment (or press Ctrl+D).

Note

Confirmation dialog boxes require you to affirm one more time that you do indeed want to delete the transaction. Usually, you will see one of two types of confirmation dialog boxes. The first asks if you are sure that you want to delete the transaction. The second tells you that deleting this transaction may affect other transactions. If you are deleting an invoice, and payments have been applied to it, QuickBooks tells you that payments have been applied to the invoice and that deleting this invoice will cause the payments to be unapplied. This would cause a credit to appear in the customer's account. Otherwise, you are simply asked if you are sure that you want to delete this invoice. Deleting a payment transaction displays a confirmation dialog box informing you that the payment has been applied to invoices and that deleting the payment will cause the invoice to have unpaid balances.

3. Delete the transaction by choosing OK. You return to the Accounts Receivable register. Selecting Cancel returns you to the Accounts Receivable register without deleting the transaction.

CPA TIP: Deleting Invoices and Bad Debt Expenses

When an account becomes a bad debt and is uncollectible, you must write off the Accounts Receivable. A bad debt is accrued when you determine a debt, usually an Accounts Receivable, is no longer collectible. You may receive notification of a customer's filing for bankruptcy, or you find the customer no longer seems to exist. In Chapter 9, "Receiving and Depositing Customer Payments," you were shown a method of charging off a bad debt, and in order to keep your bookkeeping correct, it is highly recommended that you use this method. By deleting an invoice, you no longer have a record of it, and so would have a difficult time if the debt became collectible at a later time. Moreover, deleting an invoice can also cause your various financial statements to be misstated. Your sales and bad debt expense (or other account you use for bad debt transactions) will be understated, because you deleted this invoice, and your inventory will be overstated. Any payments that you may have received from this transaction also will be unapplied.

If for some reason you must delete several invoices, or a single very large invoice, you may want to examine your allowance for doubtful accounts. If you do not now have an allowance for doubtful accounts, see your CPA for help to set up one. This account is used to estimate the value of the accounts that will become bad debts throughout the year. Usually the amount is based on an estimated percentage of your total Accounts Receivable for the year. This ensures that your Accounts Receivable balance is not overstated due to any bad debts that you have not charged off of your Accounts Receivable.

Viewing a Transaction History

A history of a transaction can be viewed from the Accounts Receivable register. A transaction history displays a summary of a selected transaction and all related transactions in the Accounts Receivable register. QuickBooks displays the transaction's history in chronological order. Table 10.3 lists the transaction history that QuickBooks displays.

Table 10.3. Transaction History Displayed

Transaction Type	Related Transactions Displayed by Transaction History
Invoice	Payments applied to the invoice
	Payments with invoice (payment invoice item)
	Deposits of payments with invoice
	Discounts applied for early payment
	Credit memos
Payment	Invoices that the payment has been applied
	Credit memos created by QuickBooks for overpayments
	Deposit transactions that include the payment
Deposit	Payments included in the deposit transaction
Credit Memos	Invoices paid by the credit
Discount	Invoices that the discount is applied
Cash Sale	Deposit that includes the payment

To view the transaction history, follow these steps:

1. Select the transaction whose history you want to view, and from the Edit menu, choose Transaction History (or press Ctrl+H). The Transaction History dialog box appears, as shown in figure 10.5.

2. Choose Edit Invoice to edit the original transaction. The title of this button varies depending, again, on the transaction that you are viewing.

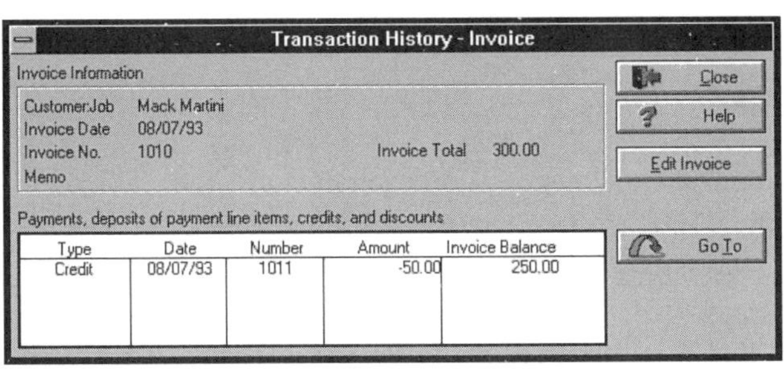

Fig. 10.5
The Transaction History - Invoice dialog box. The actual name of the window varies depending on the history of the transaction you are viewing.

3. Choose the Go To button to open the window of the selected history item, in the transaction history item list. If there are several items in this list, use the up- and down-arrow keys to select the item that you want to view.

4. Choose Close to return to the Accounts Receivable register.

Both the Create Credit Memos and Create Invoices windows contain a Tx History button; as you can see in figure 10.6, this button also allows you to view the transaction history. Use this button only when viewing the invoice or credit memo from the Accounts Receivable register. If you use this button when you create the invoice or credit memo, you will see a window pop-up telling you that there is no transaction history for this item. After all, you haven't finished the item, nor received a payment on it.

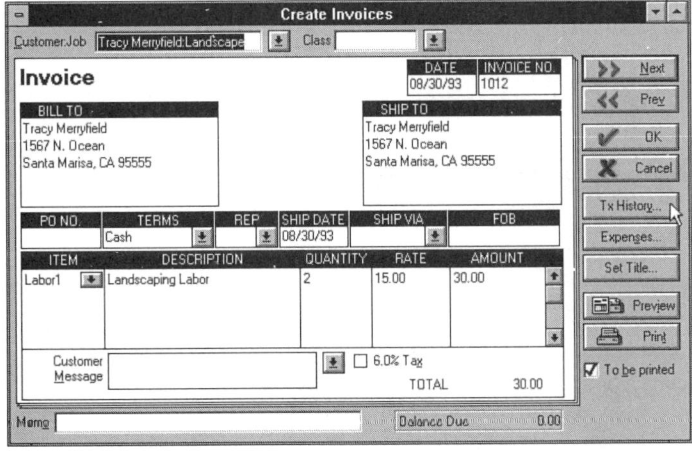

Fig. 10.6
In the Create Invoices window, notice the Tx History button shown with the mouse pointer on it. Selecting this button displays the Transaction History dialog box.

Using QuickReport To View Customer Records

With QuickBooks' QuickReport, you can select a specific customer or customer:job, and view the report on-screen. The report shows all the related transactions, including any unpaid balances, and the customer total.

To use QuickReport, follow these steps:

1. Open the Accounts Receivable register. Select the customer/ customer:job transaction you want to view more closely.

2. Choose Q-Report. A report like figure 10.7 appears on-screen.

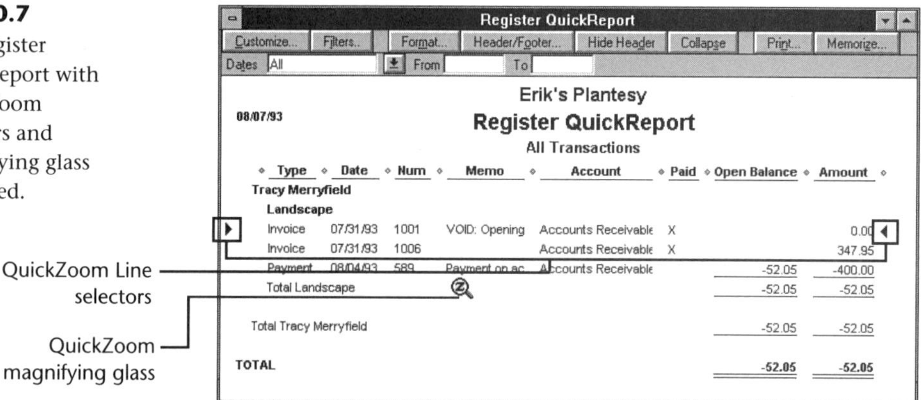

Fig. 10.7
The Register QuickReport with QuickZoom selectors and magnifying glass displayed.

3. Use the window control button to close the window.

Note

Within the QuickReport window, you can use the special QuickBooks function called QuickZoom. When the mouse cursor changes shape to a magnifying glass with the letter Z on the glass, you can double-click an item and view the original transaction. You can also access QuickZoom from the keyboard. The two black triangles, shown in figure 10.7, indicate the selected line. Use the up- or down-arrow keys to select a line, and then press the Enter key.

Adding Customer or Job Notes

QuickBooks furnishes you with a Notepad in which you can keep notes about customers or jobs. The Notepad can be accessed any time you have a customer or job transaction.

To use the Notepad, follow these steps:

1. Open a customer or job transaction.

   This can be an invoice, credit memo, payment window, or the Accounts Receivable register. If you are using the Accounts Receivable register, select a transaction related to the job about which you want to create or view a note.

2. Choose **E**dit, N**o**tepad. You will see the Notepad displayed, as shown in figure 10.8.

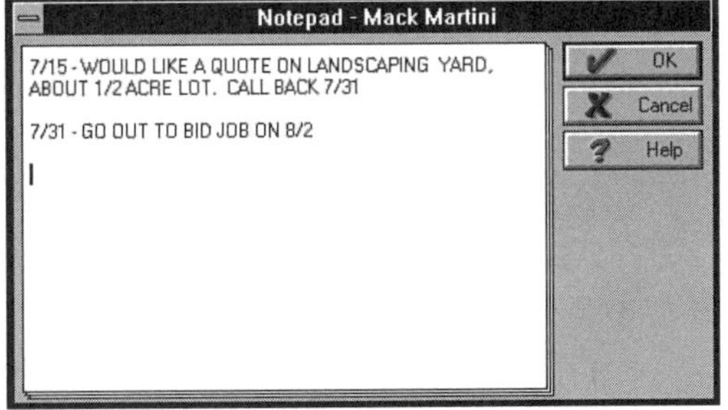

Fig. 10.8
Use the Notepad in the QuickBooks Notepad dialog box to enter notes regarding a job, payments, or other notes.

3. Type the note as you would in a word processor.

4. Choose OK to save the note. Use the Cancel button to quit without saving your note, or to delete the changes that you have made to the note. Either choice returns you to the window that you were in.

Note

Within the notepad, you can use both the mouse and keyboard to move around and to edit the text.

With the QuickReport window displayed, you can scroll up and down through the report. If the report is wider than your screen can display, you can use the left- and right-arrow keys to scroll the screen sideways. The report's title, date, and field titles, or header, are all shown at the top of the screen. As you scroll down the information, the header information does not move. The QuickReport window is also equipped with several buttons at the top of the window. These options are fully discussed in Chapter 19, "Creating and Printing Reports."

Printing the Accounts Receivable Register

At times you will need a printed copy of your Accounts Receivable register, perhaps to give to your accountant. You can print a copy of the entire Accounts Receivable register or specify a time period to be included.

To print a copy of the Accounts Receivable register, follow these steps:

1. Open the Accounts Receivable register.
2. Choose File, **P**rint Register (or press Ctrl+P). The Print Register dialog box appears, as shown in figure 10.9.

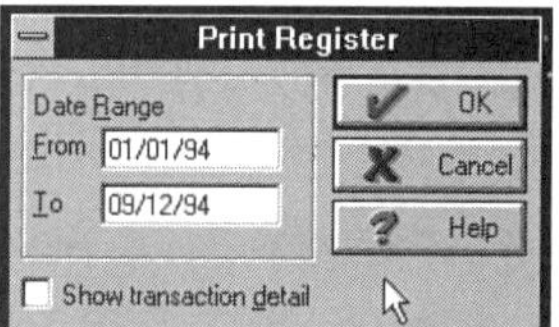

Fig. 10.9 Use the Print Register dialog box to select a range of dates if you need only a portion of the register printed.

3. Enter the beginning and ending dates for the period that you want to print. The default dates shown are the first of the year, and the current date.
4. Select the Show transaction detail check box if you want to see the maximum detail.
5. Choose OK. Select **P**rint from the Print Report window. Figure 10.10 shows the Accounts Receivable register without detail, and figure 10.11 shows the register printout with detail.

As you can see from figures 10.10 and 10.11, the printouts of the Accounts Receivable register can be quite different. Use the form that makes the most sense for your needs.

```
                              Register                          08/07/93
Accounts Receivable Register through 08/07/93:
Date      No.     Payee     Memo    Account         Amount C      Balance

07/3... 1007    Forest...           -split-          300.00        300.00

07/3... 1000    Tracy ...  Ope...   Sales             15.00 X      315.00
07/3... 1001    Tracy ...  VOI...   -split-            0.00 X      315.00

07/3... 1002    Forest...           -split-          750.00      1,065.00
07/3... 1003    Forest...           -split-          530.00      1,595.00

07/3... 1004    Forest...           -split-        7,950.00      9,545.00
07/3... 1005    Forest...           -split-          347.75      9,892.75

07/3... 1006    Tracy ...           -split-          347.95     10,240.70
08/0...         Tracy ...           Undeposi...       -1.00     10,239.70

08/0... Cash    Tracy ...           Undeposi...      -14.00     10,225.70
08/0... 589     Tracy ...  Pay...   Undeposi...     -400.00      9,825.70

08/0... 1055    Forest...  Pay...   Undeposi...   -5,000.00      4,825.70
08/0... 1009    Tracy ...           -split-          150.00      4,975.70

08/0...         Tracy ...           Undeposi...     -109.10      4,866.60
08/0...         Mack M...           Checking                     4,866.60

08/0...         Mack M...           Credit C...                  4,866.60
08/0... 1010    Mack M...           -split-          300.00      5,166.60
```

Fig. 10.10
The Accounts Receivable register without detail.

```
                              Register                          08/07/93
Accounts Receivable Register through 08/07/93:
Date      No.     Payee     Memo    Account         Amount C      Balance


07/3... 1007    Forest...           -split-          300.00        300.00

             Uncategorize...  Consultiing Fees       300.00
                              Landscaping Esti...


07/3... 1000    Tracy ...  Ope...   Sales             15.00 X      315.00


07/3... 1001    Tracy ...  VOI...   -split-            0.00 X      315.00

             Sales            Landscaping Labor        0.00
                              SUBTOTAL                 0.00

             Sales            Tree - Dog Wood ...      0.00
                              SUBTOTAL                 0.00

             Sales Tax Pa...  Sonoma County Sa...      0.00
             Cash Discounts   Discount on Invoice      0.00


07/3... 1002    Forest...           -split-          750.00      1,065.00

             Uncategorize...  Consultiing Fees       750.00
                              Landscaping Esti...
```

Fig. 10.11
The Accounts Receivable register with detail.

Summary

In this chapter, you learned to display the Accounts Receivable register and move around on-screen within the register. You learned to edit and delete an Accounts Receivable transaction. You also learned to view a transaction history, use QuickReport, use the Notepad, and print the Accounts Receivable register.

In the next part of this book, you learn the various aspects of paying your bills using QuickBooks.

In the next chapter, you learn to enter bills, change the calculated pay date, enter credits from vendors, and use reminders to pay bills.

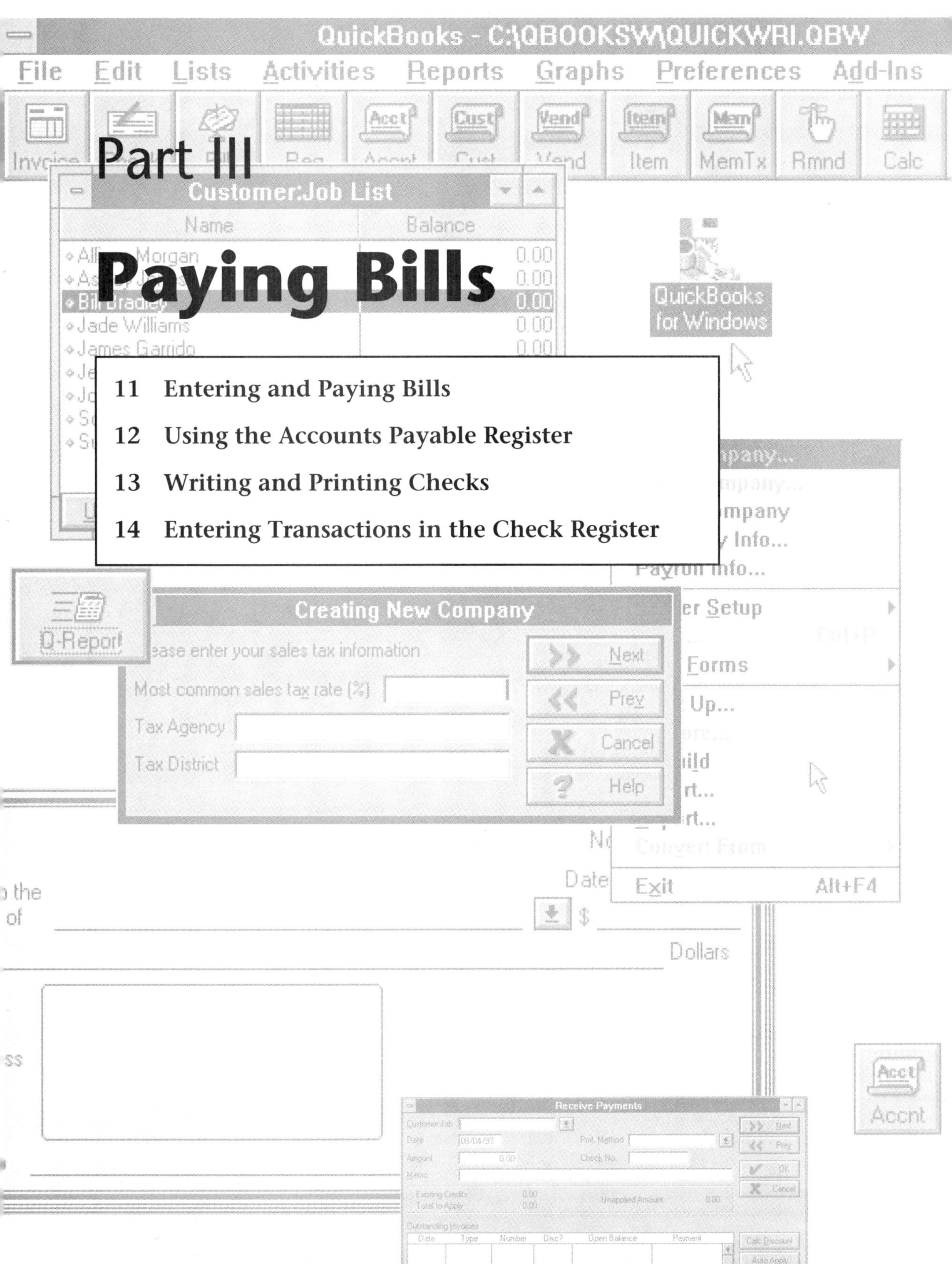

Part III

Paying Bills

11 Entering and Paying Bills

12 Using the Accounts Payable Register

13 Writing and Printing Checks

14 Entering Transactions in the Check Register

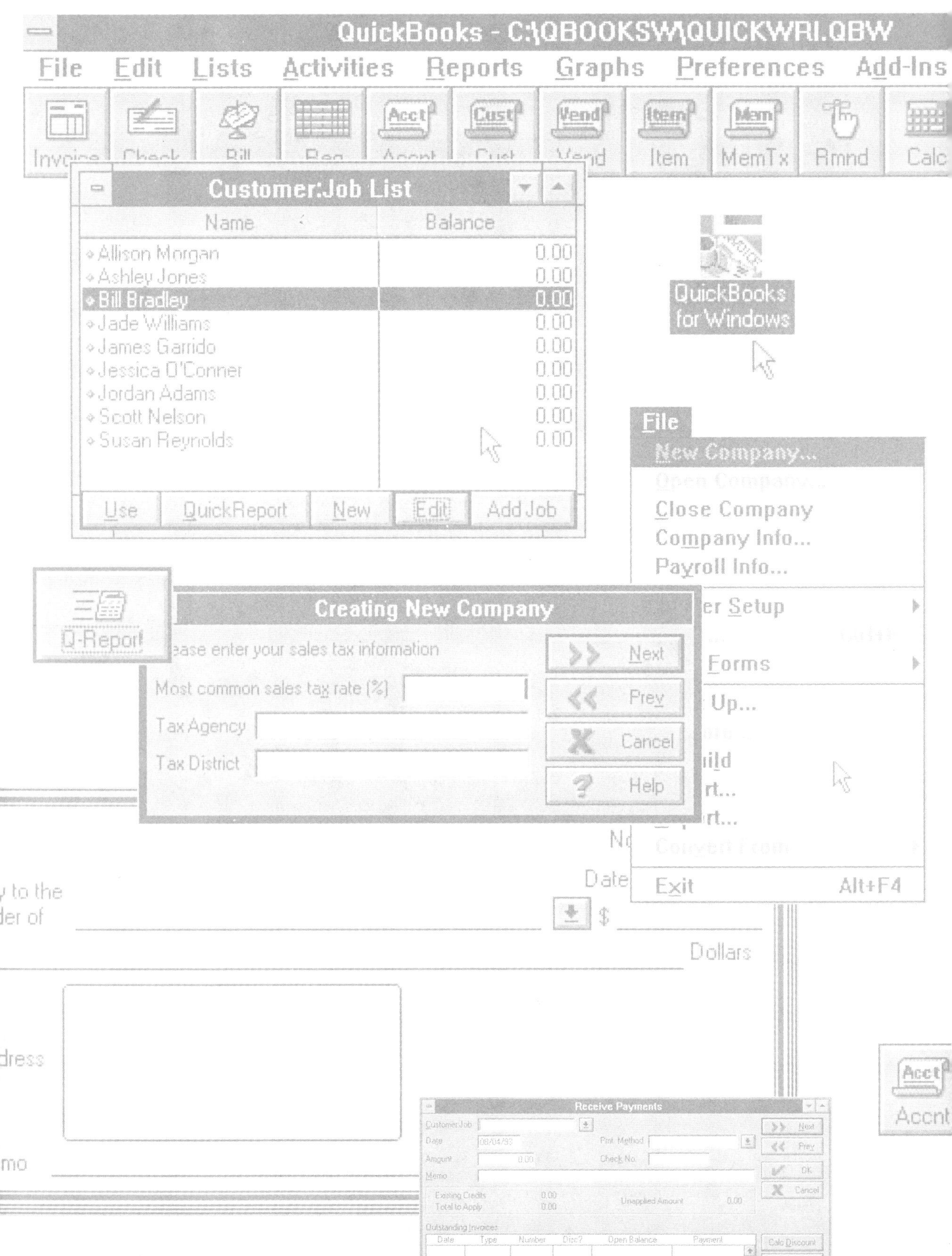
QuickBooks - C:\QBOOKSW\QUICKWRI.QBW
File Edit Lists Activities Reports Graphs Preferences Add-Ins
Invoice Check Bill Reg Accnt Cust Vend Item MemTx Rmnd Calc
Customer:Job List
Name Balance
Allison Morgan 0.00
Ashley Jones 0.00
Bill Bradley 0.00
Jade Williams 0.00
James Garrido 0.00
Jessica O'Conner 0.00
Jordan Adams 0.00
Scott Nelson 0.00
Susan Reynolds 0.00
Use QuickReport New Edit Add Job
QuickBooks for Windows
File
New Company...
Close Company
Company Info...
Payroll Info...
Exit Alt+F4
Q-Report
Creating New Company
Most common sales tax rate (%)
Tax Agency
Tax District
Next
Prev
Cancel
Help
Dollars
Receive Payments
Acct
Accnt

Chapter 11

Entering and Paying Bills

All businesses have bills that must be paid. Even a small-home business, a service business, or professional business buys services of some type, and probably office supplies. Services purchased may include office rent, utilities, and janitorial services. If you are in a product type of business, you also purchase inventory to sell to your customers, machinery to use in the manufacture of goods, and possibly freight services. The bills that you owe to vendors are liabilities and are included on your balance sheet as Accounts Payable, usually referred to as A/P.

You can set up QuickBooks to remind you when bills are due for payment, helping you take advantage of any early payment discounts that your vendors offer, and avoid any additional charges for late payment. You can easily apply vendor credits to outstanding bills, and QuickBooks can help you project your anticipated cash outflows from your business.

In this chapter, you learn how to do the following:

- Enter bills for payment
- Change the calculated pay date
- Add credits from vendors
- Use reminders to pay bills

Entering Bills

QuickBooks for Windows makes entering bills a snap. From a single screen, you can enter a bill into the Accounts Payable register, set the date it is to be paid, and assign the bill to an Expense account, a customer:job, and a class.

Use QuickBooks to enter your bills as you receive them. QuickBooks then tells you when they are due. QuickBooks also helps you forecast your projected cash flow, so that you can use your money to your best advantage—such as taking advantage of early payment cash discounts.

CPA TIP: Taking Advantage of Early Discounts

If a vendor offers terms that include a cash or sales discount, it is to your advantage to use these discounts. Businesses that fail to take discounts are not using their money wisely. A company that takes a 2 percent discount for paying an invoice within 10 days is effectively earning an interest rate of 36.5 percent. To arrive at this figure, divide the number of days that you must pay early in order to get the discount (20 days) by the number of days in a year (365 days), then divide the interest rate (2% = .02) by the number that you have from the previous calculation.

For example, you receive an invoice from a vendor for $1,000.00. The terms of this invoice are 2 percent 10 net 30, meaning that you can take a 2 percent discount from the invoice if you pay it within 10 days or pay the full amount within 30 days. If you do decide to pay the invoice before the tenth day, you will have a cash outlay of only $980.00, saving you $20.00.

If you always pay your bills when you receive them, you can continue to do so. See Chapter 13, "Writing and Printing Checks," to learn how to write and print checks to pay your bills. Remember to deduct any discounts.

To enter a bill into QuickBooks' Accounts Payable register, follow these steps:

1. Choose the Bill button from the Iconbar; or from the **A**ctivities menu, choose Enter **B**ills. The Enter Bills window appears, as shown in figure 11.1.

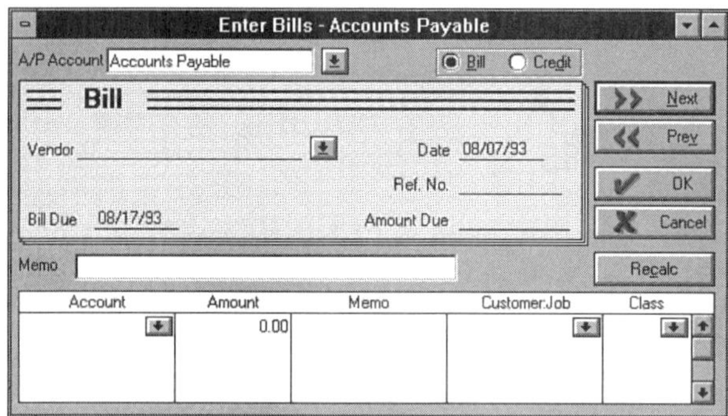

Fig. 11.1
Use the Enter Bills window to add bills to the Accounts Payable register.

2. In the A/P Account text box, enter the A/P Account to which you want to assign this bill.

   If you have a single Accounts Payable register, type in the account name.

If you use multiple accounts, or have created subaccounts for Accounts Payable, use the down-arrow button, or Alt+down-arrow to display the drop-down list; then select the account from the list. Pressing Ctrl+L displays the Chart of Accounts with all of the Accounts Payable type accounts listed.

3. Select the **B**ill option button. You learn about the Cre**d**it option later in this chapter in the section "Entering Credits from Vendors."

4. In the Vendor field, enter the vendor from whom you have received the bill. If the vendor is in the Vendor List, you can select the vendor from the drop-down list.

   Remember, you also can use QuickBooks' QuickFill to help enter the vendor name. Type the first letter, or first couple of letters of the vendor name. QuickBooks matches your entry and fills in the vendor name. If the first letter does not provide the match, type the second or third letter, and QuickBooks continues to match what you enter to the next vendor in the Vendor List. If you are entering a new vendor, QuickBooks gives you the option to **S**etUp or **Q**uick Add the vendor.

   The **S**etUp option displays the New Vendor dialog box, enabling you to enter all vendor information, such as address, phone number, and terms. **Q**uick Add, on the other hand, only enters the vendor's name in the Vendor List.

   You manually have to add the address and other vendor information in the Edit Vendor dialog box. If you do not want to take the time to enter this information now or if it is not available to you, **Q**uick Add allows you to enter the vendor name and continue with entering the bill.

5. Move to the Date field. QuickBooks automatically fills in today's date. You can enter another date in this field by typing it over today's date. You also can use the keys in the following table.

Key	Function
+	Adds one day to the date each time you press it.
–	Subtracts one day from the date each time you press it.
W	Changes the date to the first date of the current week (Sunday). Pressing W a second time changes the date to the previous Sunday.

(continues)

(continued)

Key	Function
K	Changes the date to the last date of the current week (Saturday). Pressing K a second time changes the date to the next Saturday.
M	Changes the date to the first day of the month. Pressing the M key again changes the date to the first day of the previous month.
H	Changes the date to the last day of the current month. Pressing H again changes the date to the last day of the next month.
Y	Changes the date to the first day of the current year. Pressing Y again changes the date to the first day of the previous year.
R	Changes the date to the last day of the current year. Pressing R again changes the date to the last day of the next year.
T	Changes the date to today's date.

6. Enter the vendor's invoice or statement number into the Ref No. field. QuickBooks displays this number in the Accounts Payable register, and on any reports that include this transaction.

7. Enter the due date for the bill; use the keys listed in step 5 to adjust the date. QuickBooks automatically enters a date based on the settings that you have entered in the **P**references menu. You learn more about this in the section "Using Reminders To Pay Bills."

   QuickBooks uses this date to calculate when to remind you that the bill should be paid.

8. Enter the amount of the bill in the Amount Due field, but do not add dollar signs. QuickBooks doesn't require that you enter trailing zeros. The following table gives entry examples.

Enter	QuickBooks Displays
131.54	131.54
275	275.00
31.2	31.20

9. (Optional) In the Memo text box, enter a note about the bill. This note will appear in the Accounts Payable register and in any reports that include this transaction. This could be as simple as a note about what you bought with this bill.

In the detail portion of the Enter Bills window, you can assign the bill to an Expense account, or you can prorate the bill to several Expense accounts if the bill covers a variety of items. You also can assign the bill to various customer or customer:job accounts if some of the bill is a reimbursable expense. You can then add the reimbursable expenses to the customer's invoice.

1. In the Account field in the detail portion of the Enter Bills window, enter the Expense account to which you want to assign this bill. You can use several lines to assign the bill to multiple Expense accounts. You can also press the down-arrow button (or Alt+down-arrow) to display a drop-down list of Expense accounts. If you want to select an Asset account, scroll up the list.

CPA TIP: Be Sure To Classify Accounts Correctly

Discuss with your accountant whether to assign a bill to an Expense or to an Asset account. Inventory items for resale should be properly classified in a Current Asset account, not in an Expense account.

2. In the Amount field, enter the amount of the bill to be added to this Expense account.
3. (Optional) In the Memo field, enter a memo describing this specific expense. This is for your own use and does not appear anywhere else.
4. (Optional) In the Customer:Job field, enter the Customer:Job account. You can use this field to keep track of the jobs for which you bought materials, and you can add this expense to a later customer invoice as a reimbursable expense.
5. (Optional) In the Class field, enter the Class for this transaction.

   Figure 11.2 shows a completed Enter Bills window. Notice that the total amount of this bill has been prorated among two Expense accounts and two Customer:Job accounts.

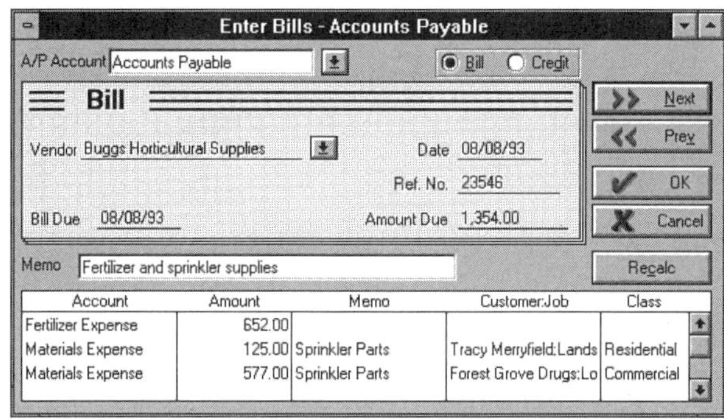

Fig. 11.2
This completed Enter Bills window has a single vendor bill that has been allocated to two Expense accounts and two Customer:Jobs. Notice how Material Expense is used on two lines to allow the allocation to the two Customer:Jobs.

6. Choose OK to save the transaction. You can also use the **N**ext button to save this transaction and open the next blank Enter Bills window. Do this if you are entering several bills at one time. The Pre**v** button enables you to go to a bill you have previously entered, letting you view or edit the transaction. Choosing OK returns you to the desktop.

   If the amount that you have entered in the expense distribution does not match the total in the Amount Due field, QuickBooks displays a Warning dialog box, as shown in figure 11.3. Choose OK, and recheck your figures in the detail distribution voucher. You may have made a data entry error in the Amount column. QuickBooks does not allow you to record a transaction whose Amount Due and expense distribution do not match each other.

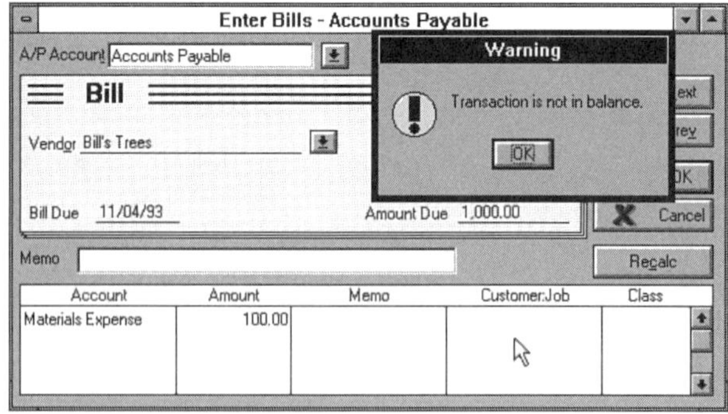

Fig. 11.3
This QuickBooks Warning dialog box tells you that this transaction is not in balance. Notice that the Amount Due is $1,000.00, and the expense is for $100.00.

Caution

The Enter Bills window also contains a button labeled Recalc. This button recalculates the Amount Due field to match the distribution of your expenses. If you have a vendor's invoice in front of you as you enter this bill, you can see the total amount at the bottom of the invoice. You don't want to make an accidental error in your expense distribution of a $100, or a $1000, and have QuickBooks recalculate the Amount Due field with the amount that you entered in your distribution. It is highly recommended that you do not use the Recalc button in the Enter Bills window. You will find the Recalc button in other windows, where it does have its uses, but not in this window.

Changing the Calculated Pay Date

When you initially install QuickBooks for Windows, bills are calculated as being due 10 days from the date received, or the date entered into the Accounts Payable. If you find that you often change the Bill Due field in the Enter Bills window, you may want to change the QuickBooks default setting.

To change the number used to calculate a bill's due date, follow these steps:

1. From the **P**references menu, choose **T**ransactions. The Transaction Preferences dialog box appears (see fig. 11.4).

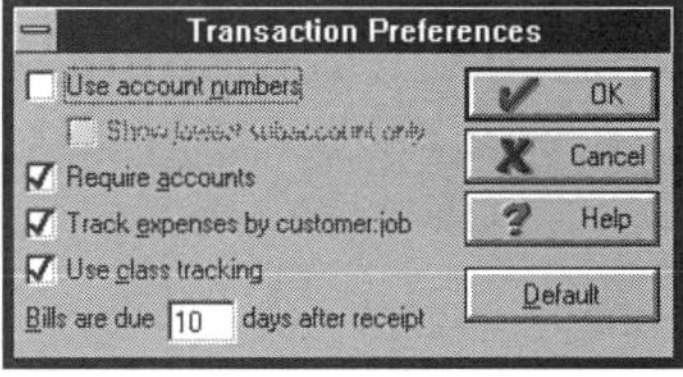

Fig. 11.4
Use the Transaction Preferences window to make selections about your account name/numbering system, and whether accounts are required.

2. Choose **B**ills are Due XX Days After Receipt and enter the number of days you require. If you generally find that your bills are due 25 days from the day that you receive them, for example, enter 25. The default setting is 10 days.

3. Choose OK to save your settings. QuickBooks now uses the new number to calculate the day that a bill is due.

Paying Bills

When you are ready to pay the bills you have entered, you only have to tell QuickBooks which bills to pay, and whether or not to pay the entire bill.

To pay bills, follow these steps:

1. From the **A**ctivities menu, choose **P**ay Bills. The Pay Bills window appears (see fig. 11.5). From this window you can choose the account from which to pay bills, which bills to choose, and the amount to pay on a bill.

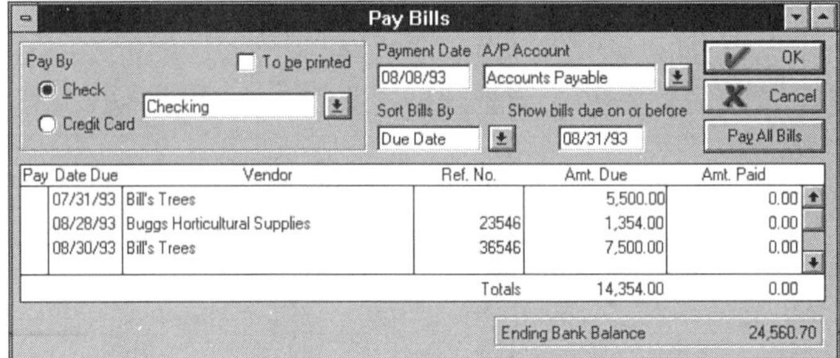

Fig. 11.5 Use the Pay Bills window to select bills to be paid at this time. You can even choose the amount that you will pay on a bill.

2. Decide how you plan to pay your bills. Select either the **C**heck or the Cre**d**it Card option button.

3. Choose the account from which the payment will be drawn in the text box beside the buttons in step 1. If you chose to pay by check in step 2, you can only select a checking account; if you chose to pay by credit card, you can only select a credit card account.

4. Select the To **B**e Printed check box if you plan to print the checks using QuickBooks. By leaving it unchecked, QuickBooks assumes that you will hand write your checks.

5. In the Payment Date field, enter the date that will appear on the checks when printed.

6. In the A/P Account text box, select an A/P Account from the drop-down list. If you enter your bills or vendor invoices into different A/P accounts, choose the account that you want pay bills for at this time. The detail box displays only bills for the selected account.

7. In the Sort Bills By text box, make your selection from the drop-down list.

   The default selection is to have all bills sorted by Due Date. You also can choose to have your bills sorted by Vendor, or by Amount Due. These options can be helpful when you want to see how much you owe a particular vendor, or to view your bills from largest to smallest.

8. In the Show Bills Due On or Before text box, enter a date. QuickBooks selects and displays all bills that are due on or before that date.

9. Choose the Pay All Bills button if you want to pay all the bills listed in the detail box. Making this selection places a check mark in the Pay field, and enters an amount in the Amt. Paid field equal to the Amt. Due field. Use this option if you want to pay all of the bills in full. When selected, the label on this button changes to Clear Payments and removes all the selection check marks if pressed.

10. Choose individual transactions for payment by entering an amount in the Amt.Paid column. You can enter the full amount of the bill, or enter a partial payment. If you do not want to pay a bill at this time, leave the amount in the Amt.Paid column as zero. Figure 11.6 shows a completed Pay Bills window.

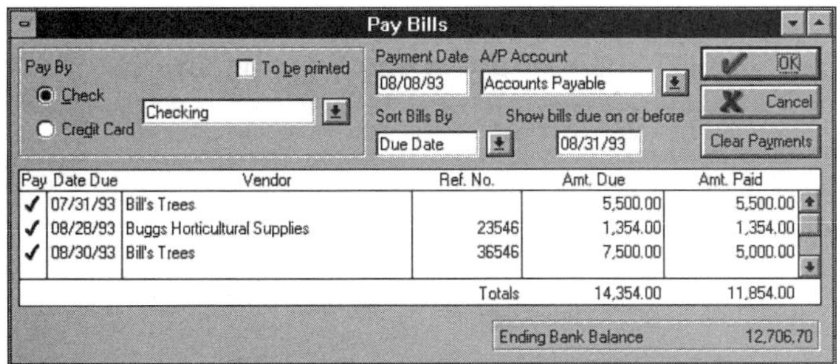

Fig. 11.6
This Pay Bills window is ready for the transactions to be recorded. Two bills will be paid in full, while the third will have a partial payment made to it.

Note

Notice that the Ending Bank Balance changes as you enter bills to be paid. This allows you to quickly see if you have enough money in your checking account to pay the bills. If the checking account balance is not adequate, you can make different decisions about how you will pay the bills now due.

QuickBooks displays totals at the bottom of both the Amt. Due and Amt. Paid fields.

11. Choose OK to save these transactions.

Entering Credits from Vendors

Sometimes you return goods or cancel a purchase, or you may receive a credit for an overcharge or overpayment from a vendor. In these cases, you need to record a credit transaction. With QuickBooks, you can keep track of credits received from vendors.

To enter a credit from a vendor, follow these steps:

1. Choose the Bill button from the Iconbar, or choose **A**ctivities, Enter **B**ills. The Enter Bills window appears (refer to fig. 11.1).
2. In the A/P Account text box, use the drop-down list to select the appropriate account.
3. Select the Cre**d**it option button. The display voucher changes. The title changes from Bill to Credit, and the Bill Due field is removed.
4. In the Vendor field, enter the vendor from whom you received the credit.
5. In the Date field, enter the date. QuickBooks automatically fills in the current date; change it if needed.
6. In the Ref. No. field, enter a reference number, such as the credit memo number.
7. In the Credit Amount field, enter the amount of the credit.

Caution

Do not enter a credit as a negative number. QuickBooks assumes that all credits are negative already, and makes the appropriate adjustments in the Accounts Payable register.

8. (Optional) In the Memo text box, type a note. This note will appear in the Accounts Payable register and on any reports that include this transaction. Generally, you want to include a note of the original invoice number from which the credit came, and possibly a short descriptive reason.

9. In the detail portion at the bottom of the window, enter the Account, Amounts, Memo, Customer:Job, and Class to which you want to assign this credit. Figure 11.7 shows the completed credit.

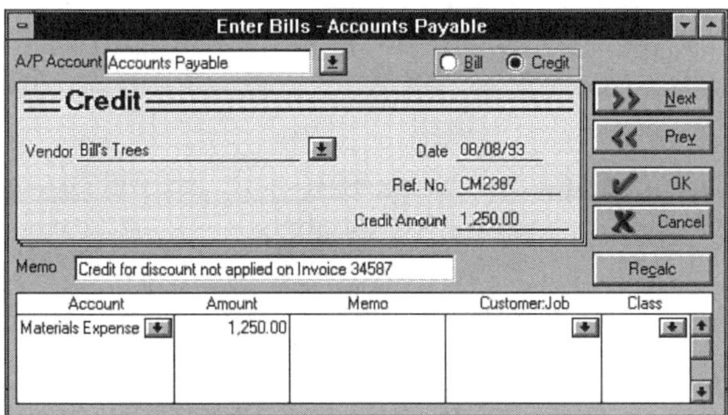

Fig. 11.7
This figure shows the completed credit in the Enter Bills window. Notice that all amounts are entered as positive numbers.

10. Choose OK to save the transaction and return to the desktop. Use **N**ext to enter another transaction or Pre**v** to view a previous transaction.

Using Reminders To Pay Bills

QuickBooks uses a Reminders List to remind you that various transactions need to be processed. One of the reminders is that bills need to be paid.

You can set up Reminders so that they are automatically displayed each time that you load QuickBooks. You also can display the Reminders List by choosing the Rmnd button from the Iconbar, or by choosing **L**ists, **R**eminders.

To change the QuickBooks Reminders, follow these steps:

1. From the **P**references menu, choose **R**eminders. The Reminder Preferences dialog box appears. As you see in figure 11.8, you can have QuickBooks display reminders for many different options.

Reminder Preferences

Show Reminders List when QuickBooks starts

For each type of reminder, QuickBooks can show a summary line, a detailed list of transactions, or not remind you.

OK
Cancel
Help
Default

Checks to Print
Show summary.
Show list of checks.
Don't remind me.
Remind me 5 days before check date.

Bills to Pay
Show summary.
Show list of bills.
Don't remind me.
Remind me 10 days before due date.

Invoices/Credit Memos to Print
Show summary.
Show list of invoices/credit memos.
Don't remind me.
Remind me 5 days before invoice date.

Memorized Transactions
Show summary.
Show list of transactions.
Don't remind me.
Remind me 5 days before due date.

Sales Receipts to Print
Show summary.
Show list of cash sales.
Don't remind me.

Money to Deposit
Show summary.
Show detail of deposit.
Don't remind me.

Fig. 11.8
Use the Reminder Preferences window to make any changes to the Reminders List.

For each option, you can choose how Reminders will be displayed, and how many days in advance you should be reminded. Two options, Sales Receipts to Print, and Money to Deposit, do not give you the option of choosing a number of days. The choices in these options are as follows:

- *Show Summary.* Displays a single line reminder, showing the type of reminder Bills to Pay and the total of all bills due.
- *Show list.* Displays a reminder line for each transaction now due.
- *Don't remind me.* Turns Reminder off for this option.
- *Remind me XX days before due date.* Reminders will display a transaction when the due date is *XX* days away.

2. Make the changes to various reminders, and then choose OK to save them.

3. Display the Reminders List by choosing the Rmnd button from the Iconbar, or by choosing **L**ist, **R**eminders. Figure 11.9 shows the Reminders window.

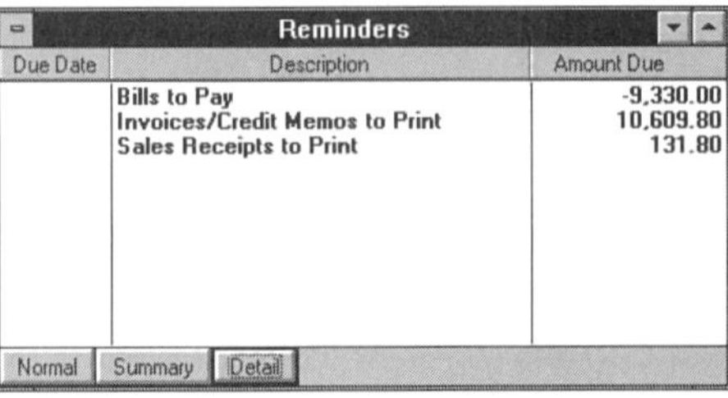

Fig. 11.9
This example shows the Reminders window, with all items shown in summary.

4. Choose the Detail button to view the Reminders list in detail. Figure 11.10 shows the Reminders list displayed with details.

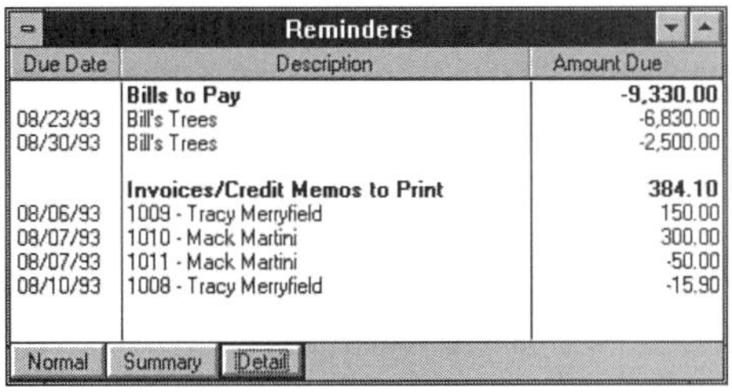

Reminders

Due Date	Description	Amount Due
	Bills to Pay	**-9,330.00**
08/23/93	Bill's Trees	-6,830.00
08/30/93	Bill's Trees	-2,500.00
	Invoices/Credit Memos to Print	**384.10**
08/06/93	1009 - Tracy Merryfield	150.00
08/07/93	1010 - Mack Martini	300.00
08/07/93	1011 - Mack Martini	-50.00
08/10/93	1008 - Tracy Merryfield	-15.90

Normal | Summary | Detail

Fig. 11.10
This example shows the Reminders window displaying details.

Summary

In this chapter, you learned to enter bills into the Accounts Payable register through the Enter Bills window, and then to pay the bills using the Pay Bills window. You also learned to add credits from vendors, and finally, to change the calculated day to pay a bill on, and to use the Reminders list to notify you when a bill is due for payment.

In the next chapter, "Using the Accounts Payable Register," you learn to display the Accounts Payable register, and to use it to enter bills and payments. You also learn to enter historical data from your old system, to add vendor notes, and to print the Accounts Payable register.

Chapter 12

Using the Accounts Payable Register

In Chapter 11, "Entering and Paying Bills," you learned how to enter and pay bills. In this chapter, you learn where the bills that you enter are recorded. The Accounts Payable register lists all transactions with your vendors: each bill received, each check written, and every credit taken.

The Accounts Payable register is similar to the Accounts Receivable register except that you can edit and enter transactions in the Accounts Payable register. After you use QuickBooks for a short time, you will be able to extract vital information about how much you owe your vendors at any given time, how much you spend with selected vendors during a period of time, and whether you paid a specific bill.

Two accounting methods for tracking Accounts Payable are available: the cash basis and the accrual basis. You can use the QuickBooks Accounts Payable register with either accounting method. Both methods are described in the next section. If you are not sure which method you should use, consult your accountant.

In this chapter, you learn to do the following tasks:

- Enter and edit bills in the Accounts Payable register
- View a transaction history
- Enter historical transactions
- Use QuickReport to view selected vendor records
- Use the Notepad to add notes to a vendor file
- Print the Accounts Payable register

Displaying the Accounts Payable Register

The Accounts Payable register lists transactions related to your vendors. These transactions include bills, credits, and payments. In the Accounts Payable register, all transactions are listed in chronological order.

To display the Accounts Payable register, follow these steps:

1. Access the Chart of Accounts by choosing the Accnt button on the Iconbar; by choosing **L**ists, Chart of **A**ccounts; or by pressing Ctrl+A.

2. Highlight the Accounts Payable account and choose the U**s**e Register button, or just double-click Accounts Payable. QuickBooks displays the Accounts Payable register, as shown in figure 12.1.

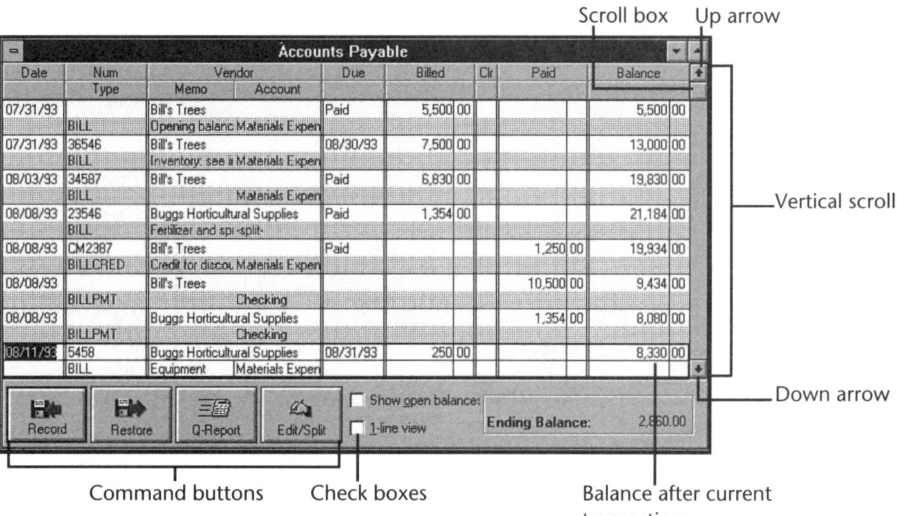

Fig. 12.1
QuickBooks enters all bills and payments to vendors in the Accounts Payable register.

Businesses can use either the cash basis or the accrual basis of accounting to track Accounts Payable. The *cash* basis method of accounting recognizes an expense when the cash is paid out, and income when it is received. If you buy inventory on August 1st, for example, but do not pay the bill until September 1st, the transaction is not recorded until September 1st. Many small businesses use the cash basis of bookkeeping because it is simple and easy to understand, especially in a manual bookkeeping system.

The *accrual* basis method of accounting recognizes an expense when you receive a product and the bill has been received; income is recognized when you earn it. In the preceding example, the expense is recognized on August 1st—the day you buy the inventory. Accountants and bankers prefer the accrual method because it can provide a better picture of the financial health of your business.

Another advantage of using the accrual basis method is that you can track vendor information with it. You can also use the QuickZoom function when you view Accounts Payable reports. This option is not available when you use the cash method. With QuickBooks, these methods work equally well.

Note

If your accountant determines that your business should use the accrual basis method of accounting to reflect income and expenses more accurately, she can make the entries needed to convert your transactions from a cash basis to an accrual basis.

Reviewing the Accounts Payable Register

The Accounts Payable register includes a transaction line for each bill that you receive from a vendor so that you can include the date of the bill, the vendor, the amount, and the account to which the expense will be assigned (such as supplies, equipment, utilities, and so on). Based on the date of the bill and the number of days within which you specify that you want bills paid, QuickBooks determines each bill's due date so that you are reminded to pay your bills in plenty of time.

Table 12.1 describes the fields that make up the Accounts Payable register:

Table 12.1. Parts of the Accounts Payable Register

Field	Function
Date	Shows the date the transaction was entered in QuickBooks.
Num	Contains the reference number for the transaction, the vendor invoice or credit memo number for bills, or the check number for payments.
Type	Displays the type of transaction. The various types of transaction codes that you see in the Accounts Payable register are listed here:
	BILL, which indicates a vendor bill or invoice.
	BILLCRED, which refers to a credit received from a vendor.
	BILLPMT, which signifies a payment against an invoice.
Vendor	Displays the vendor name for the transaction.

(continues)

III

Paying Bills

Table 12.1. Continued

Field	Function
Memo	Contains a message that you enter in the Memo field of the Enter Bills window.
Account	Shows the Expense or Balance Sheet account to which the transaction has been assigned. If you assign the transaction to more than one account, QuickBooks displays the notation `-split-` in this field.
Due	Displays the date the bill is due. The date is calculated by QuickBooks from the date the bill was entered or received, using the number of days that you have set in the Transaction Preferences dialog box. (You learn about changing the calculated due date in Chapter 22, "Customizing QuickBooks for Windows.") If the bill has been paid, QuickBooks changes the Due field to `Paid`.
Billed	Displays the total amount of the transaction. Bill amounts increase your Accounts Payable total; credit amounts (shown in red) decrease your Accounts Payable total.
Clr	Displays an X when a transaction is voided.
Paid	Shows that amount of a payment or credit transaction. The amounts in this column decrease your Accounts Payable total.
Balance	Displays a running total of the Accounts Payable balance.
Ending Balance	Shows the current total of Accounts Payable. This total changes with each new transaction entered.

The Accounts Payable Register contains four buttons:

Record	Records or saves a transaction entered or edited in the Accounts Payable register.
Restore	Changes a transaction back to the way it was before you started editing.
Q-Report	Creates a report that lists all transactions related to the selected vendor.
Edit/Split	Opens the Enter Bills window, allowing you to enter split transactions or to assign a bill to a specific customer or class.

The Accounts Payable Register also contains two check boxes.

Show open balances	Displays only the bills that you still owe.
1-line view	Displays the Accounts Payable register in a 1-line-per-transaction view. Use this check box to double the number of transactions you can display on-screen at a time.

From the Accounts Payable register, you can perform the following tasks:

- Enter bills from vendors
- Edit bills
- Pay bills
- Record a reimbursable expense
- Edit a payment
- Enter credits from vendors
- Reverse an Accounts Payable transaction
- Enter historical Accounts Payable transactions
- Add notes to a vendor account
- View vendor records
- Print the Accounts Payable register

You can enter almost all Accounts Payable transactions from the Accounts Payable register. A bill that must be distributed among several expense accounts, or noted as a reimbursable expense to a customer or class, must be entered from the Enter Bills window, as you learned in Chapter 11, "Entering and Paying Bills." After a bill is paid in full, QuickBooks enters the notation `Paid` in the Due field.

Moving Around in the Register

Within the Accounts Payable register, you can use the mouse or keyboard to move around in the window. You will find that in most cases the keyboard is easier to use.

To use the mouse to move around in the Accounts Payable register, you can do the following:

- Use the vertical scroll bar (refer to fig. 12.1) to move up or down in the register.

  Click the up- or down-arrow button to move up or down the register, one transaction at a time. Click either arrow button and hold down the mouse button to move through many transactions.

- Drag the scroll box (refer to fig. 12.1) up or down in the vertical scroll bar. Notice that the date pop-up box appears beside the scroll bar. As you move along the scroll bar, the date changes, reflecting your position within the transactions.

If you prefer, you can use the keyboard to move through the register. Table 12.2 lists the available keys to use to move quickly and easily through the Accounts Payable register.

Table 12.2. Keys To Move Through the Accounts Payable Register

Press These Keys	To Move
Up arrow	Up one transaction
Down arrow	Down one transaction
PgUp (Page Up) or Home+Home+Home	Up one screen of transactions
PgDn (Page Down) or End+End+End	Down one screen of transactions
Ctrl+PgUp	To the beginning of the current month's transactions
Ctrl+PgDn	To the beginning of the next month's transactions
Ctrl+Home or Home+Home+Home	To the beginning of the register
Ctrl+End or End+End+End	To the end of the register

Entering Bills into the Accounts Payable Register

With QuickBooks, you can enter bills directly into the Accounts Payable register. If you are familiar with your accounts and with an Accounts Payable journal, you may find that entering bills or credit directly into the register is easier than entering them in the Enter Bills window. (You learned how to enter bills and credits in the Enter Bills window in Chapter 11, "Entering and Paying Bills.")

You may find a drawback to this method: you can't enter payments to vendors. To enter a transaction for a payment to a vendor, you must use the Pay Bills window, as you learned in Chapter 11.

To enter a bill directly into the Accounts Payable register, follow these steps:

1. Access the Accounts Payable register, as explained previously. Use the scroll bar or press Ctrl+End to move to the first blank transaction line at the end of the register (see fig. 12.2).

Accounts Payable

Date	Num / Type	Vendor / Memo, Account	Due	Billed	Clr	Paid	Balance
08/08/93	23546 / BILL	Buggs Horticultural Supplies / Fertilizer and spi -split-	Paid	1,354 00			21,184 00
08/08/93	CM2387 / BILLCRED	Bill's Trees / Credit for discou Materials Expen	Paid			1,250 00	19,934 00
08/08/93	BILLPMT	Bill's Trees / Checking				10,500 00	9,434 00
08/08/93	BILLPMT	Buggs Horticultural Supplies / Checking				1,354 00	8,080 00
08/11/93	5458 / BILL	Buggs Horticultural Supplies / Equipment Materials Expen	08/31/93	250 00			8,330 00
08/11/93	5485 / BILL	Buggs Horticultural Supplies / Equipment Equipment Rent	08/31/93	110 00			8,440 00
08/11/93	BILLPMT	Bill's Trees / Checking				5,580 00	2,860 00
08/12/93	Num	Vendor / Memo Account	Due	Billed		Paid	

Record | Restore | Q-Report | Edit/Split | Show open balances | 1-line view | Ending Balance: 2,860.00

Fig. 12.2
Press Ctrl+End to move to the first blank transaction line at the end of the Accounts Payable register.

2. QuickBooks enters the current date in the Date field. If necessary, use the + or – keys to adjust the date.

3. Enter the reference number for this transaction. This number will usually be a vendor invoice or a credit memo number.

4. Type the name of the vendor or select the vendor from the drop-down list. QuickBooks uses QuickFill to help you quickly fill in the vendor name.

If you have turned on the AutoRecall feature, QuickBooks fills in the remaining parts of the transaction with a copy of the last transaction for the same vendor. This recall of information can be helpful when you enter many repetitive transactions. You can change any part of a transaction that is filled in for you. You learn about using AutoRecall to enter bills in Chapter 11, "Entering and Paying Bills."

5. Enter the date the bill is due. Or, if you are entering a credit memo, leave this field blank because QuickBooks calculates and fills in the date for you. You can change the supplied date if needed.

6. Enter the amount billed if the transaction is a bill, or enter the amount paid if this is a credit memo.

   Remember that amounts entered in the Billed column increase the amounts you owe, and amounts entered in the Paid column decrease the total owed.

7. (Optional) Type a note in the Memo field. This memo may appear in reports that include this transaction. Enter a note in the Memo field, for example, to describe the expenditures included in the invoice.

8. In the Account field, enter the Expense account to which this transaction will be allocated.

9. Choose the Edit/Split button to allocate the transaction to more than one account. QuickBooks displays the Enter Bills window. Select the accounts to allocate to the transaction, as you learned in Chapter 11, "Entering and Paying Bills."

10. Choose the Record button to record the transaction in the Accounts Payable register.

Notice the heavy line in figure 12.3, right above the transaction just recorded. This line indicates that the transaction is postdated (is dated after the current date). Any register with a postdated transaction displays that transaction below this line. You can use postdated transactions in the Accounts Payable register to record an invoice when you have not yet received the product.

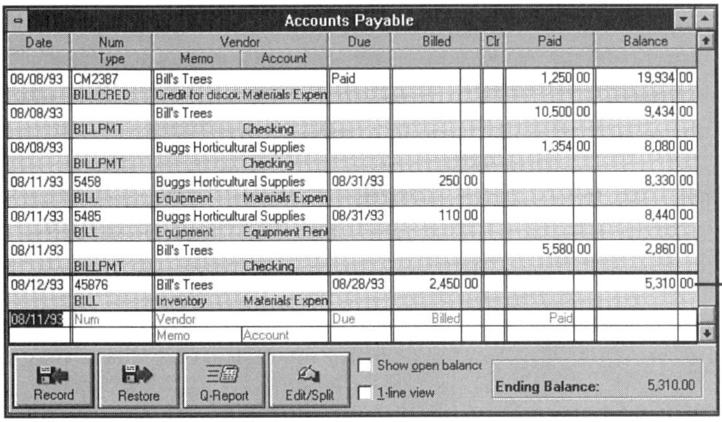

Fig. 12.3
The completed transaction. QuickBooks adds a new blank line for the next transaction.

Postdated transactions appear beneath heavy line

Editing Bills in the Accounts Payable Register

Editing a bill in the Accounts Payable register takes only a moment. You can change any part of an Accounts Payable transaction up until the time you pay the bills. After a transaction has been paid, you can't change the Due field.

If you edit the Billed or Paid columns, the transaction is no longer in balance. You must open the Enter Bills window and reallocate the distribution of the transaction.

To edit a transaction in the Accounts Payable register, follow these steps:

1. Access the Accounts Payable register, as explained previously.
2. Use the mouse or the keyboard to highlight the transaction that you want to edit. (See the section "Moving Around the Register" in Chapter 10, "Using the Accounts Receivable Register," to learn how to highlight a transaction.)
3. Make any necessary changes to the fields in the transaction.
4. Edit the Account field by using the Edit/Split button. QuickBooks opens the Enter Bills window. Make the changes required, and then choose OK to return to the Accounts Payable register.
5. Choose the Record button to save your changes.

Editing a bill that has not been paid or a credit that has not been used usually presents no problems unless you change the amount in a split transaction. After a transaction has been paid, you run into a variety of pop-up warning dialog boxes. Here are some common problems you may encounter:

- *Problem:* You change the total amount billed or paid in an unpaid transaction, and the transaction is split among several accounts.

  Reason: The transaction is out of balance. You originally allocated a certain amount of the transaction total to each of the accounts. Now the total that was allocated does not match the new total amount.

  Solution: Choose the Edit/Split button to change the distribution among the expense accounts.

- *Problem:* You change the vendor name on a transaction that has been paid. When you then choose Record, a warning is displayed, telling you that the transaction is connected to other transactions.

  Reason: This warning tells you that you paid the invoice with a check to the vendor named in the transaction. When you change the vendor name, the check that has been issued to pay this bill is no longer connected to the bill.

  Solution: First void the check that pays this transaction, and then change the vendor name. You learn how to void a check in Chapter 13, "Writing and Printing Checks."

- *Problem:* You edit the account distribution of a transaction after the bill is paid, and a warning is displayed. This warning tells you that the bill is at least partially paid and that changing it will affect how much of the bill is due.

  Reason: If you change the allocation of a paid bill, QuickBooks may have trouble keeping track of some transactions.

  Solution: Choose **Y**es to change the transaction allocation if you need to make the adjustment.

- *Problem:* You change the amount billed or paid after a transaction has been paid.

  Reason: This causes the expense allocation to become unbalanced, possibly losing an audit trail and some detail information.

Solution: Enter a credit or another bill that balances the discrepancy. You will find this method to be a cleaner method of bookkeeping than changing past transactions.

Caution

Do not use the Void or Delete option to void or delete an Accounts Payable transaction. Although QuickBooks allows you to do this, it is not a good bookkeeping practice, nor does it reverse portions of the transaction in other registers. If you must delete a transaction, add a new transaction that reverses the transaction to be deleted or voided. Enter a note in the Memo field explaining why you are reversing the transaction and include a reference to the original transaction.

Viewing a Transaction History

You can view a transaction history from the Accounts Payable register. The *transaction history* displays a summary of the selected transaction and lists all related transactions. When you choose to view a transaction history for a transaction, you can choose a related transaction and view it in its original form.

To view a transaction history for a transaction in the Accounts Payable register, follow these steps:

1. Access the Accounts Payable register, as explained previously.

2. Select the transaction for which you want to view a transaction history.

3. Choose **E**dit, Transaction **H**istory, or press Ctrl+H. QuickBooks displays the Transaction History dialog box, as shown in figure 12.4.

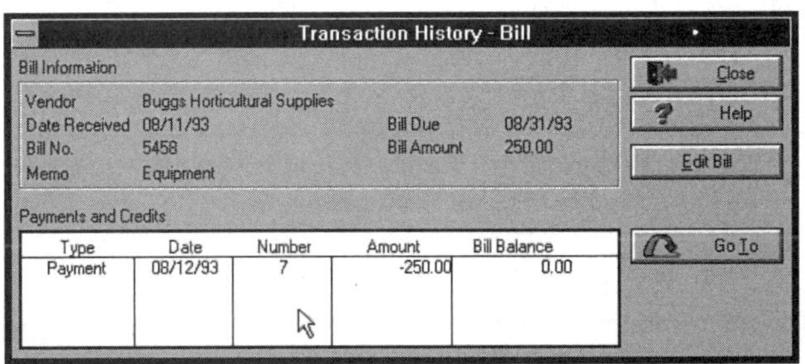

Fig. 12.4
The Transaction History dialog box shows all transactions that relate to the selected transaction.

The Transaction History dialog box shows the information for the transaction in the top portion and lists the related transactions in the bottom portion. The types of transactions listed in the Transaction History dialog box are dependent on the type of transaction you selected from the Accounts Payable register. Table 12.3 lists the transaction type and the related transactions that are displayed when you select to view a transaction history from the Accounts Payable register.

Table 12.3. Accounts Payable Transaction Types

Transaction Type	Related Transactions Shown
Bill	Payments applied to the bill
(BILL)	Credit applied to the bill
Bill Credit	Bills to which the credit was applied
(BILLCRED)	Payments applied to a bill with the credit
Bill Payment	Bills to which the payment was applied
(BILLPMT)	Credit applied to a bill and paid with the payment

4. If you want to view a transaction in its original form, highlight the transaction in the Transaction History dialog box and choose the Go **T**o command button. (In Chapter 10, "Using the Accounts Receivable Register," you learned to use the Go **T**o button in the Transaction History dialog box to jump to the related transaction.)
5. To edit a bill transaction, choose the **E**dit Bill command button. QuickBooks displays the Enter Bills window where you entered the original bill. To edit a bill payment, choose the **E**dit Bill Pmt. command button. QuickBooks displays the Bill Payments window with the original payment information.
6. To remove the Transaction History dialog box from the screen, choose **C**lose.

Entering Accounts Payable Historical Transactions

If you did not start using QuickBooks at the beginning of your fiscal year, you need to enter historical transactions for your Accounts Payable. *Historical transactions* are all those that occurred before you started using QuickBooks. Therefore, historical transactions include all Accounts Payable transactions from the beginning of your fiscal year to the date that you started using QuickBooks. For example, if your fiscal year begins on January 1st and you started your QuickBooks system on March 1st, you must not only enter those transactions that occurred from January 1st to February 28th, but also any payables that were outstanding as of January 1st. Note that when you start using QuickBooks, you can start using the Accounts Payable register immediately; you do not have to enter all the old transactions first. You can later go back and enter these historical transactions so that your Accounts Payable account accurately reflects all activity for the year.

Caution

When entering historical Accounts Payable transactions, make sure that you don't duplicate transactions that have already been entered in QuickBooks. For example, if your QuickBooks start date is March 1st, make sure that you enter only those transactions dated before March 1st, but not including March 1st. You also must be careful not to omit any transactions that are dated before your QuickBooks start date. The purpose of entering historical transactions in your Accounts Payable register is to ensure that you have a complete and accurate record of your Accounts Payable activity for your entire fiscal year.

Although you can enter historical transactions at any time, it's easier to enter them when you enter your current bills. In order for QuickBooks to correctly link a bill with its payment, enter first your bills and then your payments.

Entering Outstanding Bills

As you find the time to add historical transactions to QuickBooks, enter the outstanding bills first. You can't use the Pay Bills window to pay a bill that has not yet been entered in QuickBooks. Entering a payment directly into the Accounts Payable register creates a Bill Credit (BILLCRED), not a payment. QuickBooks does not automatically link the two together, and the result is a bill that forever remains unpaid in the Accounts Payable reports. Needless to say, this would not look good to your banker.

To enter outstanding bills, follow these steps:

1. To open the Enter Bills window, choose the Bill button on the Iconbar, or choose **A**ctivities, Enter **B**ills.

2. Enter all necessary information, as you learned in Chapter 11, "Entering and Paying Bills."

3. In the Date field, enter the date you originally received the bill. Use the + and – keys to change the date that QuickBooks automatically enters. Don't worry about the Bill Due date.

4. Save the transaction by choosing OK. If you enter several transactions in a single session, choose the **N**ext button to save the transaction and open a new blank bill in the Enter Bills window.

Entering Bills Paid This Year

After you enter bills that were outstanding before you started using QuickBooks, you will be ready to enter your payments on those bills.

To enter historical payments for bills, follow these steps:

1. To open the Pay Bills window, choose **A**ctivities, **P**ay Bills.

2. Select the historical bills to be paid in the Pay Bills window.

> **Caution**
>
> Select for payment only the historical bills that you have already entered. Do not select both historical bills and bills that are current. You must select only historical bills so that QuickBooks enters a corresponding transaction in the Checking account that shows payment of these bills.

3. Choose OK to save the payment transaction in the Accounts Payable register.

Using QuickReport To View Vendor Records

As you learned with the Accounts Receivable register, you can use the QuickReport feature with the Accounts Payable register. QuickReport displays an on-screen report for a selected vendor, showing all transactions related to that vendor.

To use QuickReport, follow these steps:

1. Access the Accounts Payable register, as explained previously, and select the vendor for whom you want to see a listing of transactions.

2. Choose the Q-Report button. You see a report like that in figure 12.5.

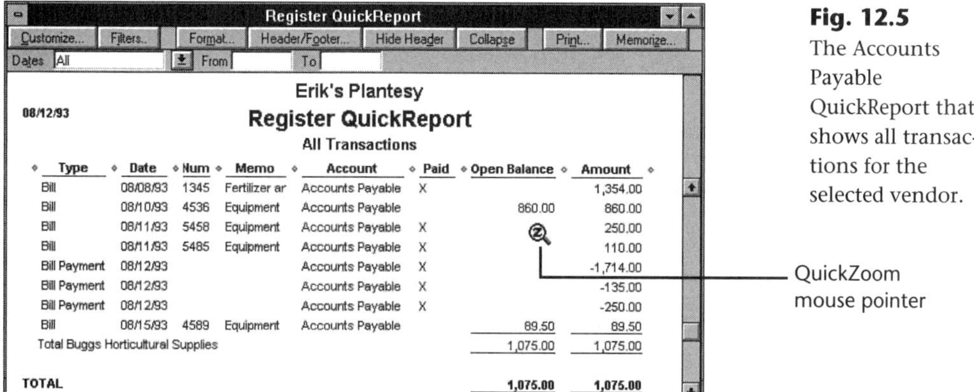

Fig. 12.5 The Accounts Payable QuickReport that shows all transactions for the selected vendor.

3. Double-click the Control menu box or press Ctrl+F4 to remove the QuickReport from the screen.

Tip
To see the original information for a transaction in a QuickReport, use QuickZoom by pointing to the transaction (the mouse pointer changes to a magnifying glass) and double-clicking.

Adding Vendor Notes

Just as with Accounts Receivable, QuickBooks provides a Notepad for you to create notes about vendors. You can list specific information about vendors you deal with—for example, whether they are strict about terms or whether they ship promptly. You can also make notes to document phone conversations.

To add a vendor note to the Notepad, follow these steps:

1. Access the Accounts Payable register, as explained previously.

2. Select a transaction that contains the vendor for whom you want to add a note.

3. Open the Notepad by choosing **E**dit, N**o**tepad. QuickBooks displays the Notepad that you see in figure 12.6.

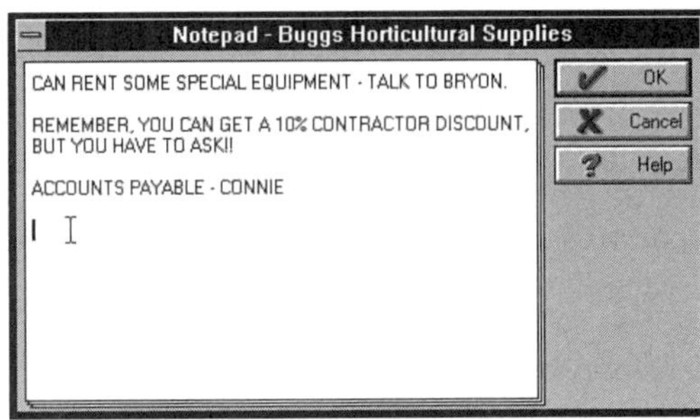

Fig. 12.6
Add a note about a vendor in the Notepad.

4. Type up to 15 lines of text in the Notepad. Use the following keys to add a note:

Keys	Function
Enter	Starts a new line of text
Ins	Inserts text in existing note
Ins again	Deactivates Insert mode
Del	Deletes characters to the right of the cursor
Backspace	Deletes characters to the left of the cursor

5. After your note is complete, choose OK or press Enter to record it in the Notepad. Choose Cancel or press Esc to discard the note.

Tip
You can also create a vendor note from the Vendor List. Just select the vendor, choose Edit, and then choose the Notes button to open the Notepad.

Printing the Accounts Payable Register

You can easily print a complete or partial copy of your Accounts Payable register. You can also select to print the register in summary format or print all of the details for each transaction in the register. A copy of the Accounts Payable register is useful if you want to check the account against vendor invoices or have your accountant look through the register.

To print a copy of the Accounts Payable register, follow these steps:

1. Access the Accounts Payable register, as explained previously.

2. Choose **F**ile, **P**rint Register, or press Ctrl+P. QuickBooks displays the Print Register dialog box.

3. In the From and To fields, enter the beginning and ending dates for the period to print. QuickBooks selects the beginning of the fiscal year to the current date. Change these dates if you require a more selective date range.

4. Choose OK to display the Print Report dialog box. Choose **Print** to print the report to your printer. Figure 12.7 shows the result of printing the Accounts Payable register with transaction detail.

Register 08/12/93

Accounts Payable Register through 08/12/93:

Date	No.	Payee	Memo	Account	Amount	C	Balance
06/2...	3564	Buggs ...	Equ...	Fertiliz...	135.00		135.00
07/3...		Bill's...	Ope...	Material...	5,500.00		5,635.00
07/3...	36546	Bill's...	Inv...	Material...	7,500.00		13,135.00
08/0...	34587	Bill's...		Material...	5,830.00		18,965.00
08/0...	4658	Buggs ...	Equ...	-split-	375.50		19,340.50
08/0...	13456	Buggs ...	Fer...	-split-	1,354.00		20,694.50
08/0...	CM2387	Bill's...	Cre...	Material...	-1,250.00		19,444.50
08/0...		Bill's...		Checking	-10,500.00		8,944.50
08/1...	4536	Buggs ...	Equ...	-split-	860.00		9,804.50
08/1...	5458	Buggs ...	Equ...	Material...	250.00		10,054.50
08/1...	5485	Buggs ...	Equ...	Equipmen...	110.00		10,164.50
08/1...		Bill's...		Checking	-5,580.00		4,584.50
08/1...	45876	Bill's...	Inv...	-split-	1,450.00		6,034.50
08/1...		Buggs ...		Checking	-1,714.00		4,320.50
08/1...		Buggs ...		Checking	-135.00		4,185.50

Fig. 12.7
A printed version of the Accounts Payable register with transaction detail.

Summary

In this chapter, you learned to display the Accounts Payable register, to enter and edit bills, and to view a transaction history. Next, you learned to enter historical transactions in the Accounts Payable register and to use the QuickReport feature. Finally, you learned to add vendor notes in the QuickBooks Notepad and to print the Accounts Payable register.

In the next chapter, you learn how to enter checks in the Write Checks window and how to edit and void checks. You also learn how to print checks and make deposits.

Chapter 13

Writing and Printing Checks

In this chapter, you learn to do the following:

- Write a check
- Use shortcuts for writing a check
- Assign accounts and jobs to checks
- Edit, void, and delete a check
- Print checks

Writing checks with QuickBooks not only saves you valuable time, but spares you from numerous opportunities to make clerical errors. When you write a check using QuickBooks, you simply enter the information using an on-screen check facsimile, and QuickBooks takes it from there. QuickBooks automatically records the check in the Check register, adjusts your account balance, and adds the transaction amount to the appropriate accounts, which you specify when you write a check. From this point, you have only to print the check, sign it, put the check in an envelope (Intuit even provides window envelopes for checks), and mail it. Refer to Chapter 1, "Preparing To Use QuickBooks for Windows," to learn how to order checks and envelopes.

If you use the QuickBooks Accounts Payable register to pay your vendors, you use the Pay Bills option to write checks for vendors. You do not use the Write Checks window; doing so creates two checks for the same bill.

If you are not using the Accounts Payable register to record and pay bills from your vendors, you can easily pay your vendors from the Write Checks window. You can also use the Write Checks window to write checks when you pay employees or a vendor for a one-time delivery. Write checks that you want to postdate and print later, such as paychecks, expense reimbursements, or refunds, from the Write Checks window.

Viewing the Write Checks Window

When you open the Write Checks window, QuickBooks automatically selects the checking account that you have set up in your Chart of Accounts. Use the Write Checks window when you want to do the following:

- Write checks directly to a vendor without adding a transaction in the Accounts Payable register
- Pay employees
- Write checks for expense reimbursements
- Review checks that you have not yet printed
- Edit or delete checks that you have not printed

To view the Write Checks window, open it by clicking the Check button on the Iconbar; by choosing **A**ctivities, **W**rite Checks; or by pressing Ctrl+W. The Write Checks window displays, as shown in figure 13.1.

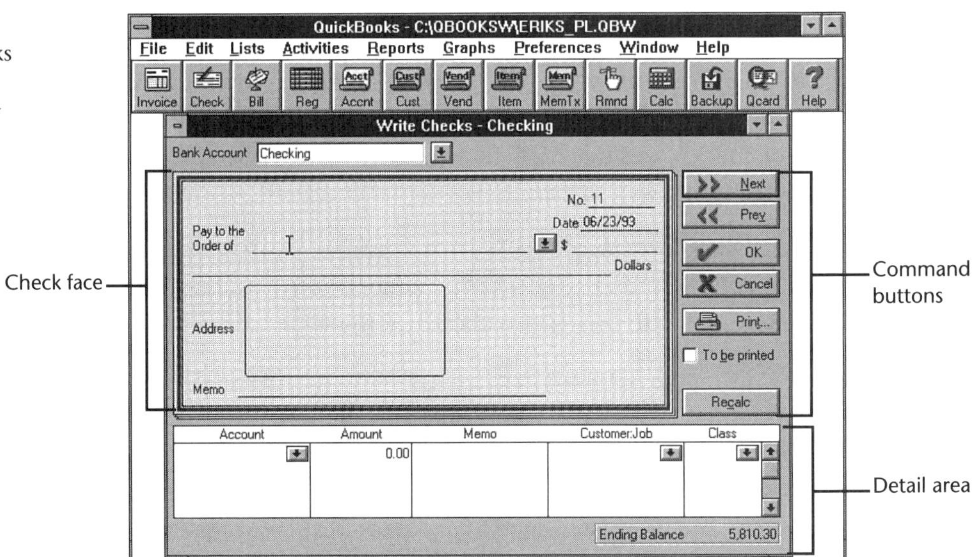

Fig. 13.1
The Write Checks window. Notice that the window title shows the name of the account: Checking.

Reviewing the Write Checks Window

The Write Checks window contains three basic parts: the check face, the detail area, and the command buttons. The parts of the Write Checks window work together to form a powerful check writing tool.

At the top of the Write Checks window is the field you use to select the checking account from which you write the check. If you have more than one checking account, select the appropriate checking account.

The *check face* is the part of the window that looks like a check. It contains all the necessary fields, or lines, that a hand-written check has. The fields on the check face are as follows:

- *No.* The check number. QuickBooks automatically enters the next check number available from the checking account. If you use a hand-written check, enter the correct number. If you plan to print the check at a later time, QuickBooks replaces the check number with *To Print* and assigns the number when the check is printed.
- *Date.* The date the check is written. You can adjust this if you want to create a postdated check.
- *Pay to the Order of.* Use this field to enter the name of the payee.
- *$.* The dollar amount of the check. QuickBooks writes out the check amount on the next line.
- *Address.* The address of the payee. This is an optional field. If the payee is a vendor, employee, or customer that exists in your company lists, QuickBooks enters this information for you.
- *Memo.* Add a note about the check payment. This memo also appears in both the Check register and any other report that contains the check transaction.

The voucher detail area of the check is similar to the detail part of the Pay Bills window, which you learned about in Chapter 11, "Entering and Paying Bills." The following fields are included:

- *Account.* Select the Expense or Balance Sheet account to assign to the payment.
- *Amount.* Enter the amount of the payment to be assigned to this particular account. The total of all dollar amounts in this column must equal the check total.
- *Memo.* Make a note concerning this specific expense.

- *Customer:Job.* Select the customer or job to which this expense relates. You can charge the expense on an invoice as a reimbursable expense. This column displays only if QuickBooks' job tracking feature is turned on. (Refer to Chapter 5, "Using QuickBooks for Windows Lists," to learn more about the job tracking feature and how to turn job tracking on and off.)
- *Class.* Select the class to which this expense relates. This column displays only if you turn on QuickBooks' class tracking feature. (Refer to Chapter 5, "Using QuickBooks for Windows Lists," to learn more about the class tracking feature and how to turn class tracking on and off.)

The Write Checks window includes command buttons as listed in the following table:

Button	Function
Next	Saves the check and opens the next blank check.
Pre**v**	Moves to a previously recorded check. Useful when you need to edit a check.
OK	Saves the check and closes the Write Checks window.
Cancel	Closes the Write Checks window without recording the check.
Prin**t**	Prints the current check.
Re**c**alc	Recalculates the amount of the check to agree with the distribution.
To **B**e Printed	Prints the check at a later time. This option check box is included with the command buttons. Selecting this check box removes the check number from the check face and replaces it with the words `To Print`.
Re**c**alc	Recalculates the check amount by adding the amounts entered in the Amount fields in the detail area of the Write Checks window.

The Ending Balance field (at the bottom of the Write Checks window) displays the balance in the checking account as of the current date. This helps you to determine whether you have enough funds in your account to write checks.

Moving Around the Write Checks Window

Moving around in the Write Checks window is simple. With a simple mouse click, you can select any field or button. The keyboard is no more complicated. You can use several keys to move about in the window, as follows:

Key	Action
Tab	Moves the cursor to the next field
Shift+Tab	Moves the cursor to the previous field
Up arrow	Moves the cursor to the previous field
Down arrow	Moves the cursor to the next field

Writing a Check

Completing the check face of the Write Checks window is easy. You write checks on-screen with QuickBooks just as you write checks in your paper checkbook.

Writing Checks from One Checking Account

If you use more than one checking account, be sure to select the correct account from which to write a check. If your business primarily writes checks from a single account and you do not often need to change the check number and check date, you may want to select the **S**tart with Payee Field on Check preference. By default, QuickBooks automatically positions the cursor in the Ban**k** Account field when you open the Write Checks window. By selecting this preference, however, QuickBooks skips the Ban**k** Account field and positions the cursor in the Pay to the Order of field when you open the Write Checks window.

To set up the Write Checks window to skip the Ban**k** Account field and place the cursor in the Pay to the Order of field automatically, follow these steps:

1. Choose **P**references, **C**hecks. The Check Preferences dialog box is displayed, as shown in figure 13.2.
2. Click the **S**tart with Payee Field on Check preference check box.
3. Choose OK to save the preference selection.

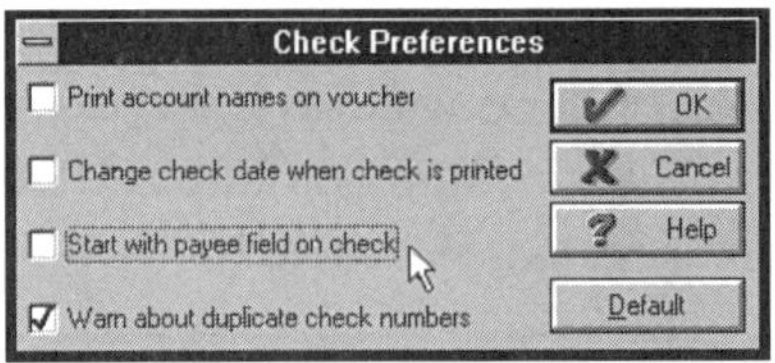

Fig. 13.2
The Check Preferences dialog box includes preferences that control the way checks are entered in the Write Checks window.

Filling Out the Check

To learn how to fill out a check, use an example to which you probably can relate: paying your office rent. Say that you pay $1,750 to the owner of your office space, Mezejewski & Wilcox, Inc. Your next office rent is due February 1, 1994. To fill out the check face of the Write Checks window, follow these steps:

1. Open the Write Checks window by clicking the Check button on the Iconbar; by choosing **A**ctivities, **W**rite Checks; or by pressing Ctrl+W.

2. If you have more than one checking account, select the checking account from which to write this check from the Ban**k** Account drop-down list box.

   If you changed your check preferences so that QuickBooks skips the Bank Account field, as explained in the preceding section, you bypass this step.

3. If the To **B**e Printed option check box is not selected, QuickBooks automatically enters the next check number in the No. field. If you are entering a check transaction for a manual check that you have written, enter the correct check number. If the To **B**e Printed option check box is selected and you will be printing the check, QuickBooks enters `To Print` in the No. field.

4. In the Date field, enter the date of the check. You would perform this optional step to postdate a check. Enter dates without typing the slashes between month, day, and year. Change the date by typing just the numbers **020194** for February 1, 1994. QuickBooks enters this as 02/01/94 on the check. The default format is MM/DD/YY.

5. Enter the payee in the Pay to the Order of field. If you previously sent a check to this vendor, use the down-arrow button, or press Ctrl+L, to display the drop-down list of payee names. Select the payee from the list by clicking the payee's name or highlighting the name and pressing Enter.

   QuickBooks' QuickFill feature also works in the Pay to the Order of field. If you type the first letter of the payee's name, QuickFill completes the first name that matches what you typed. Say that you have the following names:

   > Mallard Paints
   >
   > Metals in Sculpture
   >
   > Mezejewski & Wilcox, Inc.

   In your list of payees, QuickBooks first displays `Mallard Paints` when you type the letter **M**. When you add the letter **E**, `Metals in Sculpture` replaces the first entry. When you type the **Z**, QuickBooks enters `Mezejewski & Wilcox, Inc.` in the Pay to the Order of field in the check.

   If QuickBooks does not find a matching name in the payee list, you're asked whether you want to add it to your list.

   Another QuickBooks feature, AutoRecall, also operates when you are writing checks in the Write Checks window. AutoRecall makes entering repeat checks quick and easy. When you enter a payee in the Pay to the Order of field to whom you have written checks in the past, the AutoRecall feature automatically recalls the last transaction for this payee. In the example, if you have written previous checks to Mezejewski & Wilcox, Inc., when the name is entered in the Pay to the Order of field, AutoRecall enters the information from the last check written to this payee. Therefore, the amount, address (if entered in the last check), memo, account(s), customer:job(s), and class(es) are automatically entered when you enter this payee in the Write Checks window. You can, however, change any of the information that QuickBooks enters for you. By default, QuickBooks turns on the AutoRecall feature when you first install the program.

> **Note**
>
> You can turn off AutoRecall by choosing **D**ata Entry from the **P**references menu and then removing the check mark from the Automatically **R**ecall Last Transaction for this Name preference check box (click the check box).

6. In the $ field, enter the amount of the check, using a decimal to separate dollars and cents if necessary. Type **1750**, for example, to enter $1,750.00 for your office rent (enter **1750.49** to enter $1,750.49). QuickBooks fills in the check amount in words on the next line.

7. In the Address field, enter the address of the payee. This is optional. QuickBooks fills in the address block for you if the address was entered for this payee in the Vendor List, Employee List, or the Other Names List. You can correct any errors to the address at this time, or enter a new address. You can use up to four lines for the payee's address.

8. Enter a note in the Memo field, if necessary. This note is printed on your check, and appears in the Memo field of the Check register. You may want to include information such as an account number or a brief note.

Filling In Detail Lines

After you complete the check face, you are ready to assign one or more Expense accounts to the check transaction. By default, QuickBooks requires that you assign at least one account to a check transaction. You can, however, change QuickBooks so that you can enter transactions without assigning accounts. To do this, choose **P**references, **T**ransactions. Then remove the check mark from the Require **A**ccounts option check box (click the check box). For check transactions that are not assigned to accounts, QuickBooks assigns all income to the Uncategorized Income account, or in this case, all expenses to the Uncategorized Expense account. Note that if you do deselect this preference, you still can use the detail area of the check to assign a check amount to a specified account; however, you are not required to do so.

To assign a single account, or more than one account, to a check transaction, follow these steps:

1. Use the Tab key or the mouse to move to the first line in the detail area of the Write Checks window. QuickBooks fills in the first line of the Amount column with the total of the check amount.

2. Type the name of the account to which you want to assign this check. If you are not sure of the name, use QuickFill by typing the first letter of the account name; or click the down-arrow button or press Alt+down-arrow to display the drop-down list of accounts. Pressing Ctrl+L from the Account field displays the Chart of Accounts, which you can also use to select an account.

3. Use the Memo field to add a short note about this expense.

4. If this expense relates to a specific customer or job, click the down-arrow button in the Customer:Job field, or press Alt+down-arrow, to display the drop-down list of customers and jobs. Then select the customer or job for which this expense relates. You can later include this information on an invoice to the customer as a reimbursable expense.

5. In the Class field, select the class that you want to use to categorize this transaction. This field is optional, and is displayed only if you turned on the class tracking feature. (Class tracking is explained in Chapter 5, "Using QuickBooks for Windows Lists.")

   Figure 13.3 shows the completed check face and detail area. This check is ready to be saved or printed.

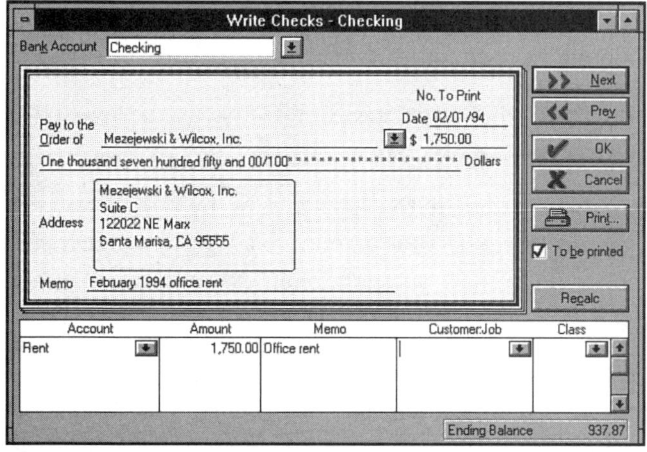

Fig. 13.3
A completed check transaction in the Write Checks window.

6. Choose OK to record the check and close the Write Checks window. To enter another check, select the **N**ext button.

Splitting a Transaction. Use the Write Checks window to assign more than one account to a check transaction. This is known as a *split transaction.* Splitting a transaction allows you to separate a single check amount into more than one type of expense. If you write a check to a vendor that covers both supplies and labor for a job, for example, you can split the check transaction to assign the appropriate amounts to a Supplies Expense account and to a Labor Expense account. In the previous example, you entered a rent check of $1750.00 and assigned the entire amount to only one account, the Rent account. In this example, the same check is split, or assigned, to two accounts: Rent and Janitorial Service.

To split a check transaction, follow these steps:

1. In the Write Checks window, complete the check face as usual.
2. Move to the first line in the detail area of the Write Checks window. In the Account field, select the first account that you want to assign to the check transaction. For this example, select Rent.
3. QuickBooks automatically enters the total amount of the check in the first Amount field. Therefore, in our example, `1,750.00` is entered in this field. Delete the entry in the Amount field by pressing the Del key. Then type the amount that you want to assign to the account that you selected in the first Account field. For our example, type **1500**, which is the amount assigned to the Rent account.
4. Type a memo, select a customer or job, or assign a class to the first expense account, as necessary.
5. Move to the next line in the detail area of the Write Checks window. In the Account field, select the account to assign to the next portion or the remainder of the check amount. In our example, select Janitorial Service from the drop-down list.
6. In the Amount field, QuickBooks automatically enters the remaining amount of the check. If you are not assigning more accounts to the transaction, press Tab to accept this amount. If you need to assign one or more other accounts to the transaction, delete the entry in the Amount field and type the correct amount.
7. For this line of the detail area, type a memo and select a customer job, or class, as necessary.

8. Repeat steps 5 through 7 for any other accounts that you need to assign to the check transaction.

9. When the entire check amount has been assigned to accounts in the detail area of the Write Checks window, choose the OK button to record the split transaction. Choose **N**ext to record the split transaction and enter another check.

Figure 13.4 shows a split check transaction with the accounts assigned in the detail area of the Write Checks window.

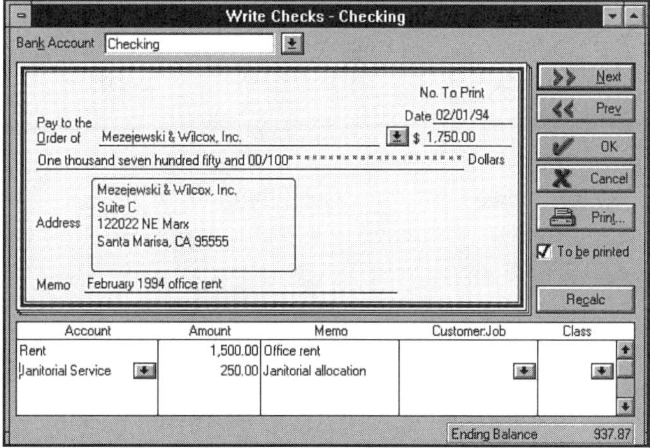

Fig. 13.4
The detail area of the Write Checks window shows the accounts assigned to a split transaction.

Calculating Payroll Checks Using Split Transactions. QuickBooks also can help you calculate the amount of a check based on the amounts you assign to accounts in the detail area of the Write Checks window. Use this option when the amount of a check is determined by the total of several amounts, like a payroll check.

To calculate a payroll check, follow these steps:

1. Access the Write Checks window by choosing the Check button on the Iconbar; by choosing **A**ctivities, **W**rite Checks; or by pressing Ctrl+W.

2. Select the checking account from which to write the check. When preparing payroll, make sure that you select the checking account from which you write payroll.

3. Enter the employee's name in the Pay to the Order of field. QuickBooks automatically fills in the address section from the information for this employee in the Employee List.

   Do not enter an amount in the $ field. This is calculated later in this section.

4. (Optional) Enter a note in the Memo field, such as the payroll period covered by the check. This note will appear on the printed check.

5. In the detail area, select the first account: Payroll Expenses:Gross Wages.

6. Enter the employee's gross wage amount for the period in the Amount field.

7. (Optional) Add a note in the Memo field.

   If you track employee wages by Customer:Jobs or classes, add the needed information in the next two fields, just as you learned in the previous section.

8. Move to the next line in the detail area of the Write Checks window.

9. In the Account field, select a payroll tax account, like Payroll Expenses:FICA, Payroll Expenses:Medicare, Payroll Liabilities:Federal Withholding, and so on.

10. In the amount field, enter the amount to be deducted from the employee's gross pay. Remember, this is a deduction. Enter it as a negative number by placing a minus (–) sign in front of the number.

11. If necessary, enter a note in the Memo field, select a customer or job in the Customer:Job field, or select a class in the Class field.

12. For all other payroll deductions, repeat steps 8 through 11. You usually have at least Federal Withholding, State Withholding, FICA (social security), FUTA (federal unemployment), and Medicare deductions. You may have additional deductions, depending on your state requirements.

13. When you are finished entering payroll deductions, choose the Recalc command button. QuickBooks totals the amounts in the Amount fields in the detail area of the Write Checks window and enters the result in the $ field in the check face.

14. Choose OK to record the check and close the window, or choose **N**ext to write another check.

Figure 13.5 shows a completed payroll check with the gross amount and payroll deductions listed in the detail area of the Write Checks window.

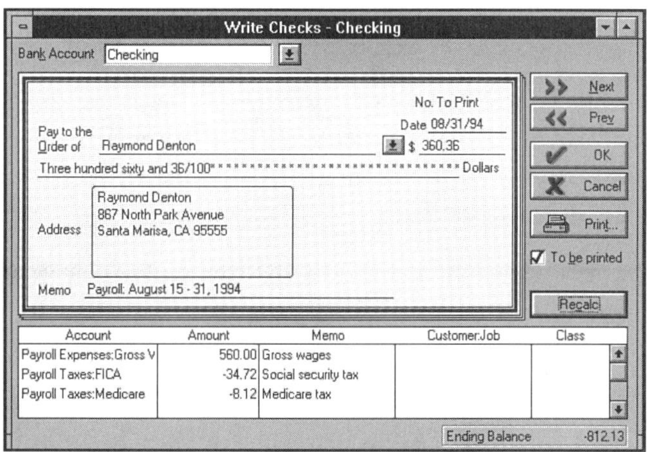

Fig. 13.5
QuickBooks calculates the check amount by totalling the amounts in the detail area of the Write Checks window.

Hiding Detail Lines. QuickBooks prints the information in the detail area of the Write Checks window on voucher checks. You may not, however, want the accounts assigned to a check to appear on the printed check voucher. If you are sending a check to a vendor to pay a bill, for example, you may not want to print portions of the voucher dealing with Customer:Jobs. Of course, if you use nonvoucher checks, QuickBooks does not print this information.

QuickBooks prints only the first 16 lines of the detail area. If you do not want to print some of the information on the check voucher, move to line 17 of the detail area and enter the information there. QuickBooks does not display line numbers in the detail area; therefore, you'll need to count down to line 17.

Editing a Check

Before you print checks that you recorded, review them one final time to ensure that the following information is correct: check amounts, payees, addresses (especially when you use window envelopes), and assigned accounts or Customer:Jobs.

QuickBooks organizes checks in chronological order. The Write Checks window displays only a single check at a time. To scroll through several checks to review each one, you can use the **N**ext or Pre**v** buttons. As you review the checks to be printed, you can make any necessary last-minute changes.

To edit a check, follow these steps:

1. Choose the Check button on the Iconbar; choose **A**ctivities, **W**rite Checks; or press Ctrl+W to access the Write Checks window.
2. Choose the Pre**v** button repeatedly to display the checks that have been written. Each time that you choose the Pre**v** button, QuickBooks displays the check with the check number immediately preceding the currently displayed check.
3. Edit a check by moving to the field that you want to change and selecting or typing new information.

   When you change a dollar amount, in either the check face or the check detail area, the transaction must balance. Say that you enter a check in the amount of $400.00, which is assigned to the Insurance Expense account. You now notice that you should have written the check for $425.00 and divided the expense between the Disability Insurance account (for $175.00) and the Liability Insurance account (for $250.00). You must not only change the amount in the $ field in the check face, but also the amounts in the detail area to assign the check transaction to the two insurance expense accounts. The amount in the $ field must be equal to the total of the Amount fields in the detail area. If not, QuickBooks displays a Warning dialog box telling you that your transaction is not in balance. QuickBooks will not record a transaction that is not in balance.
4. Choose the Pre**v** button to record the changes to the current check. QuickBooks displays the preceding check.

Voiding a Check

If a check becomes lost in the mail, or if you stopped payment on it, tell QuickBooks that this check is no longer valid. QuickBooks gives you the choice of voiding or deleting a check. Voiding a check has two advantages over simply deleting the transaction:

- Your Check register retains its numbered sequence.
- You retain the essential information about the check in your register. QuickBooks simply notes that it is void and enters the amount as $0.00.

To void a check, follow these steps:

1. Choose the Check button on the Iconbar; choose **A**ctivities, **W**rite Checks; or press Ctrl+W to access the Write Checks window.
2. Choose the Pre**v** button until the check to be voided displays in the window.
3. Choose **E**dit, **V**oid Check. QuickBooks voids the check, as shown in figure 13.6, and enters the word `VOID` as a prefix to any note that you enter in the Memo field. The check amount and the amounts in the detail area are all changed to 0.

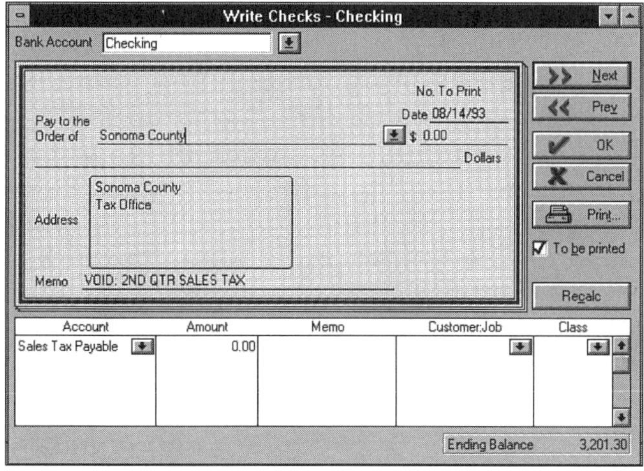

Fig. 13.6
Voiding a check in the Write Checks window.

4. Choose OK. QuickBooks adjusts the balance in your checking account to add back the amount from the voided check.

Tip
If you notice that you voided the wrong check, and you have not yet recorded the transaction (by clicking OK), choose **E**dit, **R**evert to restore the transaction.

Deleting a Check

Suppose that you want to delete a practice check or a check that you wrote inadvertently or incorrectly. QuickBooks enables you to delete checks that have been written and recorded, but have not yet printed. Because QuickBooks permanently deletes all information for the check transaction when you delete a check, you should not delete a check that has been printed. You should, instead, void printed checks. (The previous section explained how to void checks in the Write Checks window.)

To delete a check, follow these steps:

1. Access the Write Checks window, as explained previously.
2. Click the Pre**v** command button until the check that you want to delete is displayed.
3. Choose **E**dit, **D**elete Check, or press Ctrl+D. The Delete Transaction warning dialog box asks if you're sure you want to delete the transaction.
4. Delete the transaction by choosing the OK button. QuickBooks deletes the check and closes the Write Checks window. If you don't want to delete the check, choose Cancel. The check remains in the Write Checks window.

CPA TIP: Voiding Instead of Deleting

Deleting a check when you stop payment or lose a check removes the transaction information from the Check register and creates a gap in your check number sequence. Also, missing checks and transaction information affect the integrity of your financial system. To maintain system integrity, void all stopped payments, lost checks, checks written with errors, or checks printed incorrectly. Your check system is one place where you want to maintain strict control. Delete only those checks that you have written in the Write Checks window but have not been printed.

Printing Checks

After you write all the checks that you need, you can print them. With QuickBooks, you can print your checks when you have the time and are ready to send them out. This helps you to maintain an extra measure of control over your financial system.

By printing your checks all at once or in a group, you save yourself time by not having to get the checks out and into the printer, and you do not have to check the alignment each time. You also have greater control of your checks by having to access them only when they are needed, not at every miscellaneous occasion.

Ordering Checks

Before you can print checks, you must order them. Intuit provides you with several options for printing checks with both continuous-feed paper and laser printer paper.

A check and invoice form catalog comes with your QuickBooks program. Select the style of check that you want to use. Your QuickBooks checks can include the following: your name, address, account number, bank name, check numbers, and all information required by financial institutions. You even can print a standard or customized logo on your QuickBooks checks.

Intuit offers checks to fit continuous-feed printers and single-sheet printers, such as laser and inkjet printers. Payroll/voucher and standard (nonvoucher) checks are available for all printer types. When you order voucher checks, a stub or voucher is attached to the checks so that you can include the additional information on the check. Refer to Chapter 1, "Preparing To Use QuickBooks for Windows," for a complete description of the check styles that Intuit offers.

CPA TIP: Numbering Your Checks

You occasionally will need to write some manual checks, such as when you're away from the office. You either can take one of your QuickBooks checks with you or continue to write checks from your manual checkbook. After you write a manual check, simply enter the check transaction in the QuickBooks Check register.

If you also will be using your manual checkbook, you should start the QuickBooks check numbering in a higher range than your manual checkbook's numbering system. If your manual checkbook currently is in the 3000 range, for example, start your QuickBooks checks in the 5000 or 6000 range: 5001, 5002, 5003, or 6001, 6002, 6003, and so on.

Intuit includes sample checks in your QuickBooks package. Review the sample checks and experiment with them to determine which check type works best for your business. Intuit guarantees the following:

- Your checks will be accepted by your bank.
- Your checks will work with your printer.
- Your order will be printed without errors as submitted.

For current prices and shipping information, refer to the Intuit catalog, or print the Intuit Checks and Invoices Order Form. Choose **A**ctivities, Supplies **O**rder Form.

Note

You can also order checks through your financial institution or through check printing companies such as The Deluxe Check Printers, Inc., provided the checks fit your printer and include preprinted numbers. If you use the double-window envelopes from Intuit, the windows may not line up with checks ordered from vendors other than Intuit.

CPA TIP: Compare Cost of Checks

Look into the cost of preprinted computer checks from your bank before you order checks from Intuit, because your bank may offer a more economical price. Just make sure that the checks you order are compatible with your printer and the QuickBooks program.

Positioning Checks in Your Printer

With QuickBooks for Windows, it is easy to correctly position your checks in your printer, whether you use a continuous-feed printer or laser printer.

Tip
If you do not want to use one of your preprinted checks for a test, print the sample check on plain paper. Then overlay the sample check on one of your preprinted checks to see how the text lines up.

If you use a continuous-feed printer, place your checks in the printer just as you would regular paper. With a laser or inkjet printer (page-oriented), you can still print a single check if needed. Just use your printer's envelope feeder. Check the manual for your specific printer.

If the printing on your checks does not line up with the preprinted lines on your checks, QuickBooks can easily help you adjust the alignment of the printing. QuickBooks comes with several sample standard-style checks that you can use to check the alignment of your printer. If you bought a different style of check, test the printing with one of your own.

To test your printer's alignment with your checks, follow these steps:

1. Choose **F**ile, **P**rinter Setup. Then choose **C**heck Printer. The Check Printer Setup dialog box appears, as shown in figure 13.7.

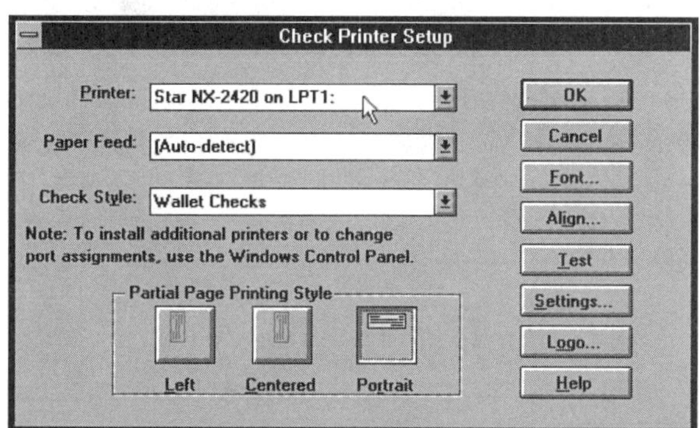

Fig. 13.7
The Check Printer Setup dialog box allows you to select your check printer and test the alignment of your preprinted checks.

2. Select the printer on which you will print checks. The printer that you plan to use to print checks must be installed through the Windows control panel. If you correctly install the printer, the name appears in the **P**rinter drop-down list box.

3. Select the paper feed for your check printer from the P**a**per Feed drop-down list box. QuickBooks selects Auto-detect by default. This option works with most printers. If QuickBooks has problems with your particular printer, try the Continuous or Page-oriented option.

4. In the Check St**y**le box, select the style of checks that you use: Standard, Voucher, or Wallet.

5. Use the Partial Page Printing Style box to choose the position that matches the way you load a partial page of checks in your printer. There are three selections:

Selection	Position of Checks
Left	If you place checks on the left side of the paper tray or feed bin.
Centered	If you place checks in the center of the paper tray or feed bin.
Po**r**trait	If you place checks in the same way that you place plain paper.

If you use a continuous-feed printer, only the portrait option is available, and it is selected by default. Generally, you need to make a selection only if a page-oriented printer is selected as the check printer.

Caution

When printing checks, be sure that you specify partial pages, and how many, when you print less than a full page of laser checks. If you don't, QuickBooks prints your checks incorrectly; you will need to void each check and then reprint them.

6. Choose the **T**est button to print a test check. QuickBooks prints a test check for "Jane Doe."

   Carefully check the alignment of all the fields and the check lines. You must decide whether they printed where you want, or whether they are too high, too low, or too far to the right or the left.

   If your test check prints just as you want, choose the OK button to save your selections. If the test check needs to be adjusted, continue to step 7.

7. Choose the Al**i**gn button. The Check Printer Alignment dialog box displays, as in figure 13.8.

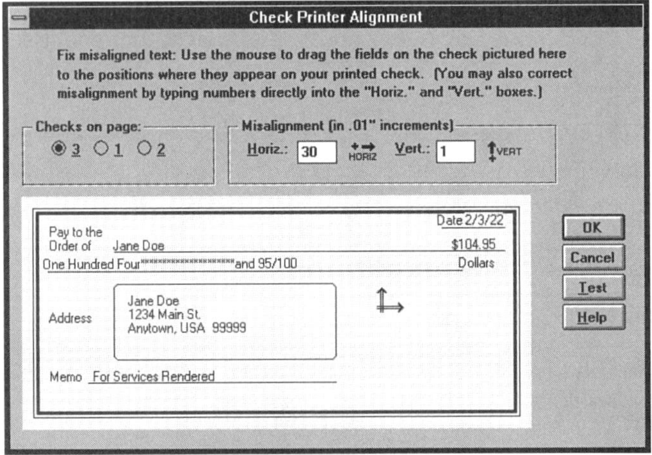

Fig. 13.8
Use the Check Printer Alignment dialog box to adjust the alignment of text on a check.

Notice the alignment cursor in figure 13.8. It displays as double arrows, with each at a right angle to the other. This cursor helps to align text on the check face in the Check Printer Alignment dialog box.

8. Press and hold the left mouse button as you drag the text of the test check to the position that it actually printed on your sample. Then release the left mouse button to leave the text where you positioned it. QuickBooks automatically enters the appropriate values in the **H**oriz. and **V**ert. fields. If the text was too far to the right, and a little too far down, for example, move it to this position now. Figure 13.9 displays the text in its printed position. QuickBooks uses this information to adjust the text on the printed check.

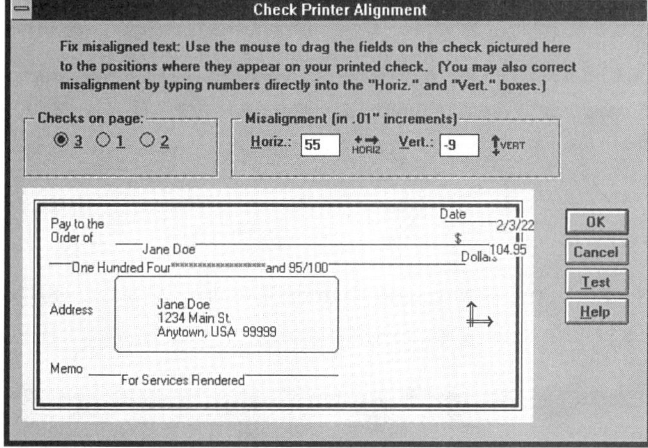

Fig. 13.9
The text, as printed, on the test check.

9. Choose the **T**est button to try the new alignment. QuickBooks prints the same test check again. Repeat steps 7 and 8 until the text on the test check is properly aligned.

10. Choose the OK button to leave the Check Printer Alignment dialog box and save your new alignment settings.

Note

If the printing needs only a small adjustment vertically or horizontally, increase or decrease the values in the **H**oriz. or **V**ert. fields by one or two. Repositioning the text by extremely small increments is difficult when using the mouse.

Printing Checks

Now that you have set up your check printer and properly aligned your checks, you are ready to print checks. After you write several checks in the Write Checks window, you can print them. QuickBooks enables you to selectively print checks; you don't have to print every check that you have written. After you print the checks, QuickBooks enters the check number of each printed check in the appropriate transaction line in the Check register. You can write checks for an entire month and print them at once. Alternatively, you can print only once or twice a month, or only when the checks are due.

QuickBooks prints checks in chronological order; the earliest-dated check prints first, followed by later-dated checks.

Note

You can prevent an unauthorized person from printing checks by using a password. Assigning passwords to check printing is explained in Chapter 21, "Managing QuickBooks for Windows Files."

To print checks, follow these steps:

1. Choose **F**ile, Print **F**orms, and then choose Print **C**hecks. The Select Checks to Print dialog box displays, as shown in figure 13.10.

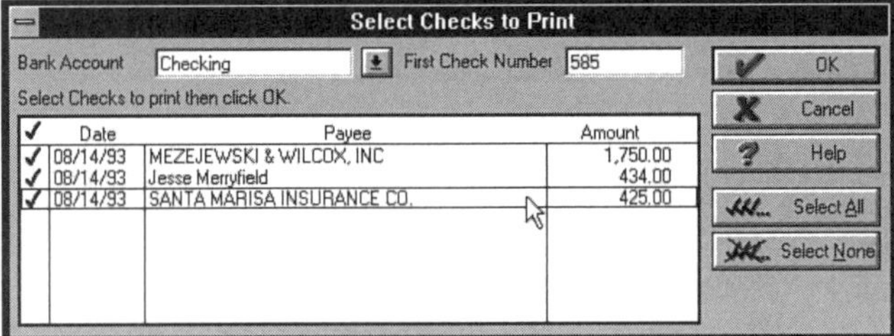

Fig. 13.10 Use the Select Checks to Print dialog box to choose the checks that you want to print at this time.

2. In the Ban**k** Account drop-down list box, select the bank account from which you write checks. If you use more than one bank account and select a different account in the Ban**k** Account drop-down list box, another list of checks displays in the Select Checks to Print dialog box.

3. In the First Check Number field, QuickBooks automatically enters the next blank check. If this number does not match the number shown on the next blank check that you loaded in your printer, change the check

number. If this difference occurs, it may be due to a hand-written check that has not yet been recorded.

4. Next, from the list of checks in the Select Checks to Print dialog box, select the checks that you want to print at this time. By default, QuickBooks selects all the checks that have been written and are ready to be printed. The check mark in the far left column indicates that a check is selected for printing.

   You can select a check by performing any of the following actions:

   - Choose the Select **A**ll button. All checks ready to be printed are selected.
   - Place the mouse pointer on a check and click.
   - Highlight a check with the up- or down-arrow key and press the space bar.

   To unselect a check, perform any of the following actions:

   - Choose the Select **N**one button.
   - Place the mouse pointer on a check and click.
   - Highlight a check and press the space bar.

5. When you have selected the checks to print, choose the OK button. The Print Checks dialog box displays, as you see in figure 13.11.

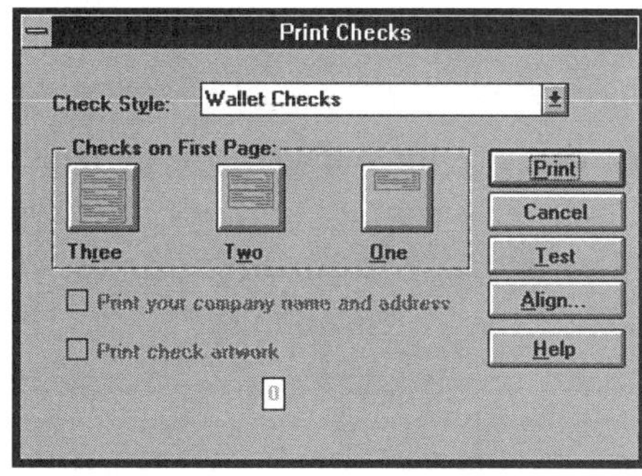

Fig. 13.11
After you select which checks you want to print, QuickBooks displays the Print Checks dialog box.

6. If the check style that appears in the Check St**y**le drop-down list box is not correct, select the correct one from the drop-down list.

7. For page-oriented printers, choose the Th**r**ee, T**w**o, or **O**ne check icon to match the number of checks that are on the first page of checks that you insert into your printer.

> **Note**
>
> If you have temporary checks that don't have your company's name or address, you can print this information on checks. To do so, select the Print Your Company Name and Address check box.

8. For voucher check styles, an extra text box—A**d**ditional Copies—appears in the Print Checks dialog box. Type the number of additional check copies that you want to print.

9. Choose the **P**rint button to print the selected checks.

   You also can print a test check before you print your real checks by choosing the **T**est button. With the **A**lign button, you can adjust the check alignment if necessary.

10. After you print your checks, QuickBooks displays the Did Check(s) Print OK? dialog box, shown in figure 13.12. Review the printed checks carefully.

If all the checks print without problems, choose the OK button. QuickBooks removes the check mark in the To **B**e Printed option check box for each check in the Write Checks window. The check then does not appear again in the Select Checks to Print dialog box (refer to figure 13.10).

If one or more of your checks printed incorrectly, perhaps the alignment wasn't right or the check forms jammed in the printer. Type the number of the first check that printed incorrectly, and then choose OK. Checks that you specify were not printed correctly remain in the Select Checks to Print dialog box (refer to figure 13.10).

Repeat steps 1 through 10 to reprint the checks that printed incorrectly.

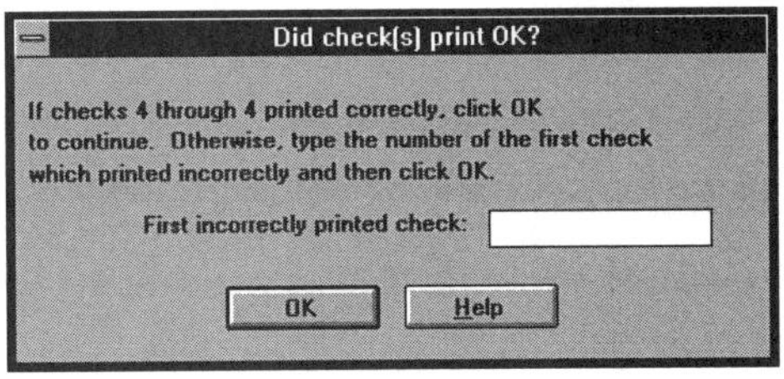

Did check(s) print OK?

If checks 4 through 4 printed correctly, click OK to continue. Otherwise, type the number of the first check which printed incorrectly and then click OK.

First incorrectly printed check:

OK Help

Fig. 13.12
If checks did not print correctly, enter the number of the first incorrectly printed check in the Did Check(s) Print OK? dialog box.

Note

If you enter historical transactions from the Write Checks window, QuickBooks indicates that you have checks to be printed. If you want a copy of the checks that you entered, print them on plain paper. If you do not want to print them, simply uncheck the To **B**e Printed option check box for each historical check transaction in the Write Checks window.

Reprinting Checks

To reprint a check, simply repeat the steps from the previous section on printing a check. QuickBooks prints the check again, just as if it had never been printed.

CPA TIP: Voiding Misprinted Checks

If one of your prenumbered QuickBooks checks does not print properly and you have to reprint it, be sure to mark *VOID* across the face of the incorrect check so that it can't be signed and cashed by an unauthorized person. You also need to void the check number in the Check register so that all your check numbers are accounted for in your QuickBooks system. See Chapter 14, "Entering Transactions in the Check Register," to learn how to void transactions in the Check register.

Printing a Logo on Checks

With QuickBooks, you can print a logo on your checks. Using logos in QuickBooks has two requirements, however:

- The logo must come from artwork from a Windows bit-map (.BMP) file.
- The logo artwork must not be larger than one square inch.

To print a logo on your checks, follow these steps:

1. Choose **F**ile, Printer **S**etup, and then choose Check **P**rinter. QuickBooks displays the Check Printer Setup dialog box (refer to figure 13.7).

2. Choose L**o**go to display the Check Logo Artwork dialog box, shown in figure 13.13.

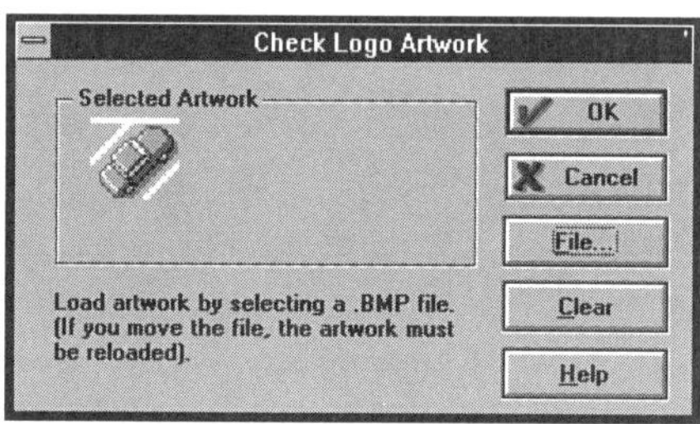

Fig. 13.13
The Check Logo Artwork dialog box displays the logo that prints on checks.

3. Choose **F**ile to display the Open Artwork File dialog box (see figure 13.14). Change the directory to the directory where your bit-map files are stored by double-clicking and scrolling to the correct path within the **D**irectories list box. Then select the bit-map file from the File **N**ame list box. (Bit-map files have the extension .BMP.) Choose OK to paste the artwork in the Selected Artwork box of the Check Logo Artwork dialog box.

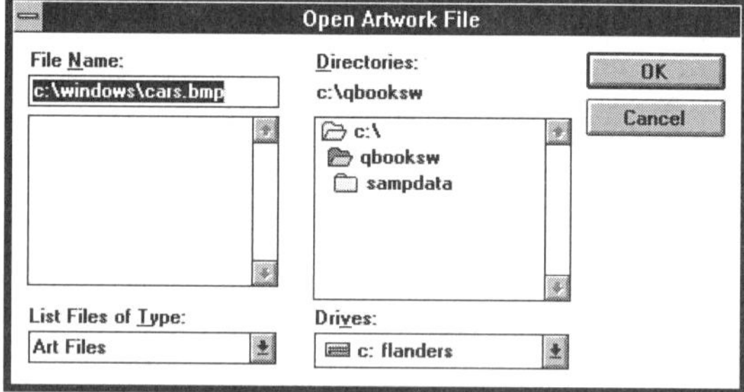

Fig. 13.14
Select your artwork bit-map file from the Open Artwork File dialog box.

4. If this logo is the one you want to print on checks, choose OK. If it isn't, choose **F**ile again and select another bit-map file.

5. When you're ready to print checks, follow steps 1 through 5 in the earlier section "Printing Checks" to display the Print Checks dialog box (refer to fig. 13.11).

6. From the Print Checks dialog box, select the Print Check Artwork check box.

> **Note**
>
> The Print Check Artwork check box isn't available if you print wallet-style checks. This check box also isn't available unless you have previously selected a bit-map file, as explained in steps 1 through 4.

7. Print the checks as usual.

Summary

This chapter discussed how to write a check and how to assign a check to an account transaction. You learned how to split the transaction to assign more than one account and to allocate an expense as a reimbursable expense to a Customer:Job account. You also learned to use the detail area to calculate the check amount and to hide detail lines so that they don't appear on printed checks. You then learned to edit, void, delete, and print checks.

In the next chapter, you learn to enter a transaction directly into the Check register. You also learn to edit and split transactions, and to enter a transfer transaction.

Chapter 14

Entering Transactions in the Check Register

While reading this book, you have seen a few references to the Check register. In the last chapter, you learned that QuickBooks automatically enters checks that you write in the Write Checks window into the Check register and updates your account balance. In this chapter, you learn exactly what the Check register is and how to use it.

Each of the Balance Sheet accounts, such as Accounts Receivable, Accounts Payable, Current Assets, Fixed Assets, and so on, also have registers similar to the Check register. You learned about the Accounts Receivable register in Chapter 10, "Using the Accounts Receivable Register," and the Accounts Payable register in Chapter 12, "Using the Accounts Payable Register."

In this chapter you learn how to do the following:

- Enter new transactions into the Check register
- Edit, delete, and void existing transactions
- Split transactions to assign more than one account
- Find and enter transfer transactions
- Enter historical transactions
- Print the Check register

Displaying the Check Register

The Check register is similar to a manual checkbook register; it has fields for the date, check number, payee, check or deposit amount, a memo or note, and the ending balance of your checking account. You can access the Check register any time that you need to view or use the register. QuickBooks makes it easy for you to switch between the Check register and the Write Checks window.

Use the Check register when you want to do the following:

- Enter manual checks that you have written, historical transactions, or summary transactions
- Enter bank fees on your checking account

- Add interest earned on the account
- Edit, delete, or void a check transaction
- Find and review a check transaction

To access the Check register window, follow these steps:

1. Access the Chart of Accounts window with one of the following procedures:
   - Choose the Accnt button from the Iconbar.
   - Press Ctrl+A.
   - From the **L**ists menu, choose Chart of **A**ccounts.
   - Choose the Reg button from the Iconbar.
2. Choose Checking account from the Chart of Accounts window by double-clicking the name of your checking account. You also can choose the Checking account by highlighting the account and choosing the Use Register button or pressing Enter. The Check register, as shown in figure 14.1, appears on-screen.

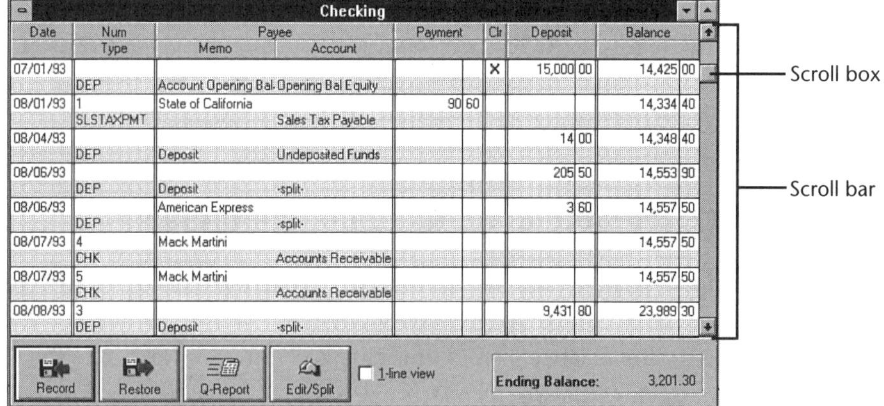

Fig. 14.1
The name of the Check register window is the same as the account name.

Reviewing the Check Register

As you can see from figure 14.1, the QuickBooks Check register resembles a manual check register. It includes a transaction line for each check or deposit so that you can enter the date, check number, payee, payment or deposit amount, and a memo. Unlike your manual register, however, the QuickBooks Check register includes fields to assign accounts and jobs to transactions. Assigning accounts and jobs to transactions provides complete tracking of your income, expenses, and customer:jobs. Also, unlike any manual check register, the QuickBooks Check register automatically keeps your balance current. Because QuickBooks uses the account name as the window title, you always know which checking account register you are displaying. In figure 14.1, the name of the checking account is simply "Checking." However, if you named your checking account "First National," that name would appear in the title bar of the Check register when you chose the account.

The Check register has many fields, which are described in the following table:

Field	Description
Date	Shows the date the transaction was entered.
Num	Shows the check number.
Type	Notes the type of transaction that occurred. You can't edit this field. Some of the type codes that you see in the Check register include:
	CHK refers to a check.
	DEP refers to a deposit.
	BILLPMT refers to a payment for a bill.
	SLSTAXPMT refers to a payment for sales taxes. (Paying sales tax is explained in Chapter 7, "Tracking Sales Tax.")
Payee	Displays the name of the check payee or the deposit source.
Memo	Displays any note that you place in the Write Checks memo field. This memo appears on any report that includes this transaction.
Account	Shows the account to which you have assigned the payment. If you have assigned the payment to two or more accounts, the field displays the word **-split-**.
Payment	Lists the amount of the check or a withdrawal from the account.
Clr	An X indicates that you have marked the transaction as cleared. The X appears after you have reconciled the account with your check statement from the bank or if the transaction has been voided.
Deposit	Lists the amount of a deposit or an addition to the account.
Balance	QuickBooks automatically calculates the balance in your account after the current transaction and enters the result here. You cannot edit this field.

Tip

If you use more than one checking account for your business, be sure to distinguish them by giving them a unique name. You may want your everyday checking to be called, "General Checking," your payroll could be "Payroll Checking," and your investment checking could be "Investment Checking."

The Check register also includes four command buttons and one option check box:

Button/Box	Description
Record	Records the selected transaction. Choose Record when you finish entering or editing a transaction in the register.
Restore	Reverts the transaction you are editing to the way it was before you started editing. You must use Restore before you record a transaction.
Q-Report	Creates a report displaying all transactions related to the payee in the selected transaction.
Edit/Split	Opens the window from which the transaction originated, such as Write Checks, Pay Bills, or Make Deposits.
1-line view	When this option check box is selected, the Check register displays a single line for each transaction. This enables you to see twice as many transactions on-screen.

QuickBooks also displays the Ending Balance and the Current Balance at the bottom of the Check register window. The Ending Balance field shows the balance in the account after all transactions. The Current Balance appears when postdated transactions are entered in the Check register. The Current Balance shows the balance in the account based on all transactions entered with dates through the current date. QuickBooks updates the values in the Ending and Current Balance fields each time a new transaction is entered or an existing transaction is edited.

Moving Around the Check Register

As you get up to speed with QuickBooks, you will want to move through the Check register quickly so that you can enter transactions as fast as possible or review prior transactions without having to move through the register line by line.

You can easily move from transaction to transaction in the Check register window by using the scroll bar on the right side of the Check register window (see figure 14.1). Just click the down arrow to move to the next transactions, or click the up arrow to move to the preceding transaction.

You also can use the scroll box to move quickly through transactions in the Check register window. To move through the register using the scroll box, follow these steps:

1. Position the mouse pointer on the scroll box.

2. Press and hold down the left mouse button as you drag (move) the scroll box up or down the scroll bar.

As you drag the scroll box, QuickBooks displays a date box to the left of the scroll box. This date represents the date of the transaction that will be at the top of the Check register window when you release the scroll box. Figure 14.2 shows the date box in the Check register.

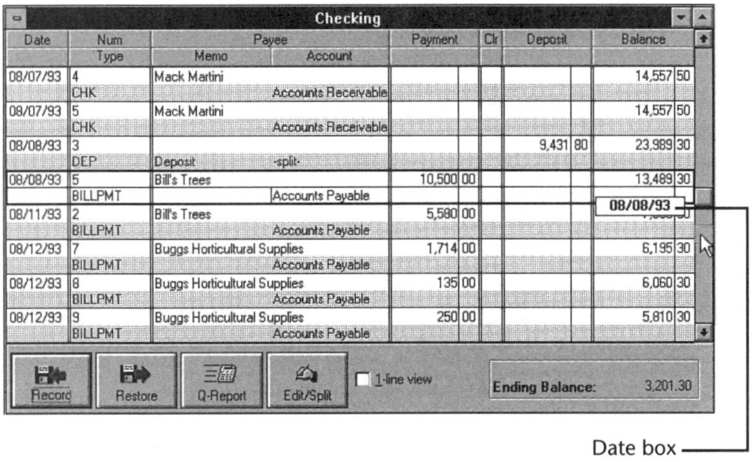

Fig. 14.2
With the mouse and scroll bar, you can move up and down the Check register window. Notice the date box beside the scroll bar.

With a few simple keystrokes, you can also navigate the Check register. Table 14.1 lists the different keystrokes that you use to move in the Check register.

Table 14.1. Keystrokes for Moving in the Check Register

Press These Keys	To Move To
Up arrow	Move up one transaction
Down arrow	Move down a single transaction
PgUp (Page Up) or Home+Home+Home	Move up one screen of transactions
PgDn (Page Dn) or End+End+End	Move down one screen of transactions
Ctrl+PgUp	Move to the first transaction of the current or prior month

(continues)

Table 14.1. Continued

Press These Keys	To Move To
Ctrl+PgDn	Move to the first transaction of the next month
Ctrl+Home	Move to the beginning of the register
Ctrl+End	Move to the end of the register

Entering Transactions

You can use QuickBooks to enter transactions directly into the Check register where they can be edited, deleted, and voided. You also can add an account to the Chart of Accounts from the Check register. This is helpful when you are assigning a new account to a transaction that you are entering in the register.

You enter check transactions in the Check register in much the same way that you enter checks in the Write Checks window. The transaction information that you enter is the same, it's just in a slightly different order.

Caution

When you add a transaction, such as a check, in the Check register, QuickBooks assumes that this transaction has been completed. The check is not added to the Checks to be printed list. If you need to print the check, you must view the check in the Write Checks window and select the To Be Printed check box. Then, QuickBooks enters To Print in the Num field for the check transaction in the Check register.

Note

Remember, you need to enter your historical transactions as soon as possible. You can enter current transactions now, but you cannot get complete and accurate reports without the historical transactions being added to the Checks register. Entering historical transactions is covered later in this chapter.

To add a transaction to the Check register, follow these steps:

1. Access the Check register as previously explained.

2. Press Ctrl+End to move to the next empty transaction line in the Check register.

3. In the Date field, QuickBooks automatically fills in the current date for you.

   To enter a different date, type over the existing date using the MM/DD/YY format. If you are entering August 16, 1994, for example, type **081694**. QuickBooks displays the date as 08/16/94. You also can press the + or – keys to quickly increase or decrease the date.

4. QuickBooks automatically enters the next check number available in the Num field. If you are using a different number, type the new number over the existing number. You also can use the + or – keys to increase or decrease the number by 1 each time you press the key. After entering the correct check number, press Tab to move to the payee field.

   If you are entering a deposit transaction, no entry is necessary in the Num field. If you are entering an automatic teller transaction, you may want to enter **ATM** in the Num field to identify the transaction.

5. Enter the payee's name in the Payee field. If the payee is a person or firm that is included in any of your QuickBooks lists, you can display the list by doing one of the following:

   - Pressing Alt+down arrow
   - Clicking the drop-down arrow
   - Pressing Ctrl+L to display the Name List window, as shown in figure 14.3

Note

Remember that when you are typing a name in the Payee field, QuickBooks helps you fill in the name with QuickFill. As you type the first letter of the payee name, QuickBooks searches the Name List for a payee name that starts with the letter that you type. QuickBooks then fills in the rest of the payee name in the Payee field. If the payee name that QuickBooks enters is not the payee that you want, continue typing until the correct name is entered in the Payee field.

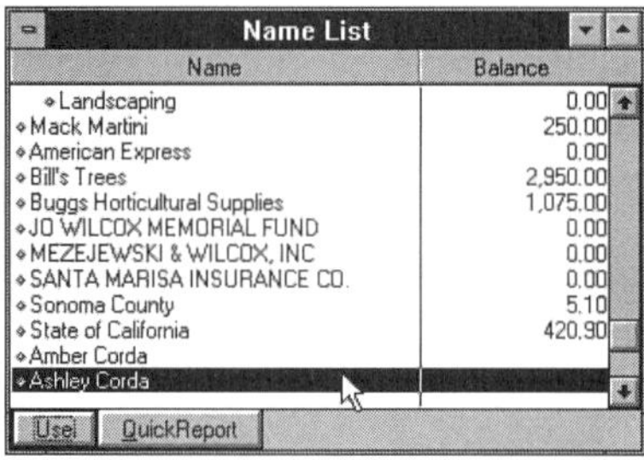

Fig. 14.3 QuickBooks displays the Name List window when you press Ctrl+L from the Payee field in the Check register.

If the person or firm that is the payee for this transaction is not listed in your QuickBooks Name List, you can add it now.

If you are entering a transaction other than a check transaction in the Check register, type the transaction description in the Payee field. For example, type **Deposit**, **Interest Earned**, **Bank Charge**, **ATM Withdrawal**, and so on.

If QuickBooks cannot find the payee in the Name List, the Name Not Found dialog box appears, as shown in figure 14.4, telling you that the name was not found.

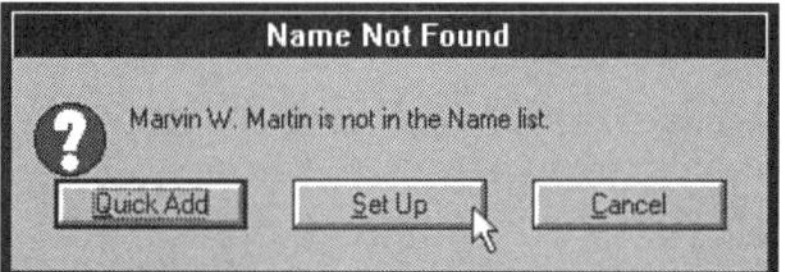

Fig. 14.4 From the Name Not Found dialog box, you can add a new name to your QuickBooks lists.

From the Name Not Found dialog box, you have three options, as shown in the following table:

Option	**Description**
Quick Add	Adds only the name to the Name List. You do not have any of the other information, such as address or phone number.
Set Up	Sets up the payee's name, address, phone numbers, credit limits, and other information. This information is saved with the name.
Cancel	Cancels the dialog box, returning you to the Check register. Use this option if you decide that you have the wrong name or want to delete the transaction.

If you select **S**et Up, the Select Name Type dialog box appears, asking you to choose the type of payee that you want to set up (see fig. 14.5).

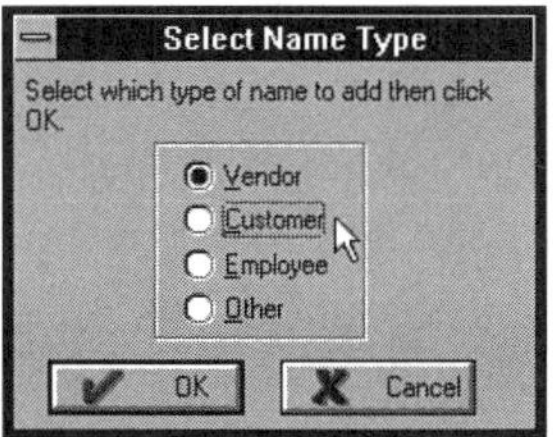

Fig. 14.5
Choose the type of payee that you are adding in the Select Name Type dialog box.

The Select Name Type dialog box gives you a choice of four different types of payees, as listed in the following table:

Payee Type	Description
Vendor	If the payee is a vendor—someone that you buy goods or services from—choose this option.
Customer	If the payee is a customer, select this option.
Employee	If the payee is an employee that you have not yet added to your Employee List, select this option.
Other	If the payee does not fit one of the preceding three categories, choose this option.

Select the appropriate option and choose OK. QuickBooks displays the appropriate dialog box for you to enter the information about the payee.

Enter the necessary information in the displayed dialog box. Choose OK to save your information, and return to the Check register.

To continue filling in the Check register:

6. Enter the amount of the transaction.

   If this is a check or other withdrawal from the checking account, enter the amount in the Payment field.

   If this is a deposit or other addition to the checking account, enter the amount in the Deposit field.

7. Type a note in the Memo field if necessary. Memos help to describe transactions but are completely optional. Any note that you enter here also appears on any report that contains this transaction.

8. Choose the account to which you want to assign this transaction. You can choose an account using any of the methods used to choose a payee name, as you learned in step 5 of this section.

   The account that you assign to a transaction must currently exist in the Chart of Accounts. If the account that you enter does not exist, QuickBooks displays the dialog box shown in figure 14.6, and gives you a change to add the account at this time.

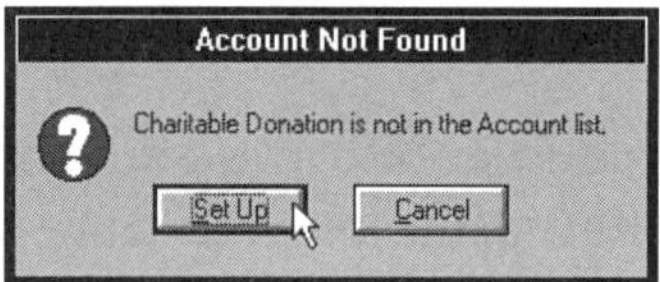

Fig. 14.6
If QuickBooks does not find the account that you enter in the Account field, the Account Not Found dialog box appears.

   To add the account, choose **S**et Up. To cancel and return to the Check register, choose **C**ancel. Choose **C**ancel only if you are going to choose another account.

   CPA TIP: Adding to Your Chart of Accounts

   Add accounts as you need them, but do not add an account just because you don't have an account with the name for which you are looking. The Chart of Accounts is the skeleton for your financial system. Add only accounts that will be useful to you. If you add accounts indiscriminately, you may end the year with many extra accounts that contain very few transactions. Try to consolidate your transactions to existing accounts.

   If you decide to set up the new account, enter the required information. Choose OK to save the new account information in the Chart of Accounts and return to the Check register.

9. Choose Record to record the transaction in the Check register. QuickBooks automatically moves the transaction up and displays the next blank transaction line.

Figure 14.7 shows the completed transaction in the Check register. Notice the dark line above check number 12, which was written to Ashley Corda. All transactions that appear below the dark line are postdated or dated after the current system date.

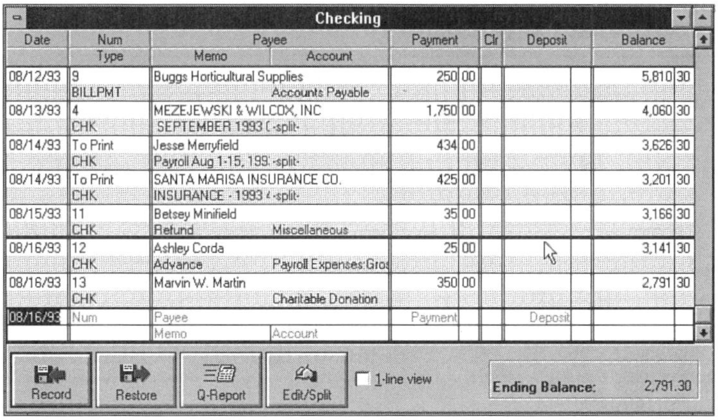

Fig. 14.7
Completed transactions in the Check register. Notice the heavy line indicating that all transactions below it are postdated.

Editing Transactions

If you need to go back and change the information in a recorded transaction, you can edit the transaction, and QuickBooks makes the necessary adjustments. For example, if you go to a recorded check transaction and change the check amount, QuickBooks recalculates the balance in your checking account. If you change the account that you originally assigned to a transaction, QuickBooks lowers the account balance in the original account and increases the balance of the account that you subsequently assign the transaction.

CPA TIP: Correcting Check Amounts

Most often, you should not adjust the total of a check that has been issued. If you need to change the check amount and the check is still in your possession, void the check and reissue it in the correct amount. Adjusting the check amount for checks that have been disbursed and have cleared the bank will cause problems with reconciling and could also cause discrepancies in the case of an audit.

To edit a Check register transaction, follow these steps:

1. Access the Check register, as previously explained.

2. Choose the transaction that you want to edit.

3. Move to the field to be edited. Use the following keys to move the cursor quickly through fields in a selected transaction:

Press These Keys	To Move
Tab	Forward one field.
Shift+Tab	Backward one field. If the cursor is currently positioned on the Date field, Shift+Tab moves you to the Edit/Split button.
Home	Beginning of the current field.
Home Home	Beginning of the first field in the current transaction.
End End	End of the last field in the current transaction.
Ctrl+Right-arrow	Forward one word within a field.
Ctrl+Left-arrow	Backward one word within a field.

Make the necessary changes to the transaction.

3. Choose Record to save your changes. If you decide that you do not want to save these changes, choose Restore.

CPA TIP: Transposing Amounts

A common source of error is in the transposition of transaction amounts. It's easy for the amount $940.00 to be entered as $490.00. During checkbook reconciliation, if the differences between your bank statement ending balance and your check register balance is a number divisible by 9, look for a transposition error in your Check register.

Splitting Transactions

Until now, you have entered transactions in the Check register that have been assigned to a single account. At times, you may want to assign a transaction to more than one account or split the transaction. You learned in Chapter 13, "Writing and Printing Checks," how to split a trans-action from the Write Checks window. You also can split a transaction from the Check register.

For example, if you went to Office Max and bought office supplies for $145.87, a facsimile machine for $678.95, and computer supplies for $79.50 with a manual check, you enter the check in the Check register and assign the transaction to several accounts.

To split a check transaction, follow these steps:

1. Access the Check register, as previously explained.
2. Press Ctrl+End to move to the next blank transaction line.
3. Enter the date, check number, payee, total amount of the check, and memo as usual.
4. Choose Edit/Split.

   QuickBooks displays the Write Checks window, as shown in figure 14.8. All of the information that you have already entered is included on the check face.

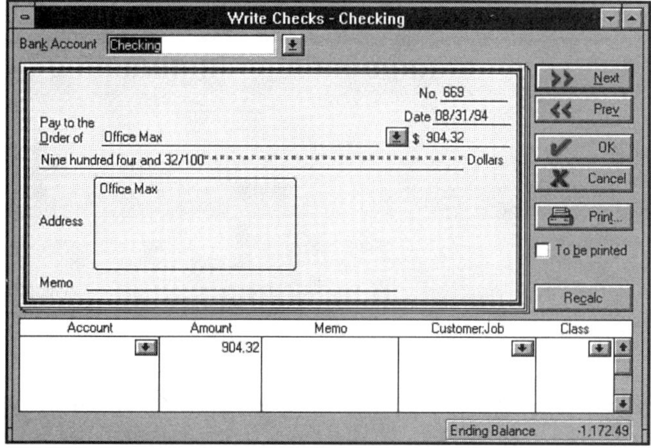

Fig. 14.8
This example shows the Write Checks window with the manual check information included.

5. In the first line of the detail area of the Write Checks window, choose the Office Supplies account in the Account drop-down list box. Then, in the Amount field, enter the dollar amount of office supplies bought: **145.87**.
6. Move to the next line of the detail area and choose the Fixed Assets account in the Account drop-down list box. In the Amount field, enter the dollar amount of the fixed asset bought: **678.95**. You may want to enter a note in the Memo field about the type of Fixed Asset bought—in this case a facsimile machine.

7. Next, move to the third line in the detail area and choose the Computer Supplies account in the Account drop-down list box. In the Amount field, enter the dollar amount of the computer supplies bought: **79.5**.

   The Write Checks window now looks like figure 14.9.

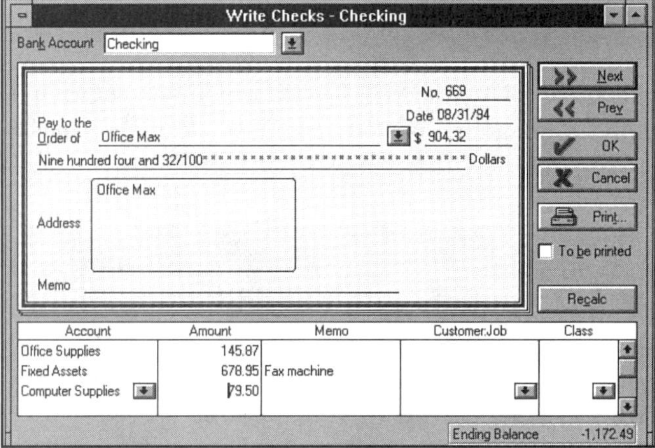

Fig. 14.9
Assigning more than one account to a check transaction.

8. Choose OK to record the split transaction and return to the Check register.

CPA TIP: Tracking Income and Expenses by Splitting Transactions

When you want to closely track your income and expenses, enter split transactions for payments to vendors in cases where you purchase different types of goods or services from a single vendor. The preceding example illustrates how a payment to a single vendor, Office Max, affects one Fixed Asset and two Expense accounts. If you do not split the transaction and instead lump the total payment into office supplies, for example, the expenses of your business are not accurately reflected.

Note

You can enter negative amounts in split transactions to represent withholdings for payroll checks or amounts deducted from a deposit. To enter a negative amount in the detail area of the Write Checks window, press the minus (–) key before you enter the amount.

Editing a Split Transaction

With QuickBooks, you can easily edit a split transaction, just as you would any other transaction.

To edit a split transaction, follow these steps:

1. Access the Check register, as previously explained.
2. Move to the transaction that you want to edit.
3. Choose Edit/Split. For check transactions, QuickBooks displays the complete transaction in the Write Checks window. For deposits, QuickBooks displays the transaction in the Make Deposits window.
4. Move to the field that you want to edit and make the necessary changes.

   Remember, if you change an amount, you must balance the transaction before QuickBooks will allow you to save the transaction.
5. Choose OK to save the edited transaction.

Deleting a Split Transaction Line

You can also delete a line from the detail area in a split transaction. If you decide not to assign part of the check to an account, delete that split transaction line from the detail area.

To delete a split transaction line, follow these steps:

1. Access the Check register, as previously explained.
2. Move to the split transaction that you want to edit.
3. Choose Edit/Split.
4. In the detail area, move to the split transaction line to be deleted.
5. From the **E**dit menu, choose Delete **L**ine; or press Ctrl+Del.
6. Balance the transaction by changing the check amount, or by adding the necessary amount to one or more of the remaining split transaction lines.
7. Choose OK to save your changes.

Deleting Transactions

QuickBooks enables you to delete a transaction that you inadvertently entered twice, entered in the wrong account register, and so on. When you delete a transaction, it is removed permanently from the Check register.

CPA TIP: Voiding Checks versus Deleting Checks

Correcting an erroneous transaction by voiding or reversing the transaction rather than deleting it is generally more acceptable. Deleting a transaction removes the check information and leaves a gap in your check-numbering sequence and also gives the impression that something may be concealed. Voiding or reversing a transaction leaves an "audit trail" (that is, a way to trace the information for the transaction) that helps reveal errors.

You should delete a recorded transaction only under the following circumstances:

- *You inadvertently enter a transaction that shouldn't be entered at all.* If you enter a deposit transaction in the Check register and subsequently don't make the deposit, for example, you should delete the transaction. Or if you enter a transaction for a bank fee in the Check register that the bank later rescinds, delete the bank fee transaction.
- *You duplicate transaction information.* For example, if you withdraw funds from an automatic teller machine and enter the transaction twice in the Check register, you should delete one of the two transactions.
- *You enter the transaction in the wrong QuickBooks register.* For example, if you enter a manual check to a vendor in the checking account set up for payroll, you should delete the transaction from the payroll account's Check register and enter it correctly in the Check register for the correct checking account.

In all other cases, you should void transactions in the Check register, so that you have complete records of all your check numbers and have established a proper audit trail in the register.

If you find that you need to delete a transaction, follow these steps:

1. Access the Check register, as previously explained.

2. Move to the transaction that you want to delete.

3. From the **E**dit menu, choose **D**elete Check; or press Ctrl+D. QuickBooks displays the Delete Transaction dialog box, as shown in figure 14.10.

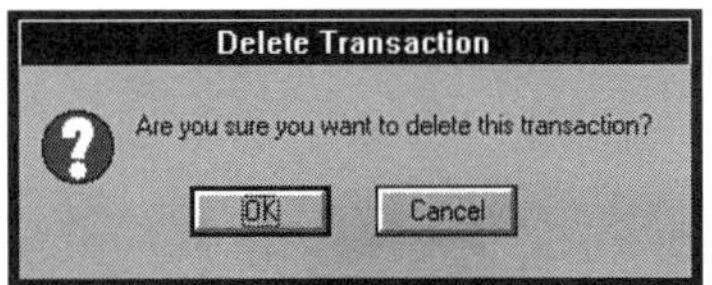

Fig. 14.10
Use the Delete Transaction dialog box to confirm the deletion of a transaction.

4. Choose OK to delete the transaction. Remember, the transaction is deleted permanently. You cannot recover it later. Choose **C**ancel to keep the transaction and return to the Check register.

Voiding Transactions

You may find that you need to void a check when you want to stop payment, when you lose a check and write another to replace it, or when a check prints incorrectly and you have to print another. Notice that you can choose to void a check from the Write Checks window, as you learned in Chapter 13, "Writing and Printing Checks."

To void a check from the Check register, follow these steps:

1. Access the Check register, as previously explained.

2. Move to the transaction that you want to void.

3. From the **E**dit menu, choose **V**oid Check. QuickBooks enters the word `VOID` in the memo field, as a prefix to any note that you have already entered, and changes the transaction amount to zero. An X is entered in the Clr field in the Check register for this transaction.

   You can reverse voiding the transaction by choosing the Restore button or **E**dit, **R**evert. You can do this only before you save the transaction changes. After you have saved the transaction, you cannot change it back.

4. Choose Record to save the changes.

Entering a Transfer Transaction

Up to now, you have used Expense accounts almost exclusively. A transfer transaction involves two Balance Sheet accounts. For instance, in the preceding example you bought a facsimile machine from Office Max. This is a transfer transaction because you have bought a fixed asset with funds from the checking account.

You enter a transfer transaction just like any other transaction, using Expense accounts. When you make the entry in the Check register, QuickBooks then makes a corresponding entry in the other Balance Sheet account.

Finding Transfer Transactions

When you enter a transfer transaction in one Balance Sheet account (source account), QuickBooks automatically records a corresponding transaction in the Balance Sheet account that you enter in the Account field (destination account). To quickly find the corresponding transfer transaction in the other Balance Sheet account, follow these steps:

1. Move to the transfer transaction in the source account's register.

2. From the **E**dit menu, choose **G**o To Transfer; or press Ctrl+G. For split transactions, you must go to the specific line that assigns a part of the transaction to another Balance Sheet account. From the **E**dit menu, choose **G**o To Transfer; or press Ctrl+G.

   QuickBooks displays the destination account's register, with the transfer transaction highlighted, as shown in figure 14.11.

Editing and Deleting a Transfer Transaction

You can edit or delete a transfer transaction just as you learned to do earlier in this chapter with transactions assigned to Expense Accounts. If you edit or delete a transfer transaction from the Check register, QuickBooks makes a corresponding change in the destination account's register. You can edit or delete a transfer transaction from either the source or destination account's register. However, if the transfer transaction is a split transaction, you must edit or delete it from the source account's register. This enables you to adjust the total of the transaction, or the distribution.

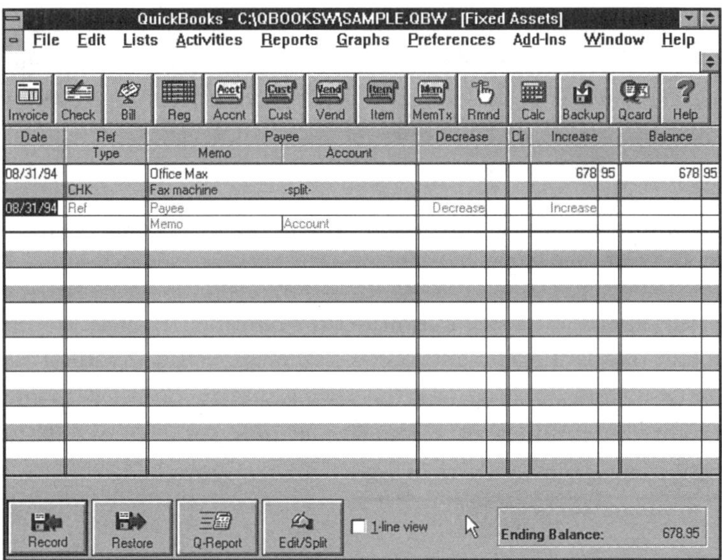

Fig. 14.11
Press Ctrl+G to go to the corresponding transfer transaction.

Entering Historical Transactions

If you're starting your QuickBooks system at any time other than the beginning of your fiscal year, you need to enter historical transactions. Historical transactions are those that are dated from the beginning of the year to the date you start your system. You can enter historical transactions in one of two ways:

- Enter each transaction directly in the Check register.
- Enter a summary transaction for income and expenses in the Check register. A summary transaction summarizes your income and expenses for a specific period. Summary transactions require fewer entries and may be the option for you if you have a significant number of historical transactions to enter to bring your QuickBooks system up to date.

There are two types of transactions that you need to consider when entering historical transactions:

- Uncleared transactions that occurred before the date of the bank statement you used when you set up your company. These transactions include checks, automatic teller machine (ATM) transactions, deposits, bank fees, interest earned, and other transactions. Review your manual check register to determine which transactions have not cleared the bank.

- Transactions that occurred since the opening date, even if they have cleared on subsequent bank statements. These transactions include checks, automatic teller machine (ATM) transactions, deposits, bank fees, interest earned, and other transactions. Review your manual check register to identify these transactions.

Entering historical transactions enables you to present a complete picture of your finances in QuickBooks.

If you want to record transactions from the beginning of your fiscal year, or since a previous bank statement date (for example, your last bank statement date), enter historical transactions the same way that you enter current transactions. Entering historical data from the beginning of the year or last bank statement brings your QuickBooks system up to date and reflects accurate totals for income and expenses.

Caution

If you are using the Accounts Payable register to track and pay bills or if you are using the Accounts Receivable register to track customer payments, enter historical transactions in those registers before you enter historical transactions in the Check register. When you enter historical transactions in the Accounts Payable and Accounts Receivable registers, QuickBooks automatically enters the appropriate transactions in the Check register. Refer to Chapter 10, "Using the Accounts Receivable Register," and Chapter 12, "Using the Accounts Payable Register," to learn how to enter historical Accounts Receivable and Accounts Payable transactions.

Enter historical transactions just as you have learned to enter current transactions. Remember to set the date of each historical transaction to the correct historical date for that transaction. QuickBooks automatically places the transaction in its correct chronological order in the Check register.

Entering a Summary Transaction

If you would rather not enter all of your year-to-date transactions individually, you can enter a few transactions that summarize your business activity since the first of the year. To enter a summary transaction, you first need to total your year-to-date transactions by Income and Expense accounts. For example, you first need to total all sales, purchases, advertising, office supplies, payroll, and so on. Total the year-to-date transactions for each account that you use in QuickBooks.

After you have accumulated totals by Income and Expense accounts, enter a split transaction in the Check register as follows:

1. Access the Check register, as previously explained.

2. Press Ctrl+End to move to the next blank transaction line.

3. In the Num field, type over the current date with the date prior to your QuickBooks start date. If you started QuickBooks on February 1, 1994, for example, enter **013194** as the date for the summary transaction.

4. Type **Year-To-Date Summary-Expenses**, **Income**, or some other descriptive phrase in the Payee field to indicate to you that the transaction is a summary of all prior transactions. Since QuickBooks does not find this name in any of its company lists, you'll need to select Quick Add and then add it as Other.

5. Do not enter an amount in the Payment or Deposit fields.

6. Choose Edit/Split.

7. In the detail area of the Write Checks window, list each of the accounts and the amounts that you have totaled. For example, if you had Payroll expenses of $5,432.65 for the year-to-date, in the Account drop-down list box, choose the Payroll Expense account and then enter **5432.65** in the Amount field. Continue for all Expense or Income accounts that you have totaled.

8. After you have entered all year-to-date totals, you must enter one more split transaction line to net the transaction to zero. In the Account field of the last detail line, choose the Open Bal Equity account. Because QuickBooks calculates the total transaction amount each time you enter another line, the amount field already should have an entry in it that balances the transaction to zero. This amount actually represents your net income or net loss (income minus expenses) for the period starting from the first day of your fiscal year to the date you started QuickBooks.

   Figure 14.12 shows the Write Checks window with a summary transaction so that you can see what it should look like before you record it. After you enter a summary transaction, your Income and Expense accounts accurately reflect all year-to-date activity. The Open Bal Equity account also adjusts to reflect activity through the current date.

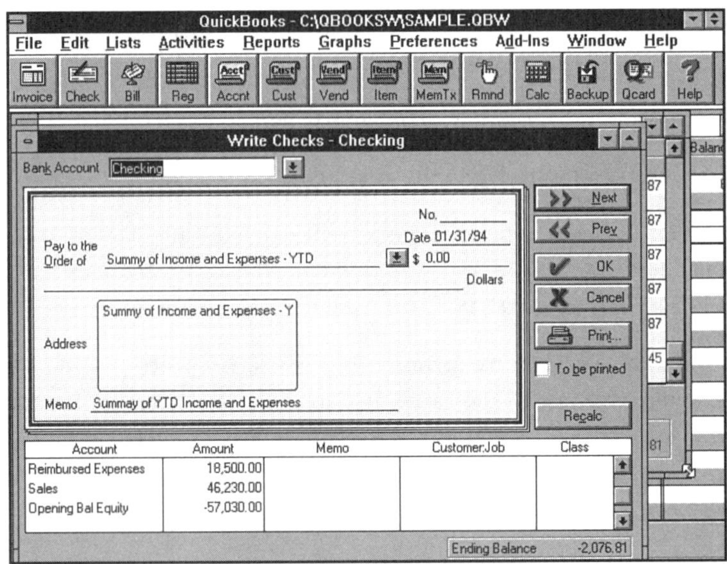

Fig. 14.12
A summary transaction entered as split transaction in the Write Checks window.

Printing the Check Register

As you have learned in this chapter, the QuickBooks Check register is easy to use. At times, you may want to take a copy of the register to another location so that you can verify transactions or give a copy to your accountant. You can quickly print a copy of the Check register by segments such as week, month, quarter, and so on or print the entire register. Be sure that you have set up your printer (from the **F**ile menu, choose Printer **S**etup and then choose **R**eport/List Printer). To print the check register, follow these steps:

1. Access the Check Register, as previously explained.
2. Choose **F**ile, **P**rint Register; or press Ctrl+P. QuickBooks displays the Print Register dialog box.
3. Select the Date **R**ange that you want to print. By default, QuickBooks selects from the beginning of your current fiscal year to today's date. If necessary, type new dates in the From and To fields.
4. To print all detail for each transaction, select the Show Transaction Detail check box.
5. Choose OK to print the Check register. Figure 14.13 shows the Check register printed with transaction detail. Figure 14.14 shows the Check register printed in summary format.

Register 11/02/93
Checking Register through 01/01/94:

Date	No.	Payee	Memo	Account	Amount C	Balance
01/0...	519	Nation...		-split-	-300.00	54,408.96
		Truck Loan			-285.00	
		Interest exp...			-15.00	

Fig. 14.13
The Check register printed with transaction detail.

Register 11/02/93
Checking Register through 01/31/94:

Date	No.	Payee	Memo	Account	Amount C	Balance
01/0...	519	Nation...		-split-	-300.00	54,408.96
01/0...	520	Bartel...	JFM...	Worker's...	-3,332.00	51,076.96
01/0...	521	Clyne ...		Accounts...	-1,000.00	50,076.96
01/0...	522	Dumani...		Accounts...	-3,278.00	46,798.96
01/0...	523	Genera...		Accounts...	-36.79	46,762.17
01/0...	524	Magic ...		Accounts...	-3,821.00	42,941.17
01/0...	525	Randy ...		Accounts...	-60.00	42,881.17
01/0...	526	Contra...	2 y...	Bond Exp...	-225.00	42,656.17
01/2...	527	State ...		MasterCard	-94.87	42,561.30
01/3...	528	Koeppl...	Feb...	Rent	-375.00	42,186.30
01/3...		Summy ...	Sum...	-split-	0.00	42,186.30

Fig. 14.14
The Check register printed in summary format.

III

Paying Bills

Summary

In this chapter, you learned about the Check register and how to enter transactions. You learned to edit, delete, void, and split transactions. You also learned to create a transfer transaction and to edit and delete a transfer transaction. Finally, you learned to enter historical data, create a summary transaction, and print the Check register.

In the next chapter, you learn to speed up your work in QuickBooks by learning how to use the calculator, find transactions, use memorized transactions and invoices, and to create groups. You also learn to copy and paste between accounts and use the Windows Clipboard.

Part IV

Maximizing QuickBooks

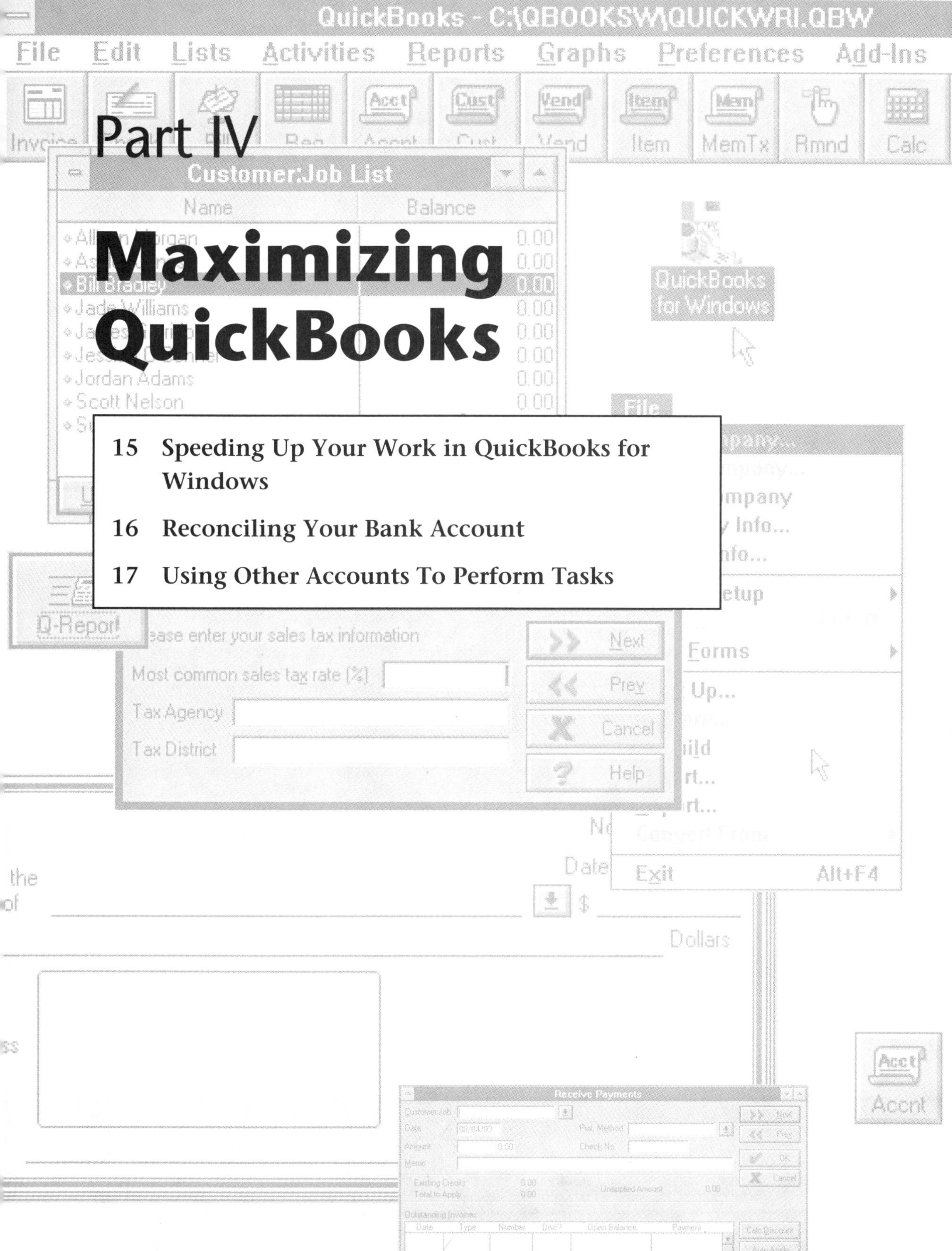

15 Speeding Up Your Work in QuickBooks for Windows

16 Reconciling Your Bank Account

17 Using Other Accounts To Perform Tasks

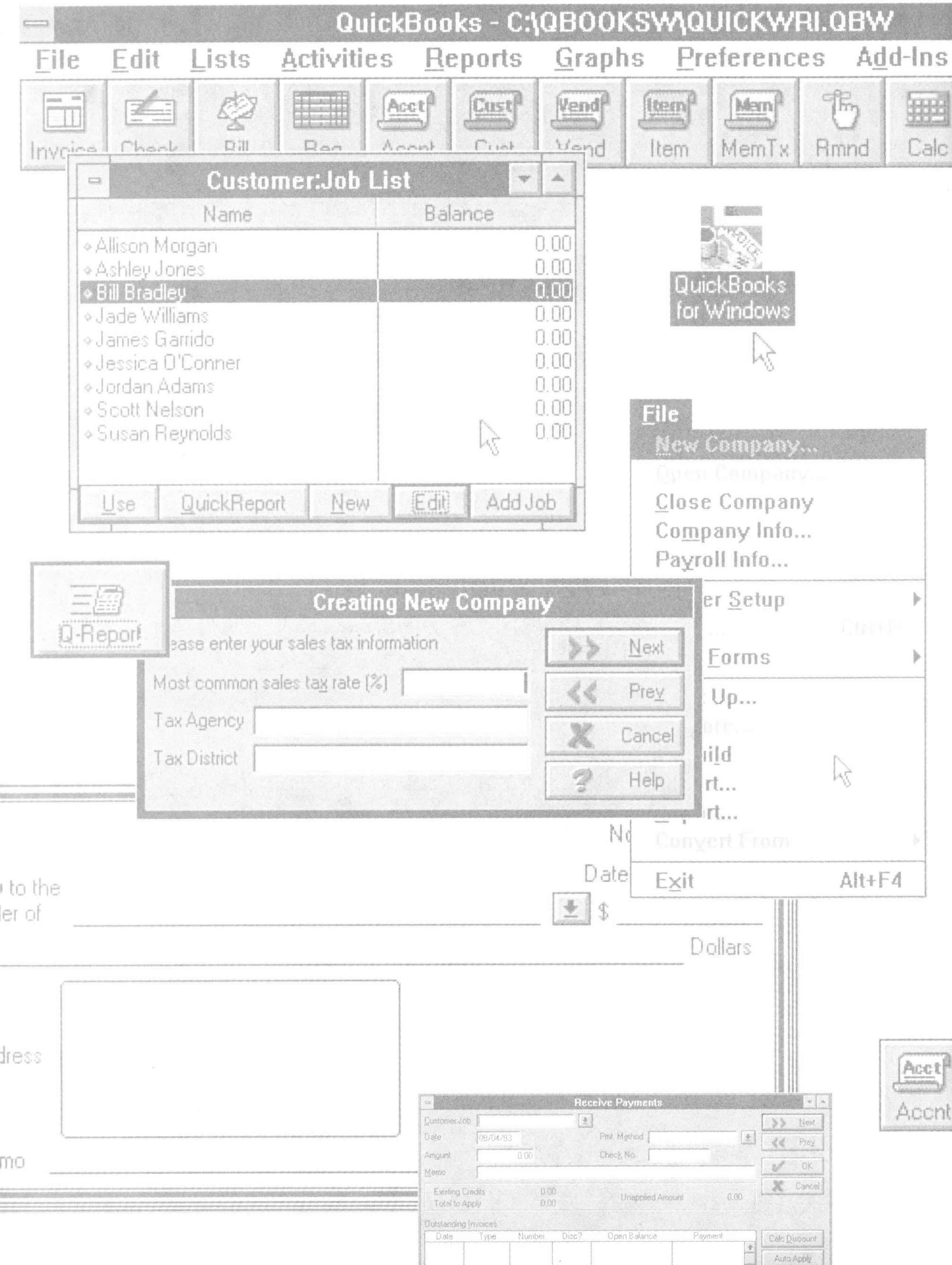
QuickBooks - C:\QBOOKSW\QUICKWRI.QBW
File Edit Lists Activities Reports Graphs Preferences Add-Ins
Invoice Check Bill Reg Accnt Cust Vend Item MemTx Rmnd Calc
Customer:Job List
Name Balance
Allison Morgan 0.00
Ashley Jones 0.00
Bill Bradley 0.00
Jade Williams 0.00
James Garrido 0.00
Jessica O'Conner 0.00
Jordan Adams 0.00
Scott Nelson 0.00
Susan Reynolds 0.00
Use QuickReport New Edit Add Job
QuickBooks for Windows
File
New Company...
Close Company
Company Info...
Payroll Info...
Forms
Exit Alt+F4
Q-Report
Creating New Company
Please enter your sales tax information
Most common sales tax rate (%)
Tax Agency
Tax District
Next
Prev
Cancel
Help
Date
Dollars
Accnt
Receive Payments

Chapter 15

Speeding Up Your Work in QuickBooks for Windows

In the first three parts of this book, you learned to enter transactions quickly and easily in any QuickBooks register. QuickBooks contains some shortcuts for finding transactions and entering recurring transactions that can help you speed up your work.

In this chapter, you learn how to:

- Use the QuickBooks calculator
- Find a transaction in the register
- Use group line items on invoices
- Memorize transactions, as well as recall, edit, and delete memorized transactions
- Create and execute a transaction group, and edit and delete transaction groups

Using the Windows Calculator

QuickBooks uses the Microsoft Windows Calculator as its on-screen calculator. You can use the calculator to perform mathematical calculations from anywhere in the program. The Windows calculator is accurate to 20 decimal places, which is usually more than adequate for most financial calculations. The Windows calculator has two modes: standard calculator and scientific calculator. The standard mode calculator is similar in both appearance and function to a standard hand-held calculator. The scientific calculator, in addition to the standard calculator functions, includes scientific, statistical, and higher level mathematical functions.

To use the Windows calculator, follow these steps:

1. From the **A**ctivities menu, choose Calc**u**lator; or choose the Calc button from the Iconbar. The Windows calculator appears, as shown in figure 15.1.

Fig. 15.1
The standard Windows calculator.

2. You can enter calculations by using the mouse, the numeric keypad, or the standard keyboard number keys.

   To use the mouse, place the mouse pointer on the number or function, and click the left mouse button. You see the number in the calculator display window. The function will be performed and the answer displayed.

   To use the numeric keypad, you must turn on the number lock (Num Lock) key. Enter the numbers as you would with a standard desktop calculator. You can use the keyboard number keys without turning on Num Lock.

   You also can use the number keys at the top of your keyboard. Type the numbers to enter for the calculation.

   Table 15.1 lists the calculator buttons, their keyboard equivalents, and their functions.

Table 15.1. The Windows Calculator Keys

Calculator Button	Keyboard Key	Function
C	Esc	Clears the current calculation
CE	Delete (Del)	Clears the current value
Back	Backspace or Left-arrow	Deletes the rightmost number from the current value
MC	Ctrl+L	Deletes the number stored in memory
MR	Ctrl+R	Recalls the number stored in memory

Calculator Button	Keyboard Key	Function
MS	Ctrl+M	Stores the current value in memory, deleting any other number currently in memory
M+	Ctrl+P	Adds the current number to the number held in memory
sqrt	@	Calculates the square root of the number displayed
%	%	Uses the current value as a percentage in a calculation
1/x	R	Calculates the reciprocal of the number displayed
+/–	F9	Changes the sign of the current value to its opposite
/	/	Divides the current value by the next number entered
*	*	Multiplies the current value by the next number entered
–	–	Subtracts the current value from the next number entered
+	+	Adds the current value to the next number entered
=	= or Enter	Performs the specified calculation on the previous two numbers
.	.	Enters a decimal point

You can use the calculator to compute the sum of a long series of numbers, and then paste the results into a QuickBooks field. To use the copy and paste functions of the Windows calculator, follow these steps:

1. Open the calculator.
2. Enter **245.37 + 536.28 + 95.43 + 383.96** into the calculator using the mouse or keypad. Press Enter. You see the result, `1261.04`, in the calculator window.

3. From the calculator menu bar, choose **E**dit, **C**opy (or press Ctrl+C). The value in the calculator window is copied to the Windows Clipboard.

4. Close the calculator by choosing **C**lose from the Window control menu, or press Alt+F4.

5. Open the QuickBooks window or the dialog box into which you want to paste the calculation.

   For example, open the Check register and move to the next blank line in the register. Enter the date, check number, and payee information into the register.

6. Move the cursor to the Payment column. Choose **E**dit, **P**aste or press Ctrl+V. You now see the calculated value pasted into the field that you indicated—the payment amount field—as shown in figure 15.2.

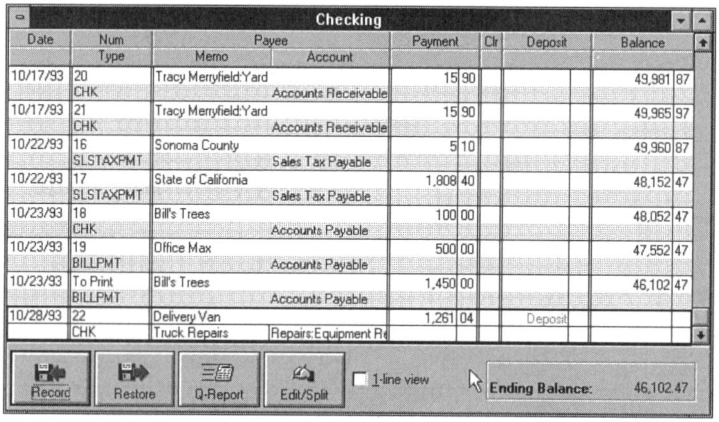

Fig. 15.2
The calculated results pasted into the Payment field of the Check register.

Checking

Date	Num / Type	Payee / Memo	Account	Payment	Clr	Deposit	Balance
10/17/93	20 / CHK	Tracy Merryfield:Yard	Accounts Receivable	15 90			49,981 87
10/17/93	21 / CHK	Tracy Merryfield:Yard	Accounts Receivable	15 90			49,965 97
10/22/93	16 / SLSTAXPMT	Sonoma County	Sales Tax Payable	5 10			49,960 87
10/22/93	17 / SLSTAXPMT	State of California	Sales Tax Payable	1,808 40			48,152 47
10/23/93	18 / CHK	Bill's Trees	Accounts Payable	100 00			48,052 47
10/23/93	19 / BILLPMT	Office Max	Accounts Payable	500 00			47,552 47
10/23/93	To Print / BILLPMT	Bill's Trees	Accounts Payable	1,450 00			46,102 47
10/28/93	22 / CHK	Delivery Van / Truck Repairs	Repairs:Equipment Re	1,261 04		Deposit	

Record | Restore | Q-Report | Edit/Split | 1-line view | Ending Balance: 46,102.47

7. Complete the transaction and save it, as you learned in Chapter 14, "Entering Transactions in the Check Register."

To use the scientific calculator, follow these steps:

1. Open the calculator.

2. From the **V**iew menu, choose **S**cientific. The calculator transforms into the scientific calculator, as shown in figure 15.3.

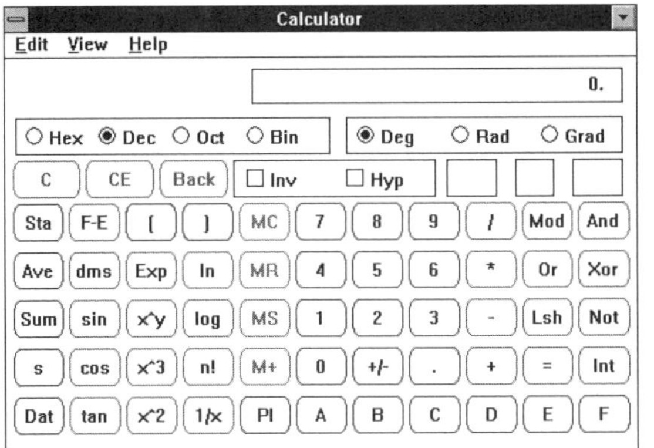

Fig. 15.3
The Windows Scientific calculator.

For almost all financial calculations, the Standard calculator will be more than adequate. See your Windows manual for more information about the scientific calculator.

Finding Transactions

In the previous chapters, you learned to scroll through the transactions to find one you need to edit, void, or delete. After using QuickBooks for several months, your registers will become so long that you can't easily scroll through them to find a transaction you want to review. To make finding a transaction faster and easier, use the **F**ind command located on the **E**dit menu. Use the **F**ind command to quickly search through your QuickBooks system for a specific transaction, such as an invoice, a check, a check amount, a certain vendor invoice, or any other transaction.

The QuickBooks **F**ind command enables you to quickly locate a transaction in any register or window. Even when you remember only bits and pieces about a transaction, you can locate it by using **F**ind.

If you are looking for a check made payable to Eastport Welding Supplies, for example, and you can only remember that *Welding* was part of the transaction name, you can tell QuickBooks to locate transactions with payees that include *Welding* in the name field. QuickBooks does not require that you search for a specific item from a specific window or register.

CPA TIP: Using Find Speeds the Search

Instead of thumbing through paid invoices, use the QuickBooks Find command to locate a transaction when a vendor is on the phone, alleging nonpayment. This gives you the opportunity to present a professional appearance, and places the phone call on the vendor's bill since you won't have to return a phone call later. Simply type the vendor's name in the Find window and search backward or forward through the Check register. QuickBooks finds and highlights each transaction for this particular vendor in seconds.

To use Find to search for a company name, follow these steps:

1. From the **E**dit menu, choose **F**ind, or press Ctrl+F. The Find dialog box appears, as shown in figure 15.4.

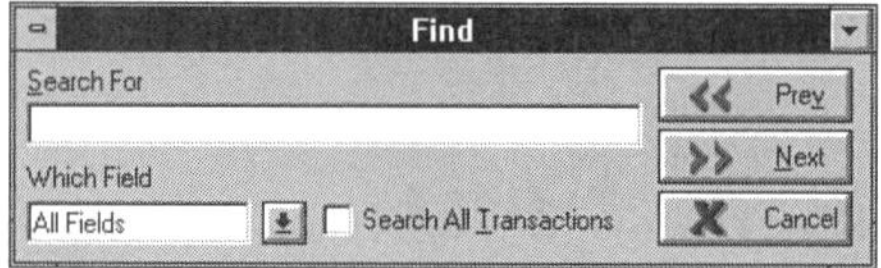

Fig. 15.4 Use the Find dialog box to search for a specific transaction.

2. In the **S**earch For text box, enter a name or other characters that are specific to the transaction you are seeking.

   QuickBooks is not sensitive to the use of upper- or lowercase letters when using Find. QuickBooks will find *WELDING* even if you enter it as *welding* in the **S**earch For text box.

3. If the item that you are searching for is only found in a particular field, select that field in the **W**hich Field text box. The default value is to search All Fields.

   To search for a specific field, type the field name into the text box, or press Alt+down-arrow, or click the down-arrow button to display the field selection list, as shown in figure 15.5.

   Select the field that will contain the value you are searching for. In this example, you are searching for a specific name, so select the Name field.

4. Check the Search All **T**ransactions check box to search outside of the account that is currently opened.

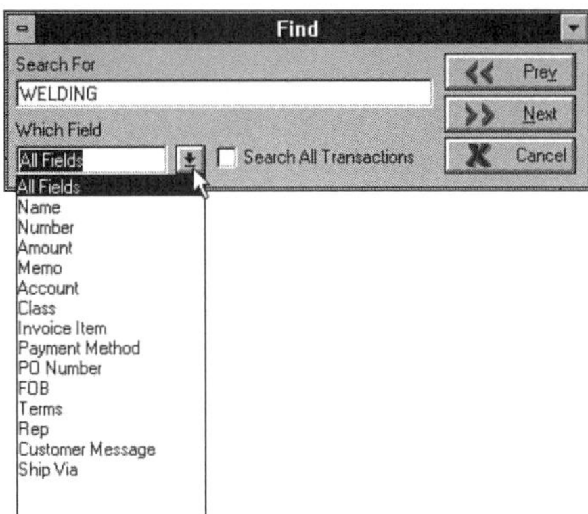

Fig. 15.5
Clicking the down-arrow button displays the Find field selection list.

Remember, accounts don't have to be displayed full-screen. Accounts are considered to be open by QuickBooks even if you have them displayed as minimized icons. Figure 15.6 shows the completed Find window. Notice that two accounts are open as minimized icons, Create Invoices and Accounts Receivable. If your QuickBooks system has been used for several months and you have extensive inventory, customer, and vendor lists, and many transactions, conducting a search on all transactions can take several minutes.

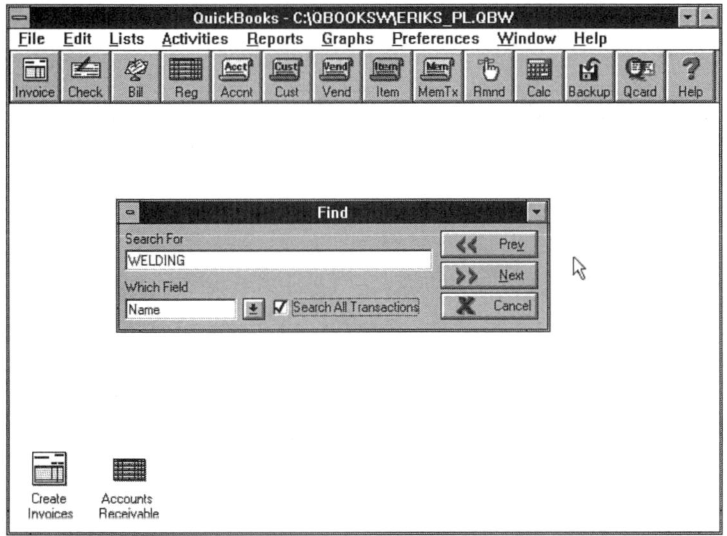

Fig. 15.6
Here the Find dialog box is ready to search. The two open accounts, Create Invoices and Accounts Receivable displayed as minimized icons, will also be searched.

5. Begin searching with Find by using the Pre**v** or **N**ext buttons.
   The buttons perform the following functions:

   Pre**v** finds the most recent transaction that meets the criteria you have entered.

   Next finds the oldest transaction that meets the criteria you have entered.

   If Find does not display the transaction you are searching for, press the button again. Pre**v** will search for the next most recent transaction, while **N**ext will search for the next oldest. To search through all transactions, you will have to use both Pre**v** and **N**ext.

   Figure 15.7 shows the transaction that it has found. Notice that the transaction is shown in the Write Checks window. This is because this particular transaction was entered directly into the Check register. The Check register is not open, but because this was a payment to a vendor, an entry is made in the Accounts Receivable register. QuickBooks uses this entry to find the transaction, and displays it in the most complete form available, in this case the Write Checks window. If you had entered the same transaction in the Pay Bills window and have not yet written a check for the payment, QuickBooks will display the results in the Pay Bills window.

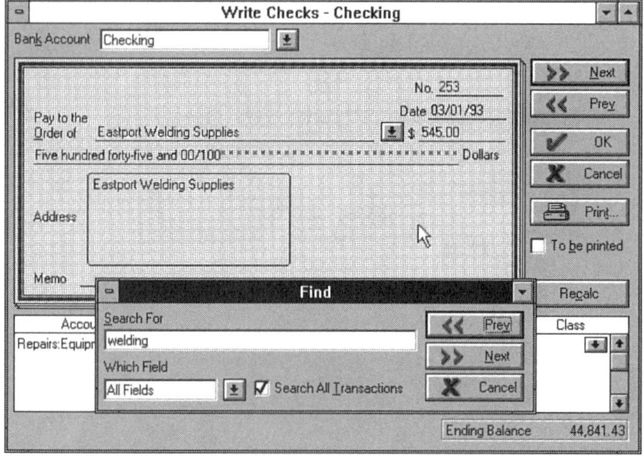

Fig. 15.7
The results of the Find command displayed on-screen. Use the **N**ext or Pre**v** buttons to search for additional transactions that meet the same criteria.

Using Memorized Transactions

You may frequently record transactions, such as your rent payment, insurance premiums, or loan payments, with the same payee, amount, and income or expense account distribution. You can quickly enter these recurring transactions in the Write Checks window, the Check register, or any other account register by using QuickBooks to memorize transactions and then recall them when needed. A memorized transaction is information you save from one transaction so that you can recall it later for other transactions.

Memorizing a Transaction

QuickBooks can memorize any transaction you enter into your system. In this section, you will learn how to memorize and recall transactions in the Check register; however, you can use the same steps to memorize and recall transactions in the Accounts Payable, Enter Bills, and Pay Bills windows. QuickBooks maintains a single list for all memorized transactions. Specifically, you will learn to memorize a payroll transaction.

CPA TIP: Use Memorized Transactions with Split Accounts

Memorized transactions provide a quick method to enter lengthy, split transactions that you always assign to the same accounts. An excellent example is the payroll check. A payroll check involves several split transactions—federal withholding, state withholding, FICA withholding, Medicare withholding, and so on—to each payroll transaction. If you memorize an employee's payroll transaction and then recall it, QuickBooks enters the employee's name and accounts for you. You then simply change the amounts assigned to the accounts, if necessary.

You also can use the payroll program QuickPay, by Intuit, to handle your payroll transactions. See Appendix B, "Using QuickPay with QuickBooks for Windows," to learn more about this add-on program.

To memorize a transaction in the Check register, follow these steps:

1. Open the Write Checks window. (Remember, you access the Write Checks window by choosing the Check button in the Iconbar; by choosing **A**ctivities, **W**rite Checks; or by pressing Ctrl+W.)

2. Enter as much of the transaction as you want to memorize. You can always edit fields later when you recall the memorized transaction.

For a payroll check, you would want to memorize the Bank Account, payee, Memo, and account distribution. If the check is a salary check, where the amounts don't change, you will enter all the amounts.

3. From the **E**dit menu, choose **M**emorize Check, or press Ctrl+M. The Memorize Transaction dialog box, as shown in figure 15.8, appears.

Fig. 15.8
Use the Memorize Transaction dialog box to name a memorized transaction.

The actual name of the Memorize command on the **E**dit menu will vary, depending on the type of transaction that you want to memorize.

4. Enter a name for the memorized transaction. Enter a name that will enable you to easily distinguish what the transaction is for. For example, type **Amber Corda/Payroll** in the **N**ame field.

5. Set up how often you want QuickBooks to remind you of this transaction, and if it is part of a group.

Setting up QuickBooks to remind you of the transaction is optional. By default, QuickBooks will never remind you of the transaction.

The Remind Me block contains two radio button options:

- *Just This **T**ransaction.* Select this option to set up this memorized transaction as a special reminder about this transaction. Then decide how often you want to be reminded, select the option from the drop-down list, and enter the date for the next reminder.

- *With Transaction**s** in Group.* Select this option to add this transaction to a group reminder. Enter the name of the memorized transaction group, or select it from the drop-down list. This option is only available if you have already created a memorized transaction group. Creating a memorized group is covered later in this chapter.

Figure 15.9 shows the completed Memorize Transaction dialog box.

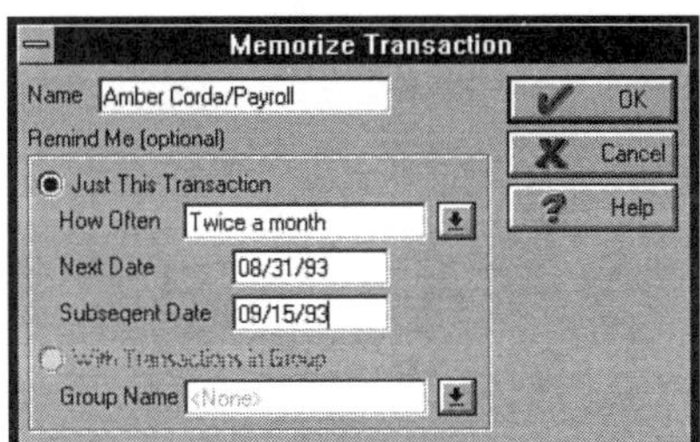

Figure 15.9
The memorized transaction window for a payroll check.

6. Choose OK to save this memorized transaction. QuickBooks will add it to the Memorized Transaction List, and return you to the Write Checks window.

You can complete the transaction and save it. You do not have to record a transaction to memorize it. You can enter the transaction information, memorize it, and then press Ctrl+Del to remove the transaction information from the register. The memorized information remains in the Memorized Transaction List.

You do not have to create a transaction in order to memorize it. You also can use a transaction that you have already recorded. Simply find the transaction you want to record and follow the steps outlined above to add the transaction to the Memorized Transaction List.

Recalling a Memorized Transaction

When you are ready to use a memorized transaction, or if QuickBooks has reminded you that it is time to recall a memorized transaction, it takes only a couple of keystrokes to recall a transaction.

To recall a memorized transaction, follow these steps:

1. Choose the MemTX button from the Iconbar; choose **L**ists, Memorized **T**ransactions; or press Ctrl+T. The Memorized Transaction List appears, as shown in figure 15.10.

2. Choose the transaction to be recalled.

   You can select the transaction by clicking it with the mouse. If you have many transactions memorized, you will see a scroll bar located on the left side of the window.

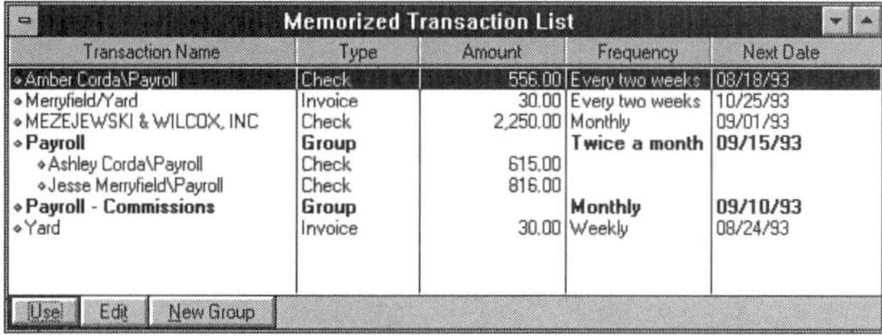

Fig. 15.10
The Memorized Transaction List.

With the keyboard, you can use several keys to move around in the window:

Use This Key	To Move
Up-arrow	Up one transaction
Down-arrow	Down one transaction
Page Up(PgUp)	Up one screen of transactions
Page Down(PgDn)	Down one screen of transactions
Home	To beginning of memorized transaction list
End	To end of memorized transaction list

Select a transaction with the keyboard by placing the black selector bar on the transaction.

3. Choose **U**se to use a memorized transaction.

   QuickBooks will display the memorized transaction in the Write Checks window for a Check register transaction, or the Create Invoice window for an invoice that has been memorized. Other transactions that are memorized will be displayed in their respective entry windows.

Editing a Memorized Transaction

To change a memorized transaction, you must first recall the memorized transaction, edit the transaction in the register or window, and then memorize the transaction again.

To edit a memorized transaction, follow these steps:

1. Open the Memorized Transaction List.

2. Select the memorized transaction that you want to change, and choose **U**se. QuickBooks displays the transaction in its window.

   You may have noticed that the Memorized Transaction List, as you saw in figure 15.10, also has an Edi**t** button. This Edi**t** button enables you to make changes to the memorized transaction name, and in the reminder options that you selected. If you decide that you want to be reminded about a transaction twice a month instead of monthly, use the Edi**t** button.

3. Edit the transaction, just as you would any other transaction. When the transaction has been changed to your requirements, memorize it again.

4. From the **E**dit menu, choose **M**emorize Check (or Invoice, etc.), or press Ctrl+M.

   QuickBooks displays the Replace Memorized Transaction window, as you see in figure 15.11. From this window you can:

   Replace the existing memorized transaction. Use this option if you are permanently changing a transaction.

   Add a new memorized transaction. Use this option to create several similar transactions.

   Cancel the action.

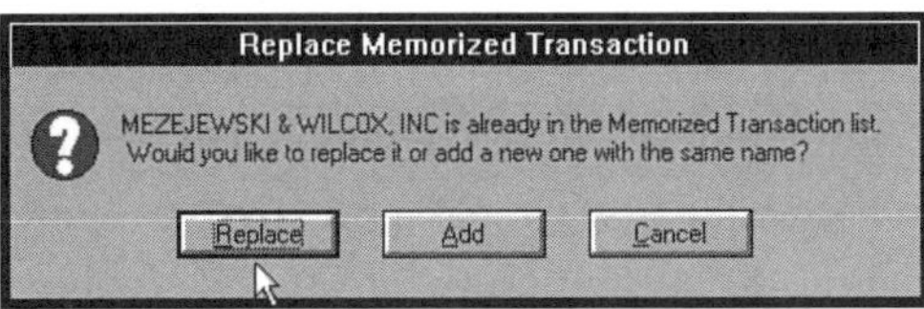

Fig. 15.11
The Replace Memorized Transaction window.

5. Choose **R**eplace to replace the transaction. QuickBooks will use this newly memorized transaction the next time that you recall this transaction.

Deleting a Memorized Transaction

If you find that you do not use a memorized transaction, you can delete it from the Memorized Transaction List. To delete a transaction from the Memorized Transaction List, follow these steps:

1. Open the Memorized Transaction List.
2. Highlight the transaction to be deleted.
3. From the QuickBooks menu bar, choose **E**dit, **D**elete Memorized Transaction, or press Ctrl+D. QuickBooks displays the confirmation dialog box with the message `Are you sure you want to delete this memorized transaction?` Choose OK to delete the transaction, or Cancel to return to the Memorized Transaction List.

Using Memorized Invoices

QuickBooks can memorize an invoice, just as it can memorize any other transaction. After an invoice has been memorized, you can recall it later and avoid typing the same information over again. If you have a customer with a standing order for every month or every quarter, you simply memorize the invoice the first time you create it, and the next time you can recall the invoice instead of typing the same information. You can memorize an entire invoice or only a few fields.

Memorizing an Invoice

Before you can memorize an invoice, you must first create the invoice or the portion that you want to memorize. You do not need to enter any fields you do not want memorized.

To memorize an invoice, follow these steps:

1. Open the Create Invoices window. (Remember, the Create Invoices window can be accessed by choosing the Invoice button from the Iconbar; by choosing **A**ctivities, Create **I**nvoices; or by pressing Ctrl+I.)
2. Enter all information that you want to save in the memorized invoice. Figure 15.12 shows an invoice ready to be memorized. This invoice is for a twice monthly yard service.
3. Choose **E**dit, **M**emorize Invoice or press Ctrl+M. The Memorize Transaction window appears (refer to fig. 15.8).
4. Enter a name that is descriptive to you in the Name field. QuickBooks automatically enters a name for you. If this name is adequate, use it.
5. Select the appropriate reminder option in the Remind Me block.

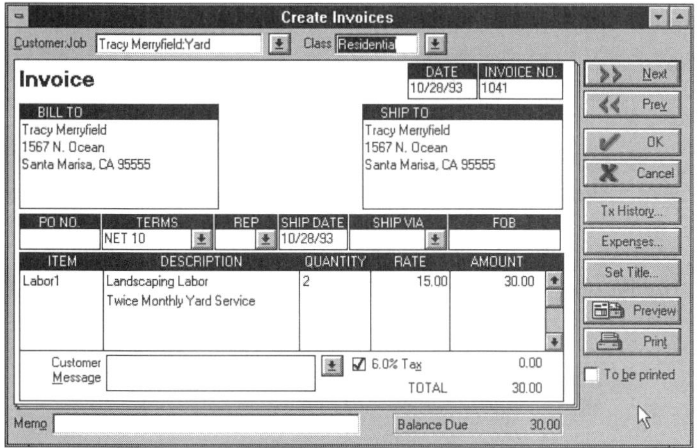

Fig. 15.12
An invoice ready to be memorized.

6. Enter the reminder option that you require for this transaction. In this example, the invoice is to be recalled and issued twice a month. Figure 15.13 shows the drop-down list for the How Often field. Select the frequency that you need for the memorized invoice.

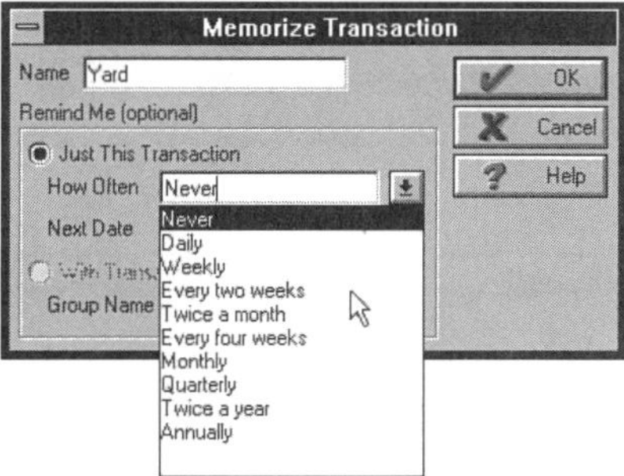

Fig. 15.13
The Memorized Transaction dialog box showing the How Often drop-down list box.

7. Enter the Next Date to recall the transaction.

Note

Each of the options in the drop-down frequency list, except Twice a Month, asks for the Next Date to recall the transaction. The Twice a Month option asks not only for the Next Date, but also for a Subsequent Date. QuickBooks will use the first date as the first day of the month the invoice is to be recalled, and the subsequent date is the second time. For example, if you want to bill on the 1st and 15th of a month, select 08/01/93 as the Next Date, and 08/15/93 as the Subsequent Date.

8. Choose OK to save the memorized invoice in the Memorized Transaction List.

Recalling a Memorized Invoice

After an invoice has been memorized, you can recall it with just a few simple keystrokes or mouse clicks. To recall a memorized invoice, follow these steps:

1. Open the Memorized Transaction List by choosing the MemTX button on the Iconbar; by choosing **L**ists, Memorized **T**ransactions; or by pressing Ctrl+T.

2. Select the memorized invoice to be recalled. Select the transaction by placing the black selector bar on the transaction.

   As you can see in figure 15.14, all items listed in the Memorized Transaction List are listed in alphabetical order by Transaction Name. You also see that each transaction Type is listed. This makes it easier to pick out an invoice or check transactions.

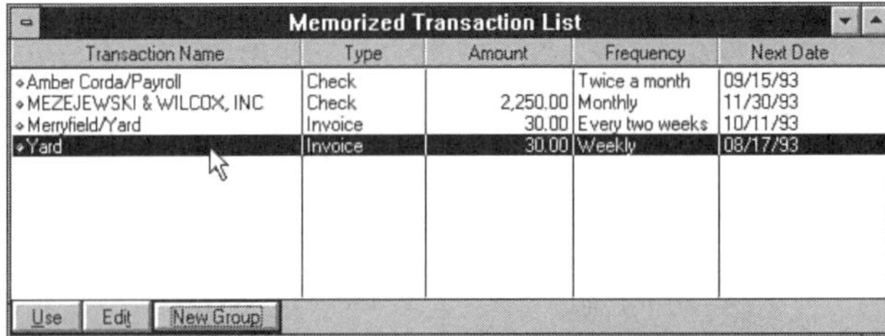

Fig. 15.14
The Memorized Transaction List.

3. Choose **U**se. QuickBooks displays the invoice in the Create Invoices window. The dates are adjusted for the new invoice, and QuickBooks selects the next invoice number. Make any further changes or additions to the invoice that you require, and save the transaction.

Editing and Deleting Memorized Invoices

If a memorized invoice is out of date, you can edit the memorized transaction, or you can delete the original and memorize a new invoice.

To edit a memorized invoice, follow these steps:

1. Open the Memorized Transaction List, choose the invoice to be edited, and choose **U**se to open the invoice in the Create Invoice window.

2. Make any changes that you need to the invoice.

3. Select **E**dit, **M**emorize Invoice or press Ctrl+M. If you have already memorized an Invoice for the selected Customer or Customer:Job, then the Replace Memorized Transaction dialog box in figure 15.15 appears.

Fig. 15.15
This dialog box appears if you have already memorized an Invoice for the Customer or Customer:Job.

4. Use the Replace Memorized Transaction window to **R**eplace the current memorized invoice with the newly edited copy. Use the **A**dd button to add the edited invoice as a new memorized invoice, use or **C**ancel to return to the Create Invoices window.

You also can delete a memorized transaction. A memorized invoice should be deleted if you no longer recall the invoice when you are reminded that it is due, or if the customer no longer requires the service. To delete a memorized invoice, follow these steps:

1. Open the Memorized Transaction List, and select the memorized invoice to be deleted.

2. Choose **E**dit, **D**elete Memorized Transaction, or press Ctrl+D.

   QuickBooks displays a confirmation dialog box asking you to confirm or cancel your decision to delete the transaction.

3. Choose OK to delete the memorized invoice, or choose Cancel to return to the Memorized Transaction List.

Using Transaction Groups

A *transaction group* contains recurring transactions that you simultaneously pay, bill, or add to a register. Transaction groups can consist of one or many transactions. You may, for example, want to set up a transaction group for bills for which you don't receive an invoice or statement, such as your rent or loan payments. You also may want to set up a transaction group for bills due at the same time each month, such as loan payments and insurance premiums.

When you create a transaction group, you assign one or more memorized transactions to a group and then name it. You may, for example, set up a transaction group named Mid-Month Items. You could include mid-month payroll, any other bills that you pay at this time, and invoices that you routinely bill out on the 15th.

QuickBooks will include this transaction group on the reminder list when it is time for you to process the Mid-Month Item transaction group. While QuickBooks will remind you of the transaction group, you must tell QuickBooks to use the group, enabling you to edit any invoices or payments.

Creating a Transaction Group

Before you can create a transaction group, you must first memorize the transactions that you want to include in the group. You can include as many transactions within a group as you need. A transaction also can be included in more than one group.

> **Note**
>
> You will find that it is easier to create several smaller groups than a single, large group. A smaller group is easier to manage and to edit. If circumstances change, you can easily find and edit a memorized transaction in a smaller group.

To create a transaction group, follow these steps:

1. Open the Memorized Transaction List.

   Currently, the Memorized Transaction List contains only the transactions that have been memorized and saved.

2. Choose **N**ew Group. This will open the New Memorized Transaction Group dialog box, as shown in figure 15.16.

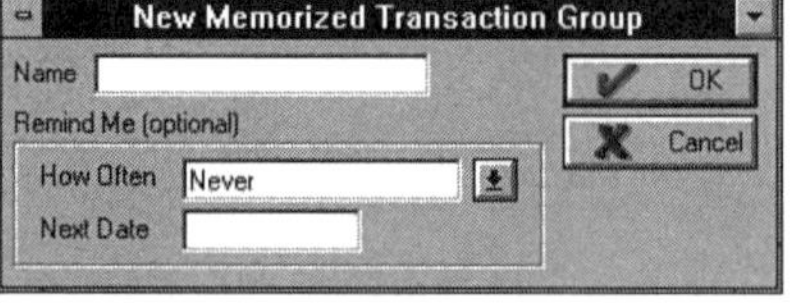

Fig. 15.16 Use the New Memorized Transaction Group dialog box to create a transaction group.

3. Enter the name for this transaction group in the **N**ame field. For example, name the group you use to do your payroll as *Payroll*.

4. Enter How Often you want QuickBooks to remind you of this transaction. For payroll, you will want to be reminded weekly or twice a month, depending on how you do payroll.

5. Enter the date when you next want to be reminded about this transaction. If you have selected the Twice a Month option, you also need to fill in the Subsequent Date. QuickBooks uses these two dates to determine when you want to be reminded for the transaction.

   The New Memorized Transaction Group dialog box is completed, as shown in figure 15.17.

   You will see the new group displayed with the group name shown in bold text at the far right-hand margin of the Transaction Name column. All members of the group appear in normal text and are indented one level.

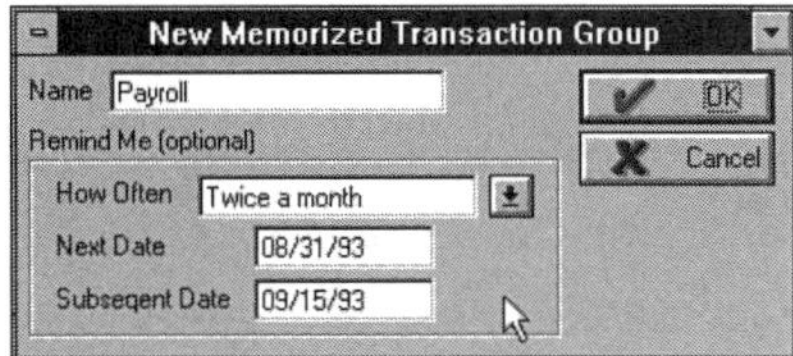

Fig. 15.17
The New Memorized Transaction Group dialog box.

6. Choose OK to save the new group. You will be returned to the Memorized Transaction List, with the newly created group displayed in the list, as shown in figure 15.18.

Memorized Transaction List

Transaction Name	Type	Amount	Frequency	Next Date
◆Amber Corda\Payroll	Check	556.00	Twice a month	08/31/93
◆Ashley Corda\Payroll	Check	615.00	Twice a month	08/31/93
◆Jesse Merryfield\Payroll	Check	816.00	Twice a month	08/31/93
◆Merryfield/Yard	Invoice	30.00	Every two weeks	10/25/93
◆MEZEJEWSKI & WILCOX, INC	Check	2,250.00	Monthly	09/01/93
◆Payroll	**Group**		**Twice a month**	**08/31/93**
◆Yard	Invoice	30.00	Weekly	08/24/93

Use | Edit | New Group

Fig. 15.18
The new transaction group in the Memorized Transaction List. Notice that the group name appears in bold text.

Using the Mouse to Add a Memorized Transaction to a Transaction Group. Now that you have created the transaction group, you must place transactions within the group. Any transaction that you add to the group transaction will be executed when the group is used. You can add a transaction to a group using either the mouse or the keyboard. To add a transaction with the mouse, follow these steps:

1. Select the transaction to be included in the newly created group. Move the mouse pointer to the transaction and click once.

   You will see the black highlight bar on the selected transaction.

2. Move the mouse pointer to the diamond shape (the transaction's handle) displayed in front of the transaction name. The mouse pointer changes shape to a four-headed arrow, as shown in figure 15.19.

Fig. 15.19
The mouse pointer ready to add a transaction to a group transaction. Notice the mouse pointer has changed shape to a four-headed arrow.

Memorized Transaction List

Transaction Name	Type	Amount	Frequency	Next Date
Amber Corda\Payroll	Check	556.00	Every two weeks	08/18/93
Merryfield/Yard	Invoice	30.00	Every two weeks	10/25/93
MEZEJEWSKI & WILCOX, INC	Check	2,250.00	Monthly	09/01/93
Payroll	**Group**		**Twice a month**	**09/15/93**
Ashley Corda\Payroll	Check	615.00		
Jesse Merryfield\Payroll	Check	816.00		
Payroll - Commissions	**Group**		**Monthly**	**09/10/93**
Yard	Invoice	30.00	Weekly	08/31/93
Yard 2	Invoice	30.00	Twice a month	10/28/93

Use Edit New Group

Four-headed arrow

3. Press and hold the left-mouse button, drag the transaction until the dashed line is underlining the group transaction that you want to add the transaction to, and then release the mouse button. As you see in figure 15.20, the selected transaction is displayed underneath the group transaction.

Fig. 15.20
Drag a selected transaction to be added as a group transaction.

Memorized Transaction List

Transaction Name	Type	Amount	Frequency	Next Date
Ashley Corda\Payroll	Check	615.00	Twice a month	08/31/93
Jesse Merryfield\Payroll	Check	816.00	Twice a month	08/31/93
Merryfield/Yard	Invoice	30.00	Every two weeks	10/25/93
MEZEJEWSKI & WILCOX, INC	Check	2,250.00	Monthly	09/01/93
Payroll	**Group**		**Twice a month**	**08/31/93**
Amber Corda\Payroll	Check	556.00	Twice a month	08/31/93
Yard	Invoice	30.00	Weekly	08/24/93

Use Edit New Group

This transaction has not yet been added to the group transaction; it is still a stand-alone transaction.

4. Place the mouse pointer on the transaction's diamond handle and click and drag the transaction to the right. You will see, as in figure 15.21, the transaction is now a sub-transaction of the group, or in other words, a member of the Payroll group transaction.

Memorized Transaction List

Transaction Name	Type	Amount	Frequency	Next Date
◆Ashley Corda\Payroll	Check	615.00	Twice a month	08/31/93
◆Jesse Merryfield\Payroll	Check	816.00	Twice a month	08/31/93
◆Merryfield/Yard	Invoice	30.00	Every two weeks	10/25/93
◆MEZEJEWSKI & WILCOX, INC	Check	2,250.00	Monthly	09/01/93
◆**Payroll**	**Group**		**Twice a month**	**08/31/93**
◆Amber Corda\Payroll	Check	556.00		
◆Yard	Invoice	30.00	Weekly	08/24/93

Use | Edit | New Group

Fig. 15.21
The new Payroll group transaction with its first member transaction added.

Notice that the Frequency and Next Date columns are now blank. The sub-transaction takes this information from the parent, or group, transaction.

Using the Keyboard to Add Memorized Transactions to a Memorized Group. You have now learned to use the mouse to add a transaction into a group transaction. To use the keyboard, follow these steps:

1. Select the transaction to be added to the group. Use the up- or down-arrow keys to place the black highlight bar on the transaction you want to add.

2. Choose Edi**t** by pressing Alt+T. The Edit Memorized Transaction window appears, as shown in figure 15.22.

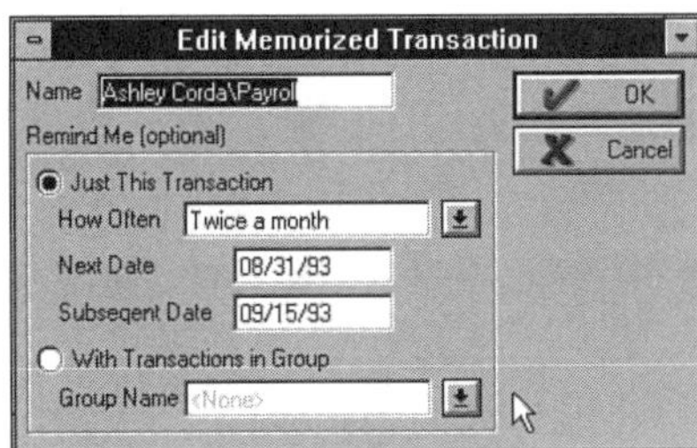

Fig. 15.22
Use the Edit Memorized Transaction dialog box to add a transaction to a group, or to change 2a stand-alone transaction's reminder frequency.

3. Select the With Transaction**s** in Group radio button. Press the Tab key until the selection box is around the button title. Press the space bar to select this option.

4. Select the Group you want to add this transaction to. You can type the name (QuickBooks will help you with QuickFill) or press Alt+down-arrow and display the Group Name drop-down list.

Figure 15.23 shows the completed window. Notice that QuickBooks only dims the original reminder information. If you later change this transaction back into a stand-alone memorized transaction, the reminder settings will become active again.

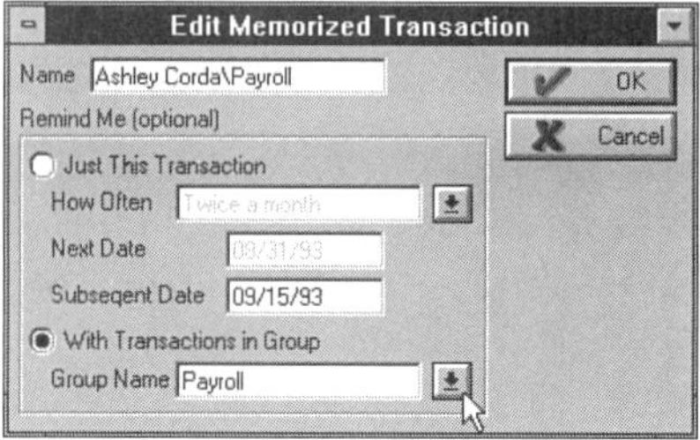

Fig. 15.23 The completed transaction information.

5. Choose OK to save the transaction as a member of the group. As you see in figure 15.24, the new transaction is added to the group and is highlighted.

Memorized Transaction List

Transaction Name	Type	Amount	Frequency	Next Date
Jesse Merryfield\Payroll	Check	816.00	Twice a month	08/31/93
Merryfield/Yard	Invoice	30.00	Every two weeks	10/25/93
MEZEJEWSKI & WILCOX, INC	Check	2,250.00	Monthly	09/01/93
Payroll	**Group**		**Twice a month**	**08/31/93**
Ashley Corda\Payroll	Check	615.00		
Amber Corda\Payroll	Check	556.00		
Yard	Invoice	30.00	Weekly	08/24/93

Use | Edit | New Group

Fig. 15.24 The Transaction Group with its second member added.

Using a Transaction Group

When QuickBooks has reminded you that it is time to process a group transaction, it only takes a few moments to recall a transaction and execute it. To use a transaction group, follow these steps:

1. Open the Memorized Transaction List.

2. Select the transaction to be executed. In this case, the group transaction Payroll is selected.

3. Choose **U**se. The Using Group dialog box appears, as shown in figure 15.25.

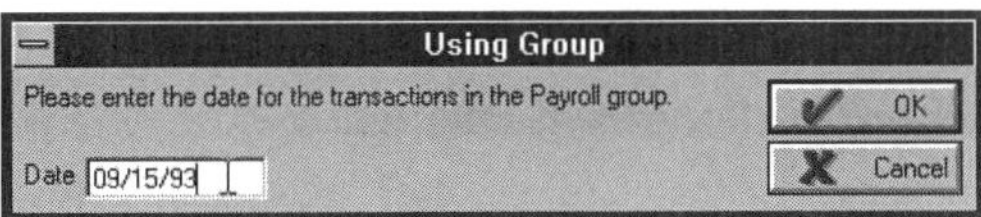

Fig. 15.25
Use the Using Group dialog box to enter the date that will appear on all of the group transactions.

From this window, you will enter the date for the transactions that will be processed as a group. QuickBooks will enter the date that was selected as the next date when you created the transaction group. If this is not the correct date, you can type in another date, or use the + or – keys to adjust the date.

4. Enter the date to be used when processing the group transaction.

5. Choose OK to process the transactions. QuickBooks will display a window titled *Working* that shows the percentage of transactions processed. QuickBooks will then display a window telling you that all transactions have been completed. Choose OK to remove the window.

In the check register, as shown in figure 15.26, you see the three payroll checks entered by QuickBooks. Notice that each of the checks is listed below the heavy line, indicating that these checks are postdated.

Checking

Date	Num / Type	Payee / Memo / Account	Payment	Clr	Deposit	Balance
08/16/93	13 CHK	Marvin W. Martin / Charitable Donation	350 00			16,071 30
08/16/93	14 CHK	Office Max / -split-	904 32			15,166 98
08/16/93	17 CHK	Office Max / -split-	1,261 04			13,905 94
08/16/93	To Print CHK	Amber Corda / Payroll for period endi -split-	556 00			13,349 94
08/31/93	255 CHK	Ashley Corda / Payroll for period endi -split-	615 00			12,734 94
08/31/93	256 CHK	Amber Corda / Payroll for period endi -split-	556 00			12,178 94
08/31/93	257 CHK	Jesse Merryfield / Payroll for period endi -split-	816 00			11,362 94
08/31/93						

Record Restore Q-Report Edit/Split 1-line view Ending Balance: 11,362.94

Fig. 15.26
The Checking account register with the completed group transactions listed.

Editing and Deleting Transactions in a Group

You can easily edit or delete a member transaction of a group. As you learned earlier in this chapter, you can edit the memorized transaction itself, or in the case of group transaction, you can edit the transaction's position within the group.

To edit the actual member transaction, refer to the section "Editing a Memorized Transaction" earlier in this chapter.

Editing Transactions in a Group. You can edit a member transaction by removing it from the group. To move a member transaction, follow these steps:

1. Open the Memorized Transaction List.

2. Select the transaction to be edited.

3. With the mouse, select the diamond handle beside the transaction. Drag the transaction to its new position. In figure 15.27, you can see a transaction that has been removed from the Payroll group and added to the Payroll-Commissions group.

Memorized Transaction List

Transaction Name	Type	Amount	Frequency	Next Date
◆Merryfield/Yard	Invoice	30.00	Every two weeks	10/25/93
◆MEZEJEWSKI & WILCOX, INC	Check	2,250.00	Monthly	09/01/93
◆**Payroll**	**Group**		**Twice a month**	**09/15/93**
◆Ashley Corda\Payroll	Check	615.00		
◆Jesse Merryfield\Payroll	Check	816.00		
◆**Payroll - Commissions**	**Group**		**Monthly**	**09/10/93**
◆Amber Corda\Payroll	Check	556.00		
◆Yard	Invoice	30.00	Weekly	08/24/93

Use | Edit | New Group

Fig. 15.27
The Memorized Transactions List after moving a member transaction from one group (Payroll) to the Payroll-Commissions group.

The same move can be performed by selecting the member transaction, and then choosing Edi**t** button. Now change the Group Name to the new group. QuickBooks automatically moves the transaction to the new group.

Removing a transaction from a group and changing it to a stand-alone transaction also can be accomplished quickly.

1. Select the transaction to be removed from the group.

2. Choose the Edi**t** button. QuickBooks displays the Edit Memorized Transaction dialog box.

3. Select the Just This **T**ransaction radio button. Make any necessary changes to the Reminder Frequency option. Choose OK. QuickBooks removes the transaction from the group.

   You can also use the mouse. Simply grab the diamond handle and drag the handle to the left. This action tells QuickBooks that this transaction is no longer a member of the group.

Deleting Transactions in a Group. QuickBooks also lets you delete transactions if you no longer have a need for them. If you find that QuickBooks is reminding you about tasks that you no longer use, delete them. To delete a transaction from a group, follow these steps:

1. Open the Memorized Transaction List.
2. Select the transaction to be deleted.
3. From the menu, choose **E**dit, **D**elete Memorized Transaction, or press Ctrl+D.

   QuickBooks will ask you to confirm the deletion by displaying the Delete Memorized Transactions dialog box.
4. Choose OK to delete the memorized transaction. Choose the Cancel button to return to the Memorized Transaction List without deleting the transaction.

> **Note**
>
> If you are not sure that you want to delete a transaction, and you do not need to be reminded about it, change the reminder frequency to Never. QuickBooks will not remind you about the transaction. You can still use it if you need to.

Editing a Transaction Group

A transaction group can be edited just like a transaction. Select the transaction group, and use the Edi**t** button to display the Edit Memorized Transaction Group window. Make the necessary changes to the group reminder frequency or name. Choose OK to save the edits.

Deleting a Transaction Group

While you can easily edit a transaction group, you cannot easily delete one. A transaction group cannot be deleted until you either delete the member transactions, or remove them from the transaction group to another transaction group, or remove them as stand-alone transactions.

To delete a transaction group, follow these steps:

1. Open the Memorized Transaction List.

2. Remove or delete all member transactions from the group. If you choose to delete the member transactions, QuickBooks asks you to confirm this action.

3. Select the transaction group, and press Ctrl+D. QuickBooks asks you to confirm the deletion of the group. Choose OK to delete the group, or choose Cancel to return to the window.

Copying and Pasting Transactions

QuickBooks can be a "forgiving" program. For some types of errors, QuickBooks doesn't even require that you enter reversing transactions to remove a transaction from some accounts. If you mistakenly enter a transaction into a register you can, in some cases, copy the transaction and paste it into the correct register.

You can only copy and paste between similar types of registers. You can copy between checking accounts, for example, but not between Accounts Payable and Accounts Receivable. To move a transaction from one account to another, follow these steps:

1. Open the register in which the transaction that was entered incorrectly resides. This is the register that should not include this transaction.

2. Select the transaction to be moved. Be sure that you have selected the transaction and not a field within the transaction.

   When you enter a new transaction with the keyboard, QuickBooks will highlight the Date field, selecting the field. If you select a transaction using the mouse, the field that you point to will be selected and displayed with a highlight. Figure 15.28 shows the selected transaction and the date field highlighted.

   To remove the highlight and select the entire transaction, either click the mouse in the field again, or press the left- or right-arrow key. The highlight will disappear, and the vertical cursor is displayed.

3. From the **E**dit menu, choose Cop**y** Check, or press Ctrl+O. QuickBooks will copy the transaction into memory. You will not notice anything on-screen.

4. Open the register that the transaction is being moved to, and open the last blank transaction line.

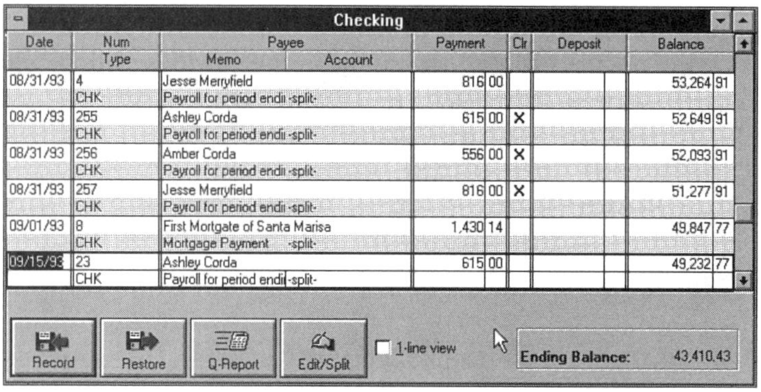

Fig. 15.28
The selected transaction. Notice that the date field is highlighted.

5. From the **E**dit menu, choose **P**aste Check, or press Ctrl+V.

   QuickBooks will paste the transaction into the selected line of the register. Figure 15.29 shows the transaction pasted into the Credit Card Account register.

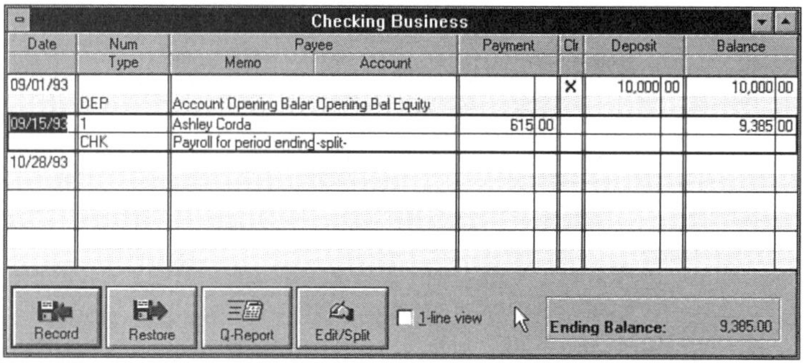

Fig. 15.29
The selected transaction moved to its correct register.

6. Choose Record to save the new transaction.

7. Delete the transaction from the original register. Select the transaction and choose **E**dit **D**elete Check, or press Ctrl+D.

Working with the Windows Clipboard

With QuickBooks for Windows, you also can easily access the Windows Clipboard. With the Windows Clipboard, you can select a field, cut or copy it to the Clipboard, and then paste the saved information back into QuickBooks, or into another application.

Using the Windows Clipboard with QuickBooks does have its limitations. You can only select a field. As you learned in the previous section, you must select an entire transaction to copy it to another account. The Windows Clipboard is limited to the selected, or highlighted, field only when copying to the Clipboard.

Using Reminders

Reminders are one of QuickBooks' most powerful tools. You use reminders to remind you when checks are due to be printed, when you need to pay bills, if you have invoices or sales receipts to be printed, if you have memorized transactions that are now due, and, best of all, that you have money to be deposited.

> **Note**
>
> Any changes that you make to the Reminders Preferences apply to all companies that you maintain with QuickBooks.

You can set Reminders to be displayed each time that you open QuickBooks, or choose the Rmnd button to display the Reminders List at any time. To edit the Reminders selections, follow these steps:

1. From the **P**references menu, choose Re**m**inders. Figure 15.30 shows the Reminder Preferences window, with all settings set at the QuickBooks default values.

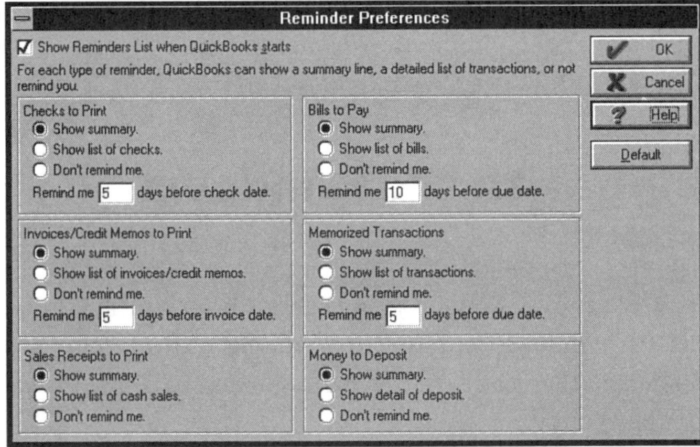

Fig. 15.30
Use the Reminder Preferences window to make any changes to your Reminders List.

2. Check the Show Reminders List When QuickBooks **S**tarts check box. This tells QuickBooks to display the Reminders List each time that you open QuickBooks. If you do not want to see the Reminders List, press the space bar or click with the mouse to uncheck the box.

3. Use the Tab key to move through the different selection blocks in the window. Change radio buttons by pressing the space bar to select an option. Enter the number of days before a transaction that you want to be reminded. If it usually takes four days for your bills to reach your vendor by mail, you will want to set the Bills to Pay option to remind you at least seven days in advance.

   You can change options for the following:

   - *Checks to Print.* This option reminds you when you have checks for bills, payroll, refunds, or other set transactions to be printed.
   - *Invoices/Credit Memos to Print.* This option reminds you that you have invoices or credit memos to be printed.
   - *Sales Receipts to Print.* This option reminds you to print the sales receipts for cash sales that were not printed.
   - *Bills to Pay.* This option reminds you of bills that are coming due for payment.
   - *Memorized Transaction.* This option reminds you of an upcoming transaction that you have previously memorized.
   - *Money to Deposit.* This option reminds you of cash that has been received, but not yet deposited to a bank or petty cash account.

   Each of the selection groups also contains a set of options chosen with a radio button. Radio button options are mutually exclusive—you can only choose one. The radio button options are:

   - *Show Summary.* This option displays a summary of the transactions in the Reminders List, such as `Checks to be Printed $1250.00`. This lets you know what type of transactions need to be processed, and what their value is.

- *Show List Of.* This option displays a listing of each individual transaction, by due date, by customer or vendor name, and amount. QuickBooks also displays the summary amount above the detailed listing.
- *Don't Remind Me.* This option removes the transaction type from the Reminders List.

QuickBooks Reminders can take most of the drudgery from processing transactions. Many transactions can be entered into QuickBooks when you either receive or have time to enter them. Then a few days or weeks later, QuickBooks will remind you that it is time to finish the transaction that you started earlier.

Summary

In this chapter, you learned to use the Windows calculator and to paste a calculated number into QuickBooks. You learned to use the Find command to search for a specific transaction, to use memorized transactions for repetitive tasks, and to create a group of memorized transactions that can be used at the same time. You also learned to move transactions between similar accounts and to use the Windows Clipboard, and then you learned to work with QuickBooks Reminders.

In the next chapter, you learn to reconcile your checking account, to adjust your balance to the banks balance, and what to do when the bank has made an error.

Chapter 16

Reconciling Your Bank Account

Each month, your bank sends you a statement listing your Checking account activity for the previous month. Every bank has its own statement format, but all statements include the following information: your beginning and ending account balances as of certain dates, deposits received, checks tendered for payment, interest earned, and service fees charged, if applicable.

Good financial management requires that you balance your checking account with your bank statement each month to account for all transactions and that the transactions you entered agree with those shown in the bank statement. Balancing your account manually can be a long and tedious process. With QuickBooks, you can quickly reconcile your checking account by using the Reconcile option from the Activities menu.

You can use the techniques in this chapter with any bank account for which you receive a statement, such as a savings account or money market account. A similar reconciliation process can also be done with credit card accounts. This subject is discussed in Chapter 17, "Using Other Accounts To Perform Tasks."

If you have gone several months without *reconciling*, or balancing, your account, you may want to start with the current month's statement and continue forward. QuickBooks will add an adjusting transaction to your account. You can go back later and correct this entry, as you learn later in this chapter in the section "Adjusting Opening Balance Differences." Your records may not be quite accurate, but they will match your bank's balance.

In this chapter, you learn to do the following:

- Reconcile your Checking account
- Adjust opening balance differences
- Mark cleared transactions
- Resolve reconciliation differences

CPA TIP: Balance Your Bank Statements Monthly

Reconcile your checking account with QuickBooks after you receive each monthly bank statement. Don't wait until you have received two or three statements before you reconcile your account. You need to catch errors or omissions in your QuickBooks Check register before you overdraw your account. As a precaution, you can set up a reserve account with your bank so that your checks are not returned for insufficient funds. You can use this reserve account as a source of funds when your checking account balance is not sufficient to cover checks presented for payment. Notice, however, that you pay an interest charge on those reserve funds that the bank deposits to your checking account. Interest starts to accrue from the date the bank transfers the reserve funds into your account. Also, if the bank has made an error in your favor, you may only have 15 to 30 days to notify the bank. Many institutions will not correct a mistake after another statement cycle has passed.

If you have reconciled your checking account prior to starting your QuickBooks for Windows system and then entered historical transactions (transactions that occurred prior to your beginning your QuickBooks company) into your Checking account, it is recommended that you reconcile forward only. Do not go back and try to reconcile previous months' data. Use the check register to manually mark each of the old transactions as cleared.

Starting To Reconcile Your Account

You are probably familiar with the mechanics of the reconciliation process. However, for those readers who are a bit rusty with the process, the next few paragraphs briefly describe how reconciling a checking (or other) account works.

To reconcile a bank account, you perform three basic steps. First, review the monthly bank statement for new transactions and errors. Verify that you recorded each transaction correctly. Enter new transactions and adjustments into your checkbook, and adjust your check register balance appropriately.

Second, determine which transactions weren't cleared by the bank and total these transactions. Be sure to check both deposits and checks.

Third, verify that the difference between the Check register balance and the ending balance on the bank statement equals the total of the uncleared transactions (the sum of uncleared deposits less the sum of uncleared checks).

If the check register balance does not equal the ending bank statement balance, and the total of the uncleared transactions does not account for the difference, repeat the first and second steps.

The best time to reconcile your Checking account is after you receive your bank statement and you have entered all your transactions in QuickBooks. If you are not using QuickBooks to print checks, make sure that you enter all manual checks in the Check register before you begin. If you have not reconciled your account for more than a month, begin by reconciling your account against the oldest bank statement and then against the next month's statement, working forward to the latest.

If you do not want to take the time to balance several months of bank statements, you can allow QuickBooks to make an adjusting entry to your check register when you have completed the balancing process. It is highly recommended that you take the few minutes each month to balance your check register to your bank statement. One of the reasons that you are using QuickBooks is to avoid inaccuracies in your financial records—not increase them.

To begin reconciling your account, follow these steps:

1. From the main menu, choose **A**ctivities, Reconci**l**e. The Reconcile window appears.

2. Choose the account to be reconciled in the A**c**count To Reconcile text box. Type the account name, or select it from the drop-down list. Figure 16.1 shows the Reconcile window after you have selected the account.

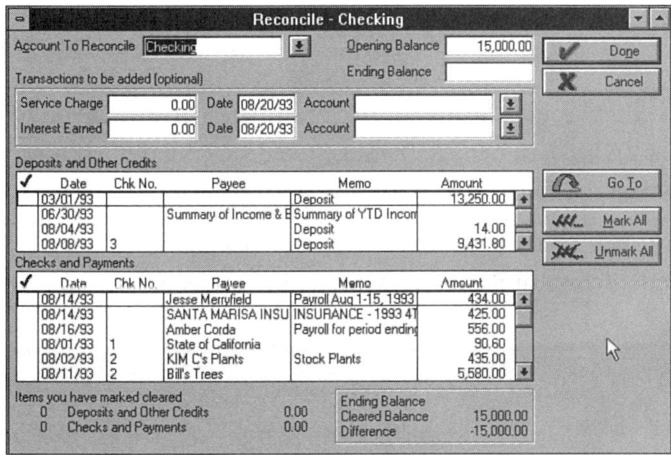

Fig. 16.1
The Reconcile window for the Checking account. QuickBooks enters the information shown from the checking account register.

Notice that the Reconcile window takes up the full screen. In order for you to see all of the Reconcile window, you must be sure to use QuickBooks in a full-screen window.

3. Enter the Ending Balance as shown on the bank statement.

4. Enter any transactions that the bank has included on the statement that you have not yet entered in your QuickBooks Check register. You may find such items as Service Charge, Bank Fees, or Overdraft charges. When you have completed the reconciliation, QuickBooks enters a cleared transaction into the check register for you. Remember that QuickBooks indicates that a transaction has been cleared by displaying an X in the transactions Clr column.

   Enter any charge that subtracts from your bank account in the text box titled Service Charge. These service charges may include items such as Automated Teller Machine (ATM) charges, service fees, or fund transfer fees. Items such as overdraft charges should be added as transactions into your checking account register. This enables you to more easily track these types of charges by categorizing them into their own Expense account.

   Enter the Date of the transaction.

   Enter the Account for this charge. QuickBooks automatically sets up an account named Bank Service Charges in your Chart of Accounts.

5. Add the interest you have earned, if any, in the Interest Earned text box. Enter this item only if you have not already recorded it in your check register.

   Enter the Date of the transaction.

   Enter the income account for tracking interest earned. If you have not set up an account named Interest Earned, or something similar, use the Uncategorized Income account.

Figure 16.2 shows these first steps completed. The ending balance, service charge, and interest earned text boxes have been filled in.

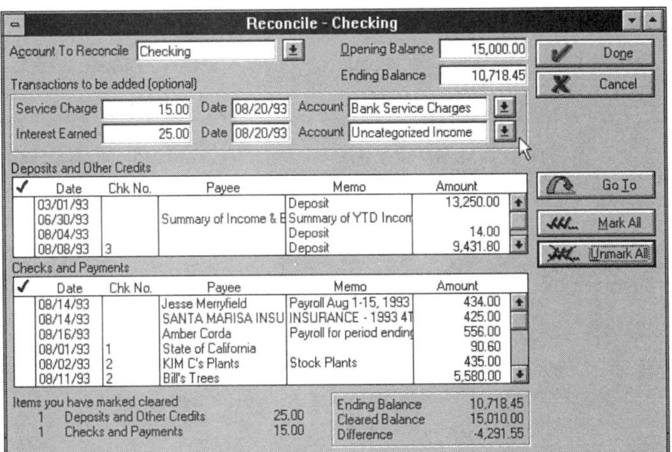

Fig. 16.2
The Reconcile window with starting entries completed.

CPA TIP: Your Account Should Draw Interest

If you normally keep a large account balance, you should have an interest-bearing checking account. You should not keep your money in an account that doesn't earn interest.

Note

Before closing your current checking account and opening a new one, check your bank service charges for each type of account. Weigh the interest factor against the fee schedule to determine the most beneficial account type for your business. If your bank does not offer interest-bearing accounts to businesses, you may want to deposit excess cash into a savings or money market account. Remember that you can set up savings and money market accounts in your QuickBooks system and use the Reconcile feature to balance each account.

Adjusting Opening Balance Differences

Before you go any further with the reconciliation process, check the **O**pening Balance text box with the beginning or opening balance on your check statement. If you have not reconciled your Checking account in several months, the opening balance probably does not agree with the bank's beginning balance.

If you have been reconciling your account regularly and have not had any problems, there are only a few reasons for your opening balance to not agree with the bank's:

- A transaction that was previously cleared in the register, and dated before the statement period, was changed between now and the date that you last reconciled your account.
- You edited the amount of a cleared transaction.
- You deleted a cleared transaction.
- You unchecked the Clr column of a cleared transaction.
- You accidentally cleared a transaction in the current statement period.

You have a choice of three options with which to proceed:

- To be accurate, you should quit reconciling at this point and find the reason for the discrepancies. After you find and correct the errors, your opening balances should agree.
- You can ignore the discrepancy for now. You can have QuickBooks create an adjusting entry for you, so that your opening balance should agree with your next statement when you complete the reconciling process. The adjusting entry adds a + or – entry to your account. Next month, your account should not be off unless you make another change as shown above.
- You can also change the opening balance in the Reconcile window to agree with the opening balance on your bank statement. This number is for reference only—QuickBooks does not use this number to calculate any balances in any of your QuickBooks accounts.

Marking Cleared Transactions

The next step to reconciling your checking account with your bank statement is to mark the transactions that have cleared the bank. A transaction is considered cleared if it has been processed by your bank and is included on the statement. To mark cleared transactions, follow these steps:

1. Check the transactions displayed in the first window titled Deposits And Other Credits. As you find a deposit, or other credit, listed on your bank statement and in the window, mark the transaction. When you have completed the deposits, move to the second window titled Checks And Payments, and do the same.

Mark a transaction by either clicking with the mouse, or highlighting by using the direction arrows and pressing the space bar. You see a check mark displayed in the far left column.

Be sure to verify that the amounts in the QuickBooks window and on your bank statement match exactly. If you find a discrepancy, verify which transaction is correct—the entry in your check register, or on the bank statement. You need to find and verify the check or deposit receipt.

2. Correct a transaction by selecting it in the display window; then choose the Go **T**o button. QuickBooks opens the transaction in the window in which it was created. Make any adjustments to the amount that are necessary to agree with the bank statement.

3. Choose the Record button in the window displaying the corrected transaction to save the transaction.

QuickBooks marks the corrected item as cleared. Continue until all transactions have been reviewed and cleared as necessary.

Entering Missing Transactions

At times, you may find transactions on your bank statement that are not listed in the uncleared transaction windows. Items not found could include Automatic Teller Machine (ATM) transactions, manual checks, or electronic transfers. To add missing transactions, follow these steps:

1. Verify each missing transaction: what was it, why has it not been entered, do you have documentation that the transaction is legitimate?

2. If you determine that the transaction is valid, enter the transaction in the Write Checks or Make Deposit window. If you have found several items that have not been entered, enter them now.

   You also can enter a transaction directly into the check register by choosing **A**ctivities, Use **R**egister (or press Ctrl+R). The Checking account register is displayed.

3. Return to the Reconcile window, and mark the transaction(s) entered as cleared.

Leaving the Reconciliation

If for some reason you cannot complete reconciling your account at this time, you can quit by selecting the Cancel button, and restart later. QuickBooks marks the checks that you have cleared so far with an asterisk (*) in the Clr column of the account register.

Unfortunately, QuickBooks does not remember the amounts that you enter as service charges, or interest earned, nor the ending balance amount that you have entered. You don't need to reenter this information.

Generally, you should not have to cancel reconciling after you have started because you can move to other windows and continue working.

Completing the Reconciliation When Your Account Balances

After you have marked all transactions on your bank statement as cleared and added any necessary transactions and cleared them, check the Difference figure in the bottom-right corner of the Reconcile window.

If the Difference amount is zero, as shown in figure 16.3, then you have successfully reconciled your check register and bank statement. Choose Do**n**e to complete the reconciliation process. The next time you view the check register, you will see that each of the cleared transactions have an X displayed in the Clr column.

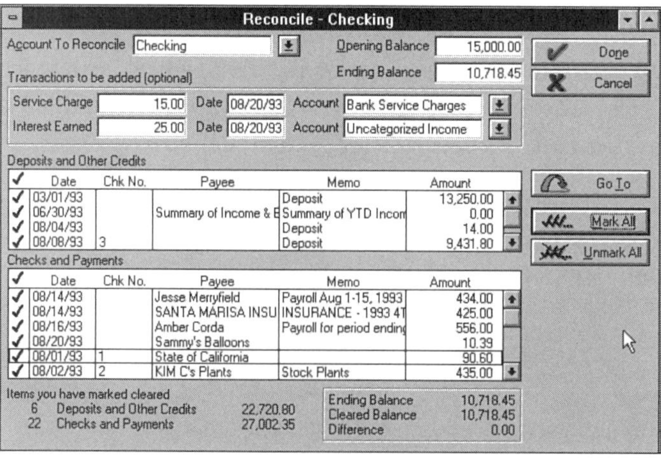

Fig. 16.3
The Reconcile window showing a zero difference at the bottom. This check register and bank statement have been successfully reconciled.

Completing the Reconciliation When Your Account Doesn't Balance

If you have finished the above steps and the Difference figure is not zero, then your account is *not* in balance. Figure 16.4 shows the Reconcile window with an account that is not in balance.

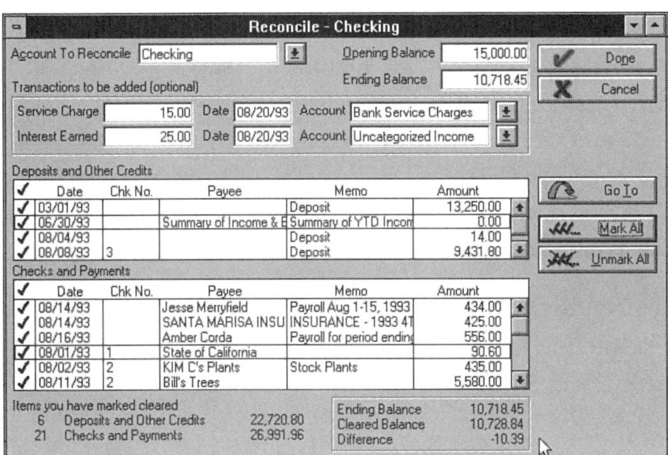

Fig. 16.4
A checking account that is not reconciled to the bank statement. Notice the difference of -10.39.

You have a choice of two alternatives when your checking account is not reconciled with the bank statement. You can hunt down the differences and correct them, or you can let QuickBooks create an adjusting transaction to make your checking account agree with the bank statement.

Resolving Reconciliation Differences

Finding and resolving any differences is the most accurate way to handle this problem. As you track through your QuickBooks transactions for the origin of the difference, check for these frequent reconciling errors:

- Clearing transactions that are not listed on the bank statement
- Not marking all transactions listed on the statement
- Missing a difference in an amount between your check register and the bank statement
- Skipping a transaction listed on the bank statement but not included in your check register

To correct a reconciling difference, follow these steps:

1. Check the number of deposits and other credits that you have listed on your bank statement. This includes all deposits you have made, and any interest payments. If the number of items listed on the bank statement agrees with the number listed in the bottom left corner of the Reconcile window, then do the same for the checks. Refer to figure 16.4 to see the number of items that have been cleared.

   QuickBooks keeps track of the number of items that you have cleared during the reconciliation. If the number of items do not agree—you have cleared six deposits, for example, and your bank statement shows seven—then you know that you need to recheck the deposits more closely. This can help you to focus in on the area where a mistake may have been made.

   Remember, the number of items marked cleared includes the service charge, and interest earned. Each of these items count as one in each category.

2. Check the total of each group of transactions. QuickBooks keeps track of the total of all deposits and the total of all checks. Many bank statements may give you the same information. Figure 16.4 also shows the dollar amount of all cleared items.

   If the number of items checked in step 1 is correct and the dollar amount checked in step 2 is not, then you know you need to closely recheck all of the amounts that have been cleared.

3. Select the erroneous transaction, and choose Go **T**o. QuickBooks opens the transaction in the window where it originated. Make any necessary changes.

4. Choose Record or OK and return to the Reconcile window.

5. Recheck the differences total. If you have found all of the errors, the difference should now be zero.

Letting QuickBooks Reconcile the Differences

You also have the option of letting QuickBooks create an adjustment in your check register to agree with the bank statement. You first must decide how large an error you can live with, and how valuable your time is.

After all, if your bookkeeper costs you $10 per hour, then having him or her spend two hours trying to track down a 50-cent error is not cost-effective. On the other hand, a $25.00 error may be significant enough for many businesses to want to track down. For a large corporation that produces several million dollars in transactions every month, a $25.00 error is *not* significant. As a business owner, you must make this decision. It is highly recommended that you make a policy addressing the dollar amount of a discrepancy that you will allow QuickBooks to adjust. This will help to ensure that you consistently follow the same rules.

If the amount is minor—under $10.00, for example—you may want QuickBooks to make the adjustment. You can always reverse the adjustment later if you find the error. To let QuickBooks make an adjustment, follow these steps:

1. Choose the Do**n**e button. QuickBooks displays the Reconcile Adjustment window, as shown in figure 16.5.

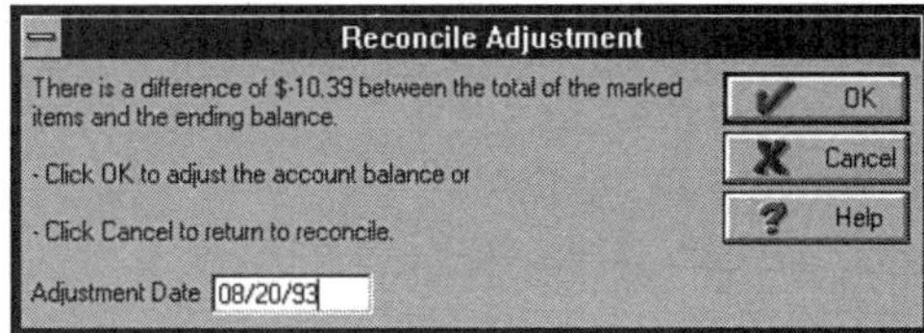

Fig. 16.5
Use the Reconcile Adjustment dialog box to create an adjusting entry in your check register.

   The Reconcile Adjustment dialog box tells you how much of an adjustment will be made, and allows you to enter the date for the adjustment.

2. Choose OK to enter the adjustment and save the reconciliation. The Reconciliation Complete dialog box, which is discussed in the next section, appears.

   Choose Cancel to return to the Reconcile window. Use this option if you decide not to enter an adjustment. You can try to find the discrepancy as you learned in the preceding section.

   Figure 16.6 shows the adjusting entry that QuickBooks has entered into the check register. Notice that the cleared transactions have an X in the Clr column.

Fig. 16.6
The adjusting entry entered into the check register.

Checking

Date	Num / Type	Payee / Memo	Account	Payment	Clr	Deposit	Balance
08/16/93	To Print / CHK	Amber Corda / Payroll for period endi	-split-	556 00	X		12,705 84
08/20/93	DEP	Interest	Uncategorized Incom		X	25 00	12,730 84
08/20/93	CHK	Balance Adjustment	Opening Bal Equity	10 39	X		12,720 45
08/20/93	CHK	Service Charge	Bank Service Charge	15 00	X		12,705 45
08/31/93	255 / CHK	Ashley Corda / Payroll for period endi	-split-	615 00	X		12,090 45
08/31/93	256 / CHK	Amber Corda / Payroll for period endi	-split-	556 00	X		11,534 45
08/31/93	257 / CHK	Jesse Merryfield / Payroll for period endi	-split-	816 00	X		10,718 45
08/20/93	Num	Payee / Memo	Account	Payment		Deposit	

Record Restore Q-Report Edit/Split 1-line view Ending Balance: 10,718.45

Note

Don't disregard reconciliation differences. If you have entered all transactions accurately in QuickBooks, you should not have a difference between the bank's balance and your QuickBooks balance. One major reason for reconciling your account is to detect your or the bank's errors. Remember, banks make mistakes, too. Reconciliation differences may be caused by the bank's error.

CPA TIP: When To Adjust a Discrepancy

If the reconciliation difference is not important, your time may be better spent on other matters, rather than tracking down a few dollars. You are the judge of what's important, based on the amount of cash flowing in and out of your account and what your average account balance is. A difference of $5 is minor if you record $100,000 of transactions each month.

Printing a Reconciliation Report

After you have finished, choose Do**n**e; QuickBooks saves all the information and displays the Reconciliation Complete dialog box (see fig. 16.7). You then can print a reconciliation report. The Reconciliation Complete dialog box gives you three options:

None — Prints no report.

Summary — Prints a summary report. Lists totals and uncleared transactions.

Full Prints a full report of all transactions, listing totals for both cleared and uncleared transactions, as well as the transactions themselves.

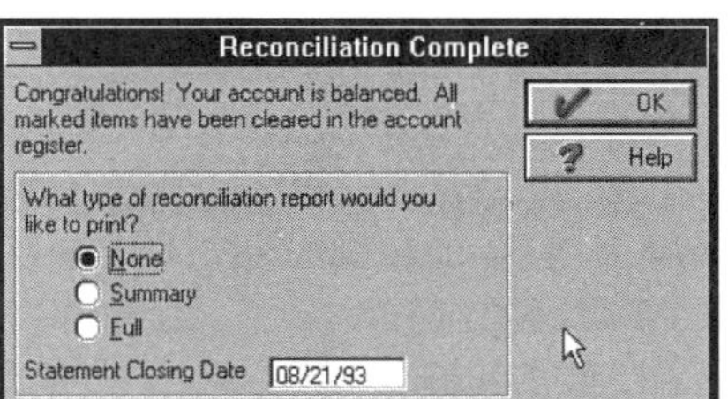

Fig. 16.7
The Reconciliation Complete dialog box.

If you do not choose a report option, QuickBooks overwrites the information the next time that you begin to reconcile the account. You will then lose any information. If you think that you may want to refer to the report at a later time, print it out. To print a reconciliation report, follow these steps:

1. Select the report option you require.
2. Choose OK. QuickBooks displays the Print Report dialog box.
3. Choose **P**rint. QuickBooks creates the report and sends it to your printer.

Summary

In this chapter, you learned how to adjust your opening balance with the bank's statement, how to mark cleared transactions, and how to enter missing transactions. You also learned how to search for and correct errors when you reconcile your account and how to print the reconciliation report.

In the next chapter, you learn how to use Balance Sheet accounts and work with Credit Card accounts. You also learn how to add fixed assets and accumulated depreciation and how to use Payroll, Liability, and Equity accounts.

Chapter 17

Using Other Accounts To Perform Tasks

Over the last 16 chapters, you learned to use three of QuickBooks' Balance Sheet accounts: Checking, Accounts Receivable, and Accounts Payable. You use the check register to track transactions that affect your checking account balance, such as checks, deposits, and automatic teller machine withdrawals. You use the Accounts Receivable register to record invoices, customer payments, credit memos, and refunds. You enter and pay bills from your vendors in the Accounts Payable register. You can accomplish most common business tasks by using QuickBooks' Checking, Accounts Receivable, and Accounts Payable accounts.

Although you can perform most of the common tasks with these three accounts, they are still only part of your complete balance sheet. You must also be able to track your fixed assets, credit card transactions, payroll liabilities, loans, and complete year-end transactions. You can add accounts to the QuickBooks Chart of Accounts to handle these tasks.

Although QuickBooks sets up some accounts for you, you need to complete the balance sheet by adding an account for each asset, liability, and retained earnings. You must have a complete and accurate balance sheet if you plan to seek financing, increase your credit line, or attract potential investors.

In Chapter 4, "Working with Accounts," you learned how to create Balance Sheet accounts and how to enter opening balances for them when you create the account.

After reading this chapter, you can perform the most common business tasks with QuickBooks. For any item you want to track, you can add an account, enter an opening balance, and record subsequent transactions in QuickBooks.

In this chapter, you learn how to do the following:

- Work with Credit Card accounts
- Use other Current Asset accounts
- Create, use, and sell fixed asset and accumulated depreciation accounts
- Use the liability accounts, including loans and payroll tax liabilities
- Work with the equity accounts such as Owners Equity and Retained Earnings
- Complete the year-end transactions

Understanding Balance Sheet Accounts

Your Balance Sheet accounts are your permanent accounts. They include all your asset, liability, and equity accounts. The Balance Sheet accounts do not include the Income and Expense accounts; they are part of your Income Statement accounts.

Assets include everything that the business owns: cash, equipment and fixtures, buildings, and vehicles. They also include everything that other people or businesses owe you—your Accounts Receivable and short- and long-term notes or loans. Assets can be broken down into current assets and fixed assets.

Current assets include: cash, checking accounts, inventory, Accounts Receivable, Notes Receivable that are due within one year, and other items that are liquid (can be easily sold).

Non-current assets include: investments in other companies, loans or notes that will not be paid within one year, buildings, equipment, vehicles, and other assets that will not be sold or otherwise converted into cash within one year.

CPA TIP: What is a Current Asset?

Generally, an asset is considered a current asset if it is to be converted into cash, used to pay a current liability, or will be consumed within one year or the business operating cycle, whichever is longer.

Liabilities include everything that is owed by the business, such as Accounts Payable, accrued payroll, prepayments by customers, notes payable, loans and mortgages, payroll taxes, and other taxes. Liabilities, like assets, also can be divided as current and long-term liabilities.

Current liabilities include such things as Accounts Payable, accrued payroll, taxes, prepaid services or layaways, or other liabilities that will be paid within one year.

Long-term liabilities include mortgages, long-term loans, notes or bonds payable, deferred income taxes, lease obligations, and pension obligations.

CPA TIP: What are Long-Term Liabilities?

Long-term liabilities often include both a current and a long-term component. The part of the long-term obligation due in the current year is considered a current liability. For example, if you have a mortgage on your building, the portion of the mortgage that is due this year becomes a current liability, although the balance remains a long-term liability.

The final part of the Balance Sheet accounts is the *Owners' Equity accounts*. Simply put, owners' equity is whatever is left over if all assets are liquidated and all liabilities paid. Equity accounts increase in one of three ways: investment by owners, net profit from operations, and retained earnings (profits from earlier periods that were not paid out to the owners). Depending on your business type—proprietorship, partnership, or corporation—your Owners' Equity accounts will be different. You may want your accountant to help you set up your Owners' Equity accounts.

The value of a Balance Sheet account varies from day to day (for example, your Checking account balance), and so its value is not considered over a period of time. Its balance is always referred to as of a specific date.

Updating Account Values

In Chapter 4, "Working with Accounts," you learned how to add accounts to your QuickBooks Chart of Accounts and how to select accounts to use them. In this section, you review how to select an account to use, and you learn how to enter an opening balance transaction (if you didn't enter an opening balance when you set up the account).

You can set the opening balance of an account when you create the account. When you first created your QuickBooks company, you may not have entered an opening balance. QuickBooks simply adds a new account with no entries. You can then add the opening balance transactions into the account register for the value of the assets or liabilities as of your QuickBooks start date. This feature is particularly useful for tracing multiple assets or liabilities within a single account.

For example, you may want to add a fixed asset account for your computer equipment. If you have chosen not to enter a dollar amount for the account balance as of the date you add the account, you can later open the computer equipment register and enter a transaction for each existing piece of equipment. Be sure to date each transaction with the starting date chosen for your QuickBooks system. For asset or liability accounts, enter the opening balance in the *Increase* column. Be sure to assign the Open Bal Equity account to any opening balance transactions that you enter.

To enter an opening balance transaction, follow these steps:

1. To open the Chart of Accounts, choose the Accnt button on the Iconbar; choose **L**ists, Chart of **A**ccounts; or press Ctrl+A.

2. Select the Fixed Asset account by double-clicking with the mouse, or highlight the account and use the U**s**e Register button. The Fixed Assets register appears, as shown in figure 17.1.

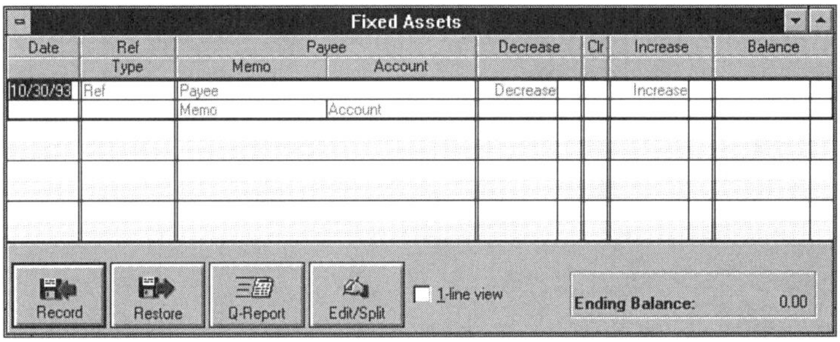

Fig. 17.1
The Fixed Assets register. Notice that QuickBooks did not enter any beginning balance transactions in this register when the account was created.

3. Enter the opening balance transaction by entering the date that you started your QuickBooks company.

4. Enter the value of your fixed assets in the Increase column.

5. (Optional) Type a memo, such as "Account Opening Balance," in the Memo field.

6. Select the Account for this transaction. When entering the value of the assets as of the beginning date of your QuickBooks company, always use the "Opening Bal Equity" account.

7. Click the Record button, or press the Enter key to save the transaction. Your Fixed Assets account now looks like figure 17.2.

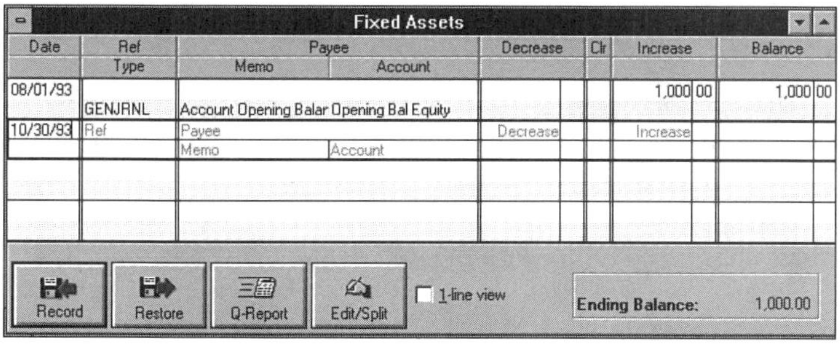

Fixed Assets

Date	Ref / Type	Payee / Memo	Account	Decrease	Clr	Increase	Balance
08/01/93	GENJRNL	Account Opening Balar	Opening Bal Equity			1,000 00	1,000 00
10/30/93	Ref	Payee / Memo	Account	Decrease		Increase	

Record | Restore | Q-Report | Edit/Split | 1-line view | Ending Balance: 1,000.00

Fig. 17.2
The Fixed Assets register with the Opening Balance adjusted to include the value of the assets.

You also can enter an adjustment to an account if the value has changed significantly. This feature is especially relevant with an investment account (stocks or bonds). Notice that QuickBooks automatically enters the transaction type "GENJRNL" into the transaction.

CPA TIP: Fixed Asset Valuation

Generally, you should not adjust the valuation of fixed assets or liabilities. Fixed assets valuations should be based on historical (meaning purchase) cost, less any accumulated depreciation. Be sure to discuss with your CPA any transactions to be recorded when you sell a fixed asset, or loose it due to destruction or theft.

Figure 17.3 shows the Investments register and an adjusting entry for a decrease in the value of the stock portfolio. Stocks and bonds that are actively traded have published values, which you can use to determine the value of a portfolio. The adjustment is assigned to the Interest Income account. You can set up another account, or assign the income, or loss, to Uncategorized Income.

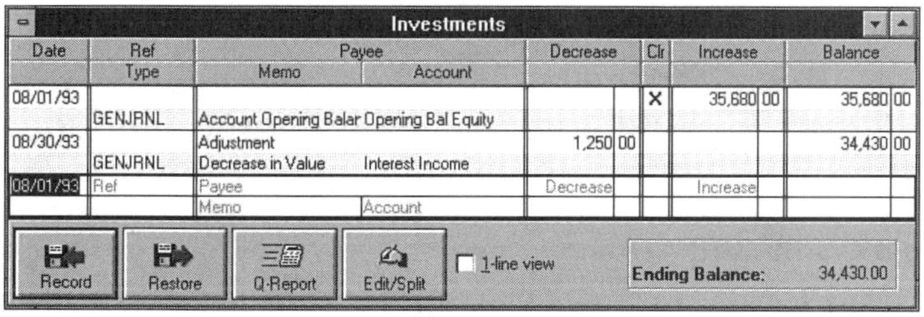

Investments

Date	Ref / Type	Payee / Memo	Account	Decrease	Clr	Increase	Balance
08/01/93	GENJRNL	Account Opening Balar	Opening Bal Equity		X	35,680 00	35,680 00
08/30/93	GENJRNL	Adjustment / Decrease in Value	Interest Income	1,250 00			34,430 00
08/01/93	Ref	Payee / Memo	Account	Decrease		Increase	

Record | Restore | Q-Report | Edit/Split | 1-line view | Ending Balance: 34,430.00

Fig. 17.3
The Investments register shows a decrease in the account value. This decrease is an unrecognizable capital loss.

CPA TIP: Investment Gains or Losses

The changes in the market value of investments usually are listed as unrealized gains or losses on a business's profit and loss statement. An unrealized gain or loss represents the amount by which an investment's value changes while you still hold the investment. Recognized gains and losses, however, represent the amount by which an investment's value changed when you sold the investment. You calculate recognized gains and losses by subtracting the cost-basis of an investment (the amount you paid for the investment, net of any commissions or fees) from the net proceeds received on the sale. If the difference is positive, you have a gain; if the difference is negative, you have a loss. Because investments are considered capital assets for income tax purposes, the resulting gain or loss also is considered a capital gain or loss.

Working with Credit Card Accounts

If you use credit cards in your business, you can add a Credit Card account for each credit card that you use to help record and keep track of purchases, payments, and finance charges. When you enter all your credit card purchases in your QuickBooks Credit Card account, you can reconcile your credit card statements and pay your bills with a few simple keystrokes.

If you use more than one credit card and want to use QuickBooks to reconcile your credit card statement, set up a separate account for each card.

CPA TIP: Credit Card Liability Accounts

A credit card transaction is a liability the moment that you use the card to pay for merchandise or services. Even if you do not have to pay for the item for 30 days, you have incurred the liability. To accurately reflect your liabilities on your balance sheet, set up a Credit Card account and enter credit transactions as you incur them. Most credit card cash advances begin accruing interest the day the advance is issued. If you're in a bind for cash, take the cash advance, and pay back the advance as soon as possible before your next statement date to avoid excessive interest charges.

Adding a Credit Card Account

When you decide to use a credit card in your business to purchase goods and services, set up a QuickBooks Credit Card account to track these expenses.

To set up a Credit Card account, follow these steps:

1. Open the Chart of Accounts.
2. Select the **N**ew button to add another account.
3. Select the **T**ype option, and choose *Credit Card* in the New Account window.
4. Enter the Name for this account. For example, if you enter an account for your company's VISA card, enter a name such as Credit Card—VISA. If your business uses more than one of the same card, be sure that you give each account a distinctive name.
5. Enter the Opening Balance for this account in the Opening Balance text box. If it is a new account, this is **0**. If you have been using the account, enter the amount from your last statement.
6. Enter the date for this opening balance. Choose OK to save the Credit Card account in the Chart of Accounts.

   Figure 17.4 shows the Credit Card register.

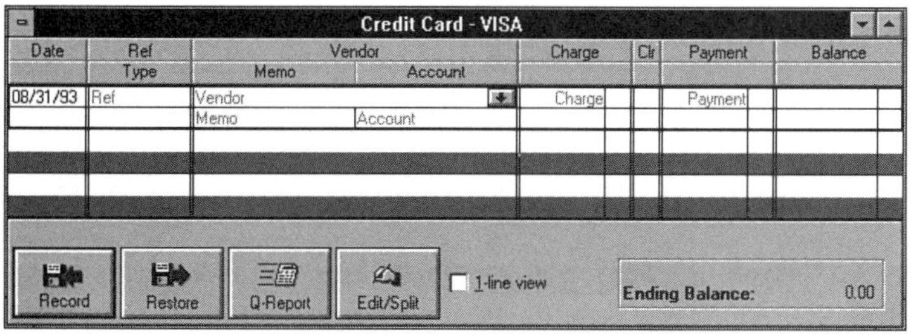

Fig. 17.4
The Credit Card—VISA register. As you use your credit card, be sure to record these transactions to keep your credit account current.

Entering Credit Card Transactions

You enter credit card transactions almost in the same way that you Write Checks in your Checking Account or Pay Bills in your Accounts Payable. You enter credit card purchases and have QuickBooks make payments directly into your Credit Card account register. When you reconcile your credit card statement, you enter finance charges into the Credit Card account register.

Be sure to add the credit card company (VISA, MasterCard, American Express, Discover, and so on) to your vendor list. This enables you to have QuickBooks prepare a check to pay credit card bills.

To add a credit card transaction in the Credit Card account register, follow these steps:

1. Choose **A**ctivities, Enter **C**redit Card Charges from the menu. The credit card entry window displays, as shown in figure 17.5.

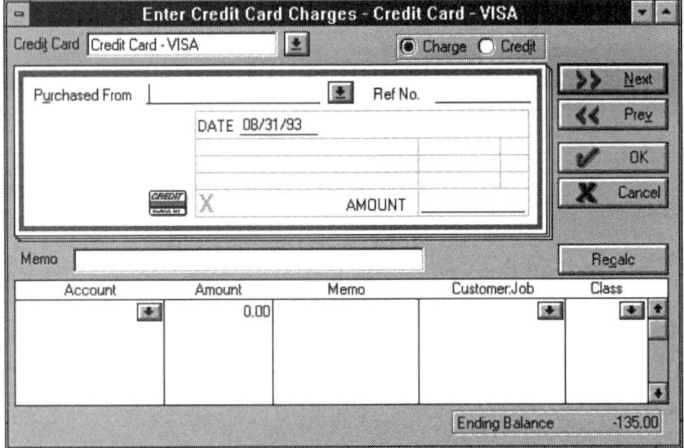

Fig. 17.5
Use the Enter Credit Card Charges window to make changes to your credit card.

2. Select the Credit Card account in the Credi**t** Card text box. If you have more than one Credit Card account, you can select the correct card from the drop-down list.

3. Choose Charge or Cred**i**t. When you enter a credit card purchase, select the Charge option. If you enter a credit card credit or refund, select the Cred**i**t option.

4. Enter the vendor from whom the purchase was made. Type the vendor name or select it from the drop-down list in the P**u**rchased from field.

5. (Optional) Enter the charge card reference number in the field marked Ref No.

6. Change the date for the transaction, if necessary. QuickBooks automatically fills in the current date. Remember, you can use the + or – keys to change the date.

7. Enter the total amount of the transaction into the Amount field.

8. (Optional) Type a note into the Memo field, if needed. This note is displayed in the Credit Card register, and on any reports that include this transaction.

9. Enter the transaction distribution in the detail area, just as you learned in Chapters 11 and 13. Enter the account for the expense, and the amount of the expense. Optionally, you also can enter a memo for each line, and assign all or part of the expense to a Customer:Job if this is a reimbursable expense, and the Class for this transaction.

10. Select OK to record the transaction and return to the QuickBooks desktop. You also can use the **N**ext button to record this transaction and open the next book window to add another credit card transaction.

Figure 17.6 shows the completed credit card window.

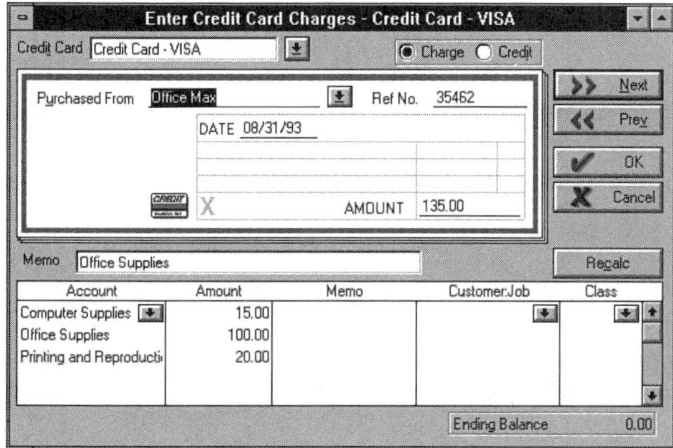

Fig. 17.6
The completed Enter Credit Card Charges window. Notice that this expense has been distributed into three different accounts.

You also can enter a simple, single expense transaction directly into the Credit Card register. To enter a credit card transaction directly into the Credit Card register, follow these steps:

1. Open the Chart of Accounts, select the Credit Card account, and choose U**s**e Register.

2. Enter the transaction, just as you have learned to enter a transaction into the Checking, Accounts Payable, or Accounts Receivable registers.

Just as you can with the other balance sheet registers, you can enter split transactions by using the Edit/Split button.

Editing, Deleting, or Voiding a Credit Card Transaction

If you find that you made an error when entering a credit card transaction, you can easily edit the transaction or delete it. To edit a credit card transaction, follow these steps:

1. Open the Chart of Accounts and select the Credit Card account that you want to use.
2. Select the Use Register button to open the register.
3. Find and select the transaction to be edited.
4. Edit the field that contains the incorrect entry. If the account field is incorrect and the transaction is a split transaction, select the Edit/Split button. The transaction is now displayed in the Enter Credit Card Charges window.
5. Choose OK from the Enter Charges window, or Record from the register window, to save your changes.

You also can delete or void a credit card transaction. To void or delete a credit card transaction, follow these steps:

1. Open the Chart of Accounts and select the Credit Card account with which you want to work.
2. Select the transaction to be voided or deleted.

Caution

As has been mentioned previously, it is generally in your best interests to void a transaction, instead of deleting it. When a transaction is voided, QuickBooks leaves a record of it in your account register, while deleting it removes all trace of the transaction. A voided transaction leaves an audit trail that can be traced if necessary.

3. Choose **E**dit, **D**elete Credit Card or press Ctrl+D to delete a credit card transaction. Remember, using the Delete option completely erases the transaction; you have no chance to recover the information.
4. Choose **E**dit, **V**oid Credit Card to void a credit card transaction. Using the Void option maintains your audit trail by keeping the transaction in the register. QuickBooks places a `VOID` notation in the memo field and changes the charge amount to zero, and places an X in the Clr column.

Reconciling Your Credit Card Account

You reconcile your Credit Card accounts in the same way that you reconcile your Checking account. When you receive your credit card statement, you check off those transactions listed in your credit card register that are also listed on your statement. When you finish the reconciliation, you can have QuickBooks write a check to the credit card company, or add the payment to the Accounts Payable account for payment later.

CPA TIP: Reconciling Your Account Helps Prevent Fraud

Reconciling your Credit Card account keeps you alert to unauthorized credit transactions. Your Credit Card account number can be used for purchases made by telephone because no signature is required. An unauthorized user needs only your account number and expiration date to make a credit purchase by phone.

To reconcile your Credit Card account, follow these steps:

1. Choose **A**ctivities, Reconci**l**e from the menu. QuickBooks displays the Reconcile window.

   If you have the Credit Card register displayed on-screen, the Reconci**l**e option displays as Reconci**l**e Credit Card. It is the same command.

2. Select the A**c**count To Reconcile, type the name of your credit card account, or select the account from the drop-down list.

   If the last account you reconciled was the Checking account, you now see fields in the Transactions To Be Added section replaced by a Finance Charges section, as in figure 17.7.

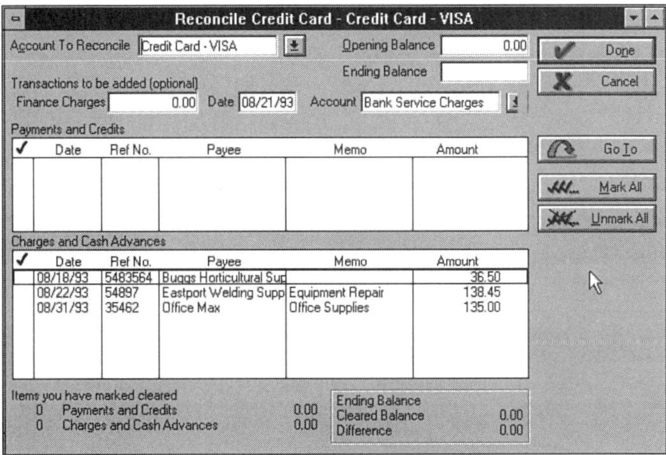

Fig. 17.7
Use the Reconcile Credit Card window to verify your credit card statement.

3. Enter the **O**pening Balance, if necessary. If you successfully reconciled this account with QuickBooks last month, the displayed amount should be the same as that shown on your credit card statement.

   If it does not match, you may have deleted or voided a previously cleared transaction, or edited the amount of a cleared transaction. You may also have accidentally marked a transaction as cleared that has not been included in the reconciliation process. Find the error and then continue.

4. Enter the Ending Balance from your credit card statement.

5. Enter any Finance Charges included on your statement that you have not previously entered in your Credit Card register in the Finance Charges text box.

6. Enter the Date for the Finance Charge transaction in the Date text box beside the Finances Charge text box.

CPA TIP: Credit Card Interest and Business Use

Although consumer interest is no longer deductible for tax purposes—because of the Tax Reform Act of 1986—you can still deduct interest charges (finance charges) that relate to purchases made in your business. You therefore should use one credit card only for business use so that you can easily identify the card's interest charges as a business interest expense. Use a different card for personal use.

7. Select the account that you want to use to track credit card finance charges. Type the account name or select it from the drop-down list.

8. Check each transaction listed on your statement and find its match in your reconciliation window. When you find the matching transaction, place a check mark in the far left column. Place the check mark by either clicking the transaction with the mouse or moving the black selector bar to the transaction and pressing the space bar.

   Be sure that you verify the amounts charged on the statement with the amount that you have entered in your Credit Card register and displayed here. If you find a discrepancy, verify the transaction with your credit card receipt. If you made an error, select the Go **T**o button. This opens the Enter Credit Card Charges window. Make the necessary corrections, and choose the OK button to save.

When you account for all transactions listed on the statement, check the amount displayed in the bottom right corner of the reconciliation window. The amount is titled `Difference`. If this amount is **0.00**, you have successfully reconciled your account. If the difference is not 0, you need to recheck each of the transactions again.

9. Optionally, you can have QuickBooks create an adjusting entry for you to force the Credit Card register to equal the statement balance. Use this option only if the difference is very small, or if you do not have the time to find the difference now.

   Figure 17.8 shows the Reconcile Credit Card window successfully reconciled.

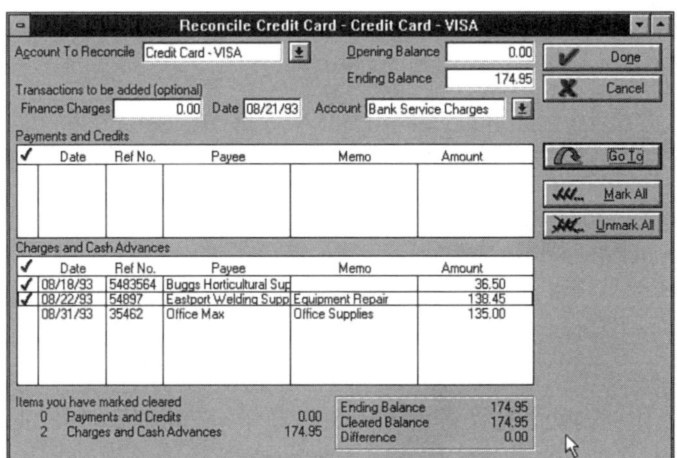

Fig. 17.8 The completed credit card reconciliation. Notice the Difference amount shows 0.00, indicating a successful balancing of this account.

10. Select the Do**n**e button to complete the reconciliation.

Making Credit Card Payments

When you finish the reconciliation process, QuickBooks displays a dialog box for you to select how you want to pay your bill. You now see the Make Payment dialog box, as shown in figure 17.9.

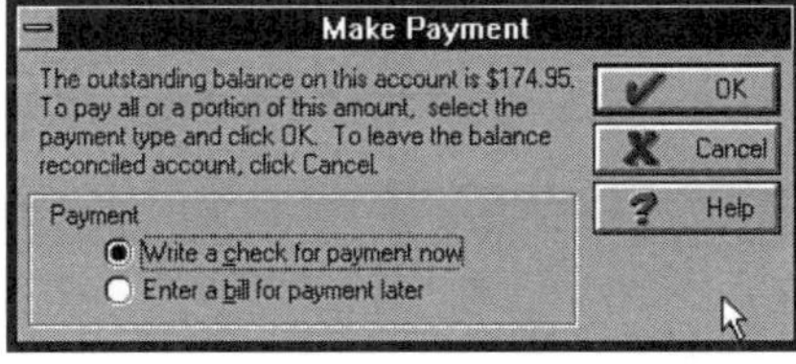

Fig. 17.9 Use the Make Payment dialog box to tell QuickBooks how you want to pay your credit card bill.

You have two options to select from in this dialog box. You can

- Write a **C**heck for Payment Now—Use this option if the payment to the credit card company is now due, or if you are using the cash basis for your accounting. QuickBooks opens the Write Check window and fills in the information for you.
- Enter a **B**ill for Payment Later—Use this option to create an entry in the Accounts Payable register with the Enter Bills window. When the bill is due, QuickBooks reminds you to enter a Pay Bills transaction.

With either selection, you enter the Vendor to be paid, and have the option to pay all or only a portion of the bill. QuickBooks enters the full amount of the payment. You can override this amount and enter a different amount.

To enter the credit card payment into your Accounts Payable register, follow these steps:

1. Select Enter a **B**ill for Payment Later. You see the Enter Bills—Accounts Payable window.
2. Enter vendor for this credit card payment. Type the name or select it from the drop-down list.
3. Enter the date if you want to change the default date of "today."
4. (Optional) Enter a Ref. No. such as the statement number.
5. Change the Bill Due date if necessary.
6. Enter the Amount Due if you want to pay an amount different than the full amount due.
7. (Optional) Type a note in the Memo field, if necessary.
8. Distribute the payment as necessary. You generally should not have to change the default distribution. Remember, you already distributed each individual charge to various Expense accounts when you entered the charges into your Credit Card register. Figure 17.10 shows the completed payment to VISA.

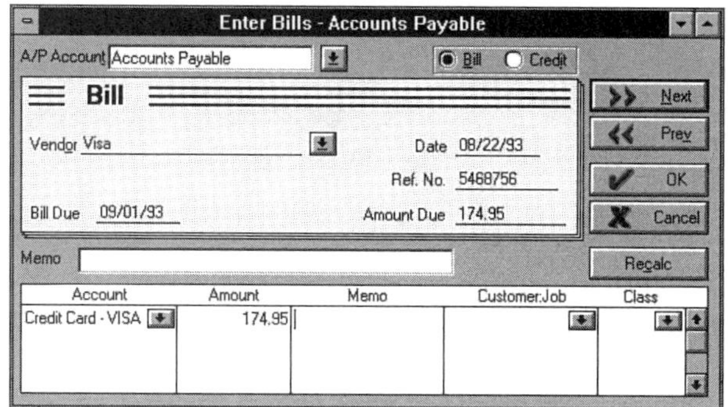

Fig. 17.10
The completed credit card payment. QuickBooks enters this payment into the Accounts Payable register.

To write a check now for the credit card payment, instead of entering a bill for payment later in the Make Payment dialog box, follow these steps:

1. Select the Write a **C**heck for Payment Now option. QuickBooks displays the Write Checks window. The check is filled in with all the necessary information.

2. Make any changes that you require. For example, if you do not want to pay the full amount, change the amount to reflect the payment that you want to make at this time.

   As you learned in Chapter 13, "Writing and Printing Checks," you can print the check now, or check the To **B**e Printed box and print the check with your next print run of checks.

3. Choose OK to save the check transaction.

Working with Current Asset Accounts

QuickBooks automatically sets up one current asset account for you, Checking. You add a current asset account to your Chart of Accounts the same way you would add any Balance Sheet account. Set up additional current asset accounts to track the following:

- Assets already in the form of cash, such as petty cash funds and cash register funds.

- Assets scheduled to be converted into cash, such as a 6-month note; or assets used during regular operations within the next 12 months, such as inventory.

The one current asset account with which you may have trouble is a prepaid Expense account. A prepaid expense is a current asset. It is not an expense until it has been used. Use prepaid Expense accounts to track expenses for items that you have paid before you actually receive the item or service.

One of the most common prepaid expenses is an insurance premium. You prepay the insurance in advance of the period covered by the premium. For proper accounting, match the expense to the time period in which you received the benefit. This requires that you set up a prepaid insurance account and reduce the prepaid account each period. When you reduce a prepaid Expense account, assign an Expense account (such as Insurance Expense) to the transaction. If you use the cash basis method of accounting, you do not have any prepaid Expense accounts. See Chapter 12, "Using the Accounts Payable Register," for an explanation of cash versus accrual accounting methods.

If you want your savings account activity reflected in cash flow reports, or if you want to use QuickBooks' Reconcile command to balance your savings account, you need to add a savings account as a QuickBooks checking account, not as a current asset account.

To add a current asset account, follow these steps:

1. Open the Chart of Accounts and select the **N**ew button. QuickBooks displays the New Account window.
2. Enter in the **T**ype text box the account type.
3. Type the name of the account in the Name text box, such as **Prepaid Insurance**.
4. Enter a Description of the account, such as **Business Insurance**, in the Description text box.
5. Leave the Bank No. blank. Bank account numbers have nothing to do with a fixed asset.
6. Select **S**ubaccount Of only if you have several prepaid insurance or insurance accounts and want to subordinate this account to another.
7. Enter the Opening Balance. This would be the amount that you prepaid.

8. Enter the date that you started your QuickBooks system or made the prepayment. Your New Account dialog box looks similar to figure 17.11.

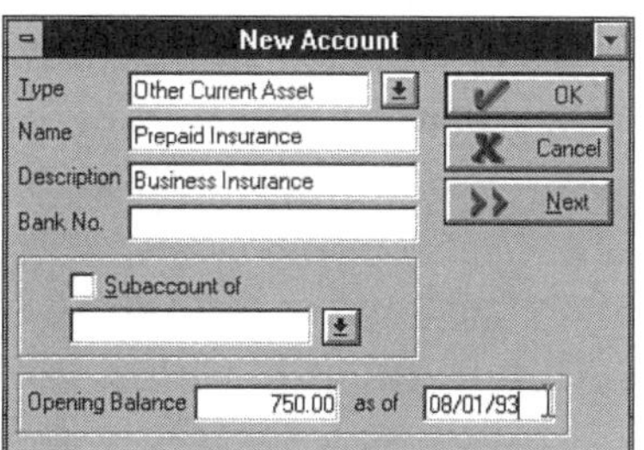

Fig. 17.11
Shown is the Other Current Asset type account named Prepaid Insurance completed in the New Account dialog box.

9. Choose the OK button to save the new account in the Chart of Accounts.

Working with Fixed Asset Accounts

Fixed Asset accounts are created to track those assets that you will not convert to cash, or expend by using in the normal course of business in the next year. Fixed assets include items such as buildings and capital equipment (machinery, store fixtures, and vehicles).

When you set up a Fixed Asset account to track assets that you use in your business (such as automobiles, furniture, and computer equipment), you not only track the value of these assets, but also the asset's related depreciation. *Depreciation* is the allocation of the asset's cost over its useful life. As you depreciate an asset, the book value of the asset declines. *Book value* can generally be described as the cost of the asset plus any setup and transportation cost minus the accumulated depreciation. An asset's book value eventually declines to zero when the asset is fully depreciated. Remember, book value does not equal market value or the amount that you may be able to sell an asset for.

Adding a Fixed Asset Account

A Fixed Asset account is added in the same way as all other Balance Sheet accounts. When you set up your Fixed Asset accounts, it is highly recommended that you set up an account for each major group of assets. You may want to create a Fixed Asset account for computer equipment, vehicles, buildings, store fixtures, and furniture.

The reason that you should create several fixed accounts is that different types of fixed assets are classified as having a certain useful life. Each life classification has a different length over which it is depreciated. Calculating the depreciation is much easier if you do not have to go back and report each asset and figure out its value again. Seek help from your accountant when first setting up your Fixed Asset accounts.

To add a Fixed Asset account, follow these steps:

1. Open the Chart of Accounts and choose the **N**ew button. QuickBooks displays the New Account window.
2. Enter the account **T**ype of Fixed Asset.
3. Type the account Name, such as **Computer Equipment**.
4. Enter a Description of the account, if necessary.
5. Add a Note, if needed. You can make a note concerning the method used to depreciate these assets.
6. Select **S**ubaccount Of if you use a separate subaccount for each fixed asset and then combine them into a single master account.
7. Enter the Opening Balance. This would be the amount that you paid for the asset, or its current book value.
8. Enter the date that you started your QuickBooks system, or that you bought the asset.
9. Choose the OK button to save the new account in the Chart of Accounts.

Adding an Accumulated Depreciation Account

Create an Accumulated Depreciation account for each Fixed Asset account that you have. You must be able to track the depreciation expense for all your fixed assets over time. This is done in the Accumulated Depreciation account. The Depreciation Expense account is an Expense account and so is reduced to zero each year when you close your books. This is covered later in this chapter, in the section "Completing the Year-end Transaction."

Accumulated Depreciation is also known as a *Contra Asset* account, an account tied to another asset account, but its value is the opposite of it. The Fixed Asset account is a positive account, whereas its associated Accumulated Depreciation account is a negative account.

Within QuickBooks, you create an Accumulated Depreciation account for each Fixed Asset account that you create. The Accumulated Depreciation account is also a Fixed Asset account, but it is a subaccount of the associated Fixed Asset.

To create an Accumulated Depreciation account for the fixed asset Computer Equipment, follow these steps:

1. Open the Chart of Accounts and choose the **N**ew button.
2. Choose the account **T**ype of Fixed Asset.
3. Enter a name for the account, such as **Accumulated Depreciation**.
4. Use the fixed asset name in the description box.
5. Check the **S**ubaccount of box.
6. Select the name of the fixed asset for which this will be the accumulated depreciation account.

> **Note**
>
> If you have begun your QuickBooks company at a date other than the beginning of your fiscal year, you may have already recorded accumulated depreciation charges. If this is true, you will then want to enter this amount in the Opening Balance text box. Enter the date as the first day for your QuickBooks company.

7. Choose the OK button.

Figure 17.12 shows the addition of the accumulated depreciation accounts to the fixed asset accounts.

> **Note**
>
> Remember that the depreciation accumulated during the year is also an expense for the year. You need to create a single Expense account called Depreciation Expense. All the year's depreciation expenses for all fixed assets are entered into this account.

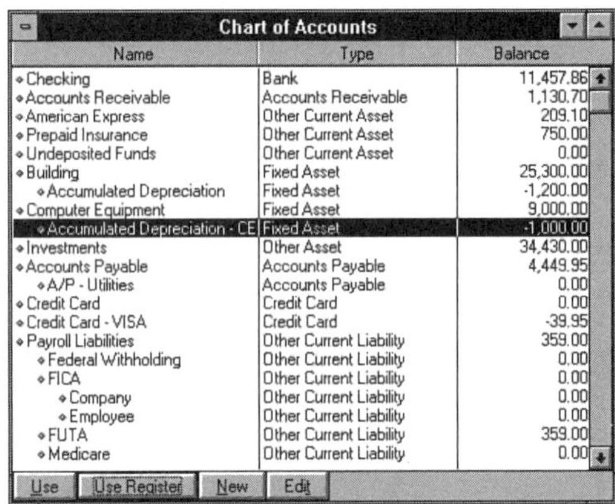

Chart of Accounts

Name	Type	Balance
Checking	Bank	11,457.86
Accounts Receivable	Accounts Receivable	1,130.70
American Express	Other Current Asset	209.10
Prepaid Insurance	Other Current Asset	750.00
Undeposited Funds	Other Current Asset	0.00
Building	Fixed Asset	25,300.00
Accumulated Depreciation	Fixed Asset	-1,200.00
Computer Equipment	Fixed Asset	9,000.00
Accumulated Depreciation - CE	Fixed Asset	-1,000.00
Investments	Other Asset	34,430.00
Accounts Payable	Accounts Payable	4,449.95
A/P - Utilities	Accounts Payable	0.00
Credit Card	Credit Card	0.00
Credit Card - VISA	Credit Card	-39.95
Payroll Liabilities	Other Current Liability	359.00
Federal Withholding	Other Current Liability	0.00
FICA	Other Current Liability	0.00
Company	Other Current Liability	0.00
Employee	Other Current Liability	0.00
FUTA	Other Current Liability	359.00
Medicare	Other Current Liability	0.00

Use | Use Register | New | Edit

Fig. 17.12
The accumulated depreciation account displayed in the Chart of Accounts. Notice that this account shows a total of $1000 in depreciation charges.

Entering Depreciable Assets

The assets you use in the course of your business—such as computers, cash registers, furniture, machinery, and buildings—are called *depreciable* assets. You must set up a Fixed Asset account for each depreciable asset.

> **CPA TIP: Depreciation and Land**
>
> If you own your plant or shop, you have one non-depreciable asset—land. Land is not consumed or worn out, and so it's not depreciable. Some expenditures related to the acquisition of land, such as parking lots and fences, however, can be depreciated because they do have limited lives.

To enter depreciable assets, follow these steps:

1. Add a Fixed Asset account for each depreciable asset group. Give each account a descriptive name, such as Computer Equipment, Furniture, or Vehicles, so that you can easily recognize a depreciable asset by its account name. If this fixed asset account includes more than one asset, enter **0** as the opening balance and continue to step 2. If the fixed asset account tracks a single asset, enter the asset's cost as the opening balance. You're now finished with this asset and can add any other fixed asset accounts.

2. In the account register, enter an individual transaction for each asset as in the next steps.

3. In the Date field, enter your QuickBooks start date, or the last day of your prior fiscal year if you are starting from the first day of the new fiscal year.

4. Type the asset's name in the Payee field, such as **Computer 486DX33**, or **HP LaserJet IIP Printer**.

5. Enter the original cost of the asset in the Increase field.

CPA TIP: Fixed Assets and Cost

Record only the historical cost. Do not use market value for a fixed asset. Market value is not an acceptable method of valuing fixed assets.

6. In the Account field, select the Open Bal Equity account from the drop-down list.

7. Press the Enter key, or choose the Record button to save the transaction.

The Open Bal Equity account is used to track all beginning balances for all Balance Sheet accounts. Balance Sheet accounts include all accounts except Income and Expense accounts. When you purchase a new piece of equipment and record the bill, credit card, or check transaction, QuickBooks automatically enters the fixed asset account in the distribution voucher of the transaction window and record the transaction. You would then see that the Account field would show the name of the account from which this fixed account was transferred. You learn more about transfer in the section "Recording Capital Investments" later in this chapter.

Entering Depreciable Transactions

Calculating depreciation for an asset can be a complex job. If you're not familiar with the concepts of depreciation and depreciation transactions, consult your accountant before you begin to calculate the depreciate as an asset.

Various formulas can be used for calculating depreciation of an asset. The Internal Revenue Service (IRS) has created a chart listing the calculated useful life of most assets used in business. When calculating depreciation for tax purposes, use the proper classification for the asset, and the formula given for calculating the depreciation for the asset. With this formula, the depreciation on an asset is greatest in its first few years of life, and the depreciation gradually drops off to zero when the asset has been completely depreciated.

> **Note**
>
> Assets are always depreciated down to a book value of $0.00, unless you sell or scrap the asset before it has been fully depreciated. You can't continue to depreciate an item after it has been fully depreciated.

QuickBooks does not calculate depreciation for you; you must calculate the depreciation amount for assets before you enter the depreciation transaction. Your accountant can tell you how to calculate depreciation for each asset and when to enter depreciation transactions. You have the option to calculate and enter depreciation monthly, quarterly, semiannually, or yearly. At a minimum, you must calculate the depreciation once a year, at the end of your fiscal year.

To enter a depreciation transaction, follow these steps:

1. Open the Chart of Accounts.
2. Select the Accumulated Depreciation account that is the subaccount of the asset for which you want to enter the depreciation transaction.
3. Select the U**s**e Register button to open the Accumulated Depreciation register.
4. Type the date for the depreciation transaction. QuickBooks enters today's date by default.
5. Enter the amount of the depreciation charge in the Decrease column.

   As explained in Chapter 4, in the section "Working with Subaccounts," the subaccounts transactions flow to the parent. A depreciation charge is subtracted from the value of the asset which is shown in the parent account. You must enter additions to the transaction charge in the Decrease column of the Accumulated Depreciation subaccount in order for QuickBooks to make the corresponding transaction in the parent fixed asset account, decreasing the book value of the asset.
6. (Optional) Type a note in the Memo field. It is recommended that you do enter a note like, "Depreciation Charge for FY 93," or "Depreciation Charge for May 94." This way you will know what period this specific depreciation transaction covers.

7. Select the appropriate expense account in the Account field. Usually this will be Depreciation Expense, unless you have set up a different account to track your depreciation expenses.

8. Choose the Record button to save the transaction.

Figure 17.13 shows both the Accumulated Depreciation register with the depreciation charge transaction and the matching entry that QuickBooks has added to the Computer Equipment Fixed Asset account.

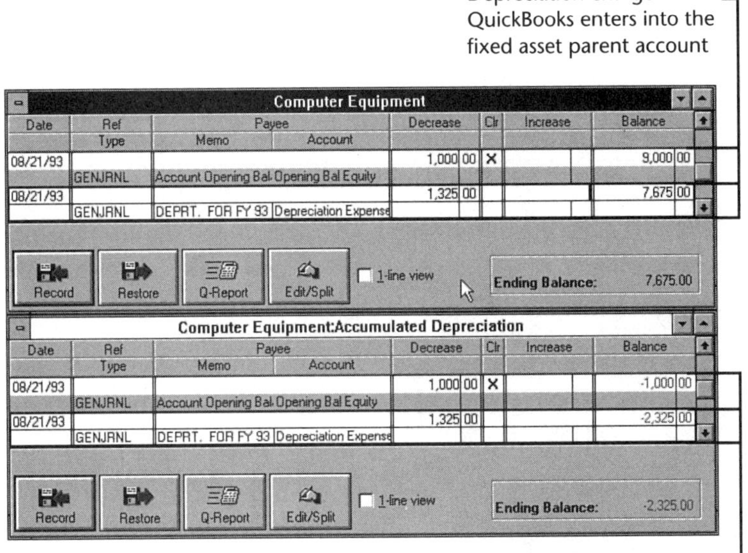

Fig. 17.13 The depreciation transaction entered into the registers. Notice the identical transactions in both registers.

It is not necessary to enter a Payee in the depreciation charge transaction. Because this transaction only involves this fixed asset account and its subaccount "Accumulated Depreciation," and the expense account "Depreciation Expense" there is no need to record any payee information. You also will notice in figure 17.13 that QuickBooks enters the transaction type of GENJRNL for this transaction.

Selling Depreciable Assets

If you sell a fixed asset, you realize either a gain or a loss on the sale. If you sell the asset for more than the current book value, you have a *capital gain*. If you sell the asset for less than book value, you have a *capital loss*.

Say that you own a delivery van that you bought three years ago. When you bought it, you paid $21,000, and you have depreciated it to a book value of $9230. If you sell the truck for $10,000, you will record a capital gain of $770. This is counted as income during this year. On the other hand, if you were able to sell the van for only $8500, you record a capital loss of $730.

When you sell assets, you want to create an account for accounting for the sale of capital equipment. You can set up a separate account for gains and another for losses. An easier method would be to set up a single account titled *Sale of Capital Assets,* and place both gains and losses in this one account.

To record the sale of the delivery van, follow these steps:

1. Open the Chart of Accounts and select the Fixed Asset account that contains records concerning the delivery van.
2. Enter the Sale date in the Date field, the name of the asset that was sold—Delivery Van—in the Payee field, and the amount originally paid for the asset in the Decrease field.
3. Move to the Account field and select the Edit/Split button. QuickBooks displays the General Journal Entry window with the first entry in the detail area displayed.
4. Move to the detail area of the General Journal Entry window and make the entries in the next steps.
5. Enter the account in which you will deposit the proceeds of the sale. Select the Undeposited Funds account, and then enter the amount of the proceeds in the Debit column—type **10000**. When you make your next deposit to your Checking account, this transaction is displayed for depositing.
6. In the next line, you reverse the amount of accumulated depreciation that you have on this particular asset. Select the Accumulated Depreciation account for the asset. In the Debit column, enter the total accumulated depreciation for the asset. Type **11770**.
7. In the next line, enter the account that you use to track capital gains or losses. Use the Sale of Capital Asset account. QuickBooks enters the amount of the gain in the Credit column. A loss would be displayed in the Credit column.

Figure 17.14 shows the completed General Journal Entry window.

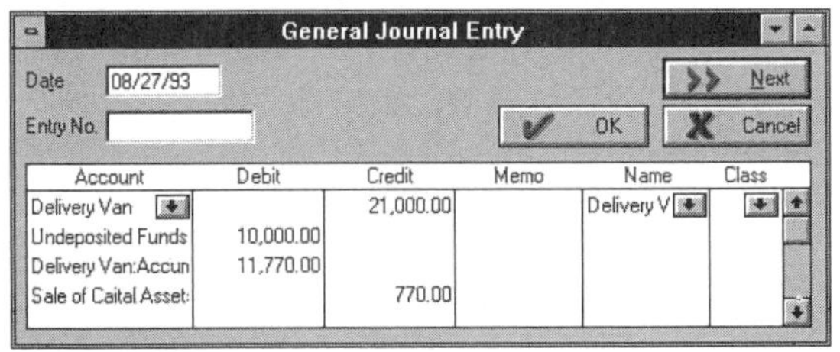

Fig. 17.14 The General Journal Entry window accounts for the sale of the delivery van.

8. Choose the OK button to save the transaction.

Figure 17.15 shows the Delivery Van Fixed Asset account, and the Delivery Van:Accumulated Depreciation account. Notice that the ending balance for each account is 0.

Delivery Van

Date	Ref / Type	Payee / Memo / Account	Decrease	Clr	Increase	Balance
08/01/91	GENJRNL	Account Opening Bal Opening Bal Equity		X	21,000 00	21,000 00
08/01/92	GENJRNL	Account Opening Bal Opening Bal Equity	11,770 00	X		9,230 00
08/27/93	GENJRNL	Delivery Van -split-			11,770 00	21,000 00
08/27/93	GENJRNL	Delivery Van -split-	21,000 00			0 00

Delivery Van:Accumulated Depreciation

Date	Ref / Type	Payee / Memo / Account	Decrease	Clr	Increase	Balance
08/01/92	GENJRNL	Account Opening Balar Opening Bal Equity	11,770 00	X		-11,770 00
08/27/93	GENJRNL	Delivery Van -split-			11,770 00	0 00
08/27/93						

Record Restore Q-Report Edit/Split 1-line view Ending Balance: 0.00

Fig. 17.15 The Delivery Van and Accumulated Depreciation accounts with the entries that QuickBooks entered from your General Journal entry.

Working with Payroll Accounts

If your business has employees, you regularly deal with payroll transactions. When you pay an employee, you normally withhold federal income tax, FICA tax, and Medicare tax. You may have additional taxes and other deductions, such as state income tax, local income tax, union dues, medical insurance, or deductions to pension accounts. As the employer, you must also make FICA, Medicare, and federal and state unemployment insurance contributions on behalf of your employee.

When you pay an employee, you establish a liability for taxes withheld and contributions on behalf of the employee. Even though you do not pay withheld taxes and contributions right away, you need to add these items to your payroll tax liability so that you can track them.

Intuit offers an add-on program called QuickPay, which you can use to calculate employees' gross pay plus all taxes and other deductions. QuickPay is not included with the QuickBooks for Windows program; you must purchase it separately. See Appendix B to learn more about how QuickPay works.

Adding Payroll Tax Accounts

When you start QuickBooks and select one of the standard business types, the program adds certain accounts to the Chart of Accounts. These payroll expense, liability, and tax accounts are listed in table 17.1.

Table 17.1. Payroll Accounts

Caption 1	Caption 2
Account Types	Accounts
Employee Wage Accounts	Payroll Expenses: Gross Wages
	Payroll Expenses: Benefits
	Payroll Expenses: Bonuses
Employee Withholding Accounts	Payroll Liabilities: Federal Withholding (Federal Income Tax)
	Payroll Liabilities: FICA:Employee (Social Security Tax)
	Payroll Liabilities: Medicare:Employee
	Payroll Liabilities: SDI (State Disability Insurance)
	Payroll Liabilities: State Withholding (State Income Tax)
Employer Tax Accounts	Payroll Taxes: FICA (Federal Income Tax employer contribution)
	Payroll Taxes: FUTA (Federal Unemployment Tax)
	Payroll Taxes: Medicare
	Payroll Taxes: SDI (State Disability Insurance)
	Payroll Taxes: SUI (State Unemployment Insurance)

This list covers most payroll situations. If you need to add another account to cover your payroll—for example, an account to track employee contributions in a 401K plan, follow these steps:

1. Open the Chart of Accounts and choose the **N**ew button.
2. Perform the following in the New Account window:
   - Select the **T**ype of "Other Current Liability."
   - Enter the name of the account, for example **Employee Contrib. 401K**, in the Name box.
   - Check the **S**ubaccount Of check box.
   - Select the Payroll Liabilities account as the parent account.

   Your new account looks like figure 17.16.

2. Choose the OK button to save the account.

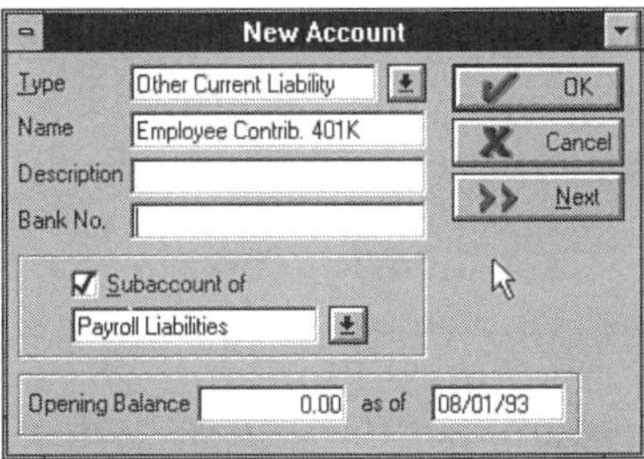

Fig. 17.16 The New Account window showing your new payroll liability account.

Assigning Payroll Liability Accounts to Transactions

When you write payroll checks, you pay the employee her gross wages, less the payroll taxes she must pay to the government; also, at designated times, you make the employee's payroll tax payment for her.

> **CPA TIP: Timing of Payroll Tax Deposits**
>
> Depending on the size of your gross payroll, you are responsible for making periodic deposits of payroll taxes, both Federal and State. You are required to make deposits for both the amount that you have withheld from employees paychecks and the matching employer's contribution for FICA (Social Security) and Medicare. Generally, the larger your payroll is the more often you must make these deposits. Be sure to talk to your accountant for information about how often you must make your payroll tax deposits. Failure to do so on a timely basis can result in penalties and fines being levied against you and your company.

In addition to the employee owing payroll taxes, you, as the employer, also owe a share of certain payroll taxes, such as Social Security (FICA) and Medicare taxes. Your share of FICA and Medicare is equal to the amount the employee must pay. Although you must pay the combined total of the company share plus the employee share whenever you make a payroll tax deposit, only part of the payroll tax deposit is actually "your" money. From an accounting perspective, you must account for the company's share of payroll tax expense by assigning those dollars to payroll tax expense accounts.

The time at which you assign payroll dollars to payroll tax expense accounts is determined by the accounting method that you use, cash or accrual. For payroll purposes, the difference between the two methods determines whether you record your company's payroll tax expense at the time you pay the employee or at the time you pay the taxing authority. Check with your accountant or tax advisor to determine which method you should use.

When you write a payroll check in the Write Checks window, you assign payroll accounts to the transaction's withholding and contribution portions in the voucher detail area. Regardless of your accounting method, the steps for writing the employee's payroll check are basically the same up to a point. To write a payroll check for the accrual basis, follow these steps:

1. Open the Write Checks window by choosing the Check button from the Iconbar; choosing **A**ctivities, **W**rite Checks; or pressing Ctrl+W.

2. Select the Ban**k** Account that you will use to draw the payroll checks.

3. Enter the employee's name in the Pay to the **O**rder of field. Enter the date for the payroll check and a memo about the payroll period covered by this check. Move to the detail voucher. Entering a memo is optional, but this is a good place to indicate what period this paycheck covers.

4. Select the Payroll Expenses:Gross Wages account. Enter the gross amount of the employee's wages in the Amount column.

5. Enter the employee's tax liabilities and other deductions in the next several lines.

   - Select Payroll Liabilities:Federal Withholding and enter the amount in the Amount column. Remember, this is a deduction from the gross wages. Enter a minus (–) sign before the dollar amount.

- Select Payroll Liabilities:FICA:Employee, and enter the amount in the Amount column.
- Select Payroll Liabilities:Medicare:Employee, and enter the amount in the Amount column.
- Select any other accounts for deductions required to be made from the employee's gross wages.

6. Choose the Recalc button to calculate the employee check total.

Figure 17.17 shows the employee check with all withholdings deducted.

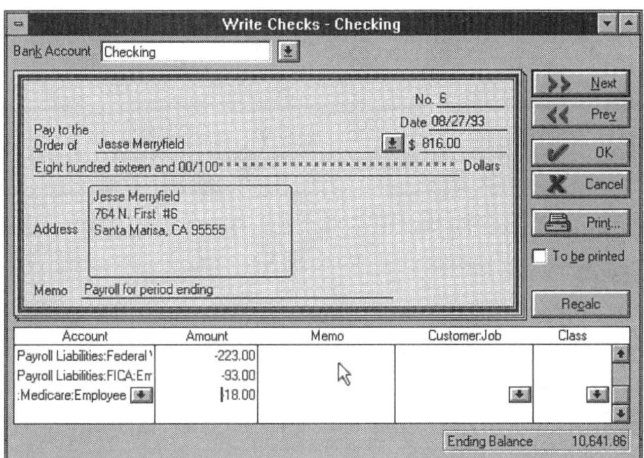

Fig. 17.17 The employee check with withholdings deducted.

> **Note**
>
> If you use the cash basis method of accounting, save this check now. You can skip the next steps and read the next section "Paying Payroll Taxes," for information about preparing your check to the taxing authority.

7. Move the cursor to line 17 and enter line items for employer expenses such as FICA, Medicare, FUTA, and SDI contributions, and the related liability for these items.

   Each expense item has a related liability item; enter amounts for expense lines as positive numbers, and amounts for related liability items as negative numbers. The two items cancel each other out and add up to 0. You also include additional expenses that you pay for your employee, such as health insurance. Figure 17.18 shows a portion of the employer's expenses and liabilities entered in the voucher. Remember, anything that you enter after line 16 does not print on a check voucher.

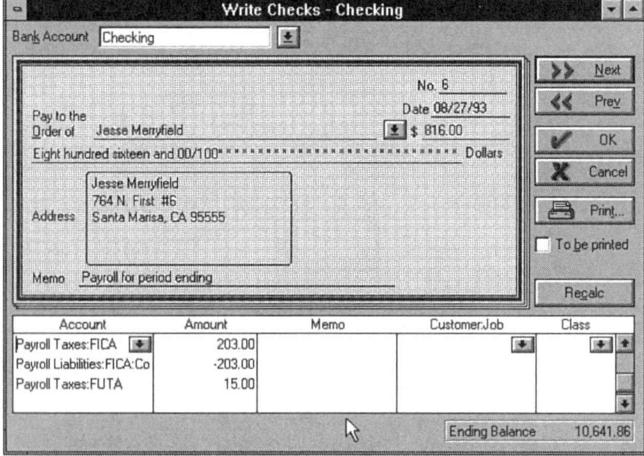

Fig 17.18 Some of the employer's expenses and liabilities show in the payroll voucher detail area.

Paying Payroll Taxes

If you use an accrual basis for accounting, you always can access a payroll tax liability account to see how much you owe. If you use a cash basis, the actual amount you owe is twice the amount in the FICA and Medicare liability accounts, plus the sum of the amounts in all the other payroll tax liability accounts.

If you use an accrual basis for accounting and it's time to pay payroll taxes, check the balances in each payroll tax liability account to determine the amount that you owe on the date that the taxes are due. Then, use the Write Checks window and write a check for that amount. In the Account field of the detail voucher area, enter the name of the payroll tax liability account to which the payment relates, such as Payroll Liability:FICA:Company for the company's portion of the FICA tax. Remember, many of the taxes are paid to the same taxing authority; use a single check and split the transaction among the various liability accounts. QuickBooks enters a transfer transaction in the appropriate payroll tax liability account to decrease the account's balance by the amount of the payment. Figure 17.19 shows a transaction to pay payroll taxes for the accrual basis.

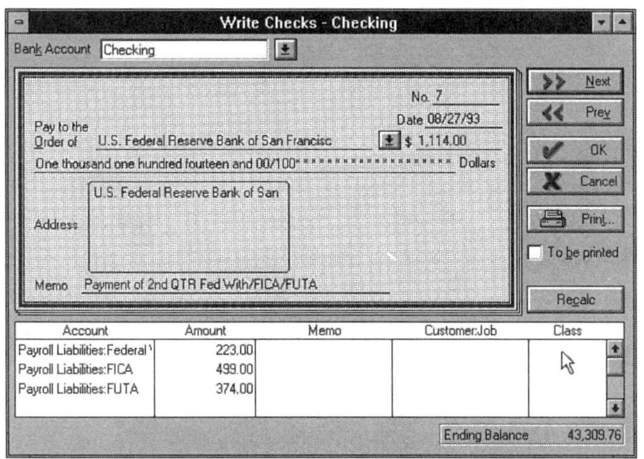

Fig. 17.19
Here is an accrual-basis payment for payroll taxes. Be sure to use the Memo field to note the period covered by this check.

If you use the cash basis for accounting, two of your liability accounts, FICA and Medicare, do not reflect the employer contribution. To write a check to the taxing authority to pay your federal payroll tax liability, follow these steps:

1. Open the Write Checks window. Fill out the check face with the date of the check, the payee, and the memo field. Do not enter the check amount at this time.

2. In the first line of the detail voucher, select the Payroll Liability:Federal Withholding account and enter the amount that was withheld from employee paychecks and is now due. Enter all other federal tax liabilities in a similar manner. Do not yet enter the FICA or Medicare tax liabilities.

3. When all the other tax liabilities have been entered, select the Payroll Liabilities:FICA:Employee account, and then enter the amount that was withheld from employee paychecks. On the next line, enter the account Payroll:FICA:Company, and enter the same amount in the Amount column. This is your matching portion of the Social Security taxes.

   Do the same for the Medicare taxes. Figure 17.20 shows the completed check and voucher.

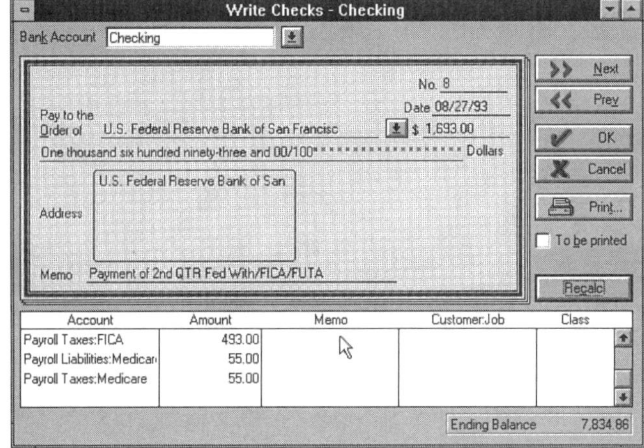

Fig. 17.20 The completed check for payment of payroll taxes, using the cash basis for accounting.

Working with Liability Accounts

Liability accounts come in two types: current liabilities and long-term liabilities. A *current liability* is a debt that will be repaid within one year. Some more common current liabilities are Accounts Payable, tax liabilities, and accrued wages. *Long-term liabilities* are loans scheduled to be paid over a period of time greater than one year. A mortgage on your store is an example of a long-term liability.

To track the money that you owe to others, add current or long-term liability accounts to the Chart of Accounts in the same way you have entered other Balance Sheet accounts. You need an amortization schedule, however, to determine the current loan balance to use as the opening balance for those accounts on which you pay both principle and interest. Ask your banker or lender for a copy of the amortization or loan payment schedule for your loan. If you use a spreadsheet program such as Lotus 1-2-3, you can create your own amortization schedule.

Adding a Liability Account

If your business enters into a loan agreement that has a term of longer than one year, you have acquired a long-term liability. For example, if you agree to buy the building in which you house your business, you will sign a mortgage contract. This mortgage is a long-term liability. A lease with a term of more than one year is also considered to be a long-term liability.

Note

Remember that if you add a liability account, you probably need to add an asset account or make an addition to an asset account. If you sign a mortgage contract, you have a long-term liability and a fixed asset (Building) to add to your Chart of Accounts.

To add a liability account, follow these steps:

1. Open the Chart of Accounts and choose the **N**ew button.
2. Select the **T**ype of account, which is Long-Term Liability.
3. Enter the Name for the liability, a description, and the bank or loan number. If this account will be a subaccount, enter that information.
4. Enter the Opening Balance. You generally find this on your loan papers or invoice.
5. Enter the date that this transaction occurred. Figure 17.21 shows the New Account window with the completed Long Term Liability account.

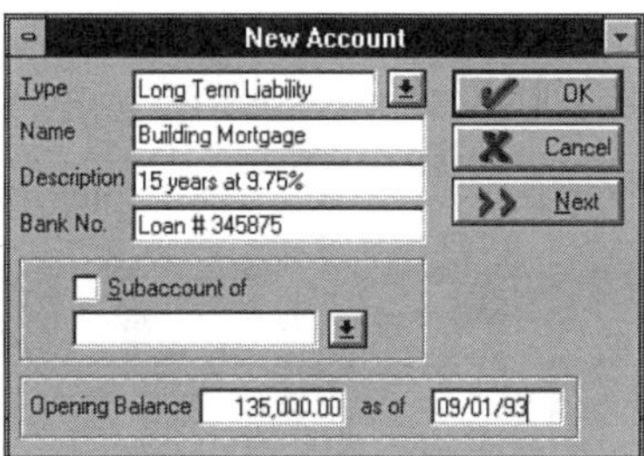

Fig. 17.21 The new Long Term Liability account. Notice that the loan information, rate, and length are included for easy reference.

6. Choose the OK button to save the new account.

Tracking Loans

When you enter a liability account's opening balance, QuickBooks records an Opening Balance transaction in the Liability Account register and enters the amount in the Increase field. QuickBooks enters transactions that increase the liability account balance in the Increase field, and transactions that decrease the liability account balance in the Decrease field.

When you enter loan payments for current or long-term liabilities in the Write Checks window, be sure to properly split the transaction between principle and interest charges. Allocate the principle payment to the liability and the interest charge to an Interest expense account.

Because the principle portion of the transaction represents a transfer transaction (transferring from one Balance Sheet account to another), QuickBooks enters the reciprocal transaction in the Liability Account register as a decrease in the total. For example, you agree to buy your building for a total of $135,000 to be repaid at an interest rate of 9.75 percent and a term of 15 years. The payment is due at the first of each month.

To enter a loan payment, follow these steps:

1. Open the Write Checks window.
2. Enter the name of the vendor or lending institution.
3. Enter the amount of your payment.
4. Type a note in the Memo field if necessary.
5. Move to the voucher detail area and enter the account distribution.
6. Select the Interest Expense account and enter the interest portion of this payment. From an amortization schedule, you would know that this was **1,096.88**.
7. Select the liability account for the principle portion of the payment, Building Mortgage. QuickBooks has already entered the principle portion of your payment, as you can see in figure 17.22.

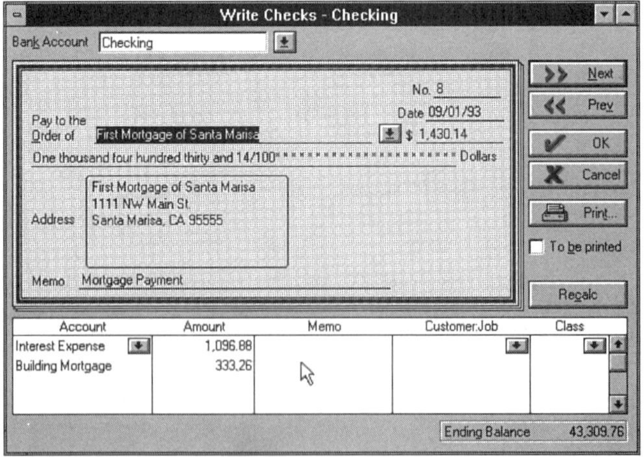

Fig. 17.22
A check written for a long-term liability. Notice the breakdown into interest expense and principle.

If your lender requires you to make payments into an escrow or impound account for taxes and insurance along with your payment, you will have additional lines for these expenses. An escrow or impound account is a special account that is set up by your lender. The payment that you make each month to the lender will include not only the principle and interest payments, but will include an additional amount to your property taxes and/or your property insurance. When you make your monthly mortgage payment, the portion of taxes or insurance will be set aside in the escrow account. When your property tax bill is due, the bill will be paid from the money that has been collected from you each month.

Working with Equity Accounts

Equity refers to the ownership interest of the business, or the assets that belong to the owners after all claims against the business are satisfied. Equity accounts help you track your company's *net worth.*

When you start QuickBooks, the program sets up the Opening Bal Equity and Retained Earnings account for you. You can add an owner's equity account, or a draw account; however, if you're not sure about equity accounts or which ones to add, consult your accountant first. Equity is one of the more difficult bookkeeping concepts. Using QuickBooks equity accounts, however, is easy when you understand what equity accounts represent.

A draw account is a special equity account that is set up expressly to record the payments made by the company to the owner of the business. Draw accounts are generally only used in sole proprietorship or partnership types of business, not in a corporation.

QuickBooks uses the Opening Bal Equity account to keep your balance sheet in balance before you enter all your assets and liabilities. After you add all your assets and liabilities in QuickBooks, the Opening Bal Equity account balance should be 0. If not, the Opening Bal Equity account balance represents your company's earnings or losses since your QuickBooks start date. You don't have to change the Opening Bal Equity account's balance unless you want your books to comply with strict bookkeeping standards. In that case, use the Retained Earnings account and enter a transfer transaction for the entire balance in the Opening Bal Equity account to the Retained Earnings account. Retained Earnings represent the business earnings that remain in the business.

For example, if your company earns $50,000 in the current year and none of the earnings are taken out of the business, the $50,000 represents the earnings retained by the business. To track prior business earnings on your balance sheet, add a retained earnings account. At the end of each fiscal year, you then transfer your business earnings for the year to the retained earnings account. This transfer is covered later in this chapter. In the next year, your balance sheet shows a current earnings line with only the current year's earnings and a retained earnings account with the prior year's earnings.

Add an owner's equity account to track investments in the business by you and others. The owner's equity account separates investments from business earnings in the equity section of the balance sheet. If you contribute more money to your business, assign the Owner's Equity account to the transaction. QuickBooks keeps track of your contributions.

Adding an Equity Account

You can add an equity account just as you add other Balance Sheet accounts. To add an Owner's Equity account so that you can track the amount of additional capital you invested in the company, follow these steps:

1. Open the Chart of Accounts and select the **N**ew button.
2. Select the account **T**ype of Capital/Equity.
3. Enter the name for the account, **Owner's Equity**.
4. Enter the date for your QuickBooks starting date. Figure 17.23 shows the completed Owner's Equity account.

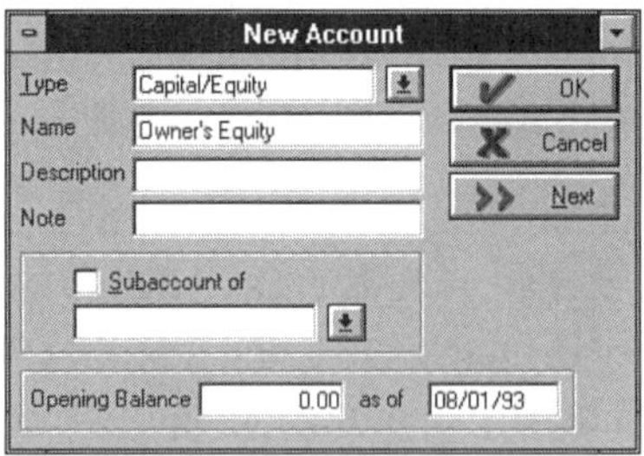

Fig. 17.23 The new equity account named Owner's Equity, ready to be entered into the Chart of Accounts.

5. Choose the OK button to save the new account.

Making Transfers from the Opening Balance Equity Account

As you already learned, any balance remaining in the Opening Bal Equity account should probably be transferred to the Retained Earnings account. To transfer the balance from the Opening Bal Equity account to Retained Earnings, follow these steps:

1. Open the Chart of Accounts and select the Opening Bal Equity account. Choose the Use Register button to open the register.

2. Enter the date for the transfer transaction. Use the start date for your QuickBooks system.

3. Enter the amount of the transfer.

   If the balance displayed in the ending balance is a positive number, enter an identical figure in the Decrease column.

   If the balance displayed in the ending balance is a negative number, enter an identical figure in the Increase column.

4. Enter a note in the Memo field, such as **Transfer to Retained Earnings**.

5. Select the Retained Earnings account in the Account field. Your transaction looks similar to the last transaction in the Opening Bal Register, shown in figure 17.24.

Opening Bal Equity

Date	Num / Type	Payee / Memo	Account	Increase	Clr	Decrease	Balance
08/01/93	GENJRNL	Account Opening Bal	Investments	35,680 00			120,501 50
08/01/93	GENJRNL	Account Opening Bal	Computer Equipment	10,000 00			130,501 50
08/01/93	GENJRNL		Depreciation Expense			13,970 00	116,531 50
08/01/93	GENJRNL	Office Max	Accounts Payable			6,300 00	110,231 50
08/01/93	GENJRNL		Building Mortgage			13,000 00	97,231 50
08/20/93	CHK	Balance Adjustment	Checking			10 39	97,221 11
08/21/93	GENJRNL	Account Opening Bal	Computer Equipment:			1,000 00	96,221 11
08/21/93	GENJRNL	Account Opening Bal	Building:Accumulated			1,200 00	95,021 11
09/01/93	Num / GENJRNL	Payee / Transfer to Retained	Retained Earnings	Increase		95,021 11	

Record | Restore | Q-Report | Edit/Split | 1-line view | Ending Balance: 95,021.11

Fig. 17.24
The transfer transaction to move the ending balance of the Opening Bal Equity account to the Retained Earnings account.

6. Choose the Record button to save the transaction. You see the ending balance change to 0.

Recording Draws

An owner's Draw account is set up for the sole use of the owner. Whenever you as the business owner write a check to yourself, it is recorded in the draw account.

Sole Proprietorships

If your business is a sole proprietorship, you may want to simply account for payments to yourself as a negative transaction in the Owner's Equity account. Ask your accountant about the best way to set up this account.

Partnerships

Partnerships have a separate drawing account for each partner. This enables you to track how much each partner withdrew from the business over the course of a year. Having these numbers easily separated can help when you distribute any profits at the end of the year. There are several correct ways to set up the partners' equity accounts. You can create a single equity account for each partner, recording capital additions and withdrawals in the one account.

Another method is to create an equity account for each partner and additional subaccounts for capital investments and draws.

Corporations

Corporations fall under slightly different rules than do sole proprietorships and partnerships. A corporation can pay a working owner a salary. Owners of a corporation are stockholders. You need to keep at least two equity accounts: Paid in Capital and Retained Earnings.

Paid in Capital represents the amount that a stockholder has paid for his shares. Retained Earnings is the amount the company has earned and not distributed as dividends.

If your business is a corporation, talk to your accountant about how to handle your equity accounts.

Recording Draws

A *draw* is a payment to an owner for services performed, or for equipment or expenses paid for by the owner from his personal money. Sole Proprietorships and Partnerships have Draw accounts. Payments made to an owner are not subject to withholding taxes or matching tax liabilities by the business. To record a draw, follow these steps:

1. Open the Write Checks window.

2. Complete the check face. Enter the owner's name as the payee. Type the amount and an optional memo.

3. Enter the owner's draw account in the first line of the detail voucher. Enter the amount of the draw. Your check should look like figure 17.25.

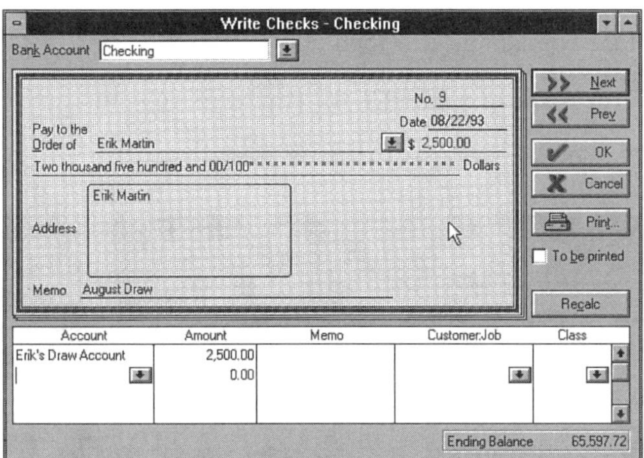

Fig. 17.25
The owner's draw check. Notice that there are no withholding taxes.

4. Choose the OK button to save the transaction.

Recording Capital Investments

An owner also can increase her capital investment in her company by contributing additional cash, equipment, or inventory. For example, an owner could contribute $10,000 in cash, or purchase a truck for $10,000 with her own funds, and then transfer ownership to the business.

Either transaction increases the owner's capital investment and needs to be recorded. To record an additional capital investment of $5,000 cash by the owner, follow these steps:

1. Choose **A**ctivities, Make **D**eposits from the menu. From the Payments to Deposit dialog box, press OK (or Enter) to open the Make Deposits window.

2. Select the account to Depo**s**it the money to.

3. Enter the owner's name in the Received From column.

4. Enter the amount of the capital investment in the Amount column.

5. Enter the Owner's Equity account in the From Account column. An additional investment by the owner is an increase to her equity account.

6. Type a memo, if needed, such as Additional Capital, in the column labeled Memo.

7. Enter the check number if applicable.

8. Enter the payment method in the Pmt Meth. column.

Figure 17.26 shows the completed deposit entry.

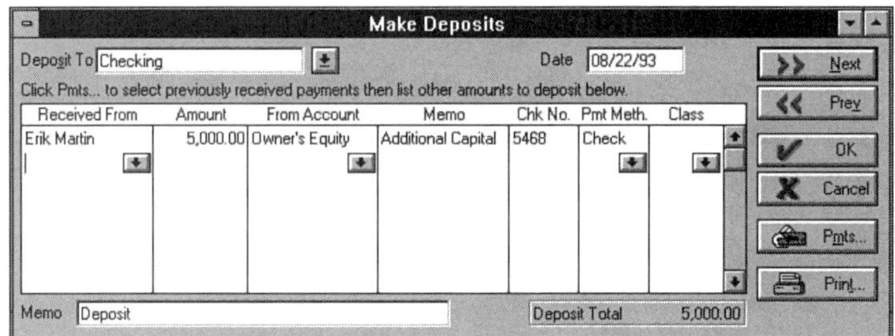

Fig. 17.26
The completed deposit entry for the additional capital investment by the owner.

Completing the Year-End Transactions

Traditionally, in most accounting systems, you must "close" your books at the end of your fiscal year. In QuickBooks, however, you do not close your books. Instead, you choose whether to continue using the same company or to "close" your books by starting a new company.

You will find advantages and disadvantages to both approaches. Whether or not you start a new company, you may still want to perform some traditional year-end activities. You may want to make adjusting entries (to account for accumulated depreciation or to transfer current-year earnings to retained earnings, for example). You may want to print certain reports so that you have a record of the financial position of your company at year-end. And you may want to freeze last year's transactions by protecting them with a password.

Closing Your Books...Or Not

In QuickBooks, you can "close" your books by starting a new company. You carry forward to the new company all the set-up work you did when you first started using QuickBooks, as well as any outstanding transactions.

The primary advantage to not closing the books in QuickBooks is that you maintain access to last year's transactions and can include them on reports to create comparative reports. In addition, changes you make to your Chart of Accounts affect last year's transactions as well as this year's transactions.

The primary advantage to closing the books is that QuickBooks removes all reconciled transactions. As a result, the company file is smaller and QuickBooks works faster.

Whether you decide to start a new company file or continue working with the existing one, you may want to take some of the traditional steps performed at year-end, such as:

- Making year-end adjusting entries to account for accumulated depreciation and to transfer current earnings to retained earnings.
- Printing reports for year-end, such as Balance Sheet, and Profit and Loss.
- Freezing last year's transactions to prevent access to them without a password.

If you do decide to start a new company file and you use QuickPay, you must make some adjustments to the names of your QuickPay files.

Making Adjusting Entries

Every business is different and has its own year-end procedures. Talk to your accountant and ask for a listing of adjusting entries for the year. This list probably consists of entries that change or add transactions to what you already entered for last year. These entries may include recording depreciation for fixed assets. Also, ask your accountant what kind of reports she wants to see. When you receive the adjusting entries from your accountant, enter them into QuickBooks. Then be sure to reconcile your Checking account through the last month of your fiscal year.

If you want the equity section of your balance sheet to separate current earnings from earnings of prior years (retained earnings), you must transfer the earnings at the end of your fiscal year to the retained earnings account.

To transfer current earnings to retained earnings at the end of the year, follow these steps:

1. Print the Balance Sheet report as of the end of your fiscal year. See Chapter 19, "Creating and Printing Reports," for further details about printing the report.

2. Access your Retained Earnings account register.

3. Open the first blank line in the Retained Earnings register.

4. Enter the date of the last day of your fiscal year.

5. Enter the amount shown as Net Income on the year-end Balance Sheet report from step 1. Enter positive earnings in the Increase field; enter negative earnings in the Decrease field.

6. Type a descriptive note in the memo field, such as **Prior year earnings**.

7. Enter an expense account such as **Earnings** in the account field. If you have not already set up this account, you need to do so now.

8. Choose the Record button to save the transaction.

9. Print the Balance Sheet again for year-end. The Net Income line should now be 0 and the Retained Earnings account should have increased by the amount of the Net Income.

Freezing Last Year's Transactions

If you decide not to start a new company file, freeze last year's transactions from changes by assigning a password to the company file. Then you do not provide adding, changing, or deleting privileges for any transaction dated earlier than the beginning of this fiscal year to anyone who does not know the owner password. See Chapter 21, "Managing QuickBooks for Windows Files," for more information on assigning passwords.

Summary

In this chapter, you learned how to complete and use your Balance Sheet accounts. You learned to add accounts such as Fixed Asset, Current Liability, and Credit Card accounts. You learned how to update the account balance by entering an opening balance transaction, and using transfer transactions. In this chapter, you also learned how to perform various tasks using other Balance Sheet accounts, such as depreciating fixed assets, assigning accrued payroll tax accounts to payroll transactions, and entering credit card purchases. Finally, you learned to handle the owner's equity accounts and to account for payments to the owner with a draw account.

In the next chapter, you learn to prepare budgets, using varied and fixed amounts, and to print a budget report.

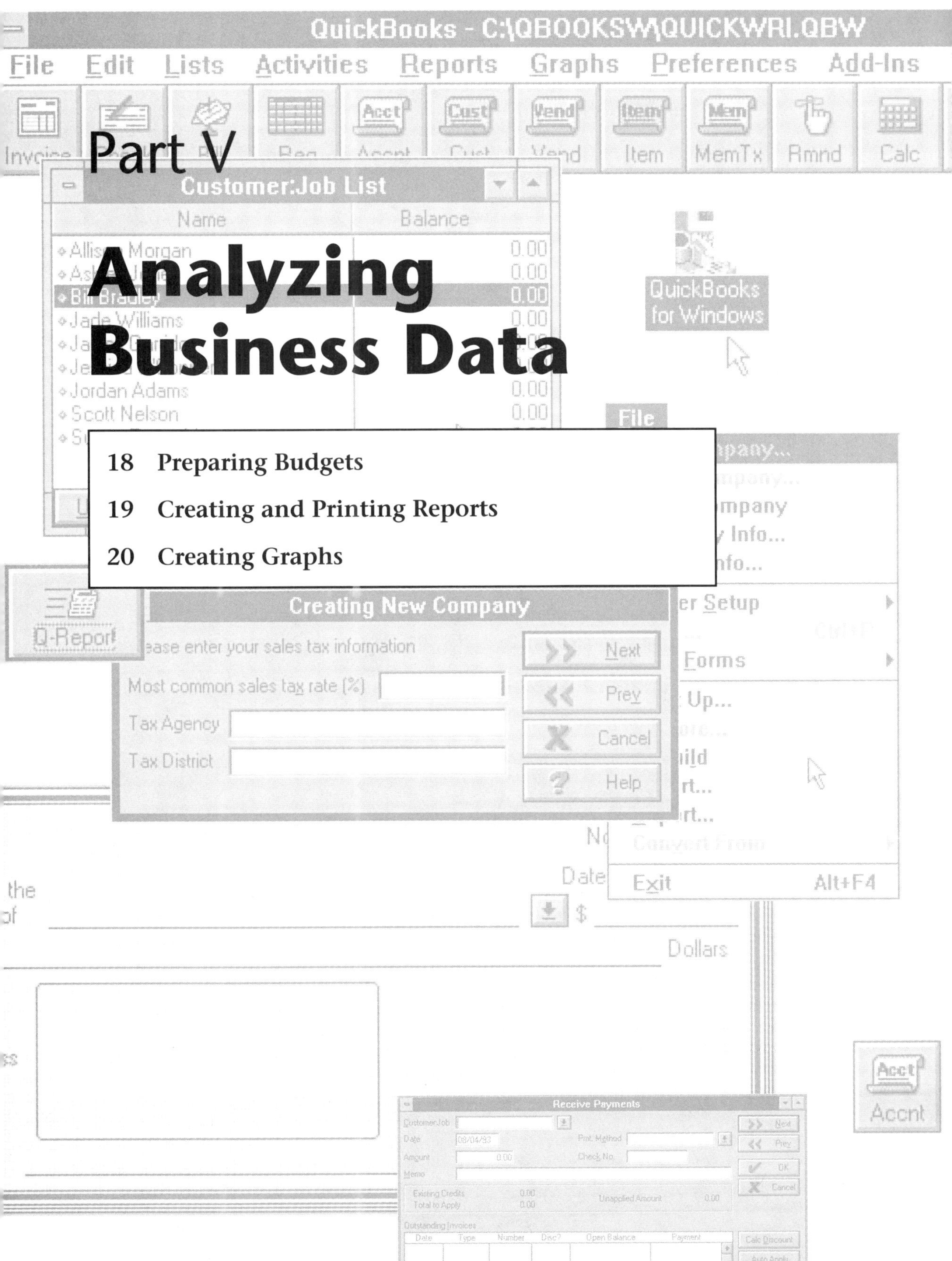

Part V

Analyzing Business Data

18 Preparing Budgets

19 Creating and Printing Reports

20 Creating Graphs

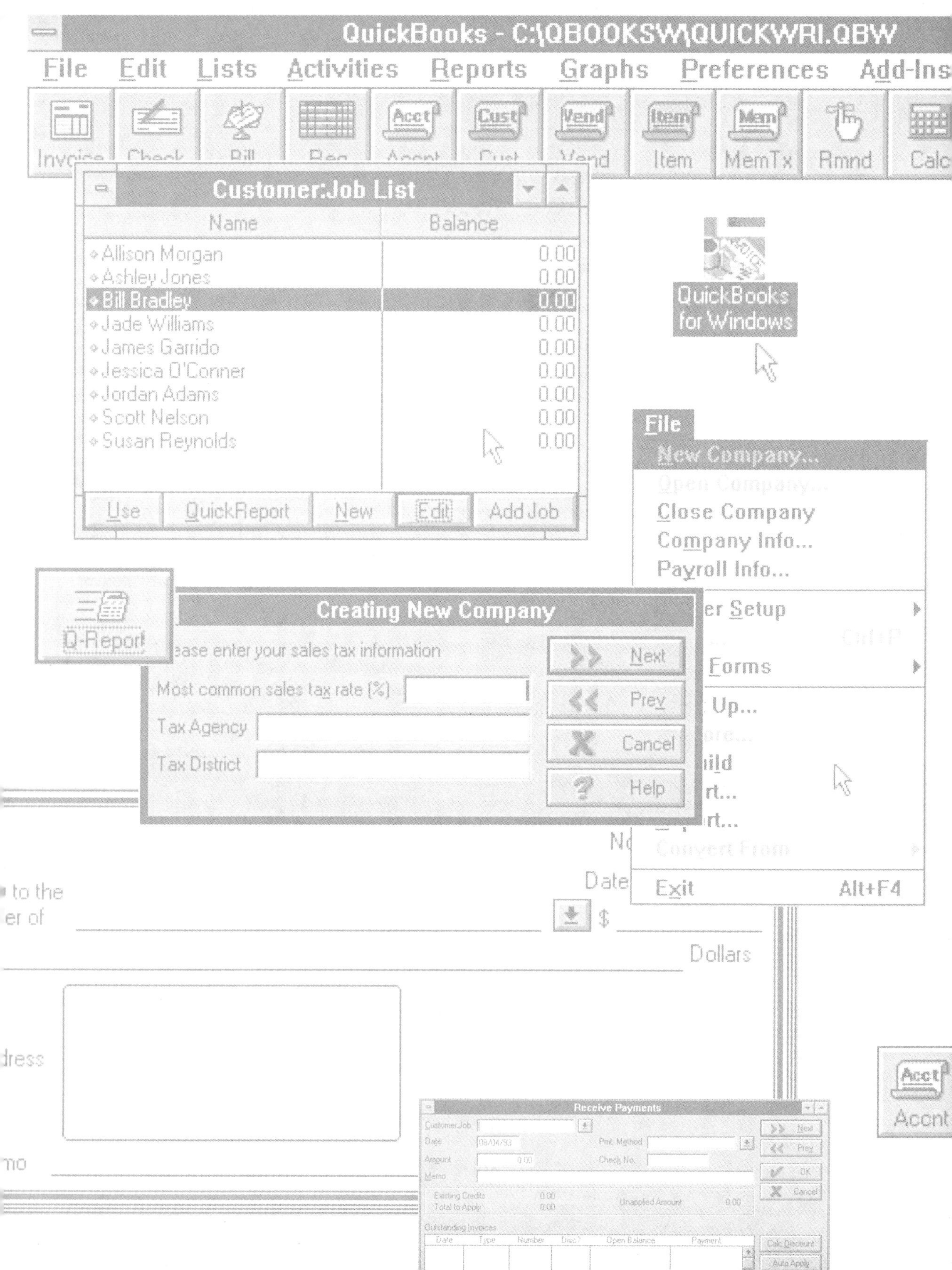
QuickBooks - C:\QBOOKSW\QUICKWRI.QBW
File
Edit
Lists
Activities
Reports
Graphs
Preferences
Add-Ins
Item
MemTx
Rmnd
Calc
Customer:Job List
Name
Balance
Allison Morgan 0.00
Ashley Jones 0.00
Bill Bradley 0.00
Jade Williams 0.00
James Garrido 0.00
Jessica O'Conner 0.00
Jordan Adams 0.00
Scott Nelson 0.00
Susan Reynolds 0.00
Use
QuickReport
New
Edit
Add Job
QuickBooks for Windows
File
New Company...
Close Company
Company Info...
Payroll Info...
Exit
Alt+F4
Q-Report
Creating New Company
Most common sales tax rate (%)
Tax Agency
Tax District
Next
Prev
Cancel
Help
Dollars
Receive Payments
Accnt

Chapter 18

Preparing Budgets

Many people talk about budgeting, few people like to follow a budget, fewer still enjoy creating a budget. The importance of budgeting your income and expenses cannot be overemphasized when it comes to sound financial management. Creating a budget helps you oversee your income and expenses in comparison to your expectations. QuickBooks provides you with the tools to create a budget and to watch the financial activity of your business with six different Budget Reports.

In this chapter, you learn how to do the following:

- Create a monthly budget
- Enter varied and constant monthly budget amounts
- Create a budget based on Customer, Job, or Class
- Edit the budget amounts
- Create a budget report

CPA TIP: Review Financial Information before Budgeting

Before you begin to create your budget, review your past and current financial information. Make sure that you have good information, including information about the current and future environment of your business, the economy in general, and the demand for your company's products or services.

Creating the Budget

The QuickBooks budgeting feature enables you to set up a budget amount for each Income and Expense account in your Chart of Accounts. Budget amounts are entered by month only; however, if you need budgets based on a different period of time, QuickBooks prorates the monthly amounts that you enter. If you want a quarterly budget, for example, QuickBooks adds the three months of the quarter to produce a quarterly total.

CPA TIP: Look at Past Performances Before Forecasting

Companies often look at historical sales or expenses to forecast future sales or expenses. To forecast sales, look at sales information for the same time periods in prior years, such as the first quarter sales for 1992 and 1993 to forecast sales for the first quarter of 1994. Don't try to forecast sales for the first quarter of 1994 by using the figures from the last quarter of 1993. Determine by what percentage sales increased from year to year. If sales in 1992 were $100,000, for example, and in 1993 were $110,000, then sales increased at a rate of 10%. Use this formula to determine your own percentage rate for past periods, [($110,000 - $100,000) / $100,000]. Use the percentage determined, 10%, to forecast your 1994 sales; $121,000, ($110,000 X 110%).

Keep in mind past and current market conditions and the overall condition of the economy when you forecast sales. If sales were down in 1993, you may want to be more conservative when forecasting sales for 1994. Remember, when preparing a budget for future events, they are not set in stone. You are forecasting the future based on the past, or as some would put it, making an educated guess. A budget is a guideline—be prepared to make adjustments if actual events dictate a need for change.

CPA TIP: When Starting a New Business, Plan Carefully

If you are starting a new business, you will not have historical sales and expense information to look at to help you establish a budget. In this case, you project sales by determining what your sales capacity is and modifying that number by the market conditions, your location, and the level of competition. If you're starting an advertising business without any other employees, for example, your sales or revenue capacity is limited to the revenue you can generate based on the number of billable hours you will be working. Modify that level of revenue to account for the market and the services you provide, where you're located in relation to potential clients, and the number of other advertising firms in your area. Remember, all of the hours that you work will not be revenue producing, or billable, hours.

When you are ready to create a budget for an account, you need to enter amounts for Income and Expense accounts differently than for Balance Sheet accounts.

Enter budget amounts for Income and Expense accounts as the amount that you expect to earn or spend for that account. To enter a budget for the expense building rent, for example, you enter the amount that you spend each month. Conversely, to enter an Income account budget, you enter the amount that you expect to earn each month from that type of income.

For Balance Sheet accounts you enter the amount that you expect the accounts ending balance will be. Your checking account, for example, is a Balance Sheet account. You need to estimate what you expect the ending balance of the checking account to be for each month. Enter this number into the budget.

Now that you are aware of some of the factors that come into play when creating a budget or forecast, you're ready to create one for your business.

Filling Varied Budget Amounts

Some of your accounts remain relatively static for periods of time, while others vary the balances from month to month. In this section, you learn to enter varied monthly budget amounts. Make sure you have income and expense information available before you start your budget.

To create a budget with QuickBooks, follow these steps:

1. From the **A**ctivities menu, choose Set Up Bud**g**ets.

   QuickBooks displays the Set Up Budgets dialog box as shown in figure 18.1. From this dialog box, you set up a monthly and yearly budget forecast.

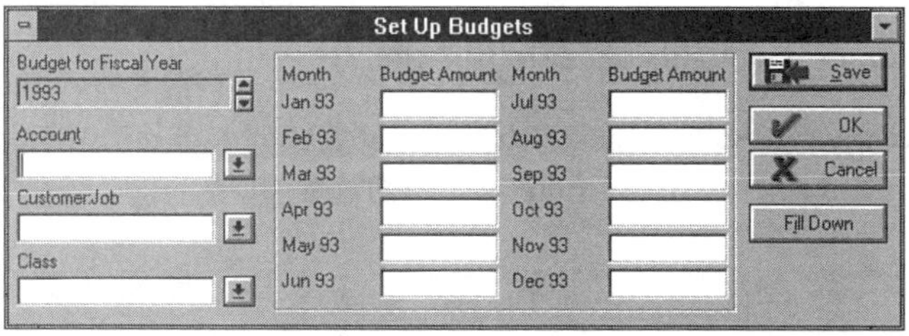

Fig. 18.1
Use the Set Up Budgets dialog box to create your budget for each Balance Sheet, Income, and Expense account.

2. Select the fiscal year for the budget. QuickBooks uses the current calendar year for the default fiscal year. If you are creating a budget for a different fiscal year, you can change the settings by:

   Using the mouse and click the up- or down-arrow buttons. Each click will adjust the displayed year by one.

   Using the keyboard is a little more difficult. Press Tab, or Shift+Tab, or the up- or down-arrow keys to move the selection indicator to the up- and down-arrow buttons displayed beside the fiscal year display. Watch the screen carefully to see when the correct button has been selected. If you can't see a change—usually a quick flash—you need to experiment by pressing the Tab key until you believe that the appropriate button has been selected. Then press the spacebar to increase or decrease the fiscal year by one year.

Note

QuickBooks allows you to have only a single budget per fiscal year. You can have a separate budget for each month, or for each fiscal year. If you are trying to prepare several budgets for the same fiscal year—such as worse case, average case, and best case—you may want to assign a fiscal year for each budget. For example, 1992 for the worst case scenario, 1993 for the average, and 1994 for the best case.

3. Select the account that you want to use to prepare a budget. For this example you will use the Sales account. You can select any Balance Sheet, Income, or Expense account to use to create a budget. In order to have a complete budget for your business, you need to set up a budget for all of your accounts.

   Alternatively, you can set up a budget for a selected account and a specific Customer:Job, or a Class. You learn more about budgeting for a Customer:Job or Class later in this chapter.

4. Enter the figures for the selected account. Figure 18.2 shows the estimated sales figures entered for each month.

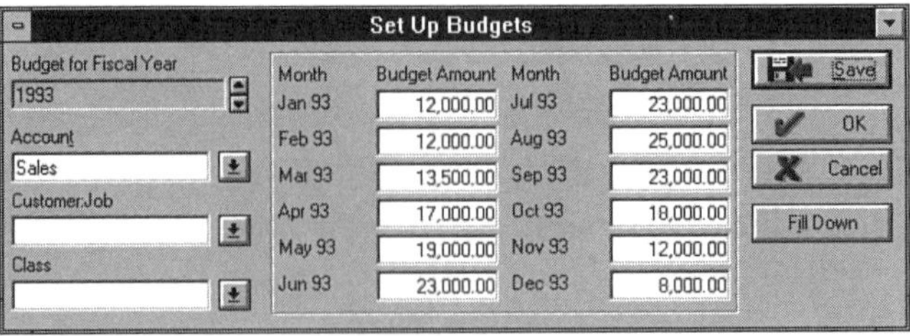

Fig. 18.2
The monthly budget set up for the Sales account, fiscal year 1993.

Sales figures are usually arrived at by looking at past years, and future expectations of the economy. If you have been in business several years, you probably have a good idea what you can expect for sales, and how they vary seasonally.

5. Choose **S**ave to save the budget.

QuickBooks has a helpful budget function called F**i**ll Down. The F**i**ll Down button will allow you to specify a certain percentage or dollar amount for QuickBooks to use to change the remaining budget months. The percentage or fixed dollar amount can be positive or negative. To see how the F**i**ll Down function works, follow these steps:

1. Choose the Sales account as you did in the previous steps.
2. Enter the January budget forecast.
3. Choose F**i**ll Down. QuickBooks displays the Fill Down dialog box, as shown in figure 18.3.

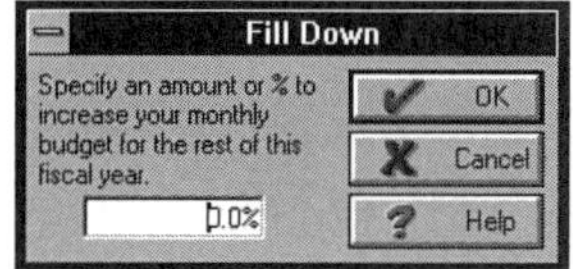

Fig. 18.3
Use the Fill Down dialog box to enter a percentage or fixed dollar amount to increase or decrease the remaining budget months.

You use the Fill Down function to quickly fill in the remaining months of a budget. The change can be specified as a percentage, or a fixed dollar amount. If you forecast a decrease, enter the change with a minus (-) sign.

4. Type **10%** for the rate of change. This tells QuickBooks that you expect your sales to increase by 10% every month.
5. Choose OK. QuickBooks fills in the remaining months. Figure 18.4 shows the Sales account budget completed. Each month has been increased by 10% more than the preceding month.

You also use the Fill Down button to vary amounts at different times of the year; you do not have to use it only at the beginning of the year. If, for example, you make the assumption that your first quarter sales will increase by 10% each month and the second quarter will increase by $1000 per month, while the third quarter will increase by 15%. Going into your slow season, sales will decrease by 15%. A variance like this is accomplished with the following steps:

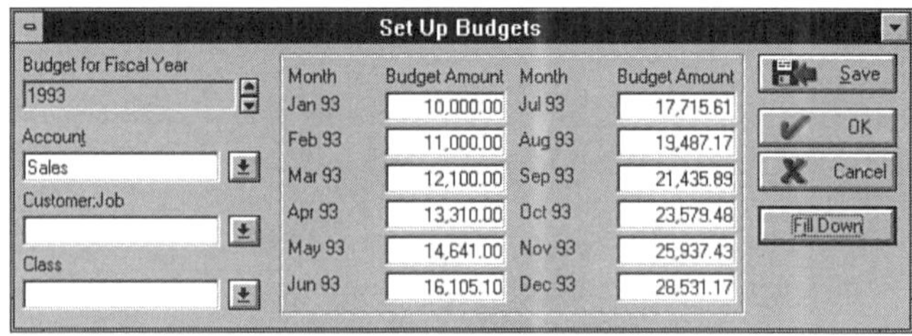

Fig. 18.4
The completed Sales budget showing a 10% increase in sales for each month.

1. Open the Set Up Budgets window for the Sales account.
2. Enter the starting amount for January as 10000.
3. Choose F**i**ll Down. Enter 10% in the text box and choose OK. Your budget now looks like figure 18.4.
4. Move the cursor to the March budget amount box. Choose F**i**ll Down. For the next quarter you expect sales to increase by a fixed amount, $1000 per month. Enter 1000 and choose OK.
5. Move the cursor to the June budget amount box, and again choose F**i**ll Down. This next quarter you expect sales to increase by 15%. Enter this percentage and choose OK.
6. Move to the September budget amount box, and choose F**i**ll Down. In the final quarter of the year, you expect sales to decrease by 10% per month. Enter–10% and choose OK.

Figure 18.5 shows the completed budget using the previous parameters.

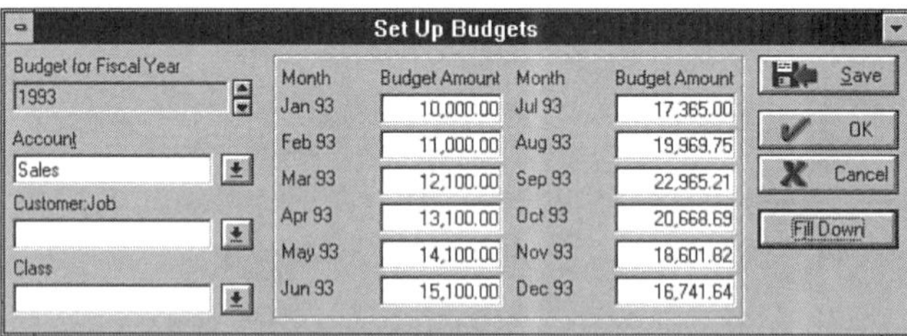

Fig. 18.5
A completed Sales budget using several variables.

Filling in Constant Budget Amounts

You also have many budget figures that do not vary from month to month. These budget accounts only take a few seconds for you to set up. To complete a budget for an account that is constant each month, follow these steps:

1. Open the Set Up Budgets window.

2. Select the Account to use for this budget. Use the expense account, Insurance.

3. Enter the fixed amount in the January budget amount box. Enter your monthly insurance payment of $250.00, as 250.

4. Choose Fill Down. Enter a 0 in the box and choose OK.

   QuickBooks completes the rest of the entries for you. The completed Insurance Expense budget is shown in figure 18.6.

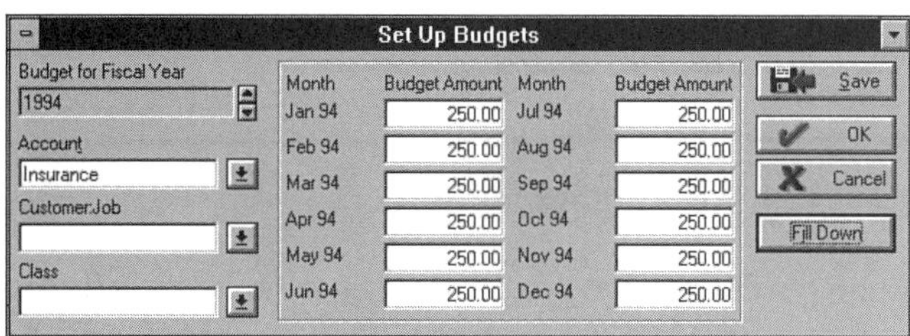

Fig. 18.6
The completed Insurance Expense budget.

5. Choose Save to save this budget.

Budgeting by Customer, Job, or Class

QuickBooks allows you to create a budget for a Customer:Job or Class. This is optional and many businesses will not need the ability to budget in this way. However, a business that may contract with a specific customer for a particular job may need this ability. A budget by Customer:Job may be especially useful to a job shop, or a construction firm who needs to know if the job that they are doing is on budget or not. This can help to determine which jobs are profitable, and how to adjust a bid to better fit real expenses the next time it comes up.

To set up a budget by Customer:Job or Class, follow these steps:

1. Open the Set Up Budgets window. Enter the account for this budget item in the Account box. For example, use the Materials Expense account.

2. Select the Customer:Job and/or Class in the next two boxes.

3. Enter the amounts that you expect to spend in the Budget Amount boxes for the months that you expect to make the expenditure.

Figure 18.7 shows a completed budget for the Materials Expense account for the Forest Grove Drugs:Lot job. This budget shows what you expect to spend over a four month period on this particular job. Since you also selected the Class option, you can create a report telling you how well you budgeted your materials for this class of customers.

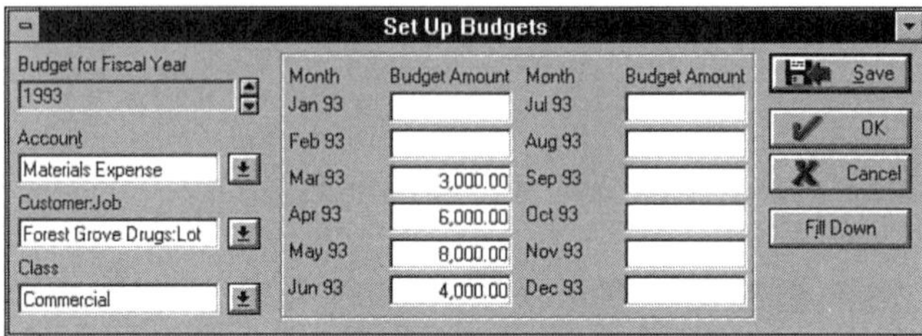

Fig. 18.7 The completed Materials Expense for a specific Customer:Job.

Changing the Budget

As the year progresses, you may find that you need to make adjustments to your projected budgets. Circumstances may have changed for the better or the worse, and you need to adjust accordingly. You should not adjust your budget for prior months, only for future months. While adjusting past months' budget, estimates may look better to another, such as your banker. Your budget for your business is to help you make better financial and business decisions. You need the information, good or bad, to help you make future decisions.

To make adjustments to your budget, follow these steps:

1. Open the Set Up Budgets window. Be sure that you select the correct fiscal year, and then Accoun**t**. If you are adjusting a budget for a Customer:Job or Class, select these also. QuickBooks displays the budget information in the various months. For this example, select the 1993 Sales budget.

2. Edit your forecast figures as necessary. For example, you just completed the month of August, with sales of $25,000, not the $19,969.75 that you were expecting.

   You also see that the rest of the year is going to be much better than you had originally anticipated. You are now forecasting a 20% growth rate through the end of the year.

3. Move the cursor to the August budget amount box. Remember, do not change this figure since the month of August has been completed. Even though using the estimated sales figures as a basis will lower the rest of the year's estimation, it is better to remain a little on the conservative side, than overly optimistic.

4. Choose F**i**ll Down. Enter the expected growth rate of 20% in the box, and choose OK. QuickBooks recalculates the budget figures for the remaining portion of the fiscal year, as you see in figure 18.8.

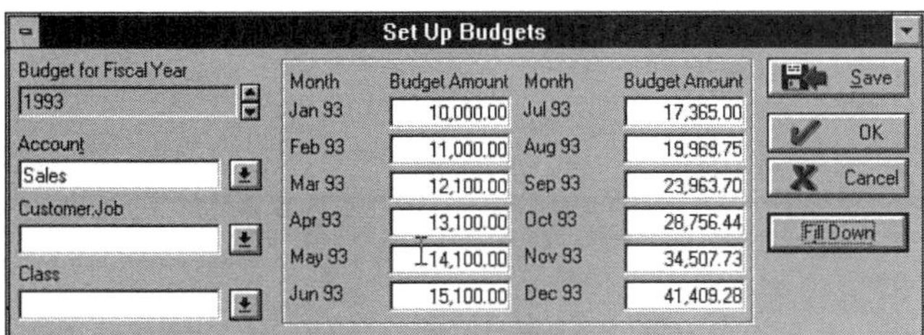

Fig. 18.8
The adjusted Sales budget. You now have a new set of budget numbers for the rest of the year.

Viewing a Budget Report

QuickBooks comes with six preset budget reports. Remember, before you can use a budget report, you must set up the budget figures for the account. For details about how to create a report, see Chapter 19, "Creating and Printing Reports." The six preset budget reports include:

P&L Budget **O**verview

P&L Budget vs. **A**ctual

P&L Budget by **J**ob Overview

P&L Budget vs. A**c**tual by Job

Balance **S**heet Budget Overview

Balance Sheet Budget vs. Actual

To view a budget report, follow these steps:

1. From the **R**eports menu, choose Bu**d**get Reports.

2. Choose the required report from the drop-down menu. QuickBooks will take a few moments to create the budget and display the report.

Figure 18.9 displays the selected report Balance **S**heet Budget Overview. The report is titled Budget for Balance Sheet Accounts. Only a portion of the report can be displayed on-screen at any one time. Use the scroll bars to view the rest of the report.

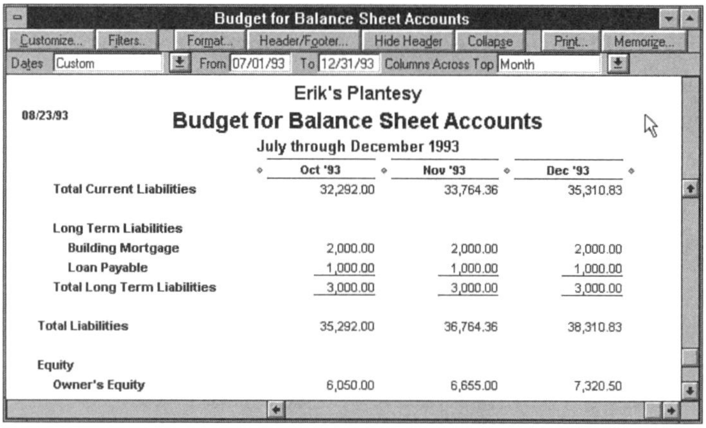

Fig. 18.9
The Budget for Balance Sheet Accounts.

Budget for Balance Sheet Accounts

Customize... Filters... Format... Header/Footer... Hide Header Collapse Print... Memorize...

Dates Custom From 07/01/93 To 12/31/93 Columns Across Top Month

Erik's Plantesy

08/23/93 **Budget for Balance Sheet Accounts**

July through December 1993

	Oct '93	Nov '93	Dec '93
Total Current Liabilities	32,292.00	33,764.36	35,310.83
Long Term Liabilities			
Building Mortgage	2,000.00	2,000.00	2,000.00
Loan Payable	1,000.00	1,000.00	1,000.00
Total Long Term Liabilities	3,000.00	3,000.00	3,000.00
Total Liabilities	35,292.00	36,764.36	38,310.83
Equity			
Owner's Equity	6,050.00	6,655.00	7,320.50

CPA TIP: Review Your Budget Reports Frequently

Review your budget reports often to compare actual results for a given period with what you forecasted or planned. You should immediately investigate any major deviations to determine whether action can be taken to correct the problem, or if conditions are so different that a budget change is necessary. Stay on top of your results. Don't let a major difference between actual and budget amounts go on for an extended period of time. Even if your sales are well above forecasted amounts, you may need to make immediate adjustments to your cash flow so that you can pay your vendors.

Summary

In this chapter, you learned how to create a budget for your business so that you can easily monitor how well your business is doing in comparison to your expectations or forecasts.

In the next chapter, you learn how to create and print the various reports that QuickBooks provides, and then how to customize a report for your specific needs.

Chapter 19

Creating and Printing Reports

You can create and print reports that summarize your company's financial activity for any given period of time. You need reports to help you analyze the results of your business operations. When you use a preset report or create a customized report, QuickBooks retrieves data from your company file and presents it in a meaningful format so that you can review the financial activity of your business at a glance. After you enter all your beginning financial data and enter transactions over a period of time, you can begin to use the QuickBooks reports.

In this chapter, you learn to do the following:

- Create a QuickReport for selected information
- Use the preset QuickBooks reports
- Customize a report
- Memorize a custom report and recall it
- Print reports to a printer or selected disk file

V

Analyzing Business Data

QuickBooks includes eight preset report categories containing fifty-two different reports, which cover most business needs. Each report category contains several reports for you to use. The preset report categories are as follows:

Profit and Loss Reports
Balance Sheet Reports
Accounts Receivable Reports
Sales Reports
Accounts Payable Reports
Budget Reports
Transaction Reports
Other Reports

An additional category is also available for your own memorized reports. You can easily customize a preset report for your specific needs at any time and save it as a memorized report. When you need to use this report again, simply select from the memorized report list instead of re-creating the report.

Customizing reports enables you to select which transactions to include in a report and determine how information appears in the report. For example, you may want to automatically limit the time period of a sales report, and display information for a specified salesperson only.

Using QuickReports To View Transactions

At various points within QuickBooks, you can create a QuickReport by clicking the QuickReport button. A QuickBooks QuickReport simply lists all the transactions related to the selected vendor, customer, employee, or account. Whenever you display the Chart of Accounts, you can create a QuickReport by selecting any income, expense, or other non-Balance Sheet account. When you select one of these accounts, the U**s**e Register button changes labels to read **Q**uickReport. You can also display a QuickReport from any account register by using the Q-Report button. You can create a QuickReport whenever you display a list or form that contains a field for a name. You saw and used the QuickReport button in the Chart of Accounts and in each Account register.

The QuickReport bases the data displays and the report title and header information on the form, account, list, or register from which you request the report. To create a QuickReport from a form such as an invoice, follow these steps:

1. Choose **A**ctivities, Create **I**nvoices from the menu to open the Create Invoices window, or click the Invoice button (or press Ctrl+I). Click the Pre**v** button to display the last invoice created.

2. Choose **R**eports, **Q**uickReport from the menu. QuickBooks creates a QuickReport for all year-to-date transactions for this customer. Figure 19.1 shows part of the resulting report.

   Notice the mouse pointer displayed as a magnifying glass with the letter Z on the lens. This is the QuickBooks QuickZoom feature. At any point that the pointer turns into this shape, you can double-click and display another QuickReport for the selected transaction.

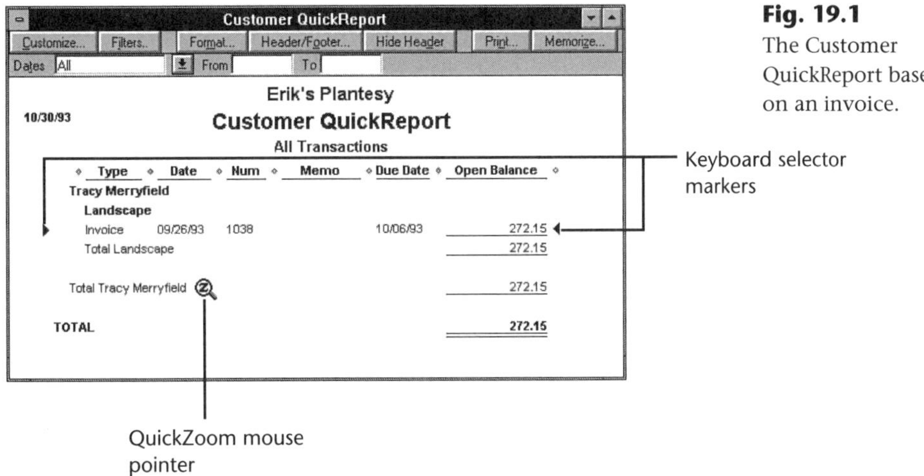

Fig. 19.1 The Customer QuickReport based on an invoice.

You can also use the up- or down-arrow keys to QuickZoom to a transaction. Along with the magnifying glass pointer, notice a set of arrowhead markers in the margins of the report, alongside the transaction. These are keyboard selector markers. Press the up- or down-arrow keys to select the transaction, and press the Enter key. QuickBooks creates the QuickReport for the selected transaction.

You can create a QuickReport from a list, Chart of Accounts, or an account register. To create a QuickReport, follow these steps:

1. Open the vendor list by choosing **L**ists, **V**endors from the menu.
2. Select the vendor that you would like to see a report on, and click the **Q**uickReport button. Figure 19.2 shows the resulting Vendor QuickReport.

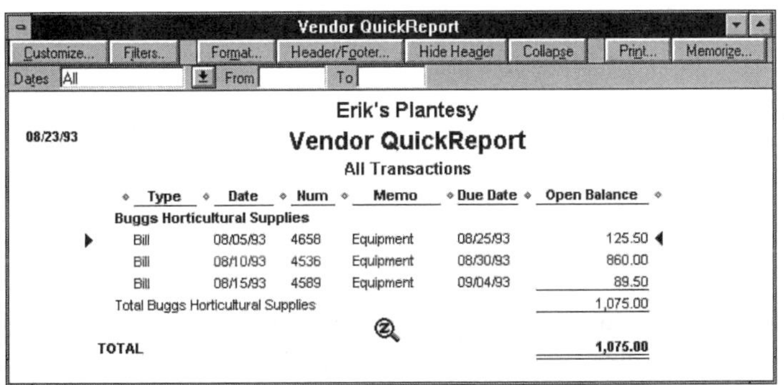

Fig. 19.2 The Vendor QuickReport.

Figure 19.3 displays the Checking account register, the Vendor List, and the Chart of Accounts. Each of these windows contains a QuickReport button. In an account register the button is called *Q-Report*; in a list it is called ***Q**uickReport*.

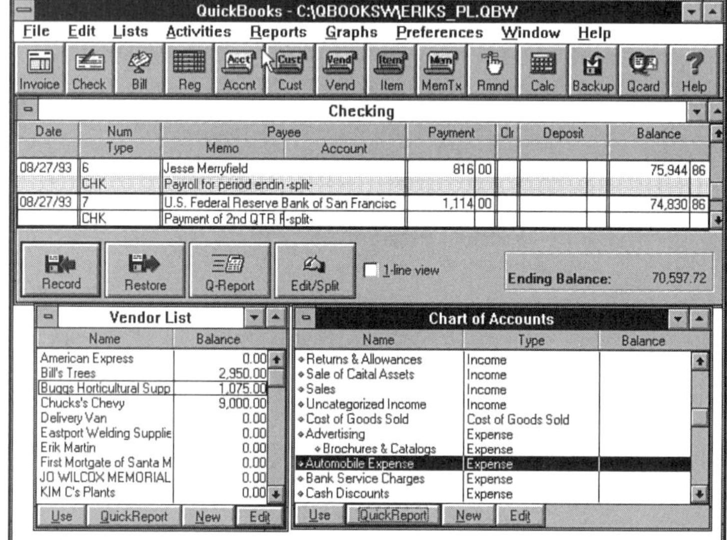

Fig. 19.3
Different windows, each containing a QuickReport button.

Using QuickBooks' Preset Reports

QuickBooks' preset reports can extract data and display a report in seconds. QuickBooks reports include the appropriate transactions based on the report that you select. The Standard Balance Sheet report is one of QuickBooks' preset reports. When you create the Standard Balance Sheet report, QuickBooks includes only Balance Sheet accounts and lists together current assets, fixed assets, current liabilities, long-term liabilities, and finally the equity accounts. Subtotal and total lines are placed as required for this type of report.

The QuickZoom feature is available for you to use from the preset reports, just as you learned for QuickReports.

When you select a QuickBooks preset report, the report is created using "today's" date as the ending date. To adjust the date or other settings, see the section, "Customizing a Report with the Report Window," at the end of this chapter.

Note

If you create this report yourself, you first have to format a report, accumulate the data, enter it into the report, add the subtotal and total fields, and finally hope that you didn't miss anything. With the preset Standard Balance Sheet report, QuickBooks performs all the work for you.

The QuickBooks reports are broken into eight categories, with a total of fifty-two preset reports. You learn about each of these categories and their preset reports in the next several sections. All the QuickBooks preset reports are accessed through the **R**eports menu option. Each option displayed on the drop-down menu displays its own cascading menu with each of the reports for the group. To use any QuickBooks preset report, follow these steps:

1. Choose Reports from the main menu.
2. Choose the report group from the drop-down menu.
3. Select the specific report that you require from the displayed menu. QuickBooks creates the required report and displays it for you.

In the next sections, each report is described briefly, and part of the report is shown. Many of these reports can run to several pages in length, especially after you have been in business for awhile.

Profit and Loss Reports

The Profit & Loss Statement summarizes all your Income and Expense accounts and subaccounts. This statement does not include transfer transactions, because they deal with two Balance Sheet accounts. The Profit & Loss Statement is a summary report and does not list individual transactions. Figure 19.4 shows the standard Profit and Loss statement for the period January through December 1993.

CPA TIP: The Profit and Loss Statement

The Profit & Loss Statement (or Income Statement) is one of your business's most used and most important financial reports. The Profit & Loss Statement reports your net income or net loss for a specific time period (a month, quarter, or year). Remember that the sales revenue shown on the Profit & Loss Statement is not necessarily the same as cash inflow from sales for the period, and that the expenses shown do not necessarily reflect the cash outflows of your business for the period. To show the cash position of your business, create the Cash Flow Forecast Report.

Fig. 19.4
The standard Profit and Loss Statement for the year ending December 31, 1993.

Erik's Plantesy
Profit and Loss
January through December 1993

		Jan - Dec '93
Ordinary Income/Expense		
Income		
Reimbursed Expenses		-18,500.00
Sale of Caital Assets		770.00
Sales		7,694.20
Uncategorized Income		9,200.00
Total Income		-835.80
Gross Profit		-835.80
Expense		
Telephone		-2,300.00
Repairs		
Equipment Repairs	1,944.49	
Repairs - Other	223.00	
Total Repairs		2,167.49
Rent		-10,500.00
Professional Fees		-3,500.00
Printing and Reproduction		500.00
Payroll Taxes		
Medicare	-158.00	
FUTA	-13.00	
FICA	-1,183.00	
Total Payroll Taxes		-1,354.00
Payroll Expenses		
Gross Wages	9,260.00	
Payroll Expenses - Other	-9,650.00	
Total Payroll Expenses		-390.00
Miscellaneous		35.00
Licenses and Permits		-250.00
Interest Expense		1,096.88
Insurance		
Disability Insurance	175.00	
Liability Insurance	250.00	
Insurance - Other	-2,000.00	
Total Insurance		-1,575.00
Equipment Rental		-4,890.00
Depreciation Expense		-12,670.00
Cash Discounts		14.25
Bank Service Charges		325.50
Advertising		-950.00
Charitable Donation		350.00
Computer Supplies		-675.00
Fertilizer Expense		-5,268.00
Janitorial Serivce		-350.00
Materials Expense		13,648.00
Office Supplies		685.00
Taxes		-5,400.00
Uncategorized Expenses		107.00
Total Expense		-31,142.88
Net Ordinary Income		30,307.08
Other Income/Expense		
Other Income		
Interest Income		-1,250.00
Total Other Income		-1,250.00
Net Other Income		-1,250.00
Net Income		29,057.08

The different types of preset Profit & Loss Statements are listed as follows:

- *The Standard Profit and Loss.* This report is probably the report that you will want to see most often. As with any QuickBooks report, you can create this report at any time; it will be up-to-date as of the day that you create it. This report summarizes income and expenses for the month-to-date. All your Income accounts are listed, along with the total for the account. All Income accounts are then totaled, and the Gross Profit displayed. Then all Expense accounts with account totals are shown and totaled. The final Net Income figure shows at the bottom of the report.

- *The Year-to-Date Comparison.* This report contains the information shown in the Standard report in one column, plus the addition of a second column showing the current year-to-Date information.

- *The Previous Year Comparison.* This report is useful for determining how your business has progressed compared to the previous year. All figures are year-to-Date, and are compared with the same period of the previous year. A column shows the dollar changes, and another shows the percentage of change.

- *By Job Profit and Loss.* This report creates a profit and loss report by jobs. This report can help to determine which jobs were profitable and which, if any, were not. A column displays for each job, and then a total for the customer. This report prints with all columns, side-by-side. If your printer can't accommodate the report, QuickBooks breaks the report into additional pages.

- *The Itemized Profit and Loss.* This report creates a report showing all income and expenses for each class. Columns are shown for each class of customers.

- *Income by Customer Summary.* This report displays a summary of net sales for each customer and job.

- *Income by Customer Detail.* This report details each sale or return, grouped and subtotaled by customer and customer:job.

- *Expenses by Vendor Summary.* This report summarizes your expenses by vendor for the current year-to-date.

- *Expenses by Vendor Detail.* This report displays detailed information about each transaction to a vendor. The report is grouped by vendor, and then lists the type of transaction, transaction date and number, account to which expended, whether the transaction has cleared, amount of the transaction, and a running balance of the account. Each group is subtotaled and finally totaled.

Balance Sheet Reports

The Balance Sheet Reports show the financial position of your company as of a certain date. The net value of all your Balance Sheet accounts is displayed and summarized. Figure 19.5 shows the summary Balance Sheet report.

Fig. 19.5
The Summary Balance Sheet for the period ending October 30, 1993.

10/30/93

Erik's Plantesy
Balance Sheet
As of October 30, 1993

	Oct 30, '93
ASSETS	
Current Assets	
Checking/Savings	47,685.26
Accounts Receivable	30,078.30
Other Current Assets	3,057.05
Total Current Assets	80,820.61
Fixed Assets	174,000.00
Other Assets	34,430.00
TOTAL ASSETS	**289,250.61**
LIABILITIES & EQUITY	
Liabilities	
Current Liabilities	
Accounts Payable	3,450.00
Credit Cards	333.55
Other Current Liabilities	222.30
Total Current Liabilities	4,005.85
Long Term Liabilities	147,666.74
Total Liabilities	151,672.59
Equity	137,578.02
TOTAL LIABILITIES & EQUITY	**289,250.61**

The different types of Balance Sheet reports follow:

- *The Standard Balance Sheet.* This report is one that most business people are familiar with. All the Balance Sheet accounts are shown. The report is in the familiar assets, liabilities, and equity format, with subtotals and totals placed as needed.

- *The Comparison Balance Sheet.* This report is similar to the standard Balance Sheet report, except that it includes a column for the same time period last year, and then comparison columns—one for dollars, and one for percent of change.
- *The Summary Balance Sheet.* This report is a more concise version of the standard report.
- *The Itemized Balance Sheet.* This report lists each account, details each transaction for the account, and subtotals the account. Figures are for month-to-date.

CPA TIP: The Balance Sheet

The Balance Sheet report measures the value of your business as of one moment in time—the date you created the report. Asset amounts represent values based on original cost, not replacement cost or earning power (unless you entered any amount other than original costs for assets). Liabilities represent the legal claims of creditors who either loaned you money or extended credit for goods or services. Owner's equity, or net worth, represents a claim resulting from the capital invested by the owners of the business and past profits retained in the business.

Accounts Receivable Reports

The various accounts receivable reports are very important to a business. They let you know how well your credit accounts are paying, and if they are not paying, you can determine who the customers are. You are extending credit to your customers, and you must be sure to stay on top of your collections and your cash flow. The A/R Summary report is shown in figure 19.6.

CPA TIP: Using the A/R Aging Reports

The information in the A/R Aging reports is essential to the effective management and control of your Accounts Receivable. You must know how long accounts have been outstanding. Use the A/R Aging reports to determine the effectiveness of your credit policy. In addition, look for signs of decline in the rate of collection, accounts that are past due, signs of problem accounts, changes in large accounts, and any accounts that may show an abnormal increase in size or an inconsistency in payments. And unless you changed your company's credit policy, your total receivables remain proportional to the level of sales. If your sales increased 15 percent from last year, for example, your receivables also should increase by roughly 15 percent.

Fig. 19.6
Use the A/R Aging Summary to quickly see if you have potential collecting problems.

10/30/93

Erik's Plantesy
A/R Aging Summary
As of October 30, 1993

	Current	1 - 30	31 - 60	61 - 90	> 90	TOTAL
Tracy Merryfield						
Yard	0.00	15.90	0.00	0.00	0.00	15.90
Landscape	0.00	272.15	0.00	0.00	0.00	272.15
Tracy Merryfield - Other	0.00	0.00	0.00	-125.00	0.00	-125.00
Total Tracy Merryfield	0.00	288.05	0.00	-125.00	0.00	163.05
Forest Grove Drugs						
Consult	0.00	25.00	0.00	1,050.00	0.00	1,075.00
Lot	0.00	0.00	0.00	-520.00	0.00	-520.00
Forest Grove Drugs - Other	0.00	29,110.25	0.00	0.00	0.00	29,110.25
Total Forest Grove Drugs	0.00	29,135.25	0.00	530.00	0.00	29,665.25
Mack Martini	0.00	0.00	250.00	0.00	0.00	250.00
TOTAL	**0.00**	**29,423.30**	**250.00**	**405.00**	**0.00**	**30,078.30**

The various A/R reports follow:

- *The Aging Summary.* This report shows all outstanding receivables grouped by customer, with subtotals for each customer. All receivables are aged in columns: Current, 1-30 days past, 31-60 days past, 61-90 days past, >90 days past due, and a Total column.

- *The Aging Detail.* This report is similar to the standard aging report, except that it groups transactions by how long balances have been outstanding; current, 1-30 days past, and so on; it then lists the details of the each transaction within the group. Each group is also totaled.

- *The Open Invoices.* This report shows only unpaid or partly paid invoices that are past due. To print a report of all unpaid invoices by customer, regardless of whether the invoices are past due, print the Open Invoices report.

  The Open Invoices by Customer report lists all open invoices, grouped by customer. Each customer listing shows a total at the end of the listing.

- *The Collections.* This report lists customers with past due balances as well as related information, such as the customer's phone number and contact person. You can use the Collections Report as a reference when telephoning customers who have past due accounts to remind them to make a payment.

- *The Customer Balance Summary.* This report shows all customers with outstanding invoices. Only the total of the customer's account is displayed along with the customer name. Customer:Job is shown as a separate item.

- *The Customer Balance Detail.* This report is similar to the summary report, with all the detail. Each invoice and payment is listed for the customer, with a total displayed for each.

Sales Reports

The QuickBooks preset sales reports can help you determine what services or goods you offer to sell, and to whom. You can also create a report that shows you how much your individual sales representatives sold. This can help if you pay a sales commission. Figure 19.7 shows the Sales by Item summary report.

10/30/93

Erik's Plantesy
Sales by Item
August 1993

	Qty	Aug '93
Parts		
T-DGWD-P	501.00	7,515.00
T-WPCHRY-F	25.00	3,125.00
Total Parts		10,640.00
Service		
Consult	321.00	8,025.00
Labor1	4,002.00	60,030.00
Total Service		68,055.00
TOTAL		78,695.00

Fig. 19.7
The Sales by Item summary can quickly show you what items have sold during a period.

The various types of Sales reports follow:

- *The By Item Summary.* This report shows you the month-to-date sales of each of the items that you sell. The report is grouped by item types, and then specific items. The quantity of each item is shown and then the dollar amount sold. Each group is totaled. This report does not include sales taxes or reimbursable expenses.

- *The By Item Detail.* This report is similar to the summary report, but includes detailed information about each invoice, credit memo, and cash sale for each item.

- *The By Customer Summary.* This report shows your sales for each customer and Customer:Job with a subtotal for each customer. A total for all sales, month-to-date, displays at the bottom of the report.

- *The By Customer Detail.* This report is similar to the customer summary report, with the addition of invoice details.
- *The By Rep Summary.* This report shows all sales listed by sales representatives. This report can be very useful if you pay by commission, or you could use it for evaluations. This report does not include sales taxes and reimbursable expenses. This report is created automatically using month-to-date sales.
- *The By Rep Detail.* This report is similar to the summary report. It includes an information line for each invoice, grouped by sales representatives. Again, this report contains month-to-date sales only.

Accounts Payable Reports

The Accounts Payable reports can help you to balance your cash flow, purchasing, and budgeting. If you notice that your own cash flow is tight and that you are starting to go beyond your normal terms with your vendors, you can take steps now to contact the vendors. Figure 19.8 shows the A/P Aging Summary report.

Fig. 19.8
The A/P Aging Report can show you if you are starting to slip past terms with any of your vendors.

10/31/93

Erik's Plantesy
A/P Aging Summary
All Transactions

	Current	1 - 30	31 - 60	61 - 90	> 90	TOTAL
ABC CO.	100.00	0.00	0.00	0.00	0.00	100.00
Bill's Trees	3,000.00	1,350.00	0.00	-1,000.00	0.00	3,350.00
TOTAL	**3,100.00**	**1,350.00**	**0.00**	**-1,000.00**	**0.00**	**3,450.00**

The various A/P reports follow:

- *The Aging Summary.* This report displays the aging of your bills by vendor. The report shows a single line entry for each vendor, with the aging of the amounts due displayed across the report.
- *The Aging Detail.* This report groups bills by their aging. All current bills are listed first, then any 1-30 days past terms, and so on. A total is shown for each group.
- *The Unpaid Bills Detail.* This report shows only unpaid or partly paid bills that are past due. To print a report of all unpaid bills sorted by vendor, regardless of whether the bills are past due, use the Unpaid Bills Detail report.

- *The Sales Tax Liability.* This report summarizes the sales tax that you collected or billed to your customers so that you can prepare the sales tax returns required by government agencies and remit the sales tax. The Sales Tax Report shows sales tax for each sales tax vendor, subtotaled by sales tax district. QuickBooks automatically creates this report for the prior month's sales.

> **CPA TIP: Sales Taxes: Cash or Accrual?**
>
> Check the regulations for the government agency for which you collect sales tax to determine the method for remitting sales tax (cash or accrual basis) and to determine how often you need to file sales tax returns. Sales tax returns must be filed on a timely basis to avoid penalties and interest charges.

- *The 1099.* This report is useful if you are required to complete a Form 1099 for any of your vendors. The 1099 report shows total cash outflows grouped by vendor. The report displays year-to-date figures. The 1099 Detail report lists each vendor, and all cash outflows to the vendor. Each vendor is subtotaled.
- *The Vendor Balance Summary.* This report shows all vendors and the unpaid balances as of the current date.
- *The Vendor Balance Detail.* This report lists all transactions, grouped by vendor. A subtotal for each vendor displays at the end of the vendor group.

Budget Reports

You can use budget reports as a check to determine whether your business is keeping up with your planned sales or expenditures. If any of the figures begins to vary from the budgeted amount, you can quickly take action. Figure 19.9 shows the Balance Sheet Budget Comparison.

> **CPA TIP: Use Your Budget Reports for Evaluation**
>
> Use the budget report to compare actual results for a given period with your budgeted forecast. Investigate any major deviations and determine whether action can or needs to be taken. Even a major increase in sales can translate quickly into a shortage of materials or goods.

Fig. 19.9
The Balance Sheet Budget Comparison report shows your Balance Sheet Accounts compared to the budgeted amounts.

Erik's Plantesy
Balance Sheet Budget Comparison
As of October 31, 1993

	Oct 31, '93	Budget	$ Over Budget	% of Budget
ASSETS				
Current Assets				
Checking/Savings				
Checking	43,309.76	38,000.00	5,309.76	113.0%
Total Checking/Savings	47,685.26	38,000.00	9,685.26	125.5%
Accounts Receivable				
Accounts Receivable	30,078.30	29,040.00	1,038.30	103.6%
Total Accounts Receivable	30,078.30	29,040.00	1,038.30	103.6%
Other Current Assets				
Prepaid Insurance	750.00	450.00	300.00	166.7%
Total Other Current Assets	3,057.05	450.00	2,607.05	679.3%
Total Current Assets	80,820.61	67,490.00	13,330.61	119.8%
Fixed Assets				
Building	160,300.00	135,000.00	25,300.00	118.7%
Computer Equipment	12,700.00	10,000.00	2,700.00	127.0%
Delivery Van	0.00	10,000.00	-10,000.00	0.0%
Total Fixed Assets	174,000.00	155,000.00	19,000.00	112.3%
Other Assets				
Investments	34,430.00	60,500.00	-26,070.00	56.9%
Total Other Assets	34,430.00	60,500.00	-26,070.00	56.9%
TOTAL ASSETS	289,250.61	282,990.00	6,260.61	102.2%
LIABILITIES & EQUITY				
Liabilities				
Current Liabilities				
Accounts Payable				
Accounts Payable	3,450.00	26,460.00	-23,010.00	13.0%
Total Accounts Payable	3,450.00	26,460.00	-23,010.00	13.0%
Credit Cards				
Credit Card	0.00	1,323.00	-1,323.00	0.0%
Total Credit Cards	333.55	1,323.00	-989.45	25.2%
Other Current Liabilities				
Payroll Liabilities				
Federal Withholding	0.00	433.54	-433.54	0.0%
Medicare	0.00	56.11	-56.11	0.0%
FUTA	215.00	127.51	87.49	168.6%
FICA	-203.00	612.06	-815.06	-33.2%
Employee Contrib. 401K	0.00	510.05	-510.05	0.0%
Payroll Liabilities - Other	0.00	2,346.23	-2,346.23	0.0%
Total Payroll Liabilities	12.00	4,085.50	-4,073.50	0.3%
Sales Tax Payable	210.30	423.50	-213.20	49.7%
Total Other Current Liabilities	222.30	4,509.00	-4,286.70	4.9%
Total Current Liabilities	4,005.85	32,292.00	-28,286.15	12.4%
Long Term Liabilities				
Loan Payable	0.00	1,000.00	-1,000.00	0.0%
Building Mortgage	147,666.74	2,000.00	145,666.74	7,383.3%
Total Long Term Liabilities	147,666.74	3,000.00	144,666.74	4,922.2%
Total Liabilities	151,672.59	35,292.00	116,380.59	429.8%
Equity				
Owner's Equity	5,000.00	6,050.00	-1,050.00	82.6%
Erik's Draw Account	-2,500.00	2,500.00	-5,000.00	-100.0%
Net Income	29,057.08	0.00	29,057.08	100.0%
Total Equity	137,578.02	8,550.00	129,028.02	1,609.1%
TOTAL LIABILITIES & EQUITY	289,250.61	43,842.00	245,408.61	659.8%

The various Budget reports follow:

- *The P&L Budget Overview.* This report shows all the budgeted figures for all Income and Expense accounts, by the month and for the year.

Remember, a budget figure is displayed only if you have set up a budget for the accounts, as you learned in Chapter 18, "Preparing Budgets."

- *The P&L Budget vs. Actual.* This report compares actual figures to budgeted figures for each Income and Expense account. Each month is grouped with a column for the actual month's figures, the budgeted figures, dollar amount over/under budget, and a percentage over/under budget.
- *The P&L Budget by Job Overview.* This report displays a complete budget for a specific job. This type of budget can help you keep on track when working on a large project for a customer. Each Income and Expense account that you budget for a job displays.
- *The P&L Budget vs. Actual by Job.* This report compares the budgeted amounts to the actual amounts spent or earned. All Income and Expense accounts are listed. The report shows year-to-date figures, actual amounts, budgeted amount, dollar amount over/under budget, and percentage over/under budget.
- *The Balance Sheet Budget Overview.* This report shows the budgeted amounts for each Balance Sheet account by month.
- *The Balance Sheet Budget vs. Actual.* This report compares the actual amounts, budgeted amounts, dollars over/under budget, and percentage over/under budget for each Balance Sheet account by month.

Transaction Reports

The various Transaction reports enable you to view a detailed listing of all transactions. Each report type groups the transactions into different configurations. The Transactions by Customer report is shown in figure 19.10.

The various Transaction reports follow:

- *The By Account.* This report shows all transactions month-to-date for each Balance Sheet, Income, and Expense account. A subtotal displays for each individual account.
- *The By Customer.* This report lists each customer's name, and then all transactions for that customer. This report is for month-to-date transactions.
- *The By Vendor.* This report displays all transactions, grouped by vendor. This report shows only month-to-date transactions.

- *The By Date.* This report shows all transactions that have been processed through QuickBooks, for the month-to-date.

Fig. 19.10
Transaction reports show you how to see your financial information in different forms.

10/31/93

Erik's Plantesy
Transactions by Customer
October 1993

Type	Date	Num	Memo	Account	Split	Amount	Balance
Tracy Merryfield							
Yard							
Check	10/17/93			Accounts Receiv...	Checking	15.90	15.90
Check	10/17/93			Accounts Receiv...	Checking	15.90	31.80
Credit Memo	10/17/93	1040		Accounts Receiv...	-SPLIT-	-15.90	15.90
Payment	10/24/93			Accounts Receiv...	Undeposited ...	-150.00	-134.10
Total Yard						-134.10	-134.10
Landscape							
Invoice	10/6/93	1016		Accounts Receiv...	-SPLIT-	1,695.00	1,695.00
Payment	10/24/93			Accounts Receiv...	Undeposited ...	-2.95	1,692.05
Payment	10/24/93			Accounts Receiv...	Undeposited ...	-1,695.00	-2.95
Total Landscape						-2.95	-2.95
Total Tracy Merryfield						-137.05	-137.05
TOTAL						**-137.05**	**-137.05**

Other Reports

The Other Reports menu includes some general accounting reports, forecasting reports, and other reports. The next several sections explain and show each report contained in the Other Reports menu. The Cash Flow Forecast report is shown in figure 19.11.

Fig. 19.11
The Cash Flow Forecast report can help you to estimate your cash flow needs over a selected period.

10/31/93

Mr. Scott's Hair Design
Cash Flow Forecast
August 1993

	Accnts Receivable	Accnts Payable	Bank Accnts	Net Inflows	Proj Balance
Beginning Balance	0.00	250.00	27,879.14		27,629.14
Week of Aug 1, '93	-537.55	6,300.00	8,485.20	1,647.65	29,276.79
Week of Aug 8, '93	0.00	8,630.00	-20,788.00	-29,418.00	-141.21
Week of Aug 15, '93	0.00	0.00	-966.39	-966.39	-1,107.60
Week of Aug 22, '93	26.75	2,206.13	61,095.05	58,915.67	57,808.07
Aug 29 - 31, '93	350.00	3,445.45	-2,803.00	-5,898.45	51,909.62
Aug '93	-160.80	20,581.58	45,022.86	24,280.48	
Ending Balance	-160.80	20,831.58	72,902.00		51,909.62

Other reports include the following:

- *The Cash Flow Forecast.* Cash is one of your most important assets. You must constantly monitor your business's cash inflow and outflow and project how much cash you will have during a future period.

The QuickBooks Cash Flow Forecast report shows projected cash receipts, disbursements, and checking account balances for the four week period.

- *The Summary.* This report is very similar to the Profit & Loss statement. The Summary report displays Income and Expense accounts, showing a total for each account and each group subtotaled. A final Net Income figure displays at the bottom of the report.
- *The Missing Checks.* You can use the Missing Checks report with any checking account, accounts receivable, or an asset account. The report shows all transactions in the account and points out gaps in the number sequence and duplicate numbers.
- *The Payroll.* The QuickBooks Payroll report summarizes all payroll transactions and any transactions related to accounts set up for payroll taxes. The report first lists your company's payroll expenses, such as gross salaries, company FICA contributions, and FUTA contributions. The Payroll report then lists payroll tax liabilities, such as federal and state withholding. The figures for this report are month-to-date. Each employee name is displayed in a single column with a cumulative total as the final column.

CPA TIP: Using the Payroll Report To Complete W-2 Forms

At the end of the calendar year, create a payroll report to help you complete employee W-2 forms. Make sure that the time period covered by the report is for the full calendar year (1/1/93 to 12/31/93, for example). The payroll report shows the total gross wages paid to each employee and their total withholdings. A W-2 form must be sent by January 31st of the following calendar year to each person you employed at any time during the preceding calendar year.

- *The General Ledger.* This report displays all transactions grouped by account. Subtotals are shown for each group. This report is similar to the Transactions by Account report.
- *The Trial Balance.* This report summarizes all your accounts in a format familiar to bookkeepers and accountants. All accounts show with their total displayed in either a Debit or a Credit column, with a final total displayed at the end of the report.

- *The Journal.* This report displays all transactions divided into their debits and credits. This report is similar to an accounting journal of all transactions. Transactions are shown for month-to-date.

- *The Transaction Journal.* This report is different from any of the other reports on the **R**eports menu. You must select a transaction from any account register, or from another report. Then choose the **R**eports, **O**ther Reports, Transaction Jo**u**rnal options from the menu. QuickBooks then creates the Transaction Journal report. This report shows all details concerning this transaction in a format that is similar to a Journal format. You see columns for the Transaction number, transaction Type, Date, Number (such as Invoice number), Name (such as Customer or Vendor), any Memos entered, Item column for line items, Account to which the transaction was recorded, Class if any, and Debit and Credit columns for the amounts of the transaction. You will notice that the Debit and Credit columns equal each other.

Customizing a Report with the Report Window

Each time you create a report, QuickBooks displays the report on-screen in the report window. Any of QuickBooks' 52 different reports can be customized, and then saved as a memorized report. You can restrict a report in its date range, customer selection, or many other options.

Use any of the preset reports as the basis for customizing your own reports. In just a short time, you can have a report on the accounts and time period that you need.

Using the Report Button Bar

The report window has its own button bar. The button bar contains two parts, as you can see in figure 19.12. The first row has several buttons; the second row has various text boxes. The second row of the button bar differs depending on the report that you create.

The button bar buttons are described in the sections that follow.

Using the Customize Report Button for Summary Reports. With the Customize button on the report button bar, you can change many of the default report settings. Some of the settings that you can change include the date range that the report covers, the report basis (accrual or cash), and the inclusion or exclusion of additional columns in the report.

By clicking the **C**ustomize button on the top report button bar, or pressing Alt+C, you display one of two Customize Report dialog boxes. The first, shown in figure 19.13, is the Customize Report dialog box that is displayed when you are working with a report that summarizes transactions for a period of time. The Profit and Loss and Balance Sheet reports are this type of report.

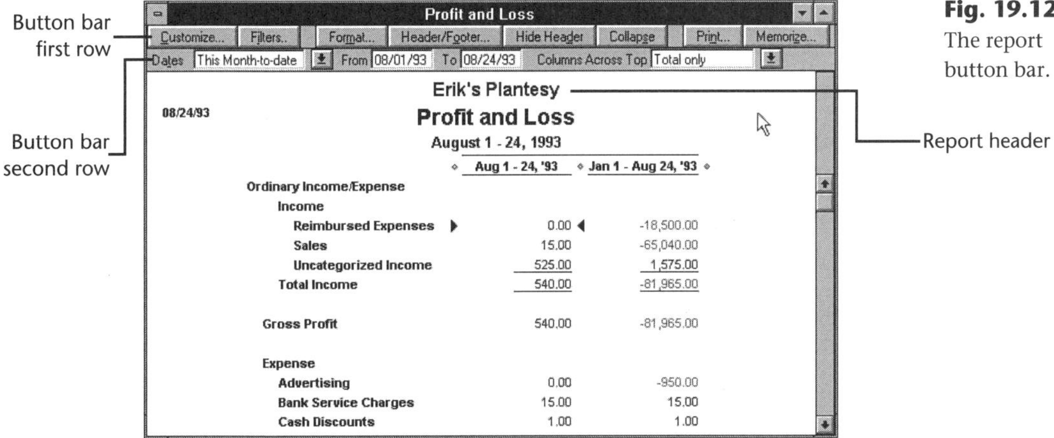

Fig. 19.12
The report button bar.

> **Note**
>
> Some items included in the Customize Report dialog box are also included on the button bar. The **F**ilters button in this dialog box displays the same dialog box that you will open when you choose the **F**ilters button on the button bar. This dialog box is discussed in the later section "Choosing Filters."

When you have made all of your choices in the Customize Report dialog box, choose OK. You return to the report window, and QuickBooks generates a new report based on the selections that you have made.

Options in the Customize Report dialog box include:

- *Report **D**ates, Fro**m**, **T**o.* Changes the report period. Select from the drop-down list of preset periods: This Month, This Year, Next Week, and so on. Use the From option if you select Custom in the Report Dates option by entering the beginning date for your report. Use the To text box to enter the ending date for the report.

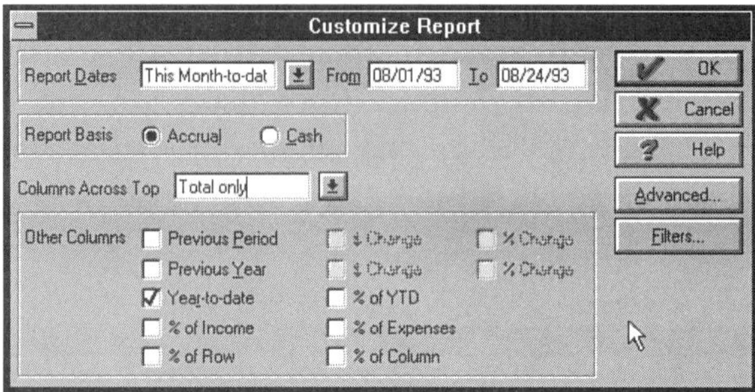

Fig. 19.13
Use the Customize Report dialog box to select the date ranges for a report, and to include or exclude other columns of information.

- *Report Basis*. Select between the two radio buttons: Accrua**l** or **C**ash. Your report uses the selected accounting basis when information is being gathered.
- *Columns Across Top*. Enables you to select additional columns for your report. For example, selecting Quarter in the P&L report shows a subtotaled column for each quarter of the year. Choose from the drop-down list.
- *Other Columns*. Places a check mark beside each column that you want to include in the report.
- ***A**dvanced button*. Displays the Advanced Options dialog box (see fig. 19.14). The Advanced Options dialog box enables you to make some final adjustments to your reports display. Use these options only if you are familiar with the report. Selecting some options in this dialog box removes rows or columns of information from your report if there has been no activity for the account or item. To return to the Customize Report dialog box, choose OK in the Advanced Options dialog box.

The following options are available in the Advanced Options dialog box:

- *Display **R**ows*. Lets you choose which rows to include in your report.
- *Display **C**olumns*. Lets you choose which columns to include in your report.

Your options for both these selections include these three radio buttons:

Active	Displays the row only if there has been activity in the account or item during the period.
All	Displays the row regardless of any activity during the period.
Non-zero	Displays the row only if there has been activity during the period and the current amount is not zero.

- *Reporting Calendar*. Enables you to choose between using your company's **F**iscal year or a Calendar **Y**ear calendar for the report period.

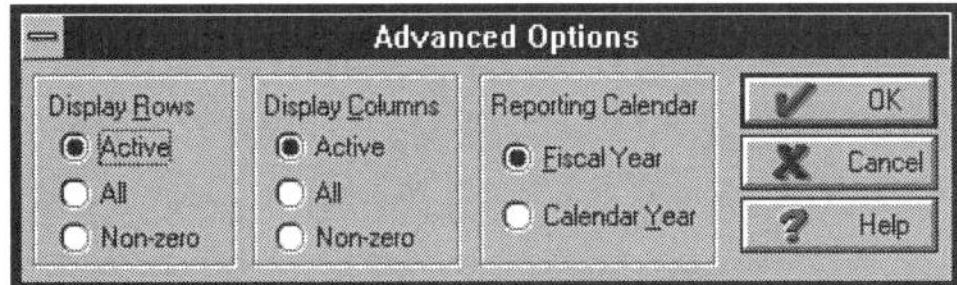

Fig. 19.14
Use the Advanced Options dialog box to restrict the display of accounts or items in a report to only active, to all, or to all non-zero accounts or items.

The Customize Report Button for Transaction Type Reports. QuickBooks uses a variation of the Customize Report dialog box discussed in the previous section for reports concerned with individual transactions. Reports that work with individual transactions include the A/R Aging Detail, the different Transaction Reports, and others. Figure 19.15 shows the dialog box displayed when you choose the **C**ustomize button in the A/R Aging Detail report window.

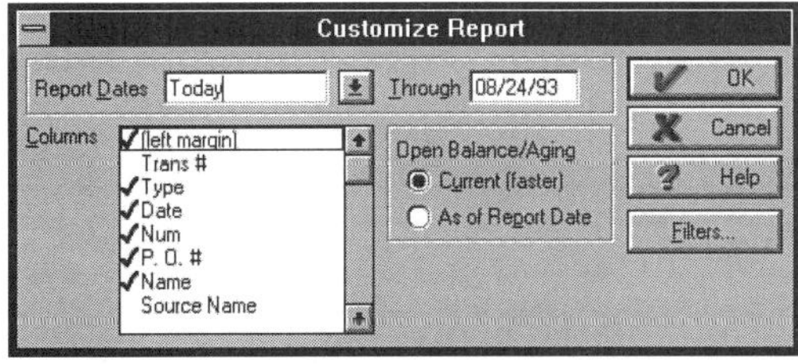

Fig. 19.15
The Customize Report dialog box for a report that displays individual transactions.

The Customize Report dialog box for an individual transaction report, such as the A/R Aging Detail, includes these options:

- *Report **D**ates.* Selects the time period that you want the report to be created for.
- ***Th**rough.* Enters an ending date for your report.
- *Open Balance/Aging.* You can select from two options that determine how QuickBooks calculates the customer's open balance on an account aging report. Your choices are:

    *C**u**rrent(faster).* Displays a customer's current open balance as of today's date. Any payments received and recorded through today's date are reflected in the open balances that are shown in this report. This report takes less time to generate than the next option.

    *As of Re**p**ort Date.* Displays the customer's open balance as of the ending date selected for this report. You can then display a report showing a customer's open balance as of a specific date. Any payments recorded from a customer after this date will not be reflected in the customer's open balance.

- ***C**olumns.* Places a check mark beside each column that you want to appear in your report. The column selection varies depending on the report that you create.

Choosing Filters. The Filter Transactions dialog box enables you to restrict, or be more selective of, the information shown in your report. You have greater control over who or what is displayed in a report.

The Filter Transactions dialog box can be accessed from the report window button bar by choosing the F**i**lters button (or press Alt+I), or from the Customize Report dialog box. Figure 19.16 shows the Filter Transactions dialog box.

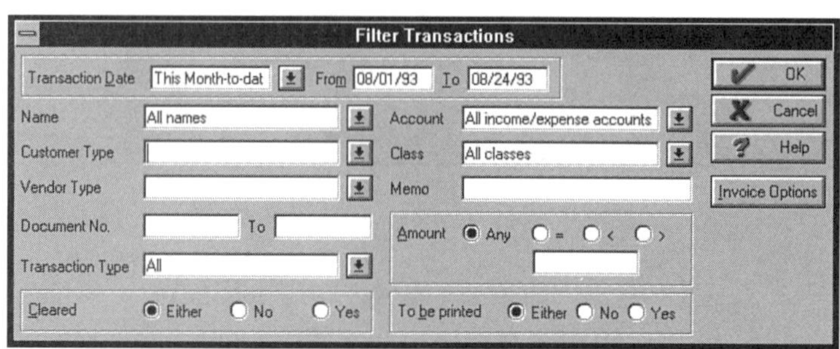

Fig. 19.16
Use the Filter Transactions dialog box to be more selective in who or what is shown in your report.

The options in the Filter Transaction dialog box include the following:

- *Transaction **Date***. Enables you to select a different date range than the reports default selection.
- *Fro**m**, T**o***. Enter dates into these text boxes if you choose Custom in Transaction Dates.
- *Name*. Enables you to create a report for selected names or selected groups. If you choose the option Selected names from the displayed Selected names dialog box, you can then place a check mark beside each name you want to include in the report. Be sure to press the OK button in the Select Name dialog box to return to the Filter Transaction dialog box.
- *Customer Type*. (Optional) Select the specific customer type that you want to include.
- *Vendor Type*. (Optional) Select a specific vendor type.
- *Document No.,To*. (Optional) Enter a beginning and ending range of numbers for checks or invoices.
- *Transaction T**y**pe*. Select a specific transaction type from the drop-down list.
- *Account*. Select specific Balance Sheet accounts, or selected groups of accounts, such as All liabilities.
- *Class*. Select a certain class of transactions. By choosing the Selected class option, you display the Select Classes dialog box. Choose the classes to be included and press OK to return to the Filter Transactions dialog box.
- *Memo*. Restricts selection to transactions with a specified text string in the memo field.
- ***C**leared*. Select the appropriate radio button: Either, No, or Yes. Use this option to restrict QuickBooks' selection of items based on whether they have been cleared by a bank or credit card statement.
- ***A**mount*. Restricts selection to an amount that meets the criteria that you enter. For example, to restrict selection to customers who have purchased more than $100 of merchandise from you, click the > radio button, and enter **100** in the text box.

- *To **B**e Printed.* Select the appropriate radio button: Either, Yes, or No. Use this option to restrict selection based on whether an item has been printed.

- ***I**nvoice Options.* Displays the dialog box shown in figure 19.17. Use this dialog box when you create a report that displays invoice transactions. This dialog box has various options to use in restricting the selection of invoices. Use the Main **O**ptions button to return to the Filter Transactions dialog box. Choose OK to accept all options and return to the Report window. QuickBooks generates and displays a new report based on your selections.

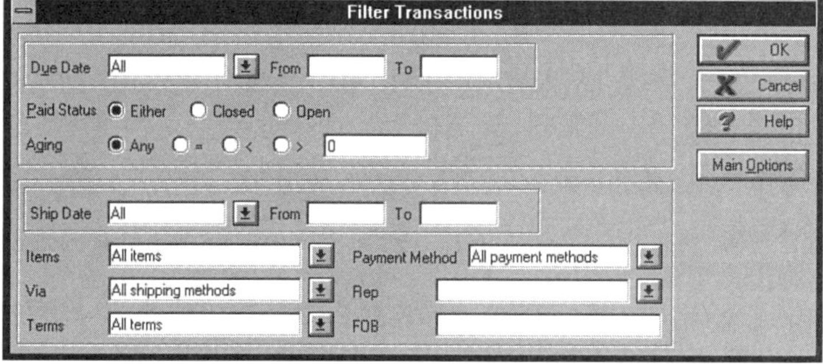

Fig. 19.17
Use the Invoice options Filter Transactions dialog box to be more selective with invoice information displayed in your report.

The Invoice options Filter Transactions dialog box includes the following options:

- *D**u**e Date.* Select a date range to use for selecting invoices.

- *F**r**om, To.* Use these text boxes to enter dates for your report if you choose Custom in the D**u**e Date text box.

- ***P**aid Status.* Select the appropriate radio button to choose an invoice, based on whether it has been paid or not.

- *A**g**ing.* Select invoices based on their aging. To see only invoices that are more than 60 days past terms, for example, click the > radio button, and enter **60** in the text box.

- *Ship Date.* Select the date range for the ship date or dates to be included.

- *Items.* Select from the drop-down list, if you want to choose only invoices that include selected items. You also can choose to display a selected group of item types, such as All Services.

- *Via.* Select from the drop-down list to include invoices with a selected shipping method.
- *Terms.* Select from the drop-down list to include only invoices that include the specified terms.
- *Payment Method.* Select from the drop-down list to include only invoices that include the specified payment method.
- *Rep.* Select a Rep to include invoices for this Rep only.
- *FOB.* Enter an FOB to include invoices with this FOB only.

Using the Format Button in the Report Button Bar. You also can change the fonts, colors, and other options that a report uses for on-screen display and printing. Choose the For**m**at button on the report window button bar to display the Format Report dialog box (see fig. 19.18). Remember, all options that discuss color display in color only if you use a color monitor, and print in color only if you are printing your report on a color printer properly supported by Windows.

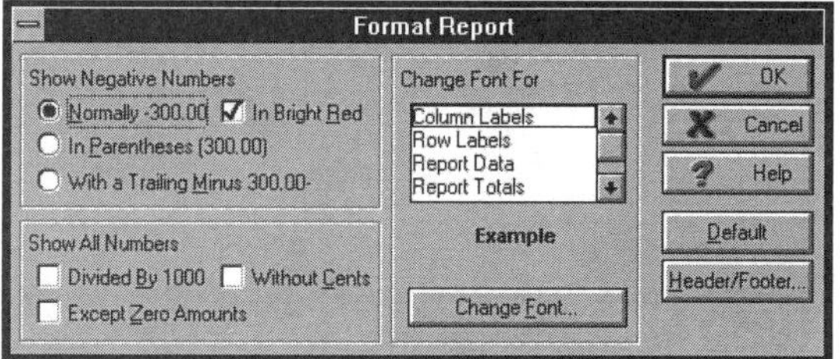

Fig. 19.18
Use the Format Report dialog box to select colors, fonts, and other display and printing formats for your report.

The following options are included in the Format Report dialog box:

- *Show Negative Numbers.* Use to specify the format for negative numbers. You can choose to have negative numbers display as: `-450.00`, `(450.00)`, or `450.00-`. You can also choose to display negative numbers in bright red on-screen by clicking thc In Bright **R**ed box.
- *Show All Numbers.* Use to format numbers in certain ways. Place a check mark in the boxes beside your choice of formats. You can choose more than one option. Your choices are as follows:

Divided **B**y 1000	Use when your report contains many very large numbers.
Without **C**ents	Use to remove the cents from amounts.

Except **Z**ero Amounts	Use to suppress zero amounts in a report. This option is not displayed for all reports.

- ***D**efault.* Use this button to reset all options to the QuickBooks default values.
- ***H**eader/Footer.* This button displays the Format Header/Footer dialog box. This displays the same button available from the button bar.
- *Chan**g**e Font For.* Use to choose the report item that you want to change the font for. A sample of the current font and color displays below the list. Use the scroll bar to display additional report items.
- *Change **F**ont.* Use to change the font of the report item selected in the list above the button. Choose this button to display the printing font control dialog box—shown as Report Data in figure 19.19. The list title changes depending on the report item selected.

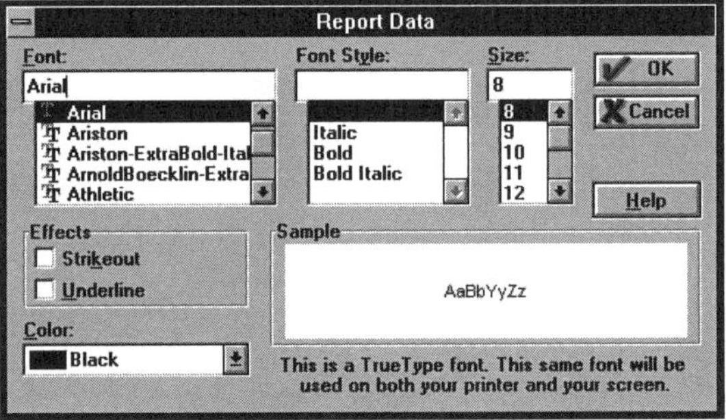

Fig. 19.19
Use the printing font control dialog box to select displayed and printed fonts and colors.

- ***F**ont.* Select the font for the report item. The options available to you depend on the font selection you have.
- *Font St**y**le.* Choose how you want the font displayed: Normal, Italic, Bold, Bold Italic.
- *Size.* Choose the size of the font.
- *Effects.* This option is available for Invoices, Statements, and Mailing Labels. Choose between Stri**k**eout and **U**nderline.

- *Color.* Choose a color from the drop-down list for the report item that you are editing. If you have a color monitor, the item displays in this color. If you have a color printer, it prints in the selected color.

- *Sample.* Displays a sample of the changes as you make them.

Using the Header/Footer Button on the Report Button Bar. If you want to make changes to the report header and footer, you must use the Header/Footer button on the report window button bar. When you choose the Header/F**o**oter button, the Format Header/Footer dialog box appears (see fig. 19.20).

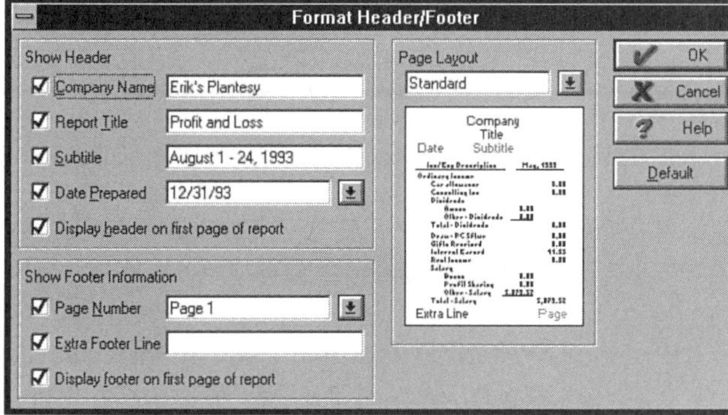

Fig. 19.20
Use the Format Header/Footer dialog box to change the display of the header and footer information of your report.

Your options in the Format Header/Footer dialog box include the following:

- *Show Header.* You have five options in this block. Removing the check mark from any of these options tells QuickBooks not to display that line in the report header. You can edit any of the header lines displayed in the text boxes by simply typing over the original text, or you can select a different date format by choosing one from the drop-down list. By removing the check mark from the Display **H**eader On First Page Of Report check box, you can suppress the header information from the first page of your report.

- *Show Footer Information.* This block has three options. You can change the page numbering display, add an additional line of text at the foot of each page by typing it into the E**x**tra Footer Line text box, and control whether or not the footer information displays on the first page of the report.

- *Page Layout.* Select this option to choose the layout format of your report. You have a selection of four options that can be displayed in the drop-down list: Standard, Left, Right, and Centered. When you choose one of these options, QuickBooks shows a sample of how your finished report will be displayed under this options text box.
- *Default.* This button returns all changes that you have made in this dialog box back to the QuickBooks default settings.

Selecting Other Report Options. There are four remaining buttons available on the first row of the report button bar (refer to fig. 19.12). These buttons include:

- *Hide Header,* or *Show Header.* The Hide Header button removes the report header from the report, allowing you to see more of the report on-screen. When selected, the button changes to the Show Header button, which displays the report header information again.
- *Collapse,* or *Expand.* The Collapse button hides details of a report, consolidating a report to just the major categories. When selected, the Collapse button changes to the Expand button, which can be used to display the report in its original format. Detail reports such as All Aging Detail or Sales Report by Item Detail do not have this option.
- *Print.* Use the Print button to display the Print Report dialog box. From this dialog box, you can print the report to the selected report printer or to a disk file, using one of several files formats.
- *Memorize.* Choose this button to memorize a report that you have customized. When selected, the Memorize Report dialog box appears (see fig. 19.21). Enter the name that you want to use for the customized report, and click the OK button.

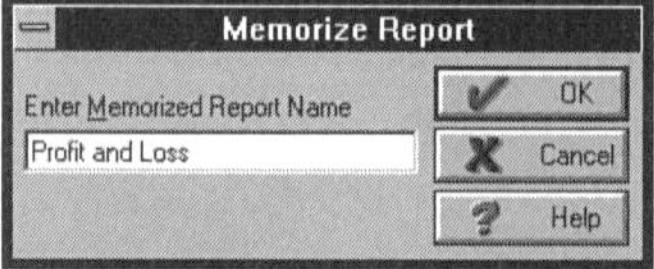

Fig. 19.21
Use the Memorize Report dialog box to name and save a customized report for reuse at a later time.

Using the Second Row of the Report Button Bar. The second row of the button bar (refer to fig. 19.12) contains options you can use to change the report date selection range, specify beginning and ending dates, and choose additional columns to display in the report. These options are also available to you from the various dialog boxes displayed when you choose one of the buttons in the first row of the report window button bar. The options available on the second row of the button bar vary depending upon the report that you have selected. Your choices may include the following:

- *Dates*. You use this option to select the date range for your report. Select the range from the drop-down list. This option is available for all reports.
- *From, To*. Many reports allow you to specify the date range for a report. Simply enter the beginning and ending dates in the From and To text boxes. QuickBooks automatically changes the Dates text box to show the Custom selection.
- *Columns Across Top*. This option allows you to add additional columns in the report. Your choices available from the drop-down list will vary with the report that you have selected. Some reports will not have this option available.
- *Aging Interval(days), Through(days past due)*. The various transaction aging reports, both A/P and A/R, show these two options instead of From and To, and Columns Across Top. You can choose a specific number of days to use in aging your payables or receivables for a report by entering this number in the Aging Interval text box. You can also enter a certain number of days in the Through text box that you want to see in detailed columns. Everything aged past the Through number of days will be shown lumped together in the > (greater than) column. For example, by entering the number 10 in the Aging Interval text box, and 60 in the Through text box, QuickBooks will show an aging report with columns titled: Current, 1-10, 11-20, 21-30 ... 51-60, >60. The most common aging is 30 day interval through 90 days.

Viewing the Entire Report On-Screen

QuickBooks always sends a report to the screen. This enables you to peruse the report before you commit it to paper. To view a report on-screen, simply select the report from the menu. QuickBooks displays it for you. To view a report on-screen, follow these steps:

1. Choose **R**eports, **P**rofit&Loss, **S**tandard from the menu. QuickBooks displays the Profit and Loss statement for the current month-to-date.

2. Click the Maximize button in the upper-right corner of the Report window, or select the window control box by pressing the Alt, left-arrow, Enter keys and choosing Ma**x**imize from the menu.

   Figure 19.22 shows the maximized report. Chances are that the report still can't be completely seen on your monitor. Use the scroll bars on the right and bottom of your screen to view the rest of the report.

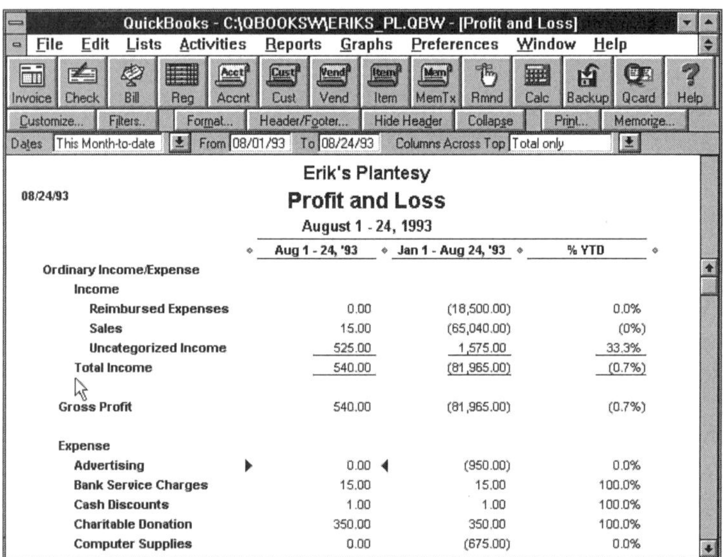

Fig. 19.22 The Profit and Loss Report, maximized.

3. Click the diamond-shaped handle that appears between columns and drag it to the left or right. Dragging to the left makes the column narrower, enabling you to display more information on a page of paper and on-screen.

Recalling a Memorized Report

Recalling a memorized report is only a few keystrokes away. Every time you memorize a report and name it, QuickBooks adds it to the Memorized Report List. When you need to recall a memorized report, follow these steps:

1. Choose **R**eport from the main menu.

2. Choose **M**emorized Reports. The Memorized Report List appears, as shown in figure 19.23.

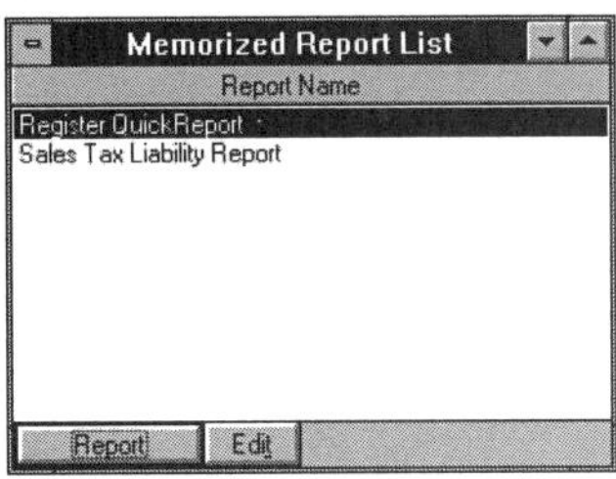

Fig. 19.23 The Memorized Reports List.

3. Select the report that you want to recall and click the Report button. QuickBooks creates and displays your memorized report.

Editing and Deleting Memorized Reports

If you use several memorized reports with very similar names, you can edit the report name or the report itself. To edit the report name, follow these steps:

1. Choose the Edi**t** button on the Memorized Report List, as described in the preceding steps 1 and 2.

2. Edit the report name displayed in the Memorized Report dialog box.

3. Click the OK button to save the report under the new name.

To edit the actual memorized report, follow these steps:

1. Open the Memorized Report List.

2. Select the report to be edited, and click the Report button.

3. Make the changes to the report that you require. You can change or add filters to restrict the report to fewer or more transactions, change the fonts or the report, or make any other change you may want.

4. Choose the Memori**z**e button from the button bar, or choose **E**dit, **M**emorize from the menu, or press Ctrl+M. The Memorize Report dialog box appears (see fig. 19.24).

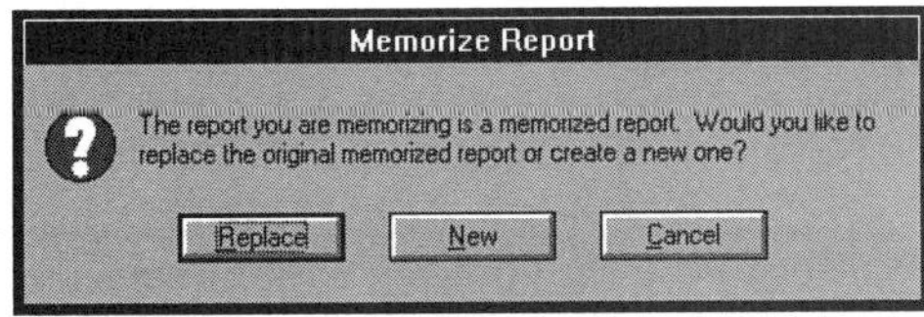

Fig. 19.24 The Memorize Report dialog box.

5. Choose the appropriate button. To replace the original memorized report with the edited version, choose **R**eplace. To save the edited report as a new memorized report, choose **N**ew, in which case QuickBooks displays the Memorize Report dialog box. Enter the new memorized report name here. Otherwise, choose the **C**ancel button and return to the report window.

Printing Reports

QuickBooks gives you many ways to print a report. A report can be printed on the selected report printer, if you need a hard copy of the report. You can also print a report to a disk file in one of three formats. This enables you to incorporate the report as part of another report or document. You can also print a report to your screen. This option enables you to view a report as it will appear on paper before you actually print it. This can help when you are not sure whether your column widths are correct, or with other potential spacing problems.

Before you can print a report to a printer, you must have selected a report printer. If you have not yet done so, follow these steps:

1. Choose **F**ile, Printer **S**etup, **R**eport/List Printer. The Report Printer Setup dialog box appears (see fig. 19.25).

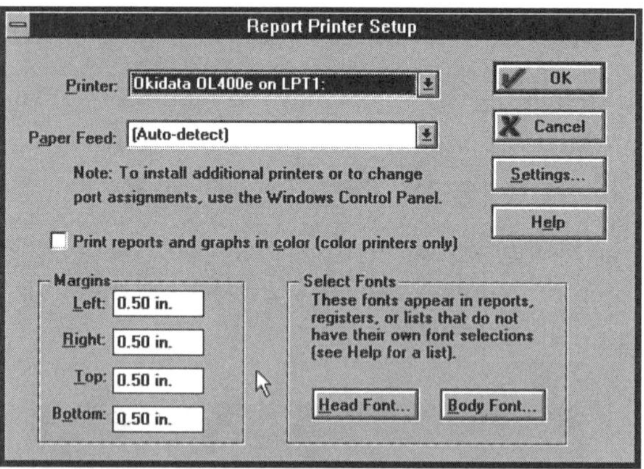

Fig. 19.25
The Report Printer Setup dialog box.

2. Choose the **P**rinter to use for your reports. Remember, you must have the printer driver installed in the Windows Control Panel before you can select it here.

3. Choose the P**a**per Feed. Generally the (Auto-Detect) option should work for your printer. You should only have to change this option to either Continuous or Page-Oriented if your printer is not completely supported by QuickBooks and Windows.

4. Check Print Reports And Graphs In **C**olor. (This option is available only if you have a printer that can print in color.)

5. Make any margin adjustments that you require.

6. Choose the **H**ead Font or the **B**ody Font button to change or set the default font for the Header or Body of a report. Choosing either button displays the Report Default Headline (or Body) Font dialog box (see fig. 19.26).

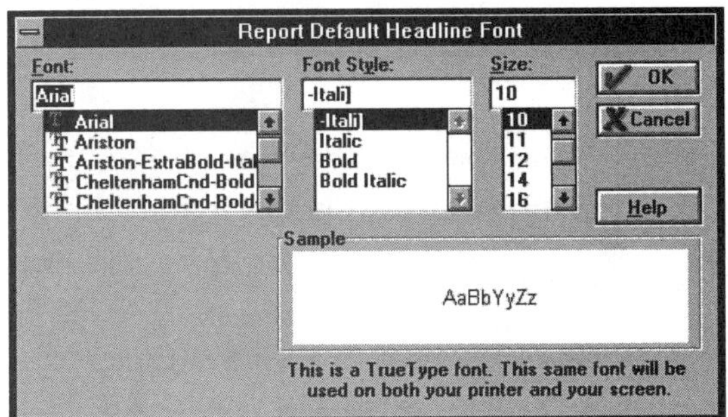

Fig. 19.26
The Report Default Headline Font dialog box.

7. Choose OK when you have made your choices. Your options for fonts may be different than those you see in figure 19.26.

8. Choose OK to save your report printer settings.

To print a report, you first must create the report. The report does not need to be displayed full-screen on your monitor; it can be a minimized report icon and still be available for printing. If you have more than one report displayed on-screen, you must select the report to be printed first by clicking it. To print a report, follow these steps:

1. Select the report to print. If you have several reports displayed as minimized icons, the selected report is the one with the box surrounding its name. If your reports are displayed full-screen, the top report is the selected report.

2. Choose **F**ile, **P**rint Report, or Ctrl+P, or, if the report is displayed in the report window, choose the Pri**n**t button. The Print Report dialog box appears (see fig. 19.27).

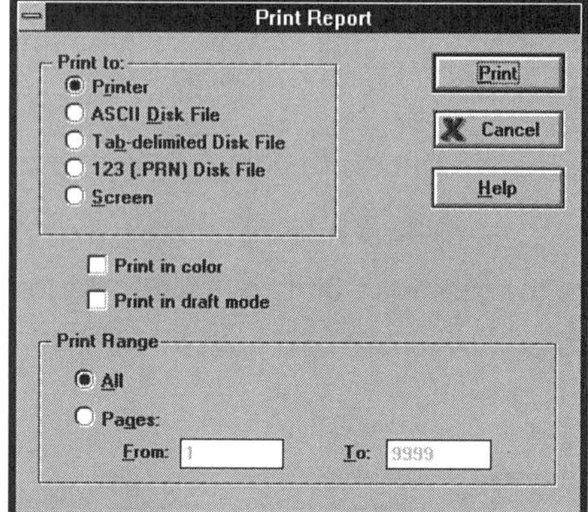

Fig. 19.27
The Print Report dialog box.

3. Choose how and where you want the report to print in the Print Report dialog box by selecting one of the options in the Print to box.

4. Choose the **P**rint button.

The Print Report dialog box has several options available:

- *Print To.* Includes a series of radio buttons telling QuickBooks where to print your report. These options are mutually exclusive; you can only select one:

  *P**r**inter.* Prints your report to the currently selected report printer.

  *ASCII **D**isk File.* Causes QuickBooks to create an ASCII text file from your report. Use this option if you plan to merge the report with another document. Any word processing program can read this file. Use a nonproportional type font to make your columns line up correctly.

  *Ta**b**-delimited Disk File.* Merges the report into a word processing software and uses proportional fonts. Columns are separated by tabs instead of spaces.

  123 (.PRN) Disk File. Merges the report into a spreadsheet program. This report type is also known as a comma-delimited text file. Columns are separated by commas; text is surrounded by quotes, while amounts are not.

Screen. Displays the report on-screen. You need to use the vertical and horizontal scroll bars to view the entire report.

- *Print in color*. Prints a report in color. This option works with a color-ready printer only.
- *Print in draft mode*. Allows a report to print more quickly, especially on a dot-matrix printer. Text is not as clear in draft mode as when using letter quality mode.
- *Print Range*. Allows you to select how much of a report to print by choosing one of the following options:

    All. Prints the entire report.

    Pages. Prints only a certain range of pages. Enter the page numbers in the **F**rom and **T**o text boxes.

If you have trouble with a report that does not fit on a standard 8 1/2-by-11-inch paper, try changing the body font for the report printer. Selecting a smaller font size helps to compress the information into a smaller area. After you change the font size, adjust the column widths for the report also.

Summary

In this chapter, you learned how to use QuickReport to view a report of transactions related to the selected name or item. You also learned about each of the preset reports that QuickBooks includes, and how to use the report button bar to customize, filter, and adjust the report settings. You also learned to create a memorized report from the customized report. Then you learned to recall, edit, and delete your memorized report. Finally, you learned to print a selected report to your printer or to a disk file.

In the next chapter, you learn to create graphs. You learn to use a graph to display information about your company, to customize the standard QuickBooks graphs, and to print the graphs on your printer.

Chapter 20

Creating Graphs

Graphs offer an excellent way to obtain an overall view of your financial picture. A quick glance at a meaningful graph can tell you more about what is happening with your company than can pouring over a report or an account register filled with figures.

Use a graph to show a summary of your financial information without displaying the details. A graph can be created for most types of financial data. Remember that a graph displays a picture about numeric information. You cannot create a meaningful graph, however, until you use QuickBooks long enough to create a base of information for a graph.

In this chapter, you learn to do following:

- Display a graph and learn about each graph type
- Create each of the types of graphs
- Customize a graph by using the button bar
- Print a graph

Overview of QuickBooks for Windows Graphs

QuickBooks displays two basic graph types for you: bar graphs and pie charts. A line graph displays the actual net worth amounts on the Net Worth Graph. Each graph appears in its own window, which is called QuickInsight.

If you display a graph, QuickBooks displays two graphs in the QuickInsight window, usually a bar graph at the top and a pie chart in the lower half of the window. The bar graph shows the item or items graphed, such as expenses, over a specified period of time. The pie chart then breaks out the various types of expenses during the specified period of time as slices of the pie.

Bar Graphs

QuickBooks uses bar graphs to show how an account changes over time. Figure 20.1 shows the Income and Expense bar graph, with income and expenses listed for each month for the year to date.

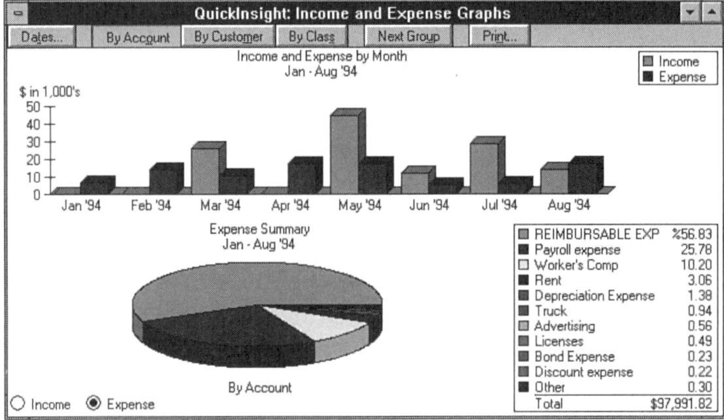

Fig. 20.1
The Income and Expense bar graph.

The bar graph best shows how a factor changes over time. The information in this graph can easily be compared with that of another factor graphed beside it, such as when income is compared to expenses. In a glance, you can see that January, February, and April produced little or no income and that May and July were very good months for cash inflows.

QuickBooks displays dollar amounts on the *Y-axis* (the vertical axis), and months, accounts, or other items on the *X-axis* (the horizontal axis) of the bar graph. The title of the graph and the date range covered by the graph appear at the top of the graph.

Pie Charts

Unlike bar graphs, pie charts do not display information over time; instead, they display a group of items as a percentage of their total. The title of the pie chart and the date range covered appears at the top of the chart, above the pie itself.

Pie charts are used by QuickBooks to show the relative percentage of an account or item to the total. If, for example, you have ten customers and one of these customers accounts for 25 percent of all your sales, the pie chart depicts this customer as a pie slice covering a quarter of the pie, while the remaining nine customers are divided among the pie's remaining 75 percent. Figure 20.2 shows the Sales Graphs and displays the pie chart for sales by sales representative for this quarter to date.

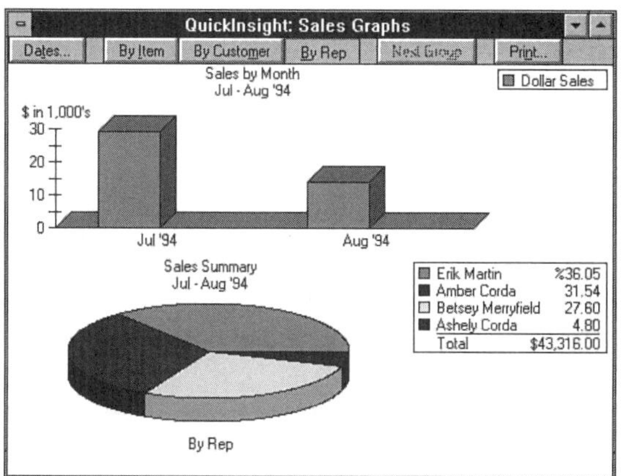

Fig. 20.2
The Sales Graph pie chart.

Other Graphs

QuickBooks uses a line-and-marker graph in the Net Worth graph. The line and markers are used to draw attention to a specific part of the graph: your net worth. This form of graph is also called a combination graph, because there are two types of graphs shown; bar, and the line and markers. Figure 20.3 shows the Net Worth graph.

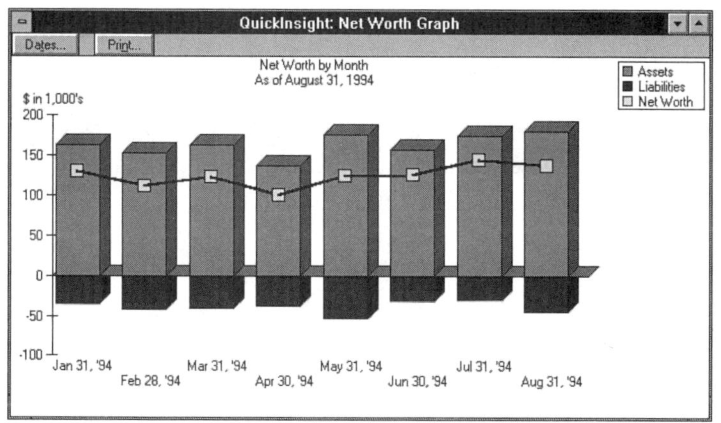

Fig. 20.3
The Net Worth Graph. Notice how the line graph stands out from the bar graph.

Creating Graphs

QuickBooks enables you to quickly and easily create a graph for certain financial information. All the various graph types are available from QuickBooks' **G**raphs menu. The following sections describe in detail each of these graph types.

Most graphs are based on year-to-date data. You can, however, change the date range that QuickBooks uses to display a graph. Generally, you do not want to include more than one year's information in a graph. Otherwise, the graph becomes too difficult to read and understand. Customizing graphs is discussed in the section, "Using the Button Bar To Customize Graphs."

Income and Expense Graphs

You may want to access QuickBooks' Income and Expense Graphs often in your business. In a glance, you can determine if you are meeting your expenses and approximately how much profit you are clearing. To create the Income and Expense Graphs, access the **G**raphs menu, and choose **I**ncome & Expenses. The QuickInsight window for Income and Expenses Graphs appears on-screen.

The bar graph portion of the Income and Expense Graphs, displayed in the upper half of the window, shows income in the left bar and expenses in the right bar. The default settings, as shown on the graph in figure 20.4, display your income and expenses for the year to date. The legend for the bar graph appears in the upper right-hand corner of the window.

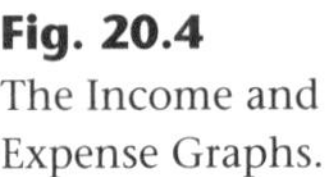

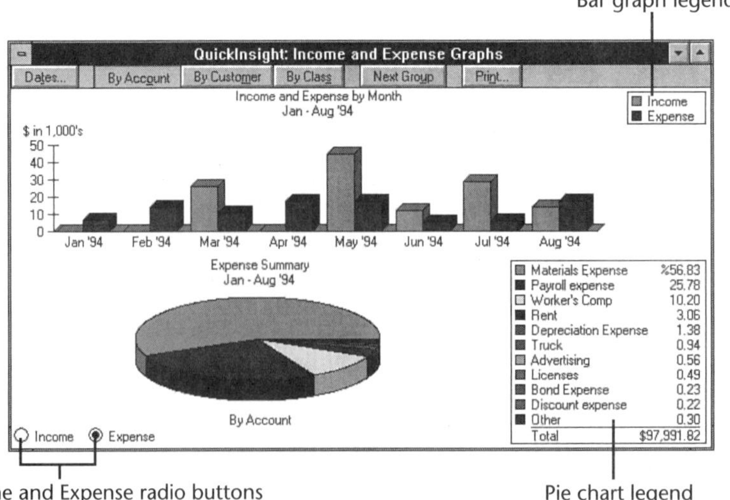

Fig. 20.4
The Income and Expense Graphs.

The pie chart, displayed in the lower half of the window, sums up all expenses over the same period of time used for the bar graph. Each Expense account is totaled for the period covered—in this case, the year to date—and appears in the pie chart as a percentage of the total. (Optionally, you can select the Income option button in the lower left-hand corner of the window to display a pie chart for the various Income accounts.)

The pie chart legend, to the right of the pie, displays the first ten largest accounts. If you have more than ten Expense accounts, the remaining, smaller accounts are lumped together in the Other group on the legend. The pie chart legend displays the color or pattern for each specific group, the name of the group represented by that color or pattern, and that group's actual percentage of the total. At the bottom of the legend, QuickBooks displays the total dollars graphed. Suppose, for example, that you incurred a total of $500 in expenses for the period graphed. This $500 is divided between four vendors: Vendor A, with $225; Vendor B, with $125; Vendor C, with $100; and Vendor D, with $50. The pie chart legend for these expenses displays the following breakdown:

Vendor A	%45.00
Vendor B	25.00
Vendor C	20.00
Vendor D	10.00
Total	$500.00

To view details of the Other group, choose the Next Gro**u**p button at the top of the window. QuickBooks reconstructs the pie chart, using only the accounts previously included in the Other group. Choose the First Gro**u**p button to change the graph back to its original configuration.

The window's button bar contain several buttons you can use to group the pie chart's information differently. The default option is By Acc**o**unt, as described earlier in this section.

Choose the By Custo**m**er button to view your expenses by those for each customer. This option can be helpful if you work on single customer:jobs and need to track expenses this way.

The By Clas**s** button breaks down the expenses of your customers by customer class. This option is available only if you use the Class option.

Sales Graphs

The Sales Graphs window shows the sales dollars earned during a month. This graph displays by default the year-to-date sales figures. To create the Sales graphs, open the **G**raphs menu, and choose **S**ales.

The bar graph portion of the Sales Graphs displays the sales dollars earned for each month for the year to date. The Sales Graphs, as shown in figure 20.5, can help you focus on just your sales figures. Notice that the Sales Graphs and the Income part of the Income and Expense Graphs look very similar. This is because the information for both graphs is gathered from the same place. By using this graph, however, you need not be distracted by expense information.

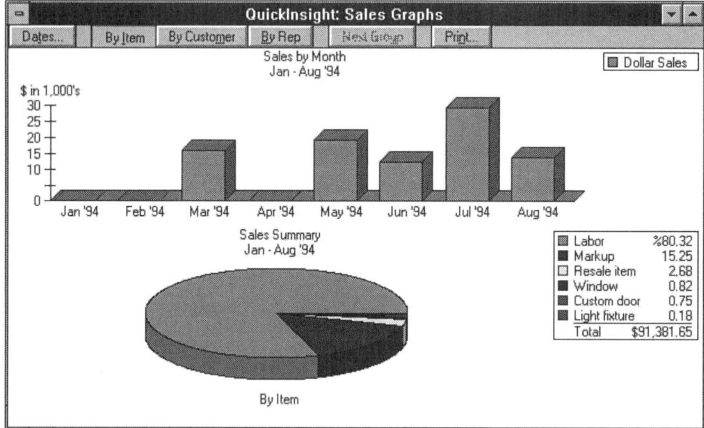

Fig. 20.5
The Sales Graphs window.

The pie chart part of the Sales Graphs also focuses on sales information alone. As shown in figure 20.5, the pie chart explains in a glance how your sales dollars came to you—in this case, by item. You can clearly see which item in your inventory brings you the greatest revenue. In the example in the figure, that item is Labor (80.32%).

You also can use this window's button bar to group your sales dollars differently. Choose the By Custo**m**er button to change the pie chart to show which customer has brought you the greatest amount of sales revenues. Remember, however, that only the largest ten customers appear; all others are grouped in the Other listing. This grouping choice can be especially helpful if you want to target some of your larger customers for a special sales promotion.

Choose the **B**y Rep button to display your sales dollars by sales representative. This representation can be useful in evaluating individual sales people. This option is not available, however, if you do not use the Product invoice type; only the Product invoice requires Rep information.

Accounts Receivable Graphs

The Accounts Receivable Graphs show you how well your customers are paying. As shown in the graph in figure 20.6, one or more of your customers are 31-60 days past terms. This should flag your immediate attention.

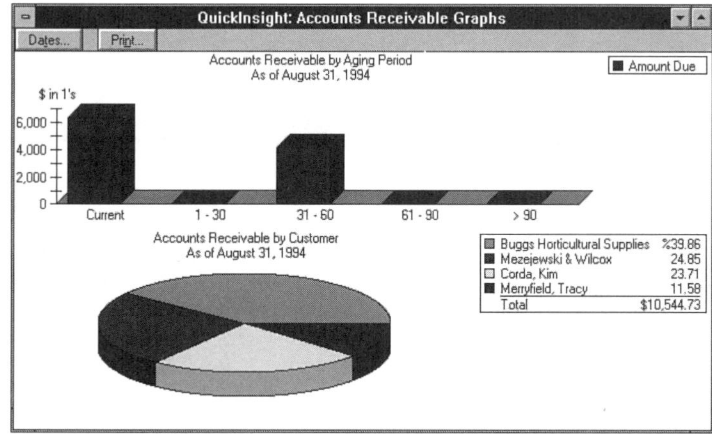

Fig. 20.6
The Accounts Receivable Graphs window.

The bar graph portion of the window displays the aging of your accounts receivable as of the current date. All currently outstanding invoices are aged at 30-day intervals. Everything more than 90 days past terms is placed in the >90 group.

The pie chart of the Accounts Receivable Graphs is grouped by customer. QuickBooks lists only the ten customers with the highest outstanding balances; all others are combined in the Others group. QuickBooks adds all invoices for each customer together to determine each customer's ranking on this list.

Accounts Payable Graphs

The Accounts Payable Graphs window shows you how well you pay your own bills. As shown in the example in figure 20.7, all your bills are current. This indicates good financial management on your part. If you are always current with your bills, you may want to make sure that your vendors give you the best terms possible, either by offering early payment discounts or by extending longer terms.

CPA TIP: Your Own Accounts Payable History

Whenever possible, try to leverage your good payment history with your vendors by asking for early payment discounts, or a larger discount on purchases, or extended terms. A customer who pays bills in a timely manner is always worth a great deal to a vendor. They may be willing to extend to you additional terms, discounts, and other inducements for your prompt payment history.

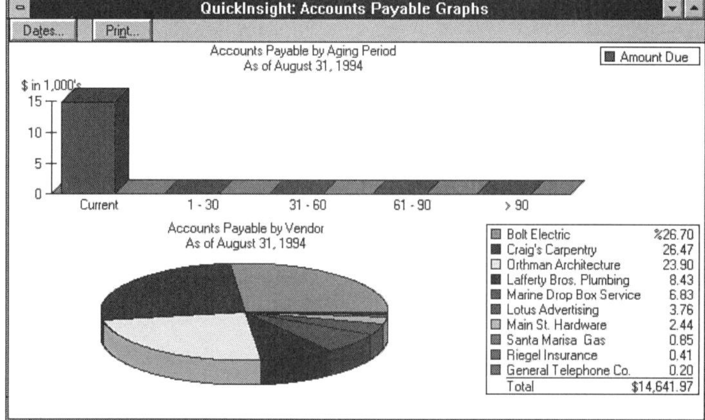

Fig. 20.7 The Accounts Payable Graphs window.

The bar graph portion presents the aging of your Accounts Payable as of the current date. All currently outstanding bills listed in the Accounts Payable are aged at 30-day intervals. All bills more than 90 days past terms are placed in the >90 group.

The pie chart of the Accounts Payable Graphs window is grouped by vendors. The ten vendors with whom you have the highest outstanding balances are listed individually, while all others are combined in the Others group. All your invoices for a particular vendor are added together to determine that vendor's ranking.

Net Worth Graph

The Net Worth Graph window contains a combination bar/line-and-marker graph only—no pie chart appears in the window. Assets appear as positive dollar amounts on the graph, while liabilities are shown as negative dollar amounts. The total net worth, or *equity*, is shown as a marker on each bar, and each marker is connected to create a line graph. The marker point is the point that equals assets less liabilities. If your business is successful, this point is somewhere on the asset bar and not on the liability bar. Figure 20.8 shows the Net Worth Graph.

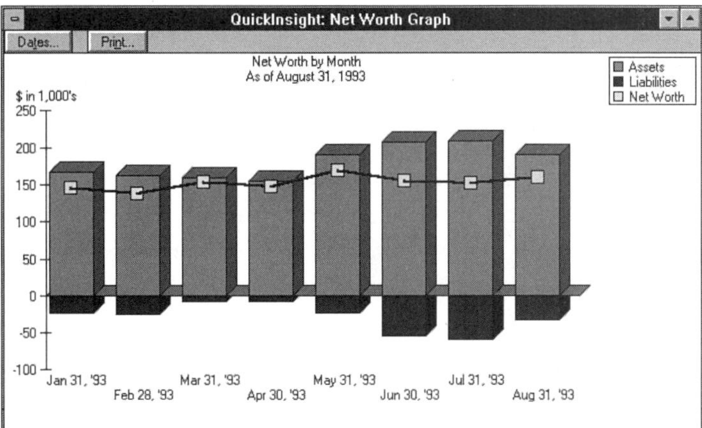

Fig. 20.8
The Net Worth Graph window.

Budget vs. Actual Graphs

The Budget vs. Actual Graphs is the final type of graphs you can create in QuickBooks. Before you can use these graphs, however, you must create a budget for your accounts, as described in Chapter 18, "Preparing Budgets."

The top bar graph in the Budget vs. Actual Graphs window shows your income—budgeted vs. actual—for the year to date. QuickBooks shows you how much your income is over or under budget for the year. This graph is created by subtracting from your actual net income for a month the month's budgeted net income. A favorable result is shown by these graphs if you earn more than you budgeted. Figure 20.9 shows the Budget vs. Actual Graphs window.

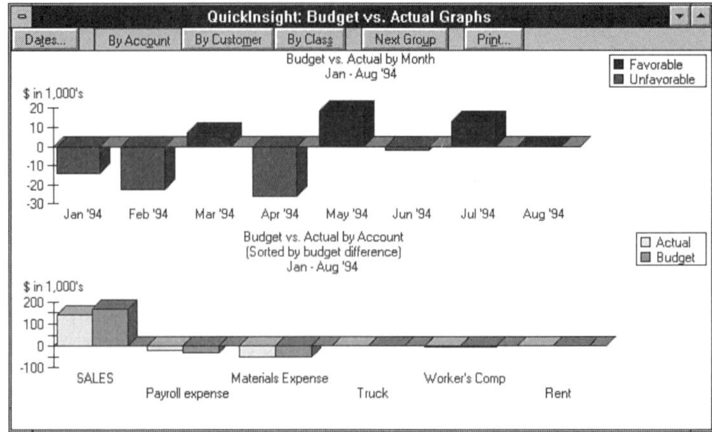

Fig. 20.9
The Budget vs. Actual Graphs window.

The second bar graph in this window shows the six Income or Expense accounts that are farthest from your budget during the period of time covered by the first graph. The accounts you are most likely to see in this group are your largest Income and Expense accounts, as well as any account encompassing a variable component (such as utilities, overtime wages, gasoline expenses, and so on). Sales and other Income accounts are almost always in this group, because they can be variable and have a sizable amount of dollars flowing through them. Your Sales account, therefore, is the most difficult account for which to create an accurate budget. Your fixed Expense accounts, on the other hand, should never appear on this graph—unless something unforeseen occurs.

The lower graph is grouped so that the account displaying the greatest variance between actual amounts and budgeted amounts appears first. The next account shows the second-greatest variance, followed by the one showing the third-greatest, and so on, going down the line to the account with the least variance. Income accounts appear above the X-axis, while Expense accounts are displayed below the X-axis.

You also can group the graph differently by choosing either the By Custo**m**ers or the By Clas**s** button. Remember, however, that you must actually create a budget for a Customer:Job or a Class before you can create a meaningful graph. Budgets were discussed in Chapter 18, "Preparing Budgets."

Using the Button Bar To Customize Graphs

As you work with each type of graph, you see and use that graph's *button bar*. The options available in these button bars vary from graph to graph, with two exceptions: the Da**t**es and Pri**n**t buttons. These two buttons appear in all graph windows. All the other buttons on these graph button bars, as described in the preceding section, enable you to either choose or group different information in the bottom graph.

By choosing the Da**t**es button, you can change the date range for the graphed information. For most of the graphs, the default date range is `This Year-to-date`. To change the graph date range, follow these steps:

1. In any graphs window, choose the Da**t**es button. The Change Graph Dates dialog box appears, as shown in figure 20.10.

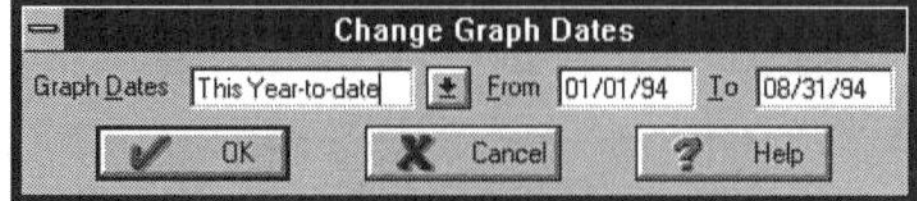

Fig. 20.10
The Change Graph Dates dialog box.

2. Choose the Graph **D**ates text box to change the default date setting.

3. Click the down-arrow button, press Alt+down-arrow, or press Ctrl+L to display the Graph **D**ates drop-down list, as shown in figure 20.11. Use the scroll bar or down-arrow key as necessary to view any options not currently visible in the drop-down list.

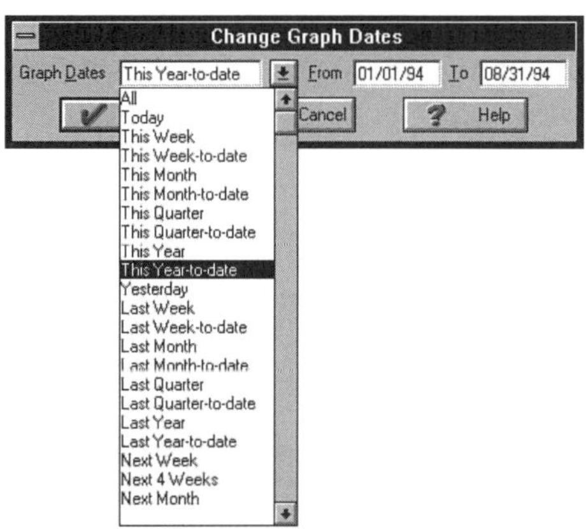

Fig. 20.11
The Graph **D**ates drop-down list, from which you can select a new default date.

4. Select an option from the drop-down list by clicking it with the mouse or highlighting the option and pressing Enter.

   If you select the Custom option from the drop-down list, you must enter the required date range in the **F**rom and **T**o text boxes to the right of the drop-down list box. Type the beginning date in the **F**rom text box and the ending date in the **T**o text box.

5. Choose OK to confirm your new date range setting; QuickBooks creates a new graph using the selected date range.

   Choose Cancel if you decide to make no changes (or change your mind about any you do make). QuickBooks returns to the original graph.

You also can change the graph display by using the **P**references menu. To change the graph display, follow these steps:

1. From the **G**raphs menu, choose **P**references. The Graph Preferences dialog box appears, as shown in figure 20.12.

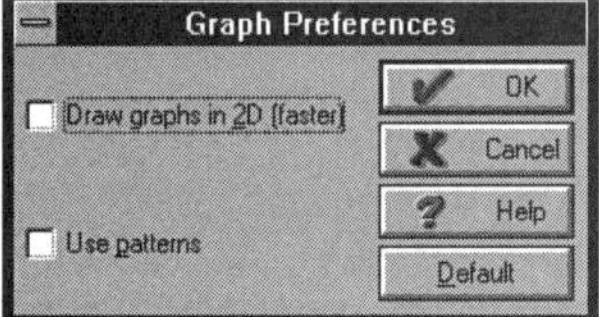

Fig. 20.12
The Graph Preferences dialog box.

   The Graph Preferences dialog box contains two check boxes. You can select either or both options.

2. Select the Draw Graphs in **2**D (Faster) check box to instruct QuickBooks to draw the graphs in a two-dimensional view instead of the three-dimensional view shown in the previous figures. On some computers, selecting this option redraws graphs on-screen much faster than if you use the three-dimensional view. Figure 20.13 shows a two-dimensional graph.

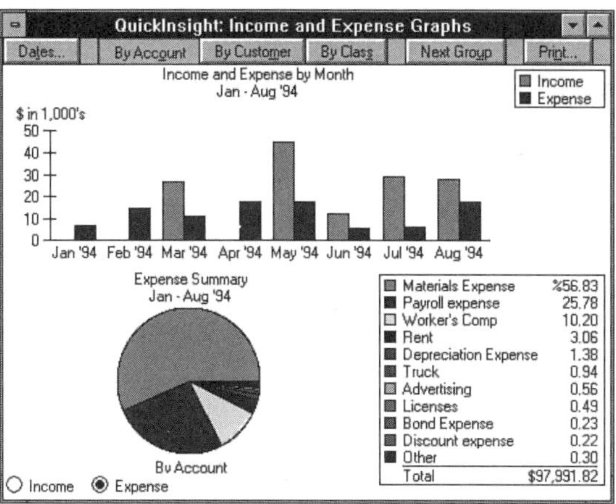

Fig. 20.13
The Income and Expense Graphs redrawn on-screen in two-dimensional view.

3. Select the Use **P**atterns check box to use various patterns instead of color to display different graph segments. If you do use a color printer to print your graph, you may be able to print the graph better by using patterns instead of shades of gray. Figure 20.14 shows the same graph with the Use **P**atterns option selected instead of the **2**D option.

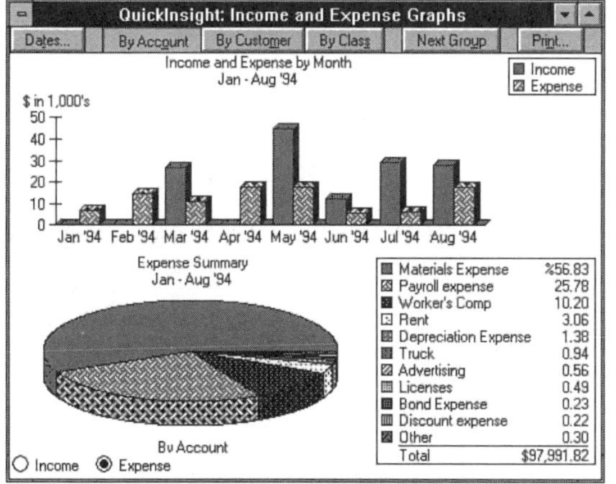

Fig. 20.14
The Income and Expense Graphs redrawn in three-dimensional view using patterns instead of colors.

4. Choose OK to redraw the graph using your selected options.

All changes you make in the Graph Preferences window become the default options used for all your QuickBooks companies.

Examining Graph Detail by Using QuickZoom

As you use your own graphs and try out the different options, you may notice the QuickZoom magnifying glass. The mouse pointer changes to this QuickZoom lens as you pass over a part of the graph that displays information in some form—graph or legend. Whenever the QuickZoom pointer appears over an item, double-click the mouse to display a detailed graph about that specific item.

To use QuickZoom in a graph window, follow these steps:

1. Open a graph window. (For example, the Sales Growth window by selecting **G**raphs, **S**ales from the menu.)

2. Move the cursor to one of the bars of the Sales by Month graph, at the top of the window, and double-click the mouse. The QuickZoom Graph window appears, containing a pie chart representing the selected bar, as shown in figure 20.15.

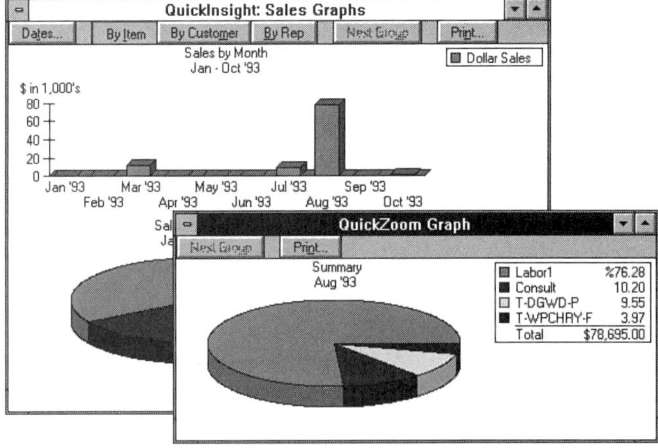

Fig. 20.15
The QuickZoom Graph window displaying a detailed pie chart about a selected bar segment.

3. View additional details about a particular summary segment displayed in the QuickZoom Graph window by double-clicking the segment. The transactions summarized by the graph appear in a report window.

4. Close the QuickZoom Graph by opening the window's Control menu and choosing **C**lose or by pressing Alt+F4.

5. Move the cursor over one of the pie chart slices in the lower area of the Sales Graphs window, and double-click. The QuickZoom Graph reappears, now displaying a detailed bar graph about the selected pie slice, as shown in figure 20.16.

6. Close the QuickZoom Graph Window as you did in step 3.

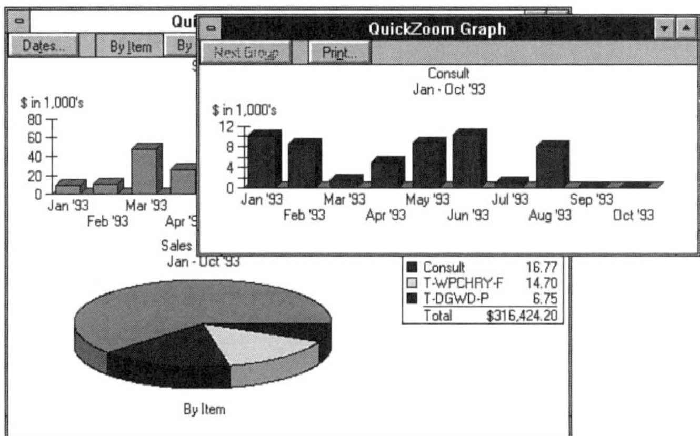

Fig. 20.16
The QuickZoom Graph window, now showing a detailed bar graph about a selected pie chart slice.

QuickZoom always displays a detailed pie chart from a bar graph and a detailed bar graph from a pie chart. You also can use QuickZoom to display a transaction report from the QuickZoom Graph window. From that transaction report, you can select an item and display it in its original window (such as the Create Invoice or Pay Bill window) by using the QuickZoom feature.

You also can display the exact number that makes up a pie slice or a bar segment. To display the exact number of a graph segment, follow these steps:

1. Move the cursor to the segment in question.

2. Click the right mouse button after the QuickZoom magnifying glass appears. The number, or *data label*, that makes up the segment is displayed in a text box beside the mouse pointer.

You also can hide selected pie chart or bar graph segments. This can be helpful if you do not want to display an item or if a single item is overwhelming other data. (Data can be overwhelmed by a single piece that is disproportionately large compared to that of the other data.) In the Expense Summary pie chart of the Sales Graphs window shown in figure 20.14, for example, the Materials Expense slice is 56.83 percent of the chart. This item is so disproportionately large compared to the other pieces that the smaller items are lost in the pie chart.

To hide a segment of a pie chart and a bar graph, follow these steps:

1. Move the cursor to the pie segment to be hidden.

2. Press and hold Shift, and then click the left mouse button.

   As shown in figure 20.17, the Materials Expense pie slice is now hidden. QuickBooks recalculates the legend percentages based on the hidden expense (or other item) not included; the percentage calculation excludes the hidden item, and QuickBooks displays the new total at the bottom of the legend.

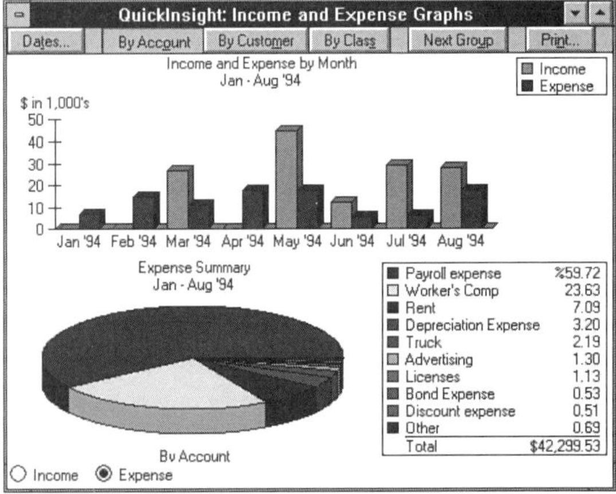

Fig. 20.17 The Income and Expense Graphs window, with the Materials Expense data hidden from the pie chart.

3. Select a bar segment from the bar graph.

4. Press and hold Shift, and then click the left mouse button.

   The graph is now displayed as shown in figure 20.18. The month selected is removed from the bar graph. Unlike on the pie chart, where the other segments fill in the missing space, the bar graph leaves the X-axis marker (the month) in place and simply removes the bar segments.

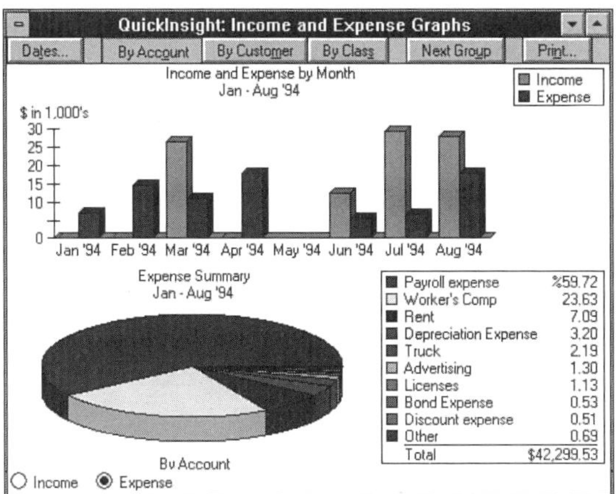

Fig. 20.18
The Income and Expense Graphs window, with the bar segments for May hidden.

5. To redisplay the hidden segments, close the graph window, and then re-create the graph by selecting from the menu again.

Printing Graphs

You also can print any graph you create. QuickBooks uses the printer selected for reports to print a graph. To print a graph, follow these steps:

1. Create the graph that you want to print, as described earlier in this chapter.

2. Choose the Pri**n**t button on the graph button bar, or press Ctrl+P. QuickBooks immediately sends the graph to the printer.

If you have a color printer and want to print a graph in color, follow these steps:

1. Check in the Windows Control Panel to make sure that your color printer is set up correctly. (If you have previously printed color pictures or reports from Windows, your printer is correctly set up and you can skip this step.)

2. Choose **F**ile, Printer **S**etup, **R**eport/List Printer from the menu. You will now see the Report Printer Setup dialog box.

3. In the printer option area of the dialog box, select the check box Print Reports and Graphs in **C**olor.

4. Choose OK to save these settings. Your graph now prints in color.

Summary

In this chapter, you learned about QuickBooks graphs and how to create them. You also learned how to use the graphs window button bar, how to hide graph segments, and how to use QuickZoom to display details about a graph segment. Finally, you learned to print a graph.

In the next chapter, you learn how to manage QuickBooks files—specifically, how to add, close, change, delete, and back up company files. You then learn how to rebuild a damaged file, how to import and export data, and how to assign passwords.

Part VI

Managing QuickBooks

21 Managing QuickBooks for Windows Files

22 Customizing QuickBooks for Windows

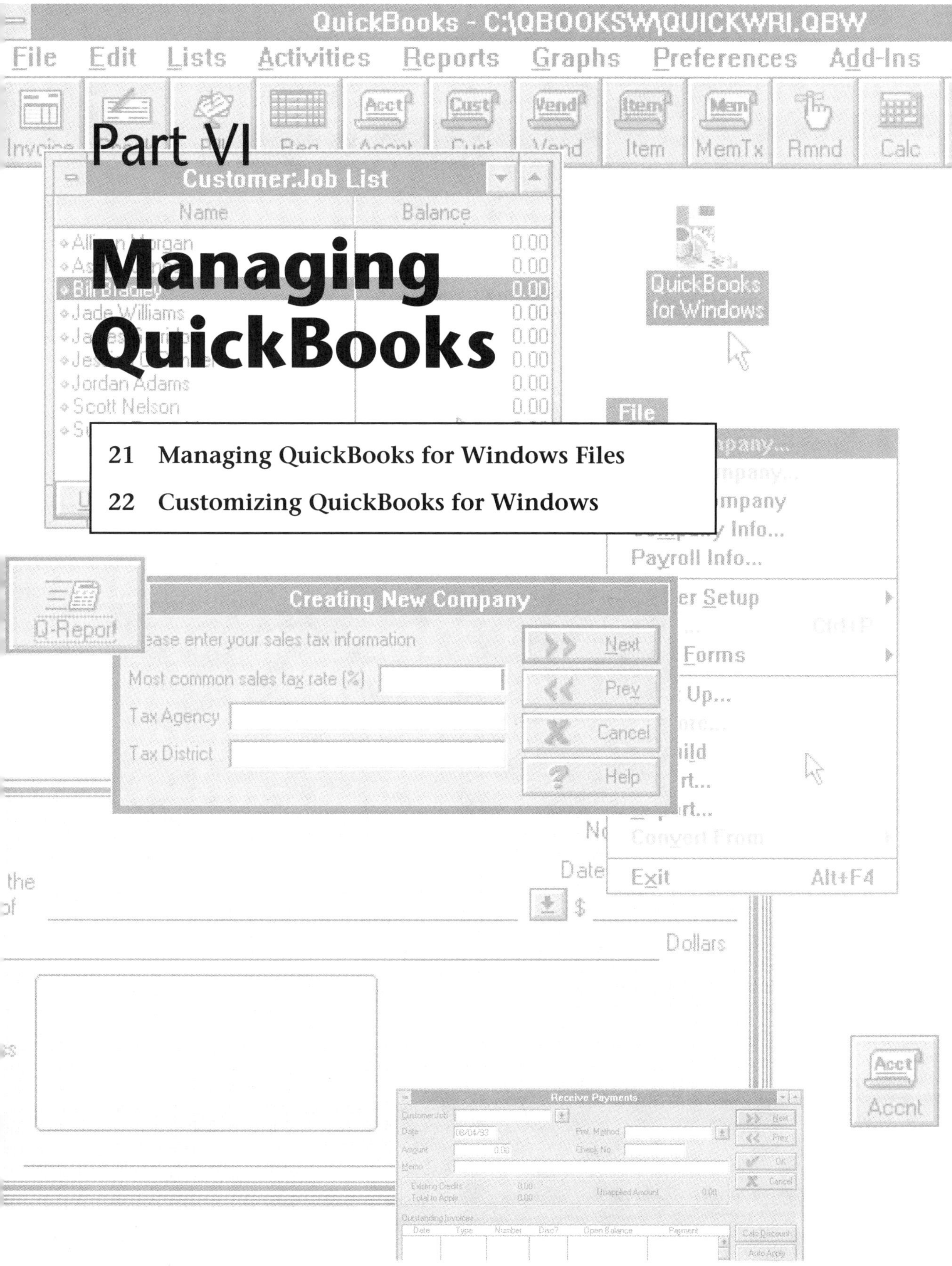

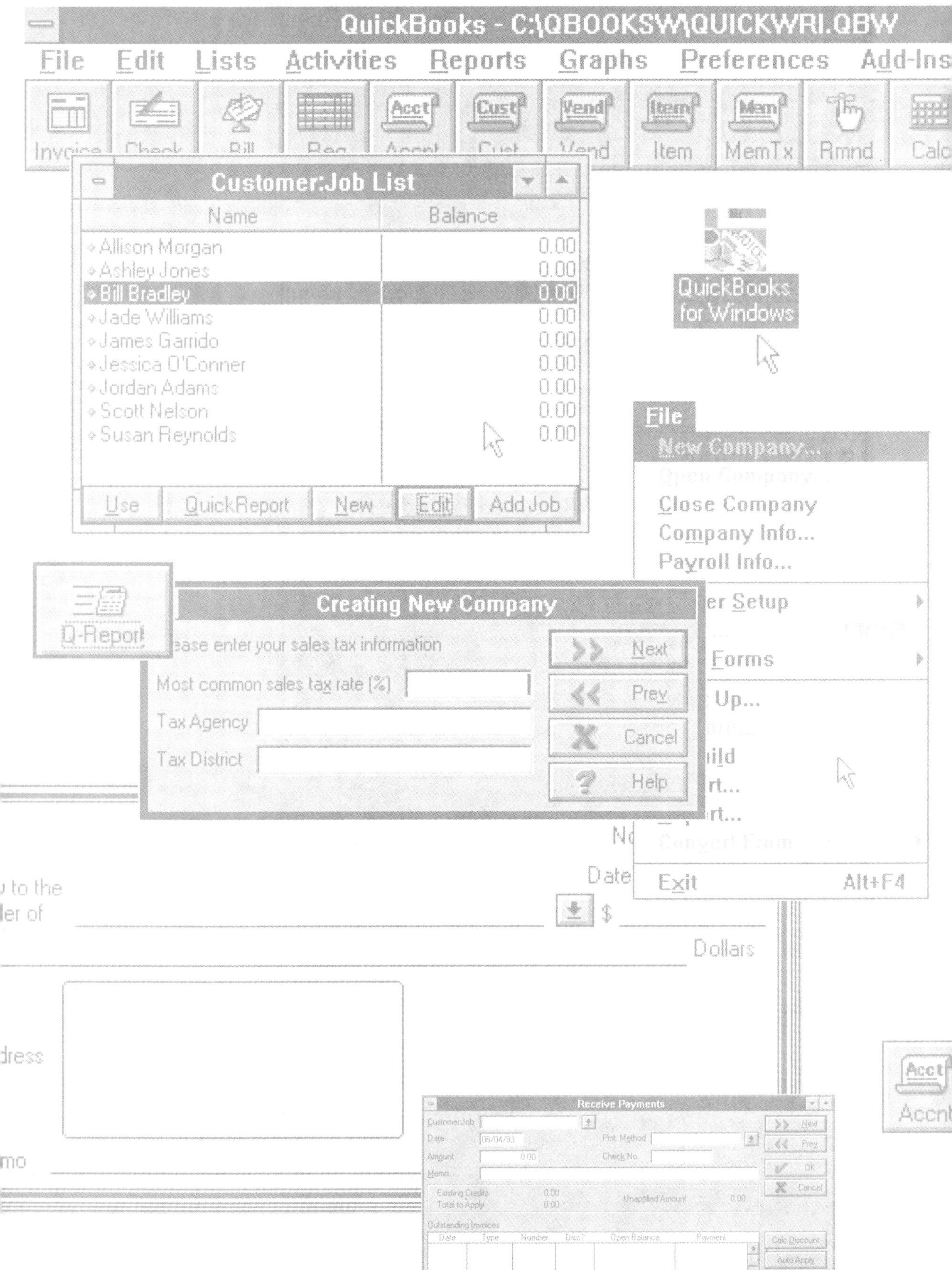

QuickBooks - C:\QBOOKSW\QUICKWRI.QBW
File Edit Lists Activities Reports Graphs Preferences Add-Ins
Invoice Check Bill Reg Accnt Cust Vend Item MemTx Rmnd Calc
Customer:Job List
Name Balance
Allison Morgan 0.00
Ashley Jones 0.00
Bill Bradley 0.00
Jade Williams 0.00
James Garrido 0.00
Jessica O'Conner 0.00
Jordan Adams 0.00
Scott Nelson 0.00
Susan Reynolds 0.00
Use QuickReport New Edit Add Job
QuickBooks for Windows
File
New Company...
Close Company
Company Info...
Payroll Info...
Exit Alt+F4
Q-Report
Creating New Company
Most common sales tax rate (%)
Tax Agency
Tax District
Next
Prev
Cancel
Help
Dollars
Receive Payments
Acct
Accnt

Chapter 21

Managing QuickBooks for Windows Files

Throughout this book, you have worked with a single QuickBooks company file. With QuickBooks, you can create additional companies so that you can maintain separate books for more than one enterprise. With multiple company files in your QuickBooks system, you can work with several companies. You can only have a single company file open at any one time.

When you create your first company, QuickBooks asks you for the name of the company. QuickBooks then assigns the company a valid DOS file name based on the company name that you entered. All QuickBooks companies use the file extension QBW. The QuickBooks company data file contains all the transactions for the company and each of the preference choices that you made from the lower half of the **P**references menu. QuickBooks keeps all the company data files in the QuickBooks directory, (C:\QBOOKSW), unless you specify a different location during the installation procedure.

Before you go much further using QuickBooks with your own company and financial information, you need to understand the importance of backing up your company files. Although you may be a careful computer user, everyone loses data at one time or another. Avoid losing important financial data by backing up your files regularly. Read the section on backing up your company files later in this chapter.

Any time you deal with financial information, it's essential that you maintain the information's integrity from unauthorized entry. Using passwords in QuickBooks enables you to control the access or to restrict certain activities to specified users of your company files.

In this chapter, you learn how to do the following:

- Add a new company file
- Open and close company files
- Back up and restore company data files
- Rebuild a company file
- Import and export data
- Use passwords to specify access

Adding Company Files

In Chapter 3, "Setting Up Your Company in QuickBooks for Windows," you learned how to add your company to QuickBooks. You use the same procedure to add another company to your QuickBooks system. When you add a new company, QuickBooks creates a file name for the company based on the name that you give to the company, and adds the company to your QuickBooks directory. You can enter your own name for the company file if you so choose. When you open a QuickBooks company the next time, the new company is added to your list.

To add a new company file, follow these steps:

1. Close the current company file, if you currently have it open. Choose **F**ile, **C**lose. QuickBooks quickly verifies the company data and then exits the company file. The Iconbar is removed, leaving only the menu.
2. Choose **F**ile, **N**ew Company. QuickBooks displays the Creating New Company dialog box shown in figure 21.1.

Fig. 21.1
The Creating New Company dialog box. Use this dialog box to add another company to your QuickBooks system.

3. Enter the Na**m**e for your new company.
4. Type the address for the company. As you learned, you can print this address on your invoices, checks, and other reports.
5. Use the drop-down list, or type the first month in the First Month in Your Fiscal Year text box. January is the default selection. In figure 21.2, you see the completed information for the new company.

Fig. 21.2
The completed information for the new company to be added to your QuickBooks system.

6. Choose the **N**ext button to display the next Creating New Company dialog box.

7. Select the Invoice type that you want to use for this company: **S**ervice, **P**rofessional, or Pro**d**uct. Choose the **N**ext button to continue. The next Creating New Company dialog box appears.

8. Choose the **Y**es button if this business must charge sales tax for its goods or services and continue to step 9. If not, choose the **N**o button and go to step 10.

9. Enter the required sales tax information in the next Creating New Company dialog box. Enter the tax rate that you commonly use in the Most Common Sales Ta**x** Rate (%) text box. For example, type **6.5** if you collect a 6.5% sales tax. Type the name of the Tax Agency and Tax District in the appropriate text boxes, if applicable. Choose the **N**ext button to move to the next Creating New Company dialog box, and continue to step 10.

10. Choose the company type that most closely matches the company you are adding. Even if none of the choices seem to be close, select either Service Business or Retail to start setting up the company accounts. It is much easier to change a few account names, and add or delete a few others than to create an entire set of accounts.

11. Choose **N**ext. QuickBooks displays the New Company Summary dialog box shown in figure 21.3. If the information is correct, choose OK.

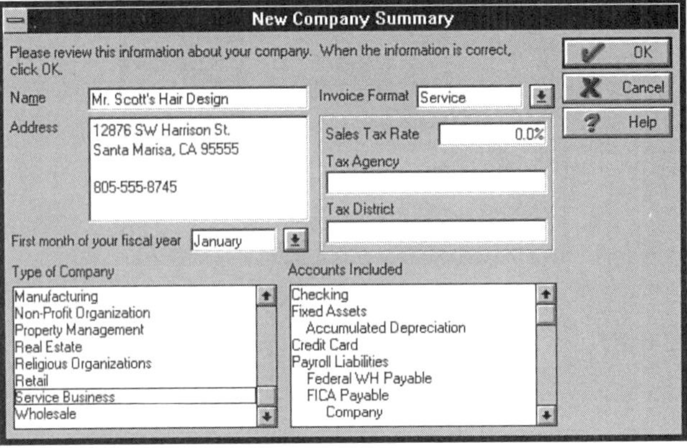

Fig. 21.3
The New Company Summary dialog box.

You can make any last minute changes to the information, if needed. Just move the cursor to the information you want to change, and type the correct information.

When you choose OK in step 10, QuickBooks displays the Filename for New Company dialog box, shown in figure 21.4.

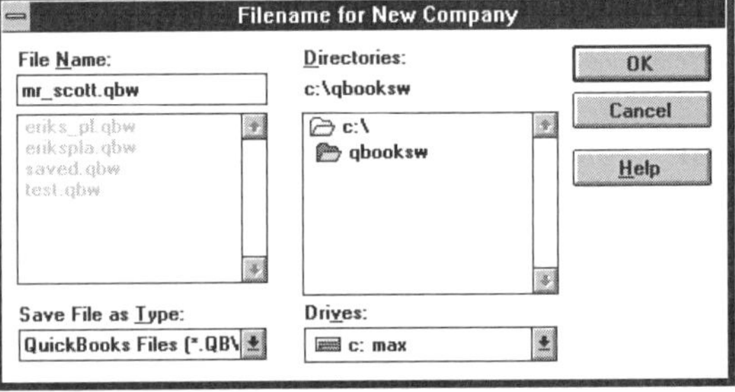

Fig. 21.4
The Filename for New Company dialog box.

QuickBooks automatically creates a valid DOS file name by using the first eight letters of the company name you entered. If you used a space in the first eight letters, QuickBooks replaces it with an underscore (_). If you used a reserved DOS character—such as a period, slash, backslash, question mark, or asterisk—in the name, QuickBooks does not include the character in the file name.

12. Choose OK if the file name is acceptable to you. You can change the file name by moving the cursor to the left side of the period. In figure 21.3, the period is located between the *t* and *q*. Do not change the file name extension, QBW, or QuickBooks will not be able to find your data file.

QuickBooks creates the data files, sets up the accounts that you specified, and then opens the company file on-screen.

Opening a Company File

After you create a company in your QuickBooks system, you can open that company and use it at any time. Remember, you can only have one company open at a time. To open a company file, follow these steps:

1. Choose **F**ile, **O**pen Company. If this option is dimmed and can't be selected, you must choose the **F**ile, **C**lose command to close the company file that is currently open.

   You can always quickly tell whether a company file is open. The Iconbar appears, and the company file name is listed in the title bar of the QuickBooks dialog box.

2. Select the company file name from the Open a Company dialog box, displayed in figure 21.5.

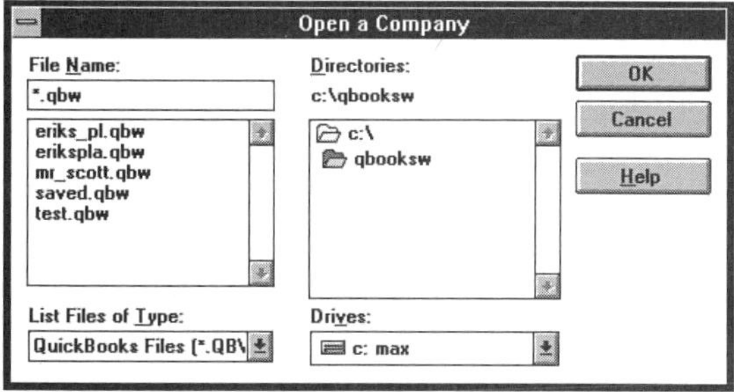

Fig. 21.5
Use the Open a Company dialog box to select the QuickBooks company file.

   The Open a Company dialog box is a standard Windows file management window. The company files that you created should be listed in the file window on the left hand side, underneath the File **N**ame text box.

   If you see the name of the company that you want to open listed in this dialog box, either double-click the name with the mouse, or press the Tab key once. This activates the file name window. Use the up- or down-arrow keys to highlight the company file name and press Enter.

The file name window contains a scroll bar you can use if you do not see the file you are looking for. If you still can't find the file that you are looking for, you may have placed it in a different directory than the one that you are currently looking in. Use the **D**irectories window to search other directories.

Closing a Company File

When you finish work in your QuickBooks company, close the file. When you close a file, QuickBooks verifies the data integrity, and saves all your transactions. Your data is now safe from a power failure and other disasters that affect your computer's RAM, or temporary memory. Closing a company file does not protect you from a hard drive failure or tampering. Only regular backups, battery backup units, and passwords protect you from these disasters.

To close your QuickBooks company files, simply choose **F**ile, **C**lose Company.

On the **F**ile menu, you may have also noticed the E**x**it option. This option is used to exit from the QuickBooks program. All of your company data is also saved at this time, too.

When you close your company file, QuickBooks remains open. You can then open another company file.

Backing Up and Restoring Company Files

Developing a routine for backing up your company data files is essential when you work with financial data. After you make the final conversion from a manual bookkeeping system with its attendant paper files to your electronic QuickBooks system, you must keep backups of this data. A power failure or hardware malfunction can cause loss or damage to your QuickBooks company files. Therefore, protect yourself from losing data by backing up your QuickBooks company files frequently. Without a current backup, you could lose months worth of information.

If your business processes many transactions a day, the loss of several days of data can cause you to lose thousands of dollars because of the cost of rebuilding your data. This assumes that you have a paper copy of all your transactions so that you can recover your data using that copy.

Part of the process of automating your company system involves setting up a backup procedure. This task can be as simple as assigning someone to create a backup copy of your QuickBooks company files on a floppy disk once a week or every day. Depending on the value that you place on your data, keeping an additional backup copy somewhere off your business premises is highly recommended. Accidents can happen, and you can't recover data from a floppy disk melted in a fire, for instance.

You may want to consider purchasing two additional hardware items that can prevent data loss: a tape drive with automatic backup software, and a battery backup unit.

Backing Up a File

QuickBooks contains its own simple procedure to back up a company data file. The QuickBooks backup does not merely copy the company file to another place. QuickBooks compresses the data into a much more compact file.

To back up your QuickBooks company files, follow these steps:

1. Choose **F**ile, **B**ack Up. QuickBooks displays the Backup Company To dialog box shown in figure 21.6.

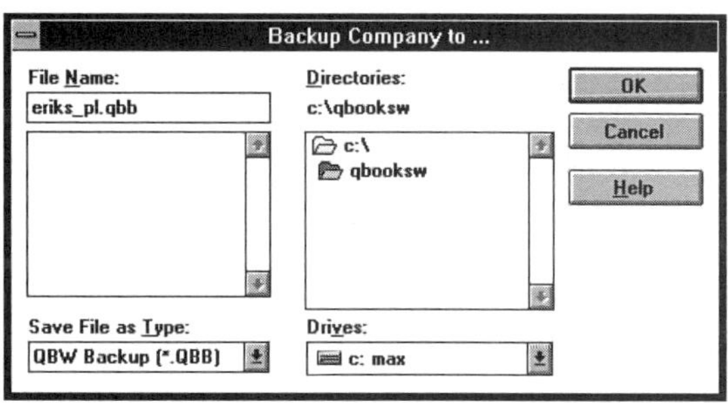

Fig. 21.6
The Backup Company to dialog box.

QuickBooks enters a file name for the backup file. By default, QuickBooks uses the same name as the company that you are backing up. QuickBooks uses the file extension QBB to indicate that this file is a backup.

2. Type a different backup file name if required. Generally, use the name that QuickBooks has entered. If you make backups of your files every day, you may want to incorporate the date, or day of the week in the file name.

   A common backup scheme calls for you to keep at least three consecutive backups available. These backups are called the Grandfather, Father, and Son backups. The oldest backup is the Grandfather, while the newest is the Son. By giving consecutive backups slightly different names, you can be sure that QuickBooks will not overwrite the previous backup information. Overwriting may never happen to you, but it is possible for an intermittent computer problem to cause a backup file to not be created completely, or to be created with bad data. If this happens, you may have to go back to one of the previous backups, the Father or Grandfather, for your backup data. While this information is not as current as a new backup, it is much better than nothing if your backup file is also damaged.

3. Select the **D**irectories option to place your backup files in the correct directory, if you use a separate backup directory.

4. Choose the Dri**v**es option to back your files up on a floppy drive or another hard drive.

   If you choose a floppy drive, be sure that you have a blank, formatted disk inserted in the drive.

5. Choose OK button to begin the backup process. QuickBooks automatically verifies your data, and then backs up your file.

   When QuickBooks finishes backing up your data, a message window tells you that the backup was successful.

To back up another company file, close the current company and open the next. Then repeat steps 1 through 5.

Restoring a File

If your QuickBooks company file becomes damaged for some reason, you need to restore your backup file. Because QuickBooks uses a proprietary backup format, only QuickBooks can restore the file.

If your hard drive fails, you must first reinstall QuickBooks from your original or backup program disks. To restore a backup file, follow these steps:

1. Close the current open company file.
2. Choose **F**ile, **R**estore. QuickBooks displays the Name of File to Restore dialog box, as shown in figure 21.7.

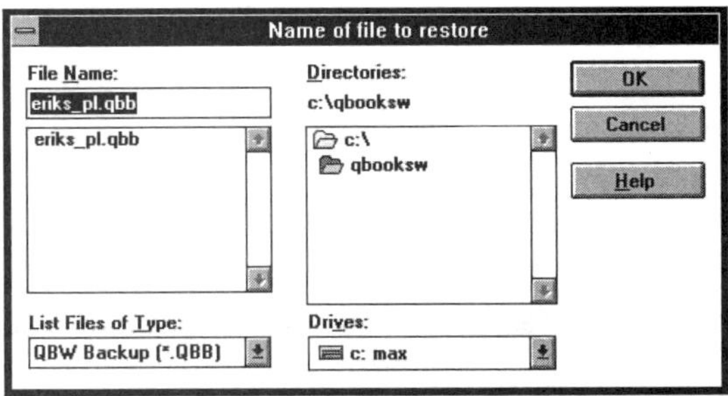

Fig. 21.7
The Name of File to Restore dialog box.

3. Select the file name of the company to be restored.
4. Choose OK. QuickBooks displays the Name Restored File dialog box, shown in figure 21.8.

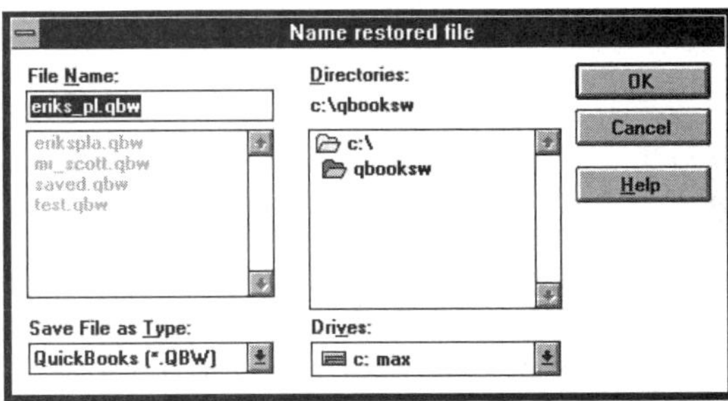

Fig. 21.8
The Name Restored File dialog box.

QuickBooks routinely uses the same name as that of the backup file, changing only the file extension from QBB to QBW. If QuickBooks finds a file with the same name, such as the original damaged file, QuickBooks asks you whether you want to replace the existing file. Choose Yes to restore the backup file over the old file. Choose No to return to the Name Restored File dialog box. Enter a new name for QuickBooks to use for the restored file.

Caution

If you are not sure that the original file is damaged, be sure to rename the restored backup file as noted in step 4. If you restore a damaged file by using the same file name, you will have no chance of recovering any of the original information.

5. Choose OK. QuickBooks restores the file.

Using the Utilities

At times, a database program such as QuickBooks can appear to lose information. This can be caused by a damaged file, a malfunctioning hard drive, a power surge, or many other factors. QuickBooks includes two maintenance functions: **V**erify Data and **R**ebuild.

Rebuilding a Company File

You can use the Rebuild command to readjust, or rebuild, the files and their data structure, possibly recovering all your information. If your company file seems to respond in unpredictable ways, try rebuilding your file. If this doesn't help, restore the file.

To rebuild a file, follow these steps:

1. Open the file that needs to be rebuilt. Be sure that all windows are closed and the desktop empty.
2. Choose **F**ile, **U**tilities Rebuild.

An information dialog box appears, informing you that you must make a backup copy of your file before you can use the **R**ebuild function. Choose OK. QuickBooks displays the Back Up Company To dialog box. Create the backup file just as you learned in the previous section of this chapter. When you have completed the backup procedure, QuickBooks continues with Rebuild. QuickBooks displays a dialog box titled Working, that shows a graph and percentage completed. QuickBooks runs through the rebuild process two times.

Verifying a Company File

The **V**erify Data option is not as extensive as the **R**ebuild option but will work in most cases, and it does not require a backup to be created beforehand.

To verify a file's data, follow these steps:

1. Open the company file that you want to verify data on. Be sure that all windows are closed and that the desktop is empty.
2. Choose **F**ile, Utilities **V**erify Data. You again see the Working dialog box.

Importing Data to QuickBooks

QuickBooks provides you with two options for transferring lists and transactions from one computer to another: Import and Export. QuickBooks uses a new file format with the file extension IIF, which stands for Intuit Interchange Format, for exporting and importing. This format is different from the QIF used by previous Quicken and QuickBooks for DOS programs.

To import data to QuickBooks, follow these steps:

1. Choose **F**ile, **I**mport. QuickBooks displays the Import dialog box, as shown in figure 21.9. All import files (iif) in the current directory display in the File Name text box.

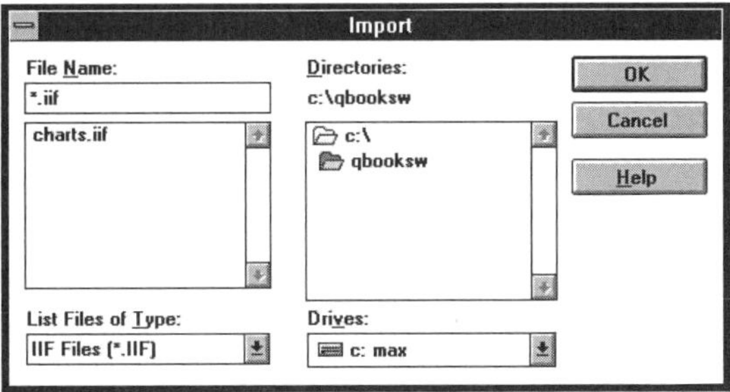

Fig. 21.9
The Import dialog box.

2. From the file list, choose the file to import, and then choose OK. QuickBooks imports the file.

Caution

Be careful when importing a file. If you are not absolutely sure what is contained in the file, create a new company with no transactions and import the file there. Importing a file can potentially overwrite your existing lists and add new transactions to your accounts that you do not want.

Exporting QuickBooks Data

You can export copies of your lists and/or transactions to another computer with QuickBooks. When you export a file, you can be very selective in what you export. To export a file, follow these steps:

1. Open the Company file from which you want to export information.
2. Choose **F**ile, **E**xport. The Export dialog box displays, as you see in figure 21.10.

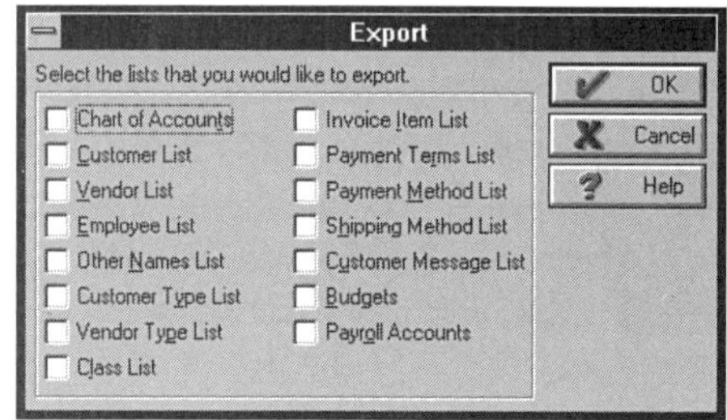

Fig. 21.10
The Export dialog box. Use this dialog box to choose the specific lists to export.

3. Choose OK. QuickBooks displays the Export File Name dialog box, as shown in figure 21.11.

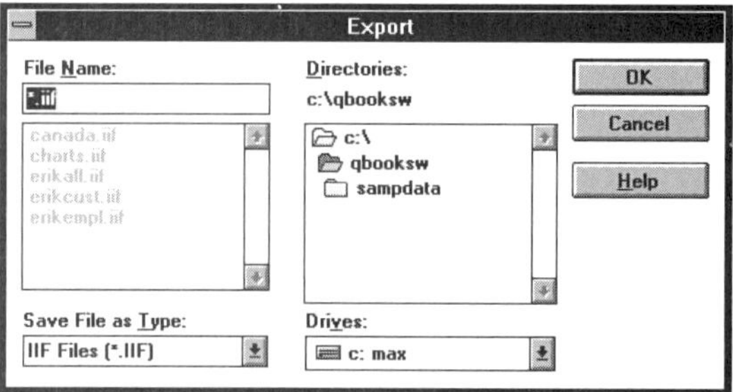

Fig. 21.11
The Export File Name dialog box.

4. Enter a name for the exported file. QuickBooks does not supply you with a suggested name; you must type one in. Remember, you are limited to an eight character valid DOS file name. You do not have to enter the file extension; QuickBooks does this for you.
5. Choose OK. QuickBooks exports the file. If you have selected all of the options, this may take several minutes.

To merge two different QuickBooks companies, you can export all transactions and lists from one company and import them to the other company.

Using Passwords

Almost all businesses consider financial data highly sensitive and confidential. If others use your computer, you may want to use passwords to prevent unauthorized access and to restrict certain activities in your company file. You can set three kinds of passwords: owner, data entry, and transaction.

The *owner password* allows full unrestricted access to all QuickBooks functions. If an owner password is created, you are asked for a password every time that you open your QuickBooks company file. You can set just an owner password if you want to.

The *data entry password* allows you to assign other people to work on your QuickBooks company files. The data entry password enables a user to enter new transactions, but not to view registers, reports, graphs, or to edit existing transactions. This is the most restrictive of the three passwords. If you set a data entry password, you must also set an owner password; otherwise you may not be able to access the remaining parts of your company file.

The *transaction password* allows you to restrict editing of transactions completed in a prior period. For example, if you place a transaction password on all transactions dated last year, QuickBooks asks for the transaction password each time that you attempt to edit a transaction from the prior period.

Caution

Assigning passwords to your QuickBooks company files provides safeguards against unauthorized access to program activities and data; however, QuickBooks' passwords do not prevent someone from using DOS or Windows to delete or rename company files. Only by providing physical security of your computer can this be prevented.

Assigning Passwords

Before you assign passwords to a company file, be sure that the current company file is the one to which you want to assign passwords. To assign passwords to your QuickBooks company file, follow these steps:

1. Choose **P**references, **P**asswords. The Password Preferences dialog box displays, as shown in figure 21.12.

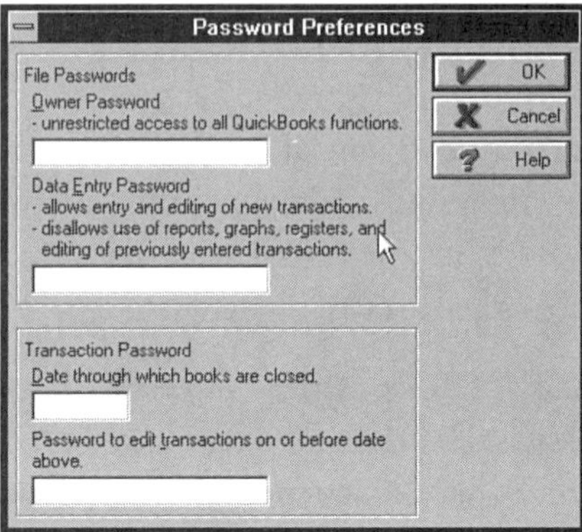

Fig. 21.12
The Password Preferences dialog box.

2. Select the Password type that you want to create.

   - Choose the **O**wner Password. Enter the password for the owner in the text box. Remember, the owner password provides for unlimited access to the company file.

   - Select the Data **E**ntry Password. Enter the password for the data entry clerk in the text box. This password allows entry of new transactions and editing of transactions entered in the current QuickBooks session.

   - Enter a transaction password only if you are closing off transactions from a prior period. Adding the transaction password restricts transactions entered prior to the date entered from being changed.

   - Enter the Date through which books are closed. This date is the date from which QuickBooks restricts editing of transactions.

   Enter the Password to edit **t**ransactions on or before date above. Enter the transaction password in the text box.

   Figure 21.13 shows the completed Password Preferences dialog box.

3. Choose OK to save the passwords.

4. Close the company file, and then open it again to activate the passwords.

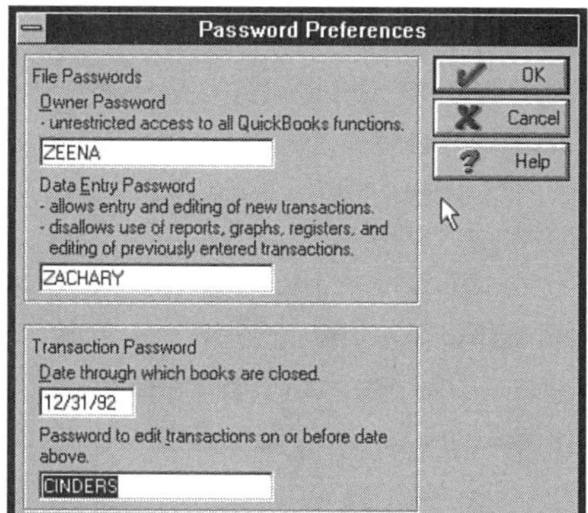

Fig. 21.13
The completed Password Preferences dialog box.

Caution

Don't forget your password. If you do not enter the correct password, you may not be able to access your company file or perform activities in your company file. Writing a password down on a piece of paper is not recommended. However, if you are not positive that you will remember the password, write it down. Be sure to put it in a secure place where others cannot find it. If you do forget your password and are unable to access your company file, call Intuit Technical Support at (415) 858-6035, Monday through Friday from 5 a.m. to 5 p.m. Pacific time.

CPA TIP: Unique Passwords

To protect your QuickBooks files from unauthorized access, assign unique passwords that are difficult for others to guess. Don't use your initials or birthdate as the password. Whatever you do assign, be sure that you will remember it.

Changing a Password

A password can be changed at any time by the holder of the owner password. Often it is recommended that you change passwords to financial information when someone with access leaves your employment or moves to another job within the company. To change a password, follow these steps:

1. Choose **P**references, **P**asswords.

2. Enter the owner's password if prompted. If the company file was opened with the data entry password, QuickBooks asks for the owner's password before allowing access to the Password Preferences dialog box.

3. Edit the passwords as needed, and choose OK to save the new passwords. Again, close the company file and reopen it to activate the new passwords.

Eliminating Password Protection

If you decide to eliminate the password protection, you can remove passwords from the company file. You must, however, enter the owner's password before you can access the Password Preferences dialog box to eliminate the passwords. To eliminate passwords, follow these steps:

1. Choose **P**references, **P**asswords.
2. Enter the owner's password if prompted.
3. Select each password and press the Delete key. When all passwords have been deleted, choose OK. Password protection has been removed from the company file.

Summary

In this chapter, you learned to add, open, and close company files. You also learned to create a backup of your company file, and to import and export company data. You then learned to add, delete, and change password protection.

In the next chapter, you learn to customize your QuickBooks company file by setting the company file preferences options, and to customize your QuickBooks program with the QuickBooks preference options.

Chapter 22

Customizing QuickBooks for Windows

In this chapter, you learn how to do the following:

- Set company file preferences
- Set QuickBooks program preferences

After you install QuickBooks for Windows, you see that all the Preference menu options are set for a predefined set of choices. The Preference options determine how your QuickBooks program appears on-screen, how you enter data into different forms, how reminders are used, and many other options. In several earlier chapters of this book, you learned how to use the Preferences menu to customize certain QuickBooks functions.

QuickBooks divides the Preferences menu into two parts: QuickBooks program preferences and company file preferences. Program preferences are effective throughout the program, regardless of the company file with which you are currently working. Company file preferences are effective only for the company that is currently open as you set the preferences.

Customizing Your Company File

The second half of the Preferences menu (everything below the line), changes the preferences for the currently open company file. Preferences changed in this part of the menu do not affect other company files. To use the same company preferences for all your company files, you must set these preferences for each company individually.

In this section, you learn about each company file preference option and how to set these preferences. (You can reset any changes made to QuickBooks' default settings by choosing the **D**efault button contained in each preference setting dialog box.)

Setting Transaction Preferences

Use the transaction preferences options to customize how you track accounts and whether you track customer:jobs or customer classes. To set transaction preferences for your company file, choose **P**references, **T**ransactions. The default Transactions Preferences dialog box appears, as shown in figure 22.1.

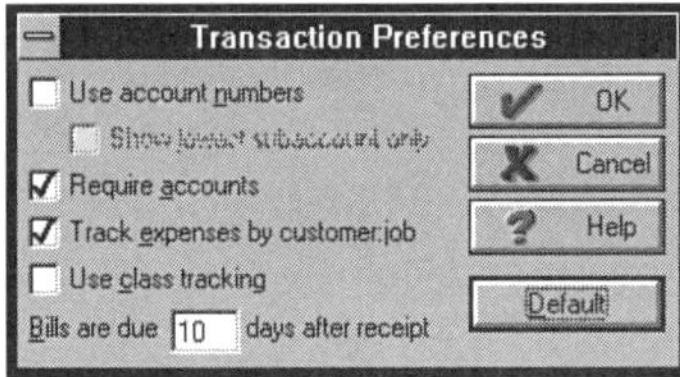

Fig. 22.1
The Transaction Preferences dialog box, used to change default preference settings for company files.

From this dialog box, you can set preferences to determine whether expenses are assigned to an account, whether your accounts are numbered, whether you track expenses by customer:job or by class, and when bills are due.

After you select your preferences for transactions, you can click the OK button to save your choices and close the dialog box.

The following preferences may be set in the Transaction Preferences dialog box:

- *Use Account **N**umbers.* If you select the check box for this preference option, QuickBooks adds a Number field to the New Account and Edit Account dialog box. QuickBooks also automatically prefixes with an account number those accounts created when you added your company. If the numbering system is not what you want, you can simply edit the account numbers in these windows. If you decide later that you do not want to use account numbers, deselect the check box for this preference. Figure 22.2 shows the Edit Account window with the Number text box displayed.

  Many companies use account numbers instead of names for their bookkeeping accounts. If you are used to such a system, you can continue to use it in QuickBooks. Otherwise, you may prefer using QuickBooks' default system of standard account names.

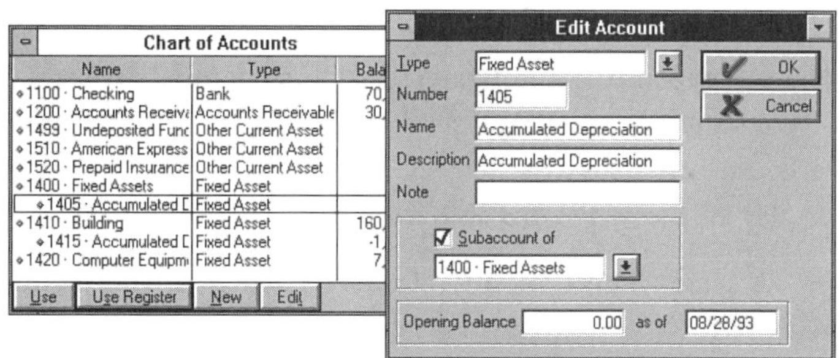

Fig. 22.2
The Edit Account window, with the account's Number field added, and the Chart of Accounts, showing all accounts prefixed by account numbers.

- *Show **L**owest Subaccount Only.* This option is available only if you first select the Use Account **N**umbers preference. If you select the check box for the Show **L**owest Subaccount Only option, QuickBooks displays only the name of the lowest subaccount on register title bars, in reports, and on detail vouchers in the WriteChecks and EnterBills windows. Figure 22.3 shows an example of an account displayed after this option is selected, and figure 22.4 shows the same account if this option is not selected. Before you can select this option, you must be sure to add account numbers to all accounts that you have added.

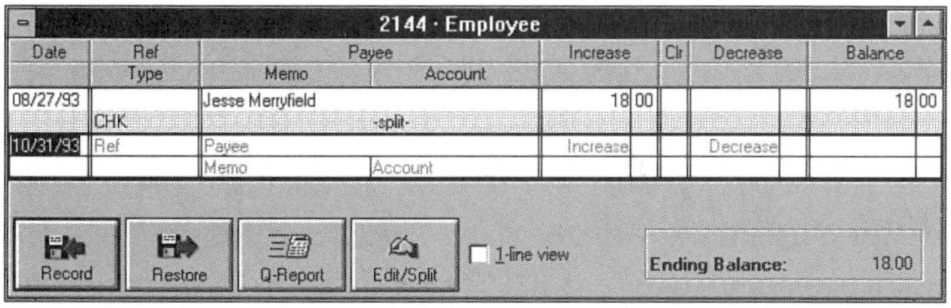

Fig. 22.3
Here you see an Employee Payroll Liability Account register showing the lowest sub-account in the window title bar.

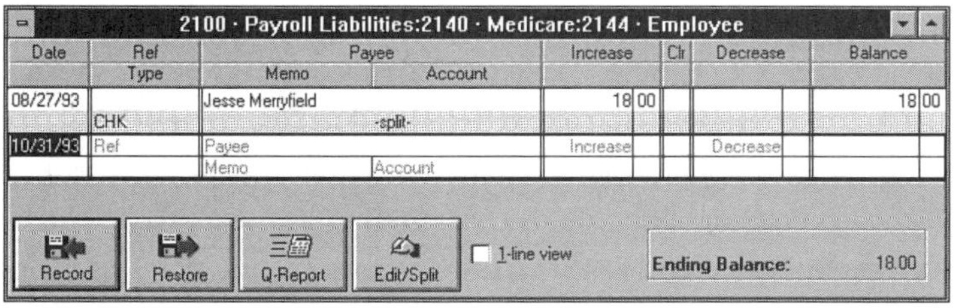

Fig. 22.4
The same Payroll Liability Account register window. Notice, however, that the window title bar now shows the primary account and then the subaccounts.

If you use a numbering system with your accounts, selecting this option can help clarify your vouchers, forms, and registers. This option also affects how customer:jobs and classes appear on-screen. Notice in figure 22.4 that you cannot see the actual account to which you assigned this expense, but in figure 22.3 the account is also listed. If you use a consistent numbering system, however, you can determine by the subaccount's number to which account it belongs, so you do not need to display all the additional account information on-screen.

- *Require **A**ccounts*. This option is selected by default as you set up QuickBooks. While the option is selected, you cannot record a transaction without assigning that transaction to an account: Balance Sheet, Income, or Expense. If you deselect the check box for this option, QuickBooks enables you to record a transaction without assigning it to an account. Recording a transaction without assigning it to an account automatically assigns the account to either Uncategorized Income or Uncategorized Expense.

- *Track **E**xpenses by Customer:Job*. This option is selected by QuickBooks as a default as you set up your company files. After this option is selected, you can track your expenses to a particular customer or job. If you bill expenses back to a customer as reimbursable, this option enables you to track these expenses and add them to an invoice. After this option is selected, all forms display a Customer:Job field in the detailed areas. If you do not want to track expenses by a Customer:Job, remove the check mark.

- *Use **C**lass Tracking*. If the check box for this option is selected, you can track income and expenses by class. QuickBooks adds to the detailed area of forms and invoices a field or text box in which you can enter the class. (Even without this option selected, however, you still can create a Class List.)

- ***B**ills Are Due **XX** Days After Receipt*. Use this option to tell QuickBooks how many days to use in calculating the due date for a bill (*XX* representing the number of days). Whatever number of days you enter in this text box, QuickBooks adds that number to the date on which you receive a bill. (Remember that, when entering a bill, you can override the date QuickBooks calculates.)

Setting Invoice Preferences

The invoice preferences enable you to change the default invoice format and two fields specific to the Product invoice form. You also can change how you track reimbursed expenses, whether to automatically apply payments, and whether QuickBooks warns you if you create a duplicate invoice number.

To change your invoice preferences, choose **P**references, **I**nvoices. The Invoice Preferences dialog box appears, as shown in figure 22.5.

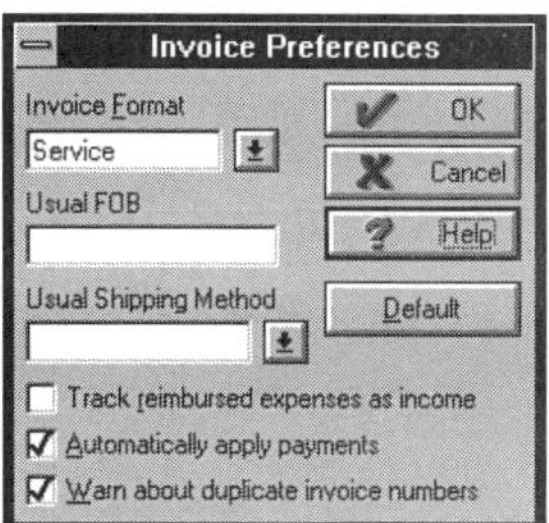

Fig. 22.5
You use the Invoice Preferences dialog box to set several preferences.

The Invoice Preferences dialog box enables you to set the following preferences:

- *Invoice **F**ormat.* QuickBooks displays as the default setting the format selected when you added your company. To change this option, select the invoice format you want from the drop-down list.

- *Usual FOB.* This field only affects the Product invoice format. If you do not use that invoice format, leave this field blank. If you do use the Product invoice format, enter the name of the city in the text box from which you usually ship goods. QuickBooks then automatically fills in the FOB field in the Create Invoices window for you. You can edit the field on the invoice if necessary.

- *Usual Shipping Method.* This option also applies only to the Product invoice format. If you do not use the Product invoice format, leave this field blank. If you primarily use a single shipping method, enter that method here, or select from the drop-down list. QuickBooks then fills in this field for you on the invoice. You can select from the drop-down list a different shipping method for a particular invoice, if necessary.

- *Track **R**eimbursed Expenses as Income.* If you select the check box for this preference, QuickBooks enables you to select an Income account in which to track reimbursement income. A check box and an additional text box are added to the New Account and Edit Account dialog box for Expense accounts, as shown for the Edit Account dialog box in figure 22.6. As you enter a reimbursable expense on an invoice, you create an entry in an Expense account. If this option is selected, QuickBooks then records the payment of the reimbursable expense in an Income account. If you deselect this preference, the income derived from the payment of the reimbursable expense goes instead to the Expense account to offset the expense.

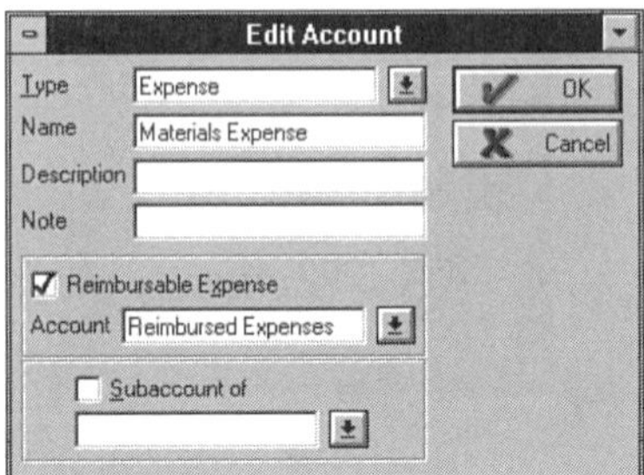

Fig. 22.6
The Edit Account dialog box. Notice the addition of the Reimbursable Expense check box; this option is selected for you.

- ***Automatically Apply Payments.*** The check box for this option is selected by default after you set up your company file. This option actually modifies the Receive Payments window. If it is selected, QuickBooks automatically applies a payment to the outstanding invoices for the selected customer:job. If the payment is less than the outstanding balance, the payment is applied to the oldest invoices first. If you deselect this option, you must specify how to apply a payment to an invoice as discussed in Chapter 9, "Receiving and Depositing Customer Payments."

- ***Warn about Duplicate Invoice Numbers.*** The check box for this option is selected by default after you add your company. If it is selected, QuickBooks warns you if you record an invoice with the same number as an already recorded invoice. If you deselect this option, QuickBooks enables you to record duplicate invoice numbers without warning.

Setting Check Preferences

By changing the Check Preferences settings you can determine what account information is printed on checks, the check's date, which field the cursor starts in the Write Checks window, and whether you receive warnings about duplicate check numbers. Open the Check Preferences dialog box by choosing **P**references, **C**hecks. The Check Preferences dialog box appears, as shown in figure 22.7.

The Check Preferences dialog box enables you to set the following preferences for checks:

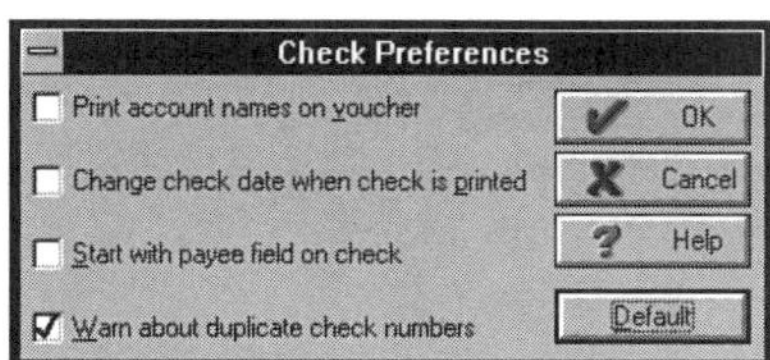

Fig. 22.7
You use the Check Preferences dialog box to set check preferences.

- *Print Account Names on **V**oucher.* This option affects only voucher or payroll style checks, not standard or wallet styles. If its check box is selected, QuickBooks prints account names on your checks, just as you entered them in the first column of the detail voucher. If you deselect this option, QuickBooks prints all the voucher information except the account names.

- *Change Check Date When Check is **P**rinted.* This option affects all check styles. If its check box is selected, QuickBooks enters the current date on a check as the check prints. If you deselect this option, QuickBooks enters the date you entered when you wrote the check.

- ***S**tart with Payee Field on Check.* This option affects the Write Checks, Enter Bills, and Enter Credit Card Charges windows. If the check box for this option is selected, QuickBooks places the cursor on the Payee or Purchased From field. If you use the same Bank account, Accounts Receivable, and Credit Card accounts and do not often change dates when entering these items, selecting this option can save you several keystrokes for every transaction. If you deselect this option, QuickBooks places the cursor in the Bank Account, Credit Card, or A/P Account field.

- ***W**arn about Duplicate Check Numbers.* This option is selected by QuickBooks by default when you set up your company files. If its check box is selected, QuickBooks warns you if you try to record a check with the same number as an already recorded check. If you deselect this preference option, you can record a check with a duplicate number with no warning from QuickBooks.

Setting Reporting Preferences

You use the Reporting Preferences options to set your report accounting basis and aging preferences. Report basis selections affect both reports and graphs. Figure 22.8 shows the Reporting Preferences dialog box. Open the dialog box by choosing **P**references, **R**eporting.

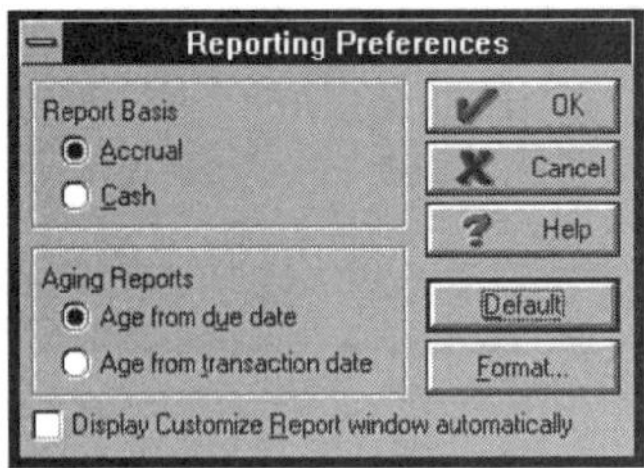

Fig. 22.8
You can use the Reporting Preferences dialog box to change some of the default formats.

You can set the following preference options in the Reporting Preferences dialog box:

- *Report Basis, **A**ccrual.* This is the default accounting basis QuickBooks selects when you set up your company. By using the Accrual accounting basis, QuickBooks includes income as of the invoice date and expenses as of the billing date. (The reporting options selected here do not affect the Sales Tax Report. See the following section for information on that option.)

- *Report Basis, **C**ash.* Selecting this option button bases all your reports and graphs on the Cash basis for accounting. QuickBooks then counts income only when a payment is received and expenses when you pay the bill, for all reports and graphs (except Sales Tax reports).

- *Aging Reports, Age from **D**ue Date.* This is the default option selected by QuickBooks when you add your company file. This preference affects all reports and graphs that show Accounts Receivable or Accounts Payable aging. After you select this option button, QuickBooks starts to count the number of days an account is past due from its due date.

- *Aging Reports, Age from **T**ransaction Date.* This option is similar to the preceding except that if you select its option button, QuickBooks ages a transaction from the date the transaction is recorded, not from its due date.

- *Display Customize **R**eport Window Automatically.* If the check box for this option is selected, QuickBooks automatically displays the Customize Report window whenever you create a report. This option is effective for any standard or memorized report or for any QuickReport. Select this option only if you find that you often need to adjust settings on the Customize window.

- *Format button.* Selecting this command button displays the Report Format Preferences dialog box, as described in Chapter 19, "Creating and Printing Reports." From this dialog box, you can change how QuickBooks displays negative numbers, other numbers, fonts, and header/footer formats. Any changes you make in this dialog box become the default settings for all reports and graphs for this QuickBooks company. If you find that you often make the same adjustments to a report format, make the changes here so that you don't need to make them again for this company.

Setting Sales Tax Preferences

Sales tax preferences are applicable only for those businesses that must collect a sales tax. If you do collect a sales tax, the Sales Tax Preferences dialog box displays the information you entered when you originally set up your company file. To open the Sales Tax Preferences dialog box, choose **P**references, **S**ales Tax. Figure 22.9 shows the Sales Tax Preferences dialog box.

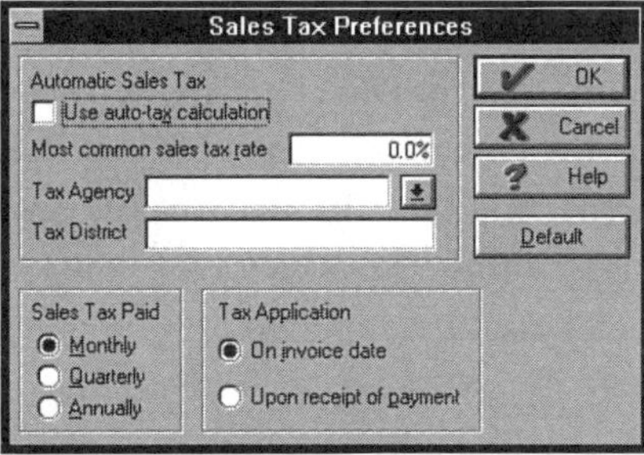

Fig. 22.9
Use the Sales Tax Preferences dialog box to adjust changes to your tax rate, the date on which sales taxes must be paid, and how the tax is calculated.

This dialog box is divided into three functional areas: Automatic Sales Tax, Sales Tax Paid, and Tax Application. The Automatic Sales Tax group concerns how you calculate a sales tax, the tax rate, and the tax authority. The Sales Tax Paid group concerns how often you must remit back to the tax authority any sales taxes collected. The last group, Tax Application, refers to when the Sales Tax Payable is calculated.

You can set the following preferences in the Sales Tax Preferences dialog box:

- *Use Auto* ***T****ax Calculation.* If the check box for this option is selected, QuickBooks automatically adds the sales tax on an invoice or sales receipt for items checked as taxable. (This applies only to customers who check the taxable box in their customer account.) Remember that if you collect a sales tax for more than one tax authority, you must add a sales tax line item for any other tax authorities beyond your primary authority.

- *Most Common Sales Tax **R**ate.* The tax rate used for the Auto Tax is entered in this text box. If your tax rate changes, enter the new rate here. If the tax rate for your sales tax is 5.25 percent, for example, enter **5.25** in the text box. QuickBooks adds the percent sign for you.
- *Tax Agency.* Enter in this text box the name of the tax agency for whom you collect the tax that you entered in the preceding text box (or select it from the drop-down list). If you have not yet entered this agency as a vendor, you can do so now.
- *Tax District.* If you collect sales tax for a different tax district under the same tax agency, enter in this text box the name of the tax district that is related to the sales tax rate you designate as the most common sales tax rate.
- *Sales Tax Paid.* Select the option button for the period that is applicable: **M**onthly, **Q**uarterly, or **A**nnually. QuickBooks uses this information to automatically set the date range on your Sales Tax Liability report and to set the Show Sales Tax Due Through field in the Pay Sales Tax dialog box. If you select **M**onthly, QuickBooks uses the last day of the previous month for the Sales Tax Liability report.

Note

If you must collect sales taxes for several agencies that require you to remit the sales taxes at different periods, you can reset the dates on the report to display your liability for the period to the specific agency. Refer to Chapter 19, "Creating and Printing Reports," for details on customizing a report.

- *Tax Application.* These options set the accounting basis for sales taxes. QuickBooks uses the settings in this area to determine the amount of your tax liability in the Sales Tax report and the amount displayed in the Pay Sales Tax dialog box for each district. If you collect sales taxes for more than one tax authority, you may need to customize a report for each tax agency if these agencies use different accounting methods for deciding when a tax is due.

- *On Invoice Date.* Select this option button if you are liable for a sales tax as of the date you write an invoice or sales receipt. QuickBooks immediately shows a liability for the tax in the Sales Tax Payable account. If you use this option, QuickBooks manages your sales tax liability on an accrual basis, even if you select a cash basis for your accounting in the Reporting Preferences dialog box.
- *Upon Receipt of Payment.* Select this option button if you are not liable for a sales tax until the date you receive payment on an invoice. If you show a sales tax on an invoice, QuickBooks does not show a liability until you receive payment on the invoice. If this option is selected, QuickBooks manages your sales tax liability on a cash basis, even if you select the accrual basis for your accounting in the Reporting Preferences dialog box.

Setting Password Preferences

If you decide that you want to set passwords for your QuickBooks company file, use the Password Preferences dialog box to set or change them. You learned how to set, edit, and delete passwords in Chapter 21, "Managing QuickBooks for Windows Files."

Customizing the QuickBooks Program

You also can customize some settings for the QuickBooks program itself. These settings are then applied to all your QuickBooks companies. All the options listed above the line in the Preference menu are applied to all company files.

This section describes these program preference options and how to use them. If you decide you do not want to keep the changes you enter to the QuickBooks default settings, you can restore the original options by choosing the **D**efault button contained in each of the preference setting dialog boxes.

Setting View Preferences

Set view preferences to change how QuickBooks displays the desktop, the Iconbar, and Qcards. Open the View Preferences dialog box by choosing **P**references, **V**iew. Figure 22.10 shows the View Preferences dialog box.

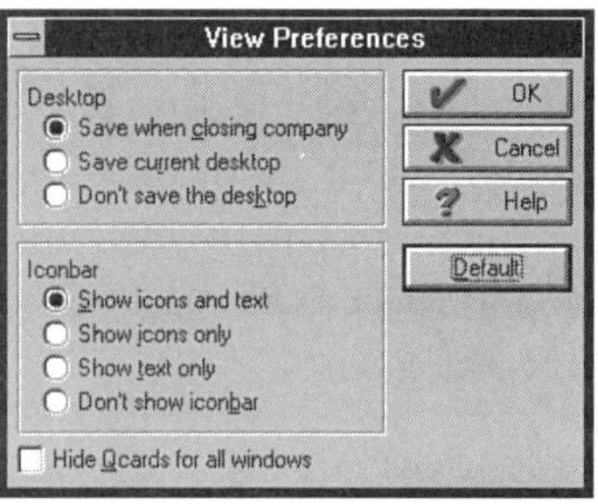

Fig. 22.10
The View Preferences dialog box is divided into three areas: DeskTop, Iconbar, and a Qcards check box.

Use the following Desktop area settings to tell QuickBooks how you want the desktop saved after you exit the program or you close a company file:

- *Save when **C**losing Company.* This is the default option QuickBooks sets as you install the program. Select this option button if you want QuickBooks to save the desktop as it is when you close the company file or exit the program. When you open QuickBooks and the company the next time, all the windows and minimized icons are in the same position on the desktop.

- *Save Cu**r**rent Desktop.* If you have a specific preference for which windows remain open and their position on the desktop, use this setting. Position all the windows you want to see each time you open QuickBooks and the company file. Choose **P**references, **V**iew, and then choose the Save Cu**r**rent Desktop option button in this dialog box. QuickBooks remembers how the desktop appears at this time and displays it the same way each time you access it. This selection affects only this company file. You can save different current desktops for different company files by selecting **P**references, **V**iew. Then simply choose OK because the Save Cu**r**rent Desktop is still selected.

- *Don't Save the Des**k**top.* If you do not want QuickBooks saved to the desktop when you close the company, select this option button. When you open the company the next time, the desktop is empty except for the menu bar and Iconbar.

The following Iconbar settings enable you to control how and whether QuickBooks displays the Iconbar:

- ***S**how Icons and Text.* This is the default setting for the Iconbar. If this option button is selected, QuickBooks displays both a picture and text for each icon. Throughout this book, the Iconbar is shown with both pictures and text.

- *Show **I**cons Only*. To reduce the size of the icons, you can select this option button to display an icon as a picture only. Figure 22.11 shows the Iconbar with icons only.

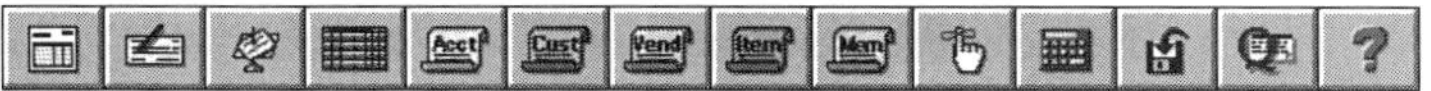

Fig. 22.11
The Iconbar, displaying icon pictures only.

- *Show **T**ext Only*. Selecting this option button reduces the size of the Iconbar even further so that the icons are displayed with text only. Figure 22.12 shows the Iconbar with text only.

Fig. 22.12
The Iconbar, displaying text only.

- *Don't Show Icon**b**ar*. Selecting this option button removes the Iconbar from the screen entirely. (All options shown on the Iconbar also are available from the menus.)

The View Preferences dialog box also displays the following check box for determining whether Qcards are displayed:

- *Hide **Q**cards for All Windows*. This option turns off the Qcards. After you install QuickBooks, Qcards appear along with each window or dialog box; each Qcard contains instructions on filling in each field or other helpful explanations. If this check box is selected, QuickBooks no longer displays the Qcards. After you become familiar with the program, you probably no longer need the Qcards. If you hire a new employee, however, you can deselect the check box so that QuickBooks again displays the Qcards, enabling the new person to more quickly become familiar with how QuickBooks functions.

Setting Data Entry Preferences

The data entry preferences regulate how QuickBooks responds as you enter data. Figure 22.13 shows the Data Entry Preferences dialog box. You can open this dialog box by choosing **P**references, **D**ata Entry.

The Data Entry Preferences dialog box enables you to set the following preference options:

- *Pressing Enter Moves Between **F**ields*. Selecting this check box enables you to use the Enter key to move between fields in the body of an Invoice, Check, or other window. Enter does not act as a Tab on buttons in a window. In Windows, pressing the Enter key is the same as clicking the OK button. This causes QuickBooks to record a transaction before you are done with it.

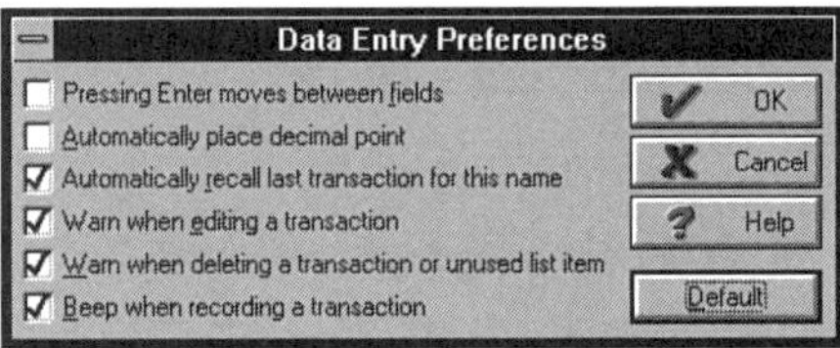

Fig. 22.13
The Data Entry Preferences dialog box.

- ***A**utomatically Place Decimal Point.* Selecting this check box instructs QuickBooks to place a decimal between the second and third number from the right if you enter a number in a numeric field without placing a decimal point yourself. If you enter **3898** and press the Tab key, for example, QuickBooks displays the number as `38.98`. If you enter **38.987**, QuickBooks leaves the number as you entered it. Deselecting this option leaves all numbers just as you type them. Some fields, such as the Invoice Quantity column, do not adjust your number. Other fields that are reserved for dollar amounts only accept the entry of a two decimal place number.

- *Automatically **R**ecall Last Transaction for This Name.* This check box is selected by default. When it is selected, QuickBooks automatically recalls a memorized transaction, or the last transaction of the same type for the name you enter. This preference does not affect invoices.

- *Warn when **E**diting a Transaction.* This preference is selected by default. If it is selected, QuickBooks warns you before it records a transaction you change and does not enable you to leave the transaction without specifically okaying the change. Deselecting this option enables you to save a change to an existing transaction without any warning from QuickBooks. It can be very easy to make an accidental keystroke in a transaction and then save it. You probably would not like to add to a check or a bill.

- ***W**arn when Deleting a Transaction or Unused List Item.* This check box is selected by default. If it is selected, QuickBooks warns you before it enables you to delete a transaction or an unused item on a list. Deselecting this option enables you to delete a transaction or an unused item without any warning if it has not been used in a transaction. QuickBooks always warns you if you attempt to delete an item that has been used in a transaction.

- ***B**eep when Recording a Transaction.* This check box is selected by default. When this preference is selected, QuickBooks beeps to confirm that a transaction has been recorded. Deselecting this option enables QuickBooks to record a transaction silently.

Setting Reminder Preferences

You work with the Reminders List and its preferences several times throughout this book. Here you learn how all the pieces fit together as a whole. Figure 22.14 shows the default Reminder Preferences dialog box. Choose **P**references, **R**eminders to display the Reminders Preference dialog box.

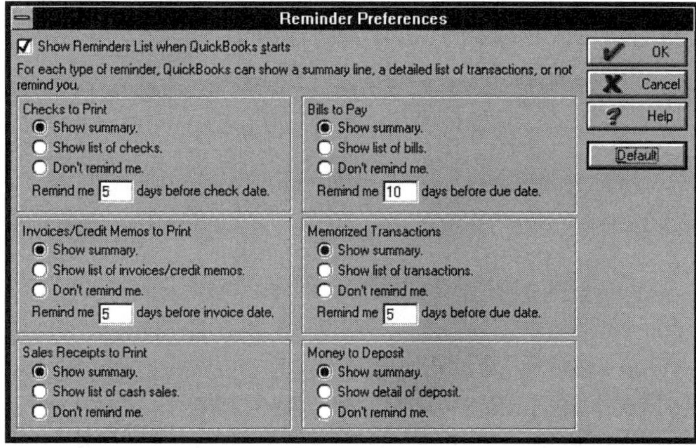

Fig. 22.14
Use the Reminder Preferences dialog box to customize how QuickBooks reminds you about various transactions.

You can set the following preferences in the Reminders Preferences dialog box:

- *Show Reminders List when QuickBooks **S**tarts.* QuickBooks places a check mark beside this option by default. Selecting this option activates the reminders, and automatically displays the reminders list each time that you open the company file. Clearing this option still allows you to view the reminders list by selecting **L**ists, **R**eminders or the Rmnd button from the Iconbar.

The Reminders Preferences dialog box also contains the following six areas:

- *Checks To Print.* Based on the preference settings in this area, QuickBooks reminds you about checks yet to be printed. These may include payroll checks, payments to vendors, and refunds.
- *Invoices/Credit Memos To Print.* Based on the preference settings in this area, QuickBooks reminds you about invoices and credit memos not yet printed. Remember that you probably have not been paid on any invoice not yet printed and presented to the customer.
- *Sales Receipts To Print.* Based on the preference settings in this area, QuickBooks reminds you about cash sales receipts to be printed.
- *Bills To Pay.* Based on the preference settings in this area, QuickBooks reminds you about bills that are now due. (These are bills you entered by using the Enter Bills window. You now need to use the Pay Bills window to select the bills to be paid at this time.)
- *Memorized Transactions.* Based on the preference settings in this area, QuickBooks reminds you when a memorized transaction is due.
- *Money To Deposit.* Based on the preference settings in this area, QuickBooks reminds you about any funds held in the Undeposited Funds account that need to be deposited into one of your Bank accounts.

Each of the preceding six areas of the Reminder Preferences dialog box contains a choice of three radio buttons, and four of these areas also contain a text box in which you can enter the number of days before QuickBooks is to remind you of a transaction. These functions are described in the following list:

- *Show Summary.* This is the default setting for all six areas. Selecting this option tells QuickBooks to display a single line entry in the Reminders List. You are shown the category and the total amount of the transactions—for example, `Bills to Pay -345.65`.
- *Show Lists.* Choosing this option button displays the single line entry shown in the preceding paragraph plus a detailed listing of each transaction with the due date, the payee, or customer, and the amount of the transaction.
- *Don't Remind Me.* Select this option button if you do not want this category to be included in the Reminders List.

- *Remind Me **XX** Days Before Check/Due Date.* Enter in the text box for this option the number of days before its due date that you want QuickBooks to remind you about a transaction. (This option is not available for Receipts To Print and Money To Deposit.)

Setting Graph Preferences

You also can set graph preference to change how a graph is displayed. Choose **P**references, **G**raphs to open the Graph Preferences dialog box, as shown in figure 22.15.

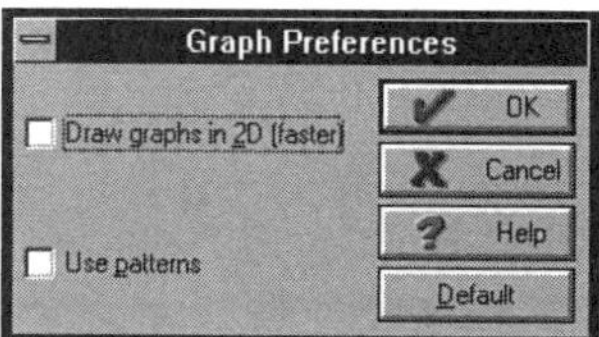

Fig. 22.15
Use the Graph Preferences dialog box to select whether to draw graphics in 3D or to use patterns.

The Graph Preferences dialog box contains only two options. You can select either or both of the following check boxes:

- *Draw Graphs in **2**D (Faster).* Selecting this check box instructs QuickBooks to draw all graphs by using only a two-dimensional view. Deselecting this option instructs QuickBooks to draw graphs in the default three-dimensional view. On some computers, selecting this option results in graphs being redrawn on-screen much faster than if displayed in a three-dimensional view.

- *Use **P**atterns.* Select this check box to use patterns instead of color to display the different graph segments. If you do not use a color printer to print your graph, you may be able to print and display the graph better by using patterns instead of shades of gray.

Summary

In this chapter, you learned how to use the Preferences menu options to customize both your company file and the QuickBooks program itself. Specifically, you learned how to customize the Transaction, Invoice, Check, Reporting, and Sales Tax Preferences options. You also learned how to set the View, Data Entry, Reminder, and Graph Preferences for the QuickBooks program.

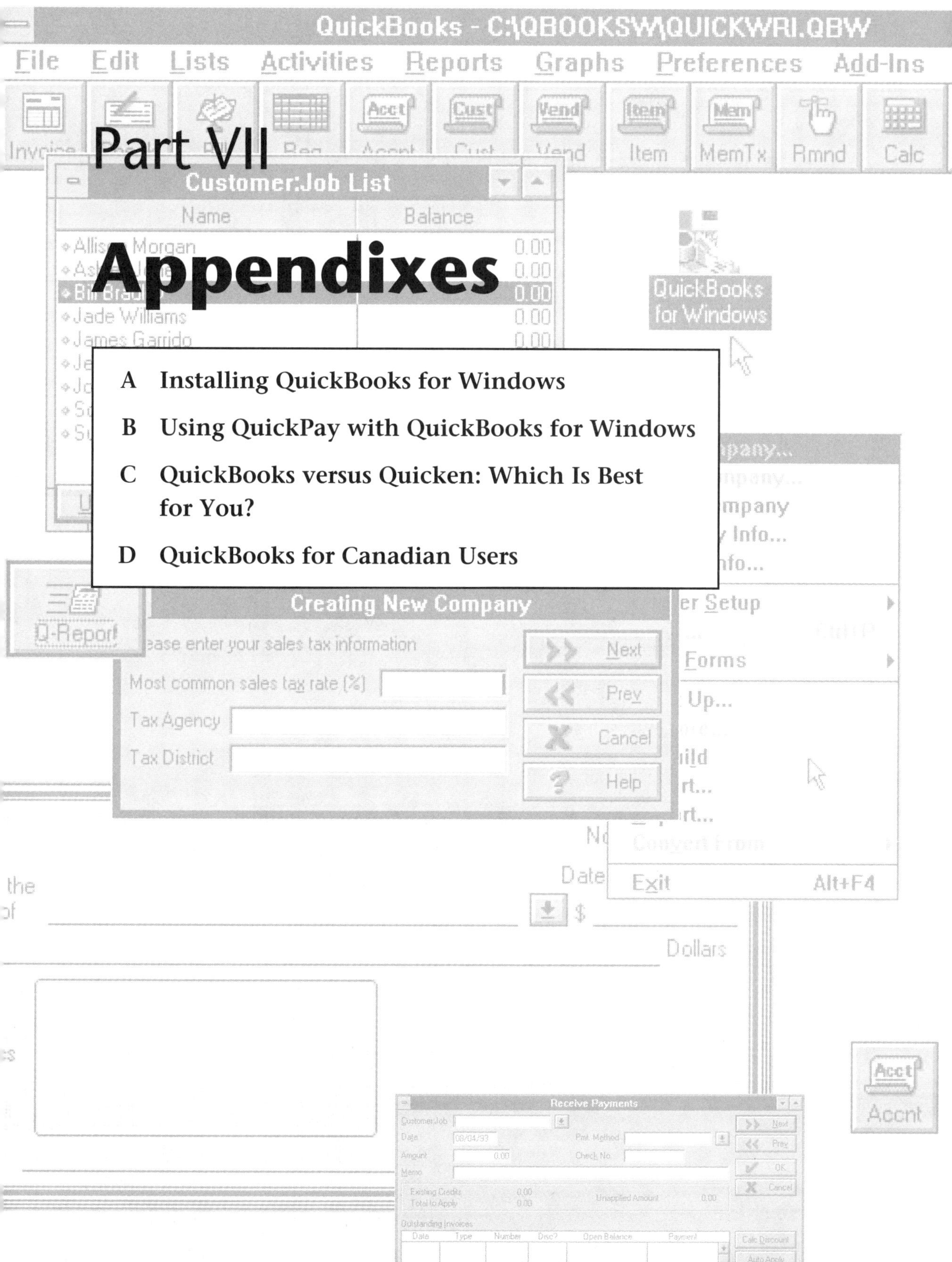

Part VII

Appendixes

A Installing QuickBooks for Windows

B Using QuickPay with QuickBooks for Windows

C QuickBooks versus Quicken: Which Is Best for You?

D QuickBooks for Canadian Users

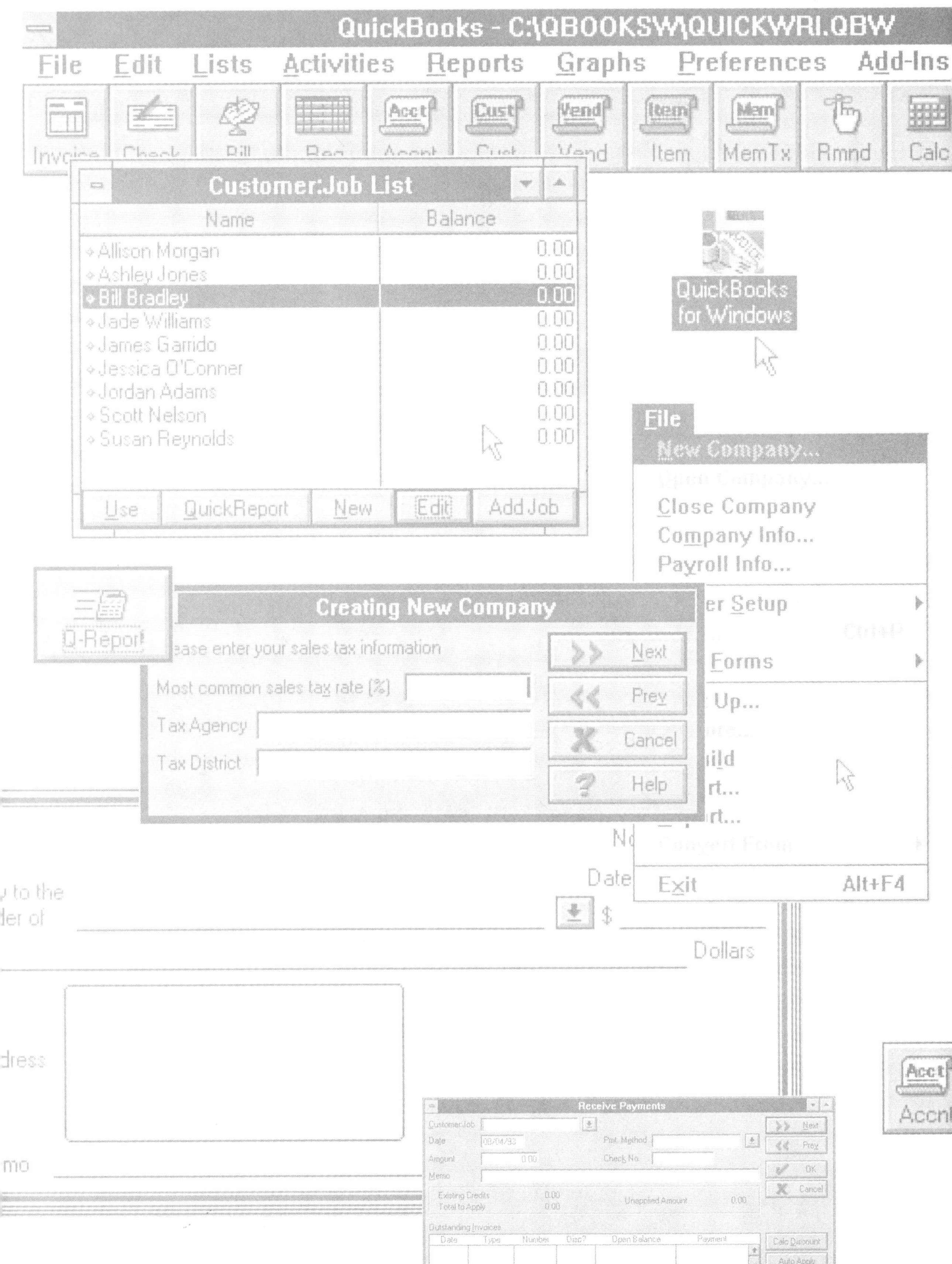

QuickBooks - C:\QBOOKSW\QUICKWRI.QBW
File Edit Lists Activities Reports Graphs Preferences Add-Ins
Acct Cust Vend Item Mem
Vend Item MemTx Rmnd Calc
Customer:Job List
Name Balance
Allison Morgan 0.00
Ashley Jones 0.00
Bill Bradley 0.00
Jade Williams 0.00
James Garrido 0.00
Jessica O'Conner 0.00
Jordan Adams 0.00
Scott Nelson 0.00
Susan Reynolds 0.00
Use QuickReport New Edit Add Job
QuickBooks for Windows
File
New Company...
Close Company
Company Info...
Payroll Info...
Setup
Forms
Up...
Exit Alt+F4
Q-Report
Creating New Company
Most common sales tax rate (%)
Tax Agency
Tax District
Next
Prev
Cancel
Help
Date
Dollars
Receive Payments
Customer:Job
Date 08/04/93
Amount 0.00
Memo
Pmt. Method
Check No.
Existing Credits 0.00
Total to Apply 0.00
Unapplied Amount 0.00
Outstanding Invoices
Date Type Number Disc? Open Balance Payment
OK
Calc Discount
Auto Apply
Acct
Accnt

Appendix A

Installing QuickBooks for Windows

Before you can use QuickBooks for Windows, you must install the program on your hard disk. This appendix explains the software and hardware requirements, and provides the steps you need to install the program.

Note

If you have QuickBooks for DOS or Quicken on your hard disk, installing QuickBooks for Windows will have *no* effect on these programs.

Reviewing the Program Requirements

The following sections review the software and hardware requirements to install and run QuickBooks for Windows.

Hardware Requirements

You need the following hardware to work with QuickBooks for Windows:

- IBM 386SX (or higher) or 100% compatible computer
- At least 2M of RAM (4M of RAM is recommended)
- One disk drive, either 5 1/4-inch or 3 1/2-inch
- Hard disk drive with at least 10M of free disk space
- VGA or SVGA monitor, or better

- Microsoft Mouse, or compatible pointing device (optional)
- Windows supported printer (if you plan to print invoices, checks, statements, lists, mailing labels, reports, or graphs)
- Microsoft Windows-compatible printer (optional)

Software Requirements

You need the following software to work with QuickBooks for Windows:

- MS-DOS or PC DOS operating system, Version 3.1 or later
- Microsoft Windows 3.1 running in Enhanced mode (To change to Enhanced mode, type **win/3** at the DOS prompt to run Windows.)
- QuickBooks for Windows program disks

Performing the Installation

Installing QuickBooks for Windows is easy and takes just a few minutes. You can install QuickBooks for Windows using Express Installation and have QuickBooks for Windows create the subdirectory and program group where the program will be installed. You also can customize the installation so that QuickBooks for Windows is installed in a different directory and/or a different program group.

Using Express Installation

To use Express Installation to install QuickBooks for Windows, follow these steps:

1. At the DOS prompt, type **win** and press Enter to start the Windows program. If you're running Windows in Real or Standard mode, type **win\3** and press Enter.
2. Make sure that the Program Manager window is active. If it is not, double-click the Program Manager icon or press Ctrl+Esc to display the Windows Task List. From the Windows Task List, choose Program Manager, or use the arrow keys to highlight Program Manager, and press Enter.
3. Insert the QuickBooks for Windows program Disk #1 in the appropriate drive.
4. From the Program Manager menu, choose **F**ile.

5. From the **F**ile menu, choose **R**un to display the Run dialog box shown in figure A.1.

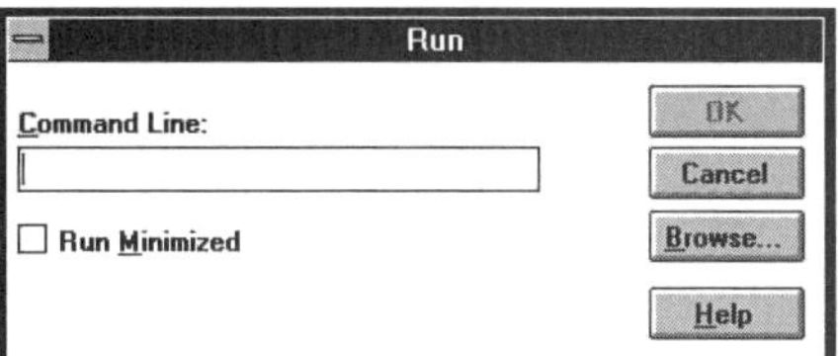

Fig. A.1
Type **a:install** (or **b:install**) in the Run dialog box.

6. Type **a:install** (or **b:install**) in the **C**ommand Line text box shown in figure A.1.

7. Choose OK or press Enter. QuickBooks for Windows displays the QuickBooks Install window shown in figure A.2.

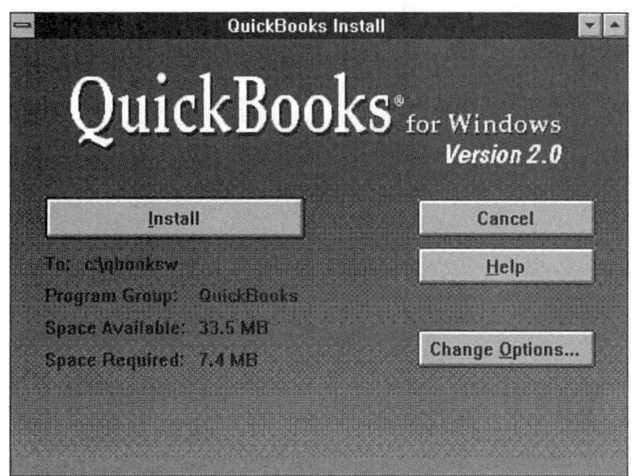

Fig. A.2
The QuickBooks Install window tells you the drive, directory, and program group where QuickBooks for Windows will be installed.

8. To choose Express Installation, choose **I**nstall.

9. QuickBooks for Windows displays a gauge to show you how installation of the program is progressing. When prompted, remove the program disk from drive A or B and insert the next disk. Choose OK when you have inserted the next disk.

10. When the installation is complete, QuickBooks for Windows displays the message `QuickBooks is installed on your computer` (see fig. A.3). Choose OK to return to Windows.

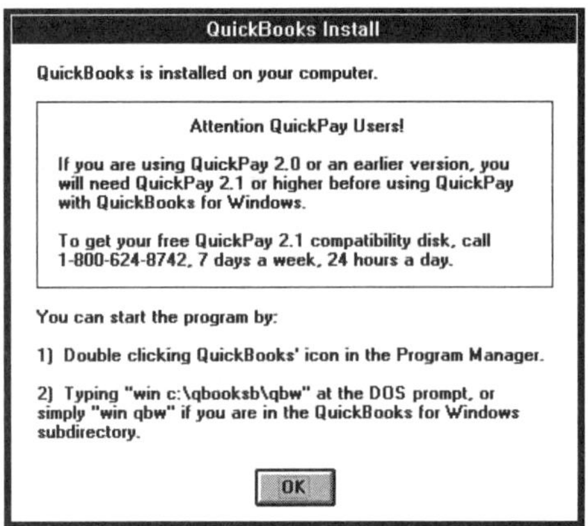

Fig. A.3 QuickBooks for Windows displays a confirmation message that the program has been installed.

Customizing Installation

To customize the installation of QuickBooks for Windows so that you can change the directory, drive, or program group where the program will be installed, follow these steps:

1. Follow steps 1 through 7 in the previous section to display the QuickBooks Install window.

2. Choose Change Options to display the QuickBooks Install Options dialog box shown in figure A.4.

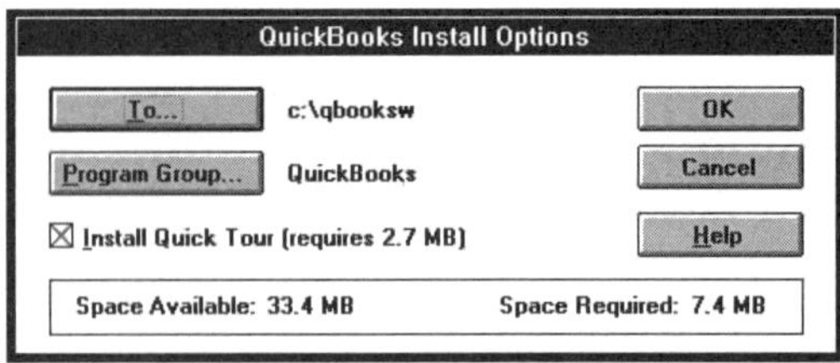

Fig. A.4 QuickBooks displays the QuickBooks Install Options dialog box when you choose Change Options from the QuickBooks Install window.

3. To install QuickBooks for Windows in a different directory or on a different drive, choose **T**o to display the QuickBooks Install Destination dialog box shown in figure A.5.

4. To change the directory, choose the desired directory from the **D**irectories list box. Click the up and down arrows at the right of the Directories box to scroll through the list of directories.

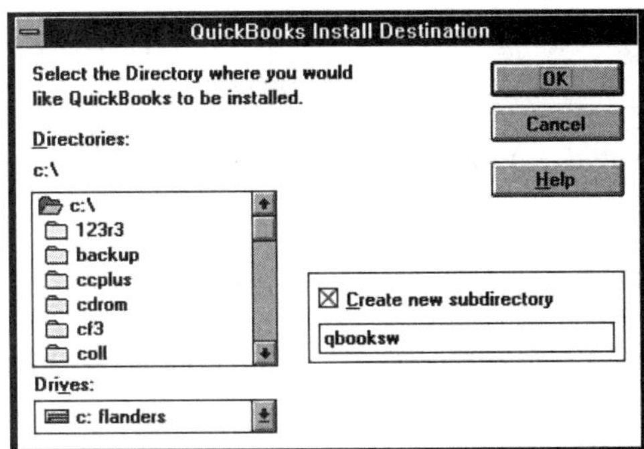

Fig. A.5
In the QuickBooks Install Destination dialog box, you can change the directory and/or drive where QuickBooks will be installed.

To create a new subdirectory other than QBOOKSW, type the desired subdirectory name in the **C**reate new subdirectory text box.

To change the current drive, click the down arrow in the Dri**v**es drop-down list to display other drives. Then choose the desired drive.

When your changes are complete in the QuickBooks Install Destination dialog box, choose OK or press Enter to return to the QuickBooks Install Options dialog box.

5. To install QuickBooks for Windows in a different program group, from the QuickBooks Install Options dialog box choose Program Group to display the QuickBooks Install Program Group dialog box shown in figure A.6.

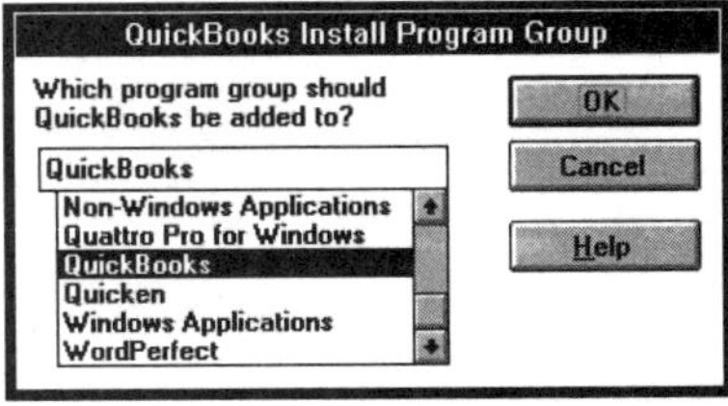

Fig. A.6
Changing the program group where QuickBooks for Windows will be installed.

6. Click the up- and down-arrow keys in the Program Group list box to find the program group where you want to install QuickBooks for Windows. Choose the program group you want to use from the list. Choose OK or press Enter to return to the QuickBooks Install Options dialog box.

7. Choose OK or press Enter from the QuickBooks Install Options dialog box. QuickBooks returns to the QuickBooks Install window.

8. Choose **I**nstall. QuickBooks for Windows displays a gauge to show you how installation of the program is progressing.

9. When prompted, remove the program disk from drive A or B and insert the next disk.

10. Choose OK when you have inserted the next disk.

11. When the installation is complete, QuickBooks for Windows displays the `QuickBooks is installed` on your computer message shown in figure A.3. Choose OK to return to Windows.

Now that your QuickBooks for Windows program is installed, you're ready to start the program and set up your company so that you can begin using QuickBooks to perform bookkeeping tasks for your business.

Appendix B

Using QuickPay with QuickBooks for Windows

QuickPay is an add-in payroll program, published by Intuit, that you can buy to work with QuickBooks. If you have employees in your business, you know what an enormous task preparing payroll checks can be, even with a system like QuickBooks. Preparing payroll not only entails calculating payroll check amounts and writing checks, but also tracking payroll taxes and filling out federal and state payroll tax forms. Although QuickPay can't fill out the tax forms for you, you can use QuickPay to track payroll taxes and to generate reports that contain the numbers you need to fill out the tax forms. In this appendix, you learn the basics of QuickPay with QuickBooks, and how QuickPay and QuickBooks interface with each other.

What QuickPay Does

QuickPay is an add-in program that you can use with QuickBooks or Quicken, but not by itself. QuickPay makes the payroll process quick and easy. After you set up employee information in QuickPay, you can enter payroll transactions with a few simple keystrokes. As you enter the data, QuickPay assigns the proper payroll accounts to each payroll transaction so that you can track gross wages, bonuses, withholdings, and payroll liabilities.

The QuickPay program performs the following payroll activities:

- Calculates gross wages each pay period
- Calculates federal, state, and local taxes (for the U.S., the District of Columbia, and Puerto Rico, but not for Guam, the Virgin Islands, or Canada)
- Calculates additional taxes or deductions, like 401K contributions, charitable donations, and union dues
- Writes payroll checks at the Write Checks window
- Tracks federal, state, and local taxes that you have withheld from employees' gross wages
- Updates the appropriate accounts in QuickBooks, such as the Gross Payroll Expense account
- Records information about employees, such as pay and commission rates, Social Security number, and number of tax exemptions
- Generates payroll reports that you can use to help fill out payroll tax forms

QuickPay handles all types of compensation: salary, hourly, commission, or any combination of these, and QuickPay accommodates weekly, biweekly, semimonthly, quarterly, or yearly pay periods. If you have other payroll items such as 401K deductions loan repayments, tips, union dues, bonuses, and car allowances, QuickPay enters them into the formula for calculating gross and net pay. (Net pay is determined by subtracting taxes and all other deductions from gross.) You can use QuickPay to perform payroll activities for an unlimited number of employees for one company or for several companies. QuickPay keeps payroll data separate for each of your QuickBooks company files. In order for you to show year-to-date totals on payroll check vouchers, QuickPay keeps track of all payroll activity by employee.

Note

QuickPay cannot print tax forms or track employees' vacation time or sick days. You can use the information accumulated by QuickPay, however, to complete tax forms such as W-2 forms, Form 940, Form 941, and so on. If you need to track paid vacation time or sick days for your employees, you may want to use another program for this purpose, or you can track paid vacation time or sick days manually.

What You Need To Run QuickPay with QuickBooks

To run QuickPay, you need the following hardware and software:

- IBM 386SX or better, 100-percent compatible computer, with a minimum of 2M (megabytes) of memory available. (Intuit recommends at least 4M of RAM.)
- Hard drive with a minimum of 900K (kilobytes) of available space.
- One high-density floppy disk, either 3 1/2 inch or 5 1/4 inch.
- Any monitor supported by Windows, VGA resolution or better.
- QuickBooks for Windows installed.
- Windows 3.1 or later using Enhanced mode.
- Up-to-date tax tables. Tax tables that are current at the time QuickPay was issued are built into the program. These tables are loaded when you install QuickPay. You must keep the tables current by subscribing to the QuickPay Tax Tables Update Service. (See the sign-up form enclosed in the QuickPay package.)

How To Run QuickPay

To run QuickPay, you must first install it on your hard drive. Before you can install QuickPay, you must have installed QuickBooks for Windows. QuickPay is an add-in program, which means that it can't run alone; it runs inside the QuickBooks program.

Caution

If you have been using Quicken to track your payroll, be sure to transfer your Quicken data into QuickBooks before installing QuickPay in your QuickBooks directory. QuickBooks must be able to find your payroll accounts before it can prepare payroll.

To start QuickPay, select the QuickPay icon from your QuickBooks program group, or start QuickBooks and choose A**d**d-Ins, **Q**uickPay from the menu bar. Figure B.1 shows the QuickPay window within QuickBooks.

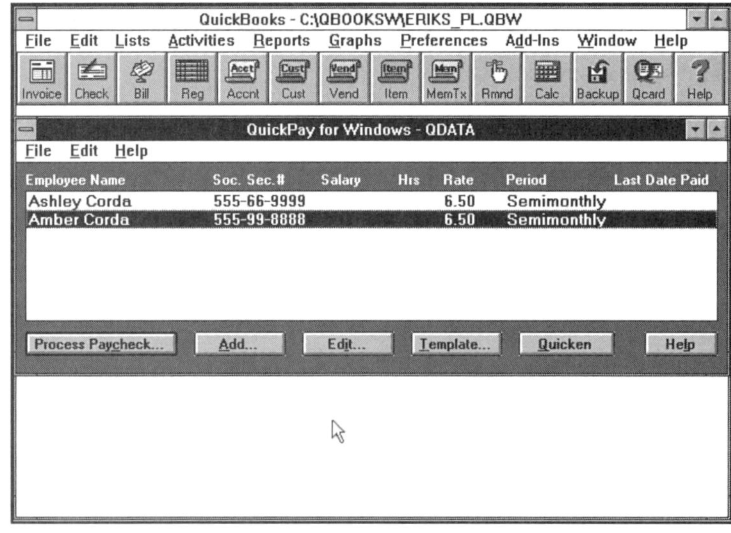

Fig. B.1 From within the QuickPay for Windows window, you can complete all payroll functions, write checks, and record information in your QuickBooks accounts.

Before you can use QuickPay, you must add in your employees' names and the information about them. To add an employee's name, follow these steps:

1. Open the QuickPay for Windows window. Choose the QuickPay icon from the QuickBooks Program Group Window, or open QuickBooks first and then choose A**d**d-Ins, **Q**uickPay from the menu.

2. Choose the **A**dd button. The Add Employee dialog box appears, as shown in figure B.2.

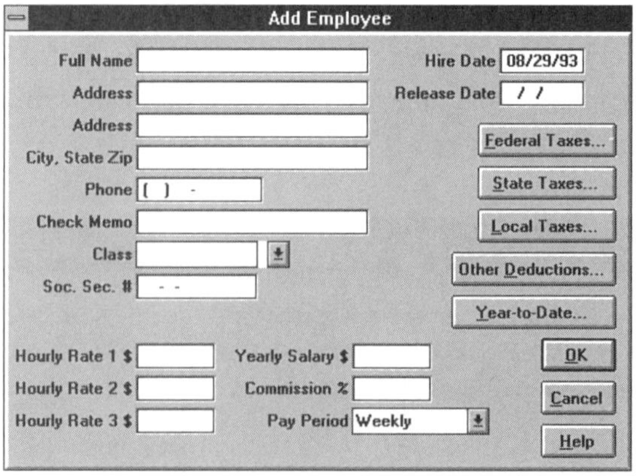

Fig. B.2 Use the Add Employee dialog box to enter all necessary information about an employee.

3. Enter the employee data in each of the appropriate text boxes. Figure B.3 shows the employee data entered in the Add Employee dialog box.

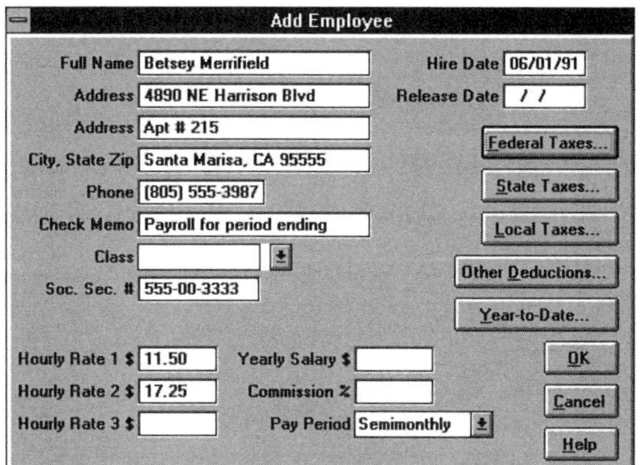

Fig. B.3
The completed Add Employee window. You are now ready to enter the employee's tax information.

4. Choose the **F**ederal Taxes button, and then enter the federal tax information. Follow the same procedure for **S**tate Taxes, **L**ocal Taxes, Other **D**eductions, and **Y**ear-to-Date information. Choosing each of these buttons displays a dialog box similar to the Federal Taxes dialog box shown in figure B.4. See the QuickPay manual for further information.

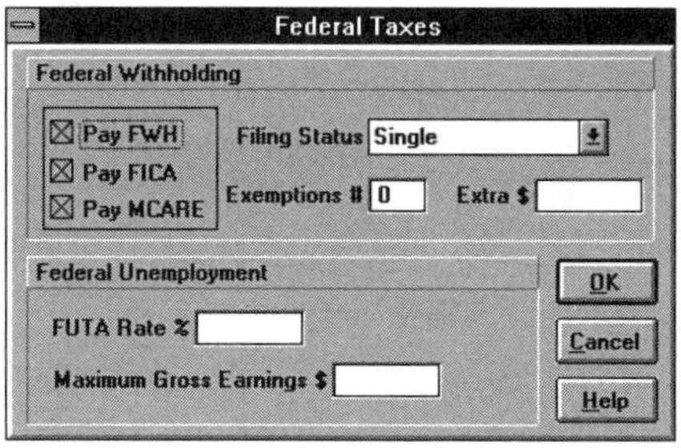

Fig. B.4
Use the Federal Taxes dialog box to enter an employee's filing status and exemptions; obtain this information from the employee's current W-2 form.

5. Choose the OK button to save the employee information.

The employee is now added to the QuickPay window.

QuickPay for Windows includes two menus—the **F**ile menu and the **E**dit menu—and several buttons. The button options are included within the menus.

The **F**ile menu includes the options listed in the following table:

Option	Function
Set up **P**assword	Allows you to set up a password for your payroll file. When this option is selected, a Password window is displayed.
Backup	Creates a backup file of your QuickPay payroll files.
Restore	Restores a backup file.
Set up Company	Sets up company payroll details for QuickPay, including general deductions that are included on all employee paychecks, and the bank account from which you draw payroll.
Return to **Q**uickBooks	Returns the user to QuickBooks.
E**x**it QuickPay	Closes the QuickPay file.

The **E**dit menu includes the options listed in the following table:

Option	Function
Process Pay**c**heck	Opens the Process Paycheck for window (after you select the employee in the window and choose this option). In this window, you enter the number of hours the employee worked and other information for the pay period.
Add Employee	Opens the Add Employee window to enter a new employee's information.
Edit Employee	Opens the Edit Employee window, which is similar to the Add Employee window. Select the employee to which you need to make a change, and choose this option.
Delete Employee	Deletes an employee from the payroll file.
Edit **T**emplate	Allows you to edit the employee template.
Undo Last Paycheck	Allows you to undo the last paycheck for the selected employee.
Sort Employee List by	Sorts the employee list by first or last name.
Preferences	Allows you to hide the Salary, Hrs, and Rate columns in the display window, and to choose to use the Enter key to move from field to field.
Template button	This is the only button that is not included as a menu item. This option allows you to create a template for the Add Employee window. If you fill in the same information for each employee, create a template with this information already completed. QuickPay then uses the template and fills in this information for you.

Caution

Do not delete an employee who worked for you sometime in the current or last calendar year. You will need to collect that employee's tax information to send him or her a W-2 form for the period worked. Delete an employee file only after your tax responsibilities have been completed. Remember, the IRS requires that you maintain employee tax records for longer than the last calendar year.

Once you have installed and opened QuickPay, you can set up your system to handle payroll for your company. You must first complete the following tasks before you can begin to pay your employees using QuickPay:

- Set up your company in QuickPay. Remember, even though your company information is entered in QuickBooks, you must set up a company in QuickPay before it can process your payroll.
- Set up personal details and tax data for each employee.
- Set up the necessary accounts and subaccounts to assign payroll transactions to.
- Enter beginning balances in QuickBooks and the year-to-date amounts in QuickPay.

Refer to the QuickPay manual for further details on completing each of these tasks. Once you have completed these tasks, just select the employee to pay, and enter the number of hours worked and any commission sales. QuickPay then calculates payroll for each employee, enters the payroll transaction in the Check register, and assigns the proper accounts to the transaction.

Appendix C

QuickBooks versus Quicken: Which Is Best for You?

Quicken has been mentioned frequently in this book, and you may be wondering which of the two Intuit programs, QuickBooks or Quicken, is most appropriate for your small business. The information in this appendix should help you make that decision.

QuickBooks and Quicken are financial software packages that enable you to enter your day-to-day transactions, write checks, keep track of income and expenses, reconcile your bank accounts, and generate financial reports and graphs. Which one should you use in your small business?

Using Quicken for Home Finances

You may be more familiar with Quicken, which has been around longer than QuickBooks and has established a strong reputation in the financial software market. Quicken is a proven product and is the most widely used software program for personal financial management.

If you're already using Quicken, you will be glad to know that you easily can convert your Quicken data to QuickBooks for Windows in just a few steps. See Chapter 3, "Setting Up Your Company in QuickBooks for Windows," to learn how to set up your QuickBooks system to use Quicken data. If you convert to QuickBooks for Windows and convert your Quicken data, your Quicken data is still intact after the conversion process. You can then use Quicken to perform activities that QuickBooks for Windows doesn't do, such as amortize loans and track investments.

Using QuickBooks for Small Businesses

Although Quicken fully accommodates the individual user for home finances, Quicken does not offer several features that small business users need. Intuit, the publisher of both Quicken and QuickBooks for Windows, has therefore devoted its energies to developing a product as sound as Quicken, but that answers the needs of the small-business user. QuickBooks for Windows and QuickBooks DOS are the result. QuickBooks offers small-business owners the ease of use that they're accustomed to in Quicken, as well as features that relate more specifically to business, such as invoicing, customer and vendor lists, and Accounts Payable tracking.

Although QuickBooks and Quicken are similar, there are a few terminology differences between the two programs, as follows:

Quicken	QuickBooks for Windows
File	Company
Accounts	Balance sheet account
Category	Income or expense account
Blanks	Fields
Category & Transfer List	Chart of Accounts
Account List	Chart of Accounts

QuickBooks writes checks and enters transactions in your Check register, just like Quicken. QuickBooks also reconciles your bank account and performs several other functions like Quicken does; however, QuickBooks does a lot of things that Quicken cannot do, such as the following:

- Offers complete invoice-writing capabilities that enable you to enter line items with item codes that link invoice transactions to accounts.
- Allows you to track reimbursable expenses so that you can bill clients and customers for reimbursable expenses on invoices.
- Tracks your Accounts Receivable so that you know at any given time how much your customers owe.

- Automatically calculates sales tax for taxable invoice items.
- Applies customer payments to invoices and calculates early payment discounts.
- Prepares a deposit summary that you can take to the bank when you deposit customer payments.
- Determines when your bills are due and tracks your Accounts Payable.
- Uses your chart of accounts to track income, expenses, and balance sheet accounts, instead of the categories, subcategories, and transfer accounts that are used in Quicken.
- Uses company lists to store data about your customers, customer types, jobs, vendors, vendor types, employees, invoice items, classes (or projects), payment and shipping methods, and payment terms. You can even store customer messages so that you don't have to retype them each time you write an invoice. Company lists speed up entry in many fields throughout the program. Company lists also serve as a database of your customers, vendors, and employees, and you can use these lists to print mailing labels or rotary file cards for your customers and vendors.
- Uses balance sheet accounts that are more representative of business, such as fixed asset and equity accounts.
- Allows you to define jobs that relate to each customer so that you can track the work that you do for each client or customer.
- Allows you to assign password protection to your QuickBooks activities. Three types of passwords are available:

  Owner password. Allows unlimited access to your company file.

  Data entry password. Allows others to enter new transactions but not view registers, reports, or graphs, nor edit transactions entered in prior periods.

  Transaction password. Restricts editing of transactions in a predefined prior period.

- Uses terminology with which small-business people are familiar. "Familiar," however, does not mean that you must be an accountant to understand the terminology in QuickBooks for Windows. On the contrary, Intuit strove for a program that does not intimidate the nonaccounting user. In QuickBooks, you don't even see common accounting terms, such as *debit* or *credit*. You *do* see the terms that you use or hear on a daily basis: Accounts Receivable and Payable, invoice, voucher, and so on.

- Offers business reports and graphs that are designed to appear in the usual and customary business format.

- Allows you to customize reports so that reports include comparison data in such areas as profit and loss statements and sales reports.

- Creates an Accounts Receivable aging status schedule for each customer that shows the portion of the customer's balance that is current and the portion that is 0 to 30 days past due, 31 to 60 days past due, 61 to 90 days past due, and more than 90 days past due.

- Generates an Accounts Payable report that shows the status of your unpaid bills.

- Generates a 1099 report that you can use to fill out 1099 Forms at the end of the calendar year for those vendors to whom you pay more than $600.

- Tracks the sales tax that you collect for each government agency and accumulates sales tax data in a report that you can use when it's time to file sales tax returns and pay sales tax.

- Displays a transaction history for transactions that you select in Accounts Receivable and Accounts Payable. A transaction history shows each transaction related to the selected transaction.

- Allows you to enter notes about customers, vendors, and employees.

As you can see, QuickBooks is designed to handle most small-business activities (with the exception of inventory control). You should know, however, that QuickBooks is *not* set up to do the following:

- Track individual investments, their market values, and their gains and losses. If it's important that you closely track your business investments, use the investment feature in Quicken and use QuickBooks for everything else.
- Amortize loans. Quicken includes a loan amortization calculator that updates the principle and interest on outstanding loans each time a payment is recorded.
- Receive electronic credit card statements. In Quicken, you can receive an electronic statement that automatically assigns categories and subcategories to purchases.
- Specify accounts as tax-related. This feature is not as important in QuickBooks as in Quicken, however, because most business transactions related to accounts and subaccounts are tax-related.

In this appendix, you learned some of the similarities and differences between QuickBooks for Windows and Quicken. Both programs are useful tools to help you track your finances. After reading this appendix, however, you may have found that QuickBooks is more suited than Quicken to your small-business needs.

Appendix D
QuickBooks for Canadian Users

QuickBooks has developed an ever-growing population of Canadian QuickBooks users. In this appendix, Canadian users learn how to customize QuickBooks for their own special needs.

Ordering Cheques, Invoices, and Other Supplies

Canadian users can use the same cheques, invoices, and other supplies from Intuit that U.S. users do. Intuit has contracted with a Canadian check printer for Canadian needs, which will save these users time and money.

For information about ordering cheques, invoices, and other supplies, call toll-free: 800-268-5779, or fax your order to 416-752-1140. Orders for cheques cannot be completed without a sample voided cheque.

Adapting the Chart of Accounts

When you added your QuickBooks company to the system, you selected a business type that included a preset Chart of Accounts. This preset list includes payroll liability and expense accounts for U.S. companies. If you plan to use QuickBooks for tracking your payroll liabilities and expenses, you'll want to change the names of these accounts. For example, edit "Payroll Taxes:FUTA to Payroll Taxes:Canada Pension Plan." For further details on using QuickBooks to handle payroll, refer to Chapter 17, "Using Other Accounts To Perform Tasks."

Tracking Goods and Services Taxes (GST)

As a Canadian business owner, you must track the GST that you collect from your customers and the GST that you must pay to your vendors. You may also have to track any provincial sales taxes that you are required to collect.

To track the GST and provincial sales taxes, you must do the following:

- Add balance sheet accounts for the GST collected.
- Create a GST line item to include GST on invoices.
- Use Auto Tax for the provincial sales tax, except in Quebec.
- Create two customized reports: the first to show your GST liability, and the second to show your GST credit.

Adding Liability Accounts for GST

In order for you to track the GST, you must create a balance sheet account for the GST that you collect, such as GST Due. Use the amount that you owe as of your QuickBooks start date as the opening balance. Select Other Current Liabilities as the account type. Refer to Chapter 4, "Working with Accounts," for further details about adding a new account. Figure D.1 shows a liability account for GST.

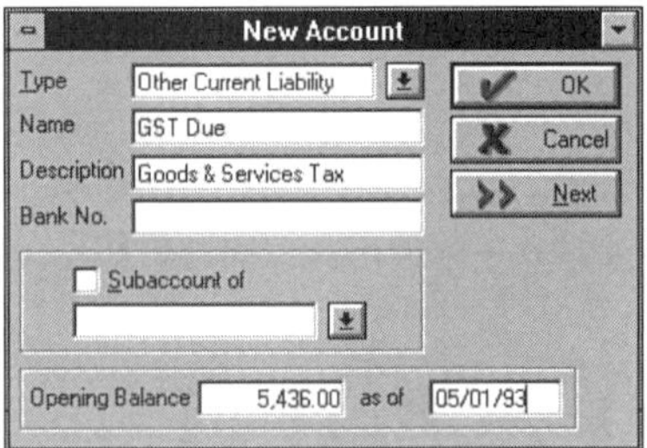

Fig. D.1 The GST Due account to be added to the Chart of Accounts.

Using Specialized Accounts in Quebec

If you are a QuickBooks user who lives in Quebec, you must keep track of the credits for provincial taxes paid. Set up two QST invoices items—one for goods and one for services—similar to the GST invoice items.

Create another current liability balance sheet account to track the QST due. Assign the QST invoice items to the QST due account.

Using Auto Tax

Use Auto Tax to track the provincial sales taxes that you collect. As you learned in Chapter 7, "Tracking Sales Tax," the Auto Tax feature automatically calculates and enters sales taxes for all items that are checked as taxable items. All taxes collected by Auto Tax are tracked in a special account called Sales Taxes Payable.

Adding a GST Invoice Item

Once you have added the current liability account to track your GST collected, you can add an invoice item for GST to the Invoice Item List. Figure D.2 shows the completed New Item dialog box with the GST invoice item. Refer to Chapter 5, "Using QuickBooks for Windows Lists," for additional details on adding an invoice item. Remember to add the percent sign in the Amount or % field. Do not check the Auto Taxable check box, or QuickBooks will include the amount of the GST calculated in the calculation of the amount of provincial sales taxes due.

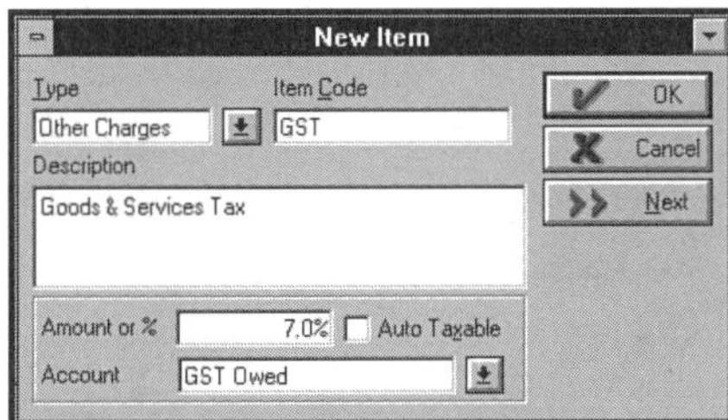

Fig. D.2
The GST Invoice Item that will be added to the Invoice Item List.

Entering GST on Invoices

Depending on your business and the province in which you live, you will fall into one of three groups:

- *You collect both GST and a provincial sales tax on the same items.* When you add items on which you collect a provincial sales tax, check the Auto Ta**x**able check box for that item. If you have not done so, you will want to edit the items, and check the Auto Ta**x**able box.

  When you write an invoice, enter all items not subject to GST first, and place a subtotal line item. Add all items that are subject to the GST, and enter another subtotal line item. Then add the GST line item. QuickBooks enters the provincial sales tax directly above the total line.

- *You collect only the GST.* When you write an invoice, enter all items that are not subject to the GST first, and enter a subtotal line item. Add all items that are subject to the GST, and enter another subtotal line item. Finally, add the GST line item.

- *You collect GST and a provincial sales tax on two different subtotals of line items.* In this case, which applies to Quebec, you will write separate invoices for taxable goods and taxable services, because you must charge different rates for each of these items.

  Enter any nontaxable items first, and enter a subtotal line item. Enter all taxable line items and enter another subtotal line item; then enter the GST line item. Next, enter two subtotal line items; the first will subtotal just the GST amount, and the second will subtotal the GST and the subtotal of all the taxable line items. Finally, enter the QST line item. Figure D.3 shows a completed sales receipt.

Fig. D.3 The completed cash sales receipt showing both GST and QST totals.

P.O. NUMBER	TERMS	PROJECT

QUANTITY	DESCRIPTION	RATE	AMOUNT	
2	Tree - Dog Wood - Pink	15.00	30.00	
1	Weeping Cherry - Flowering Pink	125.00	125.00	
	SUBTOTAL		155.00	
	Goods & Services Taxes	7.00%	10.85	GST Tax total
	SUBTOTAL		10.85	
	SUBTOTAL		165.85	
	Quebec Sales Tax	5.00%	8.29	QST Tax total

Refer to Chapter 7, "Tracking Sales Tax," for additional details on how to group items that are taxed, not taxed, or taxed at a different rate.

Entering Bills with GST

Entering bills with GST using QuickBooks is easy. When you enter a vendor bill, include the GST charged to you as an additional line item in the detail voucher of the Enter Bills window. Be sure to select the GST Due account that you have created. Assign the remainder of the bill to other accounts, as you learned in Chapter 10, "Using the Accounts Receivable Register."

Paying GST

When the time comes to pay the government the GST that you have collected, you will need to create two reports. You must be sure to have QuickBooks memorize these reports so that you can recall them later and not have to re-create them.

The first report lists the GST that you have paid to your vendors. This report lists all the GST line items that you recorded in your accounts payable for the date range that you will specify. You will notice that the amounts are negative; this is because these are amounts that your vendors charged to you. If the report includes amounts from prior periods of time, you will need to subtract that amount from the report total. This will be your input tax credit for the period.

Create the GST Paid to Vendors report by following these steps:

1. Choose **R**eports, **T**ransaction Report, By **D**ate from the menu.
2. Change the report title to "GST Paid to Vendors" by using the Header/F**o**oter button. Press OK to return to the report window.
3. Choose the F**i**lters button. The Filter Transactions dialog box appears.
4. Choose the date range for your report. Use the starting and ending dates for the tax period on which you are reporting.
5. In the Name field, choose the All Vendors option.
6. In the Account field, choose the Selected Accounts option. Then in the Select Accounts window, choose the GST Due account.
7. Press the OK button to return to the report window. QuickBooks will immediately generate a new report based on your selections and display it in the report window for you.

Your report is now similar to that shown in figure D.4. Remember to memorize this report so that you only have to change the date range the next time you want to use it.

The second report that you need to create will list the GST that you have collected from your customers.

To create the GST Collected report, follow these steps:

1. Open the report that you just created, "GST Paid to Vendors." You will use this report as the basis for the second report.
2. Choose the Header/F**o**oter button to open the dialog box. Change the report title to "GST Collected," and choose the OK button.
3. Choose the F**i**lters button. The Filter Transactions dialog box appears.
4. Select All Customers/jobs in the Name field, and click the OK button.

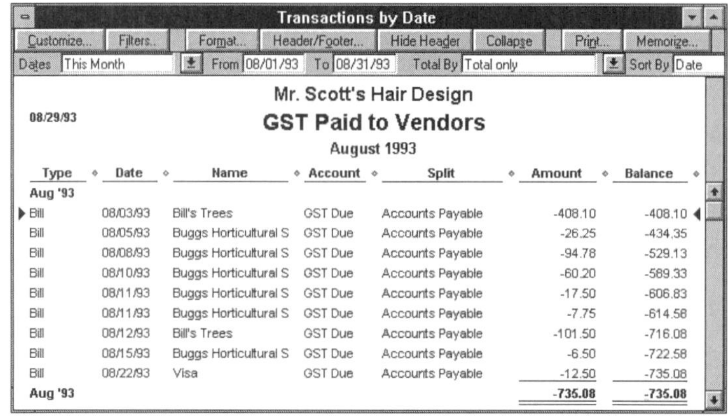

Transactions by Date

Customize... Filters... Format... Header/Footer... Hide Header Collapse Print... Memorize...

Dates This Month From 08/01/93 To 08/31/93 Total By Total only Sort By Date

08/29/93

Mr. Scott's Hair Design

GST Paid to Vendors

August 1993

Type	Date	Name	Account	Split	Amount	Balance
Aug '93						
Bill	08/03/93	Bill's Trees	GST Due	Accounts Payable	-408.10	-408.10
Bill	08/05/93	Buggs Horticultural S	GST Due	Accounts Payable	-26.25	-434.35
Bill	08/08/93	Buggs Horticultural S	GST Due	Accounts Payable	-94.78	-529.13
Bill	08/10/93	Buggs Horticultural S	GST Due	Accounts Payable	-60.20	-589.33
Bill	08/11/93	Buggs Horticultural S	GST Due	Accounts Payable	-17.50	-606.83
Bill	08/11/93	Buggs Horticultural S	GST Due	Accounts Payable	-7.75	-614.58
Bill	08/12/93	Bill's Trees	GST Due	Accounts Payable	-101.50	-716.08
Bill	08/15/93	Buggs Horticultural S	GST Due	Accounts Payable	-6.50	-722.58
Bill	08/22/93	Visa	GST Due	Accounts Payable	-12.50	-735.08
Aug '93					-735.08	-735.08

Fig. D.4 This report shows the GST Paid to Vendors report for the period August 1–31.

QuickBooks will generate and display a new report in the report window based on your new selections.

Figure D.5 shows the completed report. Again, be sure to memorize this report.

Transactions by Date

Customize... Filters... Format... Header/Footer... Hide Header Collapse Print... Memorize...

Dates This Month From 08/01/93 To 08/31/93 Total By Total only Sort By Date

08/29/93

Mr. Scott's Hair Design

GST Collected

August 1993

Type	Date	Name	Account	Split	Amount	Balance
Aug '93						
Invoice	08/06/93	Tracy Merryfield	GST Due	Accounts Receivable	10.50	10.50
Invoice	08/07/93	Mack Martini	GST Due	Accounts Receivable	21.00	31.50
Invoice	08/27/93	Tracy Merryfield	GST Due	Accounts Receivable	1.75	33.25
Invoice	08/28/93	Mack Martini	GST Due	Accounts Receivable	21.00	54.25
Invoice	08/30/93	Tracy Merryfield:Yar	GST Due	Accounts Receivable	2.10	56.35
Invoice	08/31/93	Forest Grove Drugs	GST Due	Accounts Receivable	5,468.75	5,525.10
Aug '93					5,525.10	5,525.10

Fig. D.5 The completed GST Collected report shows the period August 1–31.

When you write your cheque to the tax agency, use the Write Checks window. In the detail voucher area, select the GST Due account. This will reduce the total balance in this account.

Index

Symbols

... (ellipsis) in commands, 47
1099 report (A/P), 489
123 disk files, 510

A

A/P Report command (Reports menu), 215
A/R Aging reports, 485
A/R Summary Report, 485
accessing
  Chart of Accounts, 88-89
  Customer Message List, 157
  Customer Type List, 146
  Help system, 48
  Invoice Item List, 138
  lists, 114
  menus, 46
  Payment Method List, 151
  Payment Terms List, 154
  Ship Via List, 156
  Vendor Type List, 149
Account button (Iconbar), 88, 275
Account field (Create Invoices window), 173
accounts, 85
  adding to Chart of Accounts, 89
  assigning invoice items, 138
  assigning transactions, 332-333
  Bank account, 262
  check writing, 327-329
  color, 105-106
  combining, 104-105
  company types, 86
  current asset accounts, 437-439
  deleting, 100-101
  demoting, 102
  editing, 99-100
  Expense accounts, 84
  first-level accounts, 89, 95
  fixed asset accounts, 439-447
  Income accounts, 84
  liability accounts, 454-457
  listing, 19
  moving, 102-103
  numbering, 97-98
  payroll accounts, 448-449
  preset accounts, 67
  Quicken, 76-77
  renaming, 100
  subaccounts, 89, 95-96
  Undeposited Funds, 262
  updating values, 425-428
  see also Chart of Accounts; individual account listings
Accounts Payable, 87
  cash basis method, 308
  converting from Quicken, 79
  reports, 488-489
  setup, 21
Accounts Payable Graphs, 519-520
Accounts Payable register, 307-323
  accrual basis accounting, 308
  bills, 293
  buttons, 310
  check boxes, 311
  displaying, 307-312
  editing bills, 315-317
  entering bills, 313-314
  fields, 309-310
  historical transactions, 317-320
  navigating, 311-312
  notes, 321-322
  outstanding bills, 319-320
  printing, 322-323
  QuickReports, 320-321
  transactions, 309, 317-318
Accounts Receivable, 86
  A/R Aging reports, 485
  bad debts, 283
  converting from Quicken, 78-79
  deleting transactions, 282-283
  editing transactions, 281-282
  reports, 485-487
  setup, 21
Accounts Receivable Graphs, 519

Accounts Receivable register, 275-281
  credit memos, 282
  debit memos, 197
  invoices, 193
    current year, 202
    deleting, 196-197, 282
    editing, 195-196
    historical, 199-203
    opening balance, 200
    outstanding balance, 200
    paid, 202-203
    prior year, 202
    unpaid, 199-202
    voiding, 198
  navigating, 280-281
  notes, 287-288
  opening, 275
  printing, 288
  transaction history, 284-285
  transaction line, 276
accrual basis accounting, 308
accumulated depreciation account, 440-441
activating
  dialog box options, 44
  windows, 34
active windows, 34
Activities menu commands
  Calculator, 379
  Create Credit Memos/Refunds, 268
  Create Invoices, 170, 228, 478
  Enter Bills, 302, 320
  Enter Cash Sales, 259
  Enter Credit Card Charges, 430
  Make Deposits, 262
  Pay Bills, 300
  Pay Sales Tax, 219
  Receive Payments, 250
  Reconcile, 411, 433
  Set Up Budgets, 469
  Supplies Order Form, 224
  Use Register, 415
  Write Checks, 326, 330
address field (checks), 327
adjusting entries, 463-464
adjustments
  automatic, 418-420
  budgets, 474-475
Advanced Options dialog box, 496-497
Aging Detail reports
  Accounts Payable, 488
  Accounts Receivable, 486
Aging Summary reports
  Accounts Payable, 488
  Accounts Receivable, 486
alignment
  checks, 344
  forms, 230-233
  printing, 227
American Express, 270-273
amortization, 22
Amount of Discount text box (Calculate Discount dialog box), 255
annual sales tax payment, 208
appending company files, 534-537
applying
  payments to invoices, 248-253
  sales tax, 211-214
Arrange Icons command (Window menu), 51
arranging icons, 51
artwork, 227
ASCII disk files, 108, 510
asset accounts, 104
assets, 84, 424
  capital gains/losses, 445
  Current assets, 424, 437-439
  depreciable, 442-447
  Fixed assets, 87, 427, 439-447
  non-current assets, 424
  Other Current Assets, 86
  schedule of assets, 21
assigning
  accounts
    to invoice items, 138
    to transactions, 332-333
  bills to Expense account, 297
  passwords, 545-548
  payroll liability accounts to transactions, 449-452
ATM (Automated Teller Machine), 412
Auto Sales Tax, 138
Auto Tax, 205
  Canadian, 591
  rates, 206-209
  sales tax, 211-212
    line items, 209-210
  tax agencies, 207
  Tax District, 208
Auto Tax Calculation, 557
Auto-detect (printers), 225
Automated Teller Machine (ATM), 412
Automatic Sales Tax calculation, 69
axes (graphs), 514

B

Back Up command (File menu), 539
Backup Company To dialog box, 48, 539, 542
backups, 61, 539-540
bad debts, 283
Balance Due field (Create Invoices window), 175
balance forward system, 248
Balance Sheet accounts, 84-87, 424-425
  Accounts Payable, 87
  Accounts Receivable, 86
  adding to Chart of Accounts, 89-93
  assets, 84, 424
    Current assets, 424
    fixed assets, 439-440
    non-current assets, 424
  Bank accounts, 86
  budget amount, 469
  Capital/Equity accounts, 87
  Credit Card accounts, 87

Expense accounts, 93-95
Fixed Assets, 87
Income accounts, 93-95
liabilities, 84, 424
Long Term Liability account, 87
opening balance, 91-93
Other Current Assets, 86
Other Current Liability account, 87
Owner's Equity, 84, 425
Standard Balance Sheet reports, 480
Balance Sheet Budget Overview reports, 491
Balance Sheet Budget vs. Actual reports, 491
Balance Sheet Reports, 484-485
balances
credit balances, 256
opening balance, 93
Accounts Receivable register, 278
Balance Sheet accounts, 91-93
entering transaction, 426
invoices, 200
reconciliation process, 413-414
outstanding, 200
bank accounts, 86, 262
automatic adjustment, 418-420
differences, 417-420
interest, 413
marking cleared transactions, 414-415
missing transactions, 415
opening balance, 413-414
printing reports, 420-421
reconciling, 409-416
bank statements, 20
bar graphs, 514
Accounts Payable Graphs, 520
Accounts Receivable Graphs, 519
Budget vs. Actual graphs, 521-522
Income and Expense Graphs, 516
Sales Graphs, 518
Bill button (Iconbar), 294
bill paying, 300-302
Credit Card accounts, 435-437
Ending Bank Balance, 301
reminders, 303-305, 407
summary, 304
bills
Accounts Payable register, 320
assigning to Expense account, 297
due date, 299
editing Accounts Payable register, 315-317
GST (Goods and Service Tax), 592
oustanding payables, 319-320
recording, 293-299
sorting, 301
book value, 439
budget reports, 489-491
Budget Reports command (Reports menu), 475
Budget vs. Actual Graphs, 521-522
budgets, 467-476
adjusting, 474-475
Balance Sheet accounts, 469
constant amounts, 472-473
creating, 467-474
Expense accounts, 468
Fill Down, 471-472
fiscal year, 469
Income accounts, 468
reports, 475-476
button bars
customizing graphs, 523-525
Report, 494-505
By Account transaction reports, 491
By Customer Detail sales reports, 488
By Customer Summary sales reports, 487
By Customer transaction reports, 491
By Date transaction reports, 492
By Item Detail sales reports, 487
By Item Summary sales reports, 487
By Rep Detail sales reports, 488
By Rep Summary sales reports, 488
By Vendor transaction reports, 491

C

Calc button (Iconbar), 379
Calc Discount button (Receive Payments window), 254
Calculate Discount dialog box, 254-255
calculations
Automatic Sales Tax, 69
depreciation, 443
pay date, 299
payroll checks, 335-336
taxes, 205, 211-212
see also Auto Tax
calculator, 379-383
closing, 382
copy operations, 382
displaying, 48
scientific calculator, 382
Calculator command (Activities menu), 379
Canadian version, 589-594
cancelling bank reconciliation procedure, 416
capital gains, 445
capital investments, 461-462
capital losses, 445
Capital/Equity account, 87
Cascade command (Window menu), 51
cascading windows, 51
cash basis accounting, 308

cash discounts, 254, 294
Cash Flow Forecast reports, 492
cash sales
  American Express payment, 271-272
  recording, 259-261
  tax, 260
Change Account Color command (Edit menu), 106
Change Graph Dates dialog box, 523
Chart of Accounts, 83-88
  accessing, 88-89
  adding accounts, 89
  Balance Sheet accounts, 84, 89-93
  Canadian, 589
  Expense accounts, 84
  Iconbar, 48
  Income accounts, 84
  modifying, 99-106
    combining accounts, 104-105
    deleting accounts, 100-101
    editing accounts, 99-100
    moving accounts, 102-103
  printing, 107-109
  saving to ASCII Disk File, 108
Chart of Accounts command (Lists menu), 88, 275
charts, *see* graphs
check boxes (dialog boxes), 44
Check button (Iconbar), 326
check face (Write Checks window), 327
check preferences, 554-555
Check Preferences dialog box, 554-555
Check Printer Setup dialog box, 343
Check register, 354-356
  Current Balance, 356
  deleting transactions, 368-369
  displaying, 353-358
  editing transactions, 363-364
  Ending Balance, 356
  entering transactions, 358-362
  fields, 355
  historical transactions, 371-372
  memorized transactions, 387-389
  navigating, 356-358
  printing, 374
  setup, 21
  summary transactions, 372-373
  splitting transactions, 364-367
  transfer transactions, 370
  voiding transactions, 369
Check register window, 354
check writing, 329-337
  detail lines, 332-337
  editing, 337-338
  manual checks, 341
  selecting account, 329
checking accounts, 20, 86
  see also Bank accounts
checks
  accounts, 327
  address field, 327
  Canadian, 589
  continuous-feed printers, 341
  date, 327
  deleting, 339-340
  detail lines, 337
  dollar amount, 327
  editing, 337-338
  logos, 349-351
  manual checks, 341
  memo field, 327
  numbering, 327
  ordering, 16-19, 341-342
  Pay to the Order of field, 327, 331
  printing, 340-351
    logos, 349-351
    positioning in printer, 342-345
    reminders, 407
    reprinting, 349
    voucher styles, 348
  refunds, 269
  reprinting, 349
  voiding, 338-339
Checks command (Preferences menu), 554
Class field (Create Invoices window), 173, 177
Class List, 113, 142-146
  adding classes, 143
  deleting classes, 145-146
  editing classes, 145
  moving classes, 144-145
  subclasses, 144
Class List window, 143
class tracking, 142
classes, 69
  budgets, 473-474
  check writing, 328
  first-level classes, 142
  parent classes, 142
  subclasses, 142
clicking mouse, 31
Clipboard, 405-406
Close Company command (File menu), 71, 538
closing
  books, 462-463
  calculator, 382
  company files, 538
  dialog boxes, 45
codes (invoice items), 137, 181
Collapse button (Report button bar), 504
Collections reports (A/R), 486
color
  accounts, 105-106
  printing, 511
  reports, 503
combining accounts, 104-105
command buttons, 56
  Create Invoices window, 174-175
  Write Checks window, 328
commands
  ... (ellipses) following commands, 47

Activities menu
- Calculator, 379
- Create Credit Memos/ Refunds, 268
- Create Invoices, 170, 228, 478
- Enter Bills, 302, 320
- Enter Cash Sales, 259
- Enter Credit Card Charges, 430
- Make Deposits, 262
- Pay Bills, 300
- Pay Sales Tax, 219
- Receive Payments, 250
- Reconcile, 411, 433
- Set Up Budgets, 469
- Supplies Order Form, 224
- Use Register, 415
- Write Checks, 326, 330

Control menu
- Maximize, 39
- Minimize, 40
- Move, 37
- Restore command, 35
- Size, 39

Edit menu
- Change Account Color, 106
- Copy Check, 404
- Delete Account, 101
- Delete Check, 340
- Delete Credit Memo, 282
- Delete Invoice, 197, 282
- Delete Line, 188
- Delete Memorized Transaction, 392
- Delete Payment, 282
- Edit Credit Memo, 282
- Edit Invoice, 282
- Edit Payment, 282
- Find, 383
- Insert Line, 188
- Memorize Check, 388, 391
- Memorize Invoice, 392
- Notepad, 287
- Paste Check, 405
- Revert, 198
- Transaction History, 284, 317
- Void Check, 339
- Void Invoice, 198, 270

File menu
- Back Up, 539
- Close Company, 71, 538
- Company Info, 80
- Convert From, 71
- Exit, 60
- Export, 544
- Import, 543
- New Company, 64, 534
- Open Company, 60, 537
- Print Forms, 234, 346
- Print List, 108
- Print Register, 288, 322, 374
- Print Report, 510
- Printer Setup, 227, 245, 508
- Restore, 541
- Utilities Rebuild, 542
- Utilities Verify Data, 543

Graphs menu
- Income and Expense Graphs, 516
- Preferences, 524
- Sales, 518

Iconbar, 47-49

Lists menu
- Chart of Accounts, 88, 275
- Classes, 143
- Customer Types, 147
- Customer:Job, 115
- Employees, 130
- Invoice Items, 138
- Invoice Options, 154
- Memorized Transactions, 389
- Other Names, 134
- Payment Methods, 151
- Re-sort List, 162
- Vendor Types, 149
- Vendors, 128

Preferences menu
- Checks, 554
- Data Entry, 561
- Graphs, 565
- Invoices, 172, 553
- Passwords, 546
- Reminders, 303, 406, 563
- Reporting, 555
- Sales Tax, 206, 557
- Transactions, 98, 550
- View, 559

Printer Setup menu, Report/List Printer, 107

Reports menu
- A/P Report, 215
- Budget Reports, 475
- Memorized Reports, 506
- QuickReport, 478

selecting, 47

Window menu
- Arrange Icons, 51
- Cascade, 51
- Tile Horizontally, 51
- Tile Vertically, 51

company files, 549-559
- appending, 534-537
- backing up, 539-540
- closing, 538
- converting from DOS to Windows, 71-73
- creating, 63-69
- opening, 537-538
- passwords, 545-548, 559
- preferences
  - checks, 554-555
  - invoices, 552-554
  - reporting, 555-557
  - sales tax, 557-559
  - transactions, 550-552
- rebuilding, 542
- restoring, 540-542
- setup, 19
- verifying, 542-543

Company Info command (File menu), 80

Company Info dialog box, 80

company information
editing, 79-80
setup, 19
Comparison Balance Sheet reports, 485
Confirmation dialog box, 283
constant budget amounts, 472-473
continuous-feed printing, 225, 341
Control menu box, 35
Control menu commands
Maximize, 39
Minimize, 40
Move, 37
Restore, 35
Size, 39
Convert From command (File menu), 71
converting
DOS system to Windows system, 69-74
first-level accounts to subaccounts, 102
subaccounts to first-level accounts, 102
to QuickBooks, 15-16
Copy Check command (Edit menu), 404
copying
in calculator, 382
transactions, 404-405
corporations, 460
Create Credit Memos/ Refunds command (Activities menu), 268
Create Invoices command (Activities menu), 170, 228, 478
Create Invoices window, 169-175, 228
Account field, 173
Balance Due field, 175
Class field, 173
command buttons, 174-175
Customer:Job field, 173
Iconbar, 48
Memo field, 175
navigating, 175
Creating New Company dialog box, 64, 534-535
credit balances, 256
Credit Card accounts, 87, 428-437
deleting transactions, 431-432
editing transactions, 431-432
interest charges, 434
payments, 435-437
reconciling, 432-435
setup, 428-429
voiding transactions, 431-432
credit limits, 195
credit memos, 189, 267-269, 282
credit policies, 153
credits, recording, 302-303
current assets, 424, 437-439
Current Balance (Check register), 356
current liabilities, 424, 454
current year invoices, 202
custom installation, 572-574
Customer Balance Detail reports (A/R), 487
Customer Balance Summary reports (A/R), 486
customer list, 20
Customer Message List, 114, 157-159
customer messages (invoices), 174
Customer Number, 25
customer payments, 248-258
Customer Type List, 113, 146-148
Customer:Job option
budgets, 473-474
check writing, 328
Customer:Job field, 173, 177
Customer:Job List, 112, 115-125
customers
adding, 116-118
deleting, 121
editing information, 118-119
naming, 119
notes, 119-121
displaying, 48
jobs
adding, 122
deleting, 124
editing, 123
moving, 124-125
notes, 123
tracking, 122-126
New Customer window, 116
customers
appending Customer:Job List, 116-118
increasing credit limit, 195
Customize Report Button
Summary reports, 494
Transaction Type reports, 497-498
Customize Report dialog box, 495-498
customizing
company files
checks, 554-555
invoices, 552-554
passwords, 559
reports, 555-557
sales tax preferences, 557-559
transaction preferences, 550-552
data entry, 561-563
graphs, 523-525, 565
reminder preferences, 563-565
reports, 494-508
view preferences, 559-561

D

data entry
Accounts Payable register, 313-314, 319-320
bills, 293-299
capital investments, 461
Check Register transactions, 358-362
credit card transactions, 429-431
credits, 302-303

customizing, 561-563
depreciable assets, 442
depreciable transactions, 443-445
invoices, 175-195
individual invoices, 203
paid, 202-203
reimbursable expenses, 191-192
sales tax line items, 212-214
unpaid, 199-202
loan payments, 456
opening balance transaction, 426
passwords, 545
receivables, 248-258
reconciliation, 415
Data Entry command (Preferences menu), 561
Data Entry Preferences dialog box, 561-563
data labels (graphs), 527
Date field (invoices), 178
dates
checks, 327
Enter Bills window, 295-305
reports, 505
debit memos, 197
Delete Account command (Edit menu), 101
Delete Check command (Edit menu), 340
Delete Credit Memo command (Edit menu), 282
Delete Invoice command (Edit menu), 197, 282
Delete Line command (Edit menu), 188
Delete Memorized Transaction command (Edit menu), 392
Delete Payment command (Edit menu), 282
deleting
accounts, 100-101
checks, 339-340
classes (Class List), 145-146
credit memos, 282
customer messages (Customer Message List), 159
customers (Customer:Job List), 121
customer types (Customer Type List), 148
employees (Employee List), 133
Invoice Item List, 141
invoices, 196-197, 282
jobs from Customer:Job List, 124
line items (invoices), 188-189
memorized invoices, 394-395
memorized reports, 507-508
memorized transactions, 391-392
names, 136
payment methods (Payment Method List), 152
payment terms (Payment Term List), 155
shipping method (Ship Via List), 157
split transactions, 367
subaccounts, 100-101
transaction groups, 401-404
transactions
Accounts Receivable, 282-283
Check Register, 368-369
confirmation dialog box, 283
Credit Card register, 431-432
transfer transactions, 370
vendor types (Vendor Type List), 150
vendors (Vendor List), 129-130
demoting accounts, 102
deposits
American Express, 272-273
editing, 266-267
recording, 262-266
reminders, 407
Deposits and Other Credits window, 414
depreciable assets, 442-447
depreciable transactions, 443-445
depreciation, 439-441
Desktop, 50-53
detail lines (checks), 332-337
dialog boxes, 41-45
Advanced Options, 496-497
Backup Company To, 48, 539, 542
Calculate Discount, 254
Change Graph Dates, 523
check boxes, 44
Check Preferences, 554-555
Check Printer Setup, 343
closing, 45
Company Info, 80
Creating New Company, 64, 534-535
Customize Report, 495-498
Data Entry Preferences, 561-563
drop-down lists, 42-43
Export, 544
Export File Name, 544
Fill Down, 471
Filter Transactions, 498-501, 593
Find, 384
Format Header/Footer, 503
Graph Preferences, 524
Invoice Preferences, 172, 553-554
Invoice Printer Setup, 225
Invoice Printing Font, 227
list boxes, 41
Memorize Report, 504, 507

Name of File to Restore, 541
Name Restored File, 541
New Company Summary, 535
New Memorized Transaction Group, 396
Open a Company, 537
options, 42-44
Password Preferences, 546
Payments to Deposits, 262
Print Mailing Labels, 242
Print Register, 288
Print Report, 108, 421, 504, 510-511
Product Registration, 24
QuickBooks, 537
QuickBooks Install Destination, 572
QuickBooks Install Options, 572-573
QuickBooks Install Program Group, 573
Reconcile Adjustment, 419
Reconciliation Complete, 419-420
Reminder Preferences, 563-565
Report Printer Setup, 508, 529
Reporting Preferences, 555-557
Sales Tax Preferences, 206, 557-559
Set Up Budgets, 469
Supplies Order Form, 224
text boxes, 41
Transaction History, 318
Transaction Preferences, 98, 550-552
View Preferences, 559-561
Working, 543

discount line item (invoices), 180

discounts
cash discounts, 294
line items (invoices), 184
payments, 254-256
sales discounts, 294

displaying
Accounts Payable register, 307-312
calculator, 48
check register, 353-358
Customer:Job List, 48
Invoice Items List, 48
Memorized Transaction List, 48
Qcards, 48
registers, 48, 218
Reminders List, 48
Vendor List, 48

dollar amounts (checks), 327
down payments, 256-267
draft mode (printing), 511
dragging mouse, 31
draw accounts, 457, 460-461
drop-down lists, 42-43, 69, 114
due dates (bills), 299
duplicate check numbers, 555
duplicate invoice numbers, 554

E

early payment discounts, 254-256
Edit Account window, 100
Edit Credit Memo command (Edit menu), 282
Edit Invoice command (Edit menu), 282

Edit menu commands
Change Account Color, 106
Copy Check, 404
Delete Account, 101
Delete Check, 340
Delete Credit Memo, 282
Delete Invoice, 197, 282
Delete Line, 188
Delete Memorized Transaction, 392
Delete Payment, 282
Edit Credit Memo, 282
Edit Invoice, 282
Edit Payment, 282
Find, 383
Insert Line, 188
Memorize Check, 388, 391
Memorize Invoice, 392
Notepad, 287
Paste Check, 405
Revert, 198
Transaction History, 284, 317
Void Check, 339
Void Invoice, 198, 270

Edit Payment command (Edit menu), 282
Edit Vendor window, 129

editing
accounts, 99-100
bills, 315-317
Chart of Accounts, 99-106
checks, 337-338
classes (Class List), 145
company information, 79-80
customer information, 118-119
Customer Type List, 147
customer messages (Customer Message List), 159
Employee List, 132
Invoice Item List, 140-141
invoices, 195-196
jobs (Customer:Job List), 123
memorized invoices, 394-395
memorized reports, 507-508
Other Names List, 135-136
payment methods (Payment Method List), 152
payment terms (Payment Term List), 155
payments, 258-259, 266-267
shipping method (Ship Via List), 156

subaccounts, 99-100
text box information, 42
transaction groups, 401-403
transactions
Accounts Receivable, 281-282
Check Register, 363-364
Credit Card register, 431-432
memorized, 390-391
split transactions, 367
transfer transactions, 370
Vendor List, 128
Vendor Type List, 150
ellipses (...) in commands, 47
Employee List, 113, 130-133
appending, 131-132
deleting employees, 133
editing, 132
notes, 132-133
setup, 21
Employees command (Lists menu), 130
Employer ID number, 80
Ending Balance
Check register, 356
Reconcile window, 412
Ending Balance field (Write Checks window), 328
Ending Bank Balance, 301
Enter Bills command (Activities menu), 302, 320
Enter Bills window, 294, 320
Iconbar, 48
Recalc button, 299
Enter Cash Sales command (Activities menu), 259
Enter Cash Sales window, 260
Enter Credit Card Charges command (Activities menu), 430
entering information, *see* data entry
equity (Net Worth Graph), 521
equity accounts, 457-462
corporations, 460
draw accounts, 457
partnerships, 460
sole proprietorship, 460
Existing Credits field (Receive Payments window), 257
Exit command (File menu), 60
exiting
QuickBooks, 60-61
tutorial, 59
Expand button (Report button bar), 504
Expense accounts, 84, 87-88
adding to Chart of Accounts, 93-95
bills, 297
budget amount, 468
Budget vs. Actual Graphs, 522
Profit & Loss Statement, 481
expenses
mark up, 192-193
prepaid expenses, 438
reimbursable, 189-193
tracking, 552
Expenses by Vendor Detail reports, 484
Expenses by Vendor Summary reports, 483
Export command (File menu), 544
Export dialog box, 544
Export File Name dialog box, 544
exporting files, 544-545
Express Installation, 570-571

F

Father backups, 540
FICA tax, 70, 452
fields
Accounts Payable register, 309-310
Check register, 355
Create Invoices window, 173-175
drop-down lists, 114
lists, 114
file management, 533-548
File menu commands
Back Up, 539
Close Company, 71, 538
Company Info, 80
Convert From, 71
Exit, 60
Export, 544
Import, 543
New Company, 64, 534
Open Company, 60, 537
Print Forms, 234, 346
Print List, 108
Print Register, 288, 322, 374
Print Report, 510
Printer Setup, 227, 245, 508
Restore, 541
Utilities Rebuild, 542
Utilities Verify Data, 543
file names (converted), 72
files
company files, 63-69
converted file names, 72
exporting, 544-545
IIF format, 543
importing, 543
password protection, 585
passwords, 545-548
QIF format, 543
see also individual file type listings
Fill Down, 471-472
Fill Down dialog box, 471
Filter Transactions dialog box, 498-501, 593
Find command (Edit menu), 383
Find dialog box, 384
finding transactions, 383-386
first-level accounts, 89, 95
converting to subaccounts, 102
moving, 96
first-level classes, 142
fiscal year budget, 469

fixed assets, 87, 439-447
  accumulated depreciation account, 440-441
  valuation, 427
fonts
  printing, 227
  reports, 502
footers
  reports, 502
  statements, 238
forecasting sales, 468
Form 1099 reports, 489
Format button (Report button bar), 501, 504
Format Header/Footer dialog box, 503
formats (invoices), 170-172, 230
formatting reports, 501-503
forms
  alignment, 230-233
  printing, 225
freezing last year's transactions, 464
functions (registers), 218

G

gains from investments, 428
general journal window, 70
General Ledger reports, 493
grandfather backups, 540
graph preferences, 565
Graph Preferences dialog box, 524
graph windows, 526-527
graphs, 70, 513-530
  Accounts Payable Graphs, 519-520
  Accounts Receivable Graphs, 519
  bar graphs, 514
  Budget vs. Actual Graphs, 521-522
  creating, 516-522
  customizing, 523-525
  data labels, 527
  Income and Expense Graphs, 516-517
  legends (pie charts), 517
  line-and-marker graph, 515
  Net Worth Graph, 521
  pie charts, 514-517
  preferences, 524-525
  printing, 529-530
  QuickZoom, 526-529
  Sales Graphs, 518-519
  see also charts
Graphs command (Preferences menu), 565
Graphs menu commands
  Income and Expense Graphs, 516
  Preferences, 524
  Sales, 518
group line item (invoices), 180
groups
  adding transactions, 397-400
  deleting, 401-404
  editing, 401-403
  invoice items, 70
  line items (invoices), 188
  transactions, 395-404
GST (Goods and Services Tax), 590-594

H

Header/Footer button (Report button bar), 503
headers
  invoices, 173, 178-179
  reports, 502
headings (statements), 237-238
Help, 52-60
  accessing, 48
  menu bar, 55-56
  Qcards, 53-54
Hide Header button (Report button bar), 504
hiding
  detail lines (checks), 337
  pie chart slices, 528-529
historical bills (Accounts Payable register), 320
historical invoices, 199-203
historical transactions
  Accounts Payable register, 317-320
  Accounts Receivable register, 284-285
  Check register, 371-372
horizontal axis (graphs), 514

I

Iconbar, 47-49
  Accnt button, 88, 275
  Bill button, 294, 302
  Calc button, 379
  Check button, 326
  Invoice button, 170
  Item button, 138
  MemTX button, 389
  Qcard button, 54
  removing from screen, 49
  settings, 560-561
  sizing, 49
  Vend button, 126
icons, 35, 50-51
IIF files, 543
Import command (File menu), 543
importing files, 543
Income accounts, 84, 87-88
  adding to Chart of Accounts, 93-95
  budget amount, 468
  Budget vs. Actual Graphs, 522
  Profit & Loss Statement, 481
Income and Expense Graphs, 516-517
Income and Expense Graphs command (Graphs menu), 516
Income by Customer Detail reports, 483
Income by Customer Summary reports, 483
Income Statement, *see* Profit & Loss Statement
Insert Line command (Edit menu), 188

inserting invoice line items, 188
installing QuickBooks for Windows, 569-574
interest
  charges (credit cards), 434
  reconciliation (bank accounts), 413
Intuit
  ordering supplies, 17-19
  supplies order form, 224
investments
  capital investments, 461-462
  gains/losses, 428
Invoice button (Iconbar), 170
Invoice Item List, 180
  appending, 138-140
  Auto Sales Tax, 138
  deleting items, 141
  displaying, 48
  editing, 140-141
invoice items
  appending to Invoice Item List, 138-140
  assigning accounts, 138
  codes, 137, 181
  grouping, 70
  listing, 21
Invoice Items List, 113, 136-141
Invoice options (Filter Transactions dialog box), 500-501
Invoice Options command (Lists menu), 154
invoice preferences, 95, 552-554
Invoice Preferences dialog box, 172, 553-554
Invoice Printer Setup dialog box, 225
Invoice Printing Font dialog box, 227
invoices
  Account information, 177
  Accounts Receivable register, 282
  balances, 200
  Class field, 177
  credit memos, 189
  current year, 202
  customer messages, 174
  Customer:Job field, 177
  date, 178
  deleting, 196-197, 394-395
  duplicate invoice numbers, 554
  editing, 195-196
    memorized invoices, 394-395
    restricting access, 196
  formats, 170-172
  forms, 223-224
  GST (Goods and Services Tax), 591-592
  headers, 173, 178-179
  historical, 199-203
  job estimates, 203-204
  line items, 180-188
    deleting, 188-189
    discounts, 184
    grouping, 188
    inserting, 188
    other charges, 183-184
    part, 183-184
    payments, 187-204
    sales tax, 185-204, 209-214
    service, 183-184
    subtotal, 184-204
  memorized invoices, 392-395
  ordering, 16-19
  paid, 202-203
  payments, 248-253
  printing, 233-237
    format, 230
    positioning in printer, 229-233
    previewing, 228-229
    reminders, 407
    reprinting, 235-237
    selecting, 234-235
    testing, 227
  prior year, 202
  product invoices, 171
  professional invoices, 170
  recording transactions (Accounts Receivable register), 193
  reimbursable expenses, 189-193
  sales tax, 211-214
  service invoice, 170
  titles, 198-199
  unpaid, 199-202
  voiding, 198, 270
  writing, 175-195
Invoices command (Preferences menu), 172, 553
Item button (Iconbar), 138
Itemized Balance Sheet reports, 485
Itemized Profit and Loss reports, 483

J

job estimates, 203-204
Job Profit and Loss reports, 483
job tracking, 69
  classes, 142
  Customer:Job List, 122-125
jobs
  appending Customer:Job List, 122
  budgets, 473-474
Journal reports, 494

K

keyboard, 31-32
  calculator use, 380-381
  navigating
    Accounts Payable register, 312
    Check register, 357
    Create Invoices window, 175
  selecting
    commands, 47
    dialog box options, 44

L

legends (pie charts), 517
letterhead paper, 226
liabilities, 84, 424
- accounts, 454-457
  - combining with asset account, 104
  - GST (Goods and Services Tax), 590
  - Other Current Liability account, 87
  - payroll liability accounts, 449-452
- credit cards, 428
- current liabilities, 424, 454
- long-term liabilities, 87, 424, 454
- sales tax owed, 214-216

line items (invoices), 180-188
- deleting, 188-189
- discounts, 184
- grouping, 188
- inserting, 188
- other charges, 183-184
- part, 183-184
- payments, 187-204
- sales tax, 185-204, 209-214
- service, 183-184
- subtotal, 184-204

line-and-marker graph, 515
list boxes (dialog boxes), 41
listing
- accounts, 19
- customers, 20
- employees, 21
- invoice items, 21
- payments, 262
- printers, 225
- vendors, 20

lists, 111-114
- accessing, 114
- adding to on-the-fly, 160-161
- Class List, 113, 142-146
- Customer Message List, 114, 157-159
- Customer Types List, 113, 146-148
- Customer:Job List, 112, 115-125
- Employee List, 113, 130-133
- fields, 114
- Invoice Items List, 113, 136-141, 180
- Other Names List, 113, 133-136
- Payment Method List, 113, 151-152
- printing, 162-165
- Reminders List, 303-305
- Ship Via List, 113, 156-157
- sorting, 162
- Terms List, 113, 153-155
- Vendor List, 113, 125-130
- Vendor Type List, 113, 148-150

Lists menu commands
- Chart of Accounts, 88, 275
- Classes, 143
- Customer Types, 147
- Customer:Job, 115
- Employees, 130
- Invoice Items, 138
- Invoice Options, 154
- Memorized Transactions, 389
- Other Names, 134
- Payment Methods, 151
- Re-sort List, 162
- Vendor Types, 149
- Vendors, 128

loan amortization, 22
loans
- schedule of loans, 21
- tracking, 455-457

logos (checks), 227, 349-351
Long Term Liability account, 87
long-term liabilities, 424, 454
losses on investments, 428

M

mailing labels, 241-244
Make Deposits command (Activities menu), 262
Make Deposits window, 263
manual checks, 341
mark up (reimbursable expenses), 192-193
marking transactions cleared, 414-415
Maximize button, 40
Maximize command (Control menu), 39
maximizing
- reports, 506
- windows, 39-40

MCARE account, 70
memo field
- checks, 327
- Create Invoices window, 175

Memorize Check command (Edit menu), 388, 391
Memorize Invoice command (Edit menu), 392
Memorize Report dialog box, 504
memorized invoices, 392-395
Memorized Report dialog box, 507
memorized reports, 477
- deleting, 507-508
- editing, 507-508
- recalling, 506-507

Memorized Reports command (Report menu), 506
Memorized Transaction list, 48
memorized transactions, 387-392
- deleting, 391-392
- editing, 390-391
- recalling, 389-390
- reminders, 407

Memorized Transactions command (Lists menu), 389

MemTX button Iconbar, 389
menu bar
  accessing menus, 46
  Help menu bar, 55-56
menus, 45
  accessing, 46
  Help menu bar, 55-56
  Other Reports, 492-494
  pull-down, 47
  removing from screen, 47
messages on invoices, 174
Minimize button, 40
Minimize command (Control menu), 40
minimizing windows, 40
Missing Checks reports, 493
missing transactions, 415
modifying Chart of Accounts, 99-106
  color, 105-106
  combining accounts, 104-105
  deleting accounts, 100-101
  editing accounts, 99-100
  moving accounts, 102-103
money market account, 86
  see also Bank accounts
monthly sales tax payment, 208
Most Common Sales Tax Rate (%), 66
mouse, 30-33
  calculator use, 380
  moving accounts, 102
  navigating
    Accounts Payable register, 312
    Check register, 357
  pointer, 30
  reorganizing lists, 161-162
  resizing windows, 37
  selecting dialog box options, 44
Move command (Control menu), 37
moving
  accounts, 102-103
  classes (Class List), 144-145
  first-level accounts, 96
  jobs (Customer:Job List), 124-125
  mouse pointer, 30
  subaccounts, 96
  transactions, 404
  windows, 37-38

N

Name of File to Restore dialog box, 541
Name Restored File dialog box, 541
names (Other Names List), 134-136
navigating
  Accounts Payable register, 280-281, 311-312
  Check register, 356-358
  Create Invoices window, 175
  memorized transactions, 390
  Write Checks window, 329
negative numbers, 302, 501
net worth, 457
Net Worth Graph, 521
New Account window, 90, 94
New Company command (File menu), 64, 534
New Company Summary dialog box, 535
New Customer window, 116
New Employee window, 131
New Item window, 139
New Memorized Transaction Group dialog box, 396
non-current assets, 424
Notepad, 287-288
  Accounts Payable register, 321-322
  Customer:Job List, 119-121
  Employee List, 132-133
  Vendor List, 128-129
Notepad command (Edit menu), 287
notes
  Accounts Receivable register, 287-288
  Customer:Job List, 119-123
  Employee List, 132-133
  Vendor List, 128-129
  vendors (Accounts Payable register), 321-322
numbering
  accounts, 97-98
  checks, 327
numbers, 302, 501

O

on-line Help, 54-56
Open a Company dialog box, 537
open balances (Accounts Receivable register), 278
Open Company command (File menu), 60, 537
Open Invoices by Customer reports (A/R), 486
Open Invoices reports (A/R), 486
opening
  company files, 537-538
  registers (Accounts Receivable), 275
Opening Balance Equity account/Retained Earnings account, 459
opening balance, 93
  Balance Sheet accounts, 91-93
  bank accounts, 413-414
  entering transaction, 426
  invoices, 200
options
  dialog boxes, 42-44
  Iconbar, 47-49
  menus, 47

ordering supplies, 16-19, 223-224
- checks, 341-342
- printing order form, 224

Other Charges line item (invoices), 180, 183-184
Other Current Asset account, 86
Other Current Liability account, 87
Other Names List, 113, 133-136
- appending, 134-135
- deleting names, 136
- editing, 135-136

Other Reports menu, 492-494
outstanding Accounts Payable, 319-320
outstanding invoice balances, 200
overpayments, 256-267
owner password, 545
Owner's Equity, 84, 425
Owner's Equity accounts, 460

P

P&L Budget by Job Overview reports, 491
P&L Budget Overview reports, 490
P&L Budget vs. Actual by Job reports, 491
P&L Budget vs. Actual reports, 491
paid invoices, 202-203
paper feed (printers), 225
parent classes, 142
part line item (invoices), 180, 183-184
partnerships, 460
Password Preferences dialog box, 546
passwords, 545-548, 585
- assigning, 545-548
- changing, 547-548
- editing invoices, 196
- preferences, 559
- removing, 548

Passwords command (Preferences menu), 546
Paste Check command (Edit menu), 405
pasting transactions, 404-405
Pay Bills command (Activities menu), 300
Pay Bills window, 300
Pay Sales Tax command (Activities menu), 219
Pay to the Order of field (checks), 327, 331
paying bills, 300-302
- Ending Bank Balance, 301
- reminders, 303-305, 407
- summary, 304

payment line item (invoices), 180, 187-204
Payment Method List, 113, 151-152
payment per invoice method, 248
Payment Term List, 154-155
payments
- applying to invoices, 248-253
- balance forward system, 248
- cash sales, 271-272
- Credit Card accounts, 435-437
- credits, 302-303
- customer payments, 248-258
- discounts, 254-256
- down payments, 256-267
- editing, 258-259, 266-267
- listing, 262
- overpayment, 256-267
- prepayments, 256-267
- sales tax, 219-221
- splitting, 258
- terms, 153

Payments to Deposits dialog box, 262
payroll, 70
- accounts, 447-453
- employee list, 21
- FICA tax, 452
- liability accounts, 449-452
- QuickPay, 387
- split transactions, 335-336
- taxes, 452-453

Payroll reports, 493
pie charts, 514-515
- Accounts Payable Graphs, 520
- Accounts Receivable Graphs, 519
- hiding slices, 528-529
- Income and Expense Graphs, 517
- legends, 517
- Sales graphs, 518

point-of-sale transactions, 259
pointer (mouse), 30
positioning invoices in printers, 229-233
Preferences command (Graphs menu), 524
Preferences menu commands
- Checks, 554
- Data Entry, 561
- Graphs, 565
- Invoices, 172, 553
- Passwords, 546
- Reminders, 303, 406, 563
- Reporting, 555
- Sales Tax, 206, 557
- Transactions, 98, 550
- View, 559

prepaid expenses, 438
prepayments, 256-267
preprinted forms, 225
preset accounts, 67
preset reports, 480-494
previewing invoices, 228-229
Previous Year Comparison reports, 483
Print button (Report button bar), 504

Print Forms command (File menu), 234, 346
Print List command (File menu), 108
Print Mailing Labels dialog box, 242
Print Preview window, 229
Print Register command (File menu), 288, 322, 374
Print Register dialog box, 288
Print Report command (File menu), 510
Print Report dialog box, 108, 421, 504, 510-511
Printer Setup command (File menu), 227, 245, 508
Printer Setup menu commands, Report/List Printer, 107
printers
  Auto-detect, 225
  blank paper option, 226
  check alignment, 341-345
  continuous feed forms, 225
  form alignment, 230-233
  invoice alignment, 229-233
  letterhead paper, 226
  listing, 225
  paper feed, 225
  settings, 227
  setup, 26-27, 224-228
printing
  Accounts Payable register, 322-323
  Accounts Receivable registers, 288
  alignment, 227
  Chart of Accounts, 107-109
  Check register, 374
  checks, 340-351
    logos, 349-351
    positioning in printer, 342-345
    reminders, 407
    reprinting, 349
    voucher styles, 348
  color printing, 511
  draft mode, 511
  fonts, 227
  graphs, 529-530
  invoices, 233-237
    format, 230
    previewing, 228-229
    reminders, 407
    reprinting, 235-237
    selecting, 234-235
  lists, 162-165
  Logo button, 227
  mailing labels, 241-244
  preprinted forms, 225
  print ranges, 511
  reconciliation, 420-421, 508-511
  rotary index cards, 241-246
  statements, 237-241
  supplies order form, 224
  testing, 227
prior year invoices, 202
product invoices, 171
Product Registration dialog box, 24
professional invoices, 170
Profit & Loss Statement, 481-484
  see also Income Statement
projects, 69
pull-down menus, 47

Q

Qcard button (Iconbar), 54
Qcards, 48, 53-54, 561
QIF files, 543
quarterly sales tax payment, 208
quick keys, 31-33, 47
QuickBooks dialog box, 537
QuickBooks for Windows
  Canadian version, 589-594
  conversion, 15-16
  converting DOS system to Windows system, 69-74
  customizing, 549-565
  exiting, 60-61
  installing, 569-574
  Quicken comparison, 583-587
  QuickPay add-in, 575-581
  starting, 22-23, 29-30
  system requirements, 569-570
QuickBooks Install Destination dialog box, 572
QuickBooks Install Options dialog box, 572-573
QuickBooks Install Program Group dialog box, 573
Quicken, 73-79, 583-587
QuickFill, 114
  Auto Tax, 207
  checks, 331
QuickInvoice, 76
QuickPay add-in program, 387, 575-581
QuickReport command (Reports menu), 478
QuickReports, 70, 286, 320-321, 478-480
QuickZoom, 70, 286, 478, 526-529

R

Re-sort List command (Lists menu), 162
rebuilding company files, 542
Recalc button (Enter Bills window), 299
recalling
  memorized invoices, 394
  memorized reports, 506-507
  transactions, 389-390
receipts
  point-of-sale payments, 260
  returns, 269
Receive Payments command (Activities menu), 250
Receive Payments window
  Calc Discount button, 254
  Existing Credits field, 257

Reconcile Adjustment dialog box, 419
Reconcile command (Activities menu), 411, 433
Reconcile window, 411
Reconciliation Complete dialog box, 419-420
reconciliation, 263
  credit card accounts, 432-435
  bank accounts, 409-416
recording
  bills, 293-299
  capital investments, 461
  cash sales, 259-261
  credits, 302-303
  deposits, 262-266
  draws, 460-461
  invoice transactions, 193
  payments, 257-258
  returns, 267-270
refund checks, 269
registering QuickBooks program, 24-26
registers, 216
  Accounts Payable, 307-323
  Accounts Receivable, 275-281
  check register, *see* check register
  displaying, 48
  displays, 218
  functions, 218
  printing, 288
  Sales Tax Payable, 216-218
  transaction area, 217-222
  see also individual listings
reimbursable expenses
  invoices, 189-193
  mark up, 192-193
  setup, 190
  tracking, 189-190
Reminder Preferences dialog box, 563-565
Reminder Preferences window, 406
Reminders, 70, 406-408
  bill paying, 303-305
  customizing preferences, 563-565
Reminders command (Preferences menu), 303, 406, 563
Reminders List, 48, 303-305
removing
  Iconbar from screen, 49
  menus from screen, 47
  passwords, 548
renaming
  accounts, 100
  classes (Class List), 145
  customers (Customer:Job List), 119
  vendors (Vendor List), 128
Report Button bar, 494-505
  Collapse button, 504
  Customize Report button, 494
  Expand button, 504
  Format button, 501, 504
  Header/Footer button, 503
  Hide Header button, 504
  Print button, 504
  second row, 505
  Show Header button, 504
Report menu commands, Memorized Reports, 506
Report Printer Setup dialog box, 508, 529
Report window, 494-508
Report/List Printer command (Printer Setup menu), 107
Reporting command (Preferences menu), 555
Reporting Preferences dialog box, 555-557
reports, 477-511
  A/R Aging Report, 485
  Accounts Payable reports, 488-489
  Accounts Receivable, 485-487
  Balance Sheet Reports, 484-485
  budget reports, 475-476, 489-491
  Cash Flow Forecast, 492
  categories, 477
  color, 503
  customizing, 494-508
  dates, 505
  fonts, 502
  footers, 502
  formatting, 501-503
  General Ledger, 493
  GST (Goods and Service Tax), 592-594
  headers, 502
  Journal, 494
  memorized reports, 477
    deleting, 507-508
    editing, 507-508
    recalling, 506-507
  Missing Checks, 493
  Payroll, 493
  preferences, 555-557
  preset, 480-494
  printing, 508-511
  Profit & Loss Statement, 481-484
  QuickReports, 70, 286, 320-321, 478-480
  reconciliations, 420-421
  sales reports, 487-488
  Sales Tax Liability Report, 215
  Standard Balance Sheet, 480
  Summary reports, 493
  Transaction Journal, 494
  Transaction reports, 491-492
  Trial Balance, 493
  viewing, 505-506
Reports menu commands
  A/P Report, 215
  Budget Reports, 475
  QuickReport, 478
reprinting
  checks, 349
  invoices, 235-237
resizing windows, 35, 38
resolving reconciliation differences, 417-418
Restore command
  Control menu, 35
  File menu, 541

restoring
company files, 540-542
windows, 35-37
restricting invoice editing access, 196
Retained Earnings account, 459
Return Merchandise Authorization (RMA) number, 267
returns
credit memos, 189, 267-269
receipts, 269
recording, 267-270
Revert command (Edit menu), 198
reviewing budget reports, 476
rotary index cards, 241-246

S

sales discounts, 294
sales forecasts, 468
Sales command (Graphs menu), 518
Sales Graphs, 518-519
sales reports, 487-488
sales tax, 205-222
applying to invoices, 211-214
Automatic Sales Tax calculation, 69
Auto Tax, 211-212
liability, 214-216
line items (invoices), 180, 185-204, 209-214
payments, 219-221
preferences, 557-559
tracking, 205-210
Sales Tax command (Preferences menu), 206, 557
Sales Tax Liability Report, 215, 489
Sales Tax Payable register, 216-218
Sales Tax Preferences dialog box, 206, 557-559
sample data (Help), 59-60
saving
Chart of Accounts to ASCII Disk File, 108
Desktop, 51-53
windows, 52
savings accounts, 86
see also Bank accounts
schedule of assets, 21
schedule of loans, 21
scientific calculator, 382
screen
removing Iconbar, 49
removing menus, 47
scrolling windows, 40-41
searches, *see* finding transactions
selecting
check boxes (dialog boxes), 44
checks, 347
command buttons, 56
commands, 47
dialog boxes, 44
Help topics, 56
invoices, 234-235
lessons (Tour QuickBooks screen), 58
selection box, 280
selling depreciable assets, 445-447
service invoices, 170
service line item (invoices), 180, 183-184
Set Up Budgets command (Activities menu), 469
Set Up Budgets dialog box, 469
settings
setup
account listing, 19
Accounts Payable/Receivable, 21
Auto Tax rates, 206-209
bank statement, 20
budgets, 467-474
Check register, 21
Checking account, 20
company files, 64-69
company information, 19
Credit Card account, 428-429
customer list, 20
invoice items, 21
printers, 26-27, 224-228
Quicken data, 73-79
reimbursable expenses, 190
schedule of assets/loans, 21
vendor list, 20
Ship Via List, 113, 156-157
Show Header button (Report button bar), 504
Size command (Control menu), 39
sizing Iconbar, 49
sole proprietorships, 460
Son backups, 540
sorting
bills, 301
lists, 162
splitting
payments, 258
transactions, 334-335
Check register, 364-367
payroll checks, 335-336
Standard Balance Sheet reports, 480, 484
Standard Profit and Loss statement, 483
starting QuickBooks, 22-23, 29-30
statements
footers, 238
headings, 237-238
printing, 237-241
subaccounts, 89, 95-96
converting to first-level accounts, 102
deleting, 100-101
editing, 99-100
moving, 96
subclasses, 142-144
Subtotal line item (invoices), 180, 184-204
summarizing bills, 304
Summary Balance Sheet reports, 485

Summary reports, 493-494
summary transactions (Check register), 372-373
supplies, 16-19, 223-224
  checks, 341-342
  printing order form, 224
Supplies Order Form command (Activities menu), 224
Supplies Order Form dialog box, 224
switching windows, 50
system requirements
  QuickBooks for Windows, 569-570
  QuickPay add-in program, 577

T

tab-delimited disk files, 510
tax agencies, 207
Tax Agency text box, 66
Tax District, 208
Tax District text box, 66
tax forms
  Form 1099 reports, 489
  W-2 forms, 493
taxes
  Auto Sales Tax, 138
  cash sales, 260
  FICA tax, 452
  GST (Goods and Services Tax), 590-594
  payroll, 452-453
  rates, 206-209
  sales tax, 69, 138
  see also sales tax
terminating bank reconciliation process, 416
terminology changes when converting from DOS, 74
Terms List, 113, 153-155
test printings (invoices), 227
text boxes (dialog boxes), 41
  editing information, 42
  entering information, 42
Tile Horizontally command (Window menu), 51
Tile Vertically command (Window menu), 51
tiling windows, 51
title bar, 34, 40
titles (invoices), 198-199
Tour QuickBooks screen, 57-58
tracking
  expenses, 189-190, 552
  jobs, 69
    classes, 142
    Customer:Job List, 122-125
  loans, 455-457
  sales tax, 205-210
transaction area (registers), 217-222
Transaction History command (Edit menu), 284, 317
Transaction Journal reports, 494
transaction line (Accounts Receivable register), 276
Transaction Preferences dialog box, 98, 550-552
Transaction reports, 491-492
Transaction Type reports, 497-498
transactions
  assigning accounts, 332-333
  Accounts Payable register, 309
  Accounts Receivable
    deleting, 282-283
    editing, 281-282
  Check Register
    deleting, 368-369
    editing, 363-364
    entering, 358-362
    voiding, 369
  confirmation dialog box, 283
  copying, 404-405
  credit cards, 429-431
  Credit Card register
    deleting, 431-432
    editing, 431-432
    voiding, 431-432
  depreciable, 443-445
  entering opening balance, 426
  filtering, 498-501
  finding, 383-386
  freezing last year's transactions, 464
  groups
    adding transactions, 397-400
    deleting, 401-404
    editing, 401-403
  historical
    Accounts Payable register, 317-320
    Accounts Receivable register, 284-285
    Check register, 371-372
  marking as cleared, 414-415
  memorized, *see* memorized transactions
  missing, 415
  moving, 404
  opening balance, 93
  password, 545
  pasting, 404-405
  payroll liability accounts, 449-452
  preferences, 550-552
  splitting, 334-335
    Check register, 364-367
    payroll checks, 335-336
  summary transactions, 372-373
  transfer transactions, 370
  year-end transactions, 462-464
Transactions command (Preferences menu), 98, 550
Transactions Preferences dialog box, 550
transfer transactions, 370, 459
Trial Balance reports, 493
tutorial, 57-59

U

Undeposited Funds account, 262
unpaid invoices, 199-202
Unpaid Bills Detail reports (A/P), 488
updating account values, 425-428
Use Register command (Activities menu), 415
utilities, 542-543
Utilities Rebuild command (File menu), 542
Utilities Verify Data command (File menu), 543

V

value updates (accounts), 425-428
Vend button (Iconbar), 126
Vendor Balance Detail reports (A/P), 489
Vendor Balance Summary reports (A/P), 489
Vendor List, 113, 125-130
- appending vendors, 126-127
- deleting vendors, 129-130
- displaying, 48
- editing, 128
- notes, 128-129
- renaming vendors, 128
- setup, 20

Vendor Type List, 113, 148-150
Vendor Types command (Lists menu), 149
vendor notes (Accounts Payable register), 321-322
Vendors command (Lists menu), 128
verifying company files, 542-543
vertical axis (graphs), 514
View command (Preferences menu), 559
view preferences, 559-561
View Preferences dialog box, 559-561
viewing
- customer information, 118
- reports
  - budget reports, 475-476
  - maximizing, 506
  - on-screen, 505-506
- topics (tutorial), 59
- transaction history (A/R register), 284-285

Void Check command (Edit menu), 339
Void Invoice command (Edit menu), 198, 270
voiding
- checks, 338-339
- invoices, 198, 270
- transactions
  - Check register, 369
  - Credit Card register, 431-432

voucher check styles, 348

W

W-2 forms, 493
Window Calculator, *see* calculator
Window menu commands
- Arrange Icons, 51
- Cascade, 51
- Tile Horizontally, 51
- Tile Vertically, 51

Windows, 33-45
- Clipboard, 405-406
- converting QuickBooks DOS to Windows, 69-74

windows, 50-51
- activating, 34
- cascading, 51
- Check register, 354
- Class List, 143
- Create Credit Memos/ Refunds, 268
- Create Invoices, 169-175, 228
- Deposits and Other Credits, 414
- Edit Account, 100
- Edit Vendor window, 129
- Enter Bills, 294, 320
- Enter Cash Sales, 260
- general journal, 70
- height/width, 39
- Make Deposits, 263
- maximizing/minimizing, 39-40
- moving, 37-38
- New Account, 90
- New Customer, 116
- New Employee window, 131
- New Item, 139
- Pay Bills, 300
- Print Preview, 229
- QuickReport, 286
- Reconcile, 411
- resizing, 35, 38
- restoring, 35-37
- saving open windows, 52
- scrolling, 40-41
- switching between, 50
- tiling, 51
- title bar, 34
- Write Checks, 326-329

Working dialog box, 543
Write Checks command (Activities menu), 326, 330
Write Checks window, 326-329
- command buttons, 328
- Ending Balance field, 328
- Iconbar, 48
- navigating, 329
- splitting transactions, 334

writing
- invoices, 175-195
- checks, 329-337
  - detail lines, 332-337
  - editing, 337-338
  - manual checks, 341
  - selecting account, 329

X-Y-Z

X-axis (graphs), 514

Y-axis (graphs), 514
year-end transactions, 462-464
Year-to-Date Comparison reports, 483